SECRET HISTORY

The History of Security Intelligence
in Twentieth-Century New Zealand, Volume I

SECRET HISTORY

STATE SURVEILLANCE IN NEW ZEALAND, 1900–1956

RICHARD S. HILL
AND STEVEN LOVERIDGE

AUCKLAND
UNIVERSITY
PRESS

First published 2023
Auckland University Press
University of Auckland
Private Bag 92019
Auckland 1142
New Zealand
www.aucklanduniversitypress.co.nz

© Richard S. Hill and Steven Loveridge, 2023

ISBN 978 1 86940 985 2

Published with the assistance of
Creative New Zealand

A catalogue record for this book is available from
the National Library of New Zealand

Every effort has been made to trace copyright
holders and obtain permission to reproduce
copyright material. The publisher apologises for
any errors or omissions in this book and would be
grateful if notified of any corrections that should
be incorporated in future reprints or editions.

Book design by Kalee Jackson
Cover image: [The swaggering detective].
Photographs relating to waterfront dispute.
1910, 1951. R G Scott Collection.
Ref: PAColl-9508-3-27. Alexander Turnbull Library,
Wellington, New Zealand

This book was printed on FSC® certified paper
Printed in Singapore by Markono Print Media
Pte Ltd

Contents

Glossary, Acronyms and Initialisms

Agent: A person acting under direction from state security authorities to operate within targeted organisations or social circles.

ASIO: The Australian Security Intelligence Organisation, founded in 1949.

CIA: Established in 1947, the Central Intelligence Agency is the United States' foreign intelligence service.

Comintern: Established in Moscow in 1919, the Third Communist International (Comintern) resolved to 'struggle by all available means, including armed force, for the overthrow of the international bourgeoisie and the creation of an international Soviet republic'. It was dissolved in 1943 during the USSR's Grand Alliance with Britain and the United States.

Counter-espionage: Efforts taken to detect, analyse and suppress foreign intelligence activities.

Counter-subversion: Efforts taken to identify, surveil, and often disrupt activities classed as posing a possible threat to the state and its interests.

CPNZ: Founded in 1921, the Communist Party of New Zealand was aligned with the Soviet Union (established 1922) throughout the period covered in this book.

Espionage: The practice of obtaining sensitive and/or classified information, typically by governments seeking information on other governments.

Front organisation: An organisation established and controlled by another organisation (in the context of this book, mostly the CPNZ) for the purpose of political advantage. In some contexts, the term is stretched to refer to instances where an organisation significantly influences another rather than holding direct control.

FSU: Founded in 1930, the Friends of the Soviet Union aimed to promote knowledge of the USSR; classified as a Communist Party front, it became defunct in 1939 after the Soviet Union signed a non-aggression pact with Nazi Germany.

GRU: See RIS.

Humint: Human intelligence is a broad term referring to traditional ways of securing information from people or organisations deemed to threaten the state or its interests, as opposed to the technical field of signals intelligence (sigint). Humint techniques range from analysing publicly available sources to clandestine methods such as infiltrating undercover agents into targeted milieus and organisations.

Informant: A person who acts as a source of information for a security agency from within an organisation, circle or movement. The nature of informants' relationships with their handlers can be casual or ongoing, paid or unpaid, and the motives for providing information can vary (see MICE).

Intelligence cycle: A way of typologising the course of intelligence operations. Most models see the process as proceeding from the selection of targets, to the acquisition of information, and on to its analysis to produce the intelligence needed to inform further actions.

IWW: Founded in Chicago in 1905, the Industrial Workers of the World (the Wobblies) was an international labour organisation advocating syndicalist, industry-based direct action to achieve radical politico-economic change. It gained significant influence within the labour movements of a number of countries, including New Zealand.

JIB: See JIO/JIB.

JIC: The Joint Intelligence Committee. The 1946 Commonwealth Prime Ministers' meetings agreed to establish a 'joint intelligence system', with each participating nation replicating the British system of a JIC which would assess intelligence requirements, review intelligence agencies and be serviced by a permanent Joint Intelligence Bureau. This system was gradually implemented country by country.

JIO/JIB: The Joint Intelligence Office was established in New Zealand in 1949 under the JIC system. A civilian assessment agency, the JIO was tasked with providing integrated geopolitical reports for the JIC, and in 1953 was renamed the Joint Intelligence Bureau in line with the other participating Commonwealth countries. Renamed and refocused several times since 1975, it became the National Assessments Bureau in 2010.

KGB: See RIS.

MI5: MI5 (officially the Security Service) is the United Kingdom's domestic counter-intelligence and security agency, which also acquired Imperial and Commonwealth responsibilities. Its origin lies in the 1909 establishment of the Home Section of the Secret Service Bureau.

MI6: MI6 (officially the Secret Intelligence Service) is the United Kingdom's foreign intelligence service. Its origin lies in the 1909 establishment of the Foreign Section of the Secret Service Bureau.

MICE: An acronym encapsulating the standard motives for an individual's cooperation with intelligence authorities: money, ideology, coercion/compromise, ego.

MVD: See RIS.

NZCSO: Established in 1955, the New Zealand Combined Signals Organisation was responsible for running New Zealand's sigint operations until 1977.

NZPF: Founded in 1886, the New Zealand Police Force's duties included primary responsibility for security intelligence (except for a brief time during the Second World War) until 1956, when the New Zealand Security Service was established.

NZSP: Founded in 1901, the New Zealand Socialist Party was the first explicitly socialist political party in New Zealand. It reflected several strands of radical political and industrial thought and action which were rapidly emerging globally at the turn of the twentieth century.

NZSS/NZSIS: Formed in 1956, the New Zealand Security Service replaced the NZPF in holding primary responsibility for security intelligence and surveillance; it was officially renamed as the New Zealand Security Intelligence Service in 1969.

RIS: Russian Intelligence Services. A generic term used to cover a range of Soviet intelligence agencies, including the KGB (Committee for State Security), the MVD (the Ministry of Internal Affairs) and the GRU (the Main Intelligence Directorate).

SB: Established in 1949, Special Branch was the third division of the NZPF (alongside the Uniform and Detective Branches), tasked with security intelligence matters. It was wound down after the NZSS was founded in 1956 and officially dissolved in 1957.

SCR: Founded in 1941 in the aftermath of the German invasion of the USSR, the Society for Closer Relations with Russia was a successor organisation to the Friends of the Soviet Union.

Sedition: Conduct tending towards raising disaffection or discontent with, or insurrection against, the state.

SIB: Founded in 1941, the Security Intelligence Bureau (sometimes referred to as the Security Bureau) was a specialised Second World War security service which, after a damning review, came under increasing degrees of police management.

Sigint: Signals intelligence involves surveillance based around the interception and analysis of communication signals (as opposed to humint). In the context of the first half of the twentieth century, sigint essentially revolved around telegraphy, cable and wireless/radio transmissions.

Subversion: Activities deemed to challenge the structures, norms and values of an established order. A notably imprecise term, it lay undefined in New Zealand law until 1969, when it was legislated as 'attempting, inciting, counselling, advocating, or encouraging . . . the overthrow by force of the Government [or] the undermining by unlawful means of the authority of the State in New Zealand'.

Surveillance: Within intelligence tradecraft this term typically refers to the specific monitoring of a target by agents on the ground or by technical devices. Within this volume the term is used, consistent with its definition by Surveillance Studies scholars, to refer to the general system of gathering information, whether through overt or covert means, on people or organisations.

UKUSA: Established after the Second World War as a top-secret agreement for signals intelligence cooperation between the United States, the United Kingdom, Australia, Canada and New Zealand, it is now commonly known as 'the Five Eyes'.

UWM: Established in 1930 with the arrival of the Depression, branches of the Unemployed Workers' Movement drew inspiration from the British movement of the same name and were consolidated into a national organisation in 1931.

Vetting: The assessment of a person's suitability for access to sensitive information, taking into account such factors as loyalty to the state or vulnerability to blackmail.

Preface

This book is the first major product of a project on the New Zealand state's surveillance of people and institutions seen as actual or potential threats to its interests. It covers the period when it was primarily the role of the New Zealand Police Force to undertake this task. *Secret History* will be followed by another work canvassing the years from 1956, when the New Zealand Security Service (later, the New Zealand Security Intelligence Service, or NZSIS) was established to undertake such duties, until the end of the twentieth century.

This first part of our project has proved to be a much longer exercise than we initially envisaged, essentially because of scarcity of information. What has been called the 'secret world' of security surveillance strives to remain secret, resisting the open inquiry that most historians have had the luxury of pursuing (including ourselves in our individual past projects). The 'covert world is an inhospitable and obstructive research terrain', leading to what has been identified as a 'missing dimension' in history.[1]

A great deal of evidence has been destroyed, was never recorded in the first place, or remains classified for a number of reasons. The stated reasons focus on the need to prevent present-day enemies of the state gaining knowledge of surveillance methods, but include other factors such as protecting surveillers' identities, even those who died many decades ago. More broadly, security agencies consider that, in the words of a top New Zealand security official, 'even the smallest hints of how secret units operate can provide valuable information to opposing forces'.[2]

In view of this, it is not surprising that intelligence history remains nascent in New Zealand. The efforts of a handful of journalists, biographers, scholars and activists notwithstanding, the country lacks the detailed histories of intelligence agencies which have emerged in other countries (albeit constrained by problems relating to sources). While our attempt to fill this historiographical gap must remain 'a report on progress' – even more so than with most other historical endeavours – we have striven to capture the essence of state surveillance in the period covered in this work.

Our broad approach is chronological, but each chapter is internally thematised. After short introductory comments, we begin each with a contextual overview of the period covered. This is followed by a section on the state's surveilling agencies, and the institutional and policy framework within which they operated. The next section provides extensive coverage of the modes of surveillance that were deployed, and examples of how these worked in practice. Such matters as how well the surveillers addressed the state's objectives, and the ramifications for the type of country New Zealand professed to be, are then assessed in a separate section, followed by brief concluding remarks.

Of course, no historical research is produced within a vacuum. The emphases and findings of historical works are generally influenced by the preoccupations of the times in which they are produced. While we have our own separate personal views on the issues we canvass, we belong to the school which stresses that historians need to test their hypotheses against all available evidence, and draw conclusions based upon it; and that those conclusions should strive to be objective, however elusive a goal that may be. This approach, however difficult for an examination of state surveillance, both reflects and assists us with the main aims of this book: to provide evidence about what happened, to work out why it happened and to assess its ramifications.

Suffice to say here that we believe our findings have implications for the way New Zealanders view their past. In particular, the existence and activities of the state's surveillers challenge some cherished beliefs about the relationship between power and public in New Zealand.

While researching this book, we were grateful for the assistance of the other two members of our original project team: Dr David Burke of the University of Cambridge Intelligence Seminar, an expert on British security intelligence history, and military historian David Filer in Wellington, who investigated aspects of signals intelligence history. We also thank Grace Millar, Redmer Yska, Aaron Fox and Denis Lenihan, who joined the project to conduct research on specific aspects of security intelligence, and the results have been published on our online *Security and Surveillance History Series*.

We thank, too, the numerous people who supplied us with material as they came across it. Much of this relates to our successor book, but Graeme Dunstall and Warwick Johnston, Drs Doug Munro and Jim Rolfe, and Professors Russell Campbell and Roger Boshier brought to our attention a considerable amount of material relevant to the current volume. Others provided access to information released by the NZSIS from their own personal files and/or those of family members. The most valuable information for our current purposes was kindly provided by Nick Bollinger, Beverley and Susan Price, Max Kelly, Jackie and Tina Matthews, Keith Locke, Maureen Birchfield, Gwyn Williams, Bill Rosenberg, Murray Horton, Barbara Einhorn, Clare Taylor and Nicola Saker.

Lastly, we thank those NZSIS staff who provided assistance, most particularly the Service's archivist 'Alex', who facilitated the release of various documents and organised interviews with retired officers. We are indebted, too, to those former NZSIS staff who provided valuable information and insight into the operations of the secret world but who, like 'Alex', must remain anonymous.

We are grateful to the successive directors of the Stout Research Centre for New Zealand Studies, Professors Lydia Wevers (who, sadly, died when this book was nearing completion), Kate Hunter and Brigitte Bönisch-Brednich for their help and encouragement. We also owe similar thanks to the acting directors during a period of transition at the Centre, Associate Professor Anna Green and Professor Jim McAloon. We would like to also thank our other colleagues at the Stout Centre for their discussion and insights, especially former Research Professor James Belich, Dr Brad Patterson and Kathryn Patterson; and the Stout Centre's administrator Debbie Levy for her support. We have discussed specific issues with various visiting scholars who have passed through the Centre since we began this research, especially former J. D. Stout Fellows Sarah Gaitanos and Nick Bollinger, and we thank them for their interest and assistance. Of course, errors, omissions and interpretations are entirely our own responsibility.

We are grateful to our families and friends for their interest and assistance. Richard Hill is indebted to his wife, Nicola Gilmour, for her loving support during this project – and getting him through the dark days of health difficulties in the middle of it. He has appreciated the support and interest of the circle which meets on Friday evenings in a Wellington pub (in recent years the Hotel Bristol, which happens to feature in a footnote in this book) to discuss many issues, some of them academic. Steven Loveridge is grateful for the patience extended by friends and family members during an investigation into a history murkier than any of his previous projects.

We owe especial gratitude to Drs Bob Tristram and Nicola Gilmour, David Filer and our publishers' anonymous readers, all of whom who gave us valuable feedback on our draft manuscript. We would especially like to thank Auckland University Press: its director Sam Elworthy (who has been supportive of the project since its inception), our editor Matt Turner and proofreader Mike Wagg, designer Kalee Jackson, the press's production manager Katharina Bauer, production assistant Lauren Donald and publishing associates Sophia Broom and Kapua O'Connor. Finally, we owe our deep gratitude to the Marsden Fund of the Royal Society of New Zealand for its generous funding support for the project.

Richard S. Hill and Steven Loveridge
Stout Research Centre for New Zealand Studies
Victoria University of Wellington/Te Herenga Waka
April 2022

PART ONE:

CONTEXTUALISING

SURVEILLANCE

Introduction: Theory and Practice

Preamble

This investigation of state surveillance between 1900 and the mid-1950s seeks to cast light on a largely hidden dimension of New Zealand history, that of the 'secret world' of security intelligence.[1] During this period the country was generally depicted, at home and abroad, formally and informally, as a small country (with fewer than a million people in 1900 and some 2.2 million at the end of our period) blessed with an exceptionally 'free and open' society – a reputation that had existed since its earliest days as a colony.

Over this same period, the state possessed and employed standard processes and mechanisms for surveilling people, activities and organisations considered to pose a real or potential danger to the political order and the socio-economic system over which it presided. This imperative reflected an ancient pattern of statecraft – as examined by theoreticians as disparate as Kautilya, Sun Tzu, Niccolò Machiavelli, Carl von Clausewitz, Thomas Hobbes and Mikhail Bakunin – of rulers keeping watch for social and political elements suspected of harbouring intentions to damage, undermine or overthrow their authority.[2] Pursuing such suspicions always means that the surveilling net is cast far beyond those known to be *actual* enemies of the state and its interests to encompass much larger numbers seen as having the *potential* to be so.[3]

In the New Zealand of our period, this function of political surveillance fell, in most part, to specialised personnel within the Police Force tasked with uncovering and monitoring subversion or espionage (although we stress that the covert surveillers also drew on routine uniformed police and detective observations, material from other agencies and publicly available information).[4] Deploying men sworn into the ancient office of constable to carry out political surveillance made sense. In the final analysis, what makes constables different from other state servants is their power to coerce – to arrest and prosecute. To secure information to do so, police personnel are empowered, on a 24/7 basis, to monitor people and places and to collect material about them. In this sense, all police are surveillers.

Our concern, however, goes beyond this *general* surveilling of society. It focuses upon those men in the detective wing of policing who were tasked with surveilling the political landscape. They formed a subset of policing which we term the 'political police', although this was not a contemporary term in New Zealand. These detectives worked within a pre-existing society-wide monitoring apparatus which fed information into the political surveillance system. Eventually they established a database of 'secret files' on people and the causes they were associated with.[5]

These files were generally inaccessible to other police, and the people recorded in them were typically unaware of such monitoring, although some suspected. Those few who did find out had virtually no chance of assessing the accuracy of any reports, knowing the uses to which they were put, or finding out that they centred on political beliefs and activities rather than breaches of the law. The material that built up in such files, in other words, was of a profoundly different nature to that held on non-political suspects. Political targeting sought to contextualise the whole person, gathering up information on attendances at protests, habits and beliefs, family and friends, living and working arrangements, social and political circles, and much more besides. The files on people were increasingly cross-referenced to those on subjects (organisations, movements, activities, causes) and other targeted individuals.

The existence of such extensive surveilling of those deemed politically suspect might seem puzzling in a country such as New Zealand. From the beginning, both its colonising entrepreneurs and its officials had envisaged and portrayed it as a 'Better Britain' of the South Seas, an antipodean paradise of abundant natural resources whose subjects could thrive in an atmosphere of freedom, unfettered by the constraints of the old country.[6] In this supposedly ideal society, the means to 'get on' and improve one's lot were promised to the settlers (and Māori, if they assimilated). These opportunities were said to be based around such attributes as fairness and egalitarianism (even classlessness), social and legal justice, freedom from want and control, and (before long) the gradual introduction of the right to vote within a parliamentary democracy.[7] New Zealand, then, would be an exceptional country, an attribute often summed up in such catch cries as 'a fair go for all', 'God's Own Country', 'a free land' and (to use a term that came into currency through its adoption by Karl Popper, who wrote his classic work on the subject in New Zealand) 'an open society'.[8]

Such visions became firmly entrenched within New Zealand's 'mythscape'. That term signifies the arena in which the totality of a nation's overarching stories and ideals 'are forged, transmitted, negotiated, and reconstructed' through time. These 'myths' – 'highly simplified narratives [that] help constitute or bolster particular visions of self, society and world' – might be rooted in either actual or imagined circumstances.[9] Such subscription to exceptionalist notions, in both official rhetoric and in popular belief, cannot be dismissed as entirely chimerical. It reflects in part the attainment of real economic, political, social and other aspirations among large sectors of the population. The most recent economic history of the country places New Zealand's Pākehā (European) settler population in 1900, in aggregate, as 'probably among the best-off people in the world'.[10] The country's attainments, often state-assisted, gave credence to official rhetoric on such matters of representative democracy, education, and measures to provide greater social security.

The gradual construction of the mythscape, however, did not reflect the socio-economic inequalities inherent to the type of society which was imported. There could not be, in particular, a 'classless society', because the political economy was based on the concept of class and therefore inequality. In 1872 Marxist activist James McPherson laid out the case that burdens and benefits were grossly misallocated, to the worker's cost: 'is there any country in the world that has to keep up at the highest rate so many [capitalist] drones?'[11]

Other fractures in the national narrative can also clearly be seen. A later trope, that New Zealand possessed 'the best race relations in the world', sat in stark contrast to the dispossession and marginalisation of Māori. McPherson himself leavened his call for social justice with another demand, one that resonates across a wider history in New Zealand: that 'vast hordes of Chinese' immigrants should not be permitted to descend 'like locusts' and 'eat up the just fruits' won by European workers.[12] Moreover, while female enfranchisement in 1893 boosted the country's international fame as a 'social laboratory' towards the end of the nineteenth century, gendered constraints familiar to other times and places did not disappear with the introduction of the vote.

Governing myths are always challenged by sections of the population. There were essentially two broad and often overlapping ways of contesting them: challenging the validity of some or all of the dominant elements of the mythscape, and demanding that the authorities take steps to turn proclaimed myths into reality. The secret world has a distinctive association with both the mythscape and the public. It is, by definition, a detached relationship: 'secrecy' derives from the Latin *secretus*, meaning set apart. We contend that adding the history of the secret world and its methods to the study of New Zealand's past presents a new perspective on the complicated and blurred boundaries between myth and reality. Most significantly, as the following chapters and the succeeding volume stress, state surveillance *is* part of the history of New Zealand's state and society, and a significant one at that. In regard to practising this ancient statecraft, at least, New Zealand is not exceptional.

Intelligence as Statecraft

The essence of the secret world of political policing lies in the monitoring of perceived or actual threats to state power, the interests which state power protects and the social norms it endorses or promotes (the 'political economy'). In the nineteenth century, the Russian revolutionary anarchist Mikhail Bakunin submitted that:

> Forbidden fruit has such an attraction for men, and the demon
> of revolt, that eternal enemy of the State, awakens so easily, in

their hearts when they are not sufficiently stupefied, that neither this education nor this instruction, nor even the censorship, sufficiently guarantee the tranquillity of the State. It must still have a police, devoted agents who watch over and direct, secretly and unobtrusively, the current of the peoples' opinions and passions.[13]

The forms such surveillance has taken, however, have varied through time and across place and regimes. Many surveilling jurisdictions around the globe, past and present, possess the authority to detain people and to initiate or administer discipline to them.[14] Some jurisdictions explicitly criminalise people for their thoughts; a New Zealand teacher in interwar Japan, for example, was charged with being a 'thought criminal'.[15] While assigned members of the New Zealand Police Force (NZPF) were the major political surveillers in our period, with the ability to arrest and prosecute, their work was a far cry from that of the security police of totalitarian, authoritarian or other regimes whose powers or practices have extended to torture or killing.[16] These are generally called 'secret police', and it is partly for this reason that we have avoided that term to describe New Zealand's secret world.[17]

Our use of the term 'political policing' is a reminder that, in the broadest sense, all state policing functions to enforce the will of a society's governing bodies, as expressed through legislation, executive orders and guidelines, judicial rulings and the like; and that any threat to the state or its interests is inherently political. More specifically, however, our usage highlights police surveillance of those suspected of challenging peace and 'good order' – that far-from-neutral term which, in the final analysis, amounts to the desired or current configuration of the political economy.

In all times, those tasked with carrying out surveillance approach their duties within wider social and institutional contexts. Each chapter in this work seeks to ground surveilling policies and operations within these broader trends, reflecting developments in New Zealand and abroad. Our chronological grounding of chapters recognises the shifting context in which the surveillance agenda was formed across the first half of the twentieth century and, in turn, impresses the place of the secret world within the events of general history. The decades reviewed contain seminal developments: the volatile political realignments which played out towards 1914; the war regulations wielded during the First World War; the impact of interwar concerns about a Moscow-sponsored threat to the country (which we conceptualise as the 'latent Cold War'); the profound impacts of the Second World War; and the onset of the early Cold War from the later 1940s.

Examining the history sequentially also allows for appreciation of the evolution of the country's secret world: gradual systematisation and specialisation, sudden or longer-term responses to stimuli, ad hoc or planned developments, new institutional and policy bases, implementation of legislation. The degree of state surveillance increased enormously between 1900 and 1956, a factor reflected in the lengthening of our chapters as they move through time.[18]

We have curated our subject by various means. In particular, we have focused on the state's own protectors (while also covering its use of non-state actors to assist it), the policies and rules under which they operate, and the operations they undertake. While definitions of the state are heavily contested, policing and surveillance scholars often utilise one formulated by Max Weber. That is, the state is a polity that has successfully claimed 'the *monopoly of the legitimate use of physical force* within a given territory'.[19]

Such a definition, and variations thereof, reflect the exercise of sovereignty, which might best be defined in the final analysis as 'the power to make and enforce law'. This right was claimed under British and international law when New Zealand was annexed in 1840. It would soon be challenged by Māori tribes, which did not see their arrangements with the Crown in such light, but the state's nominal acquisition of sovereignty gradually became substantive as resistance was quelled.[20]

Within such a broad, sovereigntist definition, our use of the term 'the state' tends to be mechanism-based: namely, the totality of the various legally constituted agencies of governance and control. We pay particular attention to the political executive at the apex of the state, and those institutions which implement its surveillance policies, as well as the policies emanating from other decision-making layers of state, including the legislature and judiciary. Our key focus is placed on what is generally called human intelligence (humint): the gathering of information from human sources, by means ranging from information acquired from publicly available sources to the use of covert agents. This 'on the ground' work, collecting data on those who generally do not know they are the subjects of surveillance, is usually contrasted with the technical field of signals intelligence (sigint). This is concerned with the protection, interception and decryption of signals sent above the ground or below the sea. In the period covered in this book, sigint generally entailed interception and analysis of messages sent by wireless transmission.[21]

We emphasise that humint and sigint are not mutually exclusive, and that an intelligence-gathering enterprise is 'not an end in itself': it 'supplements other measures [and] seeks to fill in their gaps and extend their reach'.[22] Accordingly, humint practitioners will call upon sigint expertise, and (to a lesser degree) vice versa, as well as interact with many other state and private players. More broadly, the trajectories of the two broad modes of surveillance are similar, reflecting the evolving concerns of New Zealand's decision-makers on issues of state security, both internal and geopolitical.

This is an appropriate point at which to note that this study utilises a wider definition of 'surveillance' than that employed by modern intelligence practitioners. Security officials and their agents in the field tend to use the word to describe the practice of physically tracking or otherwise observing a target, an alternative term to 'watching' (surveillers in Britain's domestic Security Service/MI5 are internally referred to as 'watchers'). Our use of surveillance, however, reflects the broader definition used within the international arena of surveillance studies: scrutiny, generally covert, of persons, institutions and activities believed to present a political threat to the state and its interests.[23]

This definition expands surveillance to include the processes by which targets for monitoring are selected, the means by which information on them is gathered, and the ways in which this material is recorded, analysed, acted upon and archived. In other words, our interest goes well beyond the clandestine surveillers at the coalface to encompass the systems of state surveillance, the reasons for them, and their implications. The modes of surveillance we outline often involve the practitioners' definition of surveillance – on foot, by car or from observation post – but it will also include anything from mundane office duties, such as clipping newspaper articles, to activities more popularly associated with spying, such as bugging rooms or tapping telephones.

The military tended to be the major (if intermittent) challenger to the political executive's allocation of the humint function to the Police during our period, and it rapidly expanded its domestic role during wartime. Whatever their aspirations, however, in peacetime the defence institutions were relegated to specialist roles in areas such as sigint (as well as, of course, monitoring internal matters inside the armed forces). They are therefore not given prominence in this book, except where they are assisting the Police Force, although as with sigint *per se* their activities are also drawn upon to provide context. This rule of thumb also applies to other state agencies with specialised surveilling functions, such as those dealing with customs, censorship, and post and telegraph functions.

All of these serve as reminders that, while our focus is necessarily upon the humint activities of the NZPF, security intelligence was a holistic, state-wide concern of the political executive. Its surveilling gaze, moreover, was shaped by New Zealand's position as an isolated outlier of the British Empire and Commonwealth and, later, of the American-dominated alliance which had been firmly cemented into place by 1956. New Zealand's domestic security was always tightly intertwined with geopolitical considerations.

Producing Intelligence

At any given time, political surveillance reflects the state's contemporary assessment of the nature and scope of threats to itself and the ideologically based order it reflects and protects. Across time and place it seeks to locate and track people and organisations which it sees as subverting that order or being capable of doing so under the influence of alternative ideologies or their representatives. The way in which the state's perceptions of threat are operationalised can be envisaged as an 'intelligence cycle', a concept used to capture the fundamental processes by which the intelligence community produces its end products. This cycle forms a specialist subset of the state's broader surveillance of social and political dynamics, an enterprise itself generally dominated by the normal mechanisms of policing.

While there are some variations in envisaging the intelligence cycle, it conventionally begins when surveillance agencies *seek out and select targets* – individuals, movements, organisations – for particular attention. In the second phase of the cycle, the surveillers proceed to *collect information* on their targets through various means, including clandestine observation. During the third phase of the cycle the raw material that has been gathered is *subjected to analysis*, often at increasing levels of seniority, in a quest to assess its credibility and discover patterns and implications. In some assessments, 'it is at the analysis stage that "information" is converted into "intelligence"'.[24] If very firm conclusions about the targets can be reached, the analysis phase will produce 'finished intelligence'.

The fourth and final stage of the intelligence cycle involves the *use of analysis* by relevant authorities (within intelligence agencies or outside them, including politicians) to inform actions on countering the threats to the state which have been identified: the surveilling gaze, in other words, provides the foundation for exercising interventionary police powers. The outcomes sought from targeted surveillance, analysis and action might be short term, dealing with the current needs of state security (such as an operation to neutralise a perceived immediate threat), or longer term – especially the accumulation of material and assessments to provide a base for any necessary future investigations and interventions.

This is, of course, a schematised depiction of the secret world, whose processes both overlap and are generally far more opaque than in most bureaucracies. In the event of a perceived national emergency, for example, operational decisions may be taken on the basis of preliminary and undigested information. At the other end of the scale, investigations of suspected agents of foreign powers may take place over decades, with outcomes produced along the way – or not. Given such messiness of process within the actual secret world, the stages of the cycle may be both differently formulated and also sub-categorised in a number of ways. A former senior British intelligence practitioner, for example, posits 'four types of information that can form an intelligence product': situational awareness, explanation of what is observed 'and the motivations of those involved', assessment of 'how events may unfold under different assumptions' and '[s]trategic notice of future issues'.[25]

Whatever the schematic framework, we stress that all of them reflect dynamic and often unpredictable processes. The prioritising of targets often needed to be reassessed, for example, for a number of reasons – receipt of new information, routine review, fall-off in activity, political crisis, resurgence of dissidence in society, and so on. In its application to a targeted person, moreover, the intelligence cycle will endemically intersect with a large amount of other targeting and tracking activity. Keeping watch on a target, in fact, will generally lead to others within their political and social networks, some or all of whom, if they are not in it already, will be seen as eligible for entering the first phase of the intelligence cycle. When that happens, the cycle begins anew.[26]

The second step of the cycle – more-systematic collection of material on the targeted individual, organisation or movement – differs in intensity, scope and outcome according to many variables. Its overlap and interaction with the third, analytical phase of the cycle, moreover, is often especially important. Analysis might begin, for example, as preliminary comments in an operative's surveillance report, and end in conclusions reached during a meeting of senior police gathered in the Commissioner's office, or sometimes at a top-tier meeting in the presiding minister's office. This might lead to a variety of outcomes at the fourth stage of the cycle: a decision to intensify surveillance over the target(s) and their circles, for example, or even to mount a significant intervention, such as a raid on activists' premises or arrests.

We contextualise our investigation of the intelligence cycle in terms of three interrelated sets of enduring dynamics. First, the political and socio-economic system within which the cycle operates, and which it serves. Second, the fundamental nature of the institutions that select the targets, gather information on them, analyse it and (on behalf of or in conjunction with the political executive) decide upon its use. Third, the institutional powers and objectives of the surveillers, which both reflect and shape the essential nature of security intelligence.

The first phase of the intelligence cycle, the *search for targets*, reflects an inherent proactivity by political surveillers. This aims to detect and evaluate the seriousness of *potential* threats, as opposed to reacting once threats have been mobilised – although security officials also, of course, need to respond quickly to unforeseen 'threat activities'. Even uniformed members of the NZPF, in the period under study, frequently initiated the gathering of the information by which targets were selected. They routinely attended public meetings, marches and demonstrations to ensure public order was maintained, but also passed on to detectives any concerns they might have on grounds of security, broadly defined. If they were not already doing so, detectives, especially those specialising in surveilling the political threatscape, would attend future such gatherings, or arrange for uniformed men to don plain clothes, attend and report.

Plain-clothes policemen in attendance at such events would be searching for future targets as well as securing information on the already targeted. Their means might include asking questions of others or tailing suspects, by foot or (later) car, when they left. They might later follow up what they have observed or learnt, perhaps by intercepting mail or other communications. Such clandestine techniques, foundational to surveillance statecraft, remained fairly constant throughout our period. While they were increasingly assisted by improvements in technology, such as the ability to access phone conversations or listen in to private meetings, these represented changes in degree rather than in kind. The exception, perhaps, is radio communication which, as the following chapters track, developed from an experimental science to a readily available technology which brought new security implications and opportunities. Indeed, we postulate that a New Zealand detective involved in political policing on the first day of 1900 would, with a minimal adjustment for such matters as improvements and innovations in transport and communications, be able to readily comprehend the rhythms of political policing on the last day of 1956.

At the end of our period, as at the beginning, information gatherers might be drawn to a target through 'open-source' information, such as speeches at public events, newspaper articles, ephemeral or substantial literature produced by targeted individuals or organisations or, later, radio broadcasts. Any investigation typically included a painstaking extraction of material from such sources, which constitute a significant percentage of the material lodged in those New Zealand security files which have been released. In the United Kingdom, it has been estimated, '75 per cent of all information monitored by Special Branch officers is either publicly available or freely given' by members of the public.[27]

When it was deemed necessary or expedient, open-source information led to covert gathering. This was mostly collected by operatives (in our period, usually members of the NZPF), or by their agents or informants reporting from within targeted organisations or milieus.[28] Police surveillance techniques typically ranged from covert attendance of political gatherings to such clandestine methods as accessing phone conversations, listening in on private meetings, talking to neighbours or relatives of targets,[29] intercepting mail or other communications and illegally entering premises.[30]

As the twentieth century progressed, the overall surveilling trajectory was that of greater intrusiveness into civil society. We adapt the police concept of a dragnet to describe this phenomenon. The policing dragnet is generally characterised as a close search of targeted areas and groupings to locate suspected offenders against the criminal code. In political policing, the net is not only a permanent fixture but it also hauls in the names and details of large numbers of people and groups who are usually far from being criminals. These are metaphorically netted into hidden files because their causes and actions indicate, in police eyes, that they are either threatening the state or have the capacity to do so given a certain conjuncture of events – widespread civil discontent, for example. In times of civil or wartime emergency, in particular, the dragnet will hugely extend its reach and depth, leading to even greater swelling of the secret files.

Increasingly, the types of information gathered went considerably beyond the narrowly political. As well as their basic personal details (physical description, occupation, address, driver's licence, relatives and friends, car ownership and so on), and their political affiliations and beliefs, data gathered and filed on individuals often came to include information or speculation about mental and physical health, alcohol consumption, charisma (or lack thereof), financial circumstances, marital discord or unfaithfulness, personal relations, sexual proclivities, and so on.

This trend towards catch-all information gathering in the global history of intelligence sought to construct a holistic picture of a person, organisation or movement. Each new item of information, whatever its reliability or even its apparent inconsequence, is collected to enhance the database from which analysis is conducted and hence the chances of successful outcomes. Classically, those looking for threats to the state and/or the national interest watch for four key characteristics. These can be encapsulated in the acronym MICE: money, ideology, compromise/coercion (especially blackmail) and ego.[31]

While 'ideology' (broadly defined to include values, beliefs, causes and so on) predominated as the grounds for identifying targets in the first place, information relevant to the other three identifiers was also sought in order to assess the degree of danger targets posed (and, sometimes, the opportunities their susceptibility factors presented for 'turning' them into working for the surveillers). The lifestyle and personality of a target might, for example, be seen to render that person amenable to bribery, blackmail or flattery by domestic subversives or a foreign power.

The police mandate to keep 'peace and good order' essentially meant that any perceived challenge to broad social, economic and constitutional arrangements could be seen as justifying further scrutiny and potentially covert surveillance – were any justification required. On behalf of the political executive, then, humint practitioners conflated the interests of the existing political economy (and the beliefs which sustained it) with those of the state and society as a whole. Any threat to a part of the order of things could be perceived as a threat to its entirety. Thus, while very few targets wanted to fully overturn the institutions or legitimacy of the state and all that it stood for, advocates of many types of political or social reform were surveilled in the name of the 'public good'.

Another way of putting this is that the secret world was in essence a conservative one, following the etymology of conservatism, whose goal is to conserve what is established. Conservatism reacts adversely to any perceived threats to the existing order and is generally slow to alter its views or methods as social perspectives change, although it does adapt as long as the changes are not foundational.[32] The conservative disposition had ramifications for all stages of the intelligence cycle, but most especially the third phase, that of the formal analysis of collected information. Again, we note the overlap between phases in the cycle, with analysis (for example) often beginning in a preliminary way at the point of selecting targets and gathering raw data on them. We also stress that the formal stage of analysis – of collating and interpreting information of disparate origin and nature – is mostly undertaken at a higher level than that of the collectors. The task of drawing out the larger significance and meaning of often fragmentary and decontextualised material, in fact, is generally acknowledged to be 'the hardest and most unforgiving task in the intelligence cycle'. In particular, the practitioners are aware that their analyses hold potential consequences of great import for the state (not to mention the persons surveilled).[33]

Naturally, such assessments reflected the conservative paradigm within which the surveillers worked, with any challenges to the existing political, social and economic order considered to be threats to state security. Thus, people calling for reforms that ultimately became part of the public good through legislative enactment, or organisations with no overtly political stance, could be categorised as potential, if not actual, threats to the state and its interests. Fabian socialists at the turn of the century who wanted greater public input into local government, or members of the Left Book Club in later decades, were targets for investigation; as were promoters of birth control or a universal language, or advocates of various types of social security, including the 'cradle to the grave' welfare reforms cemented into legislation in the later 1930s.

Even if they had supported only a single-issue cause, and had not been assessed as subversive, people caught in the surveilling dragnet remained in the files, part of a pool of potential 'dupes' who might be manipulated or radicalised by enemies of the state.[34] A 1976 review of New Zealand's Security Intelligence Service observed that surveillance authorities operated on the 'undoubtably correct' basis that 'subversive activity may develop from a movement not originally subversive in concept', giving counter-subversion work 'broader dimensions' around the prioritised 'inner core'. It went on to note that '[m]ovements which are, or may be, the target for penetration by subversive groups or individuals are studied. So too are activities which might become subversive, including those of groups engaged in militant or anti-establishment protest or radical dissent.'[35] This approach represented continuity with that of the police security authorities during the period covered by this book.

The collection of information and the production of intelligence often led to no operational outcome for the state. Indeed, a recurring theme in the accounts of disenchanted former members of various intelligence agencies is the sheer accumulation of reports considered to be 'an enormous waste of time and money'.[36] That being said, as we demonstrate across the following chapters, intelligence was always utilised in a variety of ways to inform the decisions and actions of state actors. Soviet and American intelligence services, respectively, used the terms 'active measures' and 'covert actions' for their efforts to influence events, distinguishing these from passive study of targeted persons and organisations. Such measures extended to arranging disinformation campaigns, sabotage and assassinations. While intelligence interventions in New Zealand were far less extreme, they did use such proactive measures as suppressing activist or alternative literature, leaking material to journalists, and intimidating people and organisations in various ways.

The most common use of gathered intelligence in this period was to inform policing measures and further surveillance operations. Thus, political police studied targeted movements and might employ various policing powers or regulations to hamper them. Some of these measures were of a political nature, such as those targeting 'seditious utterance', but such charges were generally lightly used as they were hard to prove to judicial standards. Often, instead, public-order offences would be invoked, such as 'breaching the peace', having no 'lawful means of support', using 'offensive language', being 'idle and disorderly', 'obstructing a carriageway' and so on. The monitoring of beliefs and activities seen as possible threats to the state's integrity or existence was, therefore, treated as a subset of the general enforcement of peace and good order. The effect of this jurisdictional permeability within the policing function was that people under surveillance on political grounds were placed in the same broad category as offenders against the criminal code.

In the early years of the century, lack of operational follow-through was sometimes the result of limited resources, with only small numbers of political detectives and others available for intervention, such as working up a prosecution. The widening of the surveillance dragnet, and the casting of the surveilling gaze upon the increasing numbers it netted, prompted the development of criteria for prioritising detective actions according to the nature of the perceived threatscape. Thus, the most urgent priority for attention during socio-political turmoil might involve raiding and arresting, while a longer-term threat perception might lead to a decision to infiltrate a movement or to intensify surveillance of an organisation or persons. Most analysis, as in all intelligence services, did not lead to any immediate operationalisation.

The dragnet approach changed little in our period, other than extending the net across the proponents of new causes and, if gradually and reluctantly, ceasing intrusive surveillance of those whose ideas had become widely accepted in society and/or government policy. Along the way, however, the surveilling gaze had been assisted by technological advances; these not only enabled the widening and deepening of the surveillance net but, relatedly, also helped increase cooperation with overseas agencies. In sigint especially, but also in humint, New Zealand's intelligence links with Australia and Britain expanded over our period. After the Second World War these three countries, together with Canada, came to form an Anglo security and intelligence bloc within the five-nation security alliance that lasts to this day. The fifth partner, the United States, had become dominant, especially in the field of sigint, by the mid-1950s.

At home, the political police had effective autonomy of operation in the various stages of the intelligence cycle, a subset of the more general operational autonomy which the NZPF had forged from their political masters since the later nineteenth century. This trend was assisted by the reality of the world of mainstream politics. Even the Labour Cabinet that formed in 1935, dominated as it was by former surveillees, soon let its humint surveillers get on with the job virtually unimpeded. But few operational decisions within the secret world involved shutting down scrutiny of a targeted cause or organisation, let alone erasure of the information held in the files long after this could have had, on the most generous assessment, any operational ramifications.

Those who had been caught up in the surveillance net, then, generally never really escaped it, whatever their later personal and political trajectories. Whether or not they knew it, and they seldom did, the files generally remained in existence throughout their lifetimes, and markings on them indicate continued referencing by security operatives.[37] Information in this secret archive, including much material of uncertain veracity or faulty analysis, could be drawn upon for formal vetting for Public Service positions or informal warnings to private-sector employers about prospective or current employees. Those whose careers suffered, sometimes long after the initial targeting, often did not know why they had been rejected or ejected.

Such results were but one of many consequences of proactive policing work that tapped into the files created by the surveilling net and interpreted them within the conservative paradigm of the secret world. As we have noted, New Zealand's surveillers used methodology of ancient lineage, methods which were inherent in surveillance tradecraft worldwide. It is also equally clear that, by 1956, the widening and deepening of the surveillance dragnet meant that 'mission creep' had occurred over the decades; that state penetration of civil society had advanced well beyond the remit of the political policing of 1900.[38]

Operating Environment

The relationships between political surveillers, the public and the government, always complicated, are all the more so when the secret world lies within a police force. The institutional environment of the political police, then, is central to our exploration. Major issues raised include the degree to which the political executive is able, or seeks, to balance the surveillers' accountability to itself (on behalf of Parliament and, ultimately, the nominal head of state) with the operational autonomy sought by the surveilling institution. This is potentially a more delicate and fraught subject for the secret world, and for the politicians officially in charge of it, than for most areas of government.

Insufficient accountability to the political executive (and, more broadly, Parliament) on the part of the surveillers can lead them into operating virtually as a state within a state. The consequences might adversely affect the reputation of the state and the rights of its citizens alike: the use of dubious or illegal methods, intrusive monitoring on political or ideological grounds that fall far short of any reasonable definition of subversion, damage to the public trust and individuals' lives, and the like. Objectively this means, from the state's point of view, inefficiencies in terms of its goals. Insufficient autonomy for political police, on the other hand, can lead to (or at least give the impression of) party-political and other untoward interference by ministers and Members of Parliament. As we have noted, state-led surveilling mechanisms and operations are, by definition, political. In a liberal democracy, however, they are not supposed to reflect partisan interests (although this issue is complicated by the fact that the government's policies and legislation will most likely be seen as partisan by its opponents).

One study posits the appropriate balance between accountability and autonomy as a 'grand bargain' by which 'policymakers will not ask or force [intelligence agencies] to "cook the books" to guarantee that analysis supports their policy or political preferences', while in turn the agencies 'will not meddle in [party] politics'.[39] The location of political policing within a national police force that had gained routinised operational autonomy from its political masters, as was the case in New Zealand, might be seen as institutionalising any such 'grand bargain'. On the other hand, the political executive was generally content to leave the NZPF to get on with its job precisely because their respective outlooks on politics, in its broader sense, tended to coalesce. If they did diverge on a given issue, however, the operational autonomy that had been devolved to the constabulary was revocable.

How far such interest in, and any resultant interventions into, the secret world involved party-political considerations is difficult to trace for obvious reasons, but it is among the issues explored in this book. Ministerial interest in the NZPF's political policing function tended, indeed, to be greater than in 'ordinary policing', more especially in times of social or political turbulence or crisis. This was natural enough, given the government's day-to-day responsibility for protecting the national security of New Zealand, however comforting the cloak of British (and later American) commitments to their allies might be.

The complexities of the relationship between police surveillers and their political masters was further complicated by the judiciary and the New Zealand public. When policing became a paramilitarised enterprise early in the life of the colony, the magistracy had lost control over the constables, who were obliged to give unyielding obedience to the instructions of their superiors. While the constable's oath of office did continue to provide for a degree of judicial oversight, and the public could protest against police actions through the justice system, none of this had much practical effect on the working life of the secret surveillers.

It has been argued that the legitimacy of political surveillers in the eyes of the public is highly dependent on their being perceived 'as products of the society in which they function, not as exotic rogues'.[40] But this presupposes a significant degree of sustained knowledge among the public about the existence of the secret world and its methods when, at best, any information which does emerge into the public arena is intermittent and fragmented. What *is* certain is that, when knowledge of the secret world did surface from time to time, criticism and protest were often couched in terms of New Zealand exceptionalism. Some such unease can be traced to an older sensibility, imported from 'the Mother Country', which held that 'spying' on the citizenry reflected 'continental' police methods that were antithetical to hard-won British liberties.[41] Such methods were contrasted (if problematically) to those of 'new policing', implemented gradually throughout Britain from 1829 and later in New Zealand, which sought mass approval for, and cooperation with, policing – the principle of 'policing by consent'. This meant, as a New Zealand detective put it in 1939, winning 'the valuable help' of the great majority of the people by respectful conduct towards them.[42] In the search for public consent, police and politicians in the metropole and its settler colonies had tended to minimise or downplay the use of plain-clothes and undercover policing work. This was especially heightened in New Zealand, reflecting an official and popular emphasis on fairness and freedom.

While disparities in wealth and pockets of extreme deprivation persisted, by 1900 many New Zealanders had come to believe that the country's foundational declarations of a 'fair go for all' had moved beyond the aspirational and into the realm of the actual. This was partly underpinned by rising wages and prospects, and better working conditions as a result of the Liberals' reforms; and by comparison with the lot of friends and family who had remained in the 'old country'. Such relative socio-economic comfort sat alongside and was intertwined with those elements of the national mythscape which included a consensual mode of policing that did not involve undercover work.

How, then, did the work of political surveillers gel with such hegemonic beliefs? This is a highly pertinent question, especially given such matters as the secret world's permissive definitions of what constituted danger to the state, its proactive attempts to stymie ideas and activities defined as threats, and collateral damage to the careers and relationships of those targeted for surveillance. There are many factors involved in answering it, beginning most obviously with the central one about whether the secret world's efforts to protect a proclaimed paradise challenged or modified the country's claims to depict itself as such.

Other factors include timing. By 1900, for example, there had been a decade of government policies considerably to the left of their predecessors, and these had significant buy-in from the working population. After a staunch law-and-order party took office a dozen years later and presented strikers as a threat to the national interest, many people's perspectives on policing will have been shaped (one way or the other) by the NZPF's role in breaking the strikes. At the same time, as we stress, revelations about the secret world remained rare. Even targeted people and organisations seldom knew about the existence, let alone the depth, of the state's penetration into their lives. When instances came to light, the near monopoly of an overwhelmingly conservative press and (later) radio helped ensure that such reports alleviated public alarm, often treating them as the issues of public order that police presented them as. Public discourse about the reach and means of political surveillance was thus manipulated or forestalled. Although civil-libertarian and left-wing milieus attempted to address the subject of the secret world when the opportunity arose through judicial proceedings, politicians' allegations, leaks to special-interest media, and the like, they gained little traction. The relatively few surveillees who did have some notion of their own targeting had virtually no opportunity to confirm this, let alone peruse the secret files or comment on the interpretations placed upon their ideas, utterances, writings and activities by the political police.

But there were other, wider elements at play. From the beginning of the colony the various prospectuses for a free and open society had in effect been caveated by their creators – private and official – with disclaimers. These, in effect, had corralled personal liberties within the boundaries of those beliefs and behaviours seen to be required for good order and the national interest. With the later nineteenth century settling of the colony into widespread social conformity, large sectors of the populace undoubtedly supported the general concept that 'dangerous' or 'undesirable' elements needed to be contained by state action. An 1883 verse in a popular weekly encapsulated such views:

> Communists, Fenians, rabble and rout,
> Tagrag and bobtail, aye, send them all out;
> Dynamite, petreleuse, *sans cullotes*, fiends,
> Cut-throats, informers, infernal machines –
> Like weeds from a garden, that grow rank and dense,
> Pull them out, throw them over your next neighbour's fence.[43]

Mass endorsement of illiberal measures to safeguard the antipodean paradise was especially prominent in state-declared emergencies or crises of order, especially at times of war, industrial showdown or social turmoil: occasions when the authorities overtly justified draconian intrusions into the privacy of citizens by referencing the national good. Sentencing two men to a year's hard labour each for opposing conscription during the Second World War, for example, a judge declared their activities to be 'far more serious than cases of ordinary criminality' because they 'attack[ed] the safety of the people'.[44] Opposing such sentiments at such times remained decidedly a minority affair, and the stigma of doing so would linger long after the emergency was over. In other words, times of crisis and tension heightened the reality not only that the national narrative was mediated by the state, but also that its caveats could be accepted (or at least tolerated) by large sectors of the population.

It is difficult, however, to know how far the public would have accepted routine secret surveillance over large numbers of lives and movements in 'ordinary' times had they been aware of it. One factor militating against assuming too much buy-in is the long-standing public aversion to undercover police work, at least outside wartime conditions, which we have mentioned above. Even unmarked police cars could invoke repugnance, provoking one later commentator to insist that '[w]e should be jealous of our democratic rights, and we should oppose any form of secret police – that's what the mufti patrol is, a form of secret police'.[45] Suspicion about any kind of clandestine penetration of targeted circles extended into officialdom, including magistrates concerned about its use for 'entrapment'.[46] All the same, there was a disconnect between the notion of an open society and the operation of the secret world. Hence, while the nature and degree of covert surveillance that we reveal in this book indicates that key elements of the national mythscape need to be placed under critical scrutiny, this seldom occurred in our period: indeed, the secret world generally managed to keep its very existence hidden.

Conclusion

New Zealand's system of political policing in the first half of the twentieth century, and beyond, was shaped by the complex social and political environment within which it operated. Both the Police Force and the governments it served remained generally satisfied with the balance that had been struck between accountability to the politicians and operational autonomy for the Police. The secret world of political policing which developed largely reflected a world view that police and politicians shared and, relatedly, their congruent perception of threats to the state and its interests.

The Police role in humint was only slightly complicated by second-tier security agencies, especially the military. In fact the various institutions and currents of both humint and sigint tended to complement rather than compete with each other, despite some intermittent tensions over jurisdictional boundaries. Even when similar jurisdictions were setting up stand-alone agencies in the early Cold War, and its allies were pressuring New Zealand to do likewise, its authorities continued to address the issue of professionalisation by seeking improvements within the Police Force. However, competing visions for how secret surveillance should be carried out eventually led to the creation of a dedicated security service in 1956.

By that date, firm patterns had emerged in popular perceptions of political policing and state surveillance that were also to outlast the demise of the secret world's primary location within the Police Force. As we have noted, there was, in particular, a subdued public response on the few occasions when the breadth of the surveillance net, or the depth of its trawl into individuals' lives, came to light. Such acquiescence was shaped by the hegemonic beliefs inherent in the national mythscape, and the smoothing over of leaks by politicians, officials, radio and print media and others sought to reassure the public that nothing untoward was happening. The vigorous minority drawing attention to the civil-libertarian ramifications of what was exposed, and calling for reforms, remained very much marginalised.

Public perceptions, minority or majority, raise the issue of the extent to which the state's methods of collecting, analysing and using secretly gathered information were proportionate to the nature and degree of threats to its existence or integrity. There is inevitably friction between the secret world's activities and the ideals of liberal democracy, especially in a country whose national mythscape touts the virtues of openness, egalitarianism, freedom and fairness. This friction is most neatly encapsulated in the Roman poet Juvenal's famous question, *Quis custodiet ipsos custodes?* Who watches the watchers, who guards us from the guardians?[47]

Chapter One:
Surveilling Colonial New Zealand

Introduction

The manner in which the operational principles and dynamics of New Zealand's secret world played out between 1900 and 1956 reflected many aspects of its national and institutional characteristics. Chief among them was the institution of policing and its interaction with both politicians and public, the nature of the state and its interests, and the ideological bases of governmentality.[1] Accordingly, this chapter provides a brief historical contextualisation of policing and state social control prior to the twentieth century. During this outline, we trace the development of political policing in the colony of New Zealand (which became a Dominion in 1907), and identify practices which it built upon in the following decades.

Overview

Intelligence, and the use of surveillance to acquire it, dates back to the arrival of people in New Zealand. The Māori tribal groups who settled in the islands of Aotearoa possessed means of monitoring rival groupings, and particularly applied these when territorial invasions were being contemplated or carried out by themselves or their enemies.[2]

The expansion of the European world to the antipodes in the late eighteenth century added new dimensions to the gathering of intelligence relating to New Zealand. In 1788, for example, Charles Théveneau de Morande, a French gutter journalist, philanderer, blackmailer and spy, wrote from London to Versailles with a warning that the new British penal colony of New South Wales would have access to New Zealand timber, and this might assist the British in building sufficient naval power to contest Spanish possessions. While the French government, facing the outbreak of revolution, soon had greater worries, his reports were filed in the archives.[3]

British commerce soon moved across the Tasman Sea from New South Wales, turning New Zealand (named by a Dutch mapmaker after Abel Tasman 'discovered' it for Europe in 1642) into an informal colony. While initially there were no plans to acquire

Aotearoa, officials in London and Sydney sought to maximise profits on the new frontier: what was good for entrepreneurs was good for the Empire. This endeavour required ensuring sufficient order to facilitate activities such as whaling, sealing, and trading with Māori. To this end, Imperial and colonial authorities sought information on such matters as intertribal conflict, Māori receptivity to British commerce, and European activities which might create interracial or intertribal tension and thereby impede trade. This intelligence was gained from naval and merchant captains, missionaries (who arrived from 1814), traders, and 'adventurers' of various types, some of whom prospered by forging marriage or commercial ties with tribal or subtribal groupings.

Such reports informed a number of British interventions aimed at imposing what was sometimes aptly called 'order and commerce'. These ranged from temporary measures, such as visits by warships to show the flag (or to bombard), through to more permanent steps, such as appointing missionaries and chiefs as Justices of the Peace (JPs) of New South Wales – and eventually to establishing a British Residency in the Bay of Islands in 1833. These office-holders provided, among other things, intelligence which was collated with information provided by the likes of whaling station proprietors, explorers, travellers, traders, 'friendly Maori', and ships' captains and their crew.

The subjects of the reports ranged from behaviour by visiting or resident Pākehā likely to damage British interests to events within Māoridom that would have similar effects – especially the bloody intertribal 'musket wars' which raged intermittently between 1818 and the early 1830s to the detriment of peace and good order.[4] By the time the decision was made in London to formally acquire the territory, sufficient information existed to avoid bloodshed in the process of acquisition. The Treaty of Waitangi, signed with many chiefs in 1840, bought time to build British might and authority before the adverse ramifications of settlement for indigenous authority and resources became apparent and produced armed Māori resistance.

Throughout the colony's frontier period (until the mid-1880s), New Zealand's government, as in all settler colonies, sought to 'bring to order' both its indigenous and immigrant populations. The various police forces established from 1840 onwards were key to this task, generally comprising men sworn into the ancient British office of constable.[5] Constables were essentially 'peace officers', tasked with imposing and maintaining the peace and good order that was seen to constitute the desired state of society at the time. This sought-after social condition, often called 'order and tranquillity' among other variants, was reflected in statutes, regulations, judicial and executive decisions, and various official and informal guidelines and expectations. In attempting to secure it, members of constabularies held one key attribute that other state appointees did not: discretionary powers to coerce and detain, at any time of the day and night, on the basis of any of the state's legally codified rules of behaviour.

Successful exercise of such powers, aimed as they were at keeping the peace in the colony, generally depended on information that had been gathered, analysed and, if necessary, followed up. Put another way, effective coercive actions rested upon a general surveillance of the population, the precursor of the essential elements of the intelligence cycle.[6] Such surveillance was carried out mostly by uniformed constables on patrol, the main interface between the state and its public. Tasked with 'incessant observation',[7] the patrols (called beats in urban areas) operated under a broad remit to collect 'intelligence of whatever affects the peace of the district'.[8] As throughout the Empire, New Zealand policemen were depicted as the 'eyes and ears of the state' as well as its strong right arm.[9]

Ideally, social awareness of such overt surveillance would prevent crime and disorder but, when coercion was seen to be required, the intelligence collected by the patrollers informed its application. Moreover, the Police could also supplement its own information from other sources. From the beginning of the colony, for example, supplementary intelligence had been gained from sources such as British military forces stationed in New Zealand and local defence formations. During his first stint as Governor (1845–53), George Grey had established an intelligence network which fed him information supplied by missionaries, police, traders, schoolteachers and government agents.[10]

Even in the colony's theatres of war (primarily in the mid-1840s and throughout the 1860s) the military worked with police over the provision of intelligence. In any case the distinction between policeman and soldier was often blurred; fighting and intelligence functions in the later 1860s, after British troops withdrew, were in fact both carried out by the Armed Constabulary. The state's armed forces, and those of the 'rebels' who faced them, utilised standard military intelligence-gathering methods, gaining knowledge of their enemies by such means as infiltrating spies into or employing informants within their ranks. In the Northern War of the 1840s, government forces received some detailed assessments of movements and political opinions within Ngāpuhi from figures who dealt with the iwi – traders, missionaries and go-betweens called, at the time, 'Pakeha–Maori'.[11] Initially Māori had the superior intelligence capabilities, possessing local knowledge, but the British and colonial troops and police soon adapted, their growing intelligence capacity complementing their greater firepower.[12]

The defeat of Māori armed resistance, and the introduction of major immigration and public works policies in the 1870s, set the scene for the 'settling down' of New Zealand society. After the turbulence of wars and gold rushes, and with the swelling of the immigrant population, an increasingly stable and ordered society emerged that was both encouraged and forced along by the state. This was reflected in such factors as a dramatic decline in rates of violence and instances of social disorder.[13] By the mid-1880s the authorities were generally satisfied with the emergent state of order which was increasingly assisted by technological developments connecting the colony to global trade and communication networks. The advent of refrigerated shipping in

1882, in particular, permitted the building of an economy based on supplying the British market with as much agricultural produce as the colony could provide.[14]

The advent of social stabilisation led to a shift in policing emphasis, away from *imposing* control upon significant collectivities of subjects, Māori and Pākehā, towards that of *maintaining* the significant degree of social control which had already been achieved. In helping maintain public order, what was now a relatively benign police force could generally rely upon a significant degree of community consent for its task, or at least acquiescence in it. This reflected the fact that most people, most of the time, obeyed the standards of behaviour required of them – even though social and political requirements were ever tightening.[15] While the raison d'être of any police force was its capacity to discipline, and force majeure was always available in reserve, a post-frontier police organisation could normally place its coercive emphasis on disciplining recalcitrant individuals or small groups. It was indicative of this shift that the New Zealand Police Force was founded in 1886 as a civil agency whose men did not routinely carry firearms. This was very much in contrast to semi-military predecessors which, broadly following the Irish Constabulary model, often resembled light infantry (and sometimes cavalry) formations.[16]

Efforts to maintain order in the post-frontier environment were largely directed at those who held views and carried out activities which challenged government policies, the existing political structure and officially prescribed social norms. Most such criticism and activism emanated from the left of the political spectrum. In particular, the growth of industrial unionism and the interconnection between mass working-class organisations and socialist ideology were seen to be of greatest subversive potential. Challenges to the status quo continued despite a series of notable reforms late in the century. After the great 1890 maritime strike, a Liberal government entered office with strong working-class support, including the backing of independent Labour MPs. Preaching a common interest between labour, capital and state, this 'Lib-Lab' alliance improved labour and social relations, especially by introducing compulsory industrial conciliation and arbitration, prototypal social welfare measures and efforts to settle the 'small man' on the land. Such reforms, depicted by friends and foes alike as 'state socialist', gave New Zealand an international reputation as a progressive social laboratory.

Such complexities led to a paradoxical situation. The great majority of union members were prepared to accept the better pay and conditions they received under the Liberal regime. As a result, the surveillers lessened the intensity of their gaze upon the mass trade union movement and its leadership. But at the same time, reformist achievements encouraged elements of the left to attempt to build on such advances, so that the voices of dissent among militant unionists, socialists and other dissentients grew louder. Their activism gained stimulus by the disparity between assertions of the paradisal mythscape and socio-economic realities. Averaged out throughout the period

1893–1903, for example, 90 per cent of wealth was held by 10 per cent of the population.[17] Militant class-war trade unionists, anti-parliamentary socialists, anarchists, syndicalists and a variety of other potential (and a few actual) subversives saw Liberal ideals of harmony between all sectors of society as entrenching the grip of capital upon workers. The future, they argued, lay in educating the population into realising the hollowness of the national narrative of classlessness and taking up class struggle. The arbitration system in particular, with its delegitimisation of the strike weapon, was damned as 'labour's leg iron' even if workers might benefit from it in the short run.

Moreover, the last decades of the nineteenth century were a time of increasing global connectivity and intensifying imperial rivalries. These developments heightened awareness in New Zealand of the potential dangers that an isolated colony, vulnerable to naval attack, might face from foreign powers.[18] The list of traditionally 'unfriendly' powers had begun with the French at the founding of the colony and expanded to include others, especially Russia. It was in the context of an international 'Russian war scare', in fact, that the colony's military and policing functions had been institutionally separated in 1886.[19] Germany's adoption in the final years of the nineteenth century of a *Weltpolitik* policy aimed at transforming the country into a global power – including a decision to create a powerful navy as part of a 'full-scale challenge to British world dominance' – added fears about German expansionism to the colony's security concerns.[20]

Agencies

Throughout the period studied in this book, political policing overwhelmingly took place within a generalist Police Force oriented towards acquiring a broad knowledge of society and intervening when peace and good order was seen as potentially or actually threatened. Such interventions often followed enquiries undertaken by detectives, and these in turn were informed by general intelligence secured by the daily surveillance reports of the uniformed patrols.

This practice reflected the development of policing towards 1900. At this time almost all of the colony's police were of working-class, especially rural, backgrounds and were poorly educated. This social stratum was the preferred recruiting pool because of its general disposition to reflect the conservative values of the countryside; its acceptance of low wages was another advantage for authorities. Such recruiting was a conscious preference throughout Britain and its colonies. As Sergeant Patrick O'Neill, stationed at Dunedin's headquarters section, put it: 'If you let me select my men I would go into the country and get a lump of a farm-servant, and train him up.'[21] Over and above this, police recruiters sought young men with the unquestioning attitude towards authority that was crucial for a disciplined force run on paramilitary organisational lines. They needed, however, to be capable of internalising long-developed police perspectives on how to view society and control it, and of deploying 'wise discretion' on a daily basis. The ideal recruit, then, was 'a sort of superior labourer', as a member of the 1898 Royal Commission into the NZPF put it to the recently retired Commissioner – with his agreement.[22]

Recruits who did not fully live up to such requirements, especially those from urban areas, needed in essence to be 'reprogrammed' into appropriate perspectives and behaviour before they could go out onto the beat (there was no direct entry to detection work). One policeman recalled of his training experience in 1911 that the NCOs would seek to 'break you down' so that they could start with an empty slate upon which to inscribe 'police knowledge'.[23] This mixture of world view and know-how, embodying the ideas and ideals of the various bureaucratic and political authorities served by the Police Force, naturally reflected the dominant beliefs in state and society. However humble his class origin, on training the policeman's pre-existing inclinations were reinforced (or, sometimes, modified). He learnt to divide the populace into the reliable versus the radical, the compliant versus the criminal, the respectable versus the disreputable.

Such recruiting and inculcation processes had resonance with other police forces around the world. Indeed, they had formed the basic selection and training procedures of the archetypal forces of the Imperial metropole – first the Irish Constabulary, and then the London Metropolitan Police set up by Robert Peel in 1829. But the prevalent practices and ideologies within any polity reflected many factors, from its socio-economic base through to the intricacies of its power relations. Even forces with common roots and values, then, often had divergent ways of doing and seeing things. New Zealand's general tranquillity by 1900, for example, based on a healthy export-based economy and tightening controls over social behaviour, meant that its constables could generally behave in ways which accorded them 'public consent', in accordance with Peel's aspirational principles; and that police and politicians were now more cautious about the need to alter constabulary policy and operations than elsewhere within the British Imperial world.

One consequence of this general ethos was a pervasive resistance within the force to specialisation of tasks, including aversion to any significantly enhanced development of detection services. Thus while New Zealand policing had transitioned from a coercive to a consensual ethos as the frontier receded, it had continued to remain generalist in ethos. It was, fundamentally, a preventive body focused on the operations of uniformed surveillance patrols. While there had been modernising impulses, leading to such developments as a degree of take-up of new scientific or technological advances, there were no significant structural alterations relating to the NZPF's detection services.

Towards 1900, however, the reluctance to commit a greater degree of resources to detection was gradually being overcome. On the establishment of the Force, a more systematised detection service had been created and this had a complement of 16 designated detectives in 1888, including a Chief Detective in each of the four main centres of Auckland, Wellington, Christchurch and Dunedin.[24] Furthermore, under

Commissioner J. B. Tunbridge, appointed in 1897 after a career in detection in London, detectives gained greater status and resources within the New Zealand force. His rapid promotion of three Constables to the position of entry-grade Detective after his arrival gave an indication of things to come.[25]

With no thought given to a specialist section trained in surveilling threats to the state's interests, aspirations and security, the main responsibility for monitoring potentially subversive activities fell upon the few men in the force who carried out detection work. Some detectives were routinely assigned to political surveillance. These tended to be the elite of the plain-clothes cohort, who had themselves been selected for having 'more intelligence than the ordinary constable',[26] especially those who had exhibited (in the words of a former Police Commissioner in 1898) 'natural gifts and extraordinary powers' for finding clues and drawing conclusions from them.[27]

All detectives were, in effect, incipient intelligence specialists, and their work helped build up a body of institutional knowledge on political policing. This included surveilling people and associations seen as potential or actual threats to the state and its desired socio-political order. Those of them who specialised in such work were generally assigned to do so by the Chief Detectives. But for all their superior intelligence, all detectives remained a marginalised element within a force oriented to uniformed prevention and detention. Their opportunities in plain-clothes work were limited: if they sought promotion to the rank of commissioned officer, they had to rejoin the uniformed branch.[28]

While specialisation in political surveillance remained embryonic by 1900, the Police leadership had attempted to better professionalise detection and establish firmer operational guidelines and constraints for plain-clothes work.[29] All the same, political policing and undercover work remained problematic, given the emerging consensual policing environment in which police personnel were presented as role models, and that 'snooping' sat poorly with notions of British liberties. Surveilling foreign visitors, one of the detectives' tasks, was at least as delicate, as many targets held high social, political or military standing. As an integral part of the British Empire, New Zealand needed to avoid incidents which might exacerbate inter-imperial tensions or harm the metropole's international relations.[30] The surveillers thus had to operate within firm guidelines – expected, for example, to hold back if their targets seemed alert to the possibility of being tailed. Inevitably, police surveillers were occasionally spotted. In 1892 a nobleman who was an attaché to the Russian Embassy in Berlin, for example, had been taking photographs in Sydney and Auckland in the vicinity of coastal defences. When he observed that he was being shadowed, he complained to the New Zealand Governor that clandestine state activity of that nature did not fit the image of 'a country which professes so much liberty'.[31]

Operations

Around and after the final defeat of armed Māori insurrection in the early 1870s, Pākehā whose views and activities were seen as potentially insurrectionary or dangerous to the state and its prescribed socio-economic order became the major targets of surveillance. Such concerns date back to the early days of the colony – the 'revolt of the working men' soon after the founding of Nelson, for example.[32] The Irish-nationalist Fenian movement, too, was intensely surveilled in the 1860s because of its capacity to contribute to sectarian disturbances, its reputation for militancy and its base among Roman Catholic goldminers on the South Island's West Coast – a workforce seen to constitute the most 'unruly' portion of the Pākehā population.[33]

By the last decades of the nineteenth century the police were ramping up surveillance of the far left and the growing trade union movement (especially of industrial, as opposed to craft, unionism). This period saw an international growth of more political and radical philosophies within the labour movement – socialism, syndicalism and Communism among them. These were seen as the most potentially dangerous challenges to the state and its interests, and their monitoring was in line with governmental consciousness of mounting pressure from elements attempting to either influence or outflank it, even if these remained a small minority within the left. Intelligence helped defeat the 1890 maritime strike, for example, including by exploiting knowledge gained from within the highest planning levels of the strike leadership. This alerted the authorities to the need to marshal ancillary support (notably Special Constables and military), helping the government to place militant labour on a back footing.[34]

These years also saw a number of prominent foreign assassinations and bombings targeted against constituted authority, and New Zealand authorities grew concerned that such terrorist methods might be imported into the colony. Because many attacks had been carried out under the rubric of anarchism, that philosophy became equated with bomb-throwing: self-proclaimed anarchists came under intensive scrutiny, notwithstanding that most stood for peaceful methods of attaining their goals.[35]

Apprehension over possible espionage by foreign powers was also of growing concern. The detectives and their uniformed superiors believed that any such activities would most likely be conducted by spies masquerading as tourists, and that such travellers would focus their attention on the colony's harbour fortifications and isolated coastlines, or on locals who might assist them and any future endeavours. With international tourism in the antipodes the preserve of a wealthy few, it was easy enough to track the arrival of travellers from suspect powers. Russian and German tourists headed the list of possible spies placed under clandestine surveillance, with the latter predominating by the end of the century.[36]

Travellers from foreign powers, in fact, were often subjected to pre-arrival scrutiny. Given the general propensity for businesses to cooperate with security authorities, shipping company passenger lists could be routinely inspected by detectives for potential inbound agents. Overseas police, too, would send advance information on suspects. Pre-selected targets could thus be discreetly monitored at their port of entry, and those judged to be suspicious were followed during their travels within New Zealand, including those to inland tourist destinations such as geothermal areas. Whenever possible, detectives experienced in covert surveillance were assigned to such duties. But as such staff were few, and based mostly in the main centres, regular police in civilian clothes often carried out the shadowing, especially in tourist towns or country areas.

Other clandestine methods were in use by 1900. When there was a need to infiltrate a group of people, police might send one of their own in as well as enlisting civilian help. As we have noted, during the 1890 strike the NZPF received information from members of the striking organisations and their supporting bodies, in addition to infiltrating undercover police and civilians into them. The policemen assigned to counter-espionage duties also generally sought the help of hoteliers, coach proprietors, railway and steamer staff, and others involved in the hospitality industry.

When it came to analysing gathered information, the general level of police understanding of dissentients' aspirations could be relatively unsophisticated, with their assessments reflecting a gulf between the world they worked within and that of the political surveillee. Declassified security files reveal many examples of political policemen who were ill equipped to comprehend the impulses and motivations behind their targets' activities and beliefs, and who drew clearly faulty conclusions about their aims or motivations. A United States import, the craft-union based Knights of Labour, for example, was believed by the Dunedin police in 1895 to be the nearest thing to an anarchist grouping in the city, although there was a concession that most of the group 'would not go to the length of Anarchists'. Such an appraisal represented inadequate knowledge about both aims and means: the Knights did not seek anarchist ends or use anarchist methods.[37] Indeed, they had largely disappeared as a presence on the New Zealand left by the twentieth century precisely because most of their aims had been achieved under the Liberal government.[38]

More especially, the detective police tended to regard most advocates of reforming parts or all of the existing social, economic or political order as potentially, if not actually, coming within the category of threatening peace and good order.[39] The detectives tasked with political surveillance, and the authorities in general, found it hard to believe that radical left-wing movements could develop autochthonously within such a supposedly egalitarian colony. Ipso facto, political and industrial 'trouble' within New Zealand needed to have been inspired by imported troublemakers and alien ideas. There seemed to be even less internal cause for working people and their allies to oppose the government once the Lib-Lab reforms began to be implemented. Accordingly, the detectives intensified their search for 'contaminants' from abroad. Contact by left-wing 'ringleaders' in Britain and the Australian colonies with New Zealanders was especially monitored, but activists and polemicists from other countries with sizeable radical labour and socialist movements, such as the United States, were also on the watch list.[40]

All of this is not necessarily to say that the police staff involved in political policing at various levels did not know the difference between, say, a reformer and a revolutionary. It is, rather, to note that their formal duty to protect the state against threats inevitably segued into protecting the interests and norms that the state stood for, and that these interests were generally inimical to significant change from any quarter. Police formed, as we have noted, a 'conservative' body of men in the generally accepted sense of the word: an institution averse to any significant change in a socio-political system based on free enterprise, private ownership and socially traditional ideas. Their sharing of the moral and economic assumptions and policies held by the authorities reflected their background, their decision to take up policing work, and the subcultural ways of seeing and doing things that were inculcated into them from the beginning of their service. The strict discipline within the force did oblige its members to adapt to new legislation and policies they might not initially be comfortable with, but these did not represent any threat to the existing socio-economic order and were generally quickly normalised within society. They could thus be accommodated within a conservative world view and accepted by the secret world – even if their promulgators often remained under residual watch, or their words and deeds lodged in the files.

Assessment

The extension of the policing mandate of implementing peace and good order into the specialist field of national security brought about implications which resonated across our period. Firstly, it meant that intelligence operations were pursued alongside, and often entwined with, the policing duty of deterring, detecting or deflecting *all* challenges to the state, from the pettiest offence against property or person up to the most serious assault on its legitimacy or existence. The evidential bar was generally higher for obtaining convictions for political crime – sedition, espionage, terrorism, treason and the like – than for most offences in the criminal code. Consequently, when surveillers believed that discipline or punishment of a political target was needed, it was often far easier to deploy one of the vast array of laws and regulations at the constabulary's disposal.

While overtly political charges were sometimes invoked, then, more often the police and other sectors of the criminal justice system tended to bring political surveillees before the courts for public-order misdemeanours. The outcomes sought included removing political suspects temporarily from public life or, more commonly, deterring the accused and their circles from further political activity. On files declassified from the interwar period, blue-pencilled annotations pointed to evidence that might assist prosecution, especially where political activity elided with public disorder in such a way that a successful result was likely.[41]

Campaigners on unemployment issues would be hauled before the courts for charges such as 'insufficient lawful means of support' or being 'idle and disorderly'; language that was common in society might be designated offensive or obscene (calling strike-breakers 'scabs', shouting 'damn the police', saying 'bugger'); punitive fines could be levied on workers caught cycling home at dusk without a light, or on surveillees leaving a social gathering for being under the influence of liquor in a public place. Picketers would be declared to be obstructing a carriageway if they stayed still, or disorderly if they did not. Importers and sellers of left-wing literature could see it seized and taken out of circulation; demonstrators attacked by members of the public might find themselves before court for breaching the peace; an orator provoked by a heckler's words or a constable's actions might be arrested for a spur-of-the-moment riposte. If a holder of the office of constable put his mind to it, in fact, there was seldom an occasion when he could not find a reason to charge someone with something, and magistrates and judges were rarely sympathetic to the accused – especially when made aware of a political dimension.[42]

In other words, policemen could use their considerable legal and discretionary powers to secure exemplary punishment through their capacity to charge surveillees for offences that were not inherently political. They would have little compunction in doing so, seeing this as integral to their role of protecting the state from those seeking its undermining or overthrow. The selection of a non-political offence to charge a surveillee with might be influenced by knowing that activities generated by political beliefs (say, polemical speeches) could potentially spill over into socially, politically or economically disruptive activity (such as rioting). But it was also likely that a detective's values aligned with those of the authorities whose concept of the public good he was pledged to uphold. If asked about the propriety of selecting non-political ways of securing political results, he would have responded along the lines that he was ensuring public safety and maintaining peace and good order – catch-all terms that gave him a wide discretionary mandate.

When a significant or highly exemplary impact was sought, the political police, sometimes in conjunction with political authorities in the more serious cases, could lay criminal charges relating to specifically political offences. Laws relating to 'sedition', a term that covered a set of prohibitions imported from English law at the founding of the colony, were those most often invoked. Seditious intent was, in particular, based around the concept of raising discontent or disaffection with, or insurrection against, the state. In the 1860s, C. O. Davis was arraigned after he had allegedly 'endeavoured to stir up sedition' by publishing a 'treasonable document' supporting 'enemy' Māori against 'a loyal tribe'.[43] His acquittal, together with Fenian activism in that decade, fed into re-examination of the laws relating to staving off perceived enemies of the state. These and other issues led to an 1868 statute which attempted to supersede relevant British law regarding 'Treason' and 'Seditious Practices' by tightening the chances of a successful prosecution in New Zealand conditions.[44] Even so, sedition remained a nebulous concept.

'Subversion' was another major target of political policing, but this was even more amorphous. When efforts were made in various jurisdictions to define it as an undesirable or criminal activity, difficulties ensued – not least because the term essentially enveloped legal activities that could morph into illegal ones depending on the circumstances.[45] Indeed, subversion remained undefined in New Zealand until the Security Intelligence Service Act of 1969, when it was declared to be 'attempting, inciting, counselling, advocating, or encouraging . . . the overthrow by force of the Government [or] the undermining by unlawful means of the authority of the State in New Zealand'.[46] Before that date the use of the term generally also implied attempts to undermine those institutions or ideologies seen to underpin the public good. One analysis juxtaposes espionage, entirely 'an affair of state', with subversion, which 'may be targeted against the associations of civil society – schools, churches, trade unions, political parties, etc.'. In such light, a subversive is someone engaged in 'corrupting or weakening the moral and political fabric of society surreptitiously from within'.[47]

Detective police served a force which stressed its preventive role. In seeing a continuum between keeping an eye on a suspected burglar and tailing a possible subversive, their best outcome as policemen was to *prevent* any undesired behaviour. Accordingly, both plain-clothes and uniformed police might choose to specifically warn a criminal or political target against certain activity rather than charge them with a crime. A potential con artist drinking in a pub might be sidled up to by a detective, or questioned openly by a uniformed constable; a political activist might have their name ostentatiously taken by a uniformed man at a demonstration, or be visited at home by a plain-clothes policeman seeking a warning chat. The two branches of the NZPF often worked together on such actions. In 1915, for example, Christchurch's Superintendent John Dwyer instructed his Chief Detective to interview a labour activist to 'let him see that the Police are keeping him in view'.[48] Ultimately, the definitional and operational overlaps between political offending and criminality, then, were in the broadest sense essentially an outcome of the classical role of the sworn police: that of both *monitoring* and *countering* threats to the desired order.

Another amorphous aspect of police-based intelligence lies at the complicated interface between what is legal and what is not. A May 1930 police report on efforts to classify 'seditious literature' seized in two raids provides one example of categorisation challenges. Hundreds of seized books and pamphlets addressed topics as diverse as revolution, anti-capitalism, anti-imperialism, pacifism, social questions, child-raising and evolution. The authors were as equally eclectic: Karl Marx, Joseph Stalin and Leon Trotsky; Maxim Gorky and Leo Tolstoy; Peter Kropotkin and Emma Goldman; Bertrand Russell, Mohandas Gandhi and George Bernard Shaw; Thomas Paine and Henry Demarest Lloyd; and New Zealanders as diverse as Archbishop Francis Redwood and Labour Party MPs, including Party leader Harry Holland.[49]

Authorities did not generally favour tightening definitions of what constituted a breach of the law. Ambiguities lessened constraints on operations, and greater precision made it more difficult to secure a conviction. In some instances, indeed, political criminalisation became more flexible. In 1893, for example, the Criminal Code Act expanded the offence of seditionary behaviour to cover a wider range of often ill-defined actions, including treason.[50] In replacing it, the consolidating Crimes Act of 1908 provided for a wide range of seditious offences, covering anything from remarks bringing 'lawful authority' into question, through actions that might 'raise discontent or disaffection [or] promote feelings of ill-will and hostility between different classes', and on to organising armed insurrection or regicide. It could therefore be used to suppress activities at the lower as well as the higher end of offending, and it was especially useful for the Police in conditions of social disorder and states of emergency.[51]

But in normal circumstances the police criteria for surveilling and charging politically motivated targets tended to centre upon whether speeches or actions might threaten to provoke public disorder, so that non-political legislation could be invoked. While there was no law to prevent orators from espousing Marxism, for example, they could be closely surveilled on grounds that their words or deeds might rouse their followers into committing 'breaches of the peace'.[52] In 1870s Christchurch, for instance, police kept a close watch on James McPherson, 'the first propagandist of Karl Marx's ideas among New Zealand working people'. The two main reasons for doing so were intertwined: protests inspired by his speeches might lead to widespread breaches of the peace, and his teachings threatened to encourage rejection of the existing order.[53] Such conflation was unproblematic within an institution tasked with carrying out both security and public-order policing, if not for those targeted.

It might be argued that the development of effective evaluation criteria for security policing was inevitably hampered by its location within a generalist Police Force operating within legally oriented and lawfully constrained parameters; that viewing defence of the realm as a subset of preventing or detecting crime downgraded its significance and restricted its practitioners' access to resourcing. It might further be argued that the broad policing mandate encouraged the concept of dragnet surveillance, leading to evaluative inefficiencies; that the vast amount of small fry clogging the net tended to overwhelm monitoring and analytical resources; that the chances of detecting dupes of enemy powers or ideologies, let alone agents assisting (say) the work of 'communist dominated or infiltrated organisations', were accordingly low.[54]

There were, however, offsetting benefits in allocating security intelligence to a policing institution. These included some modicum of safeguards for the public, such as the legal framework within which policing was supposed to operate. However minimal such safeguards might be in preventing unwarranted state penetration of people's lives, they nevertheless provided some constraints on the surveillers – even if there were few, if any, effective modes of redress when these were violated. Countering this, police operational autonomy meant that those with even a small amount of knowledge of political surveillance were both few and relatively voiceless. The secret world defined efficiency in its own way, and its methods remained under minimal political or public scrutiny, despite the colony having by 1900 evolved into a classical liberal democracy in which individual rights and freedoms were officially recognised and supposed to be protected. The work of the covert surveillers, then, sat uneasily with the national narrative, clustered as it was around exemplary applications of the concepts of openness, free speech and 'fair go'. Given that the operations of the secret world mostly remained secret, such ramifications were only dimly understood by the public, if at all, at the time.

Indeed, some forms of policing were applied far more often and coercively to political than to criminal surveillees, especially those focusing on a target's professional, social and personal relationships: the lives and careers of political surveillees were impacted upon to a greater degree than those of suspected criminals. Such intrusiveness was often furthered by police activities not generally employed in the search for ordinary law-breakers. Employers, co-workers, colleagues, friends and family of targeted individuals would be visited in factories, offices and homes, actions which could lead to social ostracism or sacking. Even if such visits were not ostentatious (though many were), in a small society word soon spread and adverse consequences might well occur. Attendees of a discussion group on a subject such as 'social democracy', for example, might find the political police visiting the office-holders of voluntary societies they belonged to, leading to cold-shouldering or expulsion; sometimes landlords would be notified of tenants' supposedly subversive activities, and evict them; protests might be sabotaged by off-record suggestions to owners or managers of halls that they find an excuse to cancel already advertised meetings or make their venues unavailable for future such gatherings.

Upon eventually discovering that they had been placed under clandestine surveillance for subversive activities, many people through time have found it hard to comprehend that their activities or interests could have been seen as subversive.[55] Even from a scholarly perspective, the exercise of covert political surveillance in the past can seem puzzling at first glance. This is why, even more so than in many historical studies, an attempt needs to be made to understand the underlying assumptions and motivations of the secret world of the surveillers. This does not, of course, exonerate that world from critical investigation of its aims, methods and consequences. As we have noted, the surveillers could have great difficulty in understanding the instincts, motivations and aims of those they placed under scrutiny. This had a number of consequences for both the surveillers and the surveilled, including issues of efficiency (such as prioritising the deployment of scarce resources) on the one side, and on the other the intensive and sometimes harmful intrusion into the private lives of people whose ideas would not now be considered subversive.

Conclusion

The system of state surveillance which had evolved in New Zealand by 1900, with all its idiosyncrasies, dispositions and limits, formed the foundation of the country's security-based scrutiny of people and institutions over the next half-century and beyond, framing both future aims and methods. The colony's political policing was a subset of its general policing, and the political executive had devolved a significant degree of operational autonomy to the NZPF. But while the force's political work seldom came under explicit ministerial instruction, it followed broad governmental policies and priorities, even when relatively radical ministries might cause some disquiet within the conservative world of police culture. While New Zealand fitted the definition of a liberal democracy at the turn of the century, its essential socio-economic underpinnings had not altered. The fledgling secret world of 1900 knew what its job was: to watch out for enemy nations and radical ideologies which might seek to exploit New Zealand's openness and freedoms in order to damage the interests of the state and the economic, social and political order over which it presided – and ultimately, therefore, its legitimacy or very existence.

PART TWO:

PEACE AND WAR,

1900-1918

Chapter Two:
Searching for Spies and Seditionaries, 1900–1914

Introduction

In the early years of the new century, New Zealand authorities remained convinced of the need to root out enemy spies as well as subversives and seditionaries. The danger from encroaching rival powers was seen to be increasing, particularly as antagonisms emerged within Anglo-German relations and a naval arms race notably escalated in 1909. The New Zealand state was especially conscious of its vulnerability in the event of war. Its military was relatively small, and its coastlines were long and mostly remote from population centres; and although its security was seen to be firmly wrapped in the protective cloak of Empire, Royal Navy ships could potentially be temporarily diverted elsewhere in time of need. As the *Evening Post* soberly noted, 'Great Britain can defend the Atlantic; she can defend the Pacific just as certainly; whether she could, if pressed in both oceans, defend her possessions in each equally is a grave question.'[1]

New Zealand's authorities also felt vulnerable to internal threats from political and industrial labour, their projected scenarios ranging from minor unrest to full-scale class warfare. Certainly, the perceived threat of working-class militancy had receded as a result of the Liberal government's industrial and social reforms. From the later 1880s, indeed, paradise was being 'reforged' by the flourishing pastoral economy.[2] But state decision-makers continued to fear radical activity, seeing workers as vulnerable to influence from (mostly 'foreign') agitators who threatened to contaminate the colonial paradise.[3]

When industrial unrest did erupt, not long before the First World War, both the liberal and conservative press agreed that threats to persons and property resulted from 'violent foreigners' who were largely the 'cast-offs from London and Liverpool, and other English ports, and from Australia. They are the class of men, who, urged on by the whips of the socialists who at present control them – the Federation of Labour – and by their initial unchecked success, will stop at nothing.'[4]

With the New Zealand Police Force holding primary responsibility for detecting, surveilling and prosecuting 'enemies of the state', threats to public order and state security overlapped. In instances where there were significant 'defence of the realm' implications, however, the Police role was often supplemented by both New Zealand army and Imperial naval intelligence, as well as by postal, customs and other officials. By the outbreak of the First World War, the Police had considerably honed its surveillance capacity as a result of two factors: first, a huge wave of industrial militancy in 1912–13, and second, concern about Germany's ambitions and intentions.

That the former was as much an international phenomenon as the latter served to remind those policemen undertaking political work that, even if New Zealand had technically ceased to be a colony in 1907, their task formed part of an Empire-wide effort to ward off challenges to British hegemony. Britain's 'gigantic navy, and the military forces of the United Kingdom' were, in the words of Secretary of State for the Colonies Joseph Chamberlain in 1897, 'maintained as a necessity of empire, for the maintenance and protection of Imperial trade and of Imperial interests all over the world'. In the final analysis, a threat to one part of the Empire was a threat to its whole. Winston Churchill referred to such indivisibility in March 1914: 'The safety of Australia and New Zealand is secured by the naval power . . . of Great Britain. No European State would, or could, invade or conquer New Zealand or Australia unless the British Navy had been destroyed.'[5]

Overview

The dynamics that would later inform the Cold War are apparent in early twentieth century ideas of an emerging confrontation between capitalism and socialism.[6] Challengers to the status quo, in turn, reflected a longer lineage – Christian ideals taken from the 'Sermon on the Mount'; the influence of the Enlightenment and the Industrial Revolution; the 'Humanitarian' Revolution, at its height when New Zealand was settled; Marxian and other early socialist theorists; and so on.

Given that New Zealand's outlook on the wider world was heavily intertwined with its Imperial ties and that it was a small land on the outermost flank of the Empire, a premium was placed on Imperial unity. As Prime Minister Joseph Ward stressed at the 1907 colonial conference in London, the country's safety depended on a unified Empire and a powerful navy.[7] The change in status from colony to Dominion later that year altered little. The New Zealand authorities continued to stress both their ultra-loyalism and their economic value to Britain – part of the processes that James Belich has termed 'recolonisation'.[8] Its surveillers needed to take care that their actions neither disturbed the delicate balance of power within Europe nor disrupted the country's ongoing bid for ever greater Imperial protection.

On the other hand, as noted earlier, New Zealand's political executive was acutely conscious of the need to develop its security in an increasingly uncertain world – one in which the nearest Royal Naval station lay some 1200 nautical miles across the Tasman Sea. The colony's harbour defences had been strengthened in the last quarter of the nineteenth century, following Russian invasion scares.[9] But as rival powers, notably Japan, Germany and the United States, acquired modern navies and expanded their presence in the Pacific, New Zealand's position seemed less secure.

Such international developments strengthened an existing tendency in London to see espionage (and possibly sabotage) as an Empire-wide problem. As it later emerged, from the beginning of the new century Germany had developed war plans that included the possibility of attacking the peripheral portions of the British Empire.[10] To counter threats to the Empire, a Committee of Imperial Defence was established in the aftermath of the recent South African War to oversee policy, strategy and coordination relating to defence security across Britain's global interests. As the 'principal advisory body on home and overseas defence issues', the Committee fostered Imperial cooperation on surveillance as well as other issues.[11]

Such measures responded, in particular, to the perceived threat of German expansion, backed as it was by the building up of what soon became the world's second-largest navy.[12] The era of 'new navalism' had ramifications for the Pacific, with various powers seeking to build intelligence assessments of the region, including New Zealand. In 1888, the French squadron in Noumea had received reports from the visiting cruiser *Le Fabert* about Wellington's and Otago's naval defences. In 1911 the German cruiser *Condor*, working in concert with local German consular officials, prepared dossiers on Auckland's defences. During the 1908 visit of the United States' 'Great White Fleet', American intelligence officers compiled reports on conditions in Auckland, including local defences; the US Navy's War College had been contemplating what a potential war with the Royal Navy would look like for some time.[13]

The sense of threat spread in popular circles too. Erskine Childers' enormously popular 1903 spy novel *The Riddle of The Sands: A Record of Secret Service* had, for example, stoked fear of German deception.[14] Other such books followed, with William Le Queux's *The Invasion of 1910* prompting especial concern in 1906 (although he had previously predicted French and Russian invasions too). Such works are recorded as having an impact in New Zealand. The most curious episode of heightened tensions around the naval arms race came in 1909 when numerous New Zealanders claimed to have spotted mysterious airships in the skies. The Police investigated but discovered no concrete evidence of enemy or any other such activity in the air.[15]

All the same, despite the geopolitical threats from afar, the major perceived threat to state security in the first decade of twentieth-century New Zealand, and the years beyond, was the growing number of people opposed to some or all of the existing order, most of them members of unions or left-wing political organisations or movements. Their growth occurred in tandem with the faltering of the compulsory arbitration system. The Liberal government, accordingly, had struggled to fully contain the labour movement: strikes began to reappear from 1906, socialist groups gained traction, and in 1909 the militant Federation of Labour, popularly called the 'Red Federation' ('Red Feds'), was established.[16]

Many groupings had already loosely organised under the banner of the New Zealand Socialist Party (NZSP), the first socialist party in the country. Founded in 1901 by, among others, 'ethical socialists' from the Clarion Movement, NZSP policies altered over time and place. But the Party's unwavering opposition to the gradualist reformism of the Lib-Lab governing alliance made it a particular target for scrutiny. This stepped up when the esteemed British union orator Tom Mann briefly became the NZSP's national organiser in 1902. Such international connections particularly alarmed those detectives who tended to focus on political issues. Scrutiny of the NZSP intensified when it began to pick up influence after 1906, amidst worker disquiet – at a time of decline in real incomes – over the Arbitration Court's wage rulings. A 'greater range of revolutionary positions' began to manifest within the Party and led to periodical calls for the revolutionary overthrow of capitalism.[17]

Some NZSP members, and other parts of the labour movement, were influenced by the doctrines of syndicalism, which rejected a parliamentary route to socialism in favour of ownership of the means of production and distribution by organised labour. The most influential syndicalist strand in the country was that set up from 1906 by the United States–based Industrial Workers of the World (IWW), or 'the Wobblies'. Despite a great deal of internal factionalism, the Wobblies consistently stood for class struggle to achieve a socialist society in which the workers controlled industry and much else.[18] As its American journal said in 1903, the IWW stood for 'revolution, not reform, because we mean to abolish the foundation of all existing institutions'.[19]

Though many Wobblies (including the IWW's first general secretary, New Zealander William Trautmann) did not believe in the use of physical force, the movement advocated striking and other modes of direct action as political weapons to bring about a new global order based on collective ownership and cooperative social enterprise. In 1907, as disillusionment with the arbitration system grew, the IWW began to attract greater support and, accordingly, increased political monitoring. Special attention was paid to the 'outside agitators' who were believed to be radicalising New Zealand workers.[20]

By 1908 the NZSP had experienced a dramatic increase in membership to some 3000, assisted by skilled orators and organisers such as former Canadian Wobbly H. M. ('Fiery Fitz') Fitzgerald, who reportedly induced nearly a hundred people to form an NZSP branch on the strength of a single lecture. Another Canadian syndicalist was targeted for surveillance when he arrived in 1911: J. B. King was an especial bête noire of the employers because of his reputation for powerful advocacy of industrial sabotage as a legitimate method of political action.[21]

When the Liberal government lost office in July 1912, its Reform Party successor, under the leadership of Prime Minister William Massey, confronted and attempted to neutralise militant unionism. Ably abetted by Police Commissioner John Cullen and the Employers' Federation (led by William Pryor), the government quickly set out to send a message to the Red Feds over who ruled the country by targeting the Red Fed–backed goldminers' strike in progress at Waihī. Cullen's tactics, harking back to his formative years in paramilitary-style policing formations, involved swamping the town with dozens of police, harassing picketers and breaking up demonstrations. The Police used public-order legislation to incarcerate or otherwise repress strikers, their wives and their supporters, and introduced, organised and protected strike-breakers. On 11 November 1912, police-escorted strike-breakers attacked the picketers at the mine, reportedly with active police support, causing Cullen (who was on the spot) to find enjoyment in 'the many cut faces bleeding noses and black eyes' of the strikers. Finding their ousting 'very laughable', he predicted that 'the present state of affairs will soon terminate matters'. That afternoon he and his regional Inspector told the strike leaders that their members' safety could not be guaranteed if they continued to demonstrate in strength against the strike-breakers' daily processions to the mine. They were persuaded to temporarily cease picketing, and only three men stayed overnight to protect the miners' union hall.[22]

The next morning, in what became known as 'Black Tuesday', the strike-breakers, supposedly on their way to the mine, wheeled instead to amass outside the hall, whose overnight watch had been joined by a handful of men and women. Two miners outside the premises were attacked and, as they tried to find safety in the hall, shots were fired by persons unknown. The scabs and their police escorts, headed by Constable Gerald Wade, burst into the hall. As the picketers fled out the back, Wade was injured by gunfire, again from an unknown source. Before or after this he batoned striker Frederick Evans to the ground, and the stricken miner was severely beaten by the strike-breakers for a prolonged period. Initially denied medical assistance in police cells, he died of his injuries the next day – the only striker killed in an industrial confrontation in New Zealand's history. A scab union leader publicly acknowledged later that day that the events of the morning were prearranged, although the authorities were later to deny this.

Operating from the hall, which was later judicially declared to be illegally seized, mobs of scabs spent that day and the next few in what newspaper reports applauded as the 'cleansing' of Waihī. Working from prearranged lists, the roving bands hunted down and beat up strikers, forcing most of them and their families (including those of gaoled strikers) out of town, often having to abandon their possessions for little or no return. The Police did not intervene to prevent these events, although their command did order that homes were not to be invaded and some constables attempted to prevent beatings. Future prime minister Peter Fraser headed a furious Red Fed delegation to Prime Minister Massey to condemn the 'reign of terror' that had been instituted with police complicity. The new United Labour Party was among the many left-wing institutions alleging 'criminal connivance' by the Police Force in these violent events.

What was clear was that the scabs (some of them with criminal backgrounds), accompanied by police, had processed to the miners' hall on the very morning the strikers had been persuaded by the Commissioner to remove their guards; and that, however premeditated or otherwise the attack, it took place within a context of a great deal of covertly gathered information from inside striker circles.[23]

The crushing of the Waihī strike did not, as intended, persuade militant labour to abandon class struggle. Instead, together with the socialist movement, its leaders set about re-examining how to secure reform or (for some) revolution. Many, having seen the might of the state unleashed against striking workers and their supporters, now took a less confrontational approach by emphasising change through the ballot box. Even the country's first Marxian Club, formed in Petone in 1912, argued for 'revolution' through the election of working-class candidates.

Nonetheless, the class-struggle atmosphere of the times led to significant numbers opting for even greater militancy. The influence of the Wobblies swelled, and in the first half of 1913 they held over a hundred outdoor meetings. New organisations sprang up for the detectives to watch, some of them eschewing syndicalist or other industrial direct action in favour of political revolution. Most significantly, the 'Red Federation' of Labour gained increased support for its combination of industrial and political action as the way to alter the power dynamics between capital and labour. Its 'unity proposal' gained traction and had secured a wide catchment of support by mid-1913, when militants and moderates came together to form the United Federation of Labour and a concomitant Social Democratic Party.[24]

By then the government, acutely aware of growing politico-industrial turmoil in similar jurisdictions overseas, had become increasingly alarmed at militancy within the labour movement. In liaison with employers, farming and police leaderships, and informed by intelligence from the political police, key ministers now worked towards precipitating a showdown with those unions that operated outside the arbitration system. The government's aim was ambitious: a definitive victory which would force the militant unions back into the arbitration system. Prime Minister Massey urged the employers 'not to buy peace at any price'; they needed to be resolute in order to 'prevent a recurrence of these struggles'.[25]

The crackdown had begun with relatively small disputes at the Huntly coal mines and on the Wellington wharves early in October 1913 and escalated into a momentous strike, involving some 16,000 strikers and large numbers of supporters, which only ended in January 1914 when the miners returned to work. As New Zealand's online encyclopedia puts it, 'for several weeks the country was on the brink of violent revolution'.[26] Government planning for the confrontation ahead included mass enrolment of Special Constables ('Specials'), both foot and mounted. The main clashes between the forces representing capital and labour were at and around the wharves. In Auckland and Wellington, for example, armed sailors from warships were deployed to protect strike-breakers and property. In the capital, however, some of the most dramatic clashes in the strike centred on the barracks of the Mounted Special police on Buckle Street, which was militarised by machine guns and soldiers with fixed bayonets to repel hostile daily crowds.[27]

The Police role in breaking what became known as the 'Great Strike' (which included a general strike in Auckland in November) was assisted by an amendment to the Police Offences Act that August, which had clearly rendered illegal many of the strikers' tactics at Waihī.[28] Policemen did not, as a rule, welcome the 'assistance' of auxiliaries untrained in police work whose zealotry could provoke rather than contain disorder.[29] But the government was determined to crush labour militancy. As at Waihī, and working with Commissioner Cullen, it was prepared to invoke short-term violence in the cause of long-term 'order and commerce'. When the government sought military support, the acting army head, Colonel Edward Heard, suggested a way of getting around the convention that military aid to the civil power should be used only as a last resort. This plan was endorsed and, accordingly, large numbers of Territorials (part-time soldiers recruited under the same 1909 Defence Act which had introduced compulsory military training) were enrolled clandestinely as Special Constables, joining the civilian recruits. Their job, as with all police, was – as Commissioner Cullen put it – that of 'suppressing strikers'. The army established camps to accommodate large numbers of Specials. The Mounted Specials from the countryside were particularly hated by strikers, who dubbed them 'Massey's Cossacks'. Mostly farm workers, they were armed with long staves and sometimes firearms and horsewhips. They created havoc, especially in Auckland and Wellington, and gained a reputation for indiscriminate brutality by attacking bystanders as well as strikers and their supporters, and for vandalising property.[30]

Eventually the strike lost momentum as strikers were gaoled or lost their jobs and were outflanked; after negotiations were opened, unionists began to agree to return to work under the arbitration system. The miners' unions proved the most resolute and most remained on strike until mid-January 1914. In the aftermath of defeat, the labour and socialist movements again sought to learn from their experiences. As they regrouped, many of their leaders both placed greater emphasis on parliamentary politics and modified their industrial and extra-parliamentary approaches.

Agencies

By 1900, the government had generally been content to leave operational control of counter-subversion and counter-espionage in the hands of the Police Commissioner, his uniformed police in general and his small numbers of detective police in particular. Military officials were also involved, especially on such matters as the security of forts, and they and other officials liaised and sometimes collaborated with the Police Force in the intelligence cycle.

Over the first 14 years of the twentieth century, the Police Commissioners stepped up the monitoring of suspected seditionaries, subversives and spies, despite the relative lack of influence of political and industrial labour until towards the end of the first decade of the twentieth century. This surveilling activity reflected the priorities of a political executive under pressure from conservative forces and public fears. The detection service was a decentralised operation, with guidance and instruction passed down to the Chief Detectives via their uniformed regional superiors. At Police Headquarters in Wellington, however, the Commissioners and their immediate staff took a proactive interest in political surveillance. They might request, for example, covert watching of people who seemed suspicious by dint of newspaper reports and would order further surveillance if initial results proved inconclusive. There was, in other words, a degree of centralised direction within a decentralised political surveillance system.

London remained a major centre for guidance. In 1897, retired senior London Metropolitan Police detective J. B. Tunbridge was appointed Commissioner, the first person with extensive detective experience to take the helm of a New Zealand police organisation. His attempts to continue modernising the force focused in part on improving and giving greater prominence to plain-clothes policing. His successor from 1903, Walter Dinnie, another senior New Scotland Yard detective, continued this trend, as did his successor from 1909, Frank Waldegrave, the permanent head of the Justice Department.[31]

Along with the country's political and military leaders, these Police Commissioners closely followed security developments in the Imperial metropole, with threats to Britain seen as concerns for New Zealand. In particular, they took heed of the work of the Special Branch of the London Metropolitan Police. This had originally been set up in 1883 to target Irish dissidents, in response to a Fenian bombing campaign.[32] By the early twentieth century, the Special Branch had extended its brief to cover many other perceived threats to the state and to the social order in general. Its targets included Marxian and non-Marxian socialists, anarchists and nihilists, spies and suffragettes, anti-militarists and terrorists, revolutionists and reformists. Because of the blurred boundary between challenges to public order and state security, the Branch's watching brief increasingly included the former within the definition of the latter, paralleling and, in some cases, pioneering developments in the rest of the Empire.[33]

New Zealand's intelligence authorities saw themselves as the remotest outliers of the metropole's security network, although the scale was (of course) far different. The Special Branch, for example, had 80 members by 1914, all of them dedicated to political policing in a way that the 52 New Zealand detectives, with their manifold duties, could not be.[34] The detection capacity of the NZPF, however, had been improving since the 1880s, with systematised use of photographs and other new identification tools. In 1903, New Zealand had been one of the first countries to take up the fingerprinting method of identification, and its police developed a categorised database of fingerprints.[35]

Commissioner Dinnie, in particular, elevated the status of detectives to that of professionals with their own career structure. He established a system of 'criminal registration', utilising photographic, written and fingerprint information. He made the position of Chief Detective, previously a title for the most senior detective in a city, a rank. He sought out talent for the detection service and, in 1907, brought future (if controversial) Commissioner William McIlveney to Wellington as Chief Detective to carry out investigative duties around the country on his behalf.[36] Backup plain-clothes work by uniformed staff became more systematised, and treated as a possible apprenticeship for a career in detection. In particular, the most intelligent constables were placed on lists of men suitable for going undercover or undertaking other detection duties as called upon. In 1906 this system became more formalised with the establishment of the new rank of Acting Detective. These men would provide greater support for the permanent detectives, and their training would ensure that full appointees to the detection wing were men of tested experience; 17 constables were appointed at once.[37]

Despite pressure, however, Dinnie did not make the detective service a separate unit within the NZPF. To do so would have been to violate the ethos of a force that was essentially generalist rather than specialist. There was already considerable resentment among the patrolmen about the superior rewards of plain-clothes work, including more flexible hours and allowances, even though the latter covered such matters as paying informants. Most members of the force would have agreed that detection should be a function carried out only by fully trained policemen taken out of uniform, temporarily or otherwise, for specific services. While detectives in the larger centres would work in their own spaces within police stations, detective duties were ultimately conceptualised as integrated with those of their uniformed colleagues.

In Commissioner Dinnie's time the Finger Print Branch at Police Headquarters expanded its database and absorbed other functions, such as photography and compilation of the *New Zealand Police Gazette*; it would become the Criminal Registration Branch under Waldegrave. In 1912 Chief Detective McIlveney was instructed to take charge of this branch and reorganise it to better address and coordinate its responsibilities; among other things, it was to set an example for improving record-keeping.[38]

In 1909, Dinnie's final year in office, fears of both spies from outside New Zealand and seditionary elements within the country had led to greater efforts to extend the range and efficiency of surveillance. This included a further strengthening in numbers of the detective service. Its complement of five Chief Detectives, 30 Detectives and 14 Acting Detectives amounted to almost a three-fold increase in specialised detection capacity since the turn of the century. At the same time, greater numbers of regular constables were being given plain-clothes assignments. All of this was despite a continuing decrease in recorded crime, in line with the 'settling down' processes which had replaced the turbulence of the frontier. The greater numbers reflected an imperative to nudge the remaining pockets of social recalcitrance towards 'respectable behaviour', but it also included a capacity to more closely watch out for, and watch, subversives and spies.[39]

Problems remained, however, not least among them the disinclination of men who were already some way up the promotions ladder to apply for plain-clothes service, because moving into detection meant losing the seniority they had gained in the uniformed branch.[40] There was also loss of actual expertise due to the limited opportunities for promotion within the detection service: the absence of any rank between Detective and Chief Detective encouraged an eventual return to the uniformed branch. While such problems were essentially endemic within a generalist Police Force, they were partially addressed in 1911 through the introduction of the new rank of Detective Sergeant. This position not only gave ambitious men the prospect of attaining NCO rank within the detective branch, but also improved efficiency by providing an extra tier for sifting and analysing information, including that obtained within the intelligence cycle.

Additionally, the new management layer beneath Chief Detectives relieved them of considerable hands-on supervision, permitting more time for analysis, including threat assessment. One prerequisite for promotion to the NCO position was a decade's experience in plain-clothes work, rather than ability *per se*. Nevertheless, the quick promotion of six men to Detective Sergeant increased the branch's efficiency, and restrictions on eligibility for the position were later relaxed in any case.[41] Over and above that, greater efforts were being made in the pre-war years to ensure that only men 'possessed of superior intelligence' could become detectives in the first place, one test of this being the capacity to pass specialist examinations.[42]

While the modernising processes occurring within the plain-clothes branch increased its value to the Police Force as a whole, in a sense they helped further isolate it. There was resentment within the force at the detectives' supposedly easy way of life, and they were often depicted as acquiring an air of superiority and arrogance once they had left the rigours of the beat or patrol behind them. To counteract this, the Commissioners stressed the detectives' subordinate position within a generalist force. This was reconfirmed after the April 1912 appointment of Commissioner Cullen, whose approach to policing – as we have noted – tended to reflect an early career in the coercively oriented uniformed patrols of the Irish and New Zealand constabularies.[43] From 1913, a longer length of uniformed service was required before a constable could sit the qualification examination for admission to the detection stream. Moreover, if a successful candidate did get appointed as an Acting Detective, he had to wait for a number of years before he was eligible for promotion to full Detective. Such barriers continued to encourage bright young constables to aim for promotion to a uniformed NCO position rather than enter plain-clothes work.[44]

All the same, Cullen's career had involved extensive undercover experience, and he knew the ways in which clandestinely gathered intelligence could add value to the work of the regular police.[45] During the period of open class warfare and civil disobedience in 1912–13, he and his senior officers developed more sophisticated ways of surveilling what they saw as subversive milieus. Policemen infiltrated all strata of dissident activity, from the executive committees of unions down to rank-and-file activism in mines, factories and wharves, and secured informants within many political movements and organisations. The information gathered played a significant role in the ability of the Police, in close conjunction with the government and employers, to crush the industrial unrest of the pre-war period and stymie radical political activity.

This played out too in the burst of anti-militarist activity that accompanied New Zealand's introduction of compulsory military training for males aged 12 to 20 under the 1909 Defence Act.[46] Protesters included pacifists (who rejected all wars) and pacificists (who saw war as only a very last resort) who often drew from theological, liberal and socialist philosophies. Such protesters fell firmly under the surveilling gaze of the detective police, adding large numbers to be watched alongside those already seen as subversive or seditionary.[47] With the help of the military, police had also to track down the many youths who refused to cooperate with conscription, and those who encouraged them. Within three months of compulsory military training becoming operationalised in April 1911, 13,000 eligible youths had failed to comply, some of them on political grounds. In the event, 6876 resisters were convicted in the period up to 30 April 1914. Some of these had refused to pay their fines in protest and, in the preceding 12 months, 234 young men had been incarcerated as a result. As the prosecutions grew, opposition became more determined, accompanied by dramatic protests such as hunger strikes.[48]

As New Zealand's defence arrangements continued to rely on Britain, security intelligence too was closely linked with the Imperial metropole. Here, the lead responsibility for counter-espionage at home and abroad had rested traditionally with army and naval intelligence, and this capacity was boosted as the strategic outlook darkened. In 1903 the British War Office had established its own intelligence section, headed by former Special Branch officer William Melville. In 1909, the intelligence subcommittee of the Committee of Imperial Defence recommended an enhanced security intelligence capacity, and the Secret Service Bureau was subsequently established.[49]

This quickly split into two sections. One, led by counter-espionage head Vernon Kell, covered surveillance at home and would eventually become the Security Service (MI5), while the other handled responsibility for gathering intelligence on enemy powers, later becoming the Secret Intelligence Service (MI6).[50] Kell's section also held responsibility for counter-espionage and counter-subversion throughout the Empire, complementing Special Branch liaison with colonial and Dominion police forces.

Despite inevitable institutional friction, London's intelligence agencies worked together on such matters as developing a card-based system for keeping track of suspected political enemies of state.

New Zealand actively engaged with the burgeoning network of Imperial intelligence agencies. Besides the NZPF, the New Zealand military was similarly improving its ties with British intelligence. In 1906, on advice from London, Wellington established a Council of Defence to keep defence reforms 'in step with changes being instituted in Britain'.[51] In August 1907, Sir Joseph Ward, as minister of defence, presented the Council's first report to Parliament. Reforms included the formation of a military intelligence section within the army, described as 'naturally in many ways of a confidential – often secret – character', that would be interlinked with Imperial systems and standards:

> The collection of intelligence now in hand will shortly enable exchange to be completed with the War Office, Canada and Australia, and cannot fail to produce better preparedness in our forces. The work of this section is being made to conform to the methods laid down by the Imperial service, so that the exchanges bear more than local significance.[52]

A New Zealand naval force was officially established in 1913, though its development was delayed by the First World War, and it would subsequently develop its own intelligence unit with links to Imperial authorities.

As well as British and other (especially Australian) police forces, New Zealand detectives also liaised with state agencies within the country on intelligence matters. The army, with which the NZPF still had residual organisational links, could provide information from its own files as well as logistical support for surveilling people suspected of being enemies of the state. Such cooperation intensified, of course, in times of civil strife, as it did with government departments, especially those concerned with communications. Tracing defaulters fleeing from military service or discovering the locations of scheduled meetings of strike leaders, for example, often required the cooperation of postal officials to report on telegrams and letters of interest.

Responsibility for intercepting communications ultimately rested with the office of Governor which, in the context of warfare with Māori, had in 1845 secured the legal power to authorise interception of communications 'in extreme cases of state necessity'. Various laws had later widened such powers, such as an 1858 authorisation for the Governor to 'direct the Postmaster General or any Postmaster or other Post Officer to open, detain, or delay any Post Letter, for any purpose'. While the Electric Telegraph Act of 1865 had not specifically authorised interception, its injunction that telegraph staff should not 'improperly divulge the contents' of communications left what might constitute 'proper' divulgence undefined.[53]

In any case, police did not generally need to seek political authorisation to gain access to mail or telegrams because of their good working relationships with postmasters and telegraph operators. On request, these would frequently inspect and pass on the contents of communications sent to or from suspect individuals or organisations, and some of them would proactively notify police of any suspicions they held about items they handled. Such informal interception had become a well-entrenched means of surveillance by the twentieth century.[54]

Other officials who worked with the police surveillers included customs officers, who helped detectives monitor movements across the border of people and literature seen as subversive. Public servants tasked with promoting tourism assisted with surveillance of suspected spies in tourist areas, and sometimes attempted to counter critical commentary on New Zealand from socialists and others. The Colonial Secretary's Department (renamed Internal Affairs in 1907) had a number of functions that were often carried out in conjunction with police, such as processing naturalisation applications.

Major developments in communications technology also augmented the ability of messages and ideas to cross territory and borders – the security implications this brought resonates across the period covered by this book. In 1876 New Zealand's telegraph system was linked with the British 'All Red Line' of communications cables, enabling rapid communication across the worldwide telegraph network.[55] In 1884, New Zealand legislation had embedded firm state control of the telegraphy and telephone systems. Cable communication would later be supplemented by the development of 'wireless' transmission. In the latter half of the 1890s, Guglielmo Marconi had conducted pioneering experiments with radio waves using a telegraphic Morse key, and others assisted the development of such technology – including New Zealander Ernest Rutherford at Cambridge University. In 1903, Parliament passed a Wireless Telegraphy Act which provided a government monopoly on establishing or authorising transmitting and receiving stations for wireless telegraphy. This was the first of its kind in the world, a reflection of both the importance of communications in a remote colony and the strong role of its government.[56]

Legislation passed in the United Kingdom in 1904, with an almost identical title, heralded improved communications across the Empire. The Royal Navy had already been equipping its ships with the brand-new 'radio' technology: wireless transmission and reception by means of amplifying and detecting electrical signals in ship-to-shore communication. Protocols for wireless messaging were agreed upon at an international convention in Berlin in 1906 focusing on 'naval interests and national defence', the importance of radio in naval warfare having been demonstrated in the Russo-Japanese war of 1904–5. Meanwhile there had been trans-Tasman discussions on radio linkages, with the aim of decreasing reliance on the undersea cables, vulnerable as they were to enemy and natural forces. On 3 February 1908 New Zealand prime minister Joseph

Ward sent to his Australian counterpart, from HMS *Pioneer* in Wellington Harbour, the first international radio transmission from New Zealand.[57]

Cooperation with Australia and Pacific territories quickly developed. After an international wireless telegraphy conference in Melbourne in late 1909, the Australasian countries opted to link with the international network through Suva, Fiji. Five New Zealand radio transmitting and receiving stations were constructed from 1911 onwards: two stations at Awanui (near Kaitāia) and Awarua (south of Invercargill) and three more at Wellington, Auckland and the Chatham Islands. There were also stations on naval and merchant ships which boosted New Zealand's signals intelligence capability.[58]

Operated by the Post and Telegraph Department, the five onshore stations linked the colony into the burgeoning 'Imperial Wireless Chain'. Criticism that New Zealand was using German technology was countered by a declaration that 'British control' of the Imperial system was an adequate safeguard. The equipment at Awanui and Awarua was especially powerful, with the latter regarded as 'one of the best [sites] in the world' for both receiving and transmitting radio signals. The entire edifice possessed security intelligence dimensions, with various stations in the Imperial chain having, for example, the capacity to intercept radio traffic.[59]

By 1914, the reach of human and signals intelligence stretched from the hub of Imperial security intelligence in London to the remotest sole-charge constable or wireless station operator in New Zealand. The former might be watching for suspicious strangers, for example, or searching for absconders from military training; the latter listening for pertinent communications or sending or receiving coded messages. Thus New Zealand operators within the Imperial chain were geared to a war that now seemed quite possible.

Operations

At the beginning of the twentieth century, the New Zealand Police Force remained abreast of surveillance developments in Britain and liaised with its security authorities on a case-by-case basis. But sustained cooperation between its detectives and overseas surveillance authorities tended to be largely trans-Tasman in nature. When the Australian colonies federated into the Commonwealth of Australia on 1 January 1901, New Zealand had declined to join. Nevertheless, it retained many close ties with its neighbour, and the NZPF continued to liaise with the same police authorities as before (even though they were now in state rather than colonial forces). Contact was frequent because, in particular, the Australian continent was the main point of departure to New Zealand of both left-wing radicals and suspect foreign travellers, even if their journeys had originated elsewhere.

In 1901 two New Zealand detectives joined an 'Inter-Colonial Detective Force' formed to safeguard the Duke and Duchess of Cornwall and York during their tour of the antipodean portion of the British Empire. The presence of the royal couple was seen to present an opportunity not only for left-wing or anti-royalist protest but also for a terrorist attack by anarchists or Irish nationalists. Anarchist bomb plots in London were of recent memory (Joseph Conrad's 1907 novel *The Secret Agent* drew upon one of them). There were also institutional memories of the earlier Fenian attempt to assassinate Prince Alfred, the Duke of Edinburgh, in Sydney in 1868, and of the sectarian troubles among the Irish population which followed this on both sides of the Tasman Sea.

In addition to the two New Zealand members of the ad hoc royal protection unit, which surveilled suspects in both countries and monitored their cross-border movements, Detective William Maddern was sent across to Sydney on a temporary posting to strengthen New Zealand's border vigilance. He monitored those intending to embark for the colony who might have anti-royalist motives for disrupting or sabotaging the New Zealand leg of the visit. When each ship arrived in New Zealand, detectives boarded it to check out those Maddern had identified. More broadly, police scrutinised lists of passengers more carefully than ever. They watched all disembarkations in search of suspicious persons, such as 'foreigners . . . who may possibly be members of foreign Anarchist Societies'. In a colony-wide surveillance effort, identified targets were shadowed and their movements relayed to the uniformed police guarding the royal couple.[60]

This and other surveillance operations drew upon the pool of information built up in the central Police files, which had been created from the mid-1870s onwards, and in the regional files. The gradual systematisation of record-keeping from the last decade of the previous century onwards, the assembling of fingerprint and photography databases, and improved systems of cross-referencing all assisted greater efficiency in New Zealand's intelligence cycle. Suspected and convicted offenders had their details (including photographs, where available) circulated in the confidential *New Zealand Police Gazette*, which went to every police station in the land. Data existed on socialists of many hues; on republicans and communitarians, Fenian sympathisers and utopians; on those who wanted to unshackle unions from the arbitration system; on advocates of new forms of social and political organisation; and on many more categories of potential or actual subversives, seditionists or spies.

Socialist institutions, in particular, were monitored as soon as they were established. The police surveillers laboured to get to grips with inter- and intra-organisational dynamics on the left, fast-changing and complex as these were. Detectives were soon recording that the IWW's most successful recruiting lay among those, including members of the Socialist Party, who were attracted to the idea of revolutionary progress through the establishment of 'one big union'. A closer watch was established on the NZSP in 1908, when its first annual conference opted to endorse this position. The political detectives noted that the syndicalist focus on socio-economic transformation through industrial and other forms of direct action, rather than party politics, gelled with both the ends and means of some strands of anarchism. The term 'anarcho-syndicalism' not only became an established concept in the lexicology of the left but also in the demonology of its surveillers.[61]

Many anarchists distanced themselves from notions of political violence ('propaganda of the deed') and even those advocating industrial sabotage (such as pouring emery powder into the machinery of recalcitrant employers)[62] were in a decided minority. However, the series of high-profile assassinations and bombings abroad made 'anarchy' a synonym of chaos and terrorism. As we have noted, gaps of understanding between watchers and watched resulted, in part, from the well-evidenced fact that police sympathies generally lay far from those of socialist and militant workers and theoreticians. Indeed, although the detectives who tended to work on political surveillance were tasked with understanding the left as a prerequisite for controlling it, they seldom got to grips with its motivations and often failed to keep up with its ever-changing permutations.

What was most important to police, and to the political authorities, was to collect enough knowledge for the NZPF as a whole to be able to check the influence of militant union leaders and revolutionary socialists. In the atmosphere of increasing worker disillusionment with employers and government, this was far from easy. In 1908, Edward Tregear, who had steered major Lib-Lab reforms in the past and now headed the Department of Labour, lamented to his minister that he felt that 'fanatics' would 'win the trades unions'.[63]

Antipodean offshoots of international movements were seen as a more pressing task for surveillance than locally generated organisations, given their potential access to greater resources (literature, money, experienced activists and orators, and so on). The NZPF kept in touch with North American police forces about trans-Pacific syndicalist connections, for example, and together with their Australian counterparts traced local links with British and European socialist formations.[64] Such activity formed a specialised subset of an increasing international exchange of information (including, often, fingerprints and photographs) on suspects of all categories within the British world.[65]

The NZPF extended its surveillance in mining areas after the formation of the Wobbly-oriented Miners' Federation, following the dramatic Blackball strike of 1908. Called to address deplorable working conditions in the coal mines, the illegal action was led by Fitzgerald, local NZSP branch founder Pat ('Wild Bill') Hickey – who had been radicalised as a miner in the United States – and Patrick (Paddy) Webb, a future Labour minister of mines.[66] The strike centred around a demand for more than 15 minutes for lunch, one of many grievances. The strikers were fined an extraordinarily punitive sum after the judge's return from a 90-minute lunch break, an incident widely thereafter used to illustrate the disparities in wealth and power within a supposed workers' paradise. Hickey was instrumental in setting up a powerful national mining union which segued into the class war–based New Zealand Federation of Labour in 1909. This new organisation, envisaged as the basis of a Wobblyite one big union, came under heavy surveillance. The watching increased when many Red Feds quickly came to the conclusion that any meaningful challenge to capitalism would require political as well as mass industrial action.[67]

State surveillance was also a crucial element in Commissioner Cullen's blunt-weapon approach to breaking the strikes of 1912 and 1913. Indeed, the Police leadership was well aware that the state's success in crushing the massive Great Strike lay in no small part in information gathered clandestinely within the labour movement. The most intensive surveillance of whole sectors of New Zealand society to that date, other than during the wars between Crown and Māori forces, had swung into place as industrial conflict became imminent. Before long, police intelligence analysts were working with the usual mix of open-source and covertly gathered information. In the capital, for example, one of Chief Detective Charles Broberg's instructions was 'to ascertain if any seditious publications appear in which it would be possible to take legal action'. His men paid especial attention, accordingly, to the Red Fed newspaper *Maoriland Worker*, the populist *NZ Truth*, and large numbers of pamphlets and other ephemeral material generated on the left.[68]

This helped the detective police select strikers' and supporters' organisations for infiltration, sometimes by constables from out of town, and to secure informants within the labour movement. One police agent within the miners' ranks at Waihī went under several code names, including (on his own initiative) 'Wireless'.[69] Some informants helped the detectives out of conviction; some believed, for example, that defeat was inevitable and that prolonging industrial action in the face of state ferocity would damage workers' pay, conditions and rights into the foreseeable future. Others informed for money or ego or were perhaps coerced. Whatever their motives, police tended to place their information within a frame of reference that saw rank-and-file workers as putty in the hands of politically motivated 'Criminal Agitators', 'red Ruffians' and 'Red Firebrands' (in the words of Wellington's rabidly anti-labour Superintendent, J. W. Ellison).[70]

Armed with such information, in 1913, Cullen and his inner circle actively worked with both employers and strike-breakers, who included men 'known to the police', to defeat the Great Strike.[71] The Commissioner's strategy was two-pronged: to neutralise the militant unions' leaders (soon represented by the Red Feds in negotiations) and their socialist allies, and to demonstrate the state's willingness and capacity to crush mass opposition. Even more so than at Waihī, the intelligence cycle operated within an overtly political framework, moving away from the normal police mandate to suppress disorder. Working closely with his minister, Alexander Herdman, Cullen was at the heart of engineering the turmoil that constituted, in his own words, 'the most critical time the Dominion has ever experienced'.

Although the Commissioner directed his officers to confront the strikers with aggressive coercion, Auckland's Superintendent A. J. Mitchell saw violence as a last resort and deployed his forces accordingly – eventually losing his career as a result. As members of a disciplined organisation, the rest of the Police Force adjusted to an altered operating environment, albeit often with qualms about what they were being asked to do. Even strikers noticed the considerable disquiet within the Force at the Specials' tendency to provoke or escalate violence, especially in Wellington, where street battles raged and shots rang out during the most intense confrontations with Massey's Cossacks and the military. Cullen instituted a hunt for recalcitrant policemen, especially blaming, in particular, those associated with a police union, formed earlier in 1913, which Cullen had immediately smashed.[72]

At the heart of breaking the strike wave that occurred from October onwards, the political detectives exhibited no such unreliability. Intelligence-based forewarnings of strikers' intentions helped police take pre-emptive action: breaking up what were intended to be secret gatherings, for example, or targeting leaders and arresting them for such offences as seditionary language. Some were bound over to keep the peace, including future prime minister Peter Fraser and one of his ministers, Robert ('Fighting Bob') Semple. Others were locked away, including the IWW's firebrand speaker Tom Barker, mastermind of successful confrontations with Specials, and future Labour Party leader Harry Holland.[73] Such measures effectively removed experienced political actors from the struggle at the worksites and in the streets, including some who might have been able to negotiate ways of reducing the confrontations.

The continual flow of inside information, often covertly obtained, sometimes helped deflect violence and confrontation. The Dunedin police managed to avoid such incidents by having informants in all camps. Superintendent John Dwyer knew 'the owner of the premises where the "Strike Committee" and the "Executive of the Seamen's Union" met . . . and she kept me posted on everything that took place at these meetings'. He also had 'a friend in the "Commerce Protection Committee"', which organised strike-breakers (among other things), who 'kept me informed at what went on at their meetings'. The employers were aware that Dwyer 'knew everything that [was] going on in connection with the strike'. When they wanted to know the seamen's intentions, the Superintendent 'rang up my female friend', who told him that two delegates were to go to Wellington for a meeting to decide the next move. She was to notify him as soon as she heard the results. When he accordingly passed the news on to the Protection Committee members, 'they went away quite satisfied'.[74]

Employer and labour organisations also set about establishing their own systems of intelligence gathering and analysis. Dwyer recalled one confrontation between police and strike leaders when the employers' 'usual "spy" was present'; he 'conveyed every act and word of mine to the Commerce Protection Committee'.[75] The labour movement, too, put considerable resources into spying on police, employers and officials. Ellison reported that the local Red Feds had established a hundred-strong 'Intelligence Brigade' which operated in day and night shifts, using motorcycles and bicycles to get around. Their tasks included 'watching the Police and taking notes of buildings or premises' frequented by prominent strike-breakers.[76] A leading socialist, Robert Hogg, recorded that the 'secret intelligence bureaux' had kept the strikers 'fully seized of the position' during the strike, and revolutionary socialist Sidney Fournier later told Dick Scott that the 'telephone in parliament buildings had been tapped by the workers' throughout it.[77] Wobbly leader Tom Barker later recalled one result from the Wellington strike committee's cyclist intelligence patrols:

> The road into Wellington has steep gorges on one side and the sea on the other side. The road was fenced off from the sea by barbed wire. At night time when we got word from [the patrols] that the farmers were coming we would stretch this barbed wire across the road and then get up on the hillsides and pry big stones down on them. Not being accustomed to this kind of treatment, the farmers would make a dash for it and land up in the barbed wire . . .[78]

As Ellison's report indicates, however, police often had wind of covert operations planned by the strikers. Given this, and the constabulary and military might at the disposal of the state, the workers' intelligence efforts could do little more than provide occasional opportunities to pre-empt actions by police, employers and strike-breakers.[79]

Despite sections of the strike leadership seeking conciliation, the government was determined to use every effort to inflict a massive defeat upon the left, and exaggerated reports from infiltrators and informants both bolstered and rationalised this resolve. A Wellington spy in the strikers' ranks, for example, reported (inaccurately) that the Red Feds were contemplating 'using explosives' on wharf installations and 'cutting telegraph and telephone lines', especially the lines to the warship HMS *Psyche*.[80]

By the time of the strikes, the detectives had the advantage of a significant amount of data in their files to guide their targeting of both militant labour and the left in general. Pacifist and pacificist anti-militarism, for example, especially when linked to calls for international working-class solidarity to prevent war, had always attracted their attention. They now intensified their watch over such movements in line with the government's hard line against non-compliance with compulsory military training, in effect placing resisters and their supporters in the camp of potential seditionaries.[81] The state feared that their resistance would stimulate opposition to taking up arms, on moral, socialist and other grounds, at the very time that the threat of war seemed to be increasing.[82] The new surveillance targets necessitated by the compulsory military training system swelled the ranks of those already under clandestine monitoring, many of whom – especially those in the socialist and union movements – supported the burgeoning anti-militarist campaigns. Tracking one group would lead to useful information on the other.

In liaison with both the military's police and intelligence sections, detectives planted agents and used webs of informants in efforts to track down defaulters from compulsory military training and stymie those assisting them. They raided premises, confiscated anti-militarist literature, hunted for men of eligible age who had gone to ground, and searched for enrollees who had absconded. They also helped the military ensure that those who did enter the system were not enemy supporters. They would investigate, for example, potential or actual recruits of 'notoriously bad character' who might be intent on undermining or sabotaging war preparations.[83]

Māori had, of course, once posed the major threat to the state, but after resistance had been quelled their population had plummeted to some 40,000 around the turn of the twentieth century. The great majority of their subsistence-based communities no longer presented any physical challenge to Crown sovereignty. Areas of high indigenous population were normally watched, then, only as part of regular uniformed police surveillance. This included liaising with Native Constables on the Police payroll and constables appointed by Maori Councils, which had been established in 1900 with local government and low-level policing powers. Rural constables also gathered information from Pākehā associated with indigenous communities – storekeepers and missionaries, teachers and farmers, postal and Native Affairs staff.[84]

Māori resistance and self-determination movements were more intensively monitored, especially among tribes that had experienced the confiscation of large tracts of land after the nineteenth-century wars. The Waikato-based King Movement, which had once posed the main armed opposition to the Crown, was especially monitored because of its 'rival monarchy', its aspirations for the return of its confiscated tribal homelands, and its reluctance to cooperate with the state until its grievances had been addressed. Other areas which had rebelled and lost lands accordingly, especially in Taranaki, were also under a watching brief.

Māori movements seen to be a more immediate danger to state security were generally located in isolated areas, such as the Hokianga (the site of the 'Dog Tax Rebellion', suppressed in 1898 by a joint police–military expedition) and Te Urewera's mountains, where the prophet Rua Kēnana's millennial movement operated virtually autonomously. While they were not seen as an insurrectionary threat, their challenge to the state's policy of assimilation might, for example, help undermine the war effort in the event of conflict with Germany. The duty of rural constables to be the eyes and ears of the state had, in effect, a special brief in such areas. They cultivated 'loyalist' tribal leaders, members of Maori Councils, and informants within the oppositional movements.

From the turn of the century, Japan and Germany were increasingly seen as the major potential enemies. The former's shock military victory over Russia in 1905 had heightened awareness of a fast-rising power that was potentially menacing, even if it had been in alliance with Britain since 1902.[85] Building on long-established fears that an Asian 'yellow peril' might 'swamp' Australasia, New Zealand's mainstream press regularly depicted Japan's modernisation and militarisation as spearheading 'a flood of Asiatic barbarism' sweeping into the South Pacific.[86] New Zealand's rapturous reception of the American Great White Fleet to Auckland in 1908 partly reflected a sense that US naval power would block possible Japanese expansion in the Pacific.[87]

More prominently, threat perceptions around Germany had been spurred by antagonisms within Anglo-German relations. By 1912, the New Zealand Defence Department was receiving strategic reviews from London which noted Germany as 'our probable opponent in the next great war'.[88] Regional interests and concerns developed in parallel with global geopolitics. In the last two decades of the nineteenth century German interests in several South Pacific territories had been formalised into imperial rule. Two major possessions, New Guinea and Samoa, were annexed in 1884 and 1899 respectively, and various small island groupings, such as the Marshalls, the Mariana Islands and the Carolines, were also acquired.

Besides thwarting New Zealand's own imperialist ambitions over Samoa, these developments gave a rival power a base in relative proximity to New Zealand and Australia. Concerns escalated as strategic wireless facilities were installed. Fears especially focused on the German East Asia Squadron based at Tsingtao, China, a modern naval force capable of operating in Australasian waters. Indeed, German archival documents show that from 1901 German military planners 'regularly updated' plans relating to 'the possibility of hitting the [British] Empire at its [Australasian] periphery' in the event of war. These plans for 'ruthless warfare' included targeting coastal facilities and towns to disrupt shipping, demoralise populations and build pressure to keep troops at home.[89]

Berlin, moreover, had established a clandestine 'war intelligence' section based in Sydney (which comprised a commercial attaché, who was 'chief intelligence officer', and two businessmen) and possessing a node in Auckland.[90] Orchestrated through German consular officials, the agents of Germany ('reporters', 'confidants' and 'informants') included Karl Seegner, the German consul in Auckland. In his secret role as *Berichterstatter* (reporter) 6301, his cover signatures were 'Austin' or 'Aubert'.[91]

Reports to Berlin covered not only such matters as shipping movements, harbour installations and local defences, but also feelings towards Germany and antipodean German communities; with some 10,000 people recorded as being of German birth or extraction, this category constituted New Zealand's 'largest migrant group after those from the British Isles'.[92] Such intelligence was intended to have a military application in the event of hostilities. 'At the outbreak of war with England', all evidence of the spying network had to be 'destroyed immediately and all activities [had] to cease'.[93]

The New Zealand, Australian and British authorities were seemingly unaware of the specific details of these 'ruthless warfare' plans, and there is no known archival evidence indicating that New Zealand's police discovered any German spies. Nonetheless, suspicion of Berlin's intentions led to heightened, if broad, monitoring of the 'German' community in line with developments in geopolitical imperial rivalry. One significant advantage of allocating security surveillance to the NZPF became readily apparent at this time. As part of his normal patrolling duties, each uniformed policeman knew a great deal about the communities within his purview, including those with connections by birth or descent with Germany and Austria. He could take steps to place those with links to the German and Austro-Hungarian Empires, in particular, under closer watch, especially the small minority known to support them.

All the same, the policeman on the ground was not generally under specific instructions to target immigrant communities. From the late nineteenth century, as noted earlier, the Police leadership had believed that any spying would most likely take place among the ranks of travellers from rival powers, especially those who might be using New Zealand's fledgling tourist industry as cover. The political executive, briefed by the Police, shared this belief. Ministers took a proactive interest in the issue. In 1904, Premier Seddon noticed contradictory newspaper reports about the intended movements in the colony of Prince Bernhard of Saxe-Weimar. Suspicious, he ordered the Commissioner to make enquiries into whether the traveller was going near harbour fortifications and, if so, he had shown interest in them. This quickly prompted Dinnie to rush out a new instruction to his Inspectors: from 3 March 1904, the arrival of all 'foreign notables' in New Zealand would necessitate 'strict observation' over all forts until the visitors had left the colony. If the tourists went near any such installations, 'trustworthy and discreet' plain-clothes policemen were to shadow them and provide an urgent report to the Commissioner.[94]

Soon after this hasty directive, the policy was reviewed and found to be wanting. While the world of European spycraft was dominated by men of high social and political standing, it was now seen as unlikely that hostile foreign powers would use dignitaries to spy in New Zealand, because of their high profile. On 28 April Commissioner Dinnie altered his instructions accordingly. From that time onwards, 'all Foreigners frequenting Forts or Defences' were to be placed under observation to 'ascertain their identity, destination, and object in view'. In Wellington, Inspector John Ellison detailed Detective Tudor Boddam to this task, which should 'take precedence of all other duty he may have in hand'. With the capital's harbour forts outside the city centre, his scrutiny required cooperation from the soldiers manning the fortifications. The military were, moreover, asked to extend their vigilant eye beyond tourists identified by police and to report all strangers 'loitering' in the vicinity of fortifications.[95]

Soon, the police spy-watching brief was further expanded to include monitoring the movements of *all* foreign tourists, wherever they went and whatever they seemed to be interested in. This remained manageable: antipodean vacationing was the province of small numbers of well-heeled elites, adventurers seeking health benefits, journalists reporting on the country's prototypal welfare state experiments, wealthy people visiting family, and suchlike. Most foreign travellers focused their interest on the world-famous Rotorua geothermal area. While on the surface this might be taken to indicate that they were genuinely travelling for reasons of pleasure or health, police operated on the assumption that any such visits might be a front for espionage.

In September 1904, to take one month as an example, Boddam tracked both a Russian journalist who had been investigating the colony's progressive reforms and 'Social Conditions' and a German officer who stated that he was on furlough in New Zealand for health reasons. While neither showed any interest in fortifications, the Wellington Inspector believed that the latter might be an enemy agent.[96] While potential spies were generally assumed to have patriotic motivations, the possibility of mercenary foreign agents (including perhaps New Zealanders) was also considered. So, too, was that of women spies or accomplices, including the wives and mistresses of male travellers. When Commissioner Tunbridge heard in 1902 that an American couple might be taking photographs around Rotorua 'for improper purpose', the local constable who handled surveillance was ordered to monitor them.[97]

The main potential targets of spying, however, remained harbours and their defensive fortifications. As well as the possibility of information on defence-related installations being collected for use in warfare, both the political police and military intelligence were alert to the potential for sabotage, including that of British naval vessels docked in New Zealand harbours. One such scare arose in April 1913 when the General Officer Commanding the Military Forces notified the Police Commissioner of secret information about a possible conspiracy to destroy the battlecruiser HMS *New Zealand*. This led to police working with naval intelligence to take preventive measures in the ports it was visiting.[98]

Sabotage from the left was also seen as a possibility. During the Great Strike, for example, Ellison obtained covertly gathered information about potential sabotage of Wellington's harbour facilities by saboteurs in boats, and placed men on fixed point surveillance duties. When they 'observed [men] moving about in boats in a suspicious manner', possibly engaging in efforts to damage the warship in the harbour, a launch patrol was implemented 'to chase off' any suspects in the vicinity of the wharves.[99]

As in the days of the New Zealand Wars, counter-espionage and anti-subversion measures would sometimes converge. Detectives and uniformed men in country districts, for example, watched out for connections between foreign spies and residents fomenting disloyalty. While the main risk was seen, naturally, to lie in German-origin communities, there were other potential threatscapes. During the time of the South African War in 1901, for example, information received from the United States led to police monitoring of the movements of a couple believed to have monies at their disposal provided from the secret service fund of President Paul Kruger of the Transvaal. They allegedly intended to distribute funding to discontented sections of the population, especially those who might be persuaded to sow discord against the British. Their mission in New Zealand supposedly included an effort to liaise with disaffected Māori communities, although no such approaches were observed by the police watchers.[100]

While detectives sometimes investigated the possible intersection of foreign espionage and local subversion, most police operational work remained focused internally, especially on organised labour, socialist movements and anti-militarists. While such movements were often headed by immigrant or visiting theoreticians and 'agitators', their activities were not funded or supported from outside, bar the occasional open donation of money to a cause or organisation. The political police were perhaps fortunate that, generally, the left opposition to the existing order of things was trying to *win over* the population, its proselytising work taking place in halls or other meeting places that were relatively easy to monitor. However dominated by overseas ideas they might be, they were far easier to monitor than inconspicuous foreign spies.

Assessment

Towards 1914, Germany and Japan were seen as palpable threats to the security of New Zealand, whose authorities expanded their anti-espionage measures and contingency planning accordingly. In 1912, for example, Major-General Alexander Godley, Commandant of the New Zealand Military Forces, had plans drawn up for an invasion of German-controlled Samoa in the event of Anglo-German hostilities.[101] That the Police Force seemingly did not find any spies may in part be because the detectives concentrated their surveillance on foreign visitors rather than residents. But the fact that they were watching for espionage, and made this known (sometimes inadvertently), may have served to discourage any German New Zealanders who might have been willing to provide information useful for enemy war plans to the German consuls or other agents.

While fear of Germany's intentions grew, so too did the perceived threat to state security from New Zealand's labour and socialist movements. Their militancy increased as the broad consensus of support for the arbitration system frayed. This was now decreasingly able to satisfy workers' aspirations, which had been heightened in part because of the very establishment of the system late in the previous century.[102] While potential foreign spies or collaborators were few, the numbers of socialists and trade unionists were far larger, and their voices strident. Accordingly, watching left-wing organisations and movements formed the great bulk of the work of the detectives and other police who were given responsibilities for political surveillance. When labour and socialist militancy accelerated in 1912 and 1913, the accumulated stock of intelligence in Police files helped to direct covert surveillance over the movement. This played a significant role in crushing militant labour and its allies.

In doing so, the state deployed harshly coercive measures that harked back to methods resonant of the colonial frontier. As we have noted, in times of high stakes the state's proclivities move towards not just greater overt coercion but also actions of dubious or actual extra-legality. Intelligence gathering, already operating in the blurred spaces between legality and illegality, could easily slip into a strategy of (as critics at the time put it) 'lawless law'. While this might seem problematic for any police force pledged to uphold the rule of law in a democratic country, the subcultural norms of everyday policing around the globe encompassed activities that were not legal but seemed necessary (a proclivity that endures). Intimidation or assault of members of the public or prisoners to extract a confession, for reasons of summary or exemplary justice, was common even in the most consent-based police institutions – albeit at the lower end of the scale compared to countries where the law allowed much or meant little.

Many scholars have noted this endemic disjuncture between official pronouncements on the one hand and, on the other, the coercive and often violent reality experienced at police hands by those who, for whatever reason, challenge the general codes of behaviour that police were paid to enforce.[103] As an official historian of New Zealand policing has noted, even by the 1950s the 'policeman was still to a large degree expected to maintain his authority with his fists', whatever the Peelian rules of police behaviour might say.[104]

Such daily micro-coercions set the stage for macro-coercion in times of socio-political crisis for the state. In the industrial turmoil of 1912–13, authorisation for rule-bending and outright violence emanated from the very top of the Police and political hierarchies, which worked closely together. As Solicitor-General John Salmond's biographer notes, a 'consistent theme' in his subject's career was that legality ended 'where the State's peril began'.[105] For Salmond, whose headship of the Crown Law Office spanned the turbulent decade of 1910–20, 'extrajudicial force may lawfully supersede the ordinary process and course of law, whenever it is needed for the protection of the state and the public order against illegal violence'.[106] Salmond's contemporary, Police Commissioner Cullen, shared and applied such perspectives, even if he was rather careless about the caveat that extra-legal state coercion should be oriented towards 'illegal violence'. Hands-on policing was at several removes from the world of legal niceties.

The capacity to move well into the blurred outer limits of the law, and beyond, was always on the agenda within any threatened polity. This, of course, needed to be handled especially delicately in a democracy that prided itself on the rule of law. 'Plausible deniability' could be invoked by politicians under the convention increasingly being cemented into place as a result of the application of Peelian principles: that ministers did not interfere in police 'operations'. Under the umbrella of police autonomy, then, the state accommodated extra-legal policing methods, including those used by the political detectives and other watchers. Such methods were most especially used in times of crises in the defence of the realm, and their potential use underpinned the decision to engineer a decisive showdown with militant labour in 1913. This was a dangerous strategy. The ensuing confrontation between employers and the state on one hand, and workers and their allies on the other – the most serious ever experienced in New Zealand – threatened to segue into a full-blown insurrection. A prominent newspaper joined many other commentators warning of the possibility of 'bloody Civil War'.[107] The government's refusal to seek a negotiated outcome, and its willingness to invoke short-term (and extreme) disorder in the name of long-term order, concerned a number of people in high places, up to and including Commander of the Military Forces Colonel E. S. Heard.[108]

While some police were among those cavilling at their Commissioner's complicity in provoking rather than preventing disorder, the information gathered by the surveilling detectives played a key role in the containment of the strike and the insurrectionary proclivities which had been unleashed by the showdown. From the state's perspective, the crushing of militant labour in 1913, and the quiescence of the political and industrial left in its aftermath, had satisfactorily addressed enormous security problems. It had quashed politico-industrial activities which both challenged the existing distribution of wealth and power and had the potential to snowball into serious attempts to overturn the existing order of things. More broadly, it had also rallied conservative support to counterbalance a mood of social discontent and unrest which had the potential to sap New Zealanders' willingness to fully support the state in the event of the war that seemed ever closer.

The surveilling gaze of those watchers assigned to political policing in the early twentieth century had assisted the Force to deploy both anti-seditionary and less overtly political laws as weapons of suppression. The intensification of surveillance during the disturbances of 1912–13 had consolidated the NZPF's platform of knowledge about dissent, one which was in turn ready to be built upon when war was declared in 1914. This is not to say that the intelligence cycle in pre-war times was, by modern standards, subtle or sophisticated. The political police tended to lump protesters of many and varied hues into a credulous recruiting pool for subversives seeking to overthrow the political economy. This perspective was in part a reflection of lack of understanding and/or empathy with left-wing attitudes and stances. It indicated, too, the surveillers' difficulties in differentiating between means and ends, or their disinclination to do so. While most advocates of a society based on the socialisation of the means of production, distribution and exchange, for example, rejected violent or undemocratic ways of achieving it, their surveillers placed them on a continuum that ended in revolution – a notion that the street violence of the Great Strike reinforced. Such blanket perceptions by the surveillers of the surveilled was neither new nor quick to change in the ensuing decades.

Conclusion

In 1907, when New Zealand formally changed its status from colony to Dominion, its mechanisms for ensuring the defence of the realm continued operating within an Imperial context as if nothing had changed – essentially because it had not. In the country itself, the surveillance of suspected enemies of the state continued to rest primarily with the detectives of the NZPF. At this time, those policemen with political responsibilities were intensifying their monitoring of the left-wing component of the population and, to a much lesser degree given the few numbers potentially involved, watching out for enemy spies and collaborators. They believed that the people they identified as seditionary or subversive could readily influence significant sections of society into challenging the fundamentals of the existing order, especially in times of socio-political tension. This provided them with the rationale for watching anyone involved in progressive causes.

The role of the political detectives in countering perceived challenges to the state and its interests was assisted by their location within an institution that could follow up their surveillance with coercion. Thus, many 'agitators', strikers, orators, picketers and the like, together with their supporters, were subjected to exemplary punishment on the basis of police observations, especially in times of politico-industrial tension or strife. The most dramatic such disturbances, in 1912 and 1913, were exacerbated by decisions made at the highest levels of state (including the Police Commissioner) precisely to provide the conditions for a definitive defeat of the labour movement.

It is hard to escape the conclusion that the surveillance net thrown over the broad labour, socialist and progressive movement in early twentieth-century New Zealand, and its frequent coercive follow-up, posed a challenge to the much-touted official principles of freedom of belief and impartial justice – even if the population did not know about it at the time. In the event, the first 14 years of the twentieth century saw the state's covert surveillers establishing a firm foundation for the massive surveillance exercise facing them at the outbreak of the First World War. In this, their main targets remained those on the left, although surveillance of the German community, naturally, intensified.

Chapter Three:
Surveillance and Suppression in Wartime, 1914–1918

Introduction

On 5 August 1914, New Zealand's Governor announced that a state of war existed between the British Empire and Germany. Over the following four years the Dominion committed itself to a war effort that resulted in the mobilisation of tens of thousands of men, the passage of legislation providing extraordinary powers to the political executive, and the application of many highly coercive measures to its population. Moreover, the need to impose wartime controls and monitor resistance to them meant the surveilling tools developed in the modern era were now to have even greater application. This great increase in surveillance in New Zealand paralleled similar developments elsewhere and were described, at the end of the twentieth century, as 'the greatest intelligence explosion in history'.[1] Much wartime intelligence aimed to gain battlefield advantage or to influence grand strategy – the seminal example being the United States' entry into the war after London released an intercepted and decoded German diplomatic cable (the Zimmermann telegram) proposing a transfer of American territory to Mexico. However, all belligerent states also rapidly developed their domestic surveillance capacities to protect and enhance the war effort on the home front.[2]

The four years of war can be seen as a pivotal period between the intelligence developments of the nineteenth century and the much greater reach and sophistication of twentieth-century surveillance. A vast wartime expansion of state control brought official intrusion into many private lives and curtailed a number of hard-won civil liberties under the rationale of security.[3] The rights of individuals to take dissenting stances had always come under pressure during socio-political emergencies, most recently during the wave of industrial action prior to the war, but the scope and extent of such encroachments were now far greater. In the process, key aspects of New Zealand's paradisal values of freedom and fairness were compromised. The enormous expansion of state incursions into people's lives that was integral to its war effort, moreover, created a precedent for greater state penetration of civilian lives.

Overview

The early months of the conflict were a time of heightened anxiety, with one Member of Parliament observing 'a general feeling of insecurity throughout the country'.[4] A major point of concern focused on communities of German and Austro-Hungarian descent or nationality which might harbour pockets of disloyalty. Beliefs that 'blood' determined loyalty were widespread among those arguing that such communities should be regulated: 'We cannot afford to trust any person with German blood in his veins ... While Germany and Britain are at war the place for all Germans is Germany, failing that ... a concentration camp.'[5] Other commentators, however, noted that such communities (some of which dated back to the early years of the colony) had generally 'so closely identified themselves with the Dominion's life and nationality that there can be no question of their fidelity'.[6]

Rumours of enemy spies and agents circulated, and numerous concerned citizens reported suspicious activities – potential acts of espionage, sabotage or illicit signalling. A particular fear in the early weeks of the war was the possibility that enemy agents were communicating with German warships at large in the Pacific by means of the new, and therefore enigmatic, medium of radio. A Wellington newspaper report of September 1914 reflected public anxiety about the apparent enemy within:

> It is rumoured that undecipherable code messages picked up at New Zealand wireless stations are discovered now to have been sent by a naturalised German holding an office of responsibility in a New Zealand Government department, and that a brother of this man's (also a civil servant) left the Dominion suddenly just before the outbreak of war. This rumour is exceedingly serious. If there is truth in it, we are menaced by a very great danger. There is evidence enough of the ubiquity of German spies in Europe.[7]

The arrest of naturalised German Hugo Sewald, later that month, for the possession of illegally acquired wireless equipment heightened popular fears, with one newspaper headlining the story 'Suspected German Spy'. Sewald was charged, convicted and ultimately detained.[8]

Also in September, many newspapers reported that there had been an attack on the telegraph cable at Lyall Bay, Wellington. Sentries had reportedly fired on saboteurs attempting to cut the cable before pursuing them through the sandhills.[9] A number of the same papers, however, did not publish a rebuttal of enemy involvement in the incident by the Commandant of the New Zealand Military Forces, General Alexander Godley: 'the individuals at whom the sentries fired were endeavouring to hoax them, or were loafers who got frightened when challenged and ran away'.[10] In May 1915, with the benefit of hindsight, another newspaper could ridicule the way that 'the fun had commenced' the previous August: 'There were furtive masonic signs passing between Germans in the street, there were winking signals from lonely beaches, and on every hand the Germans were a planning and a caballing.'[11] But at the time the fears were palpable, stoked by overimaginative reporters.

Amidst this mood of insecurity, the government implemented a variety of regulations and practices to identify, assess and counter threats to the state and its interests. Many built on those in place before 1914, and some were developed in conjunction with New Zealand's allies. Others were matters of physical security at home. As a safeguard against sabotage, for example, Territorial soldiers were posted at key sites such as radio stations, cable-landing points and railway bridges and tunnels, and defensive positions were placed under heavier protection. Intensive round-the-clock coverage of such facilities prevailed through the first month of war, and the country's coastal forts remained on high alert for months afterwards.[12]

As we have seen, the increase in international tension before 1914 had led to expanded efforts by the New Zealand state to surveil people potentially associated with espionage by enemy powers. Fortified by the fact that no spy networks had been uncovered during the pre-war years, the authorities tended towards scepticism of a great deal of loose talk on such matters. On the other hand, they could not afford to ignore reports suggesting suspicious activities. The four German consuls stationed in New Zealand were obvious priorities for attention. All had their records seized, with Karl Joosten, the consul in Christchurch, briefly detained by police after an allegation that he had tried to buy waterproof clothing possibly destined for the German military.[13] All four, and those associated with them, were placed under scrutiny.

The day after the declaration of war all citizens of enemy nations were placed under strict police observation, and even policemen sceptical about the existence of widespread disloyalty had little choice but to follow regulations by at least going through the motions of surveilling those with a Central Powers genealogy.[14] Various residents or visitors who were members of the military reserve of enemy powers were arrested, along with German officials captured when New Zealand invaded Samoa. Broader groupings of 'enemy aliens' – persons born in a country at war with the British Empire, including those who had been naturalised as British citizens – were registered and monitored.[15] Individuals deemed to be 'disaffected' or 'dangerous' were rounded up and interned in specialised facilities for some or all of the war. An Alien Enemies Commission was established in mid-1915 to investigate disloyalty in German and other communities. Some measures targeted specific individuals. An extreme example was the 1915 Alien Enemy Teachers Act, which was passed to remove Professor George von Zedlitz from his chair in modern languages after Victoria University College resisted popular and political pressure to sack him.[16] In 1919 some 450 were still being held in internment.[17]

Security and surveillance measures over the country's communication networks were quickly implemented at the start of the war, and would come to affect everyone in the country, from those at the top of the machinery of government to the humblest of residents. Specific rules for ministers, for example, dictated the permissible content and transmission of their telegraphs.[18] Private access to wireless communication was seen as a security risk, and telegraphy sets were confiscated for the duration of the conflict. Among those affected were the president of the wireless association and the Chinese consul's son, whose wireless apparatus transmitted signals to a toy boat: experts had reported that the device could be adapted for nefarious purposes.[19]

Other security measures were directed towards policing printed information and telegraphic communications. Early regulations focused on preventing the distribution of material of military value to the enemy (such as troop movements and shipping details) but, perhaps inevitably, crept towards wider concerns, such as banning reports likely to cause public panic.[20] The censorship of news received from overseas by cable telegraphy was seen as particularly significant, with several filters at work before information could reach the newspapers. The great bulk of cabled news material received by New Zealand's United Press Agency had been reviewed and passed by the Official Press Bureau in Britain, and a similar sifting process occurred at the cable lay-station in Australia. In New Zealand itself a censorship regime to vet all information transmitted across its borders was quickly established, with both civilian and military input, on the British model. A telegraphic censor presided over the monitoring of international telegrams, assisted by a small number of staff in Wellington and at cable-landing stations in Auckland and Nelson.[21]

Restrictions were similarly imposed on newspaper reporting. While the mainstream press was generally compliant, it sometimes tested the limits of what authorities considered acceptable. Regulations 'gradually increased in severity and in political rather than military significance'.[22] In July 1915 regulations empowered authorities to ban the sale or possession of any book considered 'injurious to the public interest in respect of the present war'; prohibit any moving picture representing or relating to the war; prevent the printing of 'any information likely to interfere with the recruiting, training, discipline or administration' of troops; and forbid incitements 'by word, writing or otherwise' to violence, lawlessness, disorder or seditious intent.[23]

Determining which words or deeds might breach restrictive Acts and regulations developed in an ad hoc fashion, and state sanctions were regularly added in response to circumstances. To take one example, action was taken soon after an MP railed against the importation and circulation of IWW pamphlets and newspapers, calling for 'immediate steps under the Post Office Act to prevent the circulation through the post of the harmful publications in connection with the propaganda of this anarchical society – a society which openly preached sabotage'.[24] On 20 September 1915, accordingly, new regulations were brought down to prohibit 'the importation into New Zealand of the newspapers called *Direct Action* and *Solidarity*, and all other printed matter published by or on behalf of the society known as "The Industrial Workers of the World"'. Later, other titles were regularly added to the 'Prohibited Literature' list, and vigilant members of the public helped police track down people circulating such material.[25]

Controls expanded in the context of a developing illiberal mood towards individuals and sections of society deemed to be 'shirkers'. Staunchly loyalist sections of the population, in particular, were escalating their demands for the sanctioning of potential fifth-columnists, militant labour and pacifists who they argued were effectively aiding the enemy by undermining social commitment to the war effort. Towards the end of 1915, in the context of this deepening public intolerance, police intensified their monitoring of the circulation of pamphlets with pacificist messages such as *Christianity and War*.[26] Other censorship related to an air of moral revivalism that developed over the war years. All manner of social behaviours were restricted, including the favourite male pastime of drinking alcohol; 'shouting' rounds of drinks was prohibited in 1916, and six o'clock closing of all pubs and liquor outlets was introduced the following year. These measures reflected the efforts both of moral campaigners and the National Efficiency Board, which presented alcohol production and drunkenness as impediments to a fuller war effort.

From the beginning of the war, it had been the New Zealand Police Force's responsibility to monitor cinemas with a view to ensuring that 'objectionable pictures' were not shown. Pressure groups helped ensure that police took their task of surveilling movies seriously as part of their brief to uphold public morality. In March 1916 the defence minister gained permission to censor films which might hamper the war effort in areas such as recruiting. The most significant development for regulating the moving image occurred that year with the Cinematograph-film Censorship Act, which banned films that had not been approved by a government censor, whose brief was to prohibit the showing of any film 'that is against public order and decency' or 'undesirable in the public interest'. In September 1916 W. Jolliffe was appointed as film censor, and set about banning some films, cutting scenes from others, and imposing age limits on viewers where he saw it as necessary. This development lifted the burden of assessment off police personnel, whose responsibility was now to monitor movie theatres, in association with the film censorship office, for compliance with censorship decisions.[27]

Public lectures were similarly monitored to ensure their messages were appropriate. Even renowned English war correspondent Ellis Ashmead-Bartlett, notable for his dispatches celebrating the heroism of 'ANZAC' soldiers, was subjected to severe restrictions during an April 1916 lecture tour through Australasia. Before he commenced his journey, he was instructed to make no criticism of the two countries' war effort or military leaders, to invoke no '[i]nvidious comparisons' between them, and to present no reference to their censorship regimes. To ensure compliance on his New Zealand leg, he was accompanied (as an official report put it) by 'a very capable officer who never left him from the moment that he arrived to the time he left'.[28]

The most radical state intrusion into citizens' personal lives, however, was the monitoring and censoring of the country's postal system. This vast enterprise technically fell under military control, but it was mostly conducted by postal service and recruited civilian staff. In a society in which letters played a highly significant role – in 1917, between five to six million letters and postcards were processed weekly – postal censorship constituted an intensive penetration of private life. Large amounts of inward correspondence were opened and examined, most of them passed for sending on but also a good many subjected to further investigation. In the process, information in them might be copied into files and the intended recipients interviewed; a portion were confiscated and never reached their destination.[29]

As the war continued and the war effort escalated, intelligence operations adjusted in type and intensity accordingly. The introduction of conscription in mid-1916, for example, added new complications and further regulations. The Police took on major responsibility for locating thousands of men trying to evade call-up (some of the most reliable estimates put these at up to 8500 men over the duration of the war, although others more than halve that figure).[30] Whatever the numbers of defaulters and their reasons for refusing to serve, the effort to apprehend them was a difficult task, with many lying low with friends and relatives and large numbers seeking sanctuary in remote or unsettled regions – especially areas with a history of opposition to authority – or even attempting to slip out of the country.[31] The most difficult communities to penetrate, apart from some Māori regions, lay in the South Island's West Coast. In such close-knit areas, the policemen themselves were tracked. When Detective Broberg arrived in Westport, for instance, word went around town within an hour. In such circumstances the detectives often needed to call on the assistance of other officials, such as inspectors of factories or other members of the Labour Department.[32]

Not only were opponents of government policy placed under ever greater scrutiny, but so too were members of the public spreading discontent about the conduct of the war or its impact. The government's move towards conscription was vigorously opposed by a faction of political labour who sought to bring about a mass strike, echoing that of 1913, to begin in 1917. This campaign was entwined with the foundation of the Labour Party in mid-1916, the product of an alliance of various political and industrial currents with opposition to conscription forming a unifying issue.[33]

In turn, the government expanded regulations defining the scope of 'seditious utterances', aiming to stifle anti-conscription activists. From late 1916 such utterances included exciting 'disaffection against His Majesty or the Government of the United Kingdom, or of New Zealand, or of any other part of His Majesty's Dominions'; promoting 'violence, lawlessness, or disorder whether in New Zealand or in any other part of His Majesty's Dominions'; inciting class ill-will; interfering with recruiting or war production; and discouraging the prosecution of the war to a victorious conclusion.[34] The authorities drew up contingency plans to meet the industrial strike planned to protest conscription. In December 1916 Defence Minister James Allen noted:

> We have arranged for horses and forage, and at very short notice we could secure a fair number of special constables . . . We are hopeful that preparations and a knowledge of them will make the labour people see that they had better remain quiet . . . For my part I am very hopeful that we shall avoid a strike altogether.

As things turned out, a 'go-slow' in the mines and on the waterfront was pursued in lieu of more radical action, and the state used a combination of negotiations and concessions to appease some while police targeted militant leaders with surveillance, raids and arrests under anti-sedition regulations. As 1916 ended, Allen noted that anti-conscription activists were 'all pretty well muzzled by the new regulations with regard to seditious utterances'.[35]

As the war progressed, then, surveillance measures increased, although the main targets tended to change with the shifting nature of the conflict. The search for German spies and sympathisers, for example, was soon mostly superseded by the surveilling of dissenters. Increasing public dissatisfaction around the unequal distribution of war-related sacrifices, and the intractable social tensions incumbent upon mass mobilisation, added to the surveillers' repertoire – as did pockets of sympathy for Irish republicanism (especially after the Easter Rebellion in April 1916) and worsening sectarian strife between Protestant and Catholic elements. All such developments threatened unrest, and therefore held a capacity to disrupt the war effort. News of the Bolshevik Revolution in November 1917, along with calls for a 'compromise' peace settlement, also became major concerns. Māori tribes that discouraged their young men from signing up, pending redress of their grievances against the Crown, formed another surveillance target; when conscription was applied to one of those iwi, Waikato, from early 1918 its defaulters needed to be tracked down.[36] Similarly, the application of conscription to Pākehā husbands and fathers in early 1918 stirred radical rhetoric that was seen as destabilising.

Restrictions on what could be published also expanded, with concerns that imported or home-grown material might harm the war effort by feeding sectarian tensions, labour militancy and other points of social fragmentation. The censorship of published material peaked in July 1918, when Cabinet instituted a system of prior-restraint censorship by which specified publications required the approval of a censor appointed by the attorney-general before they could be printed.[37]

The surveillance and suppression regime that permeated life in wartime New Zealand did not end with the Armistice on 11 November 1918. Both internees and those serving time for hampering the war effort in various ways remained incarcerated for some time, for example. Postal censorship, too, continued until November 1920. In the longer term, restrictions on moving images remained in place, as did (for 50 years) the wartime measure of banning the purchasing of alcohol beyond 6 p.m. More broadly, wartime monitoring of greater sections of the population than ever before in the history of the country left a legacy of state surveillance that did not fully recede.

Agencies

The NZPF continued to be the primary instrument of state security during the war. Policemen were the principal surveillers on the streets and in the countryside. Although carrying out numerous extra tasks as a result of the heightened demands of wartime, the force continued to deploy its existing methods of surveillance and analysis. But the policy and operations which flowed from finished intelligence were now more often developed in conjunction with other officials. The ministers (who, from August 1915, formed part of a coalition of Reform and the Liberals) became more closely involved with surveillance policy as well. Police powers were enhanced from time to time to tackle specific measures, such as supervising enemy aliens – a category that included, after May 1916, New Zealand–born spouses of people born in enemy nations. New rules and regulations would be brought down as necessary to augment such police duties as watching for saboteurs, suppressing pacifist and socialist opposition to the war, and monitoring dissident activity that might pose a threat to the state and its interests.[38]

Most enhanced surveillance duties took place under the umbrella of the 1914 War Regulations Act and its later amendments, which empowered the political executive to prohibit acts deemed 'injurious to the public safety, the defence of New Zealand, or the effective conduct of the military or naval operations of His Majesty during the present war'.[39] Such regulations could be made without reference to Parliament, and overrode any pre-existing legislation which conflicted with them.[40]

Quite apart from such new tools and tasks of surveillance and control, police continued to watch and discipline as before the war, using methods that were time-honoured if not necessarily within their legal powers. The way in which they conducted their war effort was partly shaped by the background and philosophies of the two wartime Commissioners. John Cullen's nickname 'Czar Cullen' reflected both an imposing presence (rigid posture, penetrating eyes) and the temperament of a strict disciplinarian. His methods at Waihī in 1912 and on the streets in 1913 reflected a visceral opposition to any challenges to the political, social or economic status quo in New Zealand and a temperament inclined to punish transgressors.

For Commissioner Cullen, transgression meant virtually any deviation from the social norm. In 1916, when he was told that naturalised Viennese doctor Theodore Endletsberger was not only pro-German but also 'continually boasting about the number of British women he has seduced in New Zealand', the Commissioner responded that '[h]e is evidently a man who should be at home among his brother Huns in Belgium'. He was to be carefully watched and all his 'sayings and doings' reported to Police Headquarters. Such heavy surveillance led to his internment on Motuihe Island, where he stayed until after the war.[41] Cullen's disciplinarianism was similarly directed at policemen who did not share his outlook on such matters as how to treat enemy aliens, anti-militarists and opponents of conscription. Indeed, an informal system of spying within the Police Force, conducted by those close to him, supplemented normal police disciplinary mechanisms.[42]

In his coercive approach to those he saw as hampering the war effort, Cullen was backed by Alexander Herdman, the hard-line minister in charge of policing for most of the war. The situation changed, however, when Cullen retired in November 1916. He had reached retirement age that May, but his period of office was extended in the context of developing ways of best enforcing conscription and other measures. His disciplinary approach to foreignness now led to his appointment as commissioner of aliens, which empowered him to closely watch immigrant populations and, among other things, enforce compulsory work schemes upon sections of the community such as Dalmatian gum-diggers.[43]

With Cullen's social control and surveillance system firmly aligned with meeting wartime conditions, Herdman could now look towards a force attuned to the return of peace. His new Commissioner, John O'Donovan, who took office in December 1916, was known as a moderniser who had built a reputation as 'a remarkably able and fair-minded man' – 'one of the most gentlemanly officers in the Public Service'.[44] This key appointment marked a return to the upwards trajectory of Peelianism and professionalisation which had been somewhat dented by the pre-war and wartime national emergencies. Commissioner O'Donovan sought enhanced public consent for policing even in the difficult circumstances of wartime, including by minimising the use of coercion against the public. He would sum up his philosophy as follows: 'We keep a baton, but seldom use it; when we do, its application should be scrupulously apportioned to the need.'[45]

Reimbuing this philosophy within the NZPF was not an easy task in the wake of Cullen's punitive approach to actual and perceived transgressors. The coercive voice still held considerable sway at a time when the government was increasing rather than lowering restrictions on social behaviour. The surveilling net had accordingly been widening, with new sections of the community coming to police attention and, sometimes, apprehension. Moreover, there were practical reasons for a hesitant official and police take-up of O'Donovan's call for a shift in emphasis. His ascendancy coincided with a downturn in police numbers and expertise which stretched resources over and above the strains imposed by wartime. The focus now tended to be getting the job done, day by day, rather than adjusting the overall approach to the police role in social control.

The problem had arisen from experienced policemen resigning to go to war, the best efforts of police leadership to retain them having failed in the face of the government's need for trusted and disciplined men at the front. Able replacements were scarce, given that most young men of suitable capacity were also serving in the armed forces. A September 1916 provision for temporary constables allowed men who would not normally have been accepted into the force for health, intelligence or other reasons to be enrolled, along with retired policemen. At the end of that year, the quality of recruits further lowered when the Training Depot closed and recruiting men of military age was barred. These developments had consequences for the work of the political police.

One prospect of extra personnel lay in the recruitment of women. Women's rights advocates, moral campaigners and, eventually, parts of the labour movement had persistently advocated that the Police take on auxiliary assistance from women, who would be able to provide a combination of patrol and detective work. Such calls began early in the conflict, inspired by the 'women patrols' implemented in wartime Britain and elsewhere. Its advocates argued that women could fill roles not adequately undertaken by men, such as watching over the morals of women and girls in danger of being led astray in the altered social conditions of wartime: 'women to save women from falling'. An increase in 'fallen women', went one key argument, would lower public morale, spread venereal disease amongst the troops and workforce, and hamper the war effort in many other ways besides.

After strong opposition from the Commissioner and his senior staff, however, in 1916 the idea of women police was rejected by the government. Police objections had included the argument that women would not be able to keep secrets, something especially important in plain-clothes work. Nevertheless, the campaign for women police continued and, in the event, a minor victory was gained in 1917: the four Police Matrons employed in the main cities' central police stations were given assistants able to carry out plain-clothes work 'as helps' to constables. Towards the end of the war, too, women's 'health patrols' were established with a wide-ranging social-control brief under 'social hygiene' legislation. But the swearing-in of women to the New Zealand Police Force had to await a second global conflict.[46]

Partly because of the influx of men who would normally have been regarded as unsuitable, as well as Cullen's legacy, the new police leadership had regularly to instruct its men to be mindful of people's rights under the law. Given the deeply interventionist nature of the wartime regulations, however, this did not necessarily make much difference to the treatment of those targeted for surveillance or subjected to discipline. As we have noted, all 'consensual' forces have subcultural operating procedures which use methods that are dubious (such as entrapment) or illegal (such as physically rough treatment), and the exigencies of the wartime emergency had exacerbated the use of such methods on those considered disloyal to country and Empire. While police leaderships know about the use of such tactics, they operate on the basis of 'plausible deniability' in the event of any public scandal emerging. Such an eventuality was less likely in wartime in any case, with the press anxious not to appear disloyal to the forces of order.

Police surveillance duties were, from the beginning of the war, interlaced with those of a variety of other New Zealand institutions, most notably military police and intelligence. Such liaisons and linkages could have an impact on police approaches. Close cooperation with the army and the New Zealand section of the Royal Navy, for example, meant engaging with forces that operated under a much lesser degree of public scrutiny and accountability. Their methods could be, accordingly, careless of citizens' rights. The trajectory of wartime emergency measures meant that policemen were more inclined to be influenced by such methods than vice versa, although the presence of police could prevent serious inroads into illegal behaviour.[47]

The fact that policing and military forces had residual statutory and practical linkages, however, encouraged cooperation between the two services. Throughout the wartime years, initiatives to share information came from both sides. But military requests of the Police dominated, because of greater need – to help the army increase its rate of enrolments, for example, or to ensure that the new soldiers were loyal and reliable. Military deserters were hunted by both services, and friends and families found to have harboured them were prosecuted.[48] But there were inevitable frictions. From time to time, for example, the defence authorities complained that police were insufficiently rigorous in their vetting of recruits for the army, with the result (for example) that men of 'strong enemy sentiments' had been allowed to enrol in the ranks.

Commissioner Cullen had tended to uphold such complaints. In mid-1916 he reiterated to police staff that any applicant for the armed forces who was of 'alien enemy parentage or descent' needed to be investigated for 'the least doubt as to [his] loyalty . . . as well as that of his parents, relatives and associates'. Failure to undertake 'the most exhaustive enquiries', he stressed, was a dismissible offence. The results of all such enquiries within each Police district were now to be sent to Police Headquarters; a centralised record of perceived disloyalists was in the making.[49] When the decision had been made to introduce military conscription, the Commissioner agreed to have his men investigate any eligible man suspected by the military of disloyalty, for whatever reasons. With the vetting workload increasing greatly as a result, both police and military looked for more efficient ways of scrutinising both potential soldiers and groups targeted for special attention. In late 1916, for example, the Chief of General Staff requested that the force compile a register of 'Jugo-Slav men' of military age, together with a list of 'prominent men among the Slavs who can be depended upon to advise as to the character, loyalty etc., of their fellow countrymen'.[50]

In addition to long-established intelligence-sharing connections with Australia, the New Zealand political police liaised with security personnel in the Imperial metropole, elsewhere within the Empire and sometimes outside it. In the metropole, intelligence agencies had rapidly expanded during the first year of the war and spurred increased interest in intelligence cooperation across the Empire. In August 1915, 'arrangements for the interchange of confidential and secret intelligence' between the Central Special Intelligence Bureau in London and the antipodean intelligence authorities were initiated.[51] Eventually, in late 1916, the Australians established their own Special Intelligence Bureau, a counter-espionage agency which operated as part of the Imperial system and also came to handle counter-subversion. Australian security arrangements were further reinforced with the creation of the Commonwealth Police in 1917.[52]

In New Zealand, the watch for spies and subversives generally took place within existing structures. The British-led initiative to tighten intelligence coordination with the Dominions in August 1915, however, resulted in Colonel Charles Gibbon being 'appointed the officer to undertake the work' in New Zealand.[53] Gibbon had arrived in the country in April 1914, from a career in intelligence in India, and had been made the wartime Chief of General Staff. From this position Gibbon liaised with all institutions with state responsibilities for security, including the Police and the small Royal Navy Intelligence Centre which had been established in Wellington in 1914. This office 'managed New Zealand's World War 1 [signals] intercept activities, reporting to both London and Melbourne' and oversaw port security, searching for subversive men and literature on the wharves and in docked ships.[54]

Gibbon's role extended beyond oversight of military-based intelligence and liaison with his home country. He was allocated, too, the leading position in New Zealand's wartime censorship when he assumed the position of Chief of the General Staff. As chief censor he was assisted by senior postal officials as deputies: H. W. Harrington, with responsibility for cable traffic, and Walter Tanner in charge of post and telegraph censorship.[55] Censorship systems in the event of war had been discussed in pre-war meetings of the Committee of Imperial Defence, but arrangements had reached only initial stages by August 1914.[56] When war began, therefore, a series of measures were quickly implemented under the terms of the 1908 Post and Telegraph Act and the War Regulations Act 1914. While police would continue to open some mail of their own accord, the new system was to be located within the postal administration, which was equipped to undertake the vast efforts required for blanket coverage of any inwards and outwards mail likely to be suspect. Under Governor Lord Liverpool's authority, for example, warrants were issued permitting the opening and examining of outward mail addressed to people in enemy countries, and to people or companies on a 'Black List' kept by the British War Office.[57] In the exigencies of war, diplomatic communications were not exempt. Evidence exists, within three weeks after the outbreak of war, of letters addressed to the Austrian Consulate, and doubtless other consulates as well, being seized and analysed.[58]

Means of intercepting mail headed for or leaving private addresses within New Zealand were also quickly in place, and these were systematised under regulations issued on 17 December 1914. Officials could now, for example, prohibit the delivery of correspondence to persons or firms in New Zealand or elsewhere named in warrants under the postmaster-general's hand, with such letters being sent on to military authorities. A main postal censorship office was established in Wellington's General Post Office, but mail was also examined in Auckland, Wellington, Christchurch, Dunedin, Devonport, internment camps on Motuihe Island and Somes (now Matiu/Somes) Island, Nelson, Bluff and, after its occupation, Samoa.[59] These operations saw specialist equipment employed to facilitate the opening, copying and resealing of mail, including electric irons, carbon paper and gummed strips.[60]

The whole operation came under the ultimate control of the Defence Department and was deemed to be part of the 'military intelligence' system, given that its principal purpose was to prevent the spread of information harmful to the war effort. Although all items handled by the postal service were potentially liable to monitoring, the limits of what the system could review imposed hard constraints. Accordingly, mail addressed to hostile and neutral countries was examined on a routine basis, while internal mail and that from other countries was checked much more selectively. As lists of those whose mail should be regularly monitored were compiled, based on a great deal of intelligence from the Police Force and other authorities, the system developed into a surveillance tool with a broad, politically based definition of what was harmful.[61]

While all liaison with police and other agencies needed to go via Gibbon, in keeping with military hierarchy, the daily work of the postal censorship system was carried out by civilians working with Tanner, who had been appointed deputy chief postal censor. Initially, university staff and experts in foreign languages were appointed to conduct the work and were paid at piecework rates. These arrangements, however, resulted in considerable expenses and were reformed in October 1914.[62] Thereafter eight full-time assistant censors, distributed across the four chief centres, supervised teams of salaried Post and Telegraph clerks appointed to review letters in English, and the secretarial services of the department were utilised as well.[63] Select experts in foreign languages and handwriting were brought in as required. One such expert was the British-born Ursula Tewsley, who was fluent in German, Italian, French, Dutch and Esperanto. Employed from the beginning of the war to review material confiscated from the German consuls, she also acted as an interpreter during cross-examinations of German naval prisoners.[64]

The censorship regime was an open operation, with an official stamp informing recipients that their mail had been reviewed by a military censor. This approach had the advantage of promoting self-censorship, since letter-writers would soon consider the consequences of what they wrote after seeing an official stamp informing them that their mail had been scrutinised. No correspondence was sacrosanct; postcards were scrutinised for hidden messages, and in January 1916 a peace activist noted in the *Maoriland Worker* that even his Christmas cards were being stamped as reviewed by a censor.[65] In some instances, however, mail was clandestinely reviewed within the secret world and left unstamped. Furthermore, not all intercepted letters were sent on to their destinations – some original letters, indeed, remain in the nation's archives.[66]

Information extracted from intercepted correspondence was passed on to various state institutions. Cases are detailed below, but such material informed many covert police and military surveillance operations, ranging from checking out possible spies to locating defaulters from military registration or service or suppressing banned literature. Intelligence was also exchanged with authorities outside the Dominion. Given the close societal linkages across the Tasman, the exchange of information between Australia and New Zealand was of especial significance.

In New Zealand, the size of the task, combined with the relatively small number of postal censors (by comparison, at the end of the war, the United Kingdom had 2000 postal censors each opening 'on average over 150 letters per day'), imposed logistical limits on what the New Zealand postal censorship could scrutinise.[67] Nonetheless, the scale of operations was huge. It has been calculated that over 1.2 million items (mostly letters, postcards and packages) were examined between August 1914 and November 1920. The same study calculates the monthly average of examined items as including some 19,000 letters to and from neutral countries, 930 letters to prisoners of war held by Allied powers and more than 3000 letters to and from internees in New Zealand.[68]

Besides the obvious logistical problems, others soon became apparent. Early in the war, for example, a problem arose in relation to the neutral United States. Wishing to minimise antagonisms in Anglo-American relations, the Imperial authorities instructed that mail to and from the United States was not to be subject to censorship. In March 1915, however, New Zealand sought clearance from Britain to intercept such mail: intelligence had revealed letters to and from America that could be detrimental to the Imperial war effort, such as trade-related information of possible value to the enemy or left-wing material questioning the cause or conduct of the war.[69] London demurred at this request, but after the issue was pressed, New Zealand's censorship practices were extended to United States mail that May.[70] In particular, incoming mail from American addresses linked with pacifist and anarchist causes was opened, and parcels of radical literature were intercepted and sometimes confiscated. Such interceptions continued after America's entry to the war in April 1917.[71]

The postal and other censors working under Gibbon's overarching command worked closely with police and other humint operators in New Zealand. Sigint practitioners, however, liaised mostly with sister agencies.[72] While signals intelligence fell under the military umbrella, the specialist knowledge about transmission held within the Post and Telegraph Department was vital. In the final weeks of peace in 1914, the British Admiralty had reviewed the capabilities of all the stations in the Imperial Wireless

Chain to intercept enemy radio communication. As soon as news that the Empire and Germany were at war arrived in New Zealand on 5 August, the Dominion's own stations had commenced signals intercept duties. The following day, Commander R. A. Newton, the Royal Navy's intelligence officer in Wellington, reported among other things that 'Wireless Telegrams' in German and Dutch were being intercepted and translated.[73]

Throughout the war, New Zealand's wireless stations were an integral component of a vast sigint effort to professionalise and systematise Imperial sigint. Their Post and Telegraph operators maintained a near-continuous 'wireless watch' at the Wellington and Awarua stations, as well as part-time listening at other stations. They intercepted radio signals from German ships and land stations, listened in to suspicious traffic between neutral stations and broadly monitored all wireless traffic within their radius.[74] Although the German authorities had sabotaged their radio station near Apia before New Zealand occupied Samoa late in August 1914, this had been quickly repaired. It recommenced operations on 19 October and was run by New Zealand signallers from the Post and Telegraph Department until the Admiralty took over two years later.[75]

At the beginning of the war, the immediate priority for Australasian sigint was to locate Vice-Admiral Maximilian Reichsgraf von Spee's German East Asia Squadron, which had steamed from its base in Tsingtao and was now at large in the Pacific. With both the Australian and New Zealand troops amassing to head overseas, their governments were anxious to locate the squadron (which would sail past German Samoa just a few days after the New Zealand occupation). While the Admiralty considered the risk to be minimal, the New Zealand Cabinet considered the level of danger to its task force was unacceptable.[76] In October, coded signals between German ships were picked up in Wellington (a listening post for the Royal Navy), Awarua and Suva in Fiji, and these were sent to the Australian Commonwealth Naval Board for decoding. They revealed that the Germans knew of the departure date for New Zealand's Expeditionary Force, but also that von Spee's ships were now in the eastern Pacific and heading for South America.[77] Accordingly, but with the provision of a stronger escort in case of emergency, the main body of New Zealand troops could depart on 16 October, to link up with the Australian forces in Albany and proceed on to Egypt. Intercepted signals also informed the Royal Navy's hunt for the German squadron, leading to the destruction of most of its vessels near the Falkland Islands that December. This intercept, and the finished intelligence which flowed from it, was the most significant work carried out by New Zealand's radio stations during the war.[78]

The information gathered by the country's various interception stations continued to be shared with allies throughout the war, principally with Britain (including via key Royal Navy stations in China and at Montevideo in Uruguay), Australia and Canada. By 1939, many senior personnel in the world of sigint 'had worked as junior operators at those stations during the First World War'.[79] This Pacific-wide sigint cooperation was, in essence, repeated 'on a grander scale' during the Second World War.[80]

Operations

The pre-war Police had suspected that rival powers were looking for material relating to New Zealand's security, and countering any enemy espionage and sabotage operations was a major priority at the outbreak of the war. As we have noted, the German consular service had been part of an intelligence network tasked with collecting and forwarding security-related information to a secret war intelligence section stationed in Sydney.[81] While no documentary evidence has been located indicating police knowledge of the existence of this network, the consuls and other prominent Germans and Austro-Hungarians in New Zealand were now closely monitored. On 9 August 1914, police were ordered to seize records held within the German Consulates and hold them in Wellington, where defence personnel were among those with access. While the consular staff would no doubt already have destroyed any information on potential or actual spying or other clearly compromising activity, the seized documents were subjected to a 'careful search' for any clues on other matters – policies relating to German military reservists in New Zealand, plans for German shipping under war conditions, codes or ciphers and the like. Nothing to justify detaining consular officials was found.[82]

From the beginning of the conflict the Police monitored numbers of people who had expressed pro-enemy sentiments. In December 1914, a police report logged suspicions about Gustave Kronfeld, a trader seen as strongly sympathetic to Germany: 'I consider this man should be kept under strict surveillance.' Almost a year later, another surveillance report noted that Kronfeld had been in contact with Consul Seegner.[83] Some weeks later Seegner and his former secretary were interned. While both military and policing authorities were taciturn in commenting on the circumstances leading to their arrest, press reports stated that the two had been observed undertaking suspicious meetings.[84] Kronfeld was later interned on Motuihe Island.

As we have noted, the wartime surveilling net extended to all enemy aliens, upon whom police had to enforce a number of requirements, such as reporting commitments and travel restrictions. Political police also received orders from time to time for closer surveillance of specified members of enemy alien communities; for example, special monitoring of those working in potentially sensitive positions, including doctors, chemists and waterfront workers.[85]

Specific targeting, and the intensity of surveillance over enemy aliens, tended to wax and wane according to circumstances. Rumours that communities of Dalmatian gum-diggers in the far north were loyal to Austria, for example, attracted a series of investigations.[86] Likewise, when the British freighter *Port Kembla* sank near Farewell Spit in September 1917, the result of a mine laid by the German commerce raider *Wolf*, a renewed vigilance for spies and saboteurs began: it was initially theorised the sinking was the result of explosives smuggled onboard by radical Australian workers.[87] From time to time the government, through the Police Commissioner, sought to tighten general surveillance over possible supporters of the enemy. Inspectors were reminded in 1917, for example, of the importance of watching 'closely the movements and business transactions' of all enemy aliens, as well as 'their agents' or their children, including the possibility that they might make contact with the Central Powers through neutral countries.[88]

While people who were suspect by dint of their 'Germanic bloodline' formed a more amorphous and much larger target for surveillance, the general knowledge of local communities possessed by police personnel eased this task. For example, Hugo Sewald, the naturalised German convicted shortly into the war for possessing wireless equipment, had already been within the constabulary's purview (seemingly because he was a vagrant and perceived to be liable to be tempted by crime).[89]

Surveillance over such large sectors of the population raised difficult questions in popular and official discourse about loyalty: how far could integration into New Zealand society, and/or naturalisation, override the bonds of ethnicity and heritage? Police watchers and analysts addressed such questions on a case-by-case basis, but – partly as a result of popular pressure – their assessments were sometimes overridden at higher level. In Commissioner Cullen's time, a punitive approach to Germanness came from the top. After reviewing waterfront security in October 1916, for example, the Commissioner came to 'the opinion that no naturalised enemy subject should be employed by the Harbour Board, as I am satisfied that a German who goes through the form of getting naturalised does so merely to enable him to pose as a British subject so as to get employment, whilst he remains a German at heart just as much as he ever was'.[90]

Wartime political surveillance over both individuals and collectivities built on pre-war knowledge and monitoring techniques. The detectives knew where to look for the pacifists and pacificists, for example, because they had been monitoring them for a long time, more intensively so after the pre-war military service measures had produced considerable resistance. While many left-wingers had rallied to the patriotic cause (like their counterparts in Germany) at the beginning of the war, opposition to the conduct of the war, and even the war itself, grew over the duration. Again the political police already had a great deal of pre-war data on the dissident left upon which they could draw – those discouraging enlistment or promoting 'peace at any price' were most likely already lodged in Police records. The police surveilling task was assisted by other government agencies, especially those under military auspices, with few constraints. To take a typical case, the solicitor-general pronounced himself satisfied, at the end of 1915, that examination of the correspondence of National Peace Council founder Charles Mackie was 'fully justified'.[91]

The police role in surveilling New Zealanders expanded hugely when preparations for conscription into the armed forces began through a national registration system. This was opposed by significant sectors of society, especially within the labour and socialist movements, ranging from the few who opposed any participation in any war effort to the many who declared that any sacrifice of men should occur only if wealth was conscripted as well as labour. Allied to the latter was a strong socialist perspective which saw the war as one of imperial rivalries, fought to perpetuate capitalist exploitation of the working masses rather than liberate them from wage slavery. In October 1916 a labour movement manifesto declared that the imminent approach of conscription was 'the strongest weapon of Capitalism', signalling not only the 'further enslavement' of the working class but 'the negation of Liberty' itself.[92]

In conjunction with military and other authorities, police put enormous efforts into searching for those who declaimed, penned or otherwise shared anti-conscription sentiments. Such police activity was seen as integral to maintaining, in the words of the defence minister, the state's 'bounden duty to protect [its security] as far as possible'.[93] Close monitoring of sections of the population for breaches of the law on call-up led to a number of means of supressing the movement, including the incarceration of those seen as its ringleaders. Indeed, gaoling people at the forefront of opposition to official policies was often the optimal aim of police, military, postal and other surveillance activities. As the solicitor-general (confidentially) instructed his staff with regard to one such activist, legal proceedings should be designed to result in 'as long a term of imprisonment as practicable [with] no question of a mere fine'.[94] Temporary removal of an influential activist was designed to have a flow-on effect, including discouraging followers and possibly even the convicted person after release. There were few problems in securing convictions, given that regulations clearly stated that opposing the war effort amounted to sedition.

While the political police were surveilling significant sections of Pākehā society, they were less adept at watching Māori communities. Many tribes throughout the Dominion were initially enthusiastic about the war effort. But the high rates of volunteering from Ngāpuhi, Ngāti Porou, Te Arawa and other iwi stood beside widespread indifference or refusal in other regions. The authorities were especially concerned about disaffection among those tribes whose land had been confiscated (raupatu) after the previous century's wars.[95] Given the failure of successive governments to address their grievances, many tribal leaders in raupatu areas either failed to encourage their young men to enlist or actively discouraged them from doing so.

The main problem lay with the Waikato–Tainui federation, which had a high degree of tribal unity, in significant part because of its hosting of the King Movement. This pan-tribal grouping, the Kīngitanga, had been founded in 1858 to resist the Crown's efforts to enforce its sovereignty and acquire the fertile lands south of Auckland. Tribal memories of the bloodshed and land loss that followed invasion remained strong, and resistance to state and loyalist Māori pressure to assist the war effort was determined. Conscription had not initially been applied to Māori but, as frustrations around the inequality of sacrifice across iwi grew, it was extended to the Waikato in June 1917. After a period of administrative preparation, the first ballots were drawn in May 1918.

This created a difficult new task for the Police Force, which had long since discarded almost all of its Māori members: how to track and detain the young men who had evaded registration or call-up. The local constables in the Waikato were generally relied upon to collect information, and most were not only on friendly terms with some chiefs but could also rely on tip-offs from Pākehā sources, such as local storekeepers. As a detective stated, '[l]ocal country constables who know local conditions thoroughly are seldom far out in their deductions'.[96] But there was a paucity of informants from within the iwi, and by the end of the war few Māori defaulters had been tracked down; no Waikato conscripts served overseas.[97]

In other tribal areas, the few remaining small Māori separatist movements were monitored mainly through informants from within broader tribal communities in the region. These were mostly handled by local Pākehā constables, sometimes assisted by one of the handful of part-time Native Constables left in the Dominion. Such surveillance was especially carried out on movements whose leaders or members had suggested that the state's enemies were their friends or who had otherwise rejected assisting the war effort. This was most prominently the case with the Tūhoe prophet Rua Kēnana's millennial movement headquartered deep in Te Urewera's mountains, at Maungapōhatu. It had been under surveillance for some years, and there had been attempts to suppress it by using legal and other means of persuasion, including by Māori leaders on national and local stages. Minister Herdman finally made a move in April 1916, authorising Commissioner Cullen to head an armed invasion into the 'New Jerusalem'. After a gun battle that saw casualties on both sides, including the death of Rua's son and another follower, the movement's leaders were arrested. Although a jury acquitted the prophet on a charge of sedition, an example was made of him: a punitive gaol sentence was imposed for having 'morally' resisted arrest on a previous occasion. Thereafter, Maungapōhatu's capacity for resistance was effectively neutralised.[98]

The wartime climate meant that, outside the circles of the surveilled, there was little discussion or protest at state surveillance. One case did, however, bring some public attention and discussion to the issue. Over eight days in August 1917, an inquiry was held into allegations of secret machinations by the authorities against the Protestant Political Association (PPA). This was a mass organisation that reflected, and accelerated, the deterioration of interdenominational harmony in the latter part of the war. Headed by the demagogic Howard Elliott, among other things the Association levelled fevered warnings about the supposedly diabolical agenda of the Roman Catholic Church, urging Protestants to band together to secure their rights.[99] From its very beginning, the PPA presented a potential to threaten public order and therefore the war effort itself. The Association's formal launch coincided with the commemoration of the Battle of the Boyne, which signified the Protestant ascendancy in Ireland; and its remarkable growth, with tens of thousands joining up, portended future trouble.

Among the accusations levelled by the PPA was the claim that Catholic-controlled 'corruption within the Postal Service' had resulted in its correspondence being interfered with, an allegation made the more serious by the fact that Postmaster-General Sir Joseph Ward was a Catholic.[100] The government ordered a commission of inquiry. Magistrate H. W. Bishop was appointed to preside over the inquiry and determine:

> (a) Whether correspondence addressed to post-office box No. 912 at
> Auckland [had] been corruptly or improperly suppressed or detained
> by the officers of the Post Office;
> (b) On what grounds military censorship [had] been established over
> the correspondence of the persons using the said post-office box.[101]

Sixty-five witnesses were examined over eight days in August 1917, and prominent newspaper coverage aroused considerable public interest and led to debates in Parliament.[102] Despite severe restrictions on the powers of the commission to enquire into matters made 'obviously secret' by wartime,[103] it was soon clear that censors had been monitoring the PPA's mail for some months. Solicitor-General John Salmond testified that official attention had been drawn to the Association by various complaints concerning the circulation of a pamphlet entitled *The Hideous Guilt of Rome in the European Carnage*.[104] He had therefore advised Colonel Gibbon, in December 1916, that its Post Office Box should be monitored under the rationale that the promotion of sectarian strife 'would have a considerable effect on the recruiting of Roman Catholics' and could therefore constitute a breach of war regulations.[105] Declassified records confirm the existence of a memorandum noting these details, dated 13 December 1916.[106]

Ultimately, Commissioner Bishop found that 'there was in no degree satisfactory evidence of any impropriety or corruption on the part of the Auckland Postal officials' and that, while some mail had been held back from delivery, its quantity was 'trifling'.[107] On the second of his terms of reference, the Commissioner endorsed the solicitor-general's reason for 'recommending that censorship should be established' over the postal box: 'his belief that matter connected with this box was distinctly mischievous in tendency and was likely to very seriously interfere with the proper conduct of the war, and that therefore the Post Office should not be allowed to be the medium made for its circulation to the public'.[108]

While fostering sectarian strife clearly provided a rationale for official intrusion into private affairs, other cases of surveillance reflect a heightened wartime atmosphere of suspicion and intolerance against behaviours and attitudes held as deviant. To take one example, Danish-born Dr Hjelmar von Dannevill had previously piqued police interest by her enigmatic lifestyle and uncertain past.[109] During the war, after an anonymous tip-off, she was watched as a possible German spy. While no evidence of espionage was found, in 1917 her unconventional looks, her habit of wearing men's clothes and her relationships with other women was brought to Solicitor-General Salmond's attention. He concluded that it was 'very doubtful whether she is a man or a woman. She is very masculine in appearance and habits. There is very much reason to suspect that she may be a man masquerading as a woman.' This helped lead him to the conclusion that there was 'grave ground for suspicion that this person is a mischievous and dangerous imposter who ought in the public interests to be interned during the war'.[110]

Von Dannevill was, accordingly, extensively interviewed by police on such matters as her gender and dressing habits, her professional qualifications and her personal relationships. Salmond concluded from the results that while 'the question of sex has now been settled by medical examination, the further information received and now submitted to me in no way alters the opinion which I formerly expressed, but rather confirms it'.[111] Arrested on 26 May 1917, von Dannevill was escorted under guard to the Somes Island Internment Camp in Wellington Harbour. This example indicates both the width of the intelligence dragnet and the level of analysis in the wartime intelligence cycle.

Targets often came to the attention of police by their review of openly available source material, including newspaper reports, booklets, posters, pamphlets, leaflets and other ephemera. In some cases, this material was brought to police consideration by other officials, the public and politicians. A typical submission from a member of the public noted that the writer had been 'informed' that the Auckland Meat Company was 'run by German capital with Germans at the head of affairs, whom, it is believed, have a wireless machine on top of the building which has some strange looking enclosures of wood'.[112] While police needed to investigate all such allegations, with the most serious assigned to the overstretched political detectives, the most basic initial investigations generally revealed them to be groundless. This prompted frustration among the surveillers, especially when the accusations turned out to be (as often) rooted in prejudice against certain ethnicities or beliefs or motivated by personal malice against individuals.[113]

Complementing their frequent reliance on open-source written information to initiate or supplement surveillance operations, the police surveillers' pre-war practice of attending all public meetings that might be of potential interest remained a major means of acquiring intelligence.[114] Either uniformed or plain-clothes men, or both, would attend many a meeting in a draughty hall or rainy park. In the case of dual attendance, the presence of the regular police might be to divert attention from the undercover men circulating among the attendees in search of, say, a wanted person, or on a quest to gain a sense of their collective mood. The uniformed men, meanwhile, might be taking notes of what was being said, ready to feed these into the intelligence cycle for analysis and possible prosecution for seditious intent; or identifying speakers for follow-up attention.

For what promised to be significant meetings or rallies, police would employ stenographers to provide a fuller account of what was said. From May to July 1916, for example, Adela Pankhurst, of the renowned British suffragist family, visited New Zealand for a speaking tour centring on anti-militarism and social reform. The Police Commissioner instructed his officers to 'arrange to have all lectures delivered in your district by Miss Adela Pankhurst attended by the police, preferably in plain clothes, and if she makes any disloyal or seditious statements, or statements calculated to interfere with recruiting, the facts are to be immediately reported'.[115] Exhaustive transcripts of her speeches, and of question-and-answer sessions, were logged.[116] Similar monitoring was applied to Howard Elliott; and militant labour leader H. E. Holland, later the Labour Party leader from 1919 to 1933, noted that both detectives and stenographers had been taking notes at every public meeting he addressed as the government's battle to counter anti-conscriptionist sentiment stepped up pace.[117] Once the crime of 'seditious tendency' had been added to that of 'seditious intention' under the regulations, he told a correspondent in Australia, police only needed to lay a charge 'for a conviction to be certain'.[118]

Surveillance of suspected seditionary or subversive organisations and individuals was often followed up by use of police powers to search and seize notes, minutes, files and published material. When men of military service age were required to register their details in 1915, as part of the government's forward planning for the possibility of conscription, the political police quickly moved to counter organised opposition. That October, for example, police raided the Freedom League offices in Auckland, confiscating material held to be in breach of regulations and using it as the basis for prosecution.[119] The charges against the League's secretary Egerton Gill focused on the production of pamphlets giving advice on how to fill in National Registration Cards, recommending wording such as: 'Whilst registering as a citizen, in conformity with the Government's demand, I could not for conscientious reasons take part in military service, in employment necessitating the taking of the military oath, or in the production of materials the purpose of which is the taking of human life.'[120] The magistrate found that such advice breached regulations by discouraging enlistment, and opined that it was 'not a time to deal gently with offences of this description . . . On this occasion a heavy fine [£50] will sufficiently punish the defendant, and will at the same time draw public attention to the necessity for strict compliance with the war regulations.'[121] Similarly, on 19 December 1916, the offices of the labour newspaper *Maoriland Worker* were raided by police, some 3000 copies of the Labour Party's peace manifesto were seized, and judicial action followed.[122]

Police, postal and customs interceptions also helped the authorities to build up a wider picture of potential surveillance targets. On 28 February 1917, to take one example, Colonel Gibbon instructed his staff to 'take necessary action to ensure that all correspondence for J. W. Vandunn, Crocelann, 24 Utrecht, Holland, is examined. I should be glad to see some of the letters going to this man, as I particularly desire to know who his correspondents are.'[123] Information gained about New Zealand subscribers to organisations or journals, or recipients and senders of letters within the Dominion and abroad, was constantly added to the official records, providing an ever-expanding database on surveilled socio-political networks.

Ongoing efforts to coordinate intelligence work with allied nations also bore fruit.[124] The atmosphere of national and Imperial emergency often overrode traditional inter-agency and cross-border rivalries. The New Zealand authorities relied especially, but not exclusively, on British and Australian counterparts for 'intelligence and a range of other information on international affairs which they otherwise would have had no chance of gathering'.[125] Because a great many labour movement activists had come to New Zealand from across the Tasman, Australian police forces were often asked to provide information on their backgrounds. In 1916, for example, the Victorian Police were asked about 'extreme Socialist' Charles Hill, an American journalist of 'foreign appearance' who had formerly run a grocery shop in Melbourne.[126] The two countries swapped warnings from abroad about 'agitators' believed to be heading for Australasia. A photograph of 'dangerous Anarchist' Giuseppe Carpigo, for example, arrived in Melbourne in 1917 from Italy, to be sent on to Wellington.[127] Such suspects would have their details (including photographs where available) circulated in the confidential *Police Gazette*, alongside many other persons wanted for or suspected of criminal or political offences.

The Australian postal censors forwarded relevant parts of their weekly intelligence reports to their New Zealand counterparts, one of a number of reciprocal arrangements. These accounts would include information on intercepted letters sent by New Zealanders to Australians under surveillance. At the New Zealand end, such intelligence often led to postal or police surveillance of the senders. In this way the activities of Edwin J. (Ted) Howard, a leading Christchurch labour organiser and socialist who wrote editorials for the *Maoriland Worker* under the pseudonym 'the Vag', came to fall under greater scrutiny.[128]

The main value in the information flow from Australia, however, was that it enabled the New Zealand political police to spread their surveillance net over citizens who had not yet come to any significant attention. In one typical case, censorship authorities across the Tasman forwarded extracts from a letter sent from New Zealand to an Australian resident. These showed that the sender, Frank Lonnigan, was a defaulter living under a false name in Westland. The New Zealand censors then forwarded the details to police for follow-up action.[129] In another case, a report from Brisbane in August 1918 included transcriptions from a letter sent to a Queensland man by Pat Tooker of Reefton:

> The police have been watching me very closely lately. They charged
> me with harbouring deserters from Military service, and perhaps

they were right. They claimed I was feeding no less than four, how awful. They have a letter of mine in custody, but the affair seems to have been dropped – insufficient evidence I think. They searched the bush all around here, but it failed to reveal much desired camp. Don't mention any names when you write, Pat, as I have very good reason to believe they open some of my letters although your last came through unopened. I would hate to be the means of providing information to our enemies . . .

The Australian authorities had added their assessment of this intercept, noting that:

1) The writer evidently is an undesirable. He is endeavouring to shield shirkers in New Zealand and encourages them to escape from the Military.
2) Addressee's name has been noted and his correspondence will be watched.[130]

In some instances the Australian censors discovered serious breaches of security within New Zealand, such as that of mail that had been smuggled out of a defaulters' camp without undergoing the compulsory checking required.[131] They also assisted the New Zealand authorities in occupied Samoa, passing on, for example, details taken from correspondence sent from Sydney to Chief Malietoa Tanumafili (an official adviser to the occupation administration) that criticised New Zealand rule and questioned the future of the territory.[132]

Inter-agency cooperation within New Zealand frequently extended to the judicial authorities. The solicitor-general had declared, under regulations of 25 September 1915 banning the importing or distributing of 'documents inciting violence, lawlessness and disorder', that being 'an active agent of the I.W.W. or other anarchist and criminal organisations' could incur prosecution or internment. After postal censors intercepted orders of literature from New Zealand's leading anarchist, Philip Josephs, to renowned American-based anarchist Emma Goldman, police were able to justify a search warrant on his home and business (believed to be the Wellington headquarters of the IWW) under war regulations. This was authorised by the judiciary on grounds of suspicion that he was acting 'in a manner injurious to the public safety or to the interest of His Majesty in respect to the present war'.[133]

Correspondence was seized during the raid, and a long list of literature on the premises was compiled afterwards. Such information in turn led to ongoing cooperation between police and censors. One report resulting from the search, for example, noted that 'it would appear from books found in Josephs' possession that he obtains such literature from America and supplies same to [Syd] Kingsford', an active Wobbly who had come to the censors' attention through a private tip-off. That October both he and Josephs were placed under police and postal surveillance.[134] Nor were these links one way, as New Zealand provided reciprocal information to its intelligence allies. In May 1917, for example, a letter sent from Kiel and addressed to a German vessel stationed at Guam ended up in the Dominion after being misdirected at San Francisco. On being opened, translated and analysed, its contents were forwarded to British intelligence.[135]

The difficulties of analysing collected information to produce workable intelligence were particularly challenging during the wartime emergency, given the complexities of the situation, the vast inflow of often fragmented information, and heightened emotions throughout the society being surveilled. Outside the military–postal censorship system, police were at the fore of both the majority of security analyses and any follow-ups which resulted. As in the past, they typically compiled as much information on individuals under investigation as they could gather, working outwards from the basic details (home and work addresses, physical description, occupation and so on) to cover reports of their words or deeds, and collating such material with considerable contextual background. Their analyses often included character evaluations ('an eccentric, having once been an inmate of Nelson Mental Hospital'), and most such investigations led to no action. The reasons for decisions to cease surveillance were generally summed up succinctly on the files, such as there being 'no question of this man's loyalty'.[136]

Much analysis, however, led only to interim conclusions centred around insufficient evidence of law-breaking, a reflection of the legal-oriented approach of police personnel. Police attendance at Adela Pankhurst's lectures, for example, resulted in numerous evaluations of the likelihood of securing a conviction. Some of the first-level analysts believed that her public utterances might be deemed to have a negative impact on recruiting, hence making her liable to charges. But most were cautious as 'her language was fairly moderate' and 'she said nothing in my opinion which would amount to a Breach of War Regulations'.[137] When assessments of this latter nature were sent higher up the Police hierarchy, they were generally endorsed.

The conclusions of similar analyses carried out by allied security counterparts with reference to New Zealand were usually couched in similarly tentative terms and were not always endorsed upon further investigation. In April 1918, for example, a cable from London relayed the information that Auckland's W. H. Webbe had been ordering pacifist papers from London and the United States, and warned that 'he is a possible centre for German propaganda'.[138] In his assessment Colonel Gibbon concluded, 'I do not consider that Webbe is in any way dangerous, and look upon him as a socialistic faddist.'[139]

A great deal of police analysis revolved around the task of threshing credible intelligence from the mass of information arising out of wartime's heightened threat perceptions and social passions, rather than from any basis in fact. The investigation into claims of German spies operating from the Auckland Meat Company, for example, revealed the apparent 'wireless apparatus' to be in reality the plant's refrigeration condensers.[140] Such cases stretched police resources enormously, especially given the NZPF's problems of retention and recruitment. A Police Superintendent's comments after an investigation into flashing lights alleged to be enemy signalling, but revealed to be an evening picnic, summed up many a policeman's frustration: 'This is a specimen of the will-o-wisps the police are frequently required to chase with much loss of time of men required for other really important duty.'[141]

Moreover, as we have noted, while a large number of reporting and allegations arose from genuine concerns, many contained distortions and some were malicious fabrications. A letter to a newspaper, for example, accused the Rev. Dean Power of Anglophobic remarks: 'poverty will disappear from Ireland only when she has succeeded, like New Zealand, in shaking off British rule'. An investigation was launched, with the Inspector overseeing the inquiries concluding that he was 'satisfied' that the subject of the accusations was 'a most loyal subject'. It was 'well known' that his accuser 'disagreed with the Dean in Church matters, and ever since bitterly opposes him'.[142]

Many false reports related to potential or actual collusion with the enemy. An inquiry centred on a demand that a Tauranga man be deported as a dangerous enemy alien found that the accuser was 'taking advantage of the present intense feeling to try and vent his petty spite against an old man'.[143] After investigating assertions that the president of the Women's National Reserve was pro-German, a constable concluded that these claims represented gossip motivated by jealousy.[144] Despite the similarly fanciful nature of most allegations of espionage, however, some reports were credible enough to lead to detailed police investigations. In June 1916, for example, a Bohemian on parole from internment on Motuihe Island told the police that a fellow internee, the former governor of German Samoa, was in two-way communication with enemy officials. This was said to be concealed within correspondence to his sister, using a secret code and invisible ink. Police forwarded the case to Gibbon's jurisdiction for further investigation.[145]

As the conflict dragged on, increasing sectors of the civil population became weary of the war effort and its constraints, making the covert surveillers' task more difficult. Gathering information on suspected spies and subversion had always been a generally humdrum affair: following suspects, interviewing people connected with them, watching houses, hiding outside halls, taking notes at meetings within them, and so on. But war weariness, and what was perceived of as defeatism, presented a far more inchoate set of targets. The amorphousness of this task made it an exceedingly difficult one, although when dissatisfaction turned into industrial action some targets became more readily visible. Essentially, then, surveillance operations continued to expand in the wartime emergency. The many people who were fined, gaoled, interned, harassed or otherwise felt the consequences of their surveillance formed but a small minority of the total number of surveillees.

The political police archives, accordingly, continued to expand. Police record-keeping practice, already well embedded before 1914, was to compile as much information on movements and individuals under investigation as they could gather, however irrelevant it might seem; to add into the files the names and details of people and organisations in contact with them, however casually; and to create new files on the people and institutions continuing to appear in reports. This system of information accumulation was used in policing and security intelligence agencies worldwide, with the aim of creating a broad picture out of large amounts of scattered and fragmented information. However, as the files built up as a result of the wider scrutiny required by wartime needs, the tendency to accumulate rather than sift and prioritise created logistical difficulties at the analytical stage of the intelligence cycle – one reason why many NZPF analyses provided only interim or implicit conclusions.

Assessment

The years 1914–18 saw an unprecedented expansion of state surveillance, a phenomenon that has been characterised as amounting to an international revolution in state-led intelligence. 'Driven by the necessity of total war,' as one scholar has put it, 'the Western powers yoked corporate-grade information-processing methods to industrial-scale collection capabilities, and then in turn to the ancient art of spying.'[146] Between 1914 and 1918, MI5 expanded from 14 staff to 844, and staff in Britain's Special Branch rose more than six-fold.[147]

Within New Zealand, this expansion largely played out within existing institutions; and, rather than supersede the police systems and methods in place by 1914, the government elected to enhance the powers of the general Police Force. While this can be seen as rational, it did mean some endemic inefficiency was inherited from the old system. The hierarchical nature of the NZPF, and the fact that the highest echelons of the Force were from the uniformed rather than the detective wing, meant that key decision-making on policy and cases had to be passed up the chain of command. On the other hand, such decisions were always informed by the views of the political police, and the Dominion's political executive and other agencies were generally satisfied with the results that emerged from clandestinely gathered intelligence and its analysis.

Since the working definition of subversion by the state and its surveillers during wartime effectively included disruption to any part of the war effort, and such disruption widened as the war went on, the scope for surveillance escalated. By the end of the war the Police, in liaison with other agencies, had accumulated knowledge on a huge range of movements, organisations, subjects and individuals. An initial targeting of pacifists and pacificists, and those who dissented from participation on socialist or pro-German grounds, had expanded as the war progressed. It came to include opponents of conscription, for example, and those perceived to be proactively impeding the war effort by such activities as slowing production or spreading 'defeatist' sentiments.[148]

The main institutional innovation in the war was the postal censorship operation, which (as in other belligerents) arose out of necessity and engaged in unprecedented intervention into the private lives of New Zealanders. This military-led system within the Post Office cooperated with detectives and military intelligence units as well as other agencies with intelligence responsibilities. Ways of systematising security arrangements with allied governments were also examined from time to time, leading to a closer transnational intelligence nexus within the Empire than had existed prior to 1914. Towards the end of the war, for example, consideration was being given to a wide range of potential improvements in Imperial intelligence, including arrangements to coordinate the collection and distribution of naval intelligence across the Empire,[149] security protocols on the transport of secret documents between England and New Zealand,[150] and systematisation of wireless communication between allied ships.[151] Plans for continuing and further developing Imperial intelligence-sharing arrangements would endure into the post-war world.

The expansion of state surveillance and its operational follow-up inevitably led to an erosion of a number of civil liberties. Quite apart from the massive state penetration into postal privacy, the NZPF's covert surveillers spied upon many other aspects of private life. They enforced restrictions on what books could be read or films viewed, took note of everyone they could identify at meetings challenging government policies, and sought to hamper dissent by publicised searches, seizures, prosecutions and gaoling. All of this clearly had a dampening effect on dissent from the war effort, with intelligence work often underpinning repressive actions. In the aftermath of the raid on the Freedom League, for example, some of its members resigned and by early 1916 attendance at its meetings had halved.[152] A year later, Holland lamented, 'some of the ablest and most brilliant in the Labour and Socialist movement' were languishing in gaol for spreading 'disaffection against the Government' at anti-conscription and other such meetings.[153] Future Labour prime minister Peter Fraser was among the convicted seditionists, put out of action for a year.

While prosecution was desired in some circumstances, to discourage dissent, other repressive actions were taken more discreetly. For example, a carton of some 500 leaflets from Britain's Stop the War Committee, addressed to National Peace Council leader Mackie, was intercepted by customs officials and seized before entry to New Zealand.[154] Likewise, in late 1917, Deputy Chief Postal Censor Tanner reported on a particularly successful instance of quiet repression. The case involved interception and confiscation of mail asking Christian ministers to support a peace without annexations, a campaign believed to have been undertaken by a group affiliated with the Women's International League for Peace and Freedom: 'as a result the appeal never gained any publicity whatever'.[155]

Left: Figure 1
With a detective background in the London Metropolitan Police, John Bennett Tunbridge was the Commissioner of the New Zealand Police Force between 1897 and 1903. His successor, Walter Dinnie (1903–9), was also a former senior London detective. *2007/1/6, New Zealand Police Museum*

Below: Figure 2
The Wellington Detective Branch in 1902. Some detectives were especially charged with acting as the political eyes and ears of the state. Tudor Welby Balfour Boddam and Charles Robert Broberg (first and second from the left, respectively) were particularly specialised in this area. *B. G. Thomson Collection, New Zealand Police Museum*

Left: Figure 3
Native Constable Wiremu Tereina (William Treanor), pictured *c*.1912, was based at Tāneatua. One of his duties was to keep watch on Tūhoe prophet Rua Kēnana's community (in the nearby mountains), which was suspected to be a site of subversion. Generally Native Constables, who were employed part-time in the Police, wore plain clothes when carrying out their policing duties. *I. M. Burney Collection, New Zealand Police Museum*

Right: Figure 4
Strike-breakers processioning from the mine during the 1912 Waihī miners' strike, protected by a strong police escort. *Waihi Arts Centre and Museum*

Below right: Figure 5
Awanui station, pictured *c*.1919. Operational from 1912, the station was part of the Imperial Wireless Chain, the British Empire's strategic communication network. As such it was an important component of New Zealand's early sigint capability. *1/1-010621-G, Alexander Turnbull Library, Wellington, New Zealand*

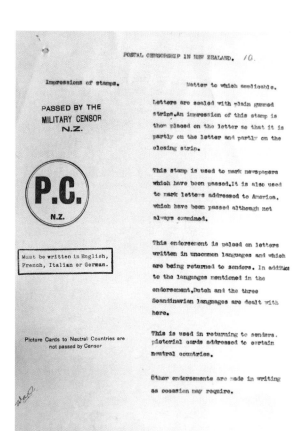

POSTAL CENSORSHIP IN NEW ZEALAND. 10.

Impressions of stamps.

PASSED BY THE
MILITARY CENSOR
N.Z.

P.C.
N.Z.

Must be written in English,
French, Italian or German.

Picture Cards to Neutral Countries are
not passed by Censor

Matter to which applicable.

Letters are sealed with plain gummed strips. An impression of this stamp is then placed on the letter so that it is partly on the letter and partly on the closing strip.

This stamp is used to mark newspapers which have been passed. It is also used to mark letters addressed to America, which have been passed although not always examined.

This endorsement is placed on letters written in uncommon languages and which are being returned to senders. In addition to the languages mentioned in the endorsement, Dutch and the three Scandinavian languages are dealt with here.

This is used in returning to senders, pictorial cards addressed to certain neutral countries.

Other endorsements are made in writing as occasion may require.

Above: Figure 6
A scene from Wellington's 'Battle of Featherston Street' during the 1913 Great Strike. The clash arrayed mounted Special Constables against crowds of strike supporters. *Richard Hill Police History Collection*

Left: Figure 7
Examples of stamps used by New Zealand's postal censors in processing private mail during the First World War. *'Administration and Miscellaneous – Censorship – Regulations postal'* [AAYS 8638/771 23/8 (R22430468)], *Archives New Zealand Te Rua Mahara o te Kāwanatanga*

Right: Figure 8
A September 1917 Police memorandum ordering surveillance and transcription of a public speech to be delivered by Howard Elliott of the Protestant Political Association. *'Censorship of correspondence, Protestant Political Association'* [AAYS 8647/10 19/6 (R3885386)], *Archives New Zealand Te Rua Mahara o te Kāwanatanga*

NEW ZEALAND POLICE.

Memorandum for

Chief Detective Boddam

Wlgtn

Inspr's

District Office, Wellington

Sept 25th , 1917

SUBJECT: Re Howard Elliott Meeting at Town Hall this date

4,000/12/15—19843]

The Commissioner directs that a shorthand writer is to be obtained, to take down the speeches verbatim, and supply a full transcription thereof. Please arrange accordingly, and instruct one of your staff to attend the Meeting.

R Marsack

Inspector

7838
'17

DETECTIVE OFFICE WELLINGTON.

SEPTEMBER 25th 1917.

Detective Torrance,

Please be at this office at 6-30 pm (Sharp) this evening at which time Mr Weston, short hand reporter will also be here. You can accompany him to the Town Hall, and you are to remain there until this meeting is over. Entrance to the Town Hall, for the Police, will be per a side door in Mercer St, Admission tickets (2) herewith.

Boddam

Chief Detective.

Above: Figure 9
Cartoon of Wellington's Detective Tudor Boddam, who was often tasked with security matters, on the lookout for German spies. *New Zealand Free Lance, 11 February 1916, p. 4*

Right: Figure 10
James (Jim) Cummings in 1920. Specialising in political policing, he would become one of the most important figures in New Zealand's security intelligence in the 1930s and the Second World War. In 1944 he succeeded his brother Denis as Police Commissioner, the operational head of political policing. *New Zealand Police Museum*

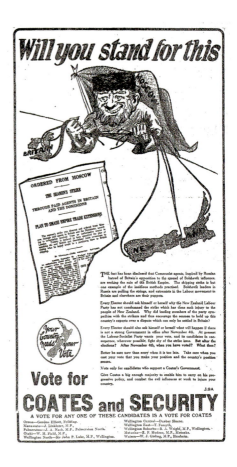

Right: Figure 13
A Reform Party advertisement for the 1925 election depicting industrial unrest as 'ordered and directed from Moscow' and implicating the New Zealand Labour Party as 'puppets'. *Evening Post, 15 October 1925, p. 15*

Below: Figure 14
Drawers of index cards from the Police cataloguing system for the secret files. These cards built up over time; the raised card lists reports relating to Auckland's waterfront union. *New Zealand Security Intelligence Service*

Further impacts included some degree of self-censorship as individuals picked their words or considered their deeds more carefully. An official surveiller of a meeting 'addressed by Mr H. Holland and others' observed a general awareness of the need for caution, noting 'the speakers are very careful in their remarks and avoid making any statements which would bring them within the scope of the War Regulations'.[156] Such self-censorship in the face of informal or formal surveillance and sanctions was one reason why wartime political policing did not lead to the high degree of controversy around intelligence work that occurred from time to time in later decades. Most of the public, in any case, seemed to accept that expanded state power was justified by the wartime emergency, if with degrees of disquiet; as one Aucklander remarked, '[i]t is hurtful to the writer to find the once customary sacred privacy of mail in transit no longer exists'.[157] However, even postal censorship occasioned little dissent. An analysis of the system noted its 'most remarkable feature' as being 'the insignificance of the agitation against it'.[158] Protests at state intrusions into people's lives were largely confined to those within the targeted sectors of the surveillance dragnet, and the complainants were quite often those who held what were seen as 'extreme' views even within their own movement.

All the same, some of the key points raised by the Protestant Political Association's lawyer H. H. Ostler in the 1917 inquiry would, although they were geared to wartime-specific postal censorship, be echoed in later controversies around intelligence work in New Zealand. Quite apart from his questioning of the legality of the censorship regime, he declared it a threat to civil liberties, denied its impartiality (claiming, for example, absence of similar censorship of inflammatory statements from Catholic publications) and opined that New Zealand's legitimate security concerns had been distorted by the perceived needs of Imperial security.[159]

Another major legacy of the war was a lasting impact on the political landscape that state surveillance monitored. The Easter Rebellion of 1916 and the Bolshevik Revolution of November 1917 were especially seen as holding the potential to radicalise and inspire local challenges to existing authorities and structures. The events in Russia, in particular, marked a global watershed whose security ramifications would come to dominate covert surveillance in New Zealand for decades. While the security police kept a close watch on those who openly welcomed news of the revolution, there was no immediate expectation that the Bolsheviks would survive – the major implication of Bolshevism, at least initially, was that it was seen as threatening to destabilise the Allied cause.[160]

On the other hand, the detectives were conscious that there was now a movement whose radically communitarian creed might inspire New Zealand leftists: Peter Fraser, for example, initially celebrated the revolution for its pursuit of a 'civilisation and social justice such as the world has hitherto only known in the dreaming of its thinkers'.[161] The authorities' dismay increased over the following years as the Bolsheviks survived internal attack and external intervention, leading to an established international hub that offered assistance to those seeking to overturn capitalist democracy.

Conclusion

Whatever the validity of Ostler's allegations, his arguments highlighted the fact that the First World War had prompted, as elsewhere, a profound increase in the level of security surveillance in New Zealand. State activity expanded as the war progressed and included a significant widening of the surveillance net and a deepening intrusion into the lives of those targeted by the political police and other surveilling authorities. Besides increases in the number of people placed under surveillance, targets evolved over the course of the war. They came to include defaulters and those offering succour to them; people opposing conscription; advocates of a negotiated peace; sectarian provocateurs; and individuals deemed sympathetic to revolutionary action.

Restrictions on civil liberties developed accordingly, and the privacy, freedom and sense of social justice so valued in New Zealand society was profoundly eroded. While many emergency measures receded after the war, some continued – such as systematic censoring of film and literature, in part for political reasons. Another legacy was an institutional capacity to scrutinise ever more sizeable sections of society. Huge databases were built up, and these helped cement in place the legacy of greater surveilling capacity over whole sectors of post-war society. In other words, wartime precedents of greater intrusion into the lives of the citizens, and hence challenges to the national imagery of freedom and fairness, had been firmly established during the wartime emergency and would continue to impact upon New Zealand's history.

PART THREE:

LATENT COLD WAR,

1919-1939

Chapter Four:
Searching for Subversives,
1919–1929

Introduction

The first post-war decade was a paradoxical time for the secret world. On one hand, Germany's defeat reduced official concerns about New Zealand's security. The level of surveillance pursued by the wartime state was, consequently, reduced. However, the legacy of the Bolshevik Revolution held profound geopolitical consequences: what has been seen as the beginning of a 'long Cold War' with international Communism began in 1919 when the Communist International (Comintern, or Third International) was established in Moscow, dedicated to promoting socialist revolution around the globe.[1]

The Russian Civil War, moreover, brought the foundation of the Union of Soviet Socialist Republics (USSR/Soviet Union) in 1922. This was presented as an exemplary model for a socialist society, one ensconced in the largest territory in the world. The spectre of 'the red menace' became a central issue in the interwar threatscape of the West. In the first decade of this 'latent Cold War', the NZPF's political policing function, backed by the enhanced database developed during the war, became more specialised and professionalised. Accordingly, the security legacy of the Great War in New Zealand, as in the West, was a considerably more surveilled society than in the pre-war years.

Overview

Surveying the chaos that followed the ceasefire on the Western Front, one historian notes that '[w]hatever it was that followed the armistice of November 11, 1918, it was not peace'.[2] The destabilisation or collapse of pre-war social and geopolitical orders meant a continuation of inter- and intra-state violence.[3] Over and above open conflict, the immediate post-war years saw revolutionary ideas and activities circulate the globe. Remembered as the 'first red scare', these years witnessed popular fears of revolution and intensive suppressive action. Perhaps the most remembered is the 'Palmer Raids'

(1919–20), in which American authorities arrested thousands of suspected subversives and deported hundreds of foreign radicals.

New Zealand's industrial relations had worsened in the final year of the war, with 40 strikes (involving 4056 workers) recorded in 1918. This escalated in the red scare years, with 75 disputes (involving 9612 workers) logged in 1920.[4] In January 1919 an Alliance of Labour, based on waterfront and transport workers and soon to be joined by other militant unions such as seamen and miners, was formed. Adopting similar policies to the United Federation of Labour, which it replaced, the new grouping alarmed the political police. The Alliance's commitment to the IWW-style syndicalism not only evoked memories of the Great Strike but tended also to be seen in the context of the international spread of Bolshevism, by now a panic-button word applied to socialist or industrial activity of many hues, and a wave of strikes around the globe.[5]

For many New Zealanders, the recent struggle against an external foe had been replaced by another against Bolshevik propaganda and subversion. In October 1919 an *Evening Post* columnist summed up many a publicly voiced sentiment on the menace posed by 'the reds': 'the internal war that goes on always is even more necessary than is external war to the safety of the State'.[6] The New Zealand government seriously contemplated the possibility of major industrial and civil unrest, and official plans for countermeasures included provisions to equip masses of 'auxiliary police', arrangements to safeguard stores of weaponry, and a re-examination of the military's role in assisting suppression of the 1913 strike.[7] Defence Minister James Allen publicly noted, in July 1919, that there was 'so much lawlessness in the country that the only thing that could save [it] from going to damnation was the drill sergeant'.[8]

The Defence Department was similarly concerned about social tension. In September 1920, it was 'reasonable to assume', it declared, 'that the authorities would [soon] be required to deal with outbreaks of Bolshevism, and strikes on a large scale in New Zealand'.[9] The perception that 'Labour Extremists' were using the strike weapon to pursue a 'Soviet system of Government' in New Zealand resulted in top-secret exchanges between Police, ministers and Defence officials throughout 1919 and 1920. These canvassed enrolling ancillary police, establishing municipal Citizens' Corps and deploying soldiers, although Defence stressed this last measure should only be a final resort.[10]

After 1920 such anxieties began to recede, though the fear of revolutionaries simmered over the decade, and episodes like the 1926 General Strike in the United Kingdom stoked fears of 'Bolshie' agitators and plots in New Zealand. Other international upheavals, notably tensions in Ireland and India and the fascist seizure of power in Italy, similarly stirred fears of disorder. The Irish Civil War (1922–23), in particular, resonated in New Zealand: the conflict was seen to challenge the integrity of the Empire, and exacerbated social tension between Irish Catholic and Protestant New Zealand. The trial of the Catholic Bishop of Auckland, James Liston, for sedition, in May 1922, showcased socio-religious division. It occurred in consequence of Liston's reported public remarks praising the 'men and women who in the glorious Easter of 1916 were proud to die for their country – murdered by foreign troops'.[11] When Liston had offered an apology for his comments, Cabinet had declined to accept it, opting instead to make a clear public statement about the need for loyalty to the Empire. In the event, the bishop was acquitted, although the jury declared that he had committed a 'grave indiscretion'.[12]

Some degree of scrutiny of Māori also continued into peacetime. Few parts of Māoridom had fully given up the hope of attaining that which had been promised in the second article of the Māori version of the Treaty of Waitangi: rangatiratanga, or control of their own affairs.[13] Some tribal groupings continued to host Maori Councils of different types, and the Police could liaise with these and their policemen when an issue potentially involving security arose.[14] The raupatu tribes remained the most watched Māori grouping, because of their enduring commitment to regain some, if not all, of the vast lands that had been confiscated from them. After the Sim Commission of 1926–27 found that land confiscation had been unjustified or excessive, the Crown opened negotiations with them. In 1928, outgoing prime minister Gordon Coates opined to his successor, Joseph Ward, that the very concession of government consideration of historical grievances would reduce Māori resistance to the state.[15]

Meanwhile, what became a major new Māori movement of interest to the state, and its surveillers, began in 1918. Founded by faith-healing prophet T. W. Rātana, and formally declaring itself a church in 1925, it evolved into a mass socio-political movement demanding a better deal for Māori. Rātana not only sought to unify Māoridom around the pursuit of socio-economic justice, itself enough to alarm the authorities, but also demanded that the promises of the Treaty of Waitangi be upheld. In the past, governments had preferred to deal with tribal leaderships in their attempts to find a modus vivendi with Māori, more especially one that would induce their people to assimilate to Western ways of behaviour and belief. With the rise of Rātanaism, a non-tribal movement headed by a charismatic leader who spoke for the morehu, the poorest and most dispossessed of the nation's indigenous people, this agenda seemed threatened. As Rātanaism began to involve itself in political action, especially once it had finally become an overtly political movement in 1928, it 'came to be seen by the government as a greater danger' than the Waikato-based King Movement.[16]

Māori issues aside, it cannot be doubted that the emergence and global outreach of the Soviet Union provided the fundamental context for the policy and operations of New Zealand's intelligence community during the interwar years.[17] At the same time, similarly to developments elsewhere, the country's labour movement was experiencing a period of heightened ideological debate over aims and methods which exhibited 'a realism, bluntness and urgency [that it had] never experienced before'.[18] Were socialist ends best achieved through revolutionary or gradualist (especially parliamentary) means, or a mixture, or something quite different? If some or all methods were to be extra-parliamentary, should they be politically and/or industrially based? What were the ultimate goals: a welfare state within a capitalist democracy, a fundamental shift of politico-economic power from capital to labour, or something in between, or something else? Could there be 'socialism in one country', or would the struggle for socialism in New Zealand need to be part of a global movement, especially in light of the acrimonious relationship between the Soviet Union and the non-Communist world?

The debates were often rancorous because the stakes were seen to be high, and for the same reason they were complex, even esoteric. The watchers, though, generally viewed them through the lens of the latent Cold War. They saw those involved in the debates as potential or actual dupes of dangerous foreign agents and ideologies. Intra-left discussions about such matters as the appropriate relationship between the labour movement and international Communism were soon, too, providing ammunition for 'red baiting' in politics and society. In 1920 Prime Minister Massey reflected establishment thinking in declaring, in the context of denouncing opposition politicians, that 'if anything like [the Soviet system] becomes established in New Zealand . . . then I say, Heaven help New Zealand'.[19] As a moderate unionist and Member of Parliament's upper house J. T. Paul noted in November 1918, 'Bolshevism' had become the 'bogey of the hour', a pejorative label used by conservative forces to tarnish the whole New Zealand labour movement. It flowed 'off the tongue with the same ease and facility', he stated, as words such as 'Red Feds' and initials such as 'IWW' had done not long before.[20]

The Labour Party proved a particularly significant site of such debates, and therefore for overt and covert monitoring. The political police were inclined to see even modestly radical proposals – such as gradual acquisition of rural land by the Crown – as evidence that the Party sought fundamental change of extremist nature. Clandestine monitoring of the Party was thus justified on the basis that even apparently moderate members might be hiding their true beliefs, and quietly subverting others. In the red scare of the immediate post-war period there were especially heightened concerns about the industrial and political left. In 1920, Auckland's Detective Sergeant Reg Ward summed up the general disposition of the political detectives in voicing a belief that many Labour Party speeches were 'carefully worded so as to avoid prosecution, but the spirit [was] revolutionary'. He was so worried about the Party that he recommended a shorthand reporter be assigned to its weekly gatherings so that a detailed record of proceedings could be subjected to in-depth analysis.[21]

In reality, the Labour Party's relationship with Communism was as cautious as it was complex and fluid. Many socialists inside the Party at this time were undergoing 'a partial reversion' to the militant views so prominent during pre-war politico-industrial struggles.[22] Numerous rank-and-file members of the party argued for solidarity with the USSR. The Labour Party's Hastings branch was not alone in calling, in 1921, for the party to affiliate with the Comintern.[23]

However, the Labour Party was moving in a distinctively reformist direction and, in 1922, affirmed that 'Labour did not support revolution' but instead 'favoured the transformation of society through education' and democratic law-making. This partly reflected the modifying effects of working within existing political parameters, as the Party garnered greater popular support: its eight parliamentary seats in 1919 rose to 17 in 1922. Its 1927 conference marked the Party's 'decisive step' towards 'retaining what it could [of its socialist platform] without jeopardising the prospect of imminent electoral success', even if that meant jettisoning some policies 'which it believed to be fundamentally right'.[24] While a minority in the Party continued to look favourably at the USSR, 'the general trend gradually came to be one of continuing interest in the experiment but disassociation from its methods'.[25]

Following many wrangles over appropriate ways and means within revolutionary circles, on 9 April 1921 a small group of comrades launched the Communist Party of New Zealand (CPNZ) in Wellington's Socialist (soon renamed Communist) Hall. This development brought together several revolutionary threads that had been developing within New Zealand from the turn of the century. One study concludes that while the CPNZ's members 'aligned themselves with the Bolsheviks emotionally they were not Bolsheviks in terms of their political ideology or practice'.[26] Nevertheless, while the Party exercised a degree of local autonomy, it operated within the discourse and policies which emerged with the Russian Revolution, and the thrust of its activities sat comfortably with those of the Comintern.[27]

The CPNZ struggled through the 1920s. In the first few years its membership sat at fewer than 50 and, while this had climbed to 120 by 1926, it then declined: it was down to 79 by 1928 and 62 by 1930.[28] Such setbacks were due in part to internal factionalism which, among other destabilising issues, saw its headquarters move to Auckland in 1922, on to the mining stronghold of Blackball in 1926, and back to Wellington in 1928. Along the way, the Party had become a branch of the Communist Party of Australia, although it subsequently regained its independence. It formally affiliated with the Comintern in its own right in 1928 and gained entitlement to send representatives to the Comintern's congresses in Moscow; Richard (Dick) Griffin attended the 1928 congress.[29]

Despite the various setbacks to the Party's hopes for wielding significant influence, the mainstream parties and newspapers continued to highlight what they depicted as 'the menace of Communism'. The political detectives, seeing the CPNZ as a toehold of the Comintern, lavished a great deal of attention on the tiny party. They especially looked for evidence of its recruiting or influencing of what they saw as naïve members of the unions, the Labour Party and the broader left. Of course, committed revolutionaries saw it as their obligation to proselytise, so there was a basis for such surveillance. On the other hand, non-revolutionary organisations did their own guarding against infiltration and poaching by the Communist Party. The Labour Party, in particular, took firm measures to distance and protect itself from Bolshevik ideas and influence.[30]

By the time of its 1925 Easter conference, Labour's relationship with the CPNZ had so cooled that the delegates voted to deny membership to anyone belonging to any other party, and this was rigorously enforced.[31] In April 1927, for example, the CPNZ's Frederick Engels Freeman sought election to Wellington City Council on the Labour Party ticket, signing Labour's loyalty pledge in the process. When this was exposed, Labour's *New Zealand Worker* highlighted the deterioration of relations between the mass socialist movement and the tiny grouping of Marxist–Leninists to its left. 'Throughout New Zealand Communists are carrying out a similar policy of falsehood, spying and treachery,' it declared, 'and they should be treated by unions and Labour Party branches as sworn enemies of the Labour Movement.'[32] Labour's loss of five seats at the 1925 election, after a vigorous Reform campaign against its 'reckless attempts to upset existing British institutions [and] make easy the road to all the evils of Communism', had made it all the more determined to disown the CPNZ.[33]

The Bolshevik Revolution also had an impact on right-wing New Zealand, elements of which focused on countering Bolshevism. Given the sheer size of this perceived enemy, some conservative forces were contemplating the use of state force to suppress radicalism in such circumstances as widespread industrial action. During the red scare, a political cartoon depicted a farmer holding a newspaper report entitled 'Bolshevism threatens New Zealand' whilst eyeing a long baton, an indication that he had been a Special in 1913 and was disposed to take up the cause again.[34] Some elements were laced with fanciful conspiracy theories and were prone to issuing alarmist statements. The Welfare League, for example, was established to counter what it called 'the activities of extreme and revolutionary Labour', whose 'most prominent leaders had announced approval of the activities of I.W.W. doctrines and Bolshevism, and the reign of terror in Russia'.[35] The Loyalty League proclaimed that the Labour Party was part of a centuries-old plot by such as the Illuminati, French revolutionaries and now Communists to overthrow the monarchy, private property, religion and marriage.[36] Similarly, the PPA tailored its activities to the red scare, proclaiming that the Labour Party was the vehicle of a Catholic–Bolshevik alliance.[37]

In some sense, the threat perceptions of the 1920s reflected socio-political proclivities which rose to prominence during the war. Weariness and the fear of chaos had brought about a strong desire for stability and a profound suspicion of agitators or reformist change. One study describes post-war New Zealand as a 'clench-buttocked community, more intolerant of dissent or disunity or diversity than ever before or since'.[38] New Zealand's only prosecution for blasphemy libel, which took place in October 1921, needs to be interpreted in the context of post-war anxieties – along with such episodes as Liston's trial and other politically charged prosecutions.[39] Communists, militant socialists, anarcho-syndicalists, Sinn Féiners, pacifists, organised labour and non-conformists, all were seen to inhabit the same dangerous universe of ideas. In the eyes of the authorities, including security intelligence operatives, the most likely reason for well-intentioned citizens of 'God's Own Country' to reject its paradisal offerings – other than through ignorance or malice – was that they had succumbed to the siren songs of outside agitators.

One legacy of the war and its immediate aftermath was greater restrictions on life than in the pre-war years. In 1921 the importation of 'any document [encouraging] violence lawlessness or disorder or express[ing] seditious intention' was banned, for example, and the Customs Department appointed an officer to police this (and, later, to prevent the arrival of indecent publications as well).[40] Politicians and civic leaders sought not only to reverse the moral laxity of wartime but furthermore to secure a definition of peace and good order that required higher standards of social behaviour than in the pre-war era. A campaign to introduce a prohibition on all liquor almost succeeded, but the 'wowsers' were consoled by the retention of six o'clock closing. The office of the film censor helped define and uphold the 'higher' moral standards of peacetime, and indeed to further tighten them. After such work in Customs, former wartime deputy chief postal censor Tanner would become Jolliffe's assistant as film censor and succeeded him in 1927.[41]

Emerging technologies meant new avenues of risk to the state. In the past, wireless telegraphy was viewed as 'an extension of, rather than alternative to, the telegraph system'.[42] Now, wireless telegraphy began to be overlapped by wireless telephony, a change from Morse code to voice transmission. In 1920 legislation enabled the use of radio for other than official and marine purposes, and provision was made to license radio receivers independently of transmitters. This paved the way for public broadcasting, albeit under strict official control. The first licensed radio broadcasting operation began in late 1921 in Dunedin, with public radio stations opening elsewhere the following year.

Controls on content were closely monitored by the postal authorities, especially as the listening audience grew: 4000 listeners in 1925 ballooned to 54,000 in 1930. From early 1923, regulations defined limits upon what could be broadcast, including a ban on 'propaganda of a controversial nature'. In 1925 the government authorised the private Radio Broadcasting Company to have, effectively, the national monopoly on broadcasting (a state of affairs that lasted until 1931). It was run by two members of the Reform Party, and there was considerable criticism that broadcasts had a pro-government bias. In 1925 the regulations were tightened to include, inter alia, both a ban on seditious material and a commitment by radio stations to send out government publicity when requested. All such developments were of interest to the political police – an early permit holder, for example, was 'ordered by the local constable to take down his first aerial for fear he may be spying'.[43]

Although tightening state surveillance could be seen as reflecting a continuation of the conservative trajectory of pre-war social and political developments, the trend had accelerated during the war. Some constraints had grown directly from the emotional strains of the conflict; the 1918 Expeditionary Forces Amendment Act, for example, had barred military defaulters from holding public office or taking part in elections for 10 years.[44] Other controls attempted to build upon the high levels of wartime loyalism: the implementation of flag saluting at schools, for example, was part of a push for civic loyalty, and loyalty pledges for teachers, introduced in 1921, sought to remove radicals from the profession.

Conversely, many restrictions sought to eradicate pockets of disloyalty. The 1919 Undesirable Immigrants Exclusion Act, for example, was an effort to screen out radical influences from abroad. The measure authorised barring entry to any non-citizen deemed 'disaffected or disloyal, or of such a character that his presence would be injurious to the peace, order, and good government', and deporting any such undesirables who were already in the country.[45] On debating the legislation Prime Minister Massey declared that 'the people who are disaffected, who favour Bolshevism and I.W.W.ism and who have sympathies with revolutionary socialism, are not wanted here. The country is better without them.'[46]

Agencies

The institutional developments of the 1920s reflected a complex mixture of lessening some wartime restrictions, continuing others and adding new ones. The success of the Police during the war at keeping tabs on dissidents and neutralising many of their activities meant that after the conflict the government was generally predisposed to retaining the NZPF as its primary surveillance agency – although alternative organisations, as we shall see, were proposed in some official quarters. Despite its stretched numbers and resources, the Police Force quickly began to use the relative luxury of emergence from a wartime threatscape to both build on the surveilling measures it had implemented during it and contemplate the lessons that had been learned.

In the early post-war red scare period, such lessons garnered immediate significance. On 29 January 1919, Commissioner John O'Donovan circulated a confidential memorandum to all officers in charge of districts:

> In view of the fact that considerable industrial and other unrest is reported from other countries and that such may extend to this Dominion it is necessary that special precautions be taken to keep in touch with the movements and actions of persons of revolutionary tendencies who are already here, or who may arrive, with a view to ascertaining whether they are advocating lawlessness or disorder or anything likely to lead to such.

When 'any such information of any value is obtained' it was to go to the Commissioner's office, and fortnightly reports were also to be prepared for him.[47]

On 3 April 1919 O'Donovan reminded his officers about these earlier instructions to monitor 'industrial unrest and persons of revolutionary tendencies'. He now also directed detective staff in each district to prepare a 'reliable and exhaustive' list of all those with 'extreme revolutionary, socialist or I.W.W. ideas or tendencies' for sending to Police Headquarters. Each entry in the alphabetised lists of names, addresses and occupations was to include an assessment on the 'degree the person is considered likely to be a menace to law and order' or if they were supported by 'fellow extremists who are already in the Dominion or who may arrive from time to time'. This was the beginning of a new process, with the detective offices instructed to maintain and update the new records, and marked the creation of a set of district-based files dedicated to security surveillance. In each office, moreover, the security files were to be in the charge of the 'detective who has been detailed to give special attention to the matter of industrial unrest and persons of revolutionary tendencies'.[48]

This instruction laid the basis for an intensive and continuing monitoring of left-wing circles through the interwar period. More sophisticated record-keeping had been developing before the war in larger jurisdictions (such as the British Special Branch and its American equivalent), part of a professionalising drive which included more efficient ways of tracking suspected subversives.[49] New Zealand was now catching up, fuelled by a sense of imminent threat, although some wartime powers were soon surrendered. Cable censorship, for example, was terminated relatively quickly, following the lead of the United Kingdom, and ended at midnight on 30 April 1919.[50]

However, the government exhibited a reluctance to abandon other powers, especially in the immediate context of the red scare.[51] A regulatory transition had begun following the Armistice, with a special parliamentary committee convened to decide which wartime measures should be abandoned and which retained, and in what form. Accordingly, a number of emergency measures were consolidated in the War Regulations Continuance Act of 1920. These addressed matters such as strikes and industrial issues, potential access to firearms and explosives, and seditious ideas and actions. Section two, for example, restated prohibitions on printing, publishing, selling, distributing or possession of material which incited, encouraged, advised or expressed any seditious intention.[52] Labour MP Daniel Sullivan protested in the House that the vague definitions contained within the continued wartime control regulations constituted a deliberate governmental ploy. Among other things, they helped ensure that there was 'not a single . . . form of protest that the workers of this country could make against intolerable conditions, that could not, under the definition provided in these War Regulations, be declared by the government to be a seditious strike'.[53] Such regulations would be used to charge accused seditionaries during the Great Depression of the 1930s and remained in force until their repeal in 1947.[54]

The military-led interception of postal correspondence also lingered after the end of hostilities, if for a much shorter length of time. In a letter to the prime minister in July 1919, Defence Minister Allen noted that 'a good deal of valuable information comes to the government through the medium of the censor, and it was thought wise not to lose this information'.[55] Deputy Chief Postal Censor Tanner provided a rationale for continuing of the system. 'During the course of the late war', he wrote, it had been necessary 'to examine secretly the correspondence of certain persons who were supposed to be disaffected, and who were working to defeat the efforts of the New Zealand Government in meeting its obligations regarding the war by advocating "go slow" or inciting to resist the Military Service Act'. Mail intercepts had given police, Tanner argued, 'the necessary opening . . . to break up organisations whilst still in the act of formation'.[56]

For a period then, censorship continued, albeit on a lesser scale than during the war. In particular, mail going to certain countries, and correspondence addressed to individuals known to have been receiving material considered seditious, was opened. A November 1919 Defence memorandum noted continuing censorship 'on correspondence to enemy countries, and also correspondence inwards and outwards for Prisoners of War, and to certain individuals in New Zealand who have been receiving literature which the Solicitor-General has considered seditious'. This continuation was met with some controversy. The National Peace Council's Charles Mackie, for example, 'one of the individuals receiving special attention' (as the military authorities described it), wrote to the minister of defence protesting that his mail was being tampered with.[57] During 1920 the issue was repeatedly raised in Parliament, with the government citing technicalities as reasons for delay in winding up the wartime regime; and large-scale postal censorship under military authority officially concluded in November 1920.[58] Upon her demobilisation, Ursula Tewsley, one of the language experts working with the censors, would subsequently translate Heinrich Zimmerman's account of James Cook's third voyage and take up a position at the Alexander Turnbull Library.

The NZPF, for its part, appreciated its wartime cooperation with the censors, military intelligence and other agencies such as Customs, noting among other things that the wartime system had greatly enhanced its knowledge base. It sought to continue such liaising.[59] Indeed, new measures were taken to extend the inspection of literature, which required cooperation between agencies. The aim was to root out what were seen as subversive publications, at the same time as efforts were taken to expand the concept of seditious activity. An October 1919 amendment to the Police Offences Act, for example, allowed arrest and prosecution of anyone who 'incites, encourages, or procures disorder, violence or lawlessness'. Public-order crimes had, as we have noted, commonly been used to ensnare political offenders in the past, and the broadened definition of offending would facilitate such use in the future.[60] The various surveilling agencies took advantage of legislative vagueness to widen their working definition of subversive publications and expand the parameters of what constituted seditious activity. With shipping still defined as an essential industry after the war, the Marine Department was among those agencies which watched radical seamen with an eye to having their actions declared seditionary.[61]

The sigint authorities, too, worked to place elements of wartime intelligence work onto a permanent footing, in the process gradually changing from wireless telegraphy to wireless telephony. In 1919, Admiral of the Fleet Lord Jellicoe arrived in New Zealand on an Imperial tour to advise the country on naval defence. His comprehensive report warned of a future Japanese threat, advocated a significant expansion in the Dominion's naval capacity and 'stressed the importance of wireless communications' for intelligence gathering, including through direction-finding radio stations.[62] In 1920 Jellicoe became Governor-General of New Zealand, adding weight to his strong recommendations.

The role of direction-finding radio had 'come into its own on the Western Front', where both sides had used it to locate enemy positions. The method involved two or more stationary receivers locating a transmitting station by means of triangulation. The Royal Navy had been working on adapting the technique to locate the position of ships at sea, and both naval and merchant shipping began using radio direction-finding extensively after the war.[63] The Dominion's naval forces operated within Imperial defence arrangements, and indeed from 1921 were constituted the New Zealand Division of the Royal Navy.

While censorship restrictions on cable, wireless and telegraphic traffic were removed in December 1918, the government retained the monopoly on radio transmission. Imperial naval and signals intelligence requirements in the South Pacific had significant implications for New Zealand stations, run by Post and Telegraph but retaining their military orientation. When the prime minister cabled the Secretary of State for the Colonies in November 1920 about updating the Awanui and Apia radio stations, he noted that the 'complete staff in these and all other New Zealand wireless telegraphy stations are trained and requalified yearly in naval procedures and would be mobilised as [the Royal Naval Volunteer Reserve] in time of war and left in these stations. This includes the stations in the Cook Islands.'[64]

The British continued to seek to more closely integrate New Zealand into the Imperial naval intelligence fold in the Pacific.[65] There were naval intelligence implications for a number of New Zealand developments – when, for example, Wellington decided to establish a direction-finding station at Cape Maria van Diemen in 1926 to support merchant ships, a facility with obvious wartime ramifications.[66] At the same time as the mutual benefits of applying new sigint technology in the Pacific region were being worked through, ways in which New Zealand could contribute to a wider Imperial sigint capacity were also under examination. In 1923, for example, a report on the state of New Zealand defences had noted that other Dominions were erecting high-power wireless stations capable of communicating directly with England. It concluded that the nation's acquisition of an equivalent capacity was a 'strategic necessity'.[67]

The possibility of a major change for humint, reflecting wartime Imperial cooperation, had also been raised. In December 1918, Governor-General Lord Liverpool received a 'secret personal letter' from the Secretary of State for the Colonies which thanked Gibbon and other authorities in New Zealand for their assistance to London's Intelligence Bureau during the war. This letter had gone on to say: 'It is hoped that it will be found possible to place the organization of Imperial Special Intelligence on a permanent footing. If this should prove possible I trust that the co-operation which has worked so well during the war may be continued in the future.' This was to be so secret for the time being 'that the existence in New Zealand of the intelligence system mentioned should not be made known to anyone other than the Minister in Charge of the Department and the officer undertaking the work'.[68] While Allen did not officially respond until 5 June 1919, he had 'no hesitation in giving assurance that in the event of the organization of the Imperial Special Intelligence Bureau being placed on a permanent footing the New Zealand Government will be only too pleased to see that the co-operation of the local bureau is continued in the future'.[69]

By August 1919, details of such a scheme were being discussed by a New Zealand intelligence committee established within the Defence Department as part of a wide-ranging examination of intelligence issues. Brigadier-General George Richardson, who had replaced Gibbon as the liaison officer with the British War Office, argued that New Zealand's main contribution to Imperial security should be to

> . . . organise an intelligence system throughout the Dominion for the purpose of gathering, classifying and recording and safeguarding information under the following heads a. Enemy aliens b. Persons using influence to establish Bolshevism c. Topographical d. Resources e. General (opinion of local citizens on military matters, strikes and Intelligence matters of general interest).

That month, an Intelligence Branch was established at Defence Headquarters, with representation outside the capital as well. Its staff created a card index system covering the categories outlined, with significant information shared with the United Kingdom.[70]

There was obviously an overlap between this organisation and the work of the Police. Finished intelligence on Richardson's list of targeted people and topics would need to rely to a significant degree on input from the political surveillers within the detective offices, especially with information relating to categories (a) and (b). All the same, the separateness of the two organisations was evident in their lines of communication with London. The Defence Intelligence Branch was to continue dealing with its War Office counterparts in the United Kingdom, and from February 1920 sent monthly intelligence reports. The NZPF continued to deal with what were essentially civil police agencies when required.

Essentially, New Zealand's Defence Department sought an arrangement in which police would provide the major legwork in gathering information for its own high-level intelligence system, the farthest part of an Imperial defence security system run from the War Office. This would mean military-led intelligence operating in civil society as part of an Empire-wide watch system. The ministers were supportive of the proposal and in late 1919 Prime Minister Massey, who was also minister in charge of policing, asked the Defence Department to handle a British request for a mutual exchange of information on seditionaries and revolutionaries.[71]

But the Defence authorities pushing this line encountered significant hurdles, even internally. Some military considered it unwise to get involved in 'labour & industrial matters' except in absolute public-order emergencies. This was long-standing policy, embedded in strict and precise guidelines on 'military aid to the civil power'.[72] Post-war unease over industrial militancy and civil discontent about unfulfilled promises did not amount to such a grave threat to the state that it required military intervention into civil society. There was disquiet in the ranks of the civil bureaucracy as well. The military authorities countered this by setting out plans which would make them partners with the Police in an overarching domestic surveillance regime that would constitute the New Zealand contribution to Imperial defence intelligence.

In February 1920, Brigadier-General Richardson proposed such a plan to Commissioner O'Donovan, outlining a 'Central Committee for Intelligence with Agents throughout the Dominion'. There would be a monthly report either 'conjointly by you and I' or by the Committee itself to both the New Zealand prime minister and the War Office. This really meant, as police historian Graeme Dunstall put it, replicating in the Dominion a system based on the 'supposedly close links between MI5 and the Special Branch' – one that was not a partnership of equals, with superior status falling to the former institution and the War Office which hosted it.[73] The director of intelligence at the War Office was told in that month that a first step had been taken to pursue this new arrangement:

> [A] Committee has been appointed here consisting of Brig-Gen G. S. Richardson. C.B., C.M.G., C.B.E., G.O. i/c Administration New Zealand Forces., and Mr J. O'Donovan, Commissioner of Police for the purpose of organizing an Intelligence System for New Zealand which shall embrace both Civil and Military Departments of State and thus be in a position to co-ordinate information from all sources.[74]

However, Commissioner O'Donovan was soon affirming the New Zealand Police Force's mandate as the principal state institution for monitoring threats to the defence of the realm. He stressed the high level of autonomy that police had built up over the last several decades, and that his officers would continue to coordinate the operations of the intelligence cycle with other departments as need arose. In other words, police detectives would continue to work in concert with Customs, Internal Affairs, Defence and other government bureaucracies on issues of joint concern such as monitoring movements of people and publications. At the core of the whole operation were the political detectives doing 'the watching and the recording of information'. [75]

The ministers, perhaps reflecting on the obvious resistance that would greet a combined military–police intelligence system, did not authorise the proposed reorganisation. Richardson arranged to meet O'Donovan in late June 1920 to again push the idea of a military–civil intelligence committee to oversee surveillance in New Zealand, stressing that this would help police better monitor the internal threatscape. The Commissioner, however, continued to reject any such arrangement. As well as arguments in principle about military intrusion into both civil society and police responsibility, there were practical issues to be considered. 'We must continue to maintain full control over all secret information obtained by our officers; no persons military or otherwise should be entitled to see anything.'[76]

Among O'Donovan's many concerns about sharing information was the sanctity of informants' identities, an imperative that remains to this day. The Commissioner expressed scepticism at a military claim that the London Metropolitan Police Special Branch handed covertly obtained information to MI5, as this 'would be a case of experts obtaining information & handing it over to amateurs'; he clearly knew that there had been a post-war power struggle between the Special Branch and defence-based intelligence agencies. It was also his understanding that no such police–military intelligence 'alliance' existed across the Tasman either.[77] Oversight of police activities should properly come only from the political executive and (consistent with national security considerations) the judiciary; and interventions should be rare in any case.

Ultimately, the ministers accepted the status quo: the NZPF remained the primary humint agency in New Zealand, although it and the military cooperated with each other on specific issues – a system which had worked well during the war, although obviously would be on a much lesser scale in peacetime. Aspirations to restructure New Zealand's intelligence community with a dedicated professional security service were now shelved (if not forgotten). All the same, the Defence Department – which also had considerable operational autonomy – did pursue its own intelligence work. It continued, for example, to maintain files on 'revolutionary agents' and 'undesirables', and updated these with information forwarded, inter alia, from the databases kept by Customs and other agencies. Its rationale was that such targets could contaminate soldiers, undermine military preparedness for a future war, and present risks to that war effort should it eventuate. More broadly, the military's interest in civil matters reflected what would today be called 'mission creep', although the curbing of its aspirations in 1920 hindered its major effort to expand its power within the secret world.[78]

The Defence Department also developed greater ties with Imperial military intelligence operations. It appointed military liaison staff with London and eventually established a strong relationship with MI5. That organisation's own duties had expanded massively and now encompassed Empire-wide strategies for countering subversion. A November 1930 memorandum to the Police Commissioner noted that 'M.I.5. duties in New Zealand are carried out at Defence Headquarters', at that time 'in the care of Captain Steele, General Staff intelligence'. His work provided an example of ongoing police–military cooperation, including joint scrutiny of 'the names of all incoming passengers' after the arrival of all vessels in the Dominion.[79]

Although it was confirmed as the primary instrument for domestic surveillance, the NZPF needed to improve its handling of intelligence in the fraught post-war environment. On 10 September 1920, the Commissioner took stock of the efficacy of his fledgling security intelligence system and issued a five-page memorandum to his officers. It stressed that they needed to pay 'increased attention' to revolutionary organisations, movements and propaganda. In Auckland, Wellington, Christchurch and Dunedin a 'discreet Detective . . . must at once be specially detailed' to security surveillance. He needed to be 'relieved of other duties to such an extent as will enable him to give such matters ample attention [and to] receive any assistance he may occasionally require'.[80] From this point onwards, New Zealand's four main cities had a detective with a virtually full-time commitment to political surveillance. Detectives outside the main districts, too, were to pay 'sufficient attention' to security matters and, where it was 'necessary and advisable', police in charge of stations in sub-districts with no detectives should also report regularly on revolutionaries and their sympathisers.

The political police were to keep tabs not only on people and organisations inside New Zealand but also those supporting suspect causes in Australia, Britain, Ireland or '[a]ny other part of the British Dominions'.[81] The detectives were to attend all shipping arrivals and departures, and to monitor, in conjunction with Customs staff, foreign revolutionaries and their sympathisers. After disembarking, these were to be tracked wherever they went throughout the country.

This September memorandum can be taken to mark the final stage of the establishment of a modern, professional political surveilling operation in New Zealand. However, while many accounts refer to a 'Special Branch' in the interwar period, this is a retrospective label that backdates developments in the years after the Second World War. Graeme Dunstall's volume in the History of Policing in New Zealand series makes the point bluntly: there was 'no separate political surveillance unit or "special branch" within the Police Force during the interwar years'.[82] An NZSIS in-house history summarises the situation: 'Detective officers were specially detailed for [security intelligence] work but no separate organisation existed within the Police for this task.'[83]

Having detectives work essentially full-time on political policing was an organisational breakthrough of considerable significance. Dedication to the job and access to better resources allowed not only specialisation but also the gatekeeping required in top-secret work. The detectives initially assigned to dedicated political policing had differing backgrounds. F. J. Beer in Dunedin and Reg Ward in Auckland were relatively new to the job, but Detective Sergeants W. E. Lewis in Wellington and Thomas Gibson in Christchurch had considerable surveilling experience.[84] Other city detectives and uniformed men, detectives in towns, and constables and NCOs in rural areas were not only drawn upon when necessary but also expected to proactively report 'suspicious' activities.[85] In one sense, then, the security service provided by the NZPF stretched down to the humblest constable. As a formal 1919 inquiry into the relationship between the detective and uniformed branches put it, while 'a detective on appointment acquired a status somewhat higher than a constable', both were 'equally necessary in order to secure an efficient police service' and needed to work in harmony.[86]

Detailed summaries from the four key political detectives, and from other stations handling security-related matters, were to be sent to the Commissioner on a monthly basis. Until then, politically sensitive information had been widely accessible within the NZPF, although an informal procedure of storing top-secret material separately from the main district and central registries had arisen (some files from the industrial troubles of 1912–13, for example, had been deemed so delicate that they remained in separate storage for many decades).[87] Under the new rules, all security-sensitive reports and letters were to be labelled 'SECRET' and generally unavailable for 'the scrutiny of other members of the Force'. This would enable the political detectives to 'report without restraint'. In fact, even the non-dedicated detectives in the main centres were not necessarily, the Commissioner stated, 'entitled to know everything that is being done in this connection'.[88] From this time onwards, then, both the regular and special reports prepared by the political policemen for the Commissioner's office were lodged systemically in registries of secret files held in both the districts and at Police Headquarters.

In the early post-war years, the NZPF also firmed up its linkages with the heart of Empire through the London Metropolitan Police's Special Branch. Until 1931, the Special Branch retained primary responsibility for counter-subversion in the United Kingdom and shared some information with, and made arrests on behalf of, MI5. Top-secret information passing between the Imperial centre and its outermost hub was channelled through the New Zealand government's offices in London, to ensure diplomatic-level security. To take one example, in 1927 an 'extremely delicate' source provided information to British security about J. Basham, a New Zealander who had been investigating the unemployed movement in the United Kingdom. When this was passed on, New Zealand's Police Commissioner ordered a 'very cautious enquiry' into the possibility that he was intending to set up a similar movement in the Dominion, one that the Police believed would be a Communist front.[89]

The NZPF also continued to develop its intelligence linkages with other security-related agencies overseas, particularly those across the Tasman (especially in the period when the CPNZ was a branch of the Communist Party of Australia) and in the United States. In 1921, for example, police sought information from the Americans about Fintan Patrick (F. P.) Walsh, 'a dangerous man of excitable temperament'; he would later become the 'most influential single figure in the New Zealand Labour Movement'.[90] International policing cooperation was relatively undeveloped, however: the organisation that eventually became Interpol, for example, was launched only in 1923. Essentially, New Zealand's security surveillance remained, for most practical purposes, inwards-looking.

Ultimately, then, perceived threats to public order 'brought political surveillance to a new level'.[91] On the surface, paradoxically, this new level of state surveillance was instituted at the same time as Commissioner O'Donovan accelerated efforts to move the NZPF back onto the modernising path that New Zealand policing (and that of similar jurisdictions) had been taking since the 1880s. John Cullen's commissionership had represented, in a sense, a throwback to frontier policing, with its emphasis on wielding coercion rather than seeking conciliation and consent, whereas O'Donovan stressed that his men were 'peace officers' seeking (and generally gaining) the consent of much of the population. While he had firmly enforced the wartime emergency measures, the Commissioner had all along been gradually moving the force back to the trajectory that had been disrupted by industrial strife and wartime emergency.

The war years, as we have noted, had witnessed a decrease in both the total police complement and the quality of policing, the result of such factors as enlistment luring personnel away and large increases in workload. After the war, additional temporary constables were taken on and former policemen were attracted back once they had regained their previous service and superannuation rights. An overdue pay rise in 1920, too, sought to entice new talent.[92] In May 1921, the training of recruits resumed, with longer courses to improve quality, and by the end of that year only 18 temporary staff remained.[93] The gradual building up of the calibre of the force had important ramifications for surveilling, given that the political police relied a great deal on reports and tip-offs from uniformed patrollers and men assigned to plain-clothes duties outside the big cities.

Detective policing had also experienced a war-related decline in quality. By the early 1920s, moreover, it was still struggling to be accepted as a calling that was integral to a generalist force based fundamentally on uniformed patrolling. A 1919 inquiry into the appropriate relationship between the two branches was dominated by senior uniformed officers. It rejected the detectives' bid for a discrete career structure that equated, for example, the position of Detective with that of a uniformed Sergeant. This both helped perpetuate discontent within detective ranks and deflected some constables of considerable potential from moving to plain-clothes work. All the same, in the wake of the report's favourable assessment of the work of the detective wing, the detectives gained a higher standing in the force. Their numbers quickly rose to 47 by 1921, up from 38 in 1918. Staffing then more or less stabilised, not exceeding 56 at any point in the decade.[94]

The moves towards modernisation of policing continued under Commissioners Arthur Wright from 1922 and, from 1926 to 1930, William McIlveney, a flamboyant man whose career had included highly successful detective work. Police professionalisation processes were overarched by the imperative to secure the consent of most of the population, the law-abiders. For the detection branch, this rested on bringing offenders to book. When this occurred through the work of the political police, however, the public did not know about their involvement. This mix of overt and clandestine policing reflected a continuation of past practices into an era of uneasy peace, but the secret world was gaining greater prominence inside the generalist Police Force – something that continued to sit uncomfortably within the dominant New Zealand mythscape. This element of policing, however, had been endorsed by the Reform government and, from 1928, by its equally conservative successor ministry, the United Party.

Operations

The ways in which the intelligence cycle is undertaken at any point in time reflect a number of factors, including the types and extent of perceived security risks; long-term organisational practices, protocols and culture; and the priorities and perceptions of the surveilling institution and its government.[95] The full scope and focus of surveillance in the 1920s remains obscured by intermittent and patchy processes in declassifying historical documentation and by the destruction of some records. In 1962, for example, the Department of Justice ordered the destruction of certain files and index cards from the 1921–31 period – those on 'Indians who were active in seeking independence for their country, but who have not come to notice since', and material on Irish Republican Army connections ('except where members of the [Communist Party] were involved', in which case they were retained).[96]

Regardless of shortfalls in evidence, the available material illustrates the ways in which surveillance priorities were set by the major strategic concerns of the era. Concerns over espionage over the 1920s did notably decline from the wartime high, but Soviet and Japanese ambitions were monitored and the surveillance of socialists took into account that the Comintern, or its offshoot the Red International of Labour Unions (Profintern), formed in 1921 with the aim of coordinating Communist activities within trade unions, might seek to use members of the CPNZ or fellow travellers as agents.[97] However, the USSR's distance from New Zealand, and the absence of any local diplomatic mission or trade presence that might act as a base for any such espionage operations, were seen to limit such threats.[98] In a 1927 report the military judged that the 'dangerous phase of the Communistic wave seems to have passed in New Zealand, and there is probably no one here now who could be considered a paid agent of the Russian Soviet'.[99]

Japan's ambitions in the Pacific were viewed with some suspicion, especially as knowledge of Japanese espionage operations began to leak out – partly through the world's first peacetime office for intercepting and decrypting diplomatic communications, established by the United States in 1919.[100] However, Japan's spying was focused elsewhere, and New Zealand's military intelligence officials merely kept a watching brief on the situation through the Naval Office in Wellington, which was linked into the British intelligence stations in Hong Kong.[101] Major-General W. G. Stevens later recalled that even in the 1930s defence intelligence constituted a 'phantom branch' that was 'entirely dependent' on material sent from Britain.[102]

Threat perceptions could also be heightened by special considerations. When the heir to the throne (Edward, Prince of Wales) undertook a month-long tour of New Zealand in 1920, he was protected by an 87-strong police escort, headed by the Commissioner himself, with the politically savvy Inspector Broberg in charge of intelligence. Security concerns centred upon threats to the safety and dignity of the prince. However, the main problems turned out to be adoring fans mobbing the 'Playboy Prince', excessive demands for handshaking, and a near strike from the Wellington section of the royal escort – who refused to sleep in cells in Dunedin when NCOs, detectives and officers were bedded in hotels.[103]

Across the decade, the selection of targets for investigation by the political police originated in various ways. Besides broad directives from the Commissioner, more specific instructions periodically arrived from central or district levels. In January 1921, for example, O'Donovan told the Auckland Superintendent that his attention had been drawn to a letter in a newspaper 'which refers to unpatriotic and seditious speeches at a conference of Unions held at Auckland under the auspices of the Alliance of Labour. Please have a report submitted on the matter.'[104] Other investigations were initiated by concern within government departments, whose permanent heads would draw some matters to the attention of their ministers. In the context of a significant industrial dispute with sugar workers in September 1920, for example, the minister of labour requested that the movements of the president of a coordinating union body 'be watched for a few weeks' to determine whether he was involving himself in the dispute; 'absolutely secret' inquiries followed.[105]

O'Donovan's instructions during the red scare to look for 'movements and persons of revolutionary tendencies' set, in many ways, the guiding tone for the decade. Under this mandate, officers and their detective officers in the districts exercised some considerable discretion in how targets for investigation were selected. Responding to O'Donovan's September 1920 memorandum, for example, Greymouth's Detective J. B. Young reported that he had, 'as yet, been unable to trace the existence of any organisation or movements in the Dominion formed expressly for the promotion or encouraging of revolutionary principles'. In lieu, he compiled and forwarded a list of men held to be in sympathy with such principles, while stressing that there was no evidence of any organised promotion of revolution. He believed that while they were 'all men holding extreme views on Labour questions [and] the controlling factors of the principal Labour Unions', they were 'organised for the purpose of improving the conditions of the working classes'.[106]

Most intelligence reports similarly focused on those who might be subject to 'contamination' by revolutionaries by dint of their connection to organised political or industrial labour. But the primary subjects of surveillance through the 1920s remained those who might be the contaminators: the Communist Party, militant unionists and the IWW, together with those in close contact or sympathy with them.[107] As the official history of policing for this period noted, although 'the scope of sedition was potentially broad, the police concentrated on the possibility of sedition from left-wing groups. This reflected both the ethos of the [Police Force] and the dominance of conservatism in New Zealand political life before 1935.'[108] As a retired Superintendent declared in the later 1920s, Police had to deal with 'Communists and Red Feds who have no respect for the laws of God or man'.[109]

It also reflected the fact that there was no mass far-right activity in the Dominion during the decade. When incidents involving potential or actual disorder from the right arose, they tended to be investigated in terms of the police mandate to maintain peace and good order rather than be viewed as threats to the state. In May 1926, for example, some 50 Canterbury University College students, many wearing black shirts, had crashed a Trade Hall meeting called to support the British General Strike. Unfurling 'a Fascisti banner', the group had sung the national anthem in competition with workers singing 'The Red Flag'. The relevant Police file shows no evidence of assessments as to whether or not the students were fascists and/or posed a danger to the state.[110]

The CPNZ was especially closely monitored, and this stepped up from time to time in response to international events: in 1926, for example, in the context of fears that Britain's General Strike might encourage Communist agitation in the Dominion, especially among the growing numbers of unemployed. To meet this possibility, Commissioner McIlveney instructed that greater attention be paid to tracking both 'Communistic Propaganda' and the movements of Communist leaders and speakers. These should preferably be known about in advance, to help inform any countermeasures that might be needed. Another escalation in covert surveillance of Communist circles occurred towards the end of the decade, after the CPNZ's affiliation with the Comintern. In January 1929 Dick Griffin, returned from the World Congress of the Communist International, became the Party's first general secretary and set out to enhance its influence. In the process, party headquarters was relocated from the isolated West Coast to the political heart of the country, Wellington.

The New Zealand Socialist Party, too, remained under close surveillance, in part because of its attempts to influence the Labour Party, even though the NZSP had morphed into the New Zealand wing of an international movement advocating communitarian-directed reform.[111] Although it was increasingly reformist, the Labour Party's often fiery rhetoric and radical past resonated in police memories, and surveillance of its key members and a number of others endured in the post-war secret world.[112] The Party's leaders were closely watched for seditionary activities, and details and activities of Labour MPs were recorded in the Police secret files. A 1921 'recording sheet' of people under watch included Harry Holland, who had addressed meetings of the Social Democratic and Labour Parties; Paddy Webb, noted as being a 'C.P. [Communist Party] sympathiser'; future prime minister Walter Nash and his assistant, for '[c]onducting revolutionary literary agency'; other leading Labour personalities such as Semple and Hickey; and Professor Thomas Hunter, who had addressed both CPNZ and Labour Party meetings.[113]

The CPNZ gained little support among Māori, but fears remained among the surveillers that increasing international attention being paid to indigenous rights might encourage a rise in self-determinationist sentiment in New Zealand that the CPNZ would then seek to exploit – and which might constitute a threat to the state in its own right. T. W. Rātana's teachings were especially worrying, as the movement campaigned not only for the Crown to honour the Treaty of Waitangi but also for 'Maori Self Government'. While successive governments had come to a modus vivendi with many tribal leaders, pending (in official plans, anyway) full assimilation, there were no precedents for dealing with Rātanaism – a mass indigenous movement that eschewed tribal structures and was growing remarkably fast. Rātana, indeed, had gained the adherence of at least a fifth of the Māori population by 1927, probably much more, and the movement would soon set out to win the four parliamentary seats reserved for Māori.[114]

The fact that some radical elements of the King Movement, the Kīngitanga, found common cause with Rātanaism caused additional concern. Most troubling of all was the fact that Rātana's precepts resonated with the fundamental tenets of social democracy and hence with a mass movement of the left. There were also worries that T. W. Rātana, who had visited Japan in 1924 and found synergies with some of its values, might present a possible beachhead for Japanese influence.[115] For such reasons, Rātanaism was increasingly viewed as 'a serious new potential mode of subversion'.[116] It had, moreover, its own social control mechanisms rivalling the state's, including its own police force of kātipa presided over by a chief of police.[117] Though they lingered, concerns about Japanese influence faded after they were forthrightly rejected by the movement.

In the traditionally oppositional regions of Te Urewera and Waikato, too, sole constables monitored the tribes with the assistance of other agencies and civilians. In the former region, for example, the Native Department helped police monitor Rua

Kēnana's followers, with an eye to pre-empting a resurgence of anti-state activities. In the latter, Kīngitanga's previous refusal to fully support the war effort ensured that a close watch was kept on it after the war.[118] Such surveillance stepped up with the re-establishment of the King Movement as 'a central force among the Tainui people' under the leadership of Te Puea Hērangi (generally known as Princess Te Puea).[119]

Supporters of nationalist and anti-colonial movements throughout the British Empire were also watched, especially as the Third International had committed itself to supporting anti-imperialist struggles in 1920.[120] This was more especially the case where, as with 'the Irish issue', such causes had a history of violent struggle. In New Zealand scrutiny would fall, for example, upon political groupings supporting Sinn Féin and other organisations struggling for a united Irish republic.[121] Particular regard was paid to overlaps between Irish republicanism, Communism and expressions of opposition or contempt for the existing Imperial and domestic socio-economic and political order. Sympathisers and members of the Mau independence movement in New Zealand–administered Samoa were placed under scrutiny.[122] As official eyes saw it, 'unrest among the natives' was 'entirely engineered by a few discontented whites and half castes who are backed up by the Labour Party in New Zealand to embarrass the government'.[123]

Wartime concerns around the loyalties of alien residents also continued into the peace and police monitored and assessed them accordingly. On 29 January 1919, the day of his 'special precautions' memorandum, the Commissioner followed up an approach from the Chief of General Staff by ordering that his men should find out whether each enemy alien in the country, together with every other alien reporting to police, sought to remain in the country; and to report whether those who wished to stay should be allowed to. The results of this exercise would be shared with the Imperial authorities.[124]

Broader politico-cultural movements perceived as being prone to contamination by revolutionists were also watched by the covert surveillers at varying levels of scrutiny. Examples include emerging campaigns for prison, hygiene and health reform, along with long-standing targets such as anti-militarist, socialist and utopian groupings of many hues: essentially all those who spoke out on behalf of the dispossessed and marginalised, or advocated collective lifestyles, or moved in rank-and-file union circles, or involved themselves in single-issue campaigns. An example of the last-mentioned category were the transnational protests about the sentencing to death of two Italian anarchists, Nicola Sacco and Bartolomeo Vanzetti, in the United States after a manifestly unjust trial in 1921: these protests were ultimately unsuccessful and Sacco and Vanzetti were executed in 1927.[125]

A number of academics came under scrutiny because of the influence they could potentially wield through their teaching, and politicians tended to show a particular interest in education. A trainee teacher, Hetty Weitzel, was convicted for selling seditious literature to an undercover policeman and consequently forfeited her chosen career. This episode led to high-level investigations into radicalism at the Wellington Teachers' Training College and, on ministerial request, an investigation into 'extreme Socialistic propaganda' allegedly disseminated through students' clubs at Victoria University College.[126] A Workers' Educational Association tutor, the 'Revolutionary Socialist' clergyman C. Marsh-Roberts, lost his job after the minister of education put pressure on the college authorities. The problem had been his 'anti-British and unpatriotic views'. Professor Thomas Hunter, who would serve as the vice-chancellor of the University of New Zealand between 1929 and 1947, and from 1938 as the principal of Victoria University College as well, was also scrutinised. He had already come under the surveillers' gaze since his foundational role in setting up the Workers' Educational Association in 1915, his links with the Social Democratic Party, and his advocacy of a rationalist approach to life. He believed that 'collective state action' was needed to address the 'social and economic reconstruction' needed to counter the harm done by 'capitalist forms of economic organisation'. His security index card remained in the secret files until it was destroyed in 1983, 30 years after his death.[127]

As we have noted, the Defence authorities were building up, in effect, parallel databases of political targets, working from these when reporting to New Zealand politicians and overseas intelligence counterparts. In 1927, for example, the Chief of General Staff sent the prime minister a list of 40 'persons who are known to have, or have had, Communistic leanings'. It included an 'agitator' married to 'a German girl named Weitzel, sister of the girl who gave trouble' at Victoria University College; a 'Labour Party man who has advocated for the Soviet form of Government'; and a '[p]lain rebel, who would take up anything against Government capitalism'.[128]

The political police continued to employ a variety of means to gather information on individuals and movements tagged as subjects of interest, ranging from securing readily available material to more covert means. The foundational base of the accumulating political files continued to be public material including literature produced by movements, organisations or individuals of interest and most especially newspaper reports. Declassified files are replete with press cuttings about meetings or rallies, articles on individuals or incidents, and letters submitted to the editor by or about persons of interest. These were sometimes marked with blue pencil, signalling an intention to follow them up with enquiries; or with marginalia that, inter alia, cross-referenced material to other layers of the archival database. In some cases, newspaper content fed into the intelligence cycle and resulted in decisions to prosecute. The rhetoric that became the basis for prosecuting Bishop Liston, for example, had not been recorded by a policeman or informant but by a journalist attending a public meeting.[129]

Other information was freely supplied by members of the public. In late 1920, for example, police enquiries were opened when the secretary of the Soldiers' Mothers League reported the sale of 'The Communist Programme of the World Revolution' in Auckland's Freemans Bay.[130] In another instance, a landlord had told police of two boarders holding anti-war, anti-royalist and anti-patriotic attitudes: '[T]hey are disloyal subjects [and] I have frequently seen them when drinking wine tap their glasses together and say "Heres Damnation to the King of England."' Such reports were frequent in the database of suspected subversives and seditionaries. In this case, it informed a revised list of Otago's 'Labour Agitators' and 'men who hold very extreme views besides one or two who might easily be termed Revolutionists'.[131]

Further information streams derived from standard policing duties and operations. A variety of public meetings, a major feature of social and political life in the interwar years, were attended by police personnel in either uniform or plain clothes.[132] Uniformed monitoring had a dual role: firstly, it was preventive, creating an official presence to influence or even intimidate the less committed and the curious. It was often observed that a uniformed presence at public meetings, for example, lowered the number of attendees.[133] Secondly, it had a prosecutorial role. If orators seemingly crossed the uncertain line between legality and illegality, the uniformed men's reports might be all there was to be fed into the intelligence cycle and any decision to prosecute. At other times, uniformed branch reports complemented those of the detectives.

In one case in early 1921, both branches attended a public address to the Otago Labour Representation Committee by Mary McCarthy, a retired schoolteacher who had recently returned from Europe. She had not only met many Communists on her trip but also had expressed bitterness towards British authorities on such matters as their suppression of strikers and Irish Catholics. Detective Beer concluded that 'she may be considered dangerous and should she deliver addresses in other centres of the Dominion it may be considered necessary to give her special attention'. This suggestion was endorsed as his report progressed upwards through the Police hierarchy.[134] Other surveillance operations also demonstrate coordination across regions. In one 1920 example an Australian member of the IWW, John B. Williams, was placed under security scrutiny upon entering New Zealand amidst suspicions that he intended to promote the establishment of syndicalist trade unions. Policemen charted his progress around the country and, among other things, linked him with a One Big Union branch launched in Auckland that May.[135]

Meetings not open to the public presented a different challenge, and covert ways of surveilling then were sometimes difficult to effect. In late 1919, for example, Wellington detectives became interested in a man 'already known to the police' for pro-Bolshevik comments he had reportedly made within the 'inner workings' of the Returned Soldiers' Association (RSA) – but not in front of Association meetings attended by policemen who were members. When a detective investigated, he found it was 'not possible to get members of that Association who are outside the Police Force to divulge what takes place at those meetings'.[136]

Such cases, obviously, would have benefited from informants within the organisation. It took time, however, to provide a significant network of police infiltrators and civilian informants to meet the needs of the latent Cold War. As Detective Beer noted, gathering information by infiltrating undercover police staff into organisations, meetings or movements was difficult because of the possibility of recognition. In particular, the city uniformed men were regularly seen on the beats that constituted their major duty, and the detectives became well known after attending a number of socialist and protest rallies and meetings. As Beer knew from personal experience, it became almost impossible for any recognised police agent to continue such infiltration work, as word would quickly spread.[137]

The political detectives, then, increasingly needed the services of informants. Some of these were recruited, while others approached the Police with offers of assistance; some required payment, others did not. The clandestine nature of their employment meant that the material they supplied was guided towards the secret files, rather than publicly aired in the courts for official prosecutions; at least until the detectives could, guided by informants' reports, gather other incriminating evidence.

The analysts contextualised informants' intelligence by referring, among other things, to observations from beat constables; detectives' reports based on what they had learnt during their rounds of factories, pubs, working men's clubs and other useful locations; memoranda by both overt and covert surveillers of public and private associations and gatherings; notes by patrol police and detectives recording informal conversations with widely disparate categories of people; and reports from other commissioned or volunteer informants. Additionally, the political detectives often trawled through the files, a task that was becoming more efficient as cross-referencing practices improved.

Too much reliance on informants created problems. Ideological zeal or personal disgruntlement could inspire or infect reports sent in by volunteers concerned at the direction being taken by their organisations and movements, as well as by those who had been shoulder-tapped because they were known to be disaffected. While informants who worked for money received modest returns, the very fact of payment might induce them to provide information tailored to impress their paymaster: embellishing or padding out their verbal or written reports, for example, or even making up some or all of the contents. Or alternatively, they might provide just enough information to string their handlers along, but never anything substantial: as one put it, he would tell them 'enough to let them think they are pumping me'.[138]

Ultimately, informants were only adjuncts in the intelligence cycle. Given their lack of training, their reports needed to be worked through carefully by their handlers and, where necessary, interrogated by others further up the chain of command. Sworn police continued to infiltrate key groups and movements, and their reports helped place those of the informants into context. They tended to be rotated quickly, to minimise the chance of discovery. In July 1929, for example, Constable George Deakin was ordered to inveigle himself into the Wellington branch of the CPNZ by posing as an unemployed worker undergoing a political awakening. Over a series of classes and meetings, he learnt about the books and pamphlets that were stocked, aspects of the branch's printing and distribution operation, the personal backgrounds and political positions of Party members, and the topics and positions raised in gatherings. This led to a raid, after which he announced that his assumed persona was moving out of town to look for work.[139]

There were some successful longer-term penetrations by undercover policemen, however. In Auckland (especially) and elsewhere, some became significant office holders within local Communist organisations. The longer the infiltration, the more valuable the information about agendas, policies, personalities and the like to feed into the intelligence cycle, and this had to be weighed against the risks of mounting such operations in a small society. A Christchurch undercover policeman was subpoenaed under his false name to provide defence evidence, for example; to make matters more complicated still, he was delegated by his 'comrades' to approach the Police to request the return of seized Party property.[140]

Such men were always conscious that their cover could be blown by recognition or remarks by a third party, perhaps another policeman not in the know. In his key memorandum of September 1920, Commissioner O'Donovan had stressed the need to erect a barrier between political policing and the general work of the force. The 'object' of specialist security detectives was to procure 'the fullest information possible regarding [subversive] matters and persons and to have thorough investigation'; in practice this meant that few, if any, uniformed men knew about any given operation. There was a logistical downside to such secrecy inside the force: a mere handful of personnel had to master the 'mountain of reports' that began to accumulate in the regional and central filing systems.[141]

This had obvious ramifications for efficiency in both the short term and long term. Much of the information gathered remained in raw form in the secret files, and such untested data could lead to misapprehensions when accessed at a later time. Even if gathered material had been analysed soon after its collection and basic (if improving) cross-referencing, this was often defective because of the size of the files, especially when coupled with other factors such as poor understanding of the motivations of the targets.

The NZPF's capacity to coerce, however, led directly to acquisition of key material. In memoirs published in 1960, Sid Scott recollected a police search in 1928, when he was the secretary of the Auckland branch of the Communist Party: '[F]ive detectives in plain clothes suddenly swooped on my place of abode [and] with two minutes warning I managed to secret some of the packages on the roof of an adjoining bakehouse.'[142] The police party did seize other papers and literature, however, and a recording sheet of this material noted not only political works such as *The A.B.C. of Communism* but also 'indecent literature' – Upton and Mary Craig Sinclair's novel *Sylvia's Marriage*, which dealt with the subject of venereal disease. Scott was eventually fined a very stiff £17.[143] Some such offending material was confiscated and destroyed, but other items went into the secret files.

Such raids had several purposes besides prosecution and removing 'dangerous' ideas from public circulation. Sometimes, after police raids had found material deemed to threaten the state, foreign 'undesirables' would be expelled from the country. By late 1926, for example, for over a year police had been monitoring 'one of the worst I.W.W. members trading in this country', Mauritius-born Eugene De Langre. He had been 'inculcating' go-slows in workplaces and engaging in other radical activities. His New Zealand activism came to an end after a Wellington police search of SS *Manuka* uncovered a substantial quantity of seditious literature in his sleeping quarters. After conviction, he was ejected from the Dominion, and a watch notice was posted in case he attempted to return.[144]

The political police especially sought documents relating to the internal matters of left-wing organisations and their wider networks. For example, in his report of a July 1929 raid on Wellington's 166D Vivian Street, Detective N. W. Baylis noted that some papers that had been seized 'are of great interest as they show where this literature is coming from and who are the supporters' of the Communist Party.[145] This correspondence was used to compile a nine-page list of names and addresses associated with the Party.[146] Such raids could have adverse ramifications for careers, even for those who were on the margins of political activity. A police analysis of Communist Party reports seized in August that year noted that they included mention of a 'sympathiser schoolteacher' and concluded that 'it may be considered advisable to pass this information on to the Education Board under whom she may be serving'.[147]

The political detectives often worked with other authorities tasked with state protection, especially those with border, judicial, postal, censorship and telegraphic responsibilities, effectively extending the intensified bureaucratic cooperation induced by the war. The Solicitor-General's Office indexed seditious literature, for example, and political police would routinely pass information about bulk importers of officially subversive literature, and the individual recipients of this material, to customs officials, as well as warning them of suspect-looking titles. A 1921 report by Auckland's Detective Sergeant Ward provides an indication of police-initiated inter-agency cooperation. He had been 'informed that socialistic literature is imported into the Dominion by Alex F McDonnell [and] I think his imports should be closely examined by the post office and customs'. After analysis, his report was then marked with blue pencil, highlighting points to be followed up.[148]

In one January 1921 operation, future prime minister Walter Nash had his luggage searched after returning from Melbourne with a load of pamphlets for his bookshop. A Wellington detective searched the package at the wharf, finding among other things Nikolai Bukharin's *Programme for World Revolution*. Nash was prosecuted for bringing material inciting revolution into the country, with the seized literature deemed by the judiciary to be as 'dangerous to the body politic as typhoid germs placed in a city reservoir'; the press proclaimed 'Bolshevik Agent Fined', and the offender, who would be in Cabinet by the middle of the following decade, was fined the not inconsiderable sum of £5 with £7 costs.[149]

Customs would in turn report to the Police Force any other intercepted literature they felt might be 'revolutionary' or otherwise threatening the national good. New 'prohibited publications' were ongoingly added to the very many socialist titles already listed. Those that were allowed, though, indicate some sifting processes that are now hard to comprehend. While Leon Trotsky's history of the Russian Revolution joined Keir Hardie's *India* in getting clearance, those not allowed in, to take one theme, included 'Sinn Fein Irish Republic Brotherhood Badges', 'Portraits of Edward or Eamon de Valera, President of the so-called Irish Republic' and a 'Map of the Irish Republic'.[150] Similarly, a later assessment did not prohibit Marx and Engels' *Manifesto of the Communist Party*, arguing it was 'well known to students of political economy and is of historical value to such students and to the general reading public'.[151]

Police liaison with the Post Office built upon those arrangements which had developed over the decades before the world war and strengthened during it.[152] As we have seen, such cooperation often occurred in the liminal spaces between what was legal and what was not. What, for example, did the prohibition on 'wilful interference' with telecommunications, written into the 1928 Post and Telegraph Act, actually mean? Whatever the answer, informal interceptions continued under the rubric of the national good.[153] The only regions where interception of letters and other communications between persons of interest was problematic for police personnel were those renowned for their radicalism, especially the South Island's West Coast. A constable stationed in the mining town of Denniston, for example, felt he was hampered by the 'Post Mistress [being] a member of a family whom I would be the first to suspect of receiving [revolutionary] literature'. For him, it was just 'not safe to make inquiries of a confidential nature at the Post-office'.[154]

Security cooperation with Australia continued in the interwar period. Postal censors' reports forwarded to New Zealand from that country, for example, provided information that was used to guide counter-subversion operations. In April 1919, labourer Henry Murphy wrote to an associate whose mail the Australian censors were monitoring. Alongside the transcribed words of the letter, the censor's report noted:

> Murphy appears to be a dangerous character of the I.W.W. type. He is an admirer of the Bolsheviki [sic] and is gradually drifting towards anarchy, revolution and outrage. This letter should be of interest to the New Zealand authorities who might not be aware of the extremist views held by the writer. His hatred of work is one

of the traits of the I.W.W. character. There are indications in the
letter, and in the style of penmanship, that the writer is an alien.

A subsequent investigation saw Murphy sentenced to 14 days' imprisonment for
failing to register under the Military Service Act and, after deportation proceedings
commenced, he agreed to leave New Zealand voluntarily.[155]

Intelligence links with Britain also furnished information to New Zealand, and
ongoing efforts were made to firm up police and military intelligence exchanges with
counterparts in London.[156] One example of such sharing occurred after a May 1927 raid
on the Arcos (All Russian Co-operative Society Ltd) building in London, where the
Soviet trade delegation was being used as a cover for subversive activity throughout the
Empire. Seized papers had revealed a New Zealand connection, and this information
was sent on to Wellington. It related to Gordon Kilpatrick, who in 1924–25 had been
general secretary of the New Zealand section of the Communist Party of Australia. He
has been described as 'probably New Zealand's first native-born Soviet agent', although
he denied that he had ever been a spy and contended that his details had been found
in the Arcos raid merely because he subscribed to the *Soviet Union Review*. At least
two policemen were present at any public meeting the Party held in Wellington, he
declared, and he and his comrades were 'not troubled in the least at their presence,
because we have nothing to hide'. Neither the overt police surveillers at his meetings,
nor the covert surveillance which complemented their reports, uncovered any reason
for charging Kilpatrick with a crime.[157]

As we have stressed, information, however acquired, required analysis to produce
the finished intelligence upon which to base official actions. This part of the intelligence cycle did not fundamentally change through the 1920s, although the organisation
of information became increasingly systematised and professionalised and this assisted
the task of assessment. Analysis of material began with the surveillers' summaries of
their inquiries, sometimes including specific assessments and recommendations. These
reports then went, at first call, to the superior officers to whom the detectives reported.
Those of consequence would move upwards through the institutional hierarchy in
various forms, condensed and/or annotated along the way. Gathered information and its
assessment would generally go into the district's monthly reports to the Commissioner,
although reports would be sent to Police Headquarters at once in cases of special or
urgent import. Higher-level analysis and its operationalisation within the intelligence
cycle, therefore, remained in the hands of uniformed officers at district and, ultimately,
headquarters level.

The sheer amount of reports that began to accumulate in local, regional
and central files threatened to introduce errors and analytical inefficiencies into
assessments.[158] Accordingly, efforts to better process and manage information were
developed, including new finding aids and *Police Gazette* references to individuals. The

central register of secret files included an index of suspected names and organisations, together with synopses of the regular and special reports received from the districts. The NCO in charge of the central registry would sift the information received from the regional offices and provide briefings for the Commissioner. Headquarters would assess and collate such material, initiating operations or circulating information to all of the Dominion's police stations – registers of known and suspected Communists, for example. A July 1929 circular listed 544 current or past subscribers to the CPNZ's newspaper and 40 active Communists in the country.[159]

However, the system remained primitive in many ways; to take just one example, only in a small number of instances were specific files on individuals opened, with extracts from the subject-based secret files being copied into personal files. All the same, the secret files enabled ongoing assessments of individuals through their component parts.[160] The moderating trend within the Labour Party, for example, was tracked. By March 1929, after a meeting of the unemployed in Wellington, a detective approvingly noted that former firebrand MPs Peter Fraser and Robert Semple had 'set out to show the meeting the foolishness' of the the one big union concept and had ridiculed its leaders and adherents in the process.[161] Likewise, military intelligence had a category for 'the Semple type who has moderated somewhat of late'; however, this remained within a broader category of men 'who may reasonably be considered to have Communistic leanings'.[162]

As this suggests, relations between the Labour Party and the CPNZ formed a subject of intense study, with surveillers increasingly exhibiting an awareness that the methods and goals of the two parties were diverging.[163] As early as mid-1921, Detective Sergeant Lewis noted the growing friction between Communism and Labourism and reported:

> From the appearance of things there is no doubt that the Labour and Communist Parties are drifting apart somewhat. This applies of course only to matters of routine, and would not apply in the matter of a strike. The Labour Party does not aim to sell literature of a dangerous kind. The Communist does. The Labour Party members state definitely that they do not believe in violence or other methods not constitutional to gain their ends. The Communist does not agree with this view, and is inclined to call the Labour members and the *Maoriland Worker*, YELLOW.[164]

This is not to say that intelligence reports and analyses were necessarily sophisticated or accurate. Detectives assigned to political surveillance were expected to learn on the job, without any specialist training. Although their selection from within the ranks for plain-clothes work had been on grounds of their greater intelligence, this was a relative concept when educational standards for entry into the Police remained low. Even the dedicated political detectives, at least in the early years of their new role, clearly avoided doing some basic homework. In Dunedin, Beer reported in July 1921 that a speaker at a labour meeting 'stated at the outset that he was a communist and a student of Carl Marks'.[165] Three years later, Auckland's Detective Sergeant Ward was referring to 'Carl Marx'.[166]

More broadly, policemen generally exhibited some difficulty in understanding the motivations and schisms within the left; some struggled, too, to believe that differences in politics could be sincere. One detective assessed Communist elements as 'students in the ways and means of agitation, irritation and revolutionaries, without any sincere desire to assist either the unemployed or the community. Their appeal is to the ignorant and indolent.'[167] Detective Sergeant Lewis's belief that the CPNZ's founding members were 'not very brainy' echoed that of other police observers, indicating preconception rather than hard analysis.[168]

Assessment

By the end of the First World War there was a long history in New Zealand of state surveillance of people and activities deemed potentially or actually subversive or seditious. The (very limited) field of literature touching on this contends, in essence, that the Dominion's interwar surveilling operations were both small in scale and scope and amateurish. One account sees the surveillance system as 'a stop-gap measure with no real structure or operating procedures'; the brevity of police intelligence summaries is presented as 'proof of the limitations of security intelligence in place at the time', rather than as efforts to understand and condense those matters seen to be of significance in the fast-growing files.[169] Another account characterises 'police surveillance of the Communist Party [as] a shoestring operation appropriate for a shoestring party'.[170]

Various limitations in the system are certainly apparent. With its own files separate from those of the general Police registry, and non-political police normally excluded from its covert surveillance operations, it is true that the political section did not generally make 'use of the majority of available bureaucratic resources to support its investigations'.[171] There was no ready way, for example, of separating out in the secret files the few who advocated overthrow of the state from the many who sought social justice through non-violent means. For such reasons, the methods of recording and categorising targeted milieus were inconsistent, subjective and often based on inadequate knowledge of the ideological intricacies, and therefore the likely future actions, of the various left currents.

That said, previous accounts tend to understate the capabilities and outreach of the arrangements for political policing that were put in place in 1919–20. A dedicated core of political detectives, together with the other police and agencies, had not insignificant means of surveilling the movements and speech of its targets, scrutinising the contents of imported literature, cultivating informants, and sharing collected information across districts and sometimes with other governments. A broad range of suspect literature was seized, along with such material as portraits of overseas leaders who might inspire subversion, and mail was intercepted. The political police cultivated and ran informants, infiltrated the inner circles of member-only organisations such as trade unions and revolutionary groupings, and developed a registry of secret files at regional and central level that both reflected and facilitated their ever-widening surveillance net. Taken together, this system of routine political surveillance has been aptly described as 'no mere continuation of the police monitoring of opposition to the war effort between 1914 and 1918'.[172] While it built upon wartime experiences, it constituted a new phase in the secret history of New Zealand's political surveillers.

As we have seen, the dragnet of the latent Cold War meant that large numbers of potential, as well as a handful of actual, revolutionaries came under various degrees of surveillance. Analysts in the intelligence cycle, therefore, faced difficulties in categorising those caught up in it. Decades later, in the early 1960s, an official review of the records from this period noted that 1660 names were recorded as Communists at a time when CPNZ membership totalled a mere 99. It concluded that, in terms of analysing the threatscape, the files were 'of no value whatsoever'.[173]

And yet this material was part of a database used through the 1920s for intelligence. The information collected, moreover, could lie dormant, to be revisited under new developments. The surveillers knew whose files to go to first in the event of sabotage, civil disorder or other emergency – such as the Depression riots of the next decade. The information gathered, too, had been employed to inform the evolution of surveillance policy, and to underpin new operations, such as those aimed at destabilising Communist causes. Although it would have been feasible to put extreme pressure on the fledgling Communist Party by brandishing war continuance regulations or employing political or police offences legislation, the Police preference was to avoid driving its activities underground. Soon after the foundation of the CPNZ, the first detective dedicated to political surveillance in Wellington noted that 'the least push would probably send the Party to the wall, but not much would be gained by that, as [it] would not disband, but would adopt hole and corner tactics, and be more difficult than ever to handle'.[174]

Indeed, toleration of words and actions that could be deemed to be illegal formed part of a long-established policing strategy. As with police forces around the world, the NZPF preferred its targeted milieus to be concentrated so that they could be better contained; as part of an unspoken quid pro quo, it tolerated low-level illegality in the likes of red-light areas, gambling environments or 'criminal pubs', where it could collect intelligence and locate those it needed to, stepping in to arrest or suppress only in serious circumstances.

While it was decided not to force the CPNZ underground, police harassment undoubtedly hampered the Party's efforts to establish itself as a force in New Zealand politics. The extant records do not indicate the use in New Zealand of the kinds of dubiously legal methods employed by the British Special Branch of the time, such as use of *agents provocateurs* to provoke law-breaking.[175] But disruption could come about in many ways: making it hard to hire halls or speak in public, for example, or raids based on tip-offs by agents or informants. When a probationary constable was infiltrated into the CPNZ's central office in 1929, to take one instance, he found sufficient evidence for a raid to be carried out. As a result, Griffin and three other leaders were convicted for distributing seditious literature and were fined or gaoled.[176] After a raid or prosecution, there was naturally much speculation about who any infiltrators of informers might have been – fomenting an atmosphere of mistrust that was sometimes itself strong enough to cause disarray within a social or political grouping.[177] Documents seized from the CPNZ headquarters in a 1930 police raid warned its members that 'police spies have been placed in workers' organisations to secure information leading to persecutions [sic]'. [178]

Surveillance of the Rātana movement provides another case where proactive measures were sometimes pursued to counter its influence. These included early efforts to obstruct the development of its centre at what became known as 'Ratana Pa', which police and other authorities (including Māori politicians, health officials and Maori Council members) deemed to lack appropriate sanitation. While hygiene problems did arise from a concentration of the movement's burgeoning numbers at the settlement, the authorities' intention of hindering the expansion of Rātanaism and its self-determinationist teachings could also be seen at work.[179]

All the same, since Māori millennial and other movements reflected indigenous motivations rather than imported ideas, their surveillance remained light compared to those numbers of non-Māori communities advocating reform or revolution. The fact that Communist, trade union and other left movements made few inroads into the isolated communities where most Māori lived similarly helped ensure relatively light surveillance of Māoridom by the political police.[180]

Dominant images of 'the roaring twenties' focus on the heady pace and spectacle of modern style, new consumerism, and the growth of mass popular culture around the cinema, 'the jazz age' and the radio show. Alongside and behind this sense of the age, however, is another strand of history, summarised in and epitomised by the secret files. The ongoing watch for, and of, those who might disrupt the New Zealand paradise spilled out into official attempts to shape its way of life – what literature was allowed, what could be seen or listened to, and what politics were deemed seditious. This strand of history is entwined with matters as significant as the development of the Labour Party and the Rātana movement, the lives of future leaders of the country and the coercion levelled against dissidents.

The establishment of a routine system of political surveillance in peacetime, of course, sits uneasily with New Zealand's dominant mythscape of a free and open society. While the salient emergency of 1914–18 was widely seen as justifying unprecedented and visible measures that constrained liberties, these had rested on assumptions that they were necessary to preserve the basis of an ideal way of life. The quieter continuation of state surveillance after hostilities ended signalled the persistent nature of the secret world.

From the point of view of the state, this was a necessary response to detect, assess and neutralise threats to domestic and Imperial security. The clandestinity embedded in the intelligence cycle, so the argument ran, was no more than an unfortunate necessity in the quest to preserve the exceptional liberties enjoyed by New Zealanders as a whole. In any case, the conservative administrations throughout the decade did not need to defend themselves on such matters because, essentially, the secret world remained secret. The surveillers themselves certainly would have rejected their successors' assessment that their secret files held 'no value whatsoever'.

Had citizens known about the developing reach of state surveillance, many of the covert methods it employed, and the proactive uses to which it was put, they might well have had difficulties reconciling these with New Zealand's dominant mythscape of a free, fair and exceptionally open society. As it was, the secret world adversely affected lives, relationships and careers. Information in the secret files might be decontextualised, or simply incorrect, and since the surveilled were generally unaware of their surveillance they did not know how any adverse consequences might have come about. By extension, they had no means of asserting a breach of natural justice and seeking remedies. Even if those mentioned in the files had knowledge of their existence, which almost all did not, there was no way of setting the record straight.

Conclusion

The history of the secret world in the 1920s parallels, in many ways, the uneasy state of the post-war world. It reflected the heightened anxieties about socio-political disorder in the new peace, notably during the red scare. While fears of imminent crisis receded, worries about the influence of revolutionary socialism from its new conceptual base in Russia (a traditional enemy of the British Empire), about domestic militant labour and socialist parties, about those advocating independence from British control, all lingered across the decade. The authorities' perception of a grand showdown between red revolutionaries and the established order led us to contextualise this period as part of a latent Cold War which prefigured the Cold War proper.

The peacetime instigation of a routine system of state surveillance likewise reflects the period's significance. While this system built upon wartime watching, and decades of political policing activities before that, it signalled a new commitment to monitoring society for 'dangerous elements'. The decision to make the NZPF the primary instrument for humint would shape the nature of intelligence work and set the course for subsequent decades, but the post-war bid to professionalise security intelligence in a dedicated agency outside of the Police was one that would, as further chapters will demonstrate, be revisited in subsequent years.

In the decade after the war, the surveillers developed a systematised knowledge base that extended far beyond interest in the scant numbers of 'Bolsheviks', anarcho-syndicalists and other perceived security concerns. From the New Zealand authorities' point of view, the revised political policing system served its purpose: monitoring a broad range of potential threats to peace and good order in an exceptionally free and open society. It prosecuted some individuals and discouraged others by such examples and by proactive interventions aimed at destabilising organisations or movements. Authorities were reassured that if the existing order came under serious threat, the Police, in tandem with the other intelligence agencies, could both track and counter the subversives and seditionaries. This approach to the uneasy peace of the 1920s became more complicated as the following decade brought new crises, threats and insecurities.

Chapter Five:
The Red Decade? 1930–1939

Introduction

Security intelligence practitioners in the 1930s built upon the system established at the start of the post-war period. Some of its evolution in the new decade reflected standard forms of institutional development, driven by such matters as technological innovation and changing leadership. But the surveilling agenda was mostly shaped by the uncertain social and political environment of the early to mid-1930s. The dire economic crisis and associated political radicalisation at the beginning of the decade produced a greatly increased demand for intelligence and, accordingly, a wider casting of the surveilling net and a deeper penetration of political policing into parts of civil society. This context is crucial for understanding the priorities and workings of the secret world during this period.

Equally so is the mid-decade accession to office of the Labour Party, which had always been within the surveilling gaze of the political police, although the intensity of the gaze had been decreasing as Labour continued to moderate its methods and aims. When Labour gained office in 1935, some adjustments to covert targeting of possible subversives needed to be made, but little changed in fundamentals: a reformist government, too, required a surveillance dragnet. And it, too, had a broad definition of what might constitute subversion and who might fall under the rubric of potential subversives. Moreover, German and Japanese militarism increasingly raised the threat of hostilities, and counter-espionage awareness among police and other security agencies stepped up accordingly.

Overview

The Great Depression began on 29 October 1929 on Wall Street and would see the market prices for New Zealand's key commodities (lamb, butter and wool) plummet and the cost of credit soar. Official unemployment figures give some sense of the resulting economic contraction. There were 2449 people registered as unemployed by February

1930, a figure which had expanded to 11,442 that December; it would reach a high of 57,352 by mid-1933.[1] Such figures actually understate the crisis, since women, men under 20 and Māori employed on Native Department development schemes were excluded from registering. Best estimates indicate that some 28 per cent of the male workforce and 46 per cent of the female workforce found itself out of work.[2]

Over the period 1929–35, successive governments' approaches to the Depression focused on retrenchment and relief schemes, operating on a no-work, no-pay philosophy.[3] Relief work was allocated by officials, and the men on the schemes (women were not eligible) were at the mercy of ongoing reductions in official spending. The situation worsened for the unemployed in 1932 when, alongside further cuts in already meagre relief rates, the Unemployment Board opened work camps to which they directed single (and later married) men, often in remote places. Here they were to labour for, at most, the low rate of 10 shillings a week. Many of the unemployed agitated against their lot, part of a broader movement of working-class discontent at falling wages and worsening conditions and anger at a capitalist system denounced for producing the slump and all its attendant human misery.

Naturally, the various socialist groupings sought not only to alleviate the plight of the poor but also to proselytise and recruit in the process. The CPNZ was increasingly linked to Moscow, which did not help its image: once Joseph Stalin had consolidated his power after Lenin's death in 1924 and ousted his chief opponent Leon Trotsky soon after, the communitarian society envisaged in Marxian principles disappeared in all but Soviet propaganda. Repression increased in scope and intensity from 1930, culminating in the show trials and 'Great Terror' later in the decade, and the international press increasingly carried news of ruthless Soviet policies towards its own people. However, the USSR continued to appeal for what it professed, rather than what it did, notably its condemnation of capitalism at a time of economic turmoil and its staunch anti-fascism at a time of Western disarray and appeasement. Indeed, as international tensions increased, those New Zealanders impressed by Soviet Communism included growing numbers who believed – once the CPNZ focused on creating an anti-fascist front – that Stalinism was the only way of stopping fascism.

Another complication in international Communism arose from Trotsky-led opposition to Stalin. Following the Comintern line, the CPNZ railed against 'Trotskyist deviations', and while no organised Trotskyist grouping emerged, some comrades took inspiration from Trotskyism as an alternative far-left position. In protest at the show trials, the upper-class union leader Major Noel Pharazyn resigned from the Friends of the Soviet Union (FSU) and became a defender of Trotsky. Likewise, Wellington educationist Max Riske and Charles White, a Māori who preached the cause across the Tasman, called themselves Trotskyists. The label could be somewhat fluid and, in the case of the union boss F. P. Walsh, has been assessed as 'smack[ing] more of fashion than commitment'.[4] Indeed, Walsh was already building a reputation in the union world for strike-breaking and ruthless crackdowns on militant labour, which earned him the soubriquet of 'the Black Prince'.[5]

The CPNZ remained small with 81 members at the start of 1932, only two more than in 1928, though this had grown to 353 by the end of 1935 as a result of Depression-led recruiting.[6] But its outreach had been hampered by internal fractiousness, with its leadership, for example, expelling a quarter of the membership in 1932.[7] The operations of the intelligence cycle further impeded its work. By mid-1933, to take one instance, the entire Central Committee had been gaoled for publishing banned literature.[8] Lastly, the CPNZ often found itself with few allies because of its strident denunciations of other left groupings. In 1928 the Communist International declared that all social democratic parties were 'social fascists' and should be vigorously opposed for misleading the workers.[9] In 1930 a Party slogan declared 'Do not expect anything of the reformist leaders; they will betray you'; in 1931 Communist demonstrators denounced Labour Party leader Harry Holland as 'a proved servant of the Boss Class'; their Party's 1935 election slogan read 'Neither Reaction nor Labour'.[10] In turn, Labour had increasingly sought to avoid any taint of association with the Soviet Union. Its annual conference in 1934 overwhelmingly voted that belonging to the FSU was incompatible with Labour Party membership.[11]

Despite all the impediments it faced, the CPNZ's influence was far greater than its small size might suggest. This was the result of the hard work it put into organising the unemployed and other causes, its strategy of infiltrating other groupings and setting up new ones, and its franchise to represent the centre of world revolution. The Party became an even more formidable force when Fred Freeman returned to New Zealand in 1933 after four years with the Comintern. Taking over the role of general secretary, he reformed its administration, policies and operations, and secured leadership positions for talented members such as Gordon Watson and Freeman's future wife Elsie Farrelly.

Now, Central Committee representatives made regular visits to local branches, directives were systematised, and internal discipline and procedures were tightened in efforts to prevent the arrests that had hampered the Party's work. There was greater caution over deploying ultra-left policies, and the Party's credentials were to be burnished by an increasing stress on the need for an international stand against fascism. In taking this up, the CPNZ would work in tactical alliance with non-Communist groupings, seeking a 'popular front' against fascism, a policy that was fully cemented into place at the Communist International conference in 1935.[12] By the time Freeman was driven out during a rolling internal purge over 1936 and 1937, he had crafted a powerful political machine.[13] Party membership had expanded, its numbers reaching 488 towards the end of the decade, by which time it had relocated its headquarters from the capital to Auckland.[14]

Of course, the CPNZ's attempts to influence the direction of a broad swathe of political, social and cultural movements were closely watched by the political police.

Some of the organisations under scrutiny were considered to be 'fronts' for the Party, although there was a flexibility in the term. Being labelled a front could mean anything from an organisation whose name was merely a façade for an essentially Communist grouping, to an association in which Communists or their sympathisers held a dominant or even significant level of influence. To take one example of what was clearly definable as a front, the CPNZ had been 'instrumental in establishing' the FSU in August 1930 as a 'fraternal' organisation oriented towards the progressive middle class.[15] Farrelly recalled attending an Auckland meeting of the FSU early in the decade, during a period of political experimentation as a university student:

> Its hall seated 200 and there were usually many people standing. The USSR appealed as 'the land without unemployment', a workers' state which, though still relatively backward, was going ahead with industrial development while the capitalist states were at a standstill . . . I went along and was rather unimpressed. The woman speaker painted a Soviet scene of unbelievable perfection. I needed something more substantial.[16]

All the same, there was a hunger among the left to hear about the Soviet Union from sources other than the hostile New Zealand newspapers and radio stations. After a reorientation to attract more working-class members, the FSU had a thousand members spread across 26 branches by 1933 – a development which fed into Labour's decision to ban its members from FSU activities the following year.[17]

Many people among the broad left were loath to criticise the USSR, in part out of a sense that the promises held out by Bolshevism had been severely compromised by both Western hostility and socio-economic backwardness inherited from the Russian Empire. Some non-Communists joined Soviet front groups knowingly, to gain knowledge or to indicate support for the concept of a radical overthrow of the capitalist past in favour of some form of socialist present. These formed part of a cohort classifiable as 'fellow travellers' of Soviet Communism, a term first coined by Leon Trotsky (whose leading advocacy of the founding principles of Marxism–Leninism led to his assassination by a Stalinist agent in 1940). The term usually referred to anyone who generally went along with Communist Party interpretations, aims and policies without actually joining up. Holding such transparent views made them relatively easy to monitor. Communist infiltrators into non-Communist organisations, generally called crypto-Communists, were more elusive to track, but the detectives did not stop looking.

In view of the potential for Communist activists to push progressive movements further leftwards as economic distress and social disorder intensified, such causes came under ever more intensive surveillance in the first half of the decade. Communist influence within mass-based movements, especially the Unemployed Workers'

Movement (UWM), came into particular focus. Various regional UWM bodies, modelled on the British organisation of the same name, were established throughout 1930 – in Wellington at the Communist Hall that April, for example. In 1931 they were consolidated into a national organisation.[18]

The UWM used militant rhetoric, organised large protests against government policy and distributed a great amount of literature that the authorities considered to be potentially subversive. Their tone was as urgent as their plight was severe. A deputation told the prime minister in January 1932: 'We have got past the stage of begging and have come now to the point where we demand that the Government should do something for us.' Indeed, 'the time has come when the unemployed realise they will fight for anything they want'.[19] The CPNZ was prominent in the Movement. Jim Edwards, for example, played a leading role in the establishment of the UWM, while also becoming involved in the CPNZ; prominent Communist Leo Sim served as the Movement's financial secretary; and workers such as Albert ('Birchie', alias Braunstein) Birchfield and his future wife Constance (Connie) were proactive in the Movement and associated causes, such as improving the lot of both unemployed and working women.[20]

Parts of the labour movement, including the Labour Party, were as worried as the surveillers that Communist influence within the unemployed movement was a powerful vehicle for promoting sectarian party politics.[21] In the 1960s, former prominent Communist leader Sid Scott offered a retrospective assessment:

> Was the 'U.W.M.', as it was commonly called, a Communist organisation? I can only answer that, like many other organisations, it was and it was not. Only a small proportion of the members were members of the Communist Party. It originated in the decisions of the Party which copied it from Britain. Yet most of the members and, at some periods most of the leaders, were not Party members. Most of them were Labour Party supporters or attached to no particular political theory.[22]

The Movement fought for better pay and conditions for relief workers, especially those in the camps, and against evictions of those who could not pay their rent, complementing the struggle of political and industrial labour to protect those still in work. Police monitoring of opposition to government policies intensified when social discontent, and political and industrial demonstrations, especially among the unemployed, escalated into street disorder and rioting. This brought the country, in one influential estimation, 'almost to the verge of civil war'. Although this was an exaggeration, the disorder certainly constituted the greatest degree of street-based civil unrest since 1913.[23]

The first major episode of violence occurred in 1931 in Auckland, when the unemployed joined a public servants' protest, and a riot occurred in Dunedin in early 1932. Various confrontations from early 1932 onwards culminated in mass riots in the main centres through to May, the most serious in Auckland in April. This led to the drafting in of military force, the deployment of volunteers and the swearing-in of a thousand Special Police. Crowd numbers in such melees could range into the thousands, and injury and damage to property was rife. Some provincial towns experienced disturbances as well; in 1932, for example, striking Huntly relief workers raided the local Farmers' Co-operative, resulting in 19 convictions.[24]

The CPNZ's presence in the unemployed riots, and especially the role of Edwards in the incident which sparked the most serious riot, led to even greater surveilling of the Party. At the same time, surveillance over left-wing currents expanded. Newspaper and broadcasting commentary reinforced the simplistic explanation that the 'red menace' was responsible for the turbulence in the streets. To take the words of the *New Zealand Observer* that April, for example, 'the real root cause of last week's turmoil can still be traced to those fomenters of discord, militant communists and "Red" agitators'.[25] The populist newspaper *NZ Truth* engaged in its characteristically sensationalist rhetoric: 'Behind the recent Auckland and Wellington riots lies the sinister hand of Communism.'[26]

The New Zealand establishment shared such sensibilities, seeing ill-intentioned ringleaders behind the disorderly consequences of social distress. In the aftermath of the Wellington riot, a magistrate spoke for most parts of the establishment in his belief that

> . . . this orgy of window smashing and looting was not the work of the genuine unemployed. It was I think the work of a small band instigated and led by members of an organisation operating within our midst – the Communists, whose doctrine appears to be the fostering of mob violence and revolutionary disorder.[27]

The political police, too, framed their surveillance activities around the assumption that Bolshevism lay behind the social turbulence. From this perspective, working and unemployed people did not protest of their own accord and in their own ways, but were led towards mass disorder by 'agitators' intent on procuring the preconditions for a revolutionary overthrow of the state and the interests it stood for. The CPNZ's literature, for example, was seen to have a dangerously seditious effect. In July 1932 Commissioner Ward George Wohlmann declared the Party's organ, *Red Worker*, to be

> . . . the mouth-piece of an anti-British and anti-social organisation inspired from a foreign source. Its object is to take advantage of existing conditions to incite and foment disorder and disregard of

the law. Even the most biased must admit that the publication of such documents is the reverse of helpful in the preservation of law and order in these unsettled times.[28]

Convicting two men for importing 'red' literature, a magistrate declared that 'distribution of this sort of literature leads to disturbances such as we have recently had on our city streets'.[29]

Some sense of the illiberal mood pervading much of the population as well as the authorities can be glimpsed in an incident which followed. Historian J. C. Beaglehole joined forces with Auckland Workers' Educational Association tutor–organiser Norman Richmond to declare that 'no evidence has been produced which would give the colour of truth to [the magistrate's] statement'. This was published in Labour's weekly *New Zealand Worker*.[30] A file was opened on Beaglehole that grew to a 'quite extensive' size, and he was soon dismissed from his academic position in Auckland. While this was ostensibly on grounds of retrenchment, in the words of Victoria University of Wellington's official historian 'it was widely, and not unjustifiably, believed to have been because of his political views'. Two decades after the sacking, a well-informed commentator believed that it was 'perfectly clear' it had resulted from what the political police 'thought [were] his political beliefs'.[31]

Beaglehole went on to miss out on the chair of history at Victoria University College in circumstances which also suggested political prejudice and pressure, the institution's council overriding the recommendation of the selection committee.[32] While he did soon get a lower position at the college, there were other such incidents in these years.[33] Soon after Beaglehole's departure, for example, his Auckland colleague Dick Anschutz was reprimanded, after ministerial intervention, for his qualified praise for the Soviet Union in a foreword to Nellie Scott's *A New Zealand Woman in Russia*.[34]

Other parts of the political landscape also reacted to Depression unrest through conspiratorially minded searches for the cause of disorder. The anti-Communist Welfare League echoed declarations that 'the agents of that sinister body' the Third International were 'organising and inciting the unemployed in this dominion'.[35] Yet others looked darkly at the banks and 'money power', sometimes with anti-Semitic undertones or intent.[36] Journalist A. N. Field, in particular, was 'New Zealand's foremost author of conspiracy theories' during the Depression.[37] Alongside publishing New Zealand editions of the infamous anti-Semitic fabrication *The Protocols of the Elders of Zion*, his *Truth About the Slump* (1931) claimed to reveal that the Depression was really a Jewish plot intended to enslave the British Empire;[38] after an initially modest reception, the publication attracted much attention, including praise in Parliament, and went through multiple print runs which circulated around the English-speaking world.[39]

Elements of the radical right suggested that the solution to the Depression lay in reactionary, and potentially authoritarian, directions, such as a local version of the

Australian New Guard, a mass fascistic organisation posing as the paramilitary vanguard against subversion and revolution.[40] Established in February 1933, the ultra-patriotic New Zealand Legion called for a radical reconstitution of the Dominion's methods of governance – by, among other things, abolishing parties in the name of national unity.[41] In the event, the Legion turned out to be a much milder version of the organised far right in similar jurisdictions. Although some of its members held fascistic views, its lack of any specific programme beyond vague calls for moral rejuvenation makes it hard to categorise precisely. Certainly, its leader, Robert Campbell Begg, declared Nazi philosophy to be 'absurd', and police did not see it as another New Guard. All the same, at its peak in late 1933 the Legion claimed some 20,000 members, garnering a degree of surveillance that fell away as it went into terminal decline a year later.[42]

The demise of the Legion reflects the changing situation from 1933, with the country beginning to slowly recover from the worst of the Depression, and protests and prosecutions for seditious offences sharply dropping.[43] At the same time, the political landscape held out the prospect of a sea change as the general election approached in December 1935 (after being postponed for a year) with the Labour Party seemingly poised to form a government in its own right. Just before the 1935 election, a 'confidential source' notified the authorities that Methodist minister Colin Scrimgeour ('Uncle Scrim'), who 'preached the Jesus-style socialism' from radio station 1ZB, would be advising his large audience on how to vote. Like other such stations, 1ZB was closely watched by Post and Telegraph officials, and 'controversial' items were censored, sometimes mid-broadcast. Although restrictions had theoretically eased by 1935, officials remained timid and, towards the forthcoming election, had banned all political electioneering and 'controversial material'.[44]

The postmaster-general authorised his departmental head to jam the programme and when, on 24 November, Scrim noted that 'the usual sources of information [were] deceiving' and his listeners 'should understand how their interests could be served', the engineer in charge (as he reported) made the broadcaster's voice 'like a chorus of duck quacks'. Post and Telegraph head George McNamara later claimed the interference to be 'wholly accidental', and Deputy Prime Minister Coates declared notions of jamming to be 'an unscrupulous attempt to make political capital by throwing suspicion on the Government'. In a subsequent enquiry, McNamara implicated Minister Adam Hamilton, the postmaster-general, although both men denied giving the specific order to disrupt the broadcast. The latter said that he had instructed that Scrimgeour was 'to be watched, and if he overstepped the mark, stopped', but did not specify as to how.[45]

Regardless, the election resulted in a landslide victory for Labour, allowing it to establish a highly reformist First Labour Government. The NZPF now, as it had done previously when the Liberals took office in 1891, needed to adjust to an altered environment – one in which an avowedly left-wing party had gained office and quickly set about instituting progressive reforms through 'a landslide of legislation'.

The new prime minister, Michael Joseph Savage, was much less radical than the previous head of the Parliamentary Labour Party, Harry Holland, who had co-written *The Tragic Story of the Waihi Strike*, edited the Red Fed paper *Maoriland Worker* and been gaoled for sedition. But some of Savage's ministers and back-benchers had once harboured seditionary intentions and seen gaol time for their words and deeds. Moreover, from the surveillers' perspective, Savage headed a mass social democratic movement which had once been under intensive scrutiny and still remained of interest because of its connections and philosophy. Sections of its rank-and-file were seen as contaminable by Communism. For many of the police, too, the policies the new government pursued remained dangerously radical. These were most famously encapsulated in the Social Security Act of 1938 which provided 'old age, invalidity, widowhood, unemployment, maternity, hospital and other benefits' and in doing so transformed the socio-political landscape.[46]

Moreover, the new minister in charge of policing was Wellington MP Peter Fraser, a former leading Red Fed who had served a year in gaol for sedition in the First World War, and had moderated his earlier socialist views only a decade or so ago. Furthermore, Fraser was effectively the second in command in the new government, 'a dominant personality in the way Savage was not'.[47] Obviously, police in general, and the political police in particular, now needed to tread carefully on such matters as surveilling people and movements whose methods and goals were broadly aligned with Labour's. The Party's rhetoric about repressive state apparatuses, some of it of recent ilk, indicated that even the scrutiny of avowed revolutionaries, members of 'front groups' (unwitting or otherwise), alleged fellow travellers and suspected crypto-Communists might have to be approached cautiously.

As one early indication of changed circumstances, Fraser ordered literature seized some years before from prominent Communist Dick Griffin to be returned, although the latter had condemned Labour's policies in the ultra-left stage of the CPNZ's history.[48] In October 1936, too, Fraser removed the restrictions that had been in place on importing books on 'political, economic and other questions'.[49] That year the Political Disabilities Removal Act, giving some rights to public servants and their representative organisations to engage in political activity, was a similarly worrying trend for some police – although others were happy that their minister soon allowed the formation of a police union, the New Zealand Police Association. Some policemen even welcomed a 'most progressive Government', seeing it as 'an example to the whole world'.[50]

Whatever the qualms of conservative elements in the police and elsewhere, the new government, fully aware that the CPNZ remained its bitterest enemy on its left, found common ground with the traditional imperatives of the surveillers. Once in office, Labour's leaders soon saw no reason for a reduction of vigilance over Communists and fellow travellers and all the sections of the left which such elements sought to influence – the peace movement, for example. Moreover, within Labour's ranks discontent soon arose among those who felt the government's policies were too moderate. In light of all such factors, there was as much need as ever to keep a general watch over the whole political environment of the left-of-centre, including inside the Labour Party.[51]

Such watching was accompanied by action on other fronts. Reviving after its battering in the Depression, much of the union movement was quickly brought into partnership with the new government, which placed matters such as arbitration and state–labour cooperation back onto the agenda. The (second) Federation of Labour replaced the old syndicalist Alliance of Labour in 1937, bringing in craft unions and gaining more power as its constituent parts benefited from the introduction of compulsory unionism the year before. Dominated by seamen's president F. P. Walsh, Fraser's close ally, the Federation of Labour helped cement most unions into collaboration with the government on such matters as wage-setting and pensions. The two men, who had both featured prominently in the secret files, operated increasingly as a 'power team', an 'alliance of mutual convenience' bent on defusing opposition to the government within organised industrial and political labour.[52] Walsh's contribution was his adeptness at keeping a lid on industrial militancy, often by means which were not necessarily savoury. He had moved a long way from Trotskyism, if he had ever been a genuine adherent. Fraser, too, had a ruthless streak within his politicking. After the election victory he 'didn't seek to pursue' the jamming incident because, the left-Labour MP John A. Lee believed, 'he would have been willing to engage in the same sort of tactics'.[53]

The new government's security concerns were entwined not just with the left, but also with the increasing geopolitical instabilities arising in the second half of the 1930s. While the government exhibited a degree of independence from the British establishment in promoting internationalism and opposing compromise with aggressor states, it also supported negotiations with Nazi Germany and welcomed the Munich settlement, in order to focus on the possible threat from Japan.[54] Tellingly, New Zealand lined up with Britain and the Commonwealth, other European nations and the League of Nations in refusing to assist the elected Republican government during the Spanish Civil War of 1936–39. The policy of non-intervention was ostensibly to prevent the war spreading, but it allowed General Francisco Franco's insurgent 'nationalist' forces to win victory with the help of the fascist powers. The Dominion followed the British lead for its own reasons, too: it feared loss of Catholic support (the Church supported Franco) and it did not wish to be seen as aligned with the CPNZ's insistent calls for intervention. Labour's 1937 conference even called for all foreign troops to leave Spain, whose legitimate government was being assisted only by the Soviet Union and international volunteers.

Popular solidarity with the Republican cause disquieted the government, especially given the success of the Communist Party's popular front strategy on the issue. The political police monitored such developments closely, including New Zealand volunteers who managed to get to Spain to fight with the International Brigades or those sending humanitarian aid from home. Attempts were made to hinder their efforts, including that of three nurses from the New Zealand Spanish Medical Aid Committee.

Just before they were due to sail to Spain, the trio was 'taken from a farewell meeting to the Auckland Central Police Station, ostensibly to check their passports'. They were 'subjected to intensive questioning' about their reasons for going. Some of the questions related to their involvement with Communist organisations and known Communists.[55] Minister of Internal Affairs W. E. (Bill) Parry, a former Red Fed who had been gaoled at Waihī, claimed that his department had only learned of their mission shortly before the function. The Police had therefore been requested, at the last minute, to check that their passports were in order for entering Spain. A close ally of Savage, Parry added that it had been necessary also to make it totally clear that the government could not accept responsibility for them. While Fraser would deny knowing anything about the nurses' mission until Parry had passed complaints about their interrogation on to him, he had been invited to their farewell several days in advance. Now, in an awkward position, Fraser would speak to the nurses by radio telephone after they boarded the ship; his friendship with the family of one of them could be utilised to deflect any potential criticism that he was infringing upon New Zealand's non-interventionist position.[56]

Worsening international tensions also led to some official concern about fascist propaganda and the potential for espionage by prospective enemy powers in New Zealand. The Police extended its surveillance net to take account of the possibility of German, Italian and Japanese operatives in the Dominion, as well as of Soviet agents. Several officials of the Italian Consulate were reportedly promoting fascism, and Wellington's Club Garibaldi was said to be adopting fascistic trappings.[57] Japan's imperial ambitions were increasingly feared, following its brutal military interventions in China dating from 1931, its alignment with the Axis powers and its potential to threaten British and Commonwealth interests in Asia and the Pacific. A war for imperial control of the region, which would inevitably involve New Zealand, could not be discounted.[58]

The major concern, however, centred on the possibility that Nazi Germany might attempt to gain both information and influence to assist its self-proclaimed expansionist plans, and both New Zealand's military intelligence and political police worked to counter this prospect. As in the years before the First World War, German visitors were closely watched, although there were now many who were not tourists. Salesmen for the I. G. Farben chemical company, for example, were believed to be agents who were recording details such as key communications routes and infrastructure for collation in Sydney.[59] The 1937–38 world tour of Count Felix von Luckner, a former prisoner of war (and escapee) in New Zealand, was suspected to be a propaganda effort to bolster the Third Reich's image. The Labour Party's own newspaper, commenting on its New Zealand leg, felt that the tour had given 'fresh stimulus to Nazi activities'.[60]

The threat of war also spurred official concerns about elements of the population that might hinder or harm a future war effort. Organised pacifism had grown in the 1930s and, in the event of war, was seen as potentially able to deter recruiting and undermine morale. Christian pacifism held a particular influence given the widespread influence of organised Christianity in New Zealand. A fifth column amidst pro-Japanese elements of the population, as well as among those of German or Italian background, was not to be ruled out. And, as always in the latent Cold War, potential Communist machinations were a persistent point of concern.

Agencies

By 1930, New Zealand's post-war system of domestic state surveillance had become firmly entrenched. The detective offices were expanding in this decade: from 54 staff in 1930 to a peak of 93 in 1938, with some two-thirds of these in the four centres.[61] In each of these centres a detective held primary, full-time responsibility for political surveillance. These included Percy James (Jim) Nalder in Auckland, N. W. Baylis in Wellington, Orme Power in Dunedin and N. W. Laugesen in Christchurch, who retired in 1933, after which he engaged in various businesses including private investigation. Beyond these four men, detectives, plain-clothes and uniformed police were assigned to specialist security work as necessary. Moreover, all members of the force were expected to remain on the alert for anything they saw as suspicious political activity. Former constable Richard Patterson, for example, later recounted that the Palmerston North police would 'keep an eye on' Leo Sim's house, a centre for Communist activity.[62]

Given that state security was of especial concern throughout the 1930s, Police Commissioners tended to take a hands-on role in political policing. When Wohlmann replaced McIlveney in June 1930, in the context of increasing social distress and political activism, among other things he instituted 'heightened police surveillance and prosecutions for inciting violence or distributing seditious literature'.[63] The practice of intercepting communications stepped up, with letters and telegrams routinely read and reported on by the political detectives, often through the agency of local police who knew the postmasters personally.[64] The working definition of potentially seditious organisations, movements, literature and speeches was extended.

As Wohlmann's concerns about Communist activity grew, police were instructed to take ever more proactive measures to hamper activists. 'Employers (including university authorities) were informed of the communist leanings of certain employees, some of whom lost their jobs.'[65] The Commissioner felt the threatscape to be so disturbing that he abandoned the former policy of tolerating the CPNZ and advised the government to ban it. While he could not persuade the government to go that far, police harassment in effect turned the Party into a 'semi-legal organisation'.[66] The Commissioner worked to revoke naturalisation of some of its comrades, and sought to prevent the return of New Zealanders who had attended Moscow's International Lenin School, which offered academic and practical training with a view to developing Communist movements around the world. One example was a 'particularly dangerous type of disloyalist', Fred Freeman, who managed to slip back into the country. In March 1932, the government banned re-entry of all 'undesirables' who had spent time in the USSR.[67]

With its public order as well as its state security hat on, the NZPF prioritised surveillance of any movement that might incite widespread disruption or violence. In March 1931, Wohlmann issued instructions for tackling significant public disorder, echoing those issued by O'Donovan over a decade before.[68] In January 1932 he brought Inspector James (Jim) Cummings to Police Headquarters to oversee investigative work in the Force, including political surveillance. Cummings had attained the rank of full Detective during the First World War and risen quickly thereafter, becoming Chief Detective in Auckland in 1923. He had gone back into uniform as an Inspector in 1930, and he would now remain at Headquarters until February 1936 – by which time the Depression-generated challenges to state security had dissipated, and were unlikely to return in view of the new government's industrial relations policies.[69]

Wohlmann took a personal hand in pre-emptively drafting public safety legislation, and this was rapidly enacted after the rioting in Auckland as the Public Safety Conservation Act 1932. This, modelled on British and Australian precedents, provided for the declaration of a state of emergency when 'public safety or public order is or is likely to be imperilled'. In that event the Governor-General (essentially on the advice of the political executive) could assume powers

> . . . to make all such regulations as he thinks necessary for the prohibition of any acts which in his opinion would be injurious to the public safety, and also to make all such other regulations as in his opinion are required for the conservation of public safety and order and for securing the essentials of life to the community.[70]

Coupled with other draconian powers, this provided a platform for greater intrusion into the socio-political life of the nation, alongside such supplementary coercive measures as the ability to swear in Special Constables at times of tension.[71]

Local bodies, too, took measures that boosted policing powers, many of which had implications for intelligence work. Responding to the 1932 riot, Auckland's mayor contemplated utilising the Dominion's equivalent to the British 'Riot Act', an action that would have made public assembly illegal and sanctioned a maximal sentence of life imprisonment with hard labour for those refusing to comply.[72] In the event, his councillors settled for milder measures, such as denying permits for protest meetings, and Wellington and Dunedin initiated similar bans. In the capital, as well as in Auckland,

Special Constables were sworn in to help police the various public-order measures put in place to quell unrest.

The easing of the Depression did not immediately remove official fears of a threatscape of mass disorder which might segue into something even more dangerous to the state and its interests. In late 1934 a Police Reserve was established to provide a permanent part-time complement of trained auxiliary police to assist regular constables on 'abnormal occasions', such as sizeable demonstrations. Opposition politicians argued that such an auxiliary force, 350 men spread over the four centres, would be 'inclined to act as spies and informers' within the community and so reduce public trust in the regular constables.[73]

The prominent Labour MP 'Fighting Bob' Semple claimed that it was the Commissioner rather than the minister who had conceived the idea of such auxiliaries. As the sergeant in charge of the Waihī police during the 1912 strike, Wohlmann had been a steadying influence until Commissioner Cullen ordered a harshly coercive approach. But in later years, and more especially in the face of Depression unrest, he had become increasingly antagonistic towards the political and industrial labour movement. He was uncomfortable when Labour took office after the 1935 election, more especially with party 'strong man' Peter Fraser taking on the role of minister in charge of the Police. This was a move clearly intended to place the conservative Police Force under firmer ministerial scrutiny, to help ensure that its conservatism did not inhibit its enforcement of the new government's requirements. Wohlmann's 'antipathy towards former Red Feds such as Fraser (who had criticised police methods and leadership)' and Semple (who had said that if Evans had shot Constable Wade at Waihī he was only 'doing his duty and should have shot more of them') played a significant role in his decision to take early retirement in 1936.[74]

Having been under sustained surveillance themselves, the new political masters had some idea of the power inherent in the possession of knowledge, and they quickly took an interest in security intelligence once in office. Fraser, in particular, 'increasingly learnt of the fruits of police surveillance and shaped its targets – focusing, for example, on a small number of communists who became union officials'. A political colleague was just one of a number to note that Fraser was not 'averse to using police information as well as other sources to keep tabs on supporters of doubtful loyalty'. A shrewd journalist was to recall that the minister 'approved of [the Police Force] so long as it was clearly understood that he was in charge of it'. Fraser 'could have the police use power in a way which if anyone else had done it would have invoked torrents of abuse from the same Peter Fraser'.[75] On such matters, however, the secret files have yielded few secrets.

The enormous social and political challenges of the first half of the 1930s had prompted some honing of police surveilling techniques. An expanded use of photography for surveillance purposes included covert operations to photograph private material, such as the correspondence of members of closely observed organisations such as the Friends of the Soviet Union.[76] But mostly, police use of photography was for identification purposes. In the past this had focused on 'mug shots' of offenders or suspects which were then circulated within the Police, including in the internal *Police Gazette*. These complemented the written descriptions that had always formed the foundation of Police identification records – 'Native of New Zealand, height 5ft 3½ in., weight 150 lbs, eyes, grey; hair, [au]burn; face, oval; nose, straight; mouth, small; faint line scar under side first joint little finger, right hand'.[77]

Declassified files from the 1930s, however, contain photographs of people at public protests and demonstrations and sometimes even of attendees in closed meetings.[78] Such images would be used in efforts to build up a comprehensive knowledge of the people involved in movements and organisations, especially those seen as seditionary 'ringleaders', and their interconnections – as well as to identify those orators, rioters and others who might be charged with public-order offences. Photographs identifying key persons could be forwarded with instructions; in March 1932, to take one example, Commissioner Wohlmann ordered Auckland police to shadow John Sandford, the Dominion organiser for the Unemployed Workers' Movement, on a speaking tour. Those assigned to the surveillance were provided with both a personal profile (including an analysis that he was 'a fairly good speaker [with] a good deal of ability as an organiser') and a photograph 'in which he is the centre figure'. His words, deeds and contacts were recorded.[79]

Wohlmann's successor from mid-1936, Denis Cummings (the brother of Jim Cummings), was 'a cautious administrator, seeking to build on long-standing practices rather than to innovate' – although he did engage with technology by introducing, for example, wireless communication within the Force. Left-wing observers had accused him of partisanship during the policing of Christchurch's tramway strike in 1932 although, in the event, his and Detective N. W. Laugesen's handling of it had avoided serious violence.[80] Denis Cummings was acutely conscious that Fraser was closely observing the work of the force. He accepted, not entirely happily, the minister's decision to allow the police union that Fraser had long campaigned for as a supporter of the rights of the police as workers.[81] The new government's propensity to improve the lot of police rank-and-file meant that the emergent Police Association and the new Commissioner could together secure improvements in police pay and conditions, a development which assisted conservative policemen to reconcile to the new political order.

Although the new administration included politicians who had previously been surveilled and harassed by police, Cummings' stress on non-partisan policing helped smooth relations between the Police leadership and the government. For their part, the ministers needed an efficient force with good surveilling capacity, including the resources and ability to keep an eye on the numerous enemies to its left. With this ambition in mind the existing legislative and regulatory framework was left in place, and the War Regulations Continuance Act was not repealed, despite the Labour Party pledging to do so in their manifesto.[82] The Commissioner built up police surveillance capacity in significant ways, including through modern equipment, in-service training and more vehicles. With the government and Commissioner more or less in synch, police were generally left to operate autonomously within broadly permissive parameters, as had become the norm in New Zealand. Minister Fraser, however, kept a close watch on the Force, and intervened more often than any previous minister since the time of Massey and Herdman.[83]

Throughout the decade, the intensity of surveillance by the other state agencies involved in protecting the state waxed and waned according to need. Judicial officials were naturally highly involved during the prosecutions of the Depression years, but so too were other departments. In May 1932, the trade and tourism commissioner in Toronto tipped off the government that a visiting American journalist was expected to produce 'sensational' stories on 'uprisings and possibility of civil war' in New Zealand that might harm the Dominion's image. Authorised to ensure, under postal regulations 'of long standing', that 'suitable action was taken', the 'Post and Telegraph Department took steps to see that exaggerated reports were not sent out'.[84]

While military intelligence constitutes a subject beyond the focus of this book, Defence continued to retain an interest in humint as well as sigint, and its intelligence capability grew as the threat of war increased.[85] In late 1933, after pressure from British and local armed forces, a New Zealand section of the Committee of Imperial Defence had been formed within the Prime Minister's Department, its tasks including overseeing intelligence. In 1936 this became the Organisation for National Security, which would later establish specialist committees on such matters as protection of 'vital points'. In March 1937 Cabinet approved the appointment of Major W. G. Stevens as its secretary, as well as that of a new Council of Defence that would coordinate the efforts of service and civil departments to monitor the intentions of perceived enemies of the state.[86]

While the Organisation for National Security's main concern was internal security, this was seen within an Imperial and Commonwealth context. At the July 1937 Committee of Imperial Defence meeting in London, representatives discussed, among other matters, the interception of wireless communications. The parties agreed that it 'appear[ed] to be of the greatest importance that the members of the British Commonwealth should consider how best they can gain experience in [wireless] interception in peace, and prepare schemes for expansion to meet war conditions'.[87] Meanwhile New Zealand Defence officials had taken part in Commonwealth sigint developments, such as a 1934 conference in Singapore to discuss coordinating the work of naval intelligence centres in the Pacific (including Wellington) in light, especially, of Japan's rising power and ambitions.[88]

As international tension increased, high-frequency direction-finding stations that could meet the requirements of Royal Navy signals messaging in time of war were established within New Zealand.[89] Looking back from many decades on, New Zealand's contemporary sigint agency (the Government Communications Security Bureau) saw 1938 as the key year in establishing a 'signals intelligence capability' in New Zealand.[90] As the outermost node of the Imperial sigint network, the Dominion received, as well as contributed, information collated in London. From the late 1930s, for example, Britain sent a weekly report on 'Communism in the Empire and Commonwealth' to the Dominions and elsewhere. Such interactions set the scene for subsequent wartime developments.[91]

By 1938 the increasing possibility of war had led to an Organisation for National Security review of New Zealand's security intelligence system, and it established a Combined Intelligence Committee. On 29 March, representatives of the three armed services (the air force had been split from the army the previous year) attended the first meeting of the Committee.[92] The Police were not invited, although matters in which they were routinely involved were discussed: censorship, the arrival and departure of aliens, the watching of those likely to instigate anti-war agitation or commit sabotage, and so on. In one sense, the existence of this Committee heralded a revival of previous military ambitions for a centralised intelligence structure in which the police role was subordinated. With the government satisfied with police performance on internal security, however, the Organisation for National Security's initiative did not lead to any change in surveilling responsibilities; in fact, the NZPF was admitted to the Committee at its next meeting.[93]

All the same, Defence authorities continued to seek better ways of coordinating intelligence of military import in the event of war. On 19 September 1938, the fifteenth meeting of the Combined Intelligence Committee recommended that

> . . . in time of war there should be established a combined Intelligence Centre to be located at Military District Headquarters in Auckland, Wellington and Christchurch. At each centre there would be an Army Intelligence Officer and either the local Intelligence Officer or a Liaison Officer from both Navy and the Air Force. All local information would be sifted at centres before being sent on to Wellington.[94]

This planning initiative effectively set the scene for what would happen when New Zealand did march to war after September 1939. While this is examined in depth in the next chapter, suffice to note here that, whatever the pre-war military blueprints had envisaged, there was inevitably overlap of Police and Defence surveillance responsibilities. When the latter eventually persuaded the government to transfer primary responsibility for intelligence activity within New Zealand to a military-led body, there were to be some bizarre consequences.

Operations

In the 1930s the intelligence cycle both reflected the practices that had become embedded in the 1920s and responded to profound developments in politics and society. At first, there was mass anger at the economic distress caused by the Depression, and this was followed by a political sea change in mid-decade when the Labour Party attained political office for the first time. From an intelligence perspective, the first of these challenges was in many ways similar to that of a decade before, another time of politico-industrial disruption. In both circumstances, police were especially concerned that militant activists, especially Communists, might be able to utilise social distress to attack the authorities and the economic system they protected – one which, in times of crisis especially, seemed to belie the New Zealand mythscape of fairness and equality of opportunity. As we have seen, this had led, in the immediate post-war years, to a discrete political police operation being established at Police Headquarters and in the detective offices, together with a secret filing system to underpin their work.

In tackling the threatscape of the early 1930s, the Commissioner took hands-on direction of surveilling priorities across the country, sometimes becoming directly involved in the investigations. He would, for example, instruct officers in charge of districts, or even the staff of individual police stations, to covertly surveil specified people and organisations. On one not untypical occasion he ordered an investigation of two men after a Wellington newspaper reported them saying that exploited workers would be 'forced to do something worse than striking'; one had averred that he had 'served on Gallipoli and [had] been taught how to throw bombs'.[95]

More normally, surveillance operations mostly arose from observations by uniformed or detective police, supplemented by a constant stream of information received from officials or the public. The social welfare officer at Wellington Hospital, for example, reported a man distributing radical leaflets;[96] a Christchurch printing company was alarmed at the nature of the political material given it to print;[97] a relief worker expressed concern at the political agitation he witnessed at a work camp.[98]

Police interventions often resulted in cautions rather than coercion. With regard to the two Wellingtonians who seemed to be advocating violence, the Commissioner had gone beyond requiring the usual reports on the 'occupation (normal), address and history' of each of them. He requested the detectives to consider whether '[i]t may also be advisable to have each of them interviewed and warned that any attempt at violence or lawlessness will be firmly dealt with, and that threats, such as those referred to in the attached article, will only get them into trouble'. In this case, as in so many, nothing substantive emerged. Detective Baylis reported that the offending words had been uttered 'just in the course of conversation' and were not intended 'to be taken seriously'. The men were in fact 'decent' people so far as the political surveillers were concerned and were warned to be more careful in the future.[99]

At the end of the First World War, Communists were viewed as one of several 'revolutionary dispositions' in the country, but they had quickly come to dominate the threatscape with the quickening of the latent Cold War. Communist influence in movements and organisations was the predominant focus of the majority of investigations, as security analysts' notes in declassified records from this period highlight; these stress that 'the organisation of most concern was the NZ Communist Party, and that persons of interest were usually leftists'.[100] Certainly, there was a deepening concern that 'Communist influence' was instigating or influencing reactions to the socio-political disruptions of the Depression. The major example of surveillance operations based on a Communist presence within a movement was that focused on the Unemployed Workers' Movement, which generated phonebook-sized files for each year in the early 1930s, slimming to thinner volumes by 1937 in the wake of the Depression.

A myriad of other associations and people came to various degrees of attention. In the early years of the decade, Labour Party activities remained a subject of study, particularly in cases where members could be associated with radicalism or unrest. For example, a full transcription was taken of Labour politician Paddy Webb's speech at a 1932 May Day demonstration, which argued that accounts of famine in Russia were manufactured by the capitalist press and warned that workers would soon be herded into a war against the Soviet Union.[101] In October that same year, police contacted the *Timaru Herald* to inquire as to the accuracy of its account of a speech given by Labour MP Clyde Carr to the UWM, which argued the Depression had been deliberately caused and perpetuated to bring down workers' living standards. The speech concluded with: 'The question is how long are you going to stand for it?'[102]

With politicians and security officials increasingly thinking in terms of a future war, concerns developed around pacifist and anti-war movements which might undermine morale, challenge mobilisation or prove vulnerable to Communist influence in a global conflict. New Zealand's No More War Movement, which had begun in 1928, formed the initial focus of surveillance of anti-militarists. The New Zealand branch of the London-based Peace Pledge Union and the Christian Pacifist Society also attracted surveillance upon their establishment in 1934 and 1936 respectively.[103] Some peace-oriented organisations were seen as virtual or actual fronts, such as the Movement against War and Fascism, regarded as being heavily within the ambit of the World Movement Against War, which the Comintern had set up in 1932.[104] Other peace activism was monitored in the general swirl of geopolitics. For example, among police surveillance targets were those protesting New Zealand trade with Japan after the outbreak of the Second Sino-Japanese War in 1937.[105]

A broad range of other groups were watched because of Communists in their ranks, or sometimes because of their openness to giving Communists a platform or accepting their help. The Howard League for Penal Reform came under scrutiny from 1934 'when the well-known unemployed activist and Communist Jim Edwards was invited to speak at a prison reform meeting in Hamilton'.[106] The members of the Rationalist Association of New Zealand came to the detectives' attention that same year partly 'because of the participation of members of the N.Z. Communist Party in their activities' and calls by associated speakers for free speech and assembly.[107] As international tension increased in the late 1930s, certain immigrant communities were especially watched for Communist influence amongst them. On the gumfields, Dargaville police noted in 1937 that 'a number of Dalmatians with Communistic leanings . . . had formed themselves into a club'.[108]

Movements that were not necessarily left of centre in a political or philosophical sense, but which were established or supported by left-wingers, fell under scrutiny – including a fledgling civil liberties association in Otago in mid-decade, and a family-planning movement which was watched closely from its beginnings in 1936.[109] Similarly, the Esperanto movement, with its promotion of a universal language, became of interest from 1931 because 'it was assumed to offer a language venue for [Communist] propaganda'.[110] That year Wohlmann requested that 'discreet inquiries' be made regarding the secretary of the Esperanto Association: 'let me have as much information as can be ascertained . . . particular regard being paid to the question of whether he is known to be a Communist sympathiser or to have otherwise displayed anti-British sentiments'.[111]

Spying rumours arose through the decade, often focused around people who were non-conformist. Manchester-born Nita Rosslyn, a showgirl who cycled long distances between variety shows, attracted such attention. Dressed in a scarlet uniform, she had toured the British Isles, Central and Southern America and Australia before arriving in New Zealand in 1935. Her air of mystery attracted rumours that the 'Girl in Red' was a spy, secreting maps in the handlebars of her bike; and in any case was perhaps a man in disguise. Had she been a spy, it would have been an inept school of spycraft that she had been taught in, given her efforts to draw public attention to herself.[112]

While it was assumed that the USSR's attempts to influence New Zealand society would generally be funnelled through the CPNZ, some police investigations concerned the possibility of other means of intervention from Moscow. For example, in 1931 the detectives investigated reports that Soviet radio transmissions were being sent to individuals for relay to other listeners around the country. This was a significant issue, in view of the rising number of radio licence holders, which had reached 150,000 in mid-decade.[113]

Another allegation of direct intervention by Moscow involved local Communists. This was made in December 1932 by an informant who named Demitro Remnizov as an agent who advocated 'Soviet style actions'. These were said to include inducing Wellington electricity workers to disrupt supply, failing which comrades would 'beat the employees in charge of the stations insensible and do the work ourselves'. During the outage, comrades would embark on 'breaking windows, burning, and blowing up buildings, especially House of Parliament'. While the informant acknowledged that such proposals were 'more or less ridiculous', he suggested Remnizov could be 'turned' by appealing to his ego or blackmailing him over allegations of financial misconduct, which had put him in a 'blue funk'. As so often happened, surveillance did not lead to any result, and Remnizov was in any case arranging at the time to be smuggled out of New Zealand.[114]

Other targets for covert surveillance where Communist influence was suspected included critics of New Zealand's administration of Samoa, a long-standing cause for sections of the New Zealand left. In August 1931, for example, the Commissioner ordered an inquiry into the reasons behind the editorial stance of the *Samoa Guardian*: was editor Percy Andrew 'known to be associated with, or to take any active interest in the Communist Movement'?[115] Members and supporters of the Samoan independence movement, the Mau, came under particularly close scrutiny, especially given the widespread anger over 'Black Saturday', in which New Zealand military police had opened fire on a procession in Apia in December 1929, killing 11 demonstrators including paramount chief Tupua Tamasese Lealofi III.[116] In 1930, 'Seditious Organisation Regulations' were applied to Samoa that were specifically aimed at the Mau.[117] Labour leader Harry Holland had taken the lead in condemning the events of 'Black Saturday' and, as the most prominent New Zealand supporter of Samoan independence, came under additional scrutiny by the political police on this issue.[118]

Although the Communist International supported Samoan as well as Māori and other indigenous self-determination causes, this was not a priority for the CPNZ. Indeed, the Comintern criticised its New Zealand comrades for insufficient effort put into such causes. In 1933 it reminded them that indigenous rights 'must be constantly driven into the minds of the working masses'.[119] But the mere fact of Soviet support in principle drew continued police scrutiny. The detectives remained vigilant, for example, over the Rātana movement, with its mass base and mix of social democratic and self-determinationist philosophy. Such vigilance stepped up as it moved ever closer towards Labour. In 1932, Rātana candidate Eruera Tirikātene won one of the four Māori seats in Parliament and voted with Labour in the House. A second seat fell to the Rātana movement in the 1935 election, and the movement formally cemented its alliance with Labour in April 1936. By then, its ties with the Labour government had led to reduced surveillance. Insofar as Māori communities and movements were of interest to the security authorities past that year, it was largely because of lingering memories of pro-Japanese sentiments within the Rātana movement and residual connections with Germany in other tribes. Te Puea, for example, was of distant German heritage, had led the Waikato opposition to conscription in the First World War, and had established 'a cordial relationship' with von Luckner, who visited Kīngitanga headquarters during his tour. There were also rumours that she had sympathies with the Japanese cause.[120]

Not long after the Nazi rise to power in Germany in early 1933, the political police were watching out for fascist activity in New Zealand. Publications with an anti-Semitic bent and/or sympathies for Nazism were studied. Inquiries were made into the editorship of *Plain Talk*, for example, a newssheet advocating monetary reform but which veered into advertising *The Protocols* and defending the Nazi Party as 'simply aimed at freeing Germany from the stranglehold of the Jew financiers'.[121]

Within a year, too, several German language and culture clubs around the country were being investigated. Although most were assessed as not constituting any threat, one Auckland club was found to be the headquarters of 'an active Nazi organisation'. It had adopted fascist salutes, featured a large portrait of Hitler and proselytised for the Third Reich. While its founding president and many others had quickly resigned, reducing its membership from nearly 220 to no more than 80, numbers later rose again and had reached some 100–120 by 1937. The club remained under continuing surveillance by Auckland detectives until it went into recess when war began.[122] A Nazi party established by members of the German community in Samoa was also monitored. Its propaganda activities were tracked, and police analysts gave some consideration to such matters as how mixed-race Samoans would fit within the Third Reich's legal and ideological structures.[123]

Police–military cooperation on counter-espionage can be seen in the strange case of Victor Penny, an amateur Auckland inventor who claimed, in the mid-1930s, to have invented a 'death ray'. Its energy could supposedly put aircraft engines and other machinery out of action. Penny told the authorities that he had been approached by German and Japanese agents offering to finance its development and, after declining, he had been violently assaulted at the Auckland bus depot where he worked. As he convalesced from very real injuries, he and his workshop were protected by police and armed auxiliaries.

After inconclusive investigations, the government decided that research on the death ray should be given state protection. Penny was taken onto the government payroll and relocated to Wellington. There, military intelligence guarded him in safe locations until he could transfer to a laboratory and quarters on Somes Island, in Wellington Harbour. While he continued his experiments, soldiers guarded Penny and his wife on the island. After Labour's electoral victory, however, the ministers responsible for defence and policing launched an investigation into Penny's state-funded experiments on his 'radio marvel' and publicly proclaimed them worthless. As a result of 'a complete lack of corroborative evidence as to the authenticity of the alleged discoveries' they had been closed down. In Parliament, Peter Fraser accused the previous government of gullibility, stating that 'a child could have seen there was nothing in it'.[124]

Through the 1930s, as before them, open-source information constituted the bulk of the material collected in the files. In some cases, investigations did not proceed beyond collection and analysis of caches of literature. For example, declassified information gathered on the Esperanto movement consists of readily available movement literature, background for enquiries into its possible links with both Communism and the peace movement. The declassification record notes that 'it seems the [Esperanto] movement was never infiltrated by any of our security services'.[125]

Public meetings and demonstrations remained major sites of surveillance, with police reporting on much more than who said what: audience reactions, for example, or the potential illegality of specific words and deeds. Sometimes the Police continued the practice of posting both overt and covert surveillers at venues. While the uniformed men or well-known detectives recorded the speakers, unrecognised plain-clothes men mingled with audiences before and after the programme, trying to extract information from unwary sources over cups of tea and plates of biscuits. But, as we have noted previously, there was only a limited pool of detectives and uniformed men with the capacity to go undercover. This number was further restricted as various infiltrators came under suspicion or were recognised. After Detective Laugesen was fingered at an October 1931 meeting of the unemployed in Christchurch, he reported that 'the usual motion was put and carried that I immediately leave'.[126]

On this occasion he was permitted to stay after he noted that the meeting had been advertised as open to all and his advocacy was accepted. Generally, however, targeted organisations were less accommodating. Earlier that year Acting Detective R. H. Waterson had outlined an attempt by police to attend a meeting of unemployed workers in Wellington's Marion Street:

> As we entered the Hall the Chairman was saying 'all those in favour of holding this meeting' and this motion was carried unanimously; We were only in the hall about ½ minute when Sandford drew the attention of the chairman to us by saying this was 'a committee meeting and the Police have no right to be here' the Chairman [Frank] 'GORDON' then stood up and said to us 'Yes, that is so I'm sorry you will have to go' Sandford interjected that they were not sorry.[127]

Tight political parties or groups often took countermeasures to guard against police infiltration, and these were increasing in sophistication. Laugesen had noted in March 1931 that he was

> ... now having difficulty in obtaining reliable information regarding the activities and intentions of the Communist Group. There are several reasons for this. The Communists do not now meet at regular places but go to the homes of the members. They will not discuss their business with persons outside the party to such a

degree as previously, and they have now adopted a rule that no Press or Police representatives shall visit any of their indoor mass meetings. I was informed to day that the Communists have adopted this measure because their more or less open methods in the past have given the Police the opportunity to frustrate their plans when an attempt was made to put them into action.[128]

Police countermeasures included surveillance outside of meetings, and this method could also be employed openly in attempts to intimidate. After the 1932 riot, prominent Communist Alexander Drennan reported that he was followed by at least one police surveiller whenever he visited Auckland.[129] Another option was to forgo quiet observation in favour of direct actions such as searching premises. As in previous decades, such raids usually followed delicate intelligence work and led to such actions as seizing documentation that could both underwrite charges and advance analysis. This is evident in the not-uncommon police raids on the CPNZ in the early 1930s, which confiscated a great deal of documentation for study. A debrief after one such swoop in Wellington, in March 1931, noted:

> Documents which purport to be copies of reports made by comrade A. Galbraith to the authorities in Russia where he recently represented the New Zealand Communist Party were found at 166d Vivian Street. These reports together with a brief outline of the main points contained in them are attached. From these it will be seen that the Communists admit that most of their activities are illegal and that they anticipate the suppression of the Party and its newspaper 'The Red Worker'.[130]

Another response was to increase the use of informants within targeted organisations, a practice which burgeoned in Depression-era protest. For example, in late March 1931, in the context of fears of a general strike, police stations around the country responded to a memorandum from Commissioner McIlveney which urged surveillers to actively recruit more informants.[131] Where the workplaces were distant from the big centres, informants' handlers were often local uniformed men. A constable in Ngāruawāhia, for example, had sources of information in all the town's main industries.[132]

Examples of ad hoc recruitment are also evident in the records. In January 1932, for example, the Auckland Superintendent told the Commissioner that he had been contacted by a relief worker who warned of a plot to stir dissent among his fellow workers and even to rob arms and ammunition. The Commissioner ordered that discreet inquiries be made: 'if he is considered reliable', secret communication channels between him and the political detectives were to be established.[133] In the event, he passed the dependability test and would go on to provide valuable inside information to Detective Nalder.

Informants were able to provide regular and fresh information from inside targeted circles. Declassified records offer good examples of regular informants' reports in the early 1930s. In 1931 Detective Laugesen noted how much he owed to his 'special agents' within the UWM: 'Per medium of reliable informants I have kept close touch with the actions of the various Unions.'[134] As always, particular care was taken to record people who were 'close sympathisers of the Communist Party'.[135] One undercover agent was a Scots seaman whose official story to his new 'comrades' was that he had jumped ship – which indeed he had. When he emerged from his four years undercover, during which time he gained a senior office-holding position in the Wellington branch of the CPNZ, he was sworn in as a constable and posted to rural districts where there was less chance of him being recognised.[136]

At their most useful, informants' reports enabled police to acquire details of the innermost workings of (especially) the CPNZ, from a decision to decline an application to join, to a document noting that only a quarter of Wellington's CPNZ members were deemed active comrades.[137] Such insider information would then inform subsequent surveilling operations. In 1934, for example, the political police had advance knowledge of Elsie Farrelly's travels to South Island centres. In Christchurch she was scheduled to stay with 'Communist Beardsley [and] Communist Jones', and it was said that she would probably visit 'Communist Saunders' in hospital; an equally detailed itinerary of her Dunedin visit was provided by another 'secret source'.[138] It was, accordingly, easy to track her and clandestinely surveil her activities.

In February 1932, to take another example, an informant within the Christchurch branches of both the UWM and the CPNZ copied 'a vast amount of correspondence [that he had] received during the last two or three days'. It included notes from a recent UWM executive meeting, information about upcoming meetings and events, lists of UWM secretaries, and observations on personal dynamics within the unemployed movement. It also referenced the arrival of 'a large bundle of Literature' and particulars of its distribution by a seaman, 'Comrade Lamb'. Between them the informant and an accomplice had

> . . . discovered that [Lamb] is the medium by which a vast amount
> of Russian and American Literature enters New Zealand. I opened
> the bundle and discovered it to contain the following:
> Soviet Policy in Russia.   (24 copies)
> The Meaning of Imperialism. (6 copies)
> Read [Red] Leader.   (4 dozen copies)
> R.I.L.U.[139]   (1 dozen copies)

Russia in Construction.	(3 copies)
Pan-Pacific Worker.	(2 dozen copies)
Soviets Today.	(2 dozen copies)
Moscow News.	(3 dozen copies)[140]

The 'greater portion of the bundle' had been sold to Professor George Lawn of Canterbury University College 'for distribution among the Students there'. Marginalia on this report indicates that a personal file had then been opened on the professor – who would, a few years later, be appointed to the directorate of the Reserve Bank.[141]

The material supplied by informants could differ from a throwaway line uttered in a pub to substantial details about ways and means to promote revolution. Material on politics could jostle with personal information about where suspect individuals were living, their occupations and preoccupations, their personal and political disagreements, their rent rates and who made the payments, their drinking or gambling or womanising or stealing, what they read and who they corresponded with, who among them were tardy in returning money from party newspaper sales, and so on.[142]

The expansion of the informant system came with various challenges. The number and quality of informants was uneven throughout the country and at different times. The Commissioner's call, in the tense times of 1931, to recruit more informants did not necessarily lead to immediate success: 'I am at present unable to discover a man suitable for the part of a secret agent as suggested in your memo', wrote the dedicated political detective Jim Nalder.[143] Meanwhile, he had to rely on information from less than satisfactory sources, including 'a man who was not fit to be recommended as a Temporary Constable'.[144]

The system represented a more intrusive, complicated and risky form of surveillance that left police one step removed from the information being delivered, raising reliability issues. Targeted organisations, too, continued to hamper the effectiveness of police surveillance by restricting important internal information to top-level members. In mid-1931, Christchurch's Detective Laugesen lamented that heightened security concerns within CPNZ circles had made it 'impossible to secure an informant connected with the inside working of the local group of Communists'. He did have 'informants who will supply me with information' on what transpired at 'the indoor mass meetings from which Press & Police are now excluded', but even here it was 'difficult to obtain reliable information and there are occasions on which my informants are not able to be present'.[145]

The most successful informants tended to seek office within targeted organisations, especially those providing access to correspondence and files. Such positions risked greater scrutiny and exposure though, given that tightly disciplined institutions, especially the CPNZ, were aware that comrades willing to take charge of membership, correspondence and literature distribution should be watched closely.

The January 1932 minutes of the Party's conference, for example, state that a man who had become the secretary of its Christchurch branch had been discovered to be reporting back to the Police Force.[146]

To protect their sources, police needed to be careful in their use of the information received. When Baylis pondered an informant's suggestion to 'smash up' a proposed illegal demonstration 'at its starting point', he 'thought this would be very effective' as a deterrent but had to weigh up several factors, including the man's own security.[147] Police actions that indicated 'obvious foreknowledge' were generally likely to lead a targeted organisation to suspect enemies within, although there were always other possible explanations for police possession of knowledge – monitoring mail, or a 'secret search' of premises, for instance. Suspicions about a traitor in the midst sometimes led to an embarrassing exposure, or at least to other counterproductive outcomes such as tougher security within the grouping, 'need to know' information-sharing or the tightening of recruitment procedures.[148]

In short, the increasing use of informants brought significant challenges to security analysis. Sources might well have ideological motivations that distorted their perceptions and reports. They might embellish or even fabricate reports for these or other reasons, such as financial reward. They might conflate the serious and the trivial or, because they were not trained in spycraft, take remarks out of context. A comment to the effect that policemen be 'included in the payment when the reign of terror began' might, for example, be presented, decontextualised, as a statement of intent. Large numbers of such supposed threats to authority, often made at private gatherings after considerable drinking, were not followed up once the detectives had carried out preliminary sifting or elementary investigations. Regardless of the outcome, the informers' reports sat in the secret files, searchable by later investigators looking for matters such as patterns of behaviour or personality and intent.[149]

In October 1931, Dunedin's Detective Sergeant H. Nuttall noted the limits of informant-based intelligence on the Militant Workers' League: 'owing to the secrecy with which these meetings are being held, I knew it was impossible to get [redacted name] into the meetings'.[150] By this time, electronic listening devices were being used by covert surveillers in the United States and other jurisdictions, but they were expensive, large and clumsy. Furthermore, if they malfunctioned there was a strong danger of discovery.[151] In lieu of such devices being acquired in New Zealand, the NZPF sometimes sought to establish listening stations, or 'facilities for overhearing', as a Christchurch detective put it when setting about finding out what was happening at CPNZ committee meetings.[152] This was Nuttall's solution, too, for surveilling the Militant Workers' League. Access to a small room in the Good Templars' Hall, where the meetings were regularly held, was arranged. A hole was drilled through the adjoining wall into the main hall and was concealed with a picture. Two or three policemen were then stationed to eavesdrop and take notes during meetings. This ongoing operation produced extensive reports and Nuttall concluded that, spurred on by the League, each one of the wider unemployed movement's leaders was a 'red hot militant and there is no knowing how far they will go'.[153]

There was conjecture at the time as to whether police instructed their clandestine sources to act as *agents provocateurs*, supporting or even inciting words or deeds that would discredit the targeted grouping and/or provide grounds for arrests. Prominent Communist Sid Scott noted an incident during the Auckland unemployed riot:

> Outside a jeweller's window was my old anarchist, or ex-anarchist, friend – he of the Viking moustache. Men were stuffing trinkets into their pockets. When he saw me, he came up to me and said, motioning towards the window, 'Get in for your chop boy.' He put one hand in a side pocket and bulged it out to suggest that the pockets were full. 'See', he said. But I was not one hundred percent naïve and did not believe for one moment that he had anything in his pockets. I just said dryly 'no thanks!' and passed on down the street. There were people who said that this man was a police provocateur. I do not know. I do know that such men existed, that there were spies, and provocateurs in the ranks of such organisations as the U.W.M.[154]

Among a number of suspected *agents provocateurs* was George Sargeef, a Russian seaman who had lived in New Zealand for a dozen years by the time of the riots. In 1968, John A. Lee recalled that Sargeef had tried to encourage him into a confrontation with police, causing suspicion that he was an undercover instigator of behaviour designed to discredit the unemployed cause. Jim Edwards, too, thought Sargeef was suspect, but he and others could not find firm evidence.[155] If the man were a 'police provocateur', it did not stop him being hauled before the courts in mid-1932 for possessing gelignite and bombs (which he unsuccessfully argued were for fishing) as well as counterfeiting equipment.[156]

As the threatscape expanded with the intensification of the Depression, New Zealand's political police ramped up their contacts with overseas agencies. After leading Communist Alex Galbraith departed for London in July 1930, bound for the USSR, the British authorities were notified. They reported back that he was 'probably going to attend a course at the Lenin School in Moscow' to undertake revolutionary training.[157] The following year, Nalder requested information from New South Wales authorities about Patrick Quill, 'the most dangerous agitator that we have in Auckland', a man seen as especially effective for his cause because he 'does his agitating in a secret and quiet way'.[158]

Von Luckner's world tour also resulted in intelligence exchanges between Australasian agencies and MI5. Reports sent by New Zealand's Police Commissioner, for example, noted that members of the entourage included two suspected Gestapo agents. He assured fellow agencies that the entourage was under surveillance throughout its time in the Dominion. While no spying activity was uncovered, it later transpired that a Nazi agent had indeed been assigned to the party. Among other things, he had reported back that the German government's investment in the tour was receiving poor dividends, with von Luckner proving an insufficiently enthusiastic propagandist about Nazi Germany.[159]

Signals intelligence links within the Commonwealth increased considerably as international tensions picked up. From 1934, for example, intelligence reports from the Far East Combined Bureau in Hong Kong (Britain's main decryption station in Asia), the Combined Intelligence Bureau in Singapore, and Australian naval intelligence all warned of the danger of Japanese espionage in the South Pacific.[160] New Zealand made reciprocal contributions to their watching. In 1938 the government approved the establishment of its 'first highly technical form' of sigint interception capabilities, with intercept stations being installed at the Auckland and Awarua radio facilities. Post and Telegraph staff began intercepting, in particular, Soviet 'naval and general traffic' and forwarding it for analysis to the Far East Combined Bureau, where New Zealand radio officers were also trained.[161]

During the Munich crisis that September, the station at Awarua 'observed the changes in call signs of German marine stations, indicating naval movements or intentions'; the Royal Navy passed on its appreciation for this data to the Post and Telegraph Department, via the Organisation for National Security.[162] In May 1939 the New Zealand authorities, in response to a British request, outlined the possibilities that their location gave them. In particular, Awarua was able to intercept 'traffic to and from the Philippine Islands, Honolulu and the Netherlands East Indies', as well as from stations in Japan and its territories.[163]

Although there was little actual sigint analysis carried out in New Zealand, the analytical phase of the intelligence cycle became increasingly important in the world of humint. Methods of processing the information that had been collected, however, differed little during the 1930s from those of the previous decade; there were basic ways of doing things, and changes were incremental rather than fundamental. A debriefing report summarised the operation of the cycle with reference to material acquired in a March 1931 raid on the CPNZ: 'From letters and other documents seized a good deal of useful information respecting the personnel and activities of the Party has been obtained. These items of information are being carefully followed up and the results tabulated for reference.'[164]

Categorisation of information in the secret files was pursued painstakingly to form the basis of current and future analysis. Christchurch detectives, monitoring the turnover of the local UWM committee members, annotated the names of new members with comments such as 'Communist' or 'Expelled Communist', providing descriptions such as 'Unemployed' alongside those they had as yet no political information on.[165] In June 1931, a 40-page list of the names and addresses of people said to be Communists and their sympathisers, organised by districts, was produced; the Commissioner circulated it throughout the force for noting or possible action.[166]

Such collated material was added to and updated periodically. Investigations of the Wellington branch of the CPNZ in 1932, for example, led to fresh analyses of personalities and dynamics within the Party, and information on such matters as accusations against comrades for breaching discipline or misappropriating party funds.[167] With so much material coming in during the Depression years, and the changing political, social and economic dynamics after 1935, ongoing efforts were made to ensure that the analysis stage of the intelligence cycle had manageable data and tools, and improvements in methods of recording, tabulation and filing were made from time to time to facilitate accessibility, tracking and analysis. In particular, significant numbers of personal files, initially based on information copied from within the subject files, were created for the most prominent surveillees.[168]

Police analyses of acquired information were a mix of factual data and supposition. They were often rooted in latent Cold War attitudes, giving substantial explanatory power to a Communist presence in any radical grouping.[169] In August 1931, for example, Commissioner Wohlmann stated that the UWM was 'merely an offshoot of the Communist Party through which the Party endeavours to carry out its orders from Moscow to exploit the unemployed in the interests of the communist movement and against Capitalism'.[170] Any link or association with the Communists was a point of interest and a focus of reports. For example, in a January 1932 letter to the minister of justice, the Police Commissioner drew from a 'secret file' to cite a leading figure in the Militant Workers' League as stating:

> The Militant Workers are not Communists in so far as being actual Members of the Communist Party is concerned but they had everything in common and that the Militant Workers League was actually an auxiliary of the Communist Party with the same sympathy and aims the final overthrowing of capitalism by militant means, as they had seen in the past that constitutional methods were useless.[171]

Beyond the focus on Communists, watchers' attitudes towards their targets were often reflected within their reports. One typical report declared an activist to be 'a pest' for his 'vicious' remarks, such as reminding an audience of the killing of Evans at Waihī in 1912.[172] It was not unusual for police and their informants to use dismissive language in their reports, such as the 'usual absurd demands' of the UWM,[173] or to assume a sinister intent behind trade union advocacy for a better deal for the unemployed.

Where nothing untoward was found in the behaviour of a targeted individual, watchers could seem puzzled. Of a militant's time spent working on the Waitaki hydro scheme, a constable reported, '[a]part from his Socialistic tendencies, [Albert] Birchfield's conduct was quite good'.[174]

While the surveillers may have found it hard to comprehend intra-left schisms, they did generally record the existence of disputes and splits when they arose. In 1937, a letter from Gordon Watson in Sydney to a London colleague was intercepted, and a section about public servant William Ball ('Bill') Sutch was copied out: he had given 'an excellent account' of the Soviet Union, 'flaying sundry Trotskyists' along the way.[175] In February 1938, a police report noted that since Jim Edwards' expulsion from the CPNZ two years before, the party had denounced him as a Trotskyist and forbidden members to associate with him. Conversely, 'few of his talks at Quay St have been free of what may be called "verbal sniping" of communism'.[176]

The relationship between Labour Party members and the Communist movement was clearly a point of interest, with statements pored over. In a September 1932 report, for example, Detective Laugesen noted of two Labour MPs: 'I do not think that [Ted] Howard is very sympathetic toward the Communist Party or its organisations, but I think T. Armstrong M.P. is sympathetic. I have only heard him speak once from the Labour Defence League's platform but on that occasion he gave them considerable support.'[177] Likewise, CPNZ antagonism towards the Labour Party was closely observed. In April 1932, for example, leading Communist Dick Griffin was recorded as attacking the Labour Party for an hour over its policy on relief measures: 'He pointed out how the slave camps were filled with men and the Labour Party were not doing anything to stop it.'[178]

Political police awareness of such antagonisms informed some collaborations with Labour leaders to foil Communist attempts to disrupt meetings. In January 1931, Peter Fraser arranged for a police presence at a meeting of the Wellington Trades and Labour Council and, from the chair, had policemen eject CPNZ hecklers. A sergeant reported of the incident that

> . . . in future it will be necessary to have ample Police at these meetings as the communist party cannot be allowed to do what they did at the Trades Hall yesterday. Since the meeting I have spoken to Mr Fraser and he stated that he was well satisfied with the action of the Police as without them he would not have been able to control the meeting from the start. I informed him that in the future when about to hold public meetings he should make application to the Inspector of Police for assistance and ample protection could be provided.[179]

Such fledging cooperation in the Depression era helped set the scene for the entente between the Labour government and the political police from the middle of the decade.

Assessment

The intelligence system that had been consolidated in the 1920s continued without fundamental change into the following decade, but its level of scrutiny intensified in line with the rapidly expanding threatscape perceived by the authorities. In particular, the widespread suffering caused by the Depression was viewed as a recruiting tool for the CPNZ; as in the past, but on a much larger scale, mass disaffection and subversion were seen to be intertwined evils.

As the threat of 'the red menace' was seen to increase, surveillance became increasingly wedded to proactive policing aimed at disrupting targeted organisations. Information received by observing meetings, for example, might be used to procure a search warrant for Communist or other premises and the searchers often found literature liable to be taken out of circulation under section 34 and other parts of the Police Offences Act: 'Every possible effort should be made to suppress the publication of documents which incite lawlessness, disorder or violence or express a seditious intention.'[180] The Christchurch Superintendent believed, as he told the Commissioner, that securing convictions under police offences legislation 'will have a good effect among the militant section of the unemployed'.[181]

Sometimes prosecutions were pursued under seditionary legislation, as for example in October 1931 when Leo Sim was sentenced to a huge £50 fine or three months' imprisonment for possessing seditious literature.[182] But many charges were laid for more petty matters: offensive language, selling papers on a Sunday or without a printer's mark, unauthorised bill-posting and the like.[183] Such charges, along with those relating vaguely to encouraging unlawful behaviour, were seen as a valuable tool for warning people off political activism. Deterrence could also extend to procedural manipulation; for example, detectives made sure that when militant unemployment campaigners applied for relief work their entitlement was challenged.[184] They also examined applications to the Charitable Aid Board and ensured that 'very searching questions' were asked of those applicants under surveillance.[185]

As well as such behind-the-scenes activity, constabulary power was wielded in a very palpable fashion to warn off protesters and campaigners. The mere fact that a policeman held the powers invested in the office of constable could be a sufficient deterrent. In April 1931, for example, a Sergeant ordered three Communists to leave a Wellington worksite where they were promoting a general strike, and they did so.[186] In their efforts to curb socialist influence among workers and unemployed people, police would intervene with a show of force when the UWM and other groups organised opposition to the eviction of families unable to pay their rent.[187] When the political police found out from an intercepted letter that Jim Edwards would be speaking at Raetihi, Detective Nalder visited the town and found a reason – his call to resist an eviction – to make a high-profile arrest. Not only was this designed to deter others, but in addition further intelligence was gained from the contents of letters he had been carrying when detained.[188]

Prosecution of out-of-work political activists under idle and disorderly legislation was common, with gaol awaiting those who could not raise the money for a fine – or who wanted to make a public statement about their commitment. Municipal rules and regulations were often resorted to. One police assessment of how best to prosecute an orator in Petone recommended section 98 of the borough's bylaws:

> There are several sections dealing with street speaking but I think the one quoted is the most applicable. It reads as follows:-. 'No person shall be deemed to be making a proper use of any street, private street, footpath, footway, or public place, unless he shall be in good faith using the same for the purpose of a thoroughfare'.[189]

A man who had denied he was a Communist in order to gain better support from the more conservative elements among the unemployed was prosecuted in the same borough for public speaking, as only the CPNZ had a permit to do so.[190]

During the 1930s, surveilling of the Public Service stepped up as members expressed support for various left-of-centre causes. The Finance Act, passed during the turbulent events of 1932, included a measure for the dismissal of 'disloyal officers of certain public services' who had, among other things, brought the government 'into disrepute' by their statements or had been 'gravely inimical to peace, order or good government'.[191] Though it was repealed by the Labour government in 1936, some public servants were drummed out by measures short of actual dismissal. These included Jock Barnes, whose radicalism was hardened by this experience; he would go on to become co-leader of the union struggle in the momentous 1951 waterfront dispute.[192] The public servant Bill Sutch first came to attention in 1932 when he visited the Soviet Union. His comments on peace issues and sympathies for the Soviet Union were observed, and he was suspected of leaking secret Committee of Imperial Defence material to the British left-wing newspaper *The Week* in 1937.[193]

As police intervention into political activity increased, countermeasures by groups and movements under scrutiny were sharpened. Reports are replete with comments such as the following: 'He seems to have developed the art of breaking off at the point and allowing his listeners to correctly guess his meaning'.[194] Such tactics were a problem for a security service which handled all parts of the intelligence cycle up to and including prosecution. Although prosecuting police could typically count on the unquestioning support of the judicial as well as civil authorities, the justice system needed to keep up a show of impartiality.[195] This led to some frustration among the political police. When Detective Laugesen suggested prosecuting prominent Communist Sidney Fournier on an indecent language charge, for saying 'bloody-well' in a speech in Christchurch, his Superintendent ruled that 'use of one indecent word . . . is not a matter that the magistrate would approve of our bringing such a case before him'. The target would continue to be surveilled until a more substantial misdemeanour was uncovered.[196]

All the same, significant numbers of CPNZ members were convicted during the Depression years. The Party's leadership stratum was especially targeted, with three of its central committee arrested in 1930, and four each in 1931 and 1932; all seven members were imprisoned in 1933.[197] In October 1931, Christchurch detectives had nothing to report in their regular bulletin on Communist activity as 'all militant members are now in custody'.[198] An Inspector optimistically affirmed the following month that since both CPNZ and UWM 'activities have been checked at so many points by the Police', it appeared that 'the great majority of the workers cannot see where anything is to be gained' by supporting them.[199] The intensive interest of the political police in the CPNZ made it, as we have noted, effectively a semi-legal organisation operating under continual harassment.

Conversely, there was little intervention into the Māori self-determination movements: rather, just a watching police brief for expressions of anti-state and pro-'enemy' sentiment. Māori unemployed and trade unionists, however, might see their political activity hampered by the political police. This might well occur through the kind of informal methods customarily used to police Māori at that time. In 1932, for example, a 'Police Agent' recounted how Huntly policemen had seized money that unemployed Māori had raised through holding a social function. They had handed it to the mayor, and when it was eventually returned there were strings attached that aimed to minimise local activism.[200]

There were often trade-offs between political and general policing. The objective of upholding good order, for example, might be set aside in the short term in the interests of a greater, security-related good. In November 1931, information gathered from the police listening station at Dunedin's Good Templars' Hall indicated that smashing shop windows and looting had been raised as a tactic at meetings. A political policeman recommended that the leaders of the Militant Workers' League be immediately contacted and deterred from any such action. His superiors, however, rejected the proposal so as to not compromise the listening operation:

> I have considered Detective Russell's report of valuable information received by him and your minute on same and I have decided to take no action regards interviewing any of the militant workers at present as some more valuable information may be obtained by Detective Russell after the meeting from the informant.[201]

The Depression-induced expansion of the range of possible converts to Communism made the hunt for evidence on those who would supposedly contaminate them more important than ever. The surveilling net spread ever more widely, especially among the unemployed movement. This had its downsides, especially given the cohabitation of political and ordinary policing: the secret files increasingly filled with information on people who might be seen essentially as threats to public order rather than to state security. A blue pencil in the margin of a report indicated where follow-up action needed to be taken, and there were many of these next to the names of those who had seemingly threatened the peace rather than the state. An enquiry, for example, was opened into a former constable whose chairing of a protest meeting had led to a police report that his rhetoric was likely to 'incite lawlessness'.[202]

The impacts and influences of the 1930s had legacies which lasted well beyond the decade. The crisis for the political economy which prevailed in the first half of the decade, followed by the growing threat of fascism in the second half, was a formative period for many on the left. Elsie Locke (formerly Farrelly) would remember how sympathy for unemployment demonstrations influenced her journey to the far left.[203] New Zealand Rhodes Scholar Ian Milner recalled Depression-era policies as a foil for socialist alternatives: '[P]aternal wisdom taught me that the poor were always with us. You were sorry for them as for a bird with a broken wing . . . But at the outset of the thirties there were far too many "birds with broken wings" . . . Moral and compassionate motives pushed me towards a socialist view of things.'[204] At the end of the twentieth century, radical lawyer and political activist Shirley Smith similarly recalled her political awakening in the 1930s: 'One never doubted that the future lay with communism . . . Once you were committed to this and believed it, it was very hard to shake.'[205]

In turn, the decade's legacies resonated within the history of the secret world. Perhaps most (in)famously, the 'Cambridge Spy Ring', recruited in the 1930s, would come to operate in some of the most sensitive areas of the British state. Furthermore, some information collected in the security files of this era possessed a prominent afterlife. Milner, for example, first came to MI5's attention in the mid-1930s due to his relationship with the Communist Party while studying at Oxford.[206] Desmond 'Paddy' Costello, too, first appeared on the British security radar in November 1934, while he was studying at Cambridge – the by-product of an investigation of prominent FSU member Agnes Costello. The resulting report noted there was no relationship between the two and described Paddy Costello as 'a very decent young man with no Communistic or similar views'.[207] But the tracking of Milner and Costello's lives in the secret files had begun and would be notably revisited in the context of later suspicions around their loyalties.

Some details of Comintern activities involving New Zealand in the mid-1930s are now available in released files from a British intelligence operation (code name 'MASK') which intercepted and decrypted wireless communications between the Communist

Party of Great Britain and Soviet intelligence. These indicate that the Comintern was transferring secret funding to the CPNZ, with Leo Sim (code name 'ANDREWS') and his wife acting as conduits for monthly payments; considerable amounts were also sent to other New Zealand addresses.[208] At this time, arrangements were made for two CPNZ members, Lewis Williams (code name 'Percival Beak') and Frank Lee, to attend the International Lenin School, provided they passed vetting on such matters as 'social origin, political standing and position reliability'.[209]

Other New Zealand agents operated outside the English-speaking world.[210] One example was William Maxwell (Max) Bickerton, a grandson of Christchurch's remarkable Professor Alexander Bickerton, who had himself been under watch by police for both his socialism and his eccentricity. 'Max' Bickerton came on the political radar when he mixed in progressive circles at Victoria University College in the post-war years. He attracted renewed attention from the NZPF in 1934 (a decade after he departed New Zealand) after his arrest in Japan on charges of assisting the underground Japanese Communist Party. After sustained police beatings in a 'tiny, filthy cell' failed to elicit a confession, and intervention by the British Consul following representations from the New Zealand authorities, he was released on bail on the lesser charge of 'harbouring dangerous thoughts'. Perhaps because of Japanese embarrassment over his allegations of torture (the case had been raised in the House of Commons), the Japanese secret police effectively allowed him to escape from their country. The police spy in the Communist Party who reported Bickerton had meanwhile been murdered.

While Bickerton did not return to New Zealand, Wohlmann and MI5 corresponded about New Zealanders with connections to him, including Winnie Harding, who had managed to survive scrutiny as a teacher at the time Hetty Weitzel was dismissed. Following internment in Hong Kong under the Japanese in the war, and a stint assisting New Zealander Rewi Alley's industrial cooperative movement ('Gung Ho') in China, Bickerton taught at the University of Peking. Back in Britain after his expulsion by the Communist regime in 1952 because of his flamboyant homosexuality, he continued to operate for the Comintern. Code named 'The Canadian', he was closely surveilled by MI5.[211]

Conclusion

The 1930s were a decade of crises, instability and political change, and the related socio-political turmoil and uncertainty had significant repercussions within the secret world. As official concern about political radicalisation and civil unrest grew in the Depression, the dragnet thrown out by the political police spread ever wider. The intention was to net, for record on the secret files, anyone who might potentially be fooled or exploited by the CPNZ and its fellow travellers. In the latent Cold War in the 1930s, Communist influence and activism became an ever more significant security concern.

In 1935, Labour entered office and began to implement policies of the kind whose advocacy had long attracted the attention of the political detectives. The Labour Party's historians stress the point that its ascent to office had never been seen as inevitable, not even by its members.[212] In this sense, the surveillers had some rapid rethinking to do with Labour's electoral victory. But Labour had long since shucked off its early flirting with revolutionism and had been steadily moderating its policies. It was now, if radical in terms of New Zealand's history, a parliamentarist party based around, as the genial and reassuring Prime Minister Savage would put it, providing social security 'from the cradle to the grave'.[213] As a small-town policeman ordered to keep watch on unemployed advocates had found out through observation, even 'an extreme Labourite' could be 'kind hearted & charitable'.[214]

The political shifts of the decade, however, cloaked continuities in the secret world. In office, Labour continued to root out Communist and other radical influence from its ranks, attempting to diminish the influence of the far left in politics and society. Cabinet was content, then, to have the police continue their surveilling gaze on elements to the left of mainstream Labour, whose leadership neglected to ask too many questions about the operations of the intelligence cycle. While the new government's policies may not have sat well with the inherently conservative ethos of police culture, the political detectives were professionals with a job to do within a tightly disciplined institution. They were doubly empowered by their own minister's growing determination to disarm opposition to his left. The First Labour Government, as things turned out, did not pay much attention to safeguarding the rights of the watched (such as they were) against the activities of the watchers.

By the second half of the decade, then, economic recovery and the new administration appeared to signal a fresh paradigm for both New Zealand and its secret world. However, as the new government both continued to fear the spread of Communism and faced the looming threat of war, it increasingly recognised the value of the political police for both counter-subversion and counter-espionage work. When war did eventuate in 1939, the surveillance mechanisms put in place some 20 years before had not changed in any fundamental sense, but they had greatly expanded their scope. The new political masters might not be fully to the liking of the secret world, but they allowed it to continue much as before. The political policing system which had emerged from the combination of wartime emergency between 1914 and 1918, and post-war challenges to the state, would now be both modified and tested by another wartime emergency.

PART FOUR:

TOTAL WAR,

1939-1945

Chapter Six:
Coercion and Dissent, 1939–1945

Introduction

In 1938 the Organisation for National Security began to take preliminary steps to prepare for war. The major enemy was seen as Japan, in view of the government's tendency to follow its allies' hopes that appeasing Germany would prevent war in Europe.[1] When Germany invaded Poland on 1 September 1939, however, Britain and France declared a state of war. Prime Minister Savage declared that 'with gratitude for the past and confidence in the future, we range ourselves without fear beside Britain. Where she goes, we go. Where she stands, we stand.'[2]

With regard to security intelligence, New Zealand's Second World War experience differed from the First in several ways, both organisationally and in terms of technological advances, especially in the area of sigint. In many ways, however, it was also a reprise of the previous conflict. Actual or potential enemies of the state within the Dominion fell into similar categories as those during the previous conflict – pacifists and pacificists, those who challenged aspects of the war effort, revolutionary and other socialists purportedly taking advantage of social or political discontent over government policies, anyone perceived to be working for or siding with enemy powers, disruptors of the peace and therefore of the war effort, and so on.

Many services and departments were involved at different levels of intensity in the uncovering and monitoring of suspected seditionaries, subversives, spies and saboteurs. In the world of humint, the police initially predominated, continuing their pre-war surveillance role. However, in a major exception to the relatively similar intelligence experience of the previous war, in 1941 primary responsibility for domestic security was transferred to a stand-alone security organisation under Defence auspices. Theoretically this constituted a vast expansion of the military's surveilling role inside the country. But, in the event, the new organisation – the Security Intelligence Bureau (SIB) – was mandated by the government to operate virtually autonomously, encroaching into military as well as policing responsibilities.

Despite the establishment of the SIB, in any case, the NZPF continued its own surveilling capacity, operating under the rationale of the nexus between dissent and disorder. While the Police Force and the Bureau cooperated on many issues, inevitable institutional rivalry fed into a dramatic fiasco for the latter in 1942. This was hugely embarrassing for the government, fatally undermined the SIB's credibility, and saw the NZPF resume its leading role in security surveillance.

Overview

The second national wartime emergency of the twentieth century brought a similarly great expansion of the state's surveillance over civil society. The fact that New Zealand had a Labour government made little difference to the nature and logic of mobilisation for total war. A series of emergency regulations, beginning just before the outbreak of hostilities, enhanced police capacities to monitor opponents of the war or its conduct, or those taking measures (such as industrial actions) that might hamper the war effort. Other agencies of state were also tasked with surveillance, again following the general lines of the First World War. Censorship of postal, press and telegraphic services was quickly put into place in an effort to protect sensitive information and suppress opposition.[3]

Earlier ideas of restructuring New Zealand security intelligence by means of a dedicated and 'professional' intelligence institution under military auspices, and interlinked with British intelligence, had revived as the possibility of war increased. After hostilities began, the New Zealand military and security authorities in London both pressed for this. They continued to do so during the 'Phoney War', which saw little fighting in Western Europe. With First World War precedents from which to work, police surveillance proved effective enough. But from May 1940, pressure for a stand-alone military agency escalated as the German military rapidly swept through Western Europe, France capitulated, the British and Allied troops evacuated the Continent in late May and early June, and the Battle of Britain began in July. With the heart of Empire threatened, the peripheries felt especially exposed.

In these circumstances, the New Zealand government opted to establish a 'Security Intelligence Organisation', and this became operative from 10 February 1941. Frictions quickly developed between the Security Intelligence Bureau (as it was soon named) and other parts of the intelligence community, especially the Police Force – which felt that its jurisdiction and expertise had been trampled upon. Inter-agency difficulties were also generated by the autocratic personality of the new organisation's director. The following year, these and other flaws led the SIB to fall victim to a professional conman claiming to be privy to a conspiracy of fifth-columnists. These had supposedly been working with enemy agents on plans for sabotage, political assassination and other preparations for an enemy landing.[4] When the deception was uncovered by the police and the information leaked to the press, political and bureaucratic support fell away from the Bureau, and the director was forced to resign in February 1943. The SIB was then placed in the hands of a senior police officer, downsized and increasingly constabularised. In November 1944 it was essentially integrated into the Police Force, and would be disbanded at the end of the war.

The SIB's establishment formed part of a range of political and bureaucratic reactions to geopolitical insecurities that had been magnified by the onset of war and its intrusion into the South Pacific. On 19 June 1940, for example, a few days before the French capitulation to Germany, the trans-Pacific liner *Niagara* fell victim to a mine laid in the approaches to the Hauraki Gulf by the German raider *Orion*, emphasising that the front line was potentially far closer than Europe.[5] Concerns about security in the Pacific region had been further amplified by Japan's tripartite pact with Germany and Italy in September 1940 and its invasion of French Indo-China. The military established a Combined Intelligence Bureau in October 1940 to cover its three services (but located in the Navy Office), and this worked with the Police Force and the SIB on matters of internal security. By the end of the year, a key Australian envoy, in 'most secret' off-record talks about which New Zealand was kept informed, was sounding out the prospects of American support if the Japanese threatened British Imperial interests in Australasia and the Asia–Pacific region.[6]

The sense that New Zealand's isolation would not protect it from enemy assault increased enormously in the months after December 1941 as Japan launched attacks on the United States' naval base at Pearl Harbor, achieved a string of military conquests in South-east Asia, and bombed Darwin, Australia. Forward defence measures were taken to defend Fiji and other British outposts in the South Pacific, and plans were initiated to guard against a possible invasion of New Zealand.[7]

New Zealand's intelligence activities were shaped not only by the shifting tides of conflict but also by their ramifications for some of the long-time targets of security intelligence. In particular, the German–Soviet (Molotov–Ribbentrop) non-aggression pact of 23 August 1939 meant that the CPNZ had quickly abandoned its anti-fascist popular front strategy and presented the war as a conflict between mutually guilty imperialists. It threw itself behind pacifist, anti-militarist and other anti-war activities which had long been under scrutiny by the political police, at the same time as fronts such as the Friends of the Soviet Union (FSU) fell apart for obvious reasons. Surveillance of the Party intensified, and members were punished. When Labour Party members protested about the conviction of Communists for subversive statements, the prime minister replied bluntly that the offenders had been 'aiming at the destruction of the Labour Movement and the Government'.[8]

The wartime emergency, and the increased sensitivity to issues of subversion that came with it, led to various types of censorship being imposed. When John A. Lee raised one case in Parliament, Fraser, who had become prime minister in March 1940 after Savage's death, declared that it was 'only right that the Censor should keep a close watch on a person who so completely puts himself in opposition to the war effort'.[9]

Regular publication of the CPNZ's *People's Voice* ceased in May 1940 when its press was seized, although during the ban some underground editions were printed and a supposedly non-Party newspaper, *In Print*, was produced. The publication of the left-wing political and literary journal *Tomorrow* ceased in June 1940 after its editor and printer were warned that publishing any content deemed subversive would see the seizing of its printing press.[10] In 1942 the Social Credit newsletter was banned from publishing any non-approved reference to government methods of financing the war, or any reference to the ban itself; its subsequent publication of an article titled 'Dictatorship in New Zealand' saw it closed down.[11]

All the state agencies engaged in censoring and surveilling expanded their scope in the course of the war, and often in an ad hoc fashion. Customs staff, for example, began intercepting ever larger amounts of suspected subversive books and periodicals. In 1940, under great pressure to release at least a portion of the seized imports, Minister Walter Nash established a secret committee to establish tighter criteria for banning literature. Titles of works released as a result included the left-wing British periodical *The New Statesman and Nation*, academic books on socialism, and Leon Trotsky's 'highly reputable work' *Karl Marx*.[12] On the other hand, large numbers of titles continued to be added to the list of those that remained banned. The Wellington Co-operative Book Society declared that, despite being on the front line of the armed struggle, England allowed more freedom to read and write than New Zealand. Forbidden works included anti-imperialist tracts such as Lenin's *Imperialism* (but not Hitler's *Mein Kampf*) and material deemed to have the potential to foment religious-based social disruption, such as anti-Catholic books.[13]

The CPNZ itself was not directly banned, despite the Commissioner's advice in early 1941 to do so after it was implicated in industrial action. It effectively became, even more than in the past, a semi-legal organisation. The crackdown induced greater secrecy within the Party and its leaders drew up plans, for example, to break its membership into cells and to establish an illegal radio station.[14] Press speculation heightened tension. In September 1940, boys exploring a cave on a farm outside Papatoetoe found a duplicating machine, a typewriter and CPNZ literature. These were seized by the police, and a journalist painted a harsh picture of the supposed operating conditions of the (literally) underground press:

> Movement within the inner radius of the cave can only be made in a stooping posture. Pieces of timber and sacks covered the sodden soil of the floor, and two pieces of asbestos board had been used to protect the duplicator and papers from the moisture dripping from the roof. An empty apple box had also been used. The depth and winding access to the cave prevented any natural light from penetrating, and candles had been employed for illumination.[15]

As it turned out, there was an innocent explanation for what appeared to be a hidden printing operation. A probationary teacher at the local school had been given reason to fear for his job after police told the education authorities of his Communist affiliations and activities. In a panic, he had concealed in the cave anything he thought might damage his case. On finding these missing from the cave, he notified local police, upon which Detective E. M. Grace had searched his home and, he said, tried to extract information from him on pain of arrest and loss of his career.[16]

The Communist Party's relationship with the war radically changed from June 1941, when Germany invaded the Soviet Union and the latter rapidly entered a military alliance with Britain. Thereafter, the Allied war effort was designated a people's war against fascism, and the CPNZ swung its support fully behind the struggle. This change of affairs presented unique opportunities for Communism in New Zealand, with establishment figures and commentators praising the Soviet Union's efforts, although such respect generally sprang from recognition of the Red Army's sacrifices rather than any liking for totalitarian governance.[17] The CPNZ experienced its high-water mark during the conflict. Party membership expanded from 690 in February 1941 to 942 in November 1945, and a much wider circle of sympathisers had formed. The 1944 Wellington mayoral elections saw Communist candidate Harold Silverstone receive nearly 10,000 votes (almost 20 per cent), and Party member Connie Birchfield received a similar number when running for Wellington Hospital Board.[18]

A series of Labour MPs, trades councils, civil libertarians and others now urged a rescinding of the ban on the *People's Voice*. The government resisted, based on intelligence reports as well as its own predilections. It argued that Communist 'devotion' to the war effort reflected support for the USSR and its revolutionist aims rather than genuine patriotism. Under continuing pressure, however, in April 1943 the government agreed to allow publication, subject to stringent conditions: no 'creating ill will between various sections of our community', for example, or 'arousing opposition to the financial or economic methods' used to fight the war.[19]

This did not necessarily mean that security police coverage of CPNZ activity lessened. In effect, the new popular front masked the ongoing realities of the long Cold War. Indeed, unaccustomed appreciation for the CPNZ in unlikely quarters made the Party, if anything, all the more targeted by the covert surveillers – for them, its new respectability was worrying. There were now new targets, too. A month after the invasion of the USSR, for example, the Society for Closer Relations with Russia (SCR) was launched. Avowedly non-partisan, though effectively a successor to the FSU, its stated aim was to promote 'closer cultural, diplomatic and economic relations between the New Zealand people and the people of the USSR'. The Society emphasised the importance of the eastern front, campaigned for aid to the Soviet Union's struggle, and called for the opening of a second front in Europe. By September 1944 it had 35 branches and, as with its predecessor, it was heavily supported by the Communist Party.[20]

As well as the Communists, a series of other groups came under surveilling scrutiny during the war. As in the last conflict, people whose nationality or ancestry linked them to enemy powers became suspects. Among other things, the police were tasked with registering and tracking the 9000 enemy aliens that had been identified, a category which included recent influxes of Jewish refugees from Germany, Austria and Czechoslovakia, who were categorised as such by dint of their status in German law.[21] Soon after the war began, those enemy aliens who were considered an immediate danger to state security were placed in the military-run internment camp on Somes Island.[22] The priority was, obviously, people identified as Nazi Party members and sympathisers, often on the basis of pre-war surveillance of members and officials of German clubs.[23]

Dr Reuel Lochore was 'responsible for the surveillance of non-British immigrants, especially those who came from parts of Europe under fascist domination. He read their mail, commissioned reports on their social and cultural gatherings and interviewed those applying for New Zealand citizenship.' On such matters he worked with police and other security authorities, including on investigations of alleged fifth-columnists working for the Axis powers. By the end of the conflict, he had found that, 'contrary to public perception, the numbers of aliens supportive of the fascist cause had been infinitesimal'. While some immigrants saw Lochore as a means to establish their anti-fascist or anti-Communist credentials, others were troubled by his interrogations, likening his intrusive scrutiny to those regimes in Europe from which they had fled.[24] Fred Turnovsky, for example, recalled undergoing a 'Kafkaesque' questioning by Lochore, where he was interrogated over his political views ('was I, or had I ever been a communist?') and personal life ('why did I not associate more with the Jewish community?').[25]

Also mirroring the last war, conscription, introduced for military-age men in July 1940, brought forth both resistance and measures to contain it. Large numbers of balloted men failed to satisfy the authorities that they 'held a genuine belief that it was wrong to engage in warfare under any circumstances'. Of the 5117 appeals lodged for exemption on conscience grounds (roughly 1.7 per cent of those balloted), 1096 were deferred because they succeeded on other grounds (mainly for undertaking 'essential work') and 944 were settled by the appellant being unfit for service. Of the remaining 3077 appeals, 606 (some 20 per cent) were accepted, 1226 (nearly 40 per cent) were assigned to non-combatant duties, and 1245 (just over 40 per cent) were rejected.[26] Those who continued to refuse service after a failed appeal were taken as shirkers and subjected to state discipline.[27]

From 1941, some 800 'defaulters' were locked away for the duration of the war (and beyond) in prisons and later purpose-built camps. Under Minister Semple's watch, this was a more severe punishment than in the previous conflict, when finite prison terms were imposed and reimposed only if the defiance continued. Among the 'strange and weird types' in detention camps (to use the National Service Department's words) were pacifists and pacificists, religious objectors and 'shirkers', and various categories of left-wing 'politicals'. This last grouping, 'recalcitrants' who exhibited 'the agitator's complex', was seen as particularly problematic for supposedly stirring up 'complacent and gullible inmates' into protest and escape. The problem was concentrated when they were sent to a bleak 'disciplinary centre' at Hautū, on the Central Plateau, but they continued to bring trouble for the authorities. Police would be brought in to track down escapees from this and the other camps, and there might be up to 30 at large at any given time.[28]

Beyond individual non-compliance with conscription, for varying motives, pacifist organisations attracted attention for their rejection of the war in its entirety. Around a thousand pacifists and anti-militarists, many associated with the Peace Pledge Union and the Christian Pacifist Society, were investigated on suspicion of breaching anti-subversionary regulations.[29] Some were gaoled, such as Christian Pacifist 'Archie' Barrington, who was charged many times before his incarceration in 1941 (for a year with hard labour) for speaking in Wellington on a pacifist platform.[30] Generally, by early 1942, with its leaders taken out of action, 'public anti-war agitation was over'.[31]

Meanwhile, in 1940 New Zealand had joined other Allied powers in categorising the Jehovah's Witnesses as a subversive organisation and placed restrictions on their activities. The Witnesses had attacked other religions (especially the 'pagan' Catholics, who they alleged were engaged in an international conspiracy to undermine the British Empire) at a time when New Zealand's 'desperate struggle for existence' required national unity. They had also condemned 'organised government' and declared New Zealand's to be 'evil'. A detective described their literature in court as 'foul and slanderous' and felt that it 'border[ed] on sedition'. While the restrictions were later eased, and some of the church's literature (such as Bibles) was allowed to be imported, it remained under surveillance and suppression until it agreed to toe the line in March 1945.[32] The degree of intervention into lives and organisations seen to be impeding the war effort, potentially or actually, was greater, and the disciplining harsher, than in Britain where the impacts of the war were far more obviously felt.[33]

Agencies

When the war began, the Police Force, headed by Commissioner Denis Cummings, continued to hold primary responsibility for domestic security intelligence. This was spearheaded by the four designated political policemen in the main centres. They had built around themselves small teams of detectives, most significantly in Auckland and Wellington, and they could also bring in other police as necessary.[34] In Auckland, for example, Detective Sergeant Nalder headed a team of five detectives, and could draw on other detectives or ask for uniformed men to don plain clothes in order to assist with covert surveillance and lower-level analysis.

Wartime demands not only greatly increased political detection work, but also placed extra pressure on those working on higher-level analysis – through, indeed, to the Commissioner himself. In September 1941 he brought his brother James to Wellington to help 'assist with wartime administration, including the control of aliens and detection of subversion'. Although this appointment might seem nepotistic, it made sense as Superintendent Jim Cummings had been in charge of anti-subversion surveillance at Police Headquarters during the Depression. A more forceful character than his brother, although equally affable on the surface, his proactive energy fitted well with the prime minister's relentless quest to suppress opposition to his wartime policies.[35]

As in the First World War, emergency regulations of various types were declared in quick succession during the Second. From 21 February 1940, for example, Public Safety Emergency Regulations allowed the police to prohibit meetings or processions, to arrest speakers or distributors of material deemed seditionary, and to conduct searches without warrants.[36] Prime Minister Fraser stressed to a delegation of aggrieved Christian Pacifists that the 'Police had been given the power to stop any meeting if that meeting was likely to be subversive or inimical to the war effort'; he endorsed the Commissioner's decision to ban the Society from hosting public sessions in town halls.[37]

In the process of hardening social control, the police also tightened coordination with a number of other departments with security responsibilities. These included censoring agencies, notably Post and Telegraph and the office of the person in overall charge of censorship, Director of Publicity J. T. Paul; and the Customs staff who watched out for subversive people and publications crossing the border. Closer liaison with military intelligence was forged as well. This covered issues such as managing sensitive information and links with British security agencies, as well as – mirroring MI5's concerns in Britain – preventing Communist penetration of the armed services.[38] Despite institutional patch protection, the crisis that beset the country at the beginning of the war led to the 'greatest degree of cooperation' between police and military.[39]

In spite of both cordial relations and efficiencies at operational levels, however, the great expansion of security work demanded by war conditions had added weight to the recently revived proposals within military circles for a professional intelligence service on the British model – a service that would therefore be under Defence auspices. As we have noted, in 1938 the defence establishment had decided, if war eventuated, to establish a military Combined Intelligence Centre, and this was implemented by centres at military district level in Wellington, Auckland and Christchurch. Police liaison with the three centres came under the control of Detective Sergeant Arthur M. Harding at Police Headquarters who, among other things, was in charge of surveilling aliens and sending selected cases to specialised panels for political assessment. A man with influential connections within the Wellington bureaucracy, since 1937 Harding had been in charge of collating intelligence in the Commissioner's office, and in that capacity he already liaised with intelligence officials in each of the armed services.[40]

There were, however, calls for a much more fundamental reorganisation of intelligence in the Dominion, especially when the three services found the concept of combined intelligence difficult to implement and the United Kingdom increasingly pushed for sound joint intelligence.[41] Fears of inadequate security arrangements heightened after the Phoney War ended, Germany rapidly swept through Western Europe and the Battle of Britain began. The vast stakes at play fuelled British concerns about enemy capability to undertake paramilitary and fifth-column activity throughout the Empire.

On 29 June 1940, the Chief of the Imperial General Staff raised the issue of German and Italian sympathisers in Australia and New Zealand and offered to send officers to discuss security arrangements, including countering internal sabotage and preparing for guerrilla warfare in territories seized by the enemy.[42] This offer was welcomed by the armed services, especially by the naval authorities, who tended to especially favour the creation of a new security service that would systematise links between relevant civil and military authorities, as well as assist them to monitor disaffection within the services. New Zealand's new War Cabinet, set up on 16 July 1940 in the wake of German successes, accepted the offer, as did the Australian government.

On 14 August 1940, naval officials formally raised their concerns over the Police Force's capacity to undertake security intelligence in the current emergency. They contended that the NZPF's approach was 'conducted on lines which are too stereotyped to meet present war conditions', proposing instead a Defence-based surveilling agency which would 'pool' the information gathered from within the three military services, as well as that collected by 'carefully selected' detectives in the NZPF, staff in the Director of Publicity's office, and the Customs Department. The public would be encouraged to report 'suspicious happenings which come under their notice' directly to the new body, a recommendation based on Australian military intelligence use of local volunteers.[43]

Meanwhile, events in Britain were in train which built on the agreement to provide advice on countering sabotage and occupation in the antipodes. An Indian-born British army officer with military policing and intelligence experience, Lieutenant-Colonel John Mawhood, had been selected to head the task of providing security intelligence advice to Australasia. His Military Mission 104 aimed to address two issues. Firstly, it would advise on preparation for 'offensive action by organising our own fifth column and allocat[ing] military activities in territories either likely to be occupied by the enemy or which are suspect'. Secondly, to help hamper enemy invasion of Australasia, it would improve security intelligence through 'defensive action against enemy fifth column and para-military activities'.[44]

Mawhood's party left Britain in early October, going first to Wellington. Here, among other things, Mawhood proposed the establishment of a new security intelligence organisation to overarch the armed forces and civil police on security matters.[45] It was envisioned that the new body would both operate as a link between the armed forces and civil police on security matters and procure its own sets of information from the Police and military combined intelligence operations (see illustration overleaf). In this way it would go quite some way towards what the various Defence authorities had advocated after the First World War. However, it would also act as a significant security agency in its own right, with staff posted around the country and abroad. While it would report to the War Cabinet through the Chiefs of Staff, this relationship would generally be hands-off, reflecting that of MI5 with the War Office, with which it would establish relations. Although its staff could liaise with 'local police', the political detectives were not mentioned in the proposal, even if the organisational chart's liaison line from the new body to the Commissioner might be taken as including them.[46]

While the existence of the new service would be publicly acknowledged, its workings would be confidential. Financial accountability would be minimal, and it would answer to the War Cabinet through the Chiefs of Staff. It would also be inconspicuous: personnel would operate in civilian clothes, use unmarked vehicles and be headquartered in a private house in Wellington. There would be a branch in each of the three military districts, and personnel would be trained at a Special Intelligence Centre to be established in Australia.[47] Given the resonance between this vision and the proposals already under discussion within military circles, the New Zealand Chiefs of Staff advised the government that such an organisation 'be set up without delay', and that a British intelligence expert be seconded to New Zealand to run it. The next day, 27 November 1940, Cabinet unanimously approved a security service within the army structure.[48]

Army headquarters in Wellington began to select recruits. Given the short time frame for selection and vetting, the rigour of the appointment procedure must be called into question, although some appointees had military intelligence backgrounds. Certainly, as an official war historian put it, the recruits 'lacked at least the training necessary for them'. The founding complement, 19 officers and NCOs and two civilians, were instructed by Mawhood and a colleague when they flew back to New Zealand in January 1941. The staff commenced duty with the Security Intelligence Bureau on 10 February, working in offices located in each of the three military districts as well as at headquarters.[49]

In seeking a head for the new institution, Mawhood had 'especially recommended' a 35-year-old Englishman, Kenneth Folkes, and the War Cabinet approved the appointment. Describing him as '[p]ale, thin, weakly looking, with semi-thick spectacles', critics compared his appearance to Heinrich Himmler, the infamous head of Nazi Germany's internal security apparatus.[50] Before the war Folkes had practised as a solicitor and then worked for a carpet firm before enlisting as a private in the British military police in July 1940. He had been quickly transferred to its Intelligence Corps, where he came to Mawhood's attention. Having passed a defence security course, that October he became a field security officer and, once he had accepted the New Zealand position, he was promoted to major; it had been a meteoric rise.[51] When Cabinet

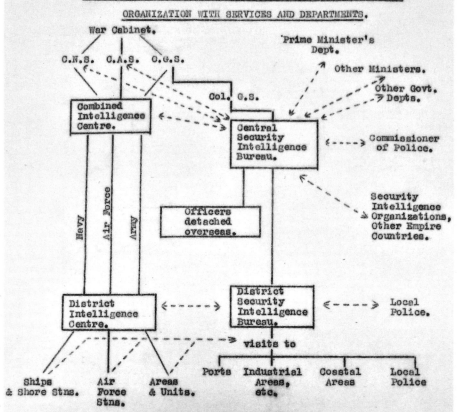

CHART SHOWING RELATION OF PROPOSED SECURITY INTELLIGENCE

ORGANIZATION WITH SERVICES AND DEPARTMENTS.

War Cabinet.

C.N.S. C.A.S. C.G.S.

Prime Minister's Dept.

Other Ministers.

Other Govt. Depts.

Col. G.S.

Combined Intelligence Centre.

Central Security Intelligence Bureau.

Commissioner of Police.

Security Intelligence Organizations, Other Empire Countries.

Navy   Air Force   Army

Officers detached overseas.

District Intelligence Centre.

District Security Intelligence Bureau.

Local Police.

visits to

Ships & Shore Stns.   Air Force Stns.   Areas & Units.   Ports   Industrial Areas, etc.   Coastal Areas   Local Police

NOTES.   (i) In order to avoid delay in obtaining information and in passing it on to the right quarter, Security Intelligence personnel must be given complete freedom of action to report direct to the person immediately concerned, confirming the report later through official channels.

(ii) They must, moreover, have ready entry into places in which they wish to make investigations. This can best be arranged by a pass signed by a Minister of the Crown.

(iii) They will operate largely in mufti.

(iv) For the above reasons stated above in Note (i), the control and administration is shown by a continuous line, while the channels for passing of information and requests for investigation are shown by dotted lines.

ANZ R21078487, 'Plans: Security Intelligence Bureau: Policy and Organisation'. A November 1940 institutional blueprint for the relationships a new security service would have with relevant departments. Such an organisation (the SIB) became operational in February 1941.

accepted Mawhood's recommendation, then, it appointed a man to head the new SIB who had far less experience than almost all security practitioners in New Zealand. He had, moreover, gained little knowledge of military protocols and practices, something that New Zealand's military soon came to regret.

Landing in the Dominion on 2 March 1941, Folkes sought to make an impression. When he arrived for his first meeting with Peter Fraser, he appropriated a selection of confidential papers from the prime minister's secretarial area while the staff were on a break and presented these to him as an indication of lax security. He quickly produced searingly critical assessments of the standard of security in police, military and other state institutions as well as in the population at large. His judgement of others for potential security breaches, however, was at odds with his extra-marital activities, which became an open secret and were of concern to the Police.[52]

Various estimations essentially summed Folkes up as arrogant, imperious and snobbish. Terry McLean, assigned to the SIB in 1941, recalled him as 'a sleazy bounder of the sort the Brits breed in profusion. He had a quick, alert mind and, if I may be forgiven the vulgarism, a quick, alert cock.'[53] Sir Jack Harris, who served with the SIB between 1942 and 1944, recollected that Folkes 'spent most of his time chasing women and the rest of the time fighting the police'. Such preoccupations made it 'difficult for those who worked for him'.[54] Folkes's secretary Molly Bishop commented on such strains when providing her own character assessment:

> Major Folkes was not a fool – he was a solicitor so did have a trained mind. He was certainly odd and didn't go out of his way to endear himself to either the armed services or the Police who regarded him and the Bureau with some suspicion . . . It seemed to me that he did nothing to try to adjust to New Zealand conditions and did not go out of his way to co-operate with the heads of the various services and [the] Police, so therefore they did not co-operate with him. At that time there were some Englishmen who regarded New Zealanders as colonials and therefore inferior human beings – he was one of them and that did not endear him to the services and police.[55]

Although institutionally located within army headquarters, the SIB operated autonomously. Its professional members, mostly NCOs or commissioned officers, had code names (such as 'Sergeant 100'), but details about staff soon began to leak out. This was a somewhat ironic development given Folkes's railing against other departments for security breaches. The personnel of the early Bureau would soon build up to around 30, distributed between the district offices (headed by Captains H. C. Meikle, G. P. Park and D. P. Lindsay in the Northern, Central and Southern Military Districts respectively) and headquarters in Wellington.[56]

Soon after the SIB's establishment, extra appointments were made from outside the military, such as journalists hired for their investigative skills and civilians to man a Radio Monitoring Service established within it. This was modelled on MI5's Radio Security Service in which volunteer operators monitored radio traffic in Britain, and later Europe, with the assistance of postal and telegraphic officials.[57] The Dominion's radio monitors trawled German, Italian and Japanese stations, listening for broadcasts relating to 'New Zealand, New Zealanders in action, or the South Pacific in general'. They formed part of a broader surveillance of radio traffic, undertaken by postal and telegraphic officials, and of a system of coast-watching stations with listening capacities across Pacific territories.[58]

The NZPF had been slow to take on sworn female staff, although in the past it had appointed some women as civilian employees and informants. The first sworn women police – 10 'temporary constables' – were enrolled in 1941, attached to detective offices but confined mostly to 'monitoring the moral welfare of females'.[59] One of them, Edna Pearce, supervised the families of interned Japanese men captured in the Pacific. She reported to Detective Sergeant Harding, who in turn liaised with Foss Shanahan from the Prime Minister's Department on such issues. They were to be exchanged for Allied equivalents, but after some of the party were killed when their aircraft crashed on take-off, she and Harding escorted the remaining Japanese internees by ship to Melbourne in 1943.[60]

The SIB also employed women in some capacities. An underground pamphlet asserted that Molly Bishop headed 'the female section' of the Bureau, for which she '[s]noops at social gatherings and poses as a member of Navy office staff'.[61] Female staff were also used to test security procedures, including by attempting 'to put it across unfortunate gallant guards at defence headquarters by stating they want to go in and see their girl friends or relatives. Obliging a lady, the guards get it in the neck when Folkes complains.' One young woman used for such duties was Joan Young, a well-connected socialite (her father was the director-general of Post and Telegraph) who was elected winner of Wellington's 1941 'Queen Carnival'.[62]

Initial proposals estimated that the new Bureau would cost £42,000 annually, and in mid-1941 its budget had been confirmed at £50,000 per annum.[63] By the start of 1942 Major Folkes's military staff had reached 54, comprising four captains and four subalterns, three warrant officers and 43 sergeants.[64] These numbers peaked at 63 that year, as security concerns escalated with German and Japanese military successes. An incomplete roll lists 111 army personnel as having served with the SIB between January 1941 and October 1945, including some privates.[65]

Contemporary assessments of the quality of SIB personnel were generally uncomplimentary, from whatever quarter they arose. A naval officer depicted the Bureau as 'a mild replica of the Gestapo', while critics on the left also described its staff as 'the Dominion's Gestapo' among many other depictions: 'hand-picked fascists', 'snoopers', 'misfits, unfits, shirkers' and the like.[66] A not untypical later account has the SIB 'staffed by people with qualities more akin to Colonel Blimp than wartime intelligence officers'.[67] Some later criticism may have been retrospectively coloured by the ignominious end to Folkes's directorship.

Wartime criticism undoubtedly reflected institutional rivalry over responsibility for state security. The naval officer cited above felt that some officials criticised the Bureau because security policing was 'abhorrent to New Zealand officials who strongly resent the mildest control over their activities'.[68] While some SIB personnel likened NZPF detectives to 'the policemen of the English comic paper', some police assessments returned the favour.[69] After an encounter with Bureau personnel, for example, Detective Sergeant A. J. White concluded that if national security was really in the hands of such men, 'the outlook for the Country or the State is not very bright'.[70] Similar criticisms came from within the Bureau itself. Terry McLean summed up his colleagues as 'a bunch of amateurs who sometimes, despite themselves, brought off a coup'. He added that one of the two 'most prominent' SIB staff during his service in Wellington was 'consumed by an ambition which led him to personal wealth, the mayoralty of Timaru and a collection of rare New Zealand books, with the contents of which I doubt he ever became familiar'; the other he described simply as 'rather a dull fellow'.[71]

It was inevitable that there would be jurisdictional tensions, given the founding vision of the SIB as an agency superimposed upon existing civil and military intelligence bodies. Such stresses would have been difficult to resolve harmoniously in the best of circumstances, let alone in a wartime emergency. The problems were exacerbated, too, by planning deficiencies on key issues, especially the exact relationship between the work of the Bureau and that of the Police and other agencies.[72] In June 1941, the Chiefs of Staff attempted to clarify the key nexus: the Bureau would deal with such matters as subversion or military security, but would hand to the Police any such matter that might be best handled by it.[73] However, the defence establishment found it wielded little control over the Bureau. That very month, in fact, the SIB was essentially mandated to operate with almost unlimited independence within Defence as well as significant operational autonomy from the prime minister and Cabinet.[74] This was an extraordinary development which, coupled with the swagger of the director and some of his staff, was to have some most unfortunate consequences.

Police had not welcomed their loss of responsibility for counter-subversion, monitoring aliens and other security matters, especially since the SIB was a new body staffed by people with little or no experience in such complex subjects. Given its responsibility for political crime, the Police continued to keep a watch on people and organisations seen as potentially or actively subversive – seeing this work in terms of its mandate to impose and protect peace and good order. Like the defence establishment, Folkes argued that the Police should only undertake 'security work' handed to it by the SIB, but he did not force his luck by attempting to secure any formal demarcation of roles. Often, therefore, parallel targeting of political suspects occurred. Indeed, the Police Force actually expanded its surveilling net during the war to cope with the many political, industrial and other challenges to maximising the war effort.[75] While the officer stationed by MI5 in Wellington was now to work with the SIB rather than the Police, the latter continued to liaise with the British Special Branch over matters of mutual concern to New Zealand and 'Home'.[76]

Demarcation difficulties and disputes characterised SIB–Police relations through 1942 as the Bureau pushed to expand its operations and powers. On 14 January 1942, Folkes had pressed upon Foss Shanahan, secretary of the Organisation for National Security, an exceedingly broad vision for the SIB: it should be an integrated 'link in the chain of Security Service[s] which is "fed" by M.I.5.'. Under this approach, the Bureau's jurisdiction would involve a comprehensive brief that covered not only obvious topics such as subversion and sabotage, but also duties currently handled by censorship, port security and other authorities. Its enlarged remit, moreover, would include tasks such as countering corruption, cracking down on those evading censorship, monitoring the movements of aliens and other foreigners of suspicious ilk, observing the activities of conscientious objectors and other pacifists 'likely to cause disaffection', keeping a watch out for illicit photography and signalling, getting to the bottom of '[r]umours and their sources' and, all in all, countering '[s]ubversion in all its forms'.[77] Obviously, many of these suggestions involved taking even further political work away from the Police.

Being fully aware that the service chiefs had been united in opposing SIB involvement in operational matters, however, Folkes was careful to suggest that any such extended brief would focus on policy advice rather than involve operations. This was sufficient to gain their agreement that an 'efficient and adequate security organization' would need to go beyond the 'skeleton' and scope of the agency proposed by Mawhood; indeed, they recommended Folkes's promotion to lieutenant-colonel, a rank befitting a comprehensive security organisation (although he was not to attain it).[78] The support of the Chiefs of Staff for bolstering national security through an enhanced SIB was stressed later that month when they warned that 'information has been received recently that the enemy are adopting all possible means to secure particulars concerning the movements of shipping and endeavouring to place their agents on the staffs of the armed forces'.[79]

While its grand plans did not eventuate, throughout 1942 the Bureau expanded its reach as well as its staff. On 26 February, for example, the War Cabinet transferred responsibility for security on the wharves from the Police to a new Port Security Control, which was under the SIB's aegis.[80] The Control's responsibilities included watching the travel of targeted persons in and out of the country and preventing such movement if necessary, handling security on troop embarkations, and gathering information on and from people passing through the ports. The army would provide accommodation, facilities and transport for up to 45 staff drawn from both the SIB and its own Field Security Wing. The prime minister directed the Police and the Departments of Internal

Affairs, Justice and Customs to cooperate with the SIB on issues of port security, but none of the political detectives with specialist knowledge of that subject were taken into Port Security Control.[81] Lastly, in another example of the SIB's expansionist aspirations, it sought in June 1942 to relocate the Wellington headquarters and regional branch into the Defence Services Building in Stout Street, co-located with the offices of the three military intelligence heads.[82]

If the situation in mid-1942 appeared to demonstrate the SIB's predominance in national security matters, events and dynamics were already in play that would result in its downfall. These went beyond jurisdictional sensitivities and the abrasiveness of Bureau personnel. The Police had been concerned about the ramifications of the SIB's use of dubious or illegal methods, such as break-ins and thefts of documents. When Bureau staff decided to watch a 'relatively high-ranking visitor' and his entourage, all of their 'meetings and discussions with New Zealand citizens, including hotel staffs' were to be 'fully recorded' and their phone calls tapped. Such methods risked exposure. Elements in the military hierarchy were also concerned about SIB methods. Almost from the beginning, there had been embarrassment from leaks. The fact that four sergeants were doing two-man shifts in Wellington's St George Hotel in a room next to a 'suspected spy', for example, became widely known and ridiculed throughout Wellington. Senior military officials were also concerned that the SIB was actively spying upon the armed services. It was rumoured that a well-connected Bureau officer who frequented the exclusive Wellesley Club reported back on what the army heads were saying, while another Bureau member was said to have been spying on the New Zealand military administration in Fiji.[83]

By mid-1942, in fact, senior military officers were actively seeking ways of regaining full control of defence security, leaving Folkes with only civil jurisdiction except in the event that the services needed to call upon his organisation's assistance. The Police, for its part, wanted full civil jurisdiction back. McLean, perhaps reflecting the Bureau's superiority syndrome, believed that 'Folkes was much too smart up top for some of the gumdrops who were at the head of the Army and Police'. But he also felt that the major was 'much too arrogant to appreciate that, by deriding them, he was digging his own grave'.[84]

What would be the beginning of a series of extraordinary events that would lead to Folkes's downfall had already taken place in late March 1942, when fraudster and safe-cracker Sydney Ross was released from prison and contacted Minister of Public Works Robert Semple. He claimed to have been approached by a fifth-column organisation plotting to open the way for a German invasion by such means as spreading misinformation, circulating counterfeit currency, attacking infrastructure and carrying out assassinations. The conspirators had supposedly sought him out for his expertise with gelignite, which would enable them to sabotage the Arapuni and Waikaremoana hydroelectric power plants.

Ross and a fellow prisoner, burglar (and ex-policeman) Charles Remmers, who had masterminded this hoax, had chosen their story well.[85] Ever since the sinking of the *Niagara* in mid-1940, fears that fifth-columnists might be preparing the way for invasion had been heightened. Now, with Japan having joined the war and the Allies suffering huge setbacks, an invasion of New Zealand had become a palpable fear. More specifically, ongoing concern about potential fifth-column activity had been recently stoked by sensational news from Australia, where 20 members of the Australia First Movement had been arrested on allegations of conspiring to prepare for a Japanese invasion by such means as sabotage.[86]

Semple took Syd Ross to see the prime minister. Both believed his story that he had not reported the conspirators to the police as they would not believe the word of a convicted criminal, and Folkes was summoned to the meeting. Perhaps influenced by his brief career in military intelligence during the Battle of Britain, when fear of fifth-columnists and spies had been especially rampant, the SIB director also accepted Ross's account. Fraser handed the matter entirely to Folkes, who was not to discuss it with the Police or any civilian agency. He met with Ross the next day, 30 March 1942, to begin his enquiries. On 4 April he told the prime minister that the SIB's 'investigations prove that the story we heard has substance', and that they were supposedly 'leading to a clique already under notice'.[87]

Ross would now be employed by the SIB as a double agent under the identity of 'Captain Calder of the Merchant Marine'. Arrangements were made for him to operate from Rotorua where the plotters, along with foreign agents who had landed to control operations, were allegedly based.[88] The operation would be run out of Captain Meikle's Northern District headquarters in Auckland. Ross was put up in Rotorua's best hotel, even though he claimed to have told the conspirators that he was an impoverished former prisoner of war. He was provided with a car and, despite rationing, unlimited petrol, which rather drew attention to him. Outwitting his SIB minders, however, he set off on a daily basis to conduct his own 'enquiries', which later turned out to be having a good time and then reporting his hosts as spies. His progress reports to Meikle, accordingly, contained numerous names and addresses of innocent people said to be enemy agents orchestrated by an 'arch-conspirator' – Remmers himself, a dying man now living near Rotorua.[89]

Folkes was soon citing this supposed conspiracy as evidence in his push for greater jurisdictional and enforcement powers. On 10 June 1942 he warned the prime minister of imminent enemy and fifth-column plans to commit acts of subversion, sabotage and assassination, assuring him that 'every possible action has been taken by me to prove the truth or otherwise of intelligence which I have received'. He asked that the SIB, rather than the Police, be granted powers to arrest and detain the plotters as he was 'unable to adduce evidence which would fix the guilt of the parties concerned within the ordinary criminal code'. Without such powers, in fact, he 'could not undertake complete responsibility' for ensuring that the eradication of such a grave threat to New Zealand's security could be 'carried into effect'.[90] Whatever the prime minister believed about his claims, Folkes's requests for plenary powers were clearly a step too far for the ministers, and he did not get the far-reaching powers he sought.

A fortnight later, on 24 June, Folkes was getting more strident. In reporting to the Chiefs of Staff, he named a number of completely innocent individuals as conspirators: three German nationals ('unknown to the Police') and their coterie of three dozen traitors, a number of whom were said to be armed. While his men had not been given the right to make arrests, he now secured permission from the military heads for 'up to a hundred selected Army personnel' to help the SIB pre-empt both sabotage from within and an invasion through New Plymouth. The chiefs would later claim that, despite their green light for the use of soldiers, they were well aware of the absurdity of the claims and had expressed some incredulity about it.[91]

Meanwhile, ordinary police vigilance had detected something peculiar in Rotorua. On 4 June a Rotorua constable, J. Richardson, reported that he had recognised the 'Captain Calder' staying at the Grand Hotel to be the criminal Ross. He requested that the Auckland police be informed 'in case the Police there have inquiries for ROSS or a fictitious Secret Service Agent'.[92] Detective Sergeant White investigated and, after reporting on the gullibility of the SIB officers assigned to liaise with the conman, the Police Commissioner became involved. On the day Folkes asked Prime Minister Fraser for arrest powers to be given to the SIB, Commissioner Cummings advised the Inspector of Police in Hamilton that 'Major Folkes has Ross employed in his service', and that the latter should 'be kept under close and secret observation'.[93]

The Commissioner met with the prime minister on 2 July to discuss police suspicions and their evidential basis, and Fraser ordered him to continue the investigation of the alleged enemy conspiracy. Inside two days, Superintendent Jim Cummings and three of his detectives had fully established the fraudulent nature of Ross's claims. Already rattled by police attention, Ross had faked his own capture and attempted murder by German spies, a story he later said the SIB had put him up to. He had been kidnapped, he claimed, because police had tipped off the conspirators that he was a double agent. Some self-inflicted wounds, unfortunately for him, were not very impressive as evidence for his story that he had been tortured during his captivity, and nor was his account of escaping from his torturers. Ross was now interrogated by police and confronted with the overwhelming evidence against him, and his addition of new claims such as adding Communists into the plot impressed the interrogators even less. Now abandoned by the Bureau, 'Captain Calder' soon confessed. Shown file material which the SIB had been ordered to hand to the Police, he declared that the Bureau had greatly embellished his own reports on the alleged conspiracy – a conclusion that police had already reached after taking over the files. Ross was taken into custody, whereupon the SIB notified him that they had dispensed with his services.[94]

The wartime government naturally wanted this whole affair kept secret, not least in the name of upholding public confidence in the authorities during a national emergency. On 29 July 1942, however, the scandal was publicly exposed by *NZ Truth*, an organ with which some political police had a close association. The leak was almost certainly orchestrated at a senior level within the Police Force as a bid to regain full control of security intelligence.[95] The story outlined how the SIB had been 'blatantly hoodwinked' and praised the police for quickly uncovering the hoax.[96] Publicity Director J. T. Paul had attempted to stop the press on grounds that telling the story was a subversive act in itself, but the editor had refused to comply and the issue sold out. The following day, the latter was summoned to the War Cabinet and agreed to suppress any further public mention of the affair. This did not fully impede knowledge of the fiasco, with John A. Lee and others on its trail. The story of (in Fraser's words) the 'grave misfit' he had placed in charge of wartime security, and the credulity of Folkes's 'experts', resurfaced from time to time, including in the House.[97]

Meanwhile, Attorney-General H. G. R. Mason had been tasked by the War Cabinet with heading an inquiry into the episode, his terms of reference including recommendations regarding the future of the SIB.[98] The material Folkes had been ordered to transfer to the Police Force was now in turn provided to the inquiry. Over the following months, Major Folkes sought to impress the value of his organisation's work upon Mason and his staff. In the absence of any great respect for the SIB among relevant agencies, this was an uphill battle. The Army General Staff, for example, had quickly recommended that one of its own officers be selected for overall charge of all military security work, and Folkes could then 'devote his full time to Civil Security duties only', his 'advice and experience' to be called upon by the army 'when required'.[99]

To counter such internal disquiet with his and the Bureau's performance, Folkes attempted to rally external support from United States military intelligence, having an entrée through US Army Counter-Intelligence, which had recently moved to share office space with the SIB.[100] But this too led to embarrassment for the government: when Folkes made a direct approach to American naval intelligence in California, the New Zealand Legation in Washington DC was pointedly directed to the appropriate protocols for communicating with American intelligence agencies.[101]

On 18 September 1942 Mason submitted his report. It recommended that responsibility for civil security be fully returned to the police, including the port security work taken on by the Bureau earlier that year. It queried why civil security had been handed to a military body in the first place. The SIB, said the report, should be reconstituted as 'a small Security Bureau' operating as a 'point of contact' between the military services and the Police. It should be no more than a 'clearing house' for information, a hybridised organisation headed by a military officer reporting to the Chiefs of Staff but housed at Police Headquarters. The report, citing national security grounds, effectively recognised the dangers in allowing a surveillance organisation to break free from bureaucratic and political oversight. A security committee comprising military and police representatives, and chaired by the minister of defence, should now be established to provide high-level, overarching advice to ministers on security issues.[102]

While the government was pondering its options, the Chiefs of Staff were working on their own report on the Bureau's short history. Delivered on 22 December, it bluntly declared that 'Major Folkes is not fitted to control the Security Bureau'. Among other things, it emphasised his disdain for proper military procedures:

> Some months ago he approached us and asked that a number of soldiers be placed under his orders to assist in the arrest of certain persons who were alleged to be Fifth Columnists and about to engage in a huge sabotage plot which was to synchronize with an attempted invasion of New Zealand at or near the port of New Plymouth. In the course of discussion it transpired that Major Folkes had been in possession of knowledge of the alleged invasion attempt for some months but notwithstanding this he had never, as he should have done, advised the Chiefs of Staff who are responsible for the defence of the Dominion.

The report judiciously avoided mentioning that, over the protests of the Chiefs of Staff, in September 1941 the War Cabinet had confirmed that Folkes should report straight to the prime minister. The military leaders were, in effect, telling the ministers that the monumental gaffe of the Ross hoax was their own fault: 'we cannot emphasize too strongly that it is the duty of any person who possesses information of this kind to communicate it to those who are responsible for the defence of the country'. In this case, they now claimed, the 'inherent improbabilities and indeed the ridiculous nature of the alleged invasion attempt were quite patent to us' when they had first heard about them. As for Folkes and his senior officers, 'what little we know' of the 'gigantic hoax', the report continued, 'gives strong reasons for believing that the leaders of the Security Intelligence Bureau were negligent and indeed distinctly incapable'.[103]

Some rump support for Folkes and the Bureau remained, however, even inside the military services. The navy's leadership restated its consistent views on the need for a security intelligence organisation independent of the Police, and found value in much of the SIB's work, especially on port security, an appreciation shared by the Chiefs of Staff.[104] But the director of naval intelligence, Lieutenant-Commander F. M. Beasley, went much further. He averred that police had orchestrated a 'campaign against the SIB' in a quest to claw back responsibility for civil security. He later told his counterpart in Melbourne, in a 'secret and personal' memorandum, that 'we have had a showdown [and] the Police won the battle hands down'. While there had been 'many things about the S.I.B. which needed overhaul', return of security surveillance to the Police was not the answer, but the navy's strong submissions on such matters had been 'shouted down'.[105]

Meanwhile, the government procrastinated over what it should do about the Mason report. It would be a serious step, in the eyes of its allies, to disband its principal domestic security service in a time of war. Could it be reformed? Fighting to preserve his institution and career, Folkes ratcheted up claims about rival agencies impeding the work of the SIB. Writing to the prime minister on 17 February 1943, he alleged that this had especially come from 'certain officers at Army headquarters, and also at the Police headquarters'. He argued that his critics had not properly comprehended the Bureau's work as 'the accredited Representative in New Zealand of the Empire Security Service', necessarily operating in secrecy and isolation. With his position clearly in jeopardy in the face of so much opposition, Folkes now called the government's bluff. If the censure by the Chiefs of Staff was not modified to take contextual matters into account, he told Fraser, he would ask to be 'released from my present position immediately'. An implicit threat indicated his desperation: he would seek an enquiry under military law if he were to be so 'released', no doubt factoring in that he was a British officer.[106]

The prime minister, in his reply two days later, chose to interpret Folkes's letter as a resignation. 'In the circumstances I think it best to accede to your request that you be released from your present position and you are accordingly released as from today.'[107] An offer to meet the expenses for his return to the United Kingdom followed, and Folkes departed in May 1943, a little over two years after his arrival.

Prime Minister Fraser would later describe the Ross case as 'one of the most extraordinary instances of human incredulity that I have ever heard in my life' – rather underplaying his own part in handing extraordinary power and responsibilities to a 'grave misfit'.[108] In turn, a New Zealand General Staff report to the British War Office deemed Folkes and his staff as responsible for damaging the previously 'cordial' relationship between police and military surveillers, omitting to mention the Ross fiasco and its own gullibility in the final days of the extended hoax.[109] Folkes continued his military career to the end of the war and then returned to his pre-war employment with a carpet manufacturer, along the way furthering his reputation as a womaniser.[110] In November 1946, the *New Zealand Observer* published an interview with Folkes in London, in which he outlined a version of events which neatly excised his failings, presenting himself as a dutiful officer who had achieved much in improving New Zealand's security despite the 'obdurate attitude of the police'.[111] When he died in 1975, his headstone mentioned a Distinguished Service Order, although 'no record can be found of him ever receiving such an award, especially for distinguished service'.[112]

In the aftermath of the hoax, various manoeuvres over what next to do about security intelligence played out. While the Police sought return of full control of political policing, the military leaders wanted more weight given to the truncated security bureau recommended by Attorney-General Mason. Negotiations between them and the Police Commissioner over its 'proper organisation' attempted to remove areas of duplication as an expanded brief was worked through. Mason, an experienced adjudicator, mediated between the various parties, including Folkes himself.[113]

The director of intelligence had doggedly fought, with some naval support, in the no-change corner, highlighting the totality of the SIB's work rather than the one incident which had led to his disgrace. His 'resignation' finally provided the convenient opportunity for change that the government had been looking for. On the day Folkes's contract was terminated, Fraser ordered him to hand over immediate control of the SIB and all of its records to the Commissioner's brother, Superintendent Jim Cummings. This move was complemented by the appointment of an ad hoc police and military committee to consider the various reports on the Bureau and its future. Reporting on 26 February, a week after the handover, the military members of the committee had little choice but to acknowledge that the SIB staff had been 'relatively untrained' in surveillance at best and had mostly duplicated the work the Police were already doing. This, together with Mason's recommendations, formed the backdrop to the committee's recommendations to government.

The NZPF, it submitted, was the appropriate primary agency for domestic political surveillance, and the SIB should become a different, much smaller agency – in effect, the 'clearing house' proposed by Mason. This organisation, albeit much reduced in size and scope, would continue to liaise with 'overseas authorities' as well as continue certain specified tasks. The prime minister agreed with the thrust of the committee's proposals, if not with all of their details: the committee's recommendation of moving the SIB's premises to Police Headquarters, for example, was not implemented. All the same, Jim Cummings was soon formally confirmed as director of security intelligence, backdated to the day he had taken over control from Folkes, 19 February 1943.[114]

On the surface little had changed, with the new director remaining in an office attached to army headquarters and retaining direct access to the prime minister. But, in actuality, control of domestic security surveillance had been effectively returned to the jurisdiction of the Police Force. The Commissioner was now back in primary charge of advice on civil security to the government and reported directly to the prime minister and War Cabinet on top-secret issues. With the loss of most of its hands-on functions, except specified duties such as port security, the Bureau's tasks were redefined to include such matters as production of regular bulletins providing an overview of internal and external security for relevant departments of state. SIB officers would also be tasked with investigating specific incidents, often those involving the interface between military personnel on the one hand and civil society or departments of state on the other. Examples include investigations into the reasons for a 1943 brawl between army personnel and locals in Taupō; a joint investigation, with other departments and United States military police, into allegations that military aircraft from both countries were being used to smuggle uncensored mail, drugs and even deserters from the Pacific war into New Zealand; and an investigation of possible arson on a military base, which led to recommendations for a range of preventive measures.[115]

After the Cummings brothers had worked through jurisdictional rearrangements, the end result was that the SIB's role was decidedly secondary to that of the political detectives. From the beginning of the February handover, in fact, police personnel tended to ignore the Bureau to such a degree that in mid-1943 they had to be reminded by the Commissioner to cooperate with it.[116] On his part, Jim Cummings set about reconstituting the SIB as a clearing house on intelligence issues whose staff could also be assigned to specific, general or one-off tasks. While he believed that he had inherited a cast of 'amateurs', he needed the best of them to stay on, if only to provide transitional continuity, but many were shunted back into the military while others went of their own volition. McLean, for example, who had been assigned to the SIB as a result of unwanted machinations by his influential father-in-law, had previously made several applications to be transferred. He was now, along with others, released for active military service.[117] Obtaining competent replacements was not easy, as Cummings could not recruit from among the police surveillers, needed as they were for the substantive task of hands-on civil security – which they had continued doing, in any case, in the days of the Bureau.

Among those retained were the head of the Auckland office, despite critical comments in Attorney-General Mason's report to the War Cabinet: 'Why did Captain Meikle not make some of the simplest and most obvious enquiries' about the Ross claims? It seems that the government now accepted that he had been enmeshed in a system of Folkes's making, one which placed an inordinate focus on information gathering to the detriment of critical analysis. When Folkes blamed Meikle for the fiasco, claiming that he had left the Ross investigation entirely to the Auckland office, Mason's enquiry concluded that '[i]t is, of course, impossible to accept this view'; Folkes was not the kind of man to devolve anything that important – or anything much at all. Whatever Meikle's culpability, it seems that in Superintendent Cummings' eyes the knowledge he had gained of security matters in the upper half of the North Island outweighed his deficiencies.[118]

Jim Cummings established a working relationship with American intelligence and, especially, with MI5. In August 1943 the latter proposed, 'in view of past unfortunate incidents', that senior officers from the Australian and New Zealand security services should travel to England to help 'establish closer and more personal relations'.[119] Eventually, Cummings left in March 1944 on such a mission, and included the security agencies of the United States and Canada in his travel itinerary.[120]

Before his departure, the position of deputy director was created, and given (on 17 March 1944) to Detective Sergeant Nalder, a sign of increasing cooperation between the political detectives and the reconstituted SIB. Those of the Bureau's staff available to assist the police surveillers were a welcome addition to an overstretched Police

Force, able to be tapped at need.[121] On the other hand, the problem of in-house quality remained, especially in the analysis stage of the intelligence cycle, given Cummings' difficulties in obtaining good new staff. Mason's inquiry had adversely contrasted the SIB's focus on accumulating evidence to the police practice of ongoing verification and assessment. This was rather too simplistic, both overplaying police analytical ability and underplaying pockets of expertise in the SIB, but it contained a core truth.[122]

The SIB's transition from a quasi-military and effectively autonomous organisation to a clearing house for general information about security and essentially an adjunct to the Police, was made more difficult by the ongoing legacy of mistrust within the Force towards it. Hitherto, the Bureau had only told police what little it thought they should know, viewing their involvement as limited to public-order issues. Conversely, police had kept the SIB away from their own secret files, wanting to protect, among other things, the identity of their informants. Such siloing remained an ongoing problem. Even the mid-1943 direction by the Commissioner to his staff to cooperate with SIB staff also instructed them to exercise 'a careful discretion' in doing so. Thus, parallel investigations on a number of issues continued and, as a result, sometimes the Cummings brothers offered differing assessments to the government – that of the SIB and that of the Police.[123]

On 1 November 1944 Jim Cummings succeeded his brother Denis as Commissioner, but retained the title of Director of Security.[124] At this point the SIB became – in the words of the historian of wartime policing – even 'more clearly an adjunct of the Police Force'. It was now effectively run by Deputy Director Nalder, who quickly became a Senior Detective.[125] A veteran political policeman who had helped to expose the Ross hoax, Jim Nalder was a stickler for proper procedures in the intelligence cycle, and had been instrumental in procuring some transfers of police staff to the SIB. The new Commissioner moved Nalder to an office in Police Headquarters, where he took charge of all political policing, the Bureau having now become definitively 'an appendage' to the NZPF. Its records were merged into the secret files of its host institution. It was now reaffirmed more strongly than ever that the political detectives of the NZPF held 'sole responsibility for security investigation', and virtually all of the SIB's non-police staff left. The Bureau now mostly conducted enquiries on request from the political detectives, although it retained some remaining niche duties.[126]

From 23 August 1945, just over a week after the end of hostilities with Japan, things happened fast. That day army headquarters was instructed by the government that the SIB's staff, who were still on its payroll, 'must be reduced to a minimum' by 31 August, with total closure of the Bureau to occur by the end of the following month. On 30 August the Military Districts were notified that the 'functions and duties of S.I.B. are to be taken over by the Civil Police immediately', and the prime minister announced the Bureau's demise on 11 September.[127]

The SIB had been the chief security experiment of the war years, but its rise and fall occurred independently of the operation of other state machinery with intelligence functions. The Emergency Precautions Service (EPS), for example, had been established in 1935 as part of the New Zealand section of the Committee of Imperial Defence. Its job was to coordinate a national response to disasters, including the possibility of enemy attack. When the Phoney War ended, the EPS began in earnest to mobilise large numbers of civilian volunteers for various activities, such as organising them to spot and counter hit-and-run raids by the enemy. After the onset of the Pacific War in late 1941 the EPS began to prepare for a possible invasion, complementing the efforts of the Home Guard, formed in August 1940. The Home Guard had a number of intelligence duties: various of its sections sought, for example, to detect fifth-columnists, potential saboteurs of 'vital points' (a list topped by Communists, followed by members of anti-militarist organisations such as the Christian Front),[128] and coastal landings: '[h]eliographs made from car headlights blinked Morse code from the hilltops' during training.[129]

Such activities were complemented by the work of the Women's War Service Auxiliary, established in late 1940, which at its peak in 1942 had 75,000 members organised across 250 district committees. Numbers of its members helped with EPS and Home Guard surveilling activities, and the organisation itself assisted with recruiting for women's armed service auxiliaries. Some of the recruits to the Women's Royal New Zealand Naval Service ('Wrens'), formed in April 1942, were assigned to intelligence-related duties, such as 'tracking Japanese radio traffic'.[130] Over 1942–44, for example, Wrens at Rapaura worked in the new field of 'radio-finger-printing', or 'Z' intelligence. They aimed to identify the sources of Japanese naval transmissions that had been intercepted by New Zealand's network of high-frequency direction-finding stations. The Waiouru direction-finding station, which also had Wrens stationed at it, undertook some 'Y' work (deciphering intercepted signals) as well as Z duties, and the Navy Office in Wellington also carried out some of the latter.[131] After the Japanese entry into the war, the army established a Special Wireless Section 'to listen to enemy radio traffic', and from 1943 its 'intercept operators' included women from the Women's Army Auxiliary Corps.[132]

As during the previous war, a rigorous censorship regime operated, its principal aim being to suppress the flow of any information that might aid the enemy or otherwise impede the war effort. Systems for monitoring newspapers, imported and local literature, and letters and telegrams were initiated on the basis of pre-war plans. Since 1934, committees drawn from the Police, the military services, Internal Affairs, Post and Telegraph, and the Prime Minister's Department had been working on censorship and publicity issues, which they explicitly saw as interrelated – the latter a proactive counterpart to the reactive coercion implicit in the former. By February 1939 it had been agreed that, in the event of war, all such tasks would fall under a board chaired by the prime minister and be undertaken within his department. On 1 September 1939, the various plans were incorporated into the Censorship and Publicity Emergency

Regulations, which authorised suppression of information deemed subversive or injurious to public safety.[133]

Four days earlier a Fraser loyalist, former unionist and journalist J. T. Paul, had been appointed to the position of director of publicity in the event of war. His objective was to procure state-friendly press and broadcasting coverage in order (in the words of the regulations) to 'secure that the national cause is properly presented'. Publications and programmes would preferably engage in voluntary censorship but, among other things, the director held powers of prior-restraint censorship – to review and censor any war-related matters before publication. More broadly, he quickly became 'by far the most prominent figure in the censorship field' during the war.[134]

An early case questioning the boundaries of war-related restrictions on reporting and commentary arose from the trial of Harold Ostler and Travers Christie for attempting to publish the *People's Voice*. The son of a prominent judge, Ostler told the press that Solicitor-General Henry Cornish had approached him on behalf of leading members of the Cabinet who wanted to avoid the publicity of a prosecution. They were said to have suggested that the matter could be dropped if Ostler agreed to take up a 'nice safe, comfortable job' in the army. He had asked Cornish what 'those members of the Cabinet whom my father . . . prosecuted during the last war' thought about such issues, alluding to a sensitive point for a number of ministers.

Paul instructed that publication of any such allegations was banned until an 'explanation and refutation' could be published alongside it. Some days after Ostler and Christie were convicted, the former's interview with the press was printed alongside a statement from the solicitor-general. Cornish acknowledged that he had advised Ostler to reject subversive associations and join the army, but firmly denied that he had offered him any privileged treatment. The delay in reporting Ostler's claims, and Paul's direction as to newspaper content, raised debates on whether the censor had inflated notions of 'public safety' in order to guard the government from embarrassment.[135] The director of publicity, however, stressed that his decision to postpone publication, pending an official response, resulted from the requirements of the War Regulations. It was 'imperative that public confidence should not without cause be shaken in the administration of justice as affecting the war effort'.[136]

While Paul acted in effect as the government's ultimate censor, postal and telegraphic censorship was integrated into normal departmental functions, a major departure from the military-led control of the First World War – although military authorities still censored soldiers' mail sent from overseas. The principal initial aim of such censorship was, as in the previous war, to halt the flow of any information that might aid the enemy or otherwise damage the war effort. It was handled mostly by permanent Post and Telegraph officials, though retired staff were taken on when military conscription of employees created vacancies. The operations were headed by chief postal and chief telegraph censors who reported to George McNamara, the retired head of the department – the man who had ordered the jamming of Scrimgeour's broadcast just before Labour's 1935 victory. In June 1939 he had been selected to serve as the controller of censorship in the event of war. The easiest operation was censoring telegrams, a task carried out by 16 staff in Auckland and Wellington (where, respectively, the cable and radio-channel terminals were located), assisted by selected officials elsewhere.[137]

Postal censorship required (among other things) liaison with security authorities over which kinds of letters and parcels to open and, if necessary, take further action on. Its primary point of contact was with the Police, and sometimes with military intelligence. It operated out of a number of post offices scattered throughout the country, and at its peak some 250 officials were involved in censoring. The basic guidelines were contained in a 200-page book issued to Commonwealth countries by the British.[138]

At first, communications to and from enemy aliens and with people in enemy or occupied territories were an obvious priority target, but more wide-ranging controls over all international communications were quickly put in place. McNamara noted the need for caution, as 'New Zealanders are not likely to take kindly to censorship'. The censors were to use 'wise discretion' in blacking or scissoring out material from letters or telegrams, delaying their passage or suppressing them altogether. In the words of a leading figure in such work, they 'came to realise that the truth or untruth of a statement had nothing to do with its censorability', the sole criterion being that which might harm the war effort.[139]

The censorship regime quickly became far more extensive than that of the previous war, in part because of a larger population and more complex modes of communication. In one typical example, in 1940 a letter from the Auckland Carpenters' Union to the local anti-conscription organisation had been subjected to the censors' attentions. At first, those who were not subject to such censorship were not generally aware of it, as the system was less open than in the First World War. But it gradually became more widely known – especially from August 1941, when Christchurch's *Press* gave it publicity.[140] In response, McNamara stated that while some letters were 'opened just at random', others were reviewed 'quite deliberately', especially if the censors were 'working under orders from the Army, the Navy, or the Police'.[141] When intercepts appeared to indicate active rather than inadvertent hampering of the war effort, suspect recipients or senders were placed under permanent monitoring. A resulting 'Censorship List' eventually acquired some 2200 names, 'the great majority being aliens or persons of alien birth, together with a score or two of natural-born British subjects – pacifists, Jehovah's Witnesses, Communists and others suspected of disaffection'.[142]

There were also double checks in place for instances where a suspect letter may have slipped through the censorship offices. All postal deliverers, for example, were to memorise listed names on their rounds and take those without a censor's stamp back to the post office for investigation.[143] Particular attention was paid to foreign-language communications, which went to a special section in Wellington that was headed by a supervisor who was a retired chief postmaster. There would be up to six full-time translators and a number of part-timers, between them handling 22 languages. The foreign-language correspondence of each enemy alien was allocated to a specified translator, who would build up a case history useful for assessment of 'loyalty'. The supervisor carried out the censoring of the translated letters. Languages not able to be translated were dealt with in other ways – by asking consuls, sending mail on to the British authorities, returning mail to their senders, and so on.[144]

Dr Reuel Lochore, who served as senior translator, claimed that the only criterion for censoring material in letters was 'adverse military or propaganda effect'. But this brief was widely and varyingly interpreted across the country's scattered censors. At the top, McNamara talked of suppressing material 'antagonistic to British ideals'. Some post offices were known to have excessive zeal. Letters might be so full of holes as to be virtually unreadable on receipt – those referring to government policies on such matters as prices and rationing, for example.[145]

Prior to the high-pressure years of 1942 and 1943 'probably less than half of the [outgoing] letters in English were examined', but the scope then escalated. In 1942, for example, mail to and from the United States was added to that routinely accessed. This was primarily to prevent knowledge circulating in public about the extent, nature and details of the large American operations based in New Zealand. After those peak years, criticism of postal censorship, especially that relating to the internal mail, began to mount. In October 1944 a committee of inquiry, set up in response to such pressure, found few intrusions into 'free expression' in the context of the national threatscape. But it warned that 'as soon as the need for security has passed all forms of censorship should be abolished'. By then, the system was already winding down in any case due to, among other things, 'the authorities, now knowing the troublesome correspondents, being able to confine the work more than earlier in the war'. Mirroring developments across the Commonwealth, the system wound down following victory in Europe in May 1945, and thereafter 'withered away'. Unlike in the First World War, postal and telegraphic censorship did not extend long into peacetime.[146]

Sigint work was perhaps the state intelligence apparatus which gained the greater peacetime prominence as a result of its wartime operations. Its New Zealand centre was located in the Navy Office in the capital. This took overarching control of the Post and Telegraph stations, which implemented the sigint roles allocated them during pre-war planning. Awarua in the south and Musick Point in Auckland commenced high-frequency direction-finding operations, and information from the former helped to take the successful German raider *Admiral Graf Spee* out of the war. New sigint locations were established as need required; the radio station on Tinakori Hill in Wellington came to form a key node in the Admiralty's Empire-wide interception and direction-finding network.

Naval intelligence intercepted enemy signals sent to and from vessels, and liaised with both the Police and the SIB. From 1942 the army also conducted sigint activities from sites around Wellington. Its Special Wireless Section intercepted Japanese signals traffic and worked with domestic intelligence agencies listening for any illicit transmissions from within the Dominion (none were discovered). The final (of nine) sigint stations to be established in the war was built in 1943 in the vicinity of the naval station at Waiouru, an optimal site for signals interception that was far from vulnerable coastal locations. It became the largest and most important naval sigint station in the country, hosting 150 staff by the end of the war.[147]

The military's Combined Intelligence Bureau, located at the Navy Office, had been subsumed in October 1941 by a larger Combined Operational Intelligence Centre under the head of naval intelligence, Beasley. The centre included a Y operation, analysing the content of intercepted signals, and a plotting room for direction-finding operations. Its specialised sections liaised with the individual services' own intelligence operations in sigint and other fields, and it was also linked with Police and Customs. All raw intelligence collected at New Zealand's sigint stations was inserted 'into the British and American intelligence systems', with much of the analysis being conducted in Australia.[148]

Combined Operational Intelligence Centre officers visited and maintained extensive liaison with Allied intelligence units in the Asia–Pacific region, and New Zealand opened a forward sigint station in Suva. When Japan entered the war in December 1941, Japanese movements, already under watch, came to dominate the work of New Zealand's sigint operatives. The United States assumed control of Allied sigint in the entire region, and Beasley forged close links with the Americans, especially on direction-finding and Y intelligence tasks. While its capacity to crack codes proved to be limited, New Zealand's direction-finding contribution helped locate Japanese ships during key naval campaigns in 1942 and 1943.

In 1942, however, 'criminal carelessness' (as it has been described) in Wellington had risked exposing the Allied capacity to intercept and decrypt highly sensitive Axis communications.[149] Although all such intelligence was designated 'Ultra secret', the highest level of all, the Combined Operational Intelligence Centre sent a cache of documents, labelled 'Ultra', in the general mail on the Australian freighter *Nankin*. They included the locations of all Allied and enemy warships and merchant vessels in the Pacific and Indian Oceans and 'could only have come from code-breaking'. The collection fell into enemy hands when the ship was captured, en route to Britain, by a German raider that May.[150]

The contents of the documents were passed on by the German naval attaché in Tokyo at the end of July to the Japanese government, whose navy changed its main code accordingly. If the information had reached the Japanese earlier, Allied operations at the pivotal Battle of Midway (4–7 June) could have been adversely affected. This is not certain, as routine Japanese code alteration often occurred, and lags in decryption were common. All the same, there had been a major risk of the Axis powers realising the full extent to which their naval security was compromised. More concretely, as a result of the blunder, the United States Navy had no decrypts of Japanese signals available during the crucial months of October and November, a period of major engagements at Cape Esperance, Santa Cruz and Guadalcanal.[151]

New Zealand's wartime sigint contribution lessened in importance as fighting in the Pacific moved northwards in 1944–45 and, accordingly, its stations had to deal with weakened Japanese signals. By the end of the fighting, New Zealand's prime interception facilities were confined to Waiouru and Suva, with the latter's direction-finding work now shared by only two facilities within New Zealand. But over the course of the war, the Dominion's contribution to Allied sigint operations had not been insignificant.[152]

Operations

The wartime intelligence cycle was overwhelmingly shaped by the array of heightened concerns that arose around the country's enormous war effort. The task of watching for spies and seditionaries began before the outbreak of hostilities. A police intelligence summary report of 9 October 1939 assessed the situation as follows:

> [W]e are well informed regarding conditions and that there is no cause for apprehension regarding the internal state of the country . . . The public reaction to the conduct of the war is most favourable. I would say that communism and anti-war organizations are not likely to gain ground . . . There has been the usual spate of 'spy stories', a considerable number of allegedly suspicious happenings being reported. Each one has been investigated as it is not wise to ignore any but the most obviously fantastic story. A close liaison with the three Defence Services is being maintained.[153]

The country's humint experts, in other words, were satisfied that their arrangements were in order. After the outbreak of hostilities, a great deal of effort continued to be paid to searching for enemy agents and fifth-columnists. While the Ross hoax has tended to dominate attention, some cases held more substance, even if no conclusive evidence of spying was uncovered. The Nelson journalist A. N. Field, for example, described in a 1943 intelligence report as having 'devoted the last 15 years of his life to exposing what he considers to be the nefarious machinations of the Jews in international finance', was well known in fascist and far-right quarters globally. He would be 'very exhaustively investigated' during the war.[154] On the diplomatic front, an October 1941 report into potential Japanese espionage revealed in-depth penetration of communications. It concluded that '[i]t has always been thought that the Japanese Consul was acting as an Intelligence link in New Zealand but so far the intelligence regarding the R.N.Z.A.F. which he has dispatched to Tokio appears to have been gleaned from official and non-secret papers'.[155]

As war approached, the search for foreign agents increasingly included those who would soon be classed as 'enemy aliens'. By the outbreak of the war, detectives were actively reviewing all such aliens in conjunction with specifically tasked bureaucrats. Some of these aliens, especially Germans and Austrians, were placed under surveillance accordingly. Registration began with the outbreak of war and, after the Phoney War ended, special tribunals were established in June 1940 to adjudicate on loyalty, generally basing their decisions on Police assessments. Most aliens were subjected to a variety of controls, such as prohibitions on possessing radios and firearms, restrictions on movements, and internment. The number of internees fluctuated according to the course of the conflict, reaching a peak of 207 in November 1942 and gradually declining thereafter.[156] As well as individual aliens, whole interest groups or communities seen to display subversive tendencies were also placed under Police surveillance. Besides obvious examples, such as the previously covered case of the Auckland German Club, some sections of Balkan communities were placed under surveillance, such as the Croatian Benevolent Society after it disseminated Communist literature.[157]

Between 1941 and 1943, reports of possible fifth-column activity were investigated in areas as disparate as the snowfields of Taranaki and the tropical heat of Samoa.[158] All reports of disaffection with the war in various regions – Te Puke, Whakatāne, Taupō and Ōpōtiki among them – were followed up. Most were found to have little substance, such as information received in early 1942 following Japan's entry into the war. A section of the Rotorua-based Home Guard reported that two Japanese men living on the East Coast had recently sold their businesses and disappeared from sight in suspicious circumstances: storekeeper and billiard saloon owner J. Kamizono, married to 'a Maori woman from Te Araroa', and Ruatoria's H. Kimioka, who had married a 'white woman'. A baker, Kimioka was alleged to be a Japanese agent intending 'to infiltrate the Maoris . . . by promising all sorts of wild things about returning their land to them'.[159]

As that episode suggests, concerns that Māori might prove susceptible to enemy promises emerged with the outbreak of the war. Such fears focused especially on the Waikato–Tainui tribes, given their history of resistance to enrolment in the First World War, their seemingly being 'less than whole-hearted about support of the war effort' and some past links with the Japanese. Likewise, some Rātana followers harboured lingering favourable sentiments about Japan because of its ostensible policy of indigenous self-determination. The Police continued to receive reports of suspected disloyalty among them and there was a brief revival of such allegations after Japan entered the war, when the SIB commenced surveillance of Māori communities.[160]

Princess Te Puea and other members of Kīngitanga leadership circles were placed under heightened surveillance.[161] The SIB increased its scrutiny of the Kīngitanga when

Te Puea gave support to Ngāti Whātua's struggle, in 1942 and 1943, to retain its ancestral land at Ōrākei pā in Auckland. Not only had she worked alongside the CPNZ, but she counted some of its members as personal friends. The state's displeasure extended to the prime minister, who warned Te Puea that if she joined the site of struggle she could be gaoled.[162] By her own account, however, she persuaded the prime minister to 'call the dogs off' on that issue, a decision based on her importance for the war effort.[163]

Soon, in any case, remaining official doubts about the full commitment of Māori to the war effort dissipated. Former minister Apirana Ngata and many other leaders called for full Māori backing for the war as 'the price of citizenship' and progress, and a Maori Parliamentary Committee was formed and mobilised considerable support for the war effort. These efforts were headed by Rātana's former secretary, the Rātana/Labour MP Paraire Paikea, who was made a 'Member of the Executive Council representing the Native Race' in January 1941. The Māori commitment was formalised in the Maori War Effort Organisation in mid-1942, headed by Paikea until his death the following May. No information of substance regarding pro-Japanese dispositions among Māori emerged. Indeed, the people of the Waikato–Tainui federation of tribes proved among the most enthusiastic loyalists on the home front. The goodwill generated by the Māori war effort in general, helped lead to the Crown agreeing, after two decades of on–off negotiations, to settle the historical grievances of Taranaki in 1944 and Waikato in 1946.[164]

The effort to detect enemy agents or fifth-column elements went hand in hand with 'protective security' efforts to safeguard vital points, such as ports, public utilities and core government services. Vetting and monitoring of government employees with access to potentially sensitive information became a particular focus of scrutiny.[165] It sought to uncover staff considered 'dangerous or unsuitable for "security" reasons' to be employed in military or government service, with foreigners and 'disaffected persons' especially scrutinised.[166] All public servants were banned from voicing sentiments in public that were 'antagonistic to the war effort of the government', and some were dismissed for breaching this rule. In mid-1940 the names of all suspect employees were to be provided 'by secret cover' for investigation and, if necessary, dismissal. The supervisor of government night cleaners in Auckland was among those who secured police investigation of a fellow employee, in this case a messenger.[167] The SIB, too, ran investigations on public servants, including cases of alleged criminality that were normally within the province of the Police but which were deemed to have security implications. For example, Henry Berthold, a clerk in the National Service Department, was found to be accepting bribes to remove ballot cards for men eligible for military service.[168]

The surveillers also listened for dangerous broadcasts that might have escaped the scrutiny of publicity officials. Some instances of wartime anti-Communism in the secret world exhibit a dynamic more generally attributed to the early Cold War period. In 1942, for example, an investigation was launched into allegations that Colin Scrimgeour, a founding member of the Society for Closer Relations with Russia and supporter of

John A. Lee, had sought to employ Communists in the Commercial Broadcasting Service.[169] Scrim's adversarial relationship with the prime minister brought him under especially close watch; one file records that a 'precis report' of Scrimgeour's 'activities' had been sent to Fraser.[170]

Ports, so strategically vital to the country's war effort, loomed especially large in protective security. Not only might they be vulnerable to sabotage and politico-industrial action, they were also likely entry points for subversives and possibly enemy agents and formed clear targets for any enemy attack. While port security was initially covered by the NZPF, by March 1940 significant concerns were being raised. The appearance of Communist stickers on vessels, for example, led to official discussions about the possibility of sabotage or treason.[171] Concerns were further exacerbated by enemy actions in New Zealand waters and the beginning of the Pacific War.[172] Such developments contextualise the establishment of Port Security Control within the SIB. A body with wide-ranging functions, its overarching role, as its founding document put it, was to 'supply the link in the Empire Security Intelligence chain which has its headquarters at M.I.5 in London'.[173] The fact that the Bureau's foundational staff, and many of its incoming members, were from the armed services helped facilitate liaison with military leaders on joint tasks such as identifying and trying to eradicate Communist influence within the ranks of servicemen.[174]

The port control authorities proactively enforced security arrangements around the departure and arrival of troopships, oversaw access to and from the ships, and monitored and restricted sensitive information.[175] They tracked the details of all troop transport and escort vessels, their date of departure and destination, their estimated time of arrival, their complements and their types of armaments; and they watched closely for breaches of secrecy about such movements. In March 1942, for example, 223 letters which had been passed by embarking soldiers in Napier to waterside workers for posting were intercepted. An official report on the incident concluded that '[i]nformation which, from a Security standpoint, should not have been given, was liberal in the extreme'.[176]

Port Security Control operated in the civil as well as the military arena. Its staff monitored allied merchant shipping movements, checked passports, supervised movements of foreign fishing and other vessels and their crews, surveilled 'suspect and undesirable persons, including trouble makers' and helped SIB operatives investigate suspected cases of sabotage. It watched out for attempts by seamen to evade censorship, and supplied lists of each ship's crew to the postal censors so that any letters they posted locally could be examined. Port Security Control staff were authorised to take a number of actions to follow up their surveillance; the War Cabinet, for example, ordered them to 'prevent the ingress and egress of undesirable persons'.[177]

The SIB designed exercises to test both the physical security of military installations and the storage of classified documents. In one series of such operations in April–May 1941, various breaches of security protocols were found. Bureau men assigned to take on the role of 'spies', for example, were readily able to gain access to military areas in the Wellington region.[178] Obviously they were not popular with those who were caught out, but they were doing their job.[179]

Folkes's ambition to expand the scope of SIB activities led, among other things, to a widening range of protective security activities, including efforts to improve public attitudes around security. In April 1941, for example, he initiated a 'Don't Talk Campaign' on the radio, stressing 'the simple but enduring rule that any information regarding naval, military, air or shipping matters must not be discussed or repeated'.[180] There were many targets on security's radar in the search for seditious or other activities that might damage the war effort. As during the previous war, pacifists, revolutionaries (now mostly Communists) and anti-conscription activists were among the obvious targets as groups that might potentially impact the war effort. Resulting investigations were not always efficient, however, partly because of inter-agency overlaps. After the SIB's establishment, indeed, parallel investigations by different agencies often occurred. Both the political detectives and the Bureau, for example, monitored suspected Communists or fellow travellers, and possible subversives of other political persuasions were also simultaneously under surveillance by both agencies before their effective merger.[181]

As usual, the CPNZ's strength was closely monitored and its potential influence remained under ongoing analysis throughout the war. Both the Police and the SIB continued to keep a watch on the Party after it endorsed the war effort. In 1942 its Christchurch District Committee was 'very concerned at the continual attention paid to us by the police force' even at meetings to promote the war effort. The presence of beat police, detectives and 'shorthand writers', it declared, 'only serves to hamper our contribution to victory'. The government's response was: 'If meetings are consistently innocent no doubt the police will take that into full consideration in determining what surveillance, if any, is necessary.'[182] The surveillance continued; the long-term interests of state security overrode shorter-term considerations, even those as important as the war effort.

Alongside the ongoing study of the Communist Party, a series of associated groups and suspected fronts were also heavily monitored. Intelligence reports came in from the very first meeting of the SCR, for example, and files were opened on its regional branches as well as its centre.[183] The Young People's Club, a successor of the Young Communist League of the 1930s, was also targeted. An informant's report concluded, 'I am definitely of the opinion that the Young People's Club is sponsored by the Communist Party as evidenced by the dominant party numbers present and the trend of discussions.'[184]

Likewise, social, cultural and protest movements linked (in fact or in the minds of surveillers) with broader left-wing ideas had, as noted, long been monitored, such as the Esperanto movement. This scrutiny continued during the war, and intensified after reports of anti-British, pro-Communist and pacifist literature having been published in Esperanto.[185] The Christchurch Co-operative Bookshop Society was noted as stocking, alongside more mainstream fare, 'progressive', socialist and Communist literature, as were similar cooperative bookshops in the Dominion.[186] The intelligence agencies paid special attention to any revolutionary influence within trade unions (white-collar as well as blue, including the actors' union), on the waterfront and inside protest movements (such as that opposing Allied support for rightist resistance forces in Greece rather than those led by the Communists).[187] Student radicalism similarly attracted interest. When 18-year-old student Dorian Saker, literary editor of *Salient*, published a short story in the student journal that was seen as expressing cynicism about enlistment, it was declared subversive (and 'indecent'). The prime minister himself summoned Victoria University College student leaders and *Salient*'s editorial committee to a meeting, at which he elicited apologies and good-behaviour pledges; he agreed in turn 'to recommend that there be no prosecution'.[188]

Ethnic communities were generally monitored through their community associations. Yugoslav waiters at Wellington's Green Parrot restaurant had records opened on them after donating to the CPNZ, and surveillance of men employed at the restaurant continued throughout the war and beyond. A magistrate commented in 1946, before fining four of them for 'pasting posters on a tramway post', that '[f]rom their names they don't seem to be British or New Zealanders. Is this the Communist element we are getting in the country?'[189]

Pacifists, peace groups and anti-conscription movements and individuals came under particularly heavy scrutiny, both because of their potential impact on the war effort and their supposed susceptibility to manipulation by the CPNZ. As well as monitoring vocal opponents of conscription, the Police were also tasked with tracking down defaulters.[190] The military, the SIB and other state entities assisted, passing on hard information, vague rumours and much material that fell between these two extremes, some of it leading to arrests designed to be both punitive and exemplary.

The anti-conscriptionist Democratic Labour Party was investigated after its founding by John A. Lee, following his expulsion from the Labour Party in March 1940. Given Lee's high profile as an outspoken socialist and a wounded First World War veteran (he had lost much of his left arm), the new party held the potential to embarrass the government and damage support for its policies, even if it had only two MPs. Police investigations focused on the conscription issue, in which the Democratic Labour Party was prominent, and on its relationship with Communists (although its pedigree put it closer to left elements of the Social Credit movement than to the CPNZ). Once the Party's prominence faded following its defeat in the 1943 elections, the surveillers could afford to lessen their scrutiny.[191]

The Wellington Peace and Anti-Conscription Council had been especially closely watched early on in the war, partly because of its high level of support from within trade unions and the Labour Party (including MPs and office-holders).[192] In March 1940 the Labour Party declared that its members could not be associated with the Council. Among those who then left the Party was Douglas Martin, formerly a vice-president of the Miramar branch. Entries in the secret files, following those noting his presence at anti-war and unemployment meetings through the 1930s, record that he addressed meetings held under the auspices of peace organisations in early 1940. In July, an entry notes he was found guilty of making 'subversive statements' at a public meeting and gaoled for a year with hard labour.[193]

In a similar fashion, notable pacifists Ormond Burton and A. C. Barrington, both associated with the Christian Pacifist Society and the Peace Pledge Union, were targeted because of their potential influence on congregations.[194] Other pacifistic groupings closely scrutinised included the New Zealand branches of the Movement against War and Fascism, the Jehovah's Witnesses church, The National Peace Council, and a number of anti-conscription campaigns.[195]

The methods by which information was gathered during the war years did not fundamentally change from those employed before them. In spite of the high degree of censorship, much of the security information that found its way to the surveillance files came from readily available material: newspaper articles, editorials and notices, and non-proscribed literature.[196] As in the previous conflict, the files also built up a great deal of information volunteered by the public. In a typical case, from 1940, a woman reported to the Police that a fellow female passenger on a trip from Gisborne to Wellington had been 'talking against enlistment' and had subsequently sent her peace publications.[197] This resulted in enquiries into the passenger which logged her family into the secret files.[198] All reports from the public needed to be considered, even if many could be quickly discarded, especially the frequent accounts of pro-enemy sentiments. To take one of many examples, a man reported by his colleagues as having given a fascist salute and claiming Germany would be victorious was quickly deemed to be 'more silly than dangerous'.[199]

As in the past, too, the Police and the SIB attended and reported on large numbers of meetings, rallies and speeches, and in some cases typed transcripts of the entire proceedings were produced.[200] Gatherings of the Christian Pacifist Society,[201] the Peace and Anti-Conscription League[202] and other organisations within the peace movement were closely watched, as well as those of the SCR and other associations with CPNZ ties.[203] Some of the surveilled groups, especially those with significant numbers of Communists in their leadership or rank-and-file, protested at the overt levels of surveillance, deeming them to be intimidatory. In March 1942, for example, the secretary of the SCR forwarded a resolution to the minister in charge of policing requesting that his men cease attending its meetings and lectures.[204]

When a supporter protested about Constable R. P. Thomas's presence at a January 1940 event organised by Ormond Burton at Wellington's Basin Reserve ('are we going to let this "bluebottle" take down notes when we have a permit to speak?'), Burton replied: 'Let him take down what he likes. He will submit a report to his Sergeant on what I have said, and the Sergeant in turn will pass it on to his superiors and it will all be added to the case that is being made against me.' Advocating passive resistance, he warned that 'there is a general move by the authorities to put down free speech. The "Voice of the People" will be suppressed as will the Communists and ourselves, and a lot of us will be in concentration camps if this war continues.' Thomas's report concluded that '[p]arts of Burton's speech seem to be a breach of The Censorship and Publicity Emergency Regulations 1939', and the Christian Pacifist leader would, indeed, spend quite some time behind bars during the war.[205]

Other methods of gathering information utilised the coercive powers of the police with, for example, raids seizing material, notably from the CPNZ early in the war and the peace movement throughout it.[206] By such means the political police sought to deter producers and distributors of literature deemed subversive, and follow-up arrests were frequent, sometimes after applying police forensic skills in areas such as handwriting analysis to track down authors and their accomplices. Such literature was often taken out of public circulation; ideally, indeed, the raiders sought to maximise suppression of locally produced literature by finding and confiscating printing equipment.[207]

Some raids were based on reports from within suspect organisations. The police had continued to recruit and use informants to provide assessments of the internal workings and dynamics of the targeted groups. An insider report of a meeting of the Te Aro–Brooklyn branch of the Wellington CPNZ, for example, included names and descriptions of attendees, observations on business relating to the SCR, and a copy of a petition being circulated around other Party branches; it finished by noting that 'I shall attend the Nov. 7th. 1942 celebration to be held in the Trades Hall by the C.P. on Friday Nov. 6th. 1942, and report on those present and any further particular'.[208]

Revolutionary circles were most aware of the possibility of clandestine scrutiny. After insider information had led to high-profile raids, some had tightened their security consciousness. When the leaders of the Wellington branch of the CPNZ were 'expecting a raid on their premises' in 1940, their documents were taken to 'a secret hiding place' outside the city. The location was known to 'only a few' insiders, not including the woman who was informing on them.[209] The Party, moreover, introduced more rigorous vetting procedures for applicants. As one of its members, Albert Birchfield, unwittingly 'told a reliable informant' handled by Detective Samuel Browne, 'candidates were [now] carefully watched for six months before being admitted'. In one practical consequence, the police were unable to infiltrate a would-be informant into the Wellington organisation. As a result, here and elsewhere security reports were often unclear on even such basic issues as Party numbers or the precise status of people associated with it; a roommate of a typist who was 'undoubtedly' in the CPNZ, for example, 'appears to be also a Party member'.[210]

The SIB staff, with no inherited network of informants to build upon, carried out most of the surveillance work themselves while they built up contacts. In the absence of any policing-oriented experience or training, they had to learn detective techniques on the hoof, although some of them brought military intelligence experience and the police did sometimes swap information (while continuing to bar access to their own secret files). Conversely, SIB operatives had to share their intelligence with the police if they wanted an arrest made.

Some of the staff, because of their status, had personal relationships which reached into higher social circles than those of the invariably humble backgrounds of most policemen. Such entrées could be useful for investigations. Sergeant 170, for example, could get information from multiple sources on public servant W. B. Sutch. The sergeant's father-in law, Professor Sir Thomas Hunter, had himself been a subject of surveillance. However, as head of both the University of New Zealand and its constituent part in Wellington, Hunter felt a responsibility to modify free speech and due process within the terms of the war effort.[211] He told the sergeant (D. J. F. White) about Sutch's abortive application for the chair of economics at his own institution early in the war. An academic committee had unanimously selected the 'brilliant economist' for the position, but follow-up reports from 'responsible persons' had been 'condemnatory'. Hunter volunteered that he felt that Sutch had become 'something of a psychological case' because of foiled ambitions. In pursuit of a fuller picture, the SIB talked to a former schoolmate who had confirmed Sutch's inclination to spurn authority. All such information went into the files, along with rumours that Finance Minister Walter Nash had lost faith in Sutch because of his 'undisciplinary attitude'.[212]

One of the key sources of Sergeant 90 (Terry McLean) in one investigation was his own mother. She claimed that Elsie Freeman (formerly Farrelly) had undermined the editorial line of Woman Today, a magazine they had been connected with but which had ceased publication in 1939 amidst factional disputes. In another such instance, McLean's brother was friendly with significant Australian artist Noel Counihan, who had invited Terry to 'Sunday afternoon sessions' where politics were discussed. While he did not attend, he recorded other information on Counihan's political and artistic circle, and thought it 'likely' that Mrs Freeman had gone to the meetings. He was especially concerned about her 'activity in connection with the formation of Housewive's [sic] Unions', which he surmised was 'Communist undercover work'. He billed this surmise as 'the feature' of one report submitted in 1941.[213]

SIB agents developed their own methods of subterfuge. Some were basic: in August 1941, for example, an SIB operative pretending to represent a group of Bible students telephoned Rev. W. S. Rollings to determine his relationship with the SCR.[214] Other covert operations were more sophisticated, such as a complicated ruse used to flush out the details of why the Petone Woollen Mills had dismissed Elsie Freeman for 'trying to make trouble among the workers'. It, too, hinged upon a false story concocted to persuade a reluctant factory manager to talk. Such methods were seen to be justified to protect the war effort from 'the kind of woman ready to commit sabotage at any time'. Freeman was 'continually watched' for being a 'died [sic] in the wool' Communist.[215]

Another source of pertinent information for the security intelligence agencies was F. P. Walsh, a key unionist who had long been under surveillance in his own right. He was now (in the words of one of his surveillers) 'so close to the government that he is said with some truth to be the unofficial Prime Minister of New Zealand'. He was now attempting to establish his credentials with the agencies by providing information to the political police and the SIB, including on union colleagues. Although 'the tag is supposed to be', a Bureau sergeant reported, '[o]nce a Communist, always a Communist', Walsh 'plays a serious and determined part in his effort to help the war'. His anti-Communist fervour, in fact, soon came to rather endear him to his surveillers, although ongoing allegations (including by a former Labour MP) of disloyalty (and dishonesty, which held out the possibility of blackmail) kept his personal file active.[216] Although Walsh was, in John A. Lee's reckoning, 'a gangster and a thug' as well as 'a contemptible cur and a shithouse', his skills and knowledge were needed by the government. By the account of an SIB informant, for example, Walsh was 'said to be violently anti-Semitic, which probably gives him a knowledge of refugee aliens'.[217]

As we have noted, NZPF and Bureau staff did exchange material when it was necessary or expedient, but the police detectives were not disposed to share confidential information with Folkes's operatives (in part to protect their informant network). This had been of little concern to Director Folkes, who believed that a military approach secured superior results to those of policemen, who were seen as overly hamstrung by guidelines, rules and regulations. This was not entirely an imaginary perspective. After Jim Cummings was confirmed as director, he found that the secret files compiled by Folkes's men were of considerable use in police investigations, in part for their collation of a great deal of information from various departments of state – postal, aliens, censorship and so on. Such sources provided a higher quantity of material on specific sectors of society than that collected in the police secret files, as well as much more analysis based on rumour, innuendo, gossip and misapprehension.

The surveillers often received a great deal of information from allied governments and intelligence services. In April 1940, for example, the New Zealand High Commissioner in London passed on British intelligence concerns about left-wing literature being sent to the Christchurch Co-operative Bookshop Society.[218] Likewise, in 1942, Fox de Victor Ambler, a possible secret agent for the French collaborationist Vichy government, was reported to be en route to New Zealand from Fiji.[219]

Information exchange with Australia was also significant, and sometimes done off the record. In March 1943, for example, the search for enemy spies in New Zealand intensified after the director of naval intelligence in Melbourne informally tipped off his counterpart across the Tasman about 'the possibility of Chinese agents' working for Japanese intelligence 'being landed on the coast' of New Zealand. In response, Melbourne was notified that 'discreet action' had been taken, including the involvement of the Chinese consul-general. He had urged Chinese associations in New Zealand to be vigilant, reminding them that 'China is an ally of New Zealand, and it is the duty of the Chinese resident in the Dominion to cooperate and take special precaution against such evil men coming to New Zealand to carry out their nefarious deeds'.[220]

Later in the year, Australian intelligence passed on details concerning a Japanese intelligence officer experienced in organising fifth columns: 'It is suggested that Japanese [sic] will make every effort to effect the entry of this Agent to Australia in the guise of a Chinese for espionage purposes.'[221] Australasian cooperation did not always lead to results. Information from the Wrens at Rapaura was ignored by the Australians in early 1943, with a consequent loss of shipping. Neither country detected a German submarine operating in their waters between late 1944 and early 1945, although – unlike off Australia – it found no suitable shipping targets in New Zealand waters.[222]

As part of the Imperial chain, Port Security Control naturally liaised with Commonwealth countries but, with large numbers of American servicemen arriving in New Zealand from mid-1942, work with the United States security agencies burgeoned. Not only did port security operators work with various American civilian and military authorities, the SIB also liaised and cooperated with US military police.[223] One joint task was to defuse tensions between New Zealand and American servicemen over race relations and women, as well as other issues that threatened efficiency, morale and sometimes public order.[224]

A major security procedure was to check passengers and crews of arriving vessels against a Port Security Suspect Index. This was initially adapted from MI5's 'Consolidated Black List', which recorded some 15,000 individuals around the world (many connected with seafaring) who were considered part of the global threatscape. Men on the New Zealand list, which was regularly updated, were interrogated before receiving a clearance to enter New Zealand, although those who passed were still liable to scrutiny.[225]

While the information-gathering methods used by the security services did not fundamentally change after 1939, the amount of information to be processed and analysed escalated enormously amidst the pressures of war. One study proposes that there was a divergence between what might be called a police legalistic approach to collected information and the manner of analysis undertaken by the SIB:

> The police and the SIB produced intelligence summaries similar in some respects but very different in others. The role of the police was to catch criminals and waylay those in breach of security measures. Their attention focussed inwards for the most part, and

was very much predicated on judicial results: convictions in court, imprisonment or internment. The SIB viewed security intelligence from another angle, as well as blocking leaks. They tended to look at the larger picture, at what was going on overseas as well as within New Zealand.[226]

Much NZPF analysis fits this description in terms of legality: whether particular instances constituted sedition or subversion, for example, or whether the information that had been collected could further investigations into the location of defaulters or duplicators. An emphasis was placed, then, on producing practical intelligence that could inform policing measures. On the most basic level, lists and details of targets (including names, addresses and occupations) were prepared that would facilitate quick targeting: of the members of the Christian Pacifist Society, for example, or the shareholders of the Christchurch Co-operative Bookshop Society operation, or the 533 alleged comrades of the CPNZ in early 1942.[227]

However, this dichotomy between 'larger picture' and narrower legality should not be overstated. Police assessments were also invested in the likelihood of broad threats to the state and its interests, and accordingly sought to understand their targets 'in the round'. Early in the war, for example, there was concern about sabotage of war-related infrastructure from oppositional quarters. After close police investigation of the organisations and their leaders, the Commissioner concluded that the 'number of mushroom organizations which have sprung up under different names' to oppose the government's war policies would not engage in sabotage. Except for the Communists among them, he assured high-level New Zealand security officials that, despite their political beliefs, most of their members were 'otherwise well conducted reputable people'. While the most likely left-wingers to use sabotage were the Communists, he elaborated, 'even in their case I do not at present feel the situation calls for anything more than ordinary caution'.[228]

Both the police and the SIB, before and after Folkes, added unverified material to their files in efforts to build larger and more penetrative profiles on organisations and individuals, continuing the well-embedded practice of accumulating whatever information turned up in an attempt to gain a fuller picture. Police reports logged increasing amounts of detail about individuals, including their social networks, family ties and associations, especially those deemed subversive; their access to typewriters and motor vehicles; whether they were in 'financial difficulties'; their sexual mores; and so on. A similar approach was applied to organisations: their memberships, structures, major personalities, political disagreements and interpersonal animosities and much more.[229]

When such collated information was analysed within the SIB in its Folkes days, the resulting assessments could include curiously judgemental comments on norms or deviancy, or highly questionable assumptions. Details filed about Elsie Freeman's personal life, for example, record that her former husband was 'old enough to be her father'. Having given birth, moreover, 'did not prevent her from carrying out work for the party during the period normally devoted by mothers to nursing'.[230]

In 1943 Jewish refugee Helmut Einhorn also came to SIB attention when he sought to enlist in the military. When interviewed, Einhorn stressed that although he 'still had German ties' by reason of birth, culture and family and other networks, he was anxious to join the fight against fascism. While it was agreed that he had given 'no reason to suspect that he is in any way disloyal or dangerous', he was still 'considered to be pro-German to some extent' so could not serve in the European theatre. 'Even if [Einhorn] desires the defeat of Hitler', it was felt, 'he probably does not desire to see Germany humbled as in 1919'. The key to his attitude, one analyst decided, was that 'if the Nazi Party were less extremist, he would be whole-heartedly pro-German'. Indeed, his Germanness supposedly so overrode his Jewishness that 'perhaps he would rather live as a despised Jew in Germany than as a free man in N.Z.'.[231]

The men in Folkes's SIB, perhaps reflecting their lack of training, did not hold back on their personal views on governing politicians. Their files, for example, contain a series of sardonic character profiles on the prime minister and Cabinet ministers ('Pious Pete' Fraser, 'Wily Walter' Nash, 'Raging Robert' Semple and so on) which were based largely on scuttlebutt and innuendo. Their depictions of ruling politicians included such comments as '[r]ather henpecked'; 'probably less political conscience than anyone else in politics in N.Z., which is saying a good deal'; 'previously a peripatetic purveyor of pornographic phrophylactics [sic]'; and 'by the way, has the largest house in Christchurch'.[232]

Although it was not part of their official security brief in the time of Folkes's SIB, the Police continued to work on a holistic approach to the security threatscape, viewing this as part of their ongoing appraisal of threats to peace, good order and the state. The Force's political detectives were practised in placing organisations, trends and movements within both national and international contexts, and well versed in preparing analyses and summations of these for the workings of the intelligence cycle. The degree to which Folkes's SIB was wanting in basic tradecraft can be seen in Attorney-General Mason's report on the Ross hoax. It noted that the Bureau 'explains that it does not send a man to take a statement, as the Police do. [It] observes, tabulates, accumulates reports, and slowly builds up a picture. It does not check, test, and verify (as far as it can) as it goes along ... Clearly the method can accumulate ... much rubbish.'[233]

The Ross hoax represents the clearest example of the faulty, to put it lightly, intelligence the SIB produced. There is, also, a more sinister element to consider. The conman later told police investigating his enemy invasion hoax that 'the stuff contained in [the SIB's] volumes is about one page of material that I supplied to three pages of fiction made up by the Security [Bureau]'. Unreliable as Ross was, other material in the files supports an assessment that, at very best, untenable conclusions were drawn and, at worst, outright fabrication of evidence occurred, including by Folkes himself.[234] Distortion or fabrication is far from unusual in security history, but it often occurs in such contexts as informants exaggerating their findings or analysts gilding the lily. It seldom involves a serious and sustained deception of a government by professional staff, including the head himself. The untested or poorly tested raw data in SIB files also had an afterlife. Transferred into the post-war secret files of the police, and later to the New Zealand Security Service, they continued to be used in intelligence assessments that had ramifications for lives and careers.

Assessment

The extraordinary circumstances of the wartime emergency led to significant new developments in New Zealand's history of state surveillance. On the outbreak of hostilities, material accumulated through pre-war surveillance positioned the Police and other authorities to pursue actions against a range of social elements. Ministers were all for cracking down hard, especially on those to the government's left. Moreover, the massive expansion of state power soon further enhanced the reach and scope of the surveillers, with sedition, for example, now seen as potentially including any words or deeds which went against any aspect of state policy. As during the last war, the NZPF formed a major instrument of the state's security intelligence apparatus, and even after the establishment of the SIB it continued to include political policing within its remit.

Through its surveilling agencies, the state intruded ever more broadly and deeply into its citizens' private lives and, as a result, coerced many of them in different ways. Some members of peace and other movements lost their jobs or their chances of gaining a position in their field, including a number of teacher trainees. Auckland academics were warned by Prime Minister Fraser of 'the grave danger if persons prominently connected with the Universities align themselves in any way in support of anyone who was engaged in subversive activities'.[235] Non–New Zealanders could be deported under the 'undesirable immigrants' legislation promulgated in the 'red scare' years. Artist Noel Counihan, acting secretary of Wellington's Peace and Anti-Conscription Council, was transported back to Australia in June 1940. Another was 'KEVA BRONSON – COMMUNIST', a clerk declared to be 'disaffected, disloyal and likely to be a source of danger to the peace, order and good government of New Zealand'.[236]

Many different ways of silencing critics were found. In 1942, in a clear attempt to defang him, the troublesome 'Uncle Scrim' was called up for military service, even though he headed a government department, suffered from ill health, had three children and was at the high end of the age qualification for military service. In June 1943, at Fraser's instigation, he was dismissed from his position. 'Thus ended the broadcasting career of the country's most prominent broadcaster.'[237]

Right: Figure 15
A typical example of Depression-era anti-Communist propaganda, which urges New Zealanders to 'wake up' to the 'red menace' hiding in their midst. *NZ Home Pictorial, 12 August 1931, cover*

Below: Figure 16
Photograph of a demonstration in Parliament grounds, 16 September 1931, filed in Police security records. Several figures were numbered for identification purposes, including leading activist Jim Edwards (number 4, centre). *'Miscellaneous Organisations: Unemployed Workers' Movement' [ADMO 21007 26/8/90 3/1 (R24716782)], Archives New Zealand Te Rua Mahara o te Kāwanatanga*

Above: Figure 17
Photograph of a scuffle between policemen and demonstrators in Parliament grounds, September 1931. After being used in court proceedings, the image was lodged in the Police secret files with identification markers. *'Miscellaneous Organisations: Unemployed Workers' Movement'* [ADMO 21007 26/8/90 3/1 (R24716782)], *Archives New Zealand Te Rua Mahara o te Kāwanatanga*

Right: Figure 18
An August 1931 Communist-led demonstration outside Wellington Town Hall, focused around a prop coffin for victims of unemployment and eviction. Political detectives habitually surveilled such protests. 1/2-084825-G, *Alexander Turnbull Library, Wellington, New Zealand*

Right: Figure 19
Information provided to the Police
by Customs in May 1932, including
a personal description and a
photograph acquired from United
States immigration authorities.
'Communist Party of New Zealand;
Wellington Branch: Sympathisers &
Contacts' [ADMO 21007 W5933/6
21/5/10 pt1 (R24118479)], Archives
New Zealand Te Rua Mahara o te
Kāwanatanga

Below: Figure 20
Mugshots of George Sargeef
(alias Sargiff or Sargeif), a Russian
furrier and seaman, charged with
'possession of explosive with
intent and bomb with intent'.
He was sentenced to two years'
imprisonment and later gaoled
for three years for counterfeiting.
A mysterious figure, he was
suspected in some left-wing
quarters of being an *agent*
provocateur, and was later
interned in the Second World War.
New Zealand Police Gazette,
2 November 1932, p. 104

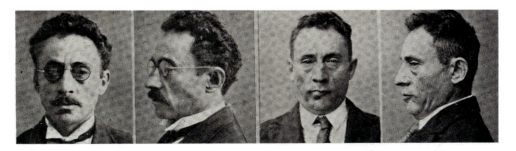

SARGEEF, GEORGE, alias SARGIFF.

P.G. 32/586.   F.P. Class $\frac{1}{25}$ $\frac{R}{R}$ $\frac{O}{OO}$ 16 ?

FREEMAN, John Derek   <u>SAMOA</u>   - 2 -

Assistant Headmaster, Ifi School, Samoa. Born Wellington NZ
16/8/1916. Parents ELSIE MAY ELIZABETH FREEMAN, and JOHN HENRY
FREEMAN (Tobacconist, 288 Lambton Quay, Wellington.)
No intention of enlisting to fight Capitalistic war. Known   40/1697
in Kelburn (whilst in residence there) as the local Communist.   51/664
Mbr Inaugural C'tee of Wellington Co-op Book Sicety.   52/424.
Assists at Public mtg addressed by E.Arya,5/3/52.   52/424.
Possible association with Modern Books,Wellington.
Details of history & antecedents. Appointed visiting lecturer in
Anthropology for 1954 at Otago University.Still left in political
matters. Serves in RNZN during war.   53/551. P.F.
Leaves N.Z.by Air from Christchurch 29.10.54 fro Sydney.   53/551. P.F
Returns N.Z. about 5-11-54.<u>Resides 128 Kelburn Parade,W'gton</u>.To take
up duties at Canberra leaving N.Z. about 1-2-55.   53/551 P.F
Association with N.L.MILLER.   54/829
Resident Aust.12 months. Returns to NZ. 13.1.57 to attend Science
Congress in Dunedin, Jan.1957.   57/8 P.F
Returns to Australia, 4.2.57.   57/8 P.F.
                                        P.F.

Above: Figure 21
This index card references filed
information on Derek Freeman
(later a leading anthropologist). The
first trace dates to 1940, triggered
by a complaint about his mother's
anti-war sentiments. A notation
('P.F.') indicates that a dedicated
personal file was opened on him.
*'Peace Organisations – Miscellaneous
Peace and Disarment [sic] – Christian
Pacifist Society Groups' [ADMO 21007
W5787/3 33/14/1/1 pt3 (R23246725)],
Archives New Zealand Te Rua Mahara
o te Kāwanatanga*

Right Figure 22
The cover of a 1944 edition of the government-published *New Zealand Listener* featuring the formerly demonised Soviet leader Joseph Stalin, now portrayed as a valued wartime ally. The journal advertises that 'the BBC will salute him on the occasion of his 65th birthday'. *New Zealand Listener, 18 December 1944, p. 1*

Below: Figure 23
1939 mugshots of professional conman Sydney Ross who, during the Second World War, hoaxed the government into believing that fifth-columnists were conspiring with enemy agents to prepare for invasion. This episode was central to the downfall of Kenneth Folkes, the first Director of the Security Intelligence Bureau. *New Zealand Police Gazette, 6 September 1939, p. 73*

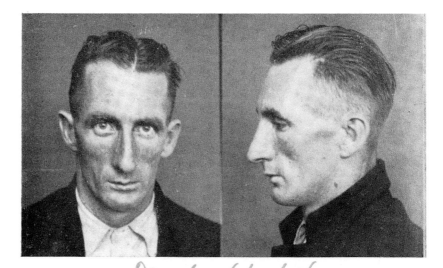

ROSS, SIDNEY GEORGE, *alias* ROSS, SYDNEY GORDON.

P.G. 39/551.

F.P. Class $\frac{29}{19} \frac{I}{O} \frac{I}{21}$

"HI, MAJOR FOOKES, COME ON UP. ARMY HEADQUARTERS' ON THE PHONE."

Above: Figure 24
Cartoon from the Communist
Party newspaper, during the period
in which it was banned, ridiculing
the Security Intelligence Bureau's
Director, 'Major Fookes' (Folkes),
who ostensibly reported to the
Defence chiefs. *People's Voice,*
5 June 1941

Right: Figure 25
Major Kenneth Folkes, head of
the Security Intelligence Bureau
from 1941 to 1943, flanked by two
of his Captains. The setting is
Mākara Beach, near the Fort Opau
defensive position. *New Zealand*
Observer, 11 October 1944, p. 6

Left: Figure 26
Wellington's APA Building. In 1941 it hosted the headquarters of the Security Intelligence Bureau. *People's Voice* said of it: 'With drawn blinds and a sentry at the door, it is the essence of secrecy. In fact, so blatantly secret that it is the laugh of the town and specially the tenants of the building.' *David Filer papers*

Below: Figure 27
The socialite Joan Young, pictured here just before she joined the new Security Intelligence Bureau. One of her duties was to test security at vital points by charming guards, earning her some condemnation as a 'skirted pimp'. *Spencer Digby/ Ronald D Woolf Collection. Gift of Ronald Woolf, 1975, B.068907, Museum of New Zealand Te Papa Tongarewa*

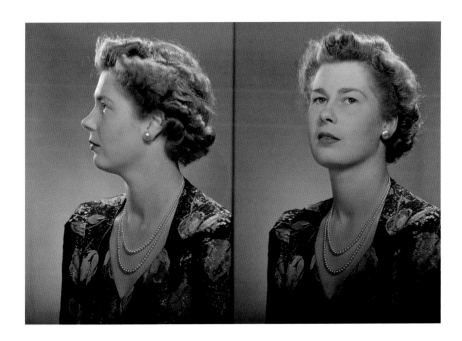

Left: Figure 28
Chief Detective J. Bruce Young in his Dunedin office, February 1936. During the war he took up senior positions and would later serve as Police Commissioner from 1950 to 1952. *Sherwood Young Collection*

Below: Figure 29
Edna Pearce, pictured front row left in the first intake of women police (1941), was one of the few women constables whose duties included matters relating to security. She worked under Detective Sergeant Harding to supervise the families of interned Japanese men during the Second World War. *2016-498-1, New Zealand Police Museum*

The general constraints on freedom, and the authorities' acts of repression through 1939–45, cannot of course be examined outside the context of total war and a cause which almost all New Zealanders regarded as necessary in view of the nature of the Axis powers. Thus, when hints of covert surveillance measures occasionally surfaced, they seemed to be at least tacitly approved by the great majority of the population. Had most people been asked, they would no doubt have agreed with the government that severe measures in the short term were necessary in the long-term interests of the sought-after ideal society. Certainly, Labour retained office comfortably in the 1943 elections (when its Rātana partner gained the last of the four Māori seats).

Once again, a national emergency had raised questions about the relationship between the dominant New Zealand mythscape and the government's interpretation of the public interest. The English writer John Middleton Murry's words early in the conflict capture the innate tension between illiberal measures needed for pursuing war and a commitment by liberal democracies to preserve citizens' liberties: 'Censorship there must be; but it is essential to the inward life of the cause they represent that the democracies should never cease to regard any limitation on freedom of expression as intrinsically an evil.'[238] Ultimately, such wartime tensions were, in New Zealand, an intensified version of the ongoing unease around state surveillance that we have observed in this history.

The war years also witnessed another round of skirmishes centred around the management of security intelligence in New Zealand. In one sense, the creation of the SIB as a professional state surveillance body, independent of the police and more networked with fellow Imperial agencies, was an administrative departure from the post-1900 norm. It also, however, reflected ideas which had been pitched in the aftermath of the First World War and had re-emerged in the late 1930s in the context of heightened threat perceptions. As in the past, the concept of military-led surveillance again had its champions within political, military and bureaucratic circles, and garnered active support from Britain. The idea also had its bureaucratic opponents, most notably in the senior levels of the NZPF. The events leading to the creation of the SIB represented, in short, another episode within a longer official discourse.

Apart from institutional patch protection, at stake was the struggle between two models of security intelligence: the ethos of police-based surveillance versus a military-style operation falling outside the criminal justice system. Police surveilling practice was, to a degree, constrained within legal parameters, even if it was operating within the blurred spaces between legality and illegality. A professional surveillance system tended, in military eyes, to be a different creature from a political policing operation. From the police perspective, to take one example, an extensive knowledge base of political criminality provided an informed platform for the surveillance of those who might be engaged in subversion or espionage.

To take another example, sworn policemen needed to situate their actions within legal and, to a degree, ethical parameters. The differences between constabularised and non-police surveillance methods can be exaggerated, but the Peelian guidelines under which police were generally expected to operate did provide some safeguards for civilian rights even in the context of a wartime emergency. If things went wrong, they were subject to discipline from superior officers (possibly acting under the unspoken rules of plausible deniability) or the judiciary. This latter possibility was not a theoretical one given that, ultimately, the role of the political police inside a general force was to prosecute offenders and therefore they routinely came under judicial scrutiny. The military were, in all practical senses, far less accountable to external scrutiny. Folkes's SIB saw itself as providing advice to the political executive on the big issues – focusing on saboteurs of the state, its policies and its infrastructure, rather than on relatively minor breaches of the law. Given that the stakes were so high, his investigators, accordingly, viewed themselves as somewhat above the law.

Police guidelines and practices also provided some rigour at all stages of the intelligence cycle. As the attorney-general put it, when the police swung into action after a constable's alert about Ross 'it took them a very short time to expose the falsity of the whole story which had occasioned security so much trouble, expense and anxiety over so many months'.[239] To be sure, the low level of competence within sections of the Bureau was partly rooted in the inexperience of its staff from top to bottom. The original SIB recruits had virtually to start from scratch, including the need to set up parallel sets of files to those held by civil and military services. Moreover, while some SIB operatives did learn surveilling skills from experienced political detectives, especially as the Bureau came under tighter Police control, Jim Cummings and Nalder still found most of them wanting.

This overall lack of both basic policing experience and detective training within SIB personnel remained a liability to surveillance efficiency, given (for example) their inability to sift the significant from the trivial – although, as we have noted, the political detectives also experienced difficulties with analysis. This points to the danger in any attempt to present a dichotomy between a political police institution operating effectively inside the law, and a non-constabularised security bureau operating ineffectively and sometimes outside of it. On the other hand, such a comparison has a broad validity, something exemplified by the political decision to effectively constabularise the Bureau in order to address issues of competence.

This, of course, resulted from the most dramatic example of SIB incompetence and loose accountability, the invasion hoax, which ended Folkes's regime. In the aftermath of the fiasco, the various authorities involved produced differing accounts of what had happened and why it had happened. Prime Minister Fraser would subsequently stress that the SIB had been set up on the 'express wish' of British authorities.[240] But this was to gloss over the crucial fact that, once he had accepted their recommendation to place Folkes at its head, and the new Director had been authorised to report to him directly, he and his ministers had exercised extraordinarily lax oversight. The deputy director of MI5 later bluntly sheeted home the ultimate blame for the SIB's spectacular fall from grace to Fraser, 'who made a complete hash of the whole business. Having taken security away from Commissioner Cummings, he eventually found that he had to hand it back.'[241]

Of course, the failure of the SIB in its original incarnation also owes much to the personality and actions of its director. Most accounts portray him as a credulous dupe of skilled hoaxers, however much their story creaked from the outset.[242] Hugh Price's book on this episode, by contrast, portrays the director of security in a much darker light. Price argues that Folkes had come to see through Ross, but cynically used the conman's claims in order to pursue expanded powers and jurisdiction for the SIB. This, not the hoax invented by criminals, was the real 'plot to subvert wartime New Zealand':

> Major Folkes and some of his men were organising an act of subversion, by which he and a few of his army intelligence officers were busy manufacturing a threat, while Folkes pressed the Prime Minister for powers to deal with it. It was a conspiracy to jolt the government into passing some very significant powers from the elected government and regular administration of law and justice, and vest them in a small junta.[243]

Aaron Fox and John Tonkin-Covell have different emphases from Price, placing any conceit and deceit on the part of the director of security within a wider institutional context. In this perspective, Folkes's underhand manoeuvres were intended to both protect and enhance the Bureau in the face of mounting concerns from police, politicians and military bureaucrats.[244] The line of argument stresses that the Police and some military leaders had been trying to discredit the Bureau because of institutional rivalry. Through the 'great opportunity' of the hoax's exposure, they could further their 'campaign' to bring down the Bureau.[245]

Senior Navy Office staff who remained sympathetic to the need for an independent Bureau located within the military argued forcefully that institutional hostility was the main driver of the events that led to Folkes's downfall. On 20 November 1942, for example, the director of naval intelligence portrayed a 'campaign against the S. I. B. [that] is, of course, inspired by the Police who all along have resented this encroachment as they consider it on their preserves'. While, he noted, the 'matter is undoubtedly aggravated by the personality of Major Folkes who has perhaps not been as tactful in his dealings as he might have been', there were mitigating factors: 'it is impossible for a man in his job to be popular with Government Departments'.[246]

Whatever the degree of institutional tensions and rivalries involved in the replacement of a military-led Bureau with a constabularised one, the fiasco that capped Folkes's tenure as head of security not only coloured impressions of the SIB experiment but also left a legacy of suspicion around the concept of a 'professional' surveillance apparatus outside police structures. This, as the next chapter indicates, meant that the ghost of the SIB haunted New Zealand's secret world for many years to come.

A much different wartime legacy, this time one that resonates into the present, was the effective integration of New Zealand's sigint operations into a powerful international Western network. The Dominion's sigint contribution to the war effort, it has been observed, could only have been significant 'within an Allied context', its 'very nature' and small size precluding any stand-alone capacity. The 'usefulness and strength' of New Zealand sigint, in short, arose from 'its practical application in cooperation with Anglo-American signals intelligence'.[247] The wartime sigint collaboration set the scene for profoundly far-reaching effects after it. Intelligence historian Nicky Hager put it this way:

> Historical ties, which made it inevitable that New Zealand's primary intelligence links would be with Britain (and thus Britain's primary ally, the United States), were reinforced by the necessity of working with these countries in the 1942–45 Pacific War . . . [Such] wartime relationships, which were built around systems for British–American cooperation, were cemented into a comprehensive and enduring post-war signals intelligence alliance in the growing cold war of the late 1940s.[248]

That Cold War, as we shall see, would have profound ramifications for both New Zealand's humint and sigint arrangements and operations, giving the country an enhanced geopolitical significance that impacted heavily within its secret world.

Wartime developments also had political ramifications. From one perspective, the alliance with Stalin's Soviet Union, epitomised in expressions of warmth towards 'Uncle Joe' and the flying of the USSR's hammer and sickle flag at official occasions, seems to be a clear and remarkable disruption of the long Cold War.[249] Nonetheless, Communism, spearheaded by the CPNZ and its fronts, remained a major security concern – one masked rather than defused by the Grand Alliance and the CPNZ's shift from opposition to support for New Zealand's war effort. One study goes so far as to conclude that within the Police there was 'almost a detectable disappointment when Germany's invasion of Russia brought the Communist Party on side'.[250] Some security reports depicted Communists as questionable allies, a view shared by the government. In October 1943, for example, SIB director Jim Cummings was briefed that the CPNZ's support for New Zealand's war effort was merely a Communist ploy, its seemingly patriotic stance no more than a cloak for efforts 'to effect a greater penetration of political, industrial and other spheres of activity'; and, more broadly, to assist the Soviet Union's international revolutionary agenda. Despite Elsie Locke's 'deceptive air of innocence [and] truly girlish expression', another report noted, she and her ilk had revealed their true colours by their talk of supporting the USSR's war aims rather than 'fighting for the BRITISH EMPIRE'.[251]

Another strand of historical continuity is reflected by the great amount of wartime material collected by the surveillers on actual, possible or potential Communists. This included two future heads of government departments (Sutch and Jack Lewin); future Labour attorney-general Dr Martyn Finlay; trade union leaders such as Jock Barnes (but no longer F. P. Walsh, now effectively Fraser's enforcer in the union movement); Members of Parliament considered unreliable, such as Lee; former Oxbridge scholars Ian Milner and Paddy Costello, suspected of being Soviet spies; activists who would later have prominent careers, such as author Dick Scott or cultural activist Rona Meek (later, Bailey); and large numbers of resisters against some or all of the government's war policies.[252] The wartime files provided, in other words, a firm foundation for Cold War surveillance.

Conclusion

The Second World War was a seminal event in the international history of the secret world. Faced with the momentous scale and stakes of the conflict, authorities harnessed their humint and sigint apparatuses to the struggle and developed them enormously in the process. The history of this side of the war effort ranges from the 'ultra-secret' work at Bletchley Park to decipher high-level enemy communications, through to the experiences of individual agents – including the Wellington-born Nancy Wake (the 'White Mouse'), who spied for the French Resistance before working for the British Special Operations Executive.[253]

Within New Zealand, wartime security intelligence fits within the longer effort to detect both enemy agents and internal elements that might act against the state's interests. Many of the targets of interest, the operations ordered and the procedures pursued similarly reflect this longer history. Developments such as the ambition to create a professional security agency beyond the Police, and much of the resulting jurisdictional jostling, likewise display older dynamics playing out in intensified circumstances.

More broadly, the contours of the alliance within which New Zealand's war and intelligence work was carried out also reflect a longer context. The country entered the conflict with a firm commitment to stand with Britain, and ensuing wartime circumstances brought greater levels of engagement with Australia and America as well. Within the work of security intelligence, these linkages were most clearly mirrored within sigint cooperation. In one sense, New Zealand's position within the larger wartime alliance with Stalin's Soviet Union appears to be a remarkable break from the hostility directed towards revolutionary organisations evinced since the nineteenth century and, more specifically, the anti-Communist attitudes which were apparent since 1917 and readily observable through the 1930s. In another sense, however, the long Cold War persisted within the Grand Alliance, continuing around and underneath enthusiastic public support for the Soviet war effort. Positive imagery lasted until the final days of the war in Europe; on 25 April 1945, for example, American and Soviet troops converged at the German town of Torgau on the Elbe River, and the image of troops fraternising brought forth much commentary on the post-war possibility of cooperation between East and West.

The history of the secret world reduces the sense of discontinuity between wartime alliance and ruptures in the post-war world. Within intelligence apparatuses, Communism remained a major security concern, and the alliance was one of necessity around a shared enemy. Adolf Hitler's suicide, five days after the friendly encounter on the Elbe, and Germany's formal surrender in early May, quickly altered the dynamics within the Grand Alliance. While post-war developments reflect decisions made at that time, they also represent a segue from the latent Cold War to the Cold War proper: in intelligence terms, the war years were a hinge between the former and the latter.

PART FIVE:

EARLY COLD WAR,

1945-1956

Chapter Seven:
Surveillance and Superpowers,
1945–1956

Introduction

Friction between Communist and Western powers had been subdued, although far from eliminated, within the Grand Alliance of the Second World War, but cooperation rapidly dissipated thereafter. Indeed, the levels of emergent suspicion and antagonism meant that open hostilities were considered to be a serious threat. Examined within a broader historical context, this development represented a new chapter in the long Cold War that dated back at least to the Bolshevik Revolution and its turbulent geopolitical aftermath. These tensions were soon openly labelled as the Cold War.

Within New Zealand, the political police continued their decades-old task of surveilling local Communists, potential or actual fellow travellers, and those suspected of being susceptible to Communist influence. A range of practices and prejudices inherited from the wartime emergency continued, and these could be ramped up if circumstances required, such as during industrial troubles (especially a momentous state confrontation with the watersiders and other unionists in 1951) or opposition to foreign policy.

This new era of domestic and international insecurity brought renewed attention to the structure of New Zealand's human intelligence apparatus, spurring moves for reform and expansion. In particular, the first decade of the post-war world saw ongoing efforts to reform state surveillance through the creation of a professional security agency independent of the Police. As with previous episodes, this ambition prompted both allies and opponents from inside and beyond the state into action. Meanwhile, although New Zealand's international ties remained principally with what was still generally called 'the Mother Country', it was rapidly being incorporated into an international security and intelligence system increasingly headed by the United States as well as Britain. This was most prominently (if, at the time, clandestinely) exemplified by New Zealand's membership of the Western signals intelligence pact that later became known as the Five Eyes.

Overview

By the end of the first decade of the post-war period, a series of developments had firmly entrenched Cold War divisions. In March 1946, Winston Churchill famously declared that an 'Iron Curtain' had descended to divide Western and Eastern Europe. In October 1947 the Comintern, which had been dissolved by Stalin in 1943, was in effect reconstituted as an organisation to further the Communist cause in Europe (the Cominform). In February 1948, fears of Soviet encroachment in Europe were fuelled by a Soviet-backed coup in Czechoslovakia. In April 1949, the North Atlantic Treaty Organization (NATO) was founded as a military alliance, primarily focused on security in Western Europe, later to be matched in May 1955 by the Soviet-led Warsaw Pact. In the wider world, independence movements and armed rebellions further fuelled fears that such instabilities would be exploited by Communists. In particular, the 1949 'fall of China' added a sense of proximity for New Zealand. In February 1950, Alister McIntosh, the head of the joint Prime Minister's and External Affairs Departments, opined that '[w]e haven't a hope in the world, in my view, of stopping the march of Communism in Asia'.[1]

New Zealand had some direct involvement in episodes of the escalating division between East and West, including a stand-off with Josip Broz Tito's partisans in Trieste and the provision of aircrews in the 1948–49 Berlin airlift.[2] More broadly, the country's defence planning operated with Cold War circumstances to the fore. Prominent among these were a September 1949 pledge to deploy troops to the Middle East in the event of hot war with the USSR; a successful referendum that year to (re)introduce compulsory military training; the signing of major collective security alliances in 1951 (ANZUS, a multilateral security agreement between Australia, New Zealand and the United States) and 1954 (the Manila Pact, establishing the South-East Asia Treaty Organization, or SEATO, to contain Communism in the region); and sending troops to Korea and Malaya as Cold War–linked conflicts broke out.[3]

Security intelligence represented a major front in early Cold War confrontations. Soviet espionage soon loomed as the subject of considerable concern for Western governments. In September 1945 Igor Gouzenko, a cypher clerk in the Soviet Embassy in Canada, defected and provided credible accounts of Soviet subversion and spying in the West.[4] Furthermore, the Venona project, a top-secret United States intelligence effort to decrypt Soviet communications which ran between 1943 and 1980, revealed extensive Soviet espionage networks in the West. Of most direct significance to New Zealand was the revelation that classified information was being leaked from within the Australian state bureaucracy.[5]

In such an atmosphere of fear and suspicion, the early Cold War saw many efforts to tighten national security in the West and, consequently, new developments in the structures and methods of security intelligence. The United States led the way with a reorganisation of its intelligence community, most notably with the establishment in 1947 of the Central Intelligence Agency (CIA), which both revived and enhanced many of the functions of the wartime Office of Strategic Services. Among other things, the Gouzenko and Venona revelations heightened American concerns about Britain's vulnerability to Soviet espionage through her Dominion intelligence partners. Australian vulnerability, in particular, was singled out by United States authorities, who noted that classified information shared with Australian officials, notably its Department of Foreign Affairs, was being transmitted through Soviet diplomatic channels. Accordingly, in June 1948 the Americans began restricting the transmission of classified information that could be shared with Australia until security improved.[6]

In response to such pressures, Britain sought to improve security in the Commonwealth. It was in this context that MI5's director-general, Sir Percy Sillitoe, visited Australia and New Zealand in early 1948. He was accompanied by intelligence officer Roger Hollis, who would later head MI5 (and eventually fall under suspicion of being a Soviet spy himself). In Australia, the Sillitoe delegation's high-level discussions, including with the prime minister, led to the foundation of the Australian Security Intelligence Organisation (ASIO) in March 1949. Modelled on MI5, ASIO was established to operate as a humint agency at the federal level and did not supplant political policing within the Australian states.[7] While it was created with spy-catching duties in mind, it inexorably took on a far broader counter-subversion mandate. Accordingly, the United States intelligence embargo was ended in early 1950. After further top-level deliberations, ASIO was followed in 1952 by the Australian Secret Intelligence Service (ASIS), which collected intelligence and conducted overseas operations on the model of MI6.

In Wellington, too, security discussions had focused on improving New Zealand's counter-espionage capability. As Sillitoe saw it, with the onset of the Cold War the Dominions 'had become a fruitful field for espionage'.[8] They, along with the colonies, were being strongly urged by the Mother Country to pay greater attention to monitoring and countering Soviet influence.[9] Such discussions informed efforts to reform New Zealand's security intelligence apparatus. However, as we outline below, any idea of founding an MI5-type arrangement met resistance. Instead, in late 1949, the political police within the New Zealand Police Force were centralised and formalised under the name Special Branch (SB). The Branch's tasks were essentially the same as those undertaken under the former arrangements, and hence similar to those assigned to its namesakes in the London Metropolitan Police and Australian states – as well as those of the domestic security services provided by MI5, ASIO, the Royal Canadian Mounted Police (and other Canadian police services), and the Federal Bureau of Investigation in the United States. It was expected that, as a separate unit inside the Police, the political detection service would undertake professional development to meet the requirements expected for intelligence-sharing with the British and the Americans.[10]

Whether SB represented an adequate defence of the state and its interests was an open question in some quarters. In February 1950 Carl Berendsen, New Zealand's ambassador to the United States, privately noted that he was 'immensely impressed' by the 'menace' of Soviet espionage and particularly the 'atomic spies': 'Now there are many who laugh at this sort of apprehension, but nobody can laugh at the Canadian spy revelations, nobody can laugh at the [Alan Nunn] May case, nobody can laugh at [several American espionage cases] and nobody can laugh at the [Klaus] Fuchs case.' He was 'far from confident that we are not ourselves victims of the same sort of thing'.[11] The following month he warned his minister that the 'aggressors of the Kremlin have at their disposal a fifth column – a Trojan horse – in every country in the world'.[12]

Such apprehensions focused on the Soviet diplomatic mission, a 1954 security assessment noting the 'post-war Soviet tendency to direct the greater part of their espionage activities through their diplomatic outposts'.[13] The mission in New Zealand had been established after formal relations were opened with the USSR in 1944 in the context of wartime cooperation and under pressure from the British. In 1946 the Soviet Legation moved into a compound on Messines Road, in the Wellington suburb of Karori, a property that had formerly served as the United States Legation. Soon after the National Party entered office in late 1949, the government closed the New Zealand Legation in Moscow, but the USSR elected to retain its presence in Wellington.

The next five years saw a stream of high-profiled allegations about and revelations of Soviet espionage in the West. In 1951, for example, British spies Guy Burgess and Donald Maclean defected to the USSR, and in 1953 Julius and Ethel Rosenberg were executed on charges of espionage in the United States. Australasian anxieties were particularly quickened with the 'Petrov affair', in April 1954, when the Third Secretary of the Soviet Embassy in Canberra, Vladimir Petrov, defected. A colonel in the newly renamed Soviet secret police (Committee for State Security, or KGB), he had been in charge of recruiting and managing spies in Australia. His wife Evdokia, also employed in Soviet intelligence, was held inside the Soviet Embassy in Canberra for a fortnight. When she was then taken to Sydney airport, a photograph of her minders 'escorting' her forcefully across the tarmac captured the scene dramatically. On prime ministerial intervention, the plane was boarded by ASIO officers at Darwin, and a second defection deal followed.[14] In exchange for asylum, the Petrovs provided a great amount of information on Soviet espionage. This included claims that 'the Soviet has some very good agents in New Zealand' and possessed a contact within the Prime Minister's Department.[15]

Two New Zealanders, Ian Milner and Walter (Wally) Clayton, were subsequently named as involved in the Soviet espionage network in Australia. The son of an ironmonger and noted for his soap-box oratory, Clayton migrated to Melbourne in 1930, joined the Communist Party of Australia and became involved in its clandestine activities. By contrast, Milner was a Rhodes Scholar from a 'respected' family who had lectured in political science at the University of Melbourne before joining the Australian

Department of External Affairs in 1944. ASIO investigations, including information from the Petrovs and Venona decryptions, pointed to Clayton being the spymaster code named 'Klod', and Milner was believed to be the agent 'Bur' who had passed classified documents during 1945 and 1946.[16]

Within New Zealand, one consequence of increasing suspicions was a greater vigilance over public servants who might have access to potentially sensitive information. This process accelerated in line with the Labour government's increasingly anti-Communist line.[17] Several studies have described the result as a milder form of 'McCarthyism', after the American senator Joseph McCarthy's demagogic accusations of disloyalty, with all their collateral damage on careers and personal lives.[18]

The year 1948 alone contains several examples. The first involves George Fraser, a former Communist who had co-founded New Zealand's Fabian Society with Jack Lewin. Fraser was employed in the Information Section of the Prime Minister's Department. His problems began when he published a Fabian pamphlet criticising American foreign policy and calling for a 'third force' to be established to counteract the influence of the two emerging superpowers. This had been ill received by the United States ambassador and embarrassed the prime minister, who was also the minister of external affairs. Fraser resisted transfer to 'the Public Service "Siberia"' but, after a number of incidents, was eventually pressured to move on to a less political department. Here, his isolation, and the atmosphere of distrust that had been generated, drove him to resign from government employment in 1949.[19]

In the second case, Gil Deynzer, a technician in the Department of Scientific and Industrial Research, a man who had worked on a secret wartime radar programme, was compulsorily transferred from his position when he refused to answer questions as to whether he held Communist affiliations. When he challenged this action, the Court of Appeal upheld the decision, noting that security procedures were necessary to maintain national credibility in intelligence-sharing arrangements.[20] The case should also be contextualised within the post-war preoccupation with 'defence security', which included New Zealand scientists and other experts who worked in coordination with overseas organisations with security implications, most notably the British Defence Scientific Advisory Committee and the Commonwealth Advisory Committee on Defence Science.[21]

Finally, in November 1948, a political scandal (dubbed the 'satchel snatch') broke out around Cecil Holmes, a documentary film-maker within the National Film Unit. Material identifying Holmes as a Communist Party member and indicating his involvement in militant union activity was stolen from his satchel in a work car outside Parliament by prime ministerial press officer Charlie Williams, who had observed him going inside to Friday-evening drinks with George Fraser's Fabian circle. The stolen documents made their way to F. P. Walsh, now in charge of post-war stabilisation policies. After pressure from Walsh, Acting Prime Minister Walter Nash leaked them to the media. They included a letter Holmes had sent to Public Service Association (PSA) president Jack Lewin, a man who himself had been under surveillance for some considerable time. As George Fraser put it, Walsh was 'out to destroy' Lewin's influence by portraying him as a tool of the CPNZ. 'PSA Hand in Glove with Commos!' thundered a *Truth* headline. Holmes was suspended from his position and, while legal action subsequently reinstated him, he left for Australia – and New Zealand lost a man of great talent.[22]

Efforts to root out Communists or fellow travellers in government service continued under the First National Government, elected in late 1949. The PSA, which retained some of the assertiveness it had acquired under Lewin, was increasingly concerned at such trends. In 1954, for example, it passed a resolution 'express[ing] alarm at the methods adopted by the secret police in investigating and reporting on public servants'.[23] All the same, popular unease at such developments tended to be intermittent because vetting assessments remained under the public radar. People whose careers suffered could generally only guess at the reasons they had missed out on a job or why their promotion prospects languished.

Fears of Communist penetration of state machinery were replicated in regard to trade unions, especially as industrial relations became a site of rising tension. In 1949, for example, the government responded to a go-slow campaign by the Carpenters' Union (in which Communists had a presence but not control) by withholding social security benefits. At the same time, the Federation of Labour, which was aligned with the government, deregistered the union.

A far more extensive clash occurred on the waterfront in 1951. That January, the Arbitration Court opted for a general wage rise of 15 per cent, something which both the Federation of Labour and the more militant Trade Union Congress (TUC, founded in 1950) found unsatisfactory. Negotiations over wages between port employers and the Waterside Workers' Union's own wage court also met difficulties. On 14 February the Union imposed an overtime ban, and the employers responded with threats to dismiss workers refusing extra hours and to replace them with men who agreed to work overtime. When negotiations stalled, the employers declared a lockout on 19 February.

The government, echoing 1913, was determined to face off against militant unionism, with Prime Minister Sidney Holland making a habit of painting industrial disputes in Cold War hues. Months earlier he had declared in Parliament that '[i]n the opinion of the Government the present hold-up is part and parcel of the "cold war" being waged throughout the world and must be treated on that basis'.[24] As arbitration stalled, Holland declared that anyone limiting the handling of goods was 'a traitor, and should be treated accordingly'.[25] The minister of labour would soon similarly seek to differentiate between 'honest trade unionists and those people who insidiously undermine the trade union movement', and stated that the 'brow beating Communist-serving agitator will be crushed'.[26]

On 21 February, with the nation's wharves at a complete standstill, Prime Minister Holland, 'fresh from a Cabinet meeting with United States Secretary of State John Foster Dulles',[27] invoked the Public Safety Conservation Act to declare a state of emergency. The Waterfront Strike Emergency Regulations, gazetted the day after the declaration, redefined refusal to do overtime as striking, and prohibited anyone from aiding or abetting a strike (which would include, infamously, providing food to the hungry families of locked-out workers); they also, among other measures, imposed 'more or less total' censorship upon the Union.[28] Police were empowered to enter premises where officers or NCOs believed a breach of the regulations had been or was 'about to be committed', and before long the military were employed on the wharves to load and unload ships. As the 'wharfies' were joined by other militant unions (eventually 22,000 workers downed tools), and members of the public defied the regulations to aid their cause, repressive measures escalated. Police were directed, for example, to proactively suppress agitation by preventing CPNZ members addressing workplace meetings.[29] The emergency regulations remained in effect over the 151 days of the dispute.

While the Public Service and trade unions were focal points for fears of Communist encroachment, comparable notions became pervasive across wider society. One study of the rise of a Cold War consciousness in New Zealand notes how international episodes were repeatedly seen as part of a broad threat that extended to the country.[30] NZ *Truth* declared in December 1948, amidst reports of Soviet espionage, that '[t]he creeping insidious blight of Communism can be as great a menace in New Zealand as in other parts of the world. It *can* happen here.'[31] Around the same time, Prime Minister Fraser was voicing similar sentiments in Parliament: 'the Government would be deceiving itself and the country if it shut its eyes to the fact that there was a Communist menace in New Zealand, as well as in other countries'.[32] Public fear of association with Communism extended to one citizen fretting over being asked to act as a witness for the passport application of 'an avowed Communist' neighbour, only doing so after a passports officer promised that he would explain the circumstances should inquiries arise.[33] Such anxieties were heightened as the nuclear arms race escalated following the USSR's successful testing of a nuclear bomb in August 1949.

Buttressing spontaneous anti-Communist sentiments, the state took proactive efforts to hamper Communist influence, establishing means of working with newspaper editors, broadcasting officials, anti-Communist trade union leaders, and the Returned Servicemen's Association and other institutions and organisations for the purposes of propagating anti-Communist material. In 1951, Minister John Marshall privately noted that this work was spearheaded by the government's Publicity Division (dubbed the 'stink factory' by its critics), which had been distributing such material 'for some considerable time'. He added he was 'encouraging and extending this work – it is most effective when it is least obvious'.[34]

This exercise was linked with Britain's Information Research Department, established in 1948, which recruited intellectuals, journalists and writers to produce material intended 'to counter Soviet propaganda in the British labour movement' and to spread 'unattributable information' (including disinformation) globally. The United States also sought to covertly influence political and cultural trends by sponsoring select figures in the world of arts and letters.[35] New Zealand's director of publicity, Sid Odell, distributed Information Research Department propaganda widely throughout society, including to universities and trade unions, along with much material emanating from official United States propaganda outlets.[36] Spin from overseas was complemented by leaks from the security police to 'friendly' outlets such as (and especially) *NZ Truth*, specialising as it did in 'red-baiting' sensationalism, and by gagging orders to prevent publication on specific issues.[37]

The media's role as Cold Warriors strengthened in 1952 after a Commonwealth-wide Defence notice ('D-notice') system was implemented following a proposal by British prime minister Winston Churchill the previous year.[38] Under Prime Minister Holland's imprimatur, an Armed Services and Press Committee comprising departmental, military, broadcasting and newspaper members met regularly from September 1952. It selected issues 'for which publicity was undesirable', including some suggested by the United Kingdom. After two years of operation, the Committee folded after it had been exposed to ridicule for D-notices attempting to stop information about an already publicised plan to produce 'heavy water' at Wairakei for the British nuclear programme; it had quickly moved a long way from its initial conception as a systematic way of gagging the publication of classified information, such as the movements of defectors or submarines.[39]

The first decade of the post-war world was a seminal period for Communism, internationally and in New Zealand. In 1945 the CPNZ enjoyed a degree of prestige for its wartime efforts and its association with the Red Army in smashing Nazism. The Party's membership approached 2000 and its newspaper held a circulation of 14,000.[40] This, however, turned out to be its high-water mark; and a decade later, leading Party member Jack Locke and academic Wolfgang Rosenberg agreed between themselves that there were no more than 500 members at that time.[41] Furthermore, cracks were appearing within international Communism, belying prevalent notions of a Communist monolith.[42] Notable fault lines included Yugoslav and (increasingly) Chinese relations with the USSR, and there was disquiet within Western Communism at the bloody Soviet suppression of the Czechoslovakian and East Berlin uprisings of 1953. In 1956 such cracks widened significantly as Nikita Khrushchev denounced Stalin (who had died in 1953) and then ordered the brutal suppression of a momentous uprising in Hungary. In retrospect, these events – covered in our following volume – marked the definitive beginning of a fragmentation of global Communism which continued across the following decades and resonated increasingly within New Zealand Communism.

Agencies

Immediately after the war, New Zealand's tradition of an exclusively police-based human intelligence system was fully restored. On 3 September 1945, the Security Intelligence Bureau was officially disbanded and 'such of its functions, principally security intelligence, as were still current, were assumed by the Police Department as part of the ordinary duties of that Department'.[43] As before, however, these duties lay principally not in 'ordinary' policing but with political detectives who reported to the officers in charge of detective offices, part of a chain of command which went up to the Commissioner in his capacity as Director of Security.[44]

It has been generally assumed that this intelligence capacity remained largely fallow until 1948, a year of escalating Cold War tensions.[45] But the release of personal and other files casts doubt on this and indicates instead that political policing continued much as before. For example, on 6 March 1946, the day after Churchill's 'Iron Curtain' speech, a secret report from the Auckland Detective Office was sent on by the Commissioner to the prime minister. Based on report 277 from informant 'U', this provided detailed lists of delegates to the CPNZ's National Committee and identified those who had been elected to office-holding positions. The informant gave detailed accounts of debates and disputes, and outlined his discussion in a pub with the vituperative CPNZ chairman Alex Drennan ('I, of course agreed with him.'). Follow-ups to this report included the compilation of Subversive History Sheets on listed people who had sufficient traces to qualify as suspected subversives.[46] Also in 1946, when the management committee of the capital's Co-operative Book Society met, its minutes found their way into the secret files. They recorded office-holders and book selectors, and the committee's congratulations to Wolfgang Rosenberg on his appointment to an economics lectureship at Canterbury University College. These minutes became part of the record held on Rosenberg until his death some six decades later and, indeed, beyond.[47] Rosenberg, who called himself a 'Marxist with a small m', never joined the CPNZ; he was not to attain professorial status, despite his eminence in his field.[48]

By 1948, the combination of escalating threat perceptions and New Zealand's increasing integration into the Western intelligence network had prompted deliberation in official circles as to whether police-led security intelligence was the best option to cope with the demands of the Cold War. One key public servant moving towards support for a new stand-alone service was the strongly anti-Communist Foss Shanahan, whose nickname 'Foss the Boss' reflected his control of access to Prime Minister Fraser and his Cabinet. However, the concept also stirred opposition. A memorandum written within the Prime Minister's Department, likely by Alister McIntosh and dated 2 March, evoked the SIB as setting a regrettable precedent:

It had not been appreciated when the Bureau was established that a considerable portion of the duties it would undertake were substantially being discharged by the Police [Force]. Furthermore, experience of <u>this para-military</u> organisation indicated that personnel recruited on a military basis were not suitable to undertake duties of this kind in New Zealand.

The memorandum advised Fraser that the Police should retain humint as a matter of principle: 'Civil security is primarily a function of the Police [Force], which is organised to undertake duties of this kind, has personnel skilled in detection and interrogation and, to a degree also, appreciation of intelligence.'[49] One account by an author who consulted McIntosh states that Shanahan ran the stand-alone option past Prime Minister Fraser, who 'shuddered at the idea of another British requested security service', recalling the embarrassment of the Folkes fiasco.[50]

The matter was soon given further consideration once Sillitoe and Hollis had arrived in New Zealand on 19 March. Sillitoe was not asked for specific recommendations, and nor were the pair (according to Shanahan, present at the discussions) 'in any position to comment in any detail on the organisation established in New Zealand to deal with questions affecting the security of the State'. Various options for improvement were canvassed with senior officials. An internal NZSIS history records that Sillitoe 'appears to have favoured the formation of a Special Branch within the Police'.[51] His high-level career in policing before he was appointed to head MI5 in 1946 may have influenced this option.

In effect, the New Zealand government forestalled any ambitions for a stand-alone security organisation by opting for Sillitoe's recommendation for 'the establishment of a small Special Branch' within the Police Force.[52] This would gather together, into a unified body, the various political policing operations within the detective offices, a British Special Branch model. The resulting New Zealand Special Branch was conceived as representing a third division of the Police Force, alongside the Uniform Branch and the Detective Branch (renamed the Criminal Investigation Branch from 1950). There was little urgency in setting it up and, when its foundation was announced in an internal 29 December 1949 memorandum by Commissioner Jim Cummings, the change was rather downplayed as an alignment of terminology within Australasian police forces to match that of Britain's Special Branch: 'At the Conference of Commissioners of Police held at Melbourne last month it was unanimously decided that with a view to uniformity each Section of Police dealing with subversive organisations will be designated the "Special Branch".'[53]

Senior Detective Jim Nalder, who had effectively run the SIB in the latter stages of the war and remained the senior intelligence expert after it, was appointed to head SB.[54] He was appropriately elevated to commissioned rank when he became a Sub-Inspector, in May 1950, and was quickly promoted to Inspector the following March during the waterfront dispute. In districts distant from SB offices, members of uniformed or detective staff were, in a continuation of past arrangements, assigned to security work as required.[55] For some time SB's Wellington headquarters were based in Stout Street before they were relocated to a discreet building in Wellington's Majoribanks Street in 1953.

A working paper provides a breakdown of the roles and placement of SB staff in 1954:

> (a) Headquarters staff of 13 persons under the control of a Senior Detective.
> (b) Auckland District staff of 8 persons under the control of a Senior Detective.
> (c) Wellington District staff of 7 persons under the direction of a Detective Sergeant.
> (d) Christchurch District staff of 6 persons under the control of a Senior Detective.
> (e) One Detective Sergeant at Dunedin employed full time on Special Branch work.
> (f) One Acting Detective at Hamilton employed practically full-time on Special Branch work.

The total SB complement of 36 comprised, in addition to the Sub-Inspector in overall charge, four Senior Detectives, five Detective Sergeants, a Sergeant, two Detectives, 10 Acting Detectives, five Constables, and eight civilians (six of whom were typists).[56]

As McIntosh and others had sought, SB was effectively a formalisation and centralisation of New Zealand's political policing in order to meet deepening Cold War concerns. Its core functions followed historical lines of surveilling radical politics and activity, now almost exclusively identified in terms of Communist encroachment. A 1951 report defining the 'Main Functions of Special Branch' noted four major objectives:

> a) Study of International Communism
> b) Study of New Zealand Communist Party and 'Front Organisations.'
> c) Evaluation of security risks (personnel) arising from screening.
> d) Co-ordination and evaluation of all reports received from agents.[57]

In April 1950, J. Bruce Young had become Police Commissioner. Having spent most of his working life as a detective, he was well attuned to the results that could be obtained from covertly gathering information and analysing it. This, and his general policing style – conciliatory rather than confrontational – helped him avoid extreme violence during the waterfront dispute, despite the government's hard line on strikers.

He did not enrol Special Constables, who had added extra tensions to past politico-industrial confrontations, even though thousands volunteered. He also discouraged excessive police use of repressive legislation on such issues as seditious utterance and the more draconian emergency regulations.

His approach recognised the efficacy of intelligence. He dispatched, for example, a memo to all districts that was not dissimilar to those made by his predecessors in times of socio-political turbulence. All were to forward lists of local CPNZ members including, where known, their business and private addresses and their ranks in the Party. Supplementary lists of additions and amendments were to be supplied on a monthly basis. In a reflection of very real fears that the Cold War might turn hot, police were also to investigate and report on non-Party members 'who would be likely to follow the Party "line" in the event of New Zealand being involved in a war which was not approved by the Communist Party'. Additionally, districts were to provide information for a 'censorship watchlist' of mailing addresses used by the CPNZ and its suspected front organisations.[58]

Young's success in preventing widespread disorder and violence during the 1951 confrontation owed a considerable amount to knowledge of how to best utilise 'systematic surveillance', including extensive use of informants.[59] As the government hardened its line after it became clear that the Federation of Labour would oppose the strategy of the militant unions, he responded to pressure. He ordered that 'everything possible' should be done to stop meetings being 'addressed by strike agitators and members of the Communist Party'.[60] Special Branch members were ordered to work alongside Post and Telegraph staff to undertake '[s]pecial monitoring in connection with illegal broadcasts', effectively shutting them down.[61] SB also leaked information to waterside and other union leaders that was intended to avert violence that would have damaged both sides' interests.[62] Such practices relied to a significant degree on in-depth surveillance within militant labour.

While the establishment of Special Branch represented the continuation of police-centred intelligence, the next few years also constituted its swan song. In late 1949 the general election put a National government into office, and this empowered a number of senior figures interested in reforming security. These included top defence planners, who urged the government to 'strengthen counter-espionage action' and to establish 'an effective security agency'.[63] Shanahan, who served as deputy secretary of External Affairs, secretary of the Cabinet, secretary of the Chiefs of Staff Committee and the working head of the Prime Minister's Department, remained a formidable advocate. Moreover, Alister McIntosh had shifted from scepticism to support. According to several accounts, the liberally inclined 'Mac' felt that police targeting of leftist public servants had been excessive, and that placing security onto a more 'professional' footing might help address this.[64] Elements of the National government were already predisposed to support the idea of a stand-alone agency, following the preference of some leading British authorities (although not Sillitoe) and the logic of the Cold War.

Further support was sought from allied security agencies. In June 1951, during the waterfront dispute, Defence Minister T. L. MacDonald met Sir Percy Sillitoe in London and discussed the situation. By Sillitoe's account, MacDonald noted that Cabinet members 'were not satisfied with the Special Branch and the security work of the New Zealand Police [and] considered that the Police had a good deal to learn about the methods of watching and penetrating Communist organisations'.[65] Sillitoe's record shows that he advised 'against setting up an independent security organisation like the A.S.I.O. in Australia and recommended instead the strengthening and further instruction of the Special Branch'. He offered to visit New Zealand or send an MI5 officer to provide further advice. Sillitoe minuted that MacDonald had thanked him for the offer, explaining that he and the prime minister 'were anxious to bring about the reform they wanted with as little fuss and publicity as possible and in particular they did not want to offend or irritate their Police Commissioner, Mr. Bruce Young'.[66]

The offer of a visit was quickly accepted, with Holland writing to British prime minister Clement Attlee that '[o]ur security service is still in process of development, and it would be very helpful to us if arrangements could be made for Sir Percy to visit New Zealand'.[67] On 5 October 1951 Sillitoe left London, ostensibly (as notes describing his plans put it) for 'a brief visit to enable him to renew his contacts with the Security authorities in New Zealand'.[68]

On 23 October he submitted a report to the New Zealand government detailing his assessment of Special Branch. The major recommendations revolved around a judgement that SB personnel lacked specialist training, especially in counter-espionage, that the Branch was short of resources, and that it was not sufficiently integrated into the 'national defence machine'. These recommendations potentially also possess a political dimension, namely the government's wish to keep on side with the Police Commissioner – the report explicitly stated that security concerns could be addressed by *internal* reform, assisted by MI5 training: 'New Zealand would be better served by the reinforcement of the Special Branch . . . than by the establishment of an independent body.' He believed that such a body, whose head, like the Police Commissioner, would need direct access to the political executive, would be problematic in a country with New Zealand's values of openness. It was part of the national ethos that policing was free from any great executive direction, in the hands of a force with a 'deservedly high reputation as the custodians of law and order'. An independent secret service reporting directly to the political executive might give the impression of political interference in the private lives of citizens, and indeed could 'rapidly acquire the reputation of a Gestapo'.[69]

Other Sillitoe recommendations, however, indicated that he wanted the recalibrated SB to be, in effect, a secret service, albeit still nestled within the NZPF and thereby using the good reputation (as a rule) of the Police as a cover for its political surveillance. While the Police Commissioner would continue reporting to his own minister, the SB head would also have direct access to the prime minister, who would give him 'directions'. The new head of security would also join the Commissioner, senior bureaucrats and military heads in advising on national security issues, fitting into an intelligence assessment structure that had already been established. There were some safeguards to protect the citizenry in Sillitoe's report: prime ministerial directions to the new-look SB should be notified to the Commissioner, with the implication that he could query their wisdom if necessary, and the military's domestic security responsibilities would be 'strictly limited to the protection of Service establishments and installations'.[70]

All the signs point to the advice contained in Sillitoe's report being a fait accompli. The report, produced within a week, accepted SB's assessments on the Communist threatscape and its handling, and Holland had discussed its final shape with Sillitoe the day before its production.[71] It has been recounted that, like Fraser before him, the prime minister keenly remembered the ignominious downfall of Folkes, with all its ramifications for both state security and governmental credibility. A 'source who knew some of the circumstances', moreover, believed that by now that the prime minister had gained a sense of undue British influence within ASIO – a not unreasonable perception.[72]

A less charitable (or supplementary) explanation is lodged in the American State Department's files. This assesses Holland as exhibiting 'weak leadership', displaying an 'inability to make firm decisions with sufficient promptitude [or] to assume or delegate responsibility with adequate force or decisiveness'. One implication might be that revamping the existing surveillance model was the easiest path to take and getting the imprimatur of MI5 would dampen disquiet among New Zealand's closest allies. In other words, a compromise.[73]

Sillitoe reported home that the New Zealand government had fully accepted his report and had thanked him for 'the successful outcome of his visit'. In turn, on 5 November, Prime Minister Holland notified Sillitoe that not only had the government already accepted his report's recommendations but action was also being taken to implement them.[74] Such reforms were further discussed at top-secret meetings held by the Advisory Committee on Security in late 1951 and early 1952.[75] In effect an interdepartmental review of the country's security requirements, these gatherings were chaired by Shanahan in his role as secretary of the Cabinet. Other attendees included Inspector Jim Nalder and Colonel Herbert 'Bill' Gilbert (as representatives of the NZPF and military intelligence respectively), McIntosh, Dr Reuel Lochore (who had been placed in charge of security in the Prime Minister's Department in 1949) and representatives of British security. These included MI5's Michael Serpell, who had accompanied Sillitoe on his mission and stayed behind to assist in implementing the report's recommendations.[76]

By 1952, then, SB appeared to have secured its institutional footing against those angling for establishing a new security service. Subsequent scandals, however, would see SB stumble, providing further impetus for a reconstitution of security surveillance in New Zealand. Having often been absent on sick leave in 1952, Police Commissioner Young died in office that December. Eric Compton, who had just jumped some three dozen seniors in the force to gain the new position of Assistant Commissioner, succeeded to the commissionership, a decision confirmed in March 1953. Compton's rapid elevation had come 'seemingly out of nowhere', though some linked it to his membership of the same evangelical Christian sect as the minister. Certainly, Young had disapproved of this meteoric rise and especially his elevation to second in command of the Force.[77] Although he encouraged specialisation within the Force, insiders felt that Compton did not fully appreciate the needs of his surveilling staff.

As noted, women were being sworn in as constables from 1941. While they could not be detectives, some were deployed on ancillary work in SB – stenography, filing, general office duties – and they might also sometimes be asked to carry out surveillance in appropriate circumstances. When uniforms were being introduced for woman police officers in late 1952, SB's Cybil Carey modelled them for the commissioned officers: but she was not allowed to pose for publicity photographs since her identity as a policewoman was never made public because of her work for Special Branch.[78] Despite their usefulness in SB, Compton ordered its policewomen to return to the beat, a matter which 'caused quiet consternation in security circles'.[79] Even the rapid promotion of Nalder to Assistant Commissioner in March 1953 (he had become a Superintendent only the previous November) led to few benefits for SB, which was left in the hands of a senior NCO.

Some six months after his appointment was confirmed, the new Commissioner would face considerable public disquiet over security issues. Before Young died, he had confided in Bob McCormick, who worked on the mass-circulation NZ Truth, about his suspicions that Compton was orchestrating corruption inside the Force. The journalist's subsequent investigations centred on corrupt practices within the detective service. At the end of September 1953 NZ Truth 'unleashed a blistering attack on police leadership', publishing the first in a series of articles in which, among other things, Compton was accused of misusing Special Branch powers and resources.[80]

A major allegation was that SB Detective J. S. (Stan) Wrigley had set up a pair of 12-metre masts and a very high-frequency (VHF) aerial at Compton's private residence in the Wellington suburb of Khandallah, connecting them to a hidden monitor in his house. Another accusation was that the Commissioner had been involved in phone tapping. When the government issued 'categorical' denials of NZ Truth's allegations, the tabloid displayed, in a front-page feature, pictures of phone-tapping equipment. Its stories were informed by leaks from Wrigley, who had signed an affidavit 'confirming illegal bugging of private telephones', smuggled the equipment out of SB headquarters for photographing, and already been promised a job at the paper.[81] Intrigue and uncertainty surrounded the claims. While 'wilful interference' of telecommunications, for example, was illegal under the 1928 Post and Telegraph Act, a 1948 amendment had added the stipulation 'without the authority of the Minister', implying some margin within which lawful interference could occur.[82]

All the same, there was much political fallout from the revelations and the recriminations that followed them; in October 1953 a commission of inquiry was announced. This was scarcely designed to get to the bottom of the most serious allegations: the terms of reference were deliberately narrow, and the prime minister 'warned the press that the activities of Special Branch were out of bounds at the inquiry'.[83] Moreover, the inquiry – conducted by Sir Robert Kennedy – was further restricted by there being no immunity from prosecution offered to witnesses who 'pimped', as the prime minister put it.[84] Despite the government's (and Kennedy's) attempts to take the focus off security matters during the hearings, Wrigley testified that Compton had personally given him eavesdropping equipment, adding 'I may require you to use it'.[85]

Kennedy's final report emerged in November 1954 and it was, not unpredictably, anodyne where it was not obfuscatory. While Compton had authorised tapping of Wellington bookmakers' phones in 1944, any such practices were said to have ceased in 1948 when it became clearly illegal without securing high-level permission.[86] Kennedy accepted the official story that the radio installations at Compton's property had been mounted to monitor police car radios (since 1946 the Police had been developing internal radio communications systems) and improve the Commissioner's access to overseas religious broadcasts. The official police historian for this period finds this, understandably, implausible. She offers alternative explanations which are, essentially, related to security surveillance. On 1 April 1953 the Force had established a VHF radio station on Wellington's Wright's Hill, where the military also operated. The Khandallah installations were most likely to be backup for this station, which was used for security surveillance as well as the base for internal police radio communications. It is plausible that the stations may have been monitoring both the Soviet Legation, near Wright's Hill, and suburban leftists who held radio licences.[87]

While the Kennedy Commission's findings did not reveal any smoking gun, neither did they clear the air. With SB's activities out of range of the inquiry, its involvement in intercepting phone calls remained obscure and under a cloud. Compton's position, moreover, was now fully compromised. Among the report's critics, NZ *Truth* railed against its 'white enamelled certificate of fitness for the police' and campaigned for the Force to be cleaned up. After a narrow electoral victory that year, Holland took the Police portfolio and played for time by appointing a three-man Police Commission (including Assistant Commissioners Nalder and Peter Munro) to run the Force for six months, although to the disquiet of most observers it was to be chaired by Compton.[88] Further pressure came from within the Force itself. In January 1955 almost all commissioned officers in the country tried to pass a motion of no confidence in Compton. After he had refused, as chair of the Police Commission, to accept the motion, the officers took their concerns straight to the prime minister. Clearly, Compton's retention of his position was no longer politically tenable, but he clung on. Finally, in April 1955, under enormous pressure he elected to take voluntary retirement on exceedingly generous terms that provoked much public backlash and the coining of the word 'Comptonsation'.[89]

The new police chief was the widely respected Secretary of Justice Samuel Barnett. This appointment, and the fact that Barnett was titled Controller-General rather than Commissioner, were firm indications that the government was seeking to clean up a tarnished Force. Barnett's 'passion for excellence' led to thorough reform of recruiting and training. He was assisted by senior education official D. G. Ball, whose review of quality and training was followed by his appointment as the first Director of Police Training. Among the new measures was the provision of an elite cadet intake aimed at enticing better-educated school leavers. By the time a new training school opened in Trentham in February 1956, however, the sun was fast setting on Special Branch.[90]

Although its operations had been off limits to Kennedy's commission of inquiry, SB had become entangled in major allegations against Compton. When Prime Minister Holland tasked Barnett with reviewing and, where necessary, reforming the Force, he had specifically singled out the political detectives for special attention. The investigations into the Branch were supplemented by consultation with British security authorities during his travel to Britain in the latter part of 1955. His 'elementary investigation' had convinced him that SB 'was not fulfilling its functions satisfactorily' and needed to be reconstituted.[91] A draft 'Directive on Constitution and Operation of the New Zealand Security Service' was prepared in December 1955, seemingly with strong endorsement from Lochore. It was clearly influenced by Sillitoe's 1951 recommendation, envisioning that security intelligence should continue to sit within the Police – a Force that Barnett was now in the process of modernising. While Sillitoe had retired in 1953, some of his reasons for rejecting a fully stand-alone agency still held resonance: among other things, 'the reassurance of the public'.[92]

Barnett submitted his full report on Special Branch to the prime minister on 13 March 1956. He had found its record gravely wanting compared to fellow institutions overseas. On his trip to Britain he had 'spent a deal of time' meeting MI5's leaders and examining how their service was constituted and operated. By contrast, SB was burdened by an accumulation of police-oriented policy decisions, to the detriment of customised surveillance practices. He wrote that '[i]n general terms the defects of our security service are these':

1. The Branch is leaderless.
2. It has no charter or, as the modern phrase has it, no directive.

3. It has not the personnel to cope with its real functions.

4. It is burdened with work it should not be asked to undertake.

5. It has not the "aids" of a modern security service and, if it did have them, it might be politically inexpedient, and in practice almost impossible, to operate some of them.[93]

The final point alluded to what was increasingly being discussed in policing quarters: the appropriateness of nestling secret surveillance within a rules- and consent-based policing system.

The 13 March report signalled the exhaustion of any support for SB in its current form. However, major questions remained over what would replace it. Barnett recommended a 'reconstituted' Special Branch which would be more professional and technically skilled and which would remain under the control of the head of the Police. As a former head of the country's judicial system and a man with a reputation as a progressive reformer, Barnett was loath to give the security service full autonomy; keeping it under the NZPF structure would provide a necessary degree of regulatory and judicial oversight. However, he also recommended that the new organisation should be far more firmly delineated from the uniform and detective police, removing any working connection with other policing activities. Barnett's recommendations, then, amounted essentially to a halfway house between full police control and full autonomy.

A few days after he received Barnett's report, Prime Minister Holland wrote to Attorney-General John Marshall seeking advice. While he agreed about the poor state of SB, he thought the proposals 'somewhat empty and nebulous' and invited Marshall's views.[94] In an undated reply Marshall recommended a totally reorganised 'Security Service' that would essentially be fully independent of regular policing, wherever it sat administratively. Its director would recruit highly intelligent and educated men who would undergo training in Australia. This would include the use of 'technical aids which are available for the detections [sic] & securing of information' – an issue that the attorney-general wanted to discuss further, clearly not wishing to be on record as supporting illegal information-gathering methods. The new service should be headed by 'a suitable man from England'.[95] In his memoirs, Marshall reflected on his vision for a new organisation: 'The service should be neither seen, nor heard, nor publicly identified. Its expenditure should be buried in the Justice Department estimates. The staff should be highly qualified, and academically trained, and before being appointed they should be subjected to rigorous investigation as to their integrity, loyalty, reliability and judgment.'[96]

Under ministerial direction, officials drafted another 'Directive on Constitution and Operation of the New Zealand Security Service', and Holland ran this past Marshall on 18 May 1956. The document displayed the evolution in official and ministerial thinking about how to constitute the country's surveilling system. While the Controller-General of Police would hold general supervision over the organisation, the new Security Service would be 'one arm of the National Defence Forces'. All the same, it still fell within the purview of the head of the Police Force. But, as was clearly envisaged, Barnett would be able to delegate 'executive responsibility' to the head of the security service. Any such delegation of power, however, would require Holland's approval and, implicitly, the appointee would have a close relationship with the prime minister.[97] By 27 May the prime minister had given 'general approval' to the directive and authorised preliminary work to proceed.[98]

Towards the end of May 1956, then, a degree of ambiguity remained around what relationship a new security service would have with the Police, and over the next few months this issue remained a topic of bureaucratic debate and manoeuvring. In late May and on 23 August further assessments on the state of New Zealand security were received, respectively, from MI5's George Leggett (stationed in Canberra) and ASIO's deputy director, George Richards. Both concurred with the general assessment that SB was 'totally inadequate' and was 'not giving, and cannot give in its present form, satisfactory security service'.[99] Both assessments recommended the creation of a brand-new security organisation, offering variations on how this might be constituted.

Richards recommended that security work would be best carried out by an organisation outside of the Police, explicitly stating it should 'not be subject to the routine administrative and disciplinary controls of the Police Force' or existing departmental controls. These 'might hamper its operations, or embarrass the free exercise of its directions'. The new organisation 'should be given a "cover" other than that of the Police Force for its headquarters formation'.[100] Leggett leaned more towards Barnett's outlook, as laid out in his March report, recommending a new organisation that was effectively one step removed from the NZPF. While it would thus be 'independent of the rigid rules and conventions of the police force', it would still be accountable to the Controller-General and would draw funds out of the Police budget ('where they can be conveniently hidden').[101]

A further complication was that the idea of maintaining intelligence duties under the Police umbrella still possessed some rump support, notably from Lochore, the head of security in the Prime Minister's Department. In a report dated 25 July 1956, he argued that Barnett's mandate to reorganise security intelligence could be met by a reconstituted Special Branch, essentially echoing the draft directive prepared in December 1955. Arguing that surveilling measures should be proportional to the 'scale of attack', he saw subversion as a minor problem and Communist encroachment as effectively contained. He argued that the 'besetting sin' of intelligence agencies was their tending to 'make intelligence the final aim, and collect it irrespective of whether it is useful or not', and warned that this needed to be studiously avoided.

To that end, he recommended that operational restraint would be needed in several areas. Telephone tapping was described as potentially useful, but controversial, and so should not presently be used. Bugging devices, too, were stated as unnecessary in current circumstances. For now, 'no steps should be taken to acquire these techniques and training until the situation is clearer'. Conversely, Lochore was envisioning an organisation that could undertake tasks which a Peelian police force should only use sparingly. The employment of undercover agents was noted as having 'always been the chief [operational] method and should continue', and he advised that a locksmith on the staff 'may be useful' for covertly entering premises.[102]

However, Lochore's rearguard attempt made little impact among the bureaucrats planning the restructuring of security. In his later life, in a period of advancing cognitive decline and paranoia, Lochore told historian Michael King that he had wanted to head the new service himself, but had been sidelined. He added that events had been engineered by both 'a senior New Zealand civil servant' and Roger Hollis, who became the director-general of MI5 in 1956, to plant Soviet moles in New Zealand's new security organisation.[103] As we have noted, Hollis was later believed in various quarters to have been a Soviet spy; this allegation has lingered for decades.[104] By implication, if Hollis had been a spy, there were serious ramifications for New Zealand's security. That aside, it seems that Lochore's bid to head the surveilling system could only have worked if the organisation remained under police accountability. But, in the event, the implication of what was being discussed was that the security service would leave the Police umbrella.

After May 1956, then, designs moved in the direction of an MI5-style security organisation entirely outside of police structures. This direction was reinforced by geopolitical turbulence, most notably in the Hungarian uprising of October–November that year. By then, the authorities were well advanced on planning the specifics of an independent New Zealand Security Service (NZSS), later to be renamed the New Zealand Security Intelligence Service. The constitution, responsibilities and functions of the NZSS were set out in a draft document, prepared in October, which drew heavily from British and Australian security models.[105] Further discussions revolved around cloaking administration, employment and operational details. After government approval was obtained, on 28 November 1956 an unheralded Order-in-Council established New Zealand's stand-alone service in a suitably obscure way: the Public Service Act of 1912 was declared not to apply to '[e]mployees of the New Zealand Security Service'.[106]

Meanwhile, Marshall had been tasked with locating a suitable person to head the Service. He eventually offered the position, in October 1956, to a former army colleague, Acting Brigadier Bill Gilbert, who had been the military member of the Advisory Committee on Security and was now stationed in London. When he accepted the offer, the man who would eventually become known as 'The Brig' began training with MI5.[107] C. B. Robson, who had been on the Advisory Committee on Security and worked on security planning issues for Barnett, would go on to become the founding deputy director of the NZSS.

Finally, in late November Barnett stated his intention that SB was to be totally dissolved: 'I do not think there is room for, and for other reasons I think it undesirable that this small country should have two organisations operating in this field, and I want the Security Service to stand on it [sic] own, independent of the Police Force as soon as may be.'[108] This arrangement differed from Australia's, where police forces had retained intelligence branches upon ASIO's establishment. A transitional period now followed as the NZSS took over SB records and became fully operational. This exercise ended on 1 August 1957, with the disbandment of SB and the reassignment of most of its personnel to other parts of the Force. Even after the formal dissolution of SB, however, the NZPF retained intelligence linkages with other institutions, and it continued to undertake its own intelligence surveillance activities along the porous boundaries between crime and disorder on the one hand and subversion on the other. These subjects are picked up in our subsequent volume.

Other components of state intelligence also experienced internal and external pressures for greater professionalism and transnational security integration during the early Cold War. This was especially true of sigint, which remained even more hidden from the public eye than humint. With the major external enemies definitively defeated in 1945, there was an immediate fall-off in sigint activity; 'the Wellington intelligence centre was disbanded and the New Zealand–run signals intelligence stations were either returned to the Post and Telegraph Department or closed'.[109] The 'British officer who came to look after Y intelligence in 1946' was 'surprised at what he found when he arrived. There was virtually nothing left', except for a sigint capacity at the military radio stations at Waiouru, where a number of personnel who had been active in wartime intelligence continued to work in communications roles.[110]

As with humint, however, a Cold War–fuelled international revival in sigint activity followed, building on the extensive advances that had been made during the war. A leading historian of signals intelligence in Britain sees such developments as '[o]ne of the most important legacies of the Second World War'.[111] New Zealand's adjustment to the post-war global security situation took place, naturally, under the British umbrella, during 'secret discussions' throughout 1946. In February and March that year, at a classified sigint conference in London, Britain proposed that Commonwealth members form a global signals intelligence network under the 'broad direction of the United Kingdom'. The beginning of this conference, 22 February, has been described as the 'crucial moment in the creation of the global signals alliance' that eventually became the Five Eyes.[112]

After a fortnight of deliberation, a British-led geopolitical security bloc with Canada, Australia and New Zealand, the Commonwealth's key Dominions (although that term was gradually falling out of use), had been formulated. During the talks, and in subsequent discussions that year, broad spheres of global responsibility for 'defence intelligence' were worked out. In effect, in 1946 'the *British/Allied* arrangements of the Second World War were converted into post-war *Commonwealth* arrangements' aimed at protecting the entire Empire and Commonwealth.[113]

Rapid progress on the Commonwealth front strengthened London's hand in negotiating its security relationship with the United States, at a time when the latter was quickly becoming the dominant power in the Western bloc. During the Commonwealth conference, in fact, a top-secret British–United States Communication Intelligence Agreement was signed. This effectively updated the wartime sigint alliance that had been formalised with the 1943 'BRUSA agreement' (with which New Zealand had been associated).[114]

During 1946, it became generally agreed that the antipodean component of the Commonwealth sigint network would be centred in Australia, where 'a multi-national signals intelligence centre' would be established; Britain and New Zealand, however, would share 'an equal role' with the host country.[115] A series of discussions focused on establishing a network of direction-finding and interception stations in Australia, together with a New Zealand offshoot which might also run the direction-finding station in Suva, Fiji.[116] By the end of 1946, a broad consensus on how to approach all such matters had emerged. At that point a British delegation, led by the director of the Government Communications Headquarters (GCHQ), visited Australia and New Zealand to discuss implementation of the plans. The main New Zealand representative at the talks was Bill Gilbert.[117]

Another step was taken in 1948 when a convention on British–American sigint was concluded. These post-war arrangements are now generally known as the UKUSA Agreement and sometimes presented as a single landmark treaty. The reality, however, is 'a complex network of different alliances which were built up from many different overlapping agreements' and which were updated and amended from time to time.[118] Regardless of this more complicated nature, the 'agreement' has consistently revolved around facilitating cooperation in intelligence gathering and exchange, primarily in the field of sigint. Canada, Australia and New Zealand were initially party to these arrangements as 'collaborating Commonwealth countries' but formally joined in 1949 (Canada) and 1956 (New Zealand and Australia). What was now a five-nation security alliance became internally and later publicly known as the 'Five Eyes'.[119]

New Zealand was very much the most junior participant in the new alliance (albeit higher than a few Commonwealth nations like South Africa and India which were brought into the fold for specific purposes). Over the next three decades, for example, New Zealand's communications with United States sigint agencies went through Australia and Britain.[120] As last in the pecking order of UKUSA's permanent membership, New Zealand authorities were anxious to be seen as a dependable partner, but they were also conscious of opportunities to assert themselves.[121] In December 1946, for example, Wellington agreed in principle to participate in the new Australian sigint centre (in Melbourne), but only so long as New Zealand had a 'full and effective share in the control of the organisation'.[122]

At home, the Navy Department headed the country's sigint expansion, operating from its complex at New Zealand's military hub at Waiouru. In early 1947 it acquired an air force radio receiving station for development into the centre of sigint activity in New Zealand, as its designation NR1 (Navy Receiver 1) indicated (the navy's nearby previous main radio receiving station was renamed NR2).[123] NR1 had become fully functional by November 1948 and would be the headquarters of New Zealand sigint for some three decades.[124] In the following years, ideas of better integrating New Zealand's signals interception operations with Australian and, more broadly, UKUSA systems were periodically examined, including with GCHQ staff in 1952.[125] Incremental steps were taken to this effect, with, for example, experienced New Zealand radio operators being sent to Australian sigint headquarters in Melbourne in the mid-1950s to be trained in the 'special communications work' that UKUSA required.[126]

By 1954, however, it was already becoming clear that NR1's value to the UKUSA alliance was decreasing, especially because of its limited effective range; and that New Zealand was receiving few intelligence benefits in return, lacking (among other things) its own analytical capacity with regard to intercepted information.[127] The in-house chronicler of sigint, looking back, concluded that 'little of enduring nature was achieved' until 1954.[128] At this point, Cabinet took officials' advice that the nation's sigint system needed to be better designed if it were to bring significant intelligence benefits to the country. Accordingly, in August 1954 the head of the Defence Signals Branch in Melbourne was invited to send a team to assist 'in determining the potential of the [NR1] intercept station' (or HMNZS *Irirangi*, as it was now called) and to advise on how best to shape 'New Zealand's participation in the British Government Sigint Organisation'.[129]

As a result, John Burrough, the senior GCHQ officer at the Defence Signals Branch, together with a technical officer, arrived in New Zealand towards the end of 1954. After discussions in Wellington and at the military and intercept facilities in and around Waiouru, Burrough came to conclusions that broadly aligned with those already emerging within the New Zealand defence and sigint establishments. These centred on the proposition that the country's sigint efforts should be more fully integrated with the other members of UKUSA, including such matters as providing trained staff to overseas interception bases.

The Burrough Report of 15 December 1954 recommended, firstly, that sigint cease to be a purely joint services provision, since it had civil as well as military implications; its costs needed to be 'borne by civilians' as well as by the armed forces. Secondly, New Zealand's contribution to UKUSA needed to be ramped up to an around-the-clock operation manned (and soon headed) by civilians, albeit working under Navy Office auspices. It proposed, accordingly, the creation of a new organisation, the New Zealand Combined Signals Organisation (NZCSO), to run sigint activities in New Zealand.[130]

Burrough's findings and recommendations were approved by Cabinet on 14 February 1955, and the NZCSO would run the country's sigint operations for over

20 years.[131] A British officer was seconded to help set it up as 'part of a Commonwealth-wide network'. Its initial staff were mostly based in Waiouru where, among other things, it maintained HMNZS *Irirangi* and liaised with naval and army staff. Overseas training and secondments were to follow, especially to Australia's Defence Signals Branch (later, Directorate), a secret interception station in Singapore, and locations in the Pacific region. Ultimately, a third of NZCSO's staff would be stationed overseas, both enhancing New Zealand's value to British-centred signals intelligence (and, by extension, to the UKUSA network) and gaining advanced training at the same time.[132]

The Burrough Report had pointed to the need for better use of signals intercepts made within New Zealand, and recommended a full-time position in Wellington to both coordinate the collection of information gained from signals technology and disseminate it to the relevant New Zealand authorities.[133] Successive holders of the resulting position of distribution officer, who nominally oversaw all of NZCSO's operations, were military personnel located in Defence Headquarters. But the country's operational sigint hub remained at the facilities in the Waiouru area, which were integrated into and oriented towards the UKUSA network. Taking its cue from Melbourne, NZCSO focused on the broader Pacific region.[134]

The distribution office in Wellington was designed to work within another post-war development that reflected New Zealand's willingness to integrate itself within wider alliances. While only New Zealand had supported the initial British desire for full defence intelligence centralisation in London at the Commonwealth Prime Ministers' meetings in London in May–June 1946, both Australia and New Zealand had officially endorsed the consensus which had emerged. This was a British-led compromise position to the effect that each Dominion should establish a 'joint intelligence system' to overarch its 'defence intelligence' capacity. This entailed each replicating the British system of a high-level Joint Intelligence Committee (JIC) serviced by a permanent Joint Intelligence Bureau (JIB) undertaking the analysis required by the JIC.[135]

The JIBs would prepare intelligence assessments that, via the JICs, would feed into big-picture assessments for the Imperial and Commonwealth joint intelligence network. Among other things, the bureaus would provide integrated reports from varied sources on 'the military, geography, communications, peoples, administration and economic resources of foreign countries' that fell 'within their agreed areas of responsibility'. While they would have military input, the JIBs would be civilian assessment agencies, and the naval, army and air force intelligence agencies would continue as separate entities within each service.[136]

During a trip to Singapore and Australasia in early 1947 to advance the scheme, its 'principal architect', Major-General Kenneth Strong, who was director of Britain's JIB, had no difficulty persuading Australia to establish a Melbourne-based joint intelligence system. In New Zealand, he also found that officials were amenable to joining the 'speedy, reliable and continuous communications between all Empire Joint Intelligence

Bureaux' that Strong sought. While the Chiefs of Staff had initially felt that such intelligence should be entirely in the hands of the armed services, after Strong's visit they eventually came to agree that a civilian assessment body, albeit one that would draw on military sources, would produce maximal outcomes.

After long deliberations at home and abroad, in 1948 the Chiefs of Staff advised the government, accordingly, that a top echelon (JIC) should overarch New Zealand's defence intelligence. In addition, specialist assessment staff should be appointed to 'a small research and procurement section' called a Joint Intelligence Office (JIO). It would not be designated a bureau because it would have subordinate status to Australia's JIB, for which it would 'in effect operate as a collecting post'.[137] While this plan was accepted, it stalled at bureaucratic and political levels. Vic Jaynes, then the deputy director of naval intelligence, later noted that 'by 1949 nothing had been done and we were facing increasing pressure to honour [the] intelligence commitment' made, in principle, to assist the Australian-based operations.[138] Prompted by another visit by Strong, Foss Shanahan, in his capacity as secretary of the Chiefs of Staff Committee, raised the proposal for a New Zealand JIC–JIO structure again with the prime minister. After being assured that it would require minimal personnel and resources, Fraser acceded, and on 23 February 1949 Cabinet approved its formation 'on a provisional basis'.[139]

The JIC would comprise the military directors of intelligence and senior departmental representatives. Jaynes was appointed to take charge of the Joint Intelligence Office which reported to it. Although his small staff included military appointees, it was – as he stressed – a civilian body engaged in the collecting and collating of 'Strategic Intelligence' within New Zealand and its 'zones of immediate strategic interest' in the Pacific. While it was to 'maintain cohesion' with the Chiefs of Staff, it was 'decidedly under the influence of the Prime Minister's/External Affairs Department' which administered it. This meant, before long, it was being watched over by the government's security expert, Reuel Lochore.[140]

The primary function of the Commonwealth joint intelligence assessment network was to 'collate, evaluate and distribute factual intelligence relating to topography, communications, ports and harbours, landing beaches, aviation facilities, defences, economics, industrial and manpower resources and social and constitutional organisations of countries'. Each of the participants carried out these functions within agreed areas of responsibility.[141] As Nicky Hager notes, such data, gleaned from both open and secret sources, were 'the types of geographical military information which would be needed to fight future wars'. Strong had strongly advocated that 'total war required total intelligence'.[142]

New Zealand's area of responsibility operated out of its principal naval station, NR1, which monitored a vast area of the South Pacific from the Antarctic to the equatorial north. The JIO's first major exercise was to be a national survey of New

Zealand, Fiji and other territories to compile the kind of 'codified Intelligence data' whose absence had hampered the work of the Organisation for National Security in the late 1930s. This would assist a new such organisation 'should the need for its re-institution arise'.[143] The JIO secured foundational information from disparate sources in New Zealand, such as wartime surveys, government departments (including a research unit within External Affairs), the political police, the directorates of naval, military and air intelligence and the country's sigint operators.[144] It gained external material from the Joint Intelligence Bureaus in London, Ottawa and Melbourne. Once a link had been established through the New Zealand Joint Staff Mission in Washington DC, it also obtained material from the CIA and the American armed forces as well.[145]

As early as July 1950, New Zealand's JIC was reporting that '[q]uite apart from the local value of the Joint Intelligence Office', it had become 'an integral link in the Commonwealth organisation for "JIB" Intelligence'.[146] By extension, the JIO's evaluations were of increasing significance in the broader UKUSA intelligence grouping. Soon, in response to growing Western fears about the Sino-Soviet bloc's threat to colonial and other South-east Asian regimes, the organisation's interests extended into that region – although such efforts were headed by the Australian JIB's sub-office in Singapore.[147]

By 1952 the JIO, itself effectively operating as an informal sub-office of the Australian JIB, was seen to have proven its worth, despite its small staff of four, and it was established on a permanent basis. Jaynes, now a civilian, was confirmed as its director. It set about both forging operational autonomy from Australia and tightening its links with its other counterparts in the five-nations alliance. In 1953, after permission from Britain, the JIO was renamed the Joint Intelligence Bureau (JIB), signifying full partnership in the network of intelligence assessment bureaus centred in London; it was 'structured and organised to parallel other Commonwealth JIBs'. At the time when SEATO was being established in 1954, New Zealand's JIB was making formal arrangements for the exchange of intelligence with the CIA.[148] From now on, leading External Affairs staff were given the role of 'Intelligence Liaison Officers' to the CIA during their terms of duty at New Zealand's embassy in the United States.[149]

Other intelligence liaisons also burgeoned during the early Cold War period, some of them outside the exclusive UKUSA grouping. For example, Australian and New Zealand representatives (including Jaynes) attended the final two meetings, in 1953 and 1955, of a 'three-party' intelligence conference (France, Britain and the United States) which had first met in Singapore in 1951.[150] Some domestic developments followed precedents established by New Zealand's intelligence partners, especially the United Kingdom. In May 1950, for example, Wellington followed London's example in establishing a committee to monitor security threats to its own confidential transmissions; this was dominated by military signals officials, but chaired within the Prime Minister's Department by Lochore.[151]

During these years, too, New Zealand's three military services continued to apply their own long-standing humint and sigint capacities, at home and abroad, to new developments in the five-nation security alliance and other 'defence security' arrangements. This can be seen, to take one example, in 1955, the year in which the NZCSO was established. In 1949 New Zealand had joined the Anglo-New Zealand-Australia-Malaya (ANZAM) contingency plan to protect British-ruled Malaya from a Communist-led, nationalist revolt. Now a Special Air Service (based on its British namesake) was inaugurated inside New Zealand's army to assist the new British Commonwealth Far East Strategic Reserve in Malaya. Its role as an elite combat force fighting the 'Communist Terrorists' was 'to follow the guerrillas into the deep jungle and to destroy them'. Its participation in, among other things, forcibly 'regrouping' villagers into guarded camps required extensive use of intelligence, and its commander had a 'close liaison' with Malaya's Police Special Branch.[152]

By 1956 New Zealand was firmly embedded as a junior partner in the British-led Commonwealth human intelligence world as well as in the American-led secret world of UKUSA. These networks represented a vast expansion of sigint and humint arrangements across the 'Anglo world', propelled at first by the struggle against fascism in the Second World War and then that against Communism in the Cold War. New Zealand held responsibility for sigint monitoring of vast regions for UKUSA, entered combat zones in faraway places, and carried out intense surveillance of civil society at home. It had adjusted the structures which carried out such functions and, as our next volume demonstrates, its continuing surveilling gaze was shaped both by the ancient tradition of spycraft and by responses to the new threatscape that the state perceived at home and abroad.

Operations

Unsurprisingly, the pressing concerns of the early Cold War were highly influential in determining intelligence operations in the first post-war decade. A sense of priorities within the political police can be seen in one response to a November 1951 memorandum from the Deputy Commissioner of Police to senior personnel asking '(a) what are the major threats to security in New Zealand, and (b) their order of importance'.[153] SB Senior Detective J. J. Halcrow, broadly reflecting other responses, stated:

> The most dangerous political elements may be broadly described as 'Leftists' of extreme views, i.e., those elements favouring and fighting for, as an ultimate aim, the establishment of a Soviet form of government in this country. Extreme 'Rightists' – Nazi or Fascist elements – could likewise menace the security of this country but

there appears to be little, if any, real grounds for apprehension in
that respect at the present time or indeed in the near future.

He also noted other perceived threats and their relative significance, including pacifists
who might 'attempt to hamper the defence of, and war potential of, New Zealand';
militant trade union leaders, who fomented discord and were, 'in some instances'
at least, 'working towards the establishment of a Soviet State in New Zealand'; and
'[a]liens whose sympathies lie towards a Soviet form of government', especially
'nationals of the Soviet Union and China'.[154]

This last point, of course, reflected vigilance against espionage, in an age of
dramatic spy scandals – a time of concerns about whether New Zealand might
represent a vulnerable point to access classified matters shared between allies.
For example, a 1954 security assessment warned that it 'may well be easier for the
Russians to [extract sensitive material] from the smaller government machines of
Commonwealth countries than in their larger and more complicated counterpart in
London'.[155] By now New Zealand was generally seen as the weakest link in the five-
nation security grouping.

Efforts to detect and assess Soviet intelligence efforts centred on monitoring its
legation, noted as suspiciously 'over-large' with a 'total strength' listed as 16 (including
seven wives) in 1946, 24 (including 12 wives) in 1951 and 30 (including 15 wives) in
1956.[156] The main surveilling task was to keep a close eye on Soviet personnel, any
of whom might be working for Soviet intelligence or have intelligence-related duties
allocated to them; and especially to monitor their contact with locals, in particular
those who might have access to sensitive information. Going by precedent in other
countries, cultivation of left-leaning public servants and intellectuals was seen as the
major target of what were generically referred to as 'Russian Intelligence Services' (RIS)
officers. Apart from sections of society that might willingly collaborate with the USSR,
the political police also worked on the assumption that the public's general disposition
towards trust and openness, and a general disbelief that New Zealand might be targeted
by foreign spies, might well produce exploitable vulnerabilities.

The debriefing of Vladimir Petrov in 1954 had added weight to concerns about
the Soviet Legation's role as a spy base. While 'Soviet intelligence procedure precluded
Petrov, stationed in another country, from learning precise details of the conduct of
operations in New Zealand', his past access to sensitive communications and his
conversations with Soviet couriers who had been in New Zealand had allowed him
to name certain legation staff as spies.[157] A secret report that August, analysing the
significance of the debriefs, concluded that Petrov's accounts of agents and their
handlers 'imply that the Soviet intelligence effort in New Zealand is meeting with
success and that information regarded by the Russians as useful is making its way back
to Moscow'. The report went on to say:

[I]t is to be expected that the priority tasks of both the Soviet Intelligence Services [operating] in New Zealand will for some time have been the recruiting of sympathetic persons at a suitable stage in their careers for the penetration of Government departments and establishments where information required by the Russians can be found. Knowing that active Communists and open Party members are today automatically subject to security attention, the Russians will have concentrated on recruiting persons who have either left the Communist Party or who have never joined it. Such persons may be found in intellectual and professional groups. It must be expected that some may be Public Servants, possibly of some seniority.[158]

New Zealand's political police had increasingly, since the war, focused attention on the loyalty of personnel in potentially sensitive or influential areas of the state machinery. In 1948 Prime Minister Fraser told Parliament that 'whenever people are members of the Communist Party, whether active members, passive members, or in close association or sympathy with the Communists, and owe no allegiance to their country, then there is no place for these people in positions where the security of the country is affected'.[159] Concerns about public servants passing sensitive information, unwittingly or otherwise, tightened under the National administration. This was more especially so after an examination of the adequacy of security following the 1951 waterfront dispute, during which contact between radical union leaders, their sympathisers in the Public Service, and Communists had been observed. On 6 December 1951, an amendment to the Public Service Act was passed which established a process for transferring public servants out of sensitive positions in the interests of 'national security', although it also provided a means of reviewing any such decisions.[160]

More significantly, that same day the Official Secrets Act passed, superseding the application of the British Official Secrets Act 1911 within New Zealand. Applying to all New Zealanders, it was of particular relevance to public servants, who had to sign up to its provisions. The Act tightened regulations around such matters as accessing and circulating officially generated information, banning citizens from contact with 'foreign agents' or premises used by them, and prohibiting any activities that might be interpreted as being 'for any purpose prejudicial to the safety or interests of the State'.[161] The Act generated disquiet in a number of quarters which saw it as unnecessarily draconian; a later attorney-general characterised it as 'undeniably . . . restrictive, even oppressive'.[162]

Increasing concern about public servants' loyalties, together with such other factors as New Zealand's expanding diplomatic profile and entrenchment within transnational security alliances, escalated efforts to screen out potential security risks within the public sector. With the onset of the Korean War, for example, SB staff had to vet the large numbers of volunteers for service in Korea in case of Communist infiltration of the armed forces (although military intelligence continued to handle 'matters which are of interest only to the Armed Forces').[163] In early 1952 a customised set of vetting methods was developed. A Police recording sheet provides some examples of comments logged during the process. One subject was 'alleged to have made derogatory remarks re the Royal Family and stated her opposition to the Korean War and also Compulsory Military Training, both current in C.P. propaganda'. Another was said to have a 'known C.P. association in England', while a third was labelled 'a leftist' on the 'inference drawn by a reliable informant'.[164]

Suspicions of spying fell upon some significant figures in the public sector, with the validity of the accusations highly (and bitterly) contested through to the present. In April 1951, with the waterfront dispute raising security concerns about those public servants sympathetic to the locked-out workers, Commissioner Young sent a top-secret memorandum to the minister in charge of policing about the issue, noting that his concerns extended into the highest levels of the bureaucracy. In particular, '[s]ince I was appointed to my present position, which includes responsibility for internal security, I have not been happy concerning the question of security in the Prime Minister's Department'. He warned that police 'feel that we cannot report freely information that may be of vital importance to the Government while an employee in the Department of External Affairs is not free of security risk'.[165]

In fact, he believed that there was 'considerable reason for apprehension concerning the loyalty' of two diplomats. The first was Douglas Lake who, 'in the light of the present world situation must, in my opinion be regarded as a security risk and therefore is considered unsuitable for employment in a position where he will handle or have access to classified documents'.[166] Lake had been stationed in New Zealand's legation in the USSR before returning to New Zealand in December 1948. He had come under scrutiny for familiar reasons (association with Communists, an overly sympathetic outlook on the USSR, and so on) and also because of his wife Ruth, a linguist whom he had met and married when both worked at the legation. In 1950, the SCR had asked her to write a rebuttal of an unflattering picture of the Soviet Union presented by the *New Zealand Herald* in articles written by Jean Boswell, wife of the former head of the Moscow Legation. The pamphlet published by the SCR, *My Years in Mrs Boswell's Moscow*, presented a rosy picture of conditions under Stalinism, adding to SB's concerns about the Lake family.[167] A 1952 security vetting of Douglas Lake advised that he be transferred out of External Affairs and the Prime Minister's Department, and he was subsequently transferred to the aid section of External Affairs.[168]

The second named suspect was Desmond ('Paddy') Costello, who had been recruited in 1944 for posting to the Moscow Legation despite his 'strongly left-wing views'. A 'brilliant linguist' who was fluent in Russian, he had impressed both the prime minister and the head of External Affairs, Alister McIntosh, with 'his intelligence, toughness and integrity'; he had become chargé d'affaires in 1949.[169] However, his past membership of the Communist Party of Great Britain (joining as a student at Cambridge University in the 1930s), his open sympathies for the USSR through the 1940s, and his marriage to an active Communist (Bella, known as Bil) had all attracted scrutiny from MI5.[170] In October 1944, Hollis had recorded strong misgivings about Costello, although hard evidence was thin.[171] In March 1945, McIntosh told Costello about the suspicions surrounding him: 'The British Security Authorities have reported that you have a record of undesirable Communist activities in the past, and that your wife is apparently at present associated with the Communist Party.'[172]

In June 1950, New Zealand's Moscow Legation was closed and Costello was soon appointed First Secretary in the country's legation in Paris. However, the cloud of suspicion over Costello endured. In 1952, for example, Special Branch recorded him to be of 'possible security Interest'.[173] Both SB and British security agencies pushed for his removal from the Public Service.[174] Eventually Prime Minister Holland acceded to such pressure and Costello was, in effect, forced to resign in return for a protracted period of notice. He left government service in July 1954, taking up a position in Russian studies at Manchester University until his death a decade later, still under MI5 scrutiny.

After Petrov's allegations of a Soviet 'contact' within the New Zealand Prime Minister's Department, a review of possible candidates within the senior ranks of the Public Service settled especially upon William Ball Sutch.[175] He had long been under watch. One later assessment that has been declassified, from 1974, noted that '[s]ince 1932, when SUTCH first visited the USSR, he has been the subject of security interest and assessment both in New Zealand and overseas'.[176] It did not help that he was married to radical lawyer and political activist Shirley Smith. She had been attracted to Communism while studying at Oxford University in the 1930s, and was a subject of surveillance in her own right.[177]

From 1947 to 1951, when Sutch served as secretary-general of the New Zealand delegation to the United Nations, several security agencies monitored his political proclivities especially closely. His critical comments on United States policies, along with political leanings perceived as pro-Soviet, made him highly suspect.[178] An FBI report from this period noted that Sutch had been

> . . . described by Confidential Informant [name redacted] of known reliability, as a Communist sympathizer, but not as a known member of the New Zealand Communist Party. The Informant advised that SUTCH has reportedly maintained close connections with the Society for Closer Relations with Soviet Russia, and is described as an outstanding intellectual and 'doctrinaire Communist', who has avoided formal connections with the Communist Party.[179]

The FBI had forwarded its concerns to Wellington, warning that the United States would 'regard New Zealand's security as suspect' if Sutch were appointed to head the Department of Industries and Commerce, a position he was in line for.[180] Upon his return to New Zealand, his activities remained under surveillance. A 1953 security report notes that 'for many years his activities have been suspect'.[181]

While the spy scares of the early Cold War boosted concerns about espionage, much of the effort by the political police to uncover potential disloyalty continued to play out in the field of counter-subversion activity pursued under the police mandate to suppress and convict seditious activity. The Police Offences Amendment Act of December 1951, for example, was a clear attempt to limit protest by making it easier for police to take measures to secure convictions for sedition.[182]

Counter-subversion records from the period cover a huge range of leftist/progressive organisations and large numbers of people suspected of being Communists, fellow travellers or at risk of being influenced or manipulated by Communists. Many a trade unionist, for example, was seen as 'a dupe to the Communists' during the 1951 lockout.[183] The rationale was simple: the CPNZ was interested in all potential forums where it might propagate ideas and gain recruits, and that meant essentially that the entire left was under scrutiny – along with 'alternative' sectors of society whose views were deemed to make them possibly susceptible to those wanting to overturn the entire existing order.

The main surveillance targets fell into two broad groups. The first was those perceived to be hard core: the tiny Communist Party and its members, associates and fellow travellers, together with organisations, movements and individuals deemed to be fronts for, allied with or heavily influenced by them. As well as private and public CPNZ meetings, the surveillers looked out for secret Communist cabals. One of these, so Special Branch watchers recorded, was a group of Party members who met weekly under the guise of being a religious study group. They were replete with 'Bibles and other sacred literature [as props] to corroborate this assertion'.[184]

More common among the hard-core watched were those categorised as crypto-Communist or Communist front groupings. The influential New Zealand Peace Council, affiliated to the Soviet-funded World Peace Council, was seen as 'one of the principal Communist front organisations'.[185] The surveillers focused on Communist influence within the Council, and its relationship with the national and international Communist movement.[186] In a comparable fashion, the 'Plato Club' was viewed as 'a cover name by N.Z.C.P.' for a grouping within which it could influence others.[187] When the secretary of the 'Wellington Carnival Committee', CPNZ member Catherine Eichelbaum (later Kelly), opened a bank account for the Committee, it was recorded as being 'the principal known account' of the Wellington Communists.[188]

The Progressive Youth League (until 1949 called the Young People's Club) was the subject of substantial and sustained investigation to determine the degree to which it was being directed by Communists.[189] Quite apart from known Communists being involved in its work, its activism on political issues that happened to align with Communist agendas ensured that it remained of interest to the political police through the 1950s.[190] After resigning from the CPNZ in 1957, its former leader Sid Scott claimed that the League, while '[n]ominally "broad" and non-Party', was instead 'an adjunct of the [Communist] Party and every tactical and organisational point was decided beforehand in Room 26, St. Kevin's Arcade', the CPNZ's headquarters in Auckland.[191] Conversely, the agent tasked with infiltrating the League, the Peace Council and the SCR later rejected the idea that these organisations could be called Communist: 'In truth many members had no such loyalties.'[192]

Following the establishment of the People's Republic of China in 1949, security interest in both the Chinese community in New Zealand and visitors from China heightened.[193] Peking (later Beijing) would quickly come to be seen as a significant promoter of subversion, complementing that orchestrated from Moscow. The scoping of sensitive sites by Chinese agents was feared, and visitors from China were monitored. In 1954, for example, a Chinese seaman was followed when he left his 'tramp ship', and the report that entered the secret files was summarised on a SB recording sheet as follows: 'visits Defence area, Bluff Hill, Napier 2-9-54 in hired taxi and takes notes etc. of aerodromes, guns etc.'.[194] Delegations from Chinese trade unions or visits by Chinese cultural groups, such as the Chinese Classical Theatre Company, were as closely watched as Bolshoi Ballet tours, and their contacts within New Zealand were added into the secret files.[195] SB replicated its coverage of supposed Soviet front, fellow-traveller and 'susceptible' organisations with regard to China, especially focusing on the China Friendship Association and the circulation of Chinese publications.

The second main conceptual grouping of targets for surveillance was much broader, comprising leftist/progressive individuals, organisations and movements considered vulnerable to some degree of Communist influence, or at risk of Communist infiltration, or presenting other challenges to the state or its interests. Communist influence within trade unions was a major example and this focus was stepped up during the industrial troubles of 1949 and especially 1951. In such times of civic strife, the political detectives had a massive workload, assisted by uniformed colleagues donning plain clothes to infiltrate organisations, non-police undercover agents and a raft of informants.[196] Informants' motivations ranged from those just wanting money through to members of the labour movement who felt their cause would be severely set back if the strike continued.

The peace movement constituted another major example of targeting; it was generally seen as under some degree of Communist influence or as independently working towards ends that would benefit international Communism.[197] The Peace Pledge Union, which had developed out of the anti-militarist and anti-conscription movements before and during the Second World War, was one among a number of such organisations subject to ongoing watch.[198]

More broadly, the presence of known Communists in organisations or activities saw them considered as susceptible to Communist influence. One such was the New Zealand Council for Civil Liberties, founded in 1952 following long discussions first prompted by the government's use of emergency powers during the waterfront dispute. A report on its inaugural meeting stated that it 'was characterised by the attendance of left-wing, so-called intelligentsia in Wellington' and included a list of those 'well-known as Communists or Communist sympathisers'. At this meeting, too, an undercover constable noted that Professor Ian Campbell had been primarily responsible for the Council's constitution. This had been based on one drawn up in London the previous year by an organisation whose officers were, 'according to the records of this Office', either 'Communists or Communist sympathisers'. Campbell had been the founding secretary of the Police Association and producer of the *Police Journal* and had been praised when he left the union in 1939 for his 'splendid service' to policing.[199]

The Fabian Society and its Summer Schools were also studied; prominent attendees came from all corners of the left, ranging from Labour Party luminaries such as Walter Nash and former MP Ormond Wilson, through public servants such as Jack Lewin, to lawyers such as Nigel Taylor.[200] Other examples of the wide trawl of the political police include the Karori Children's Centre,[201] a network of organisations called Housewives' and Women's Unions,[202] the New Zealand Seamen's Social Club[203] and campaigners for equal pay for women.[204] Particular protest movements also attracted attention, including those protesting against the re(introduction) of compulsory military training, the 1953 execution of the Rosenbergs,[205] the deployment of New Zealand troops to Korea and Malaya,[206] the 1951 ratification of the Japanese Peace Treaty (which was said to integrate Japan into 'the U.S. military empire'),[207] and nuclear weapons testing.[208]

Surveillance of both leftist university staff and radical students also heightened in the early Cold War. In 1950, Special Branch was cultivating a 'number of very reliable contacts' at Canterbury University College,[209] paying particular attention to its Socialist Club (soon, the Radical Club), and its equivalent at Victoria University College was equally surveilled.[210] A degree of university-based support for the watersiders in 1951 – or, more broadly, opposition to the draconian nature of their suppression – led to intensified surveillance of university milieus. *Craccum*, the student magazine in Auckland, reported that 'the security police had searched through the student roll in the executive office and noted the names of requisitioners of the special general meeting over the Emergency Regulations and the names of members of the Peace Society and Socialist Club'.[211] A November 1952 report on the university Socialist Club in Wellington noted a high attendance of 70 people, identified significant figures present and canvassed the major subjects discussed.[212] A 1954 internal draft report on SB activities observed that '[w]e have in the past succeeded in penetrating the [Communist] Party on certain University levels'.[213]

State authorities were generally satisfied that Rātana, Kīngitanga, Tūhoe and other movements asserting rangatiratanga no longer presented a major security challenge, and Māori were seen as requiring only general surveillance. There were, however, ongoing concerns that Communists might exploit racial tension or ethnic loyalties at a time of significant Māori migration to towns and cities. In 1952, a confidential backgrounder within the government's Publicity Division declared that 'the Communist Party for its own ends, has always tried to develop the idea that the Maori People are an underprivileged and exploited racial and national minority'.[214] Organisations such as a 1951 'United Front to Save Orakei', to oppose the Crown's final steps to displace Ngāti Whātua from its ancestral pā, were seen in such light.[215] Other concerns were directed at Yugoslavs, including consular activities and attitudes towards Titoite Communism in the community.[216] In 1951, for example, the Commissioner of Police warned the director of employment that a Dalmatian worker had exhibited pro-Titoite leanings.[217]

While the great bulk of surveillance was targeted at the left and progressive causes, there was also a degree of scrutiny of a small number of far-right activists in the country. Such surveillance tended to be reactive, responding to such matters as the appearance of anti-Semitic propaganda and claims that fascists had immigrated to New Zealand among those displaced by the war.[218] During a 1953 SB investigation into the anti-Semitic nature of a Hungarian language periodical, inquiries to the head of Internal Affairs produced the reply that:

> For some time it has been fairly clear that the wartime activities of a certain number (probably not a large number) of the displaced persons in New Zealand were highly dubious. Provided, however, the people concerned show by their conduct in New Zealand that they left their political conduct behind them when they came here, it is probably the fair and possibly the only feasible course to accept the position and let by-gones be by-gones.[219]

The inadequacy of post-war screening of immigrants was a curiously open secret, with one memoir recalling Wellington in the 1950s as 'a drab but strangely cosmopolitan town, full of post-war European exiles, escaped Nazis (minor Jew hunters and concentration camp officers – the big boys went to Brazil) and a gaggle of budding poets'.[220] The 'let by-gones be by-gones' attitude is sometimes implicit within SB records. The NZSIS, which inherited SB's secret files, for example, '[hold] no information about Willi Huber', a ski-field entrepreneur who became highly regarded in the South Island. Huber had previously been a volunteer member of the Waffen-SS, the combat section of the Nazi Party's leading paramilitary institution, with direct involvement in numerous war crimes. Arriving in New Zealand in 1953 after lying about his past in his application documentation, Huber (according to various sources, and essentially confirmed by his own words) remained 'unrepentant' about Nazism in general and his own contribution to the Nazi Party to the end of his life.[221]

Whatever the target, monitoring methods changed little from those of the interwar period, apart from uptake of new technology, such as radio communication between staff. Publicly available information remained the major source of information that went into the files. The print media was scrutinised daily and numerous articles clipped, analysed and filed. As during the industrial troubles of 1912–13, a comprehensive newspaper clipping record of the 1951 waterfront dispute was compiled as it happened, and it was added to until 1957.[222] The acquisition of literature produced by targets remained another major means of readily acquired information. Soviet propaganda distributed through the SCR was a subject of sustained study,[223] while notes on contributors, content and distribution were compiled on Peace Council publications, especially its regular organ *Peace*.[224]

Information continued to be freely supplied by the public. File indexes reference many an anonymous, sometimes 'rambling', letter accusing various figures of being spies or Communists.[225] Another way of acquiring information was to mingle in left-wing circles and engage in apparently casual conversations, which sometimes secured information that fed into decisions made at the highest level of the NZPF. Commissioner Young himself undertook secret conversations with waterside leader Toby Hill in 1951, where each sought, among other things, to tease out the limits to which the other party was prepared to go.[226]

Protest material sent to the government was collected and investigated. For example, an open letter addressed to the government and a petition protesting the declaration of an emergency during the 1951 waterfront dispute were both forwarded to Special Branch 'for record and a check of the signatures to see what known Communists have signed'.[227] In another case, letters, petitions and telegrams sent to the United States ambassador calling for clemency for the Rosenbergs were copied and forwarded to SB, who compiled a list for further analysis.[228]

The production and/or distribution of material deemed to be subversive continued to take up a great deal of the watchers' time. Security interest in cooperative bookshops which stocked Communist, socialist and progressive literature along with more mainstream fare increased throughout the early Cold War period. These included Christchurch Co-operative Bookshop Society, and the society which ran Wellington's Modern Books.[229] The latter attracted in-depth attention and was referred to by the political police as the 'Communist bookshop'.[230] Subversive films constituted another medium of interest. Police records log, for example, reports about a Napier screening of *Victory of the Chinese People* and an individual receiving a copy of *Germ Warfare in Korea*, with a note that this film had not been submitted to the censor.[231]

The most concentrated efforts to suppress as well as record came during the waterfront dispute. A major effort was made to disrupt the production and dissemination of pro-watersider literature, which was banned under the emergency regulations.[232] Wellington Communist and activist Rona Bailey later recalled her experience of a police raid on her flat in the search for a printing press:

> For five months we had been living in this scary, unreal atmosphere and I was home one night when the doorbell rang. The adrenalin started pumping. I was on my own except for [my daughter], who was asleep in her bed. I went to the door to be confronted by two hefty policemen. One was the infamous Dave Paterson who was in charge of the whole area. He liked to be friendly. 'Call me Dave,' he would tell people. So this became his nickname – nobody called him anything else.

The two SB men came 'barging in and pushing me aside'. At first she had felt she 'was quite capable of taking them on', but when they entered her small daughter's bedroom

> . . . [t]hey just shoved me aside and stormed into the room. This was the one time I really wished my daughter would wake up and yell her head off but [she] slept soundly right through it. I decided to ignore the policemen completely so I went into the lounge and began compiling some folk dances for teaching the next day. I tried to stay oblivious to them as they ransacked my house . . .

Her husband had 'a very big old printing machine that he used occasionally for leaflets', and when Paterson and his colleague saw it 'their eyes lit up'. They confiscated it and a hefty £14 fine for having an unregistered press followed, although Bailey wryly noted that 'most government departments had never registered those types of machine'.[233] Despite such raids, the illegal production of bulletins and leaflets continued throughout the dispute. Printing equipment was often, as political cartoonist Max Bollinger later recalled, moved from location to location. The freezing workers' duplicator operated out of a car, and some illegal strike bulletins were produced at the homes of prominent people who were 'above suspicion from the police'.[234]

Various cultural productions came under differing levels of suspicion and surveillance. For example, in 1951 a list of contributors to *Here and Now*, a monthly publication slanted towards progressive views on topical and cultural issues, was logged.[235] Christchurch's William Morris Group, which promoted art and literature to workers, attracted similar attention, its songs and plays noted as 'rather glaringly pro-Communistic'.[236] Sometimes SB turned to very different targets; in 1952, for example, it shut down an amateur operation to import and distribute anti-Semitic propaganda and confiscated the offending material.[237] The distribution of Esperanto literature also continued to attract interest, and its enthusiasts' associations with other progressive causes was recorded.[238]

One case that has received a significant degree of historical attention revolved around *Newsquote*, a fortnightly periodical organised by three young Wellingtonians, Hugh Price, Don Brown and Doug Foy, with the assistance of others. It was semi-public, insofar as it was sent to some five dozen subscribers. Its contents comprised retyped articles, with no editorial comment, from mainstream American publications such as the *Washington Post*, the *Wall Street Journal* and the *New York Times*, many secured from the United States diplomatic mission. The idea was to provide information and perspectives not easily available. Produced on a hand-cranked duplicator, 21 issues of *Newsquote* were produced over 1952–53.

The purpose of *Newsquote* perplexed SB staff, but they could readily see that the tone of some articles (on the Korean War, for example, or the build-up to the American invasion of Guatemala) indicated reservations about aspects of American foreign policy.[239] A report in December 1952 noted: 'It is apparent from reading its contents that this journal has a "left" tenor, but whether the purpose of its publication is to supply "left" reading or whether its object is to be a guide or background to persons preparing current Communist propaganda is not at present clear.'[240] Observed links (often tenuous) between the editors and circles under suspicion, such as the Victoria University Socialist Club (recorded, wrongly, as a Communist organisation), led to mainstream American journalism being interpreted in a sinister light and *Newsquote* being filed under the heading 'Communist party – Literature'.[241]

As in previous decades, constables on the ground remained the 'eyes and ears' in gathering material for feeding into the intelligence cycle. In Māoridom, this intersected with new administrative arrangements arising from the 1945 Maori Social and Economic Advancement Act. While Māori aspirations for the full autonomy they hoped would arise out of the Maori War Effort Organisation were not fulfilled, the legislation did provide for elected Tribal Committees and, above them, Tribal Executives holding specified local-body type powers (similar to those of the Maori Council system, which, along with the part-time Native Constables, was now defunct). By 1949 the system covered most of the country, with 63 Executives and 381 Committees in place and ready to implement its last phase: voluntary Maori Wardens nominated by the Executives. These possessed some coercive powers under the 1945 legislation, with 32 approved by the Department of Native Affairs the following year. While the Wardens acted as the Tribal Executives' own eyes and ears, they also passed information to the Police on issues of security and public disorder that concerned them. Such cooperation expanded after 1955, when the NZPF began to implement a 1952 policy to recruit Māori constables.[242]

Other information was acquired by more clandestine methods. Security files contain copies of material acquired from within many targeted organisations, in some cases duplicated by photography or photostat copying. Files on the Peace Council,[243] the SCR[244] and the Progressive Youth League[245] from this period include speech transcripts, administration documents, conference content, meeting minutes and group photos. During the 1951 dispute Cabinet received, via SB and the Commissioner, a constant flow of insider information, including detailed reports of meetings of the combined national strike committee.[246] Mail was intercepted, scrutinised and copied, and sometimes held on to. When the Communist Party's Canterbury executive interrogated Elsie Locke in June 1953 about her refusal to 'uncritically accept everything' emanating from the USSR, and her apparently 'petit-bourgeois approach to life', its full report to CPNZ headquarters ended up in the secret files.[247]

Physical surveillance was most notably employed to log the movements and interactions of Soviet diplomatic staff; a trip two Soviet officials made to Hamilton in 1955, for example, was closely observed, in part to assess which one was the senior of the pair.[248] During the 1951 dispute, the daily movements of waterside leaders Toby Hill and Jock Barnes were closely shadowed, and haunts such as Wellington's Royal Oak Hotel, where Communists were known to mingle with those deemed by law to be strikers, were closely surveilled.[249] By the early 1950s policewomen working for SB were being used to report on political meetings. Josephine Brophy, who had undercover experience, was given permission to have her shopkeeper uncle escort her to meetings held under CPNZ auspices – much to his embarrassment when he was later recognised by a customer. Cybil Carey, assigned to SB as a shorthand typist soon after joining in 1951, was 'used to check on the movements of known Communist Party members'.[250] Such field procedures carried an element of risk of discovery. At a Wellington Peace Council meeting in 1953, for example, an undercover detective fell under suspicion; it was 'made quite clear . . . that my presence was not desired', he reported, and he was escorted to the door.[251]

Covert operations were mounted to document and record details of persons attending targeted meetings, with photographic records created and audio records compiled. Some political speeches at CPNZ meetings were obtained by secretly acquiring and duplicating the Party's own recordings.[252] A 1956 report noted that access to CPNZ archives had been 'effected in the past, with marked success'. While it was noted that, since 1951, the Party had stored its records in private houses, it was considered that gaining access to them 'should not be impossible'.[253]

Declassified files often mention that personal material had been 'received from a delicate source', and in many cases this meant an informant had been deployed. Detectives cultivated a great many sources in pubs, billiards halls and other places where wharfies, seamen and other militant unionists gathered. Sometimes this was in return for small one-off or continuing payments.[254] In other cases, potentially sympathetic persons were proactively sought out by the political police to inform.

In one case, they tried to locate a particular speaker at a meeting whose 'apparently anti-communist . . . beliefs' might make him a good informant.[255] Such sources could provide intimate and deeply guarded information. One file, for example, indicates that photographic reproductions had been taken by someone close to the owner – 'These photographs have been reproduced from originals in the possession of the Communist Party member, Ian Rex MITCHELL'.[256] Likewise, as the hectic and complex events of the 1951 waterfront confrontation unfolded, a 'most delicate source' within the CPNZ was able to provide reports of the Party's strategy on the trade union movement, including its intention to infiltrate the new 'scab' unions set up to replace the militant ones.[257] A December 1954 report noted that the informant system had played a significant part in the identification of 80 per cent of CPNZ membership.[258]

Complementing the role of an informant, who would generally have a relatively unstructured relationship with his or her handler, agents were recruited (or assigned, if they were already working in the NZPF), given code names and aliases, and placed under operational direction. Being an agent effectively demanded taking up a double life, whereas informants continued to live their lives much as before – unless they were uncovered. Some informants were induced to become agents, especially if the political police sought a deeper penetration of the target organisation's leadership. In January 1951 an internal SB report noted that it employed seven agents, costing £27.15.0 per week. Three years later their number had increased to eight, costing £48 per week.[259] In 1954 there were three agents in Auckland, three in Wellington and two in Christchurch. Two were National Executive members of the SCR and Peace Council respectively, while six held branch-level positions in the CPNZ and its 'ancillary organisations'.[260]

A detailed description of an agent's work in the 1950s is available in the case of George Fraser (not the previously mentioned public servant of the same name). Fraser initially worked for SB, under the code name 'C1' and the code signature 'John Ferguson', and then for the NZSS under the codes 'BB' and 'RR' and the signatures 'Richard Hobson' and 'Robert Shelton'. After nine years undercover, Fraser became disillusioned; maintaining a double life was, as a scholar of ASIO activities mentions, one of 'dissembling and mendacity'.[261] Fraser eventually published a memoir of his experience undercover which emphasises his growing doubts about the value and morality of his spying activities and the deception involved.[262]

In the course of his career Fraser, with regular direction from his handlers, infiltrated various organisations. He examined inward and outward mail for organisations he penetrated and was tasked especially with looking for correspondence arriving from overseas.[263] When he became the chair of the Hutt branch of the CPNZ, he borrowed keys so copies could be made, and accessed tape recordings of Party speeches so they could be duplicated by the detectives.[264] His cover as a committed Communist also placed him in a position to provide information relevant to counter-espionage work. He reported, for example, that Nikolai Ivanovich Burov, the Second

Commercial Attaché in the Soviet Legation, had proposed that he join the Royal New Zealand Air Force in order to spy for the Soviet Union.[265]

Fraser was also infiltrated into workplaces. He was, for example, posted to Rongotai College, where he worked as a music teacher while investigating the teaching staff. Among his targets were deputy head Doug Edwards (who proved to have no left-wing views at all) and A. H. (Bonk) Scotney, who had been a founder of Victoria University College student magazine *Salient* and was now in the SCR as well as other left-leaning organisations.[266] SB, too, arranged with university authorities to allow Fraser to enrol in classes, despite lacking the prerequisites for entry. His job was to report on suspected Communist activities on campus.[267] This included infiltrating the Socialist Club; his report on a 'buffet tea' meeting in November 1952 identified a number of the 70 attendees and summarised the major speeches.[268]

Although the aim of using penetrative agents was a political one, Fraser's work was heavily entwined with reporting on the personal lives of those he associated with, often under specific directions from his handlers. In one instance, he was tasked with secretly recording a conversation with a CPNZ member who had approached him for help with his marital problems.[269] In mid-1953, he accepted an invitation to flat with Conrad Bollinger, a man Dave Paterson saw as 'a well-disciplined communist and a security risk', though a 'reliable and well-informed source' believed he was 'more of an academic socialist than an ardent communist'.[270] Living within the household enabled Fraser to report on who had attended social gatherings at the house, who had casually dropped by, who had stayed there, and what they had said to each other. This also positioned him to initiate ostensibly casual conversations, which often moved into deeply personal matters, and such information was channelled to his handlers and went into the secret files. After Bollinger joined the CPNZ, Fraser relayed a great deal of information on his dissident stance within the Party to SB. Fraser informed Paterson of Bollinger's intention to apply for a position in the Public Service, an action which had obvious career ramifications: the 'Public Service Commission [had been] informed', the file recorded. Bollinger's employment record thereafter was closely followed.[271]

Informants could be tasked with investigating what seemed to be suspect public servants. After Gil Deynzer was transferred out of the Department of Scientific and Industrial Research, an informant was tasked to socialise with him and assess whether he had any association with the Soviet Legation.[272] In 1953 Douglas Lake and Richard Collins, another External Affairs employee whom SB deemed suspect, were among the targets of an intelligence operation using both informants and agents.[273] Both men were regular attendees of the 'Vegetable Club', an informal Friday-evening social circle established in 1952 that met at the legal offices of Duncan, Matthews and Taylor on Lambton Quay in Wellington. Its name derived from both the fact that it was organised around the bulk-purchase and distribution of fresh produce (an idea which sprang from distributing food to strikers' families in 1951) and as an ironic reference to the exclusive Wellington Club. Generally, the mixed gatherings involved discussions of political and other current events, usually associated with what one report to SB handlers called 'a fair quantity of liquor'.[274]

Although a loose and changing circle, some two dozen or so regularly attended. Most of these were left-of-centre professionals, some of whom were already on SB's radar, and the association of Lake and Collins with them was especially concerning to the Branch.[275] Keith Matthews, one of the legal partners, had been classed as a 'Communist sympathiser' (or even as a 'suspected Communist') because of his involvement in progressive causes deemed to be aligned with CPNZ agendas. For his own part, Matthews outlined his intent, in a 1951 letter, to ensure that the peace movement will contain 'so many people of differing points of view that it cannot by the remotest stretch of the imagination be called a communist body' (this letter was lodged in the secret files after it was 'found in Lambton Quay' by SB in 1957).[276] However, SB regarded it as suspicious that, since 1949, Matthews and his legal partner Nigel Taylor had been listed by the CPNZ as solicitors who could be contacted if members were 'accosted by the police', and that they had represented the watersiders in 1951. Among the huge amount of material recorded on file was a statement that Matthews' wife Jacqueline (Jackie) had 'admitted' in a private conversation to being a 'leftist'.[277] Taylor's wife Nancy, too, was seen as having similar views, and an informant had supposedly spotted a 'red flag' on the couple's lounge wall.[278] The Matthews family were so closely observed that the name of the taxi driver who took their child to a crèche was dutifully recorded.[279]

After a great deal of surveillance of the Vegetable Club, an assessment in May 1953 concluded that it was 'significant that practically all the club members are persons associated directly or indirectly with the Communist Party and "front" organisations of the Communist Party, which poses the question whether the "VEGETABLE CLUB" may not be a cover for some more sinister activity'.[280] This conclusion, based on the topics of conversation, was relayed back to SB by Fraser and by an informant (or informants). According to club members in later years, infiltrators exaggerated and decontextualised discussions; some reported remarks, which attendees later avowed were invented, would be considered at that time as breaching social mores and legal boundaries over 'indecent' language or blasphemy. Some phrases attributed to Vegetable Club members ('to hell with the POPE!', which was heavily underscored in a report, for example) later leaked out and became widely circulated in Wellington to ridicule the mindset associated with the watchers.[281] An excerpt from a typical informant's report on the Club recorded an attendee as stating that

> . . . there could be immediate peace in Korea, but the bloody American bastards had so many rotten dollars tied up in armaments that they would see to it that there was no peace there. He said

'Those bastards are so involved in it financially that they will see to it that the Communists don't get peace.' He also said to [an occasional right-wing attendee] 'It's the same with that f . . . n cobber of yours Cardinal Spellman. It seems to me he's going to be the next Pope, because of those same f . . . n stinking dollars.'[282]

The use of informants and agents continued to come with various concerns and dangers. The use of agents, as internal documentation noted, meant that 'the State is indirectly contributing to the funds of the Communist Party as all agents as good Communists must pay dues and purchase their quota of Communist literature'.[283] The maintenance of cover could also risk an agent acting as an *agent provocateur*. This can be seen when Agent Fraser's handler told him that an informant, reporting on the same circles but unaware Fraser was an agent, had described him as 'one of the most dangerous communists he's ever met' and advised that his 'movements should be watched at all times' – a clear enough example of an agent seeking to firm up credibility by trying to out-comrade the comrades.[284]

The practice was also recognised as demanding operatives distort their lives, particularly in a small and close-knit society:

> Security work is very much more difficult and trying in New Zealand in some important aspects than it is in bigger and more densely populated countries. The concealment of agents and penetration of enemy ranks is an infinitely more intricate business . . . Everyone knows everyone else in this country and, not only has one to be singularly astute to lead a double life but, should one succeed in doing so, it is exceedingly trying to be misunderstood by family and friends.[285]

Lastly, the practice was observed as carrying the risk of public distaste if exposed. As an SB report noted, 'the average law-abiding New Zealander tends to frown on anything which savours of spying or pimping'.[286]

A degree of such exposure played out in June 1955 when the *People's Voice* published a confession by Henry Guy that had been witnessed by a Justice of the Peace. A Lower Hutt drainlayer, Guy declared that he had served as a paid police agent within the Communist Party for nine months. By Guy's account, SB had preyed on his vulnerability at a time when his wife had left him and his debts were mounting. Its officers had arranged for him to spy on the Hutt branch of the Party to which he belonged in return for helping him with his plight. He was given the code name Samuel Lee and became agent 'S1'. In exchange for Guy's weekly reports, his SB handlers provided him with information regarding his wife (although he came to doubt its authenticity) and weekly payments of £5, later increased to nearly £7. Guy recounted that his handlers encouraged him to take a leadership role in the branch. His reports, mailed to a Post Office Box number, supplied information on such matters as the branch executive, topics covered at meetings, and details of attendees. His handlers were particularly interested in the personal weaknesses of Party members, and Communist links or influence within unions, the peace movement and the Labour Party.[287]

Documentation lodged in the secret files broadly aligns with his account, recording that Henry Guy officially became an informant in September 1954 and was initially paid £4 per week (later raised to £7.10s). It recounts that, after becoming suspicious of him, the branch leadership subjected Guy to surveillance and then to intimidation: by Guy's own account, his confession resulted from Party members arriving at his house with a typewriter and a Communist JP in tow. In demanding his compliance, they had supposedly told him that 'they would get me, where I went or what I did if I did not play ball'.[288] As the story gained publicity, the Council for Civil Liberties condemned any such penetration of a legal party, calling for the government to deny the allegations if they were false or overhaul SB if they were true.[289] Prime Minister Holland received a number of letters over the incident (which were forwarded to SB for analysis)[290] and questions were raised in Parliament, where the prime minister cast doubt on the account given in the *People's Voice*.[291]

SB agent George Fraser, who had already penetrated the Hutt branch, did not know about Guy's role, and vice versa. This was common in international spycraft, a means of checking veracity and loyalty, although the relatively small amount of resources available for undercover work meant that this was less typical in New Zealand – except, that is, in what were seen as significant circumstances such as the Vegetable Club. Although he was told that it had been Guy who approached police in the first place, Fraser felt 'disturbed at the fact that Special Branch had used a man's misery to its own ends'.[292]

The question around whether SB, or the NZPF as a whole, tapped phones in this period, as emblazoned upon *NZ Truth*'s front page on 7 October 1953, remains shadowy. A December 1954 in-house report on SB's objectives and capabilities stated that 'overt means and technical aids such as telephone tapping and mail censorship, which are among the main counter-intelligence weapons of Security Services abroad, are not being used in New Zealand'.[293] Use of the present tense may be significant in the context of increasing internal and external criticism of covert methods at this time. Whatever the case, ongoing suspicions and rumours abounded. In 1955, for example, Opposition leader Walter Nash reminded Parliament that Compton had acknowledged two occasions of police phone tapping. He stated that although Prime Minister Holland had declared that 'there was no tapping' past 1946, 'I have my doubts on that, because my telephone may have been tapped several times in 1951–52'. Nash further recounted that he had been approached by a man who claimed he was on the line 'to somebody at the Trades Hall [when] the conversation was interrupted by a policeman coming in and saying who he was'.[294]

Personal files from the period indicate that a number of left-wing activists and organisations and supporters of progressive causes were under the impression that their home phones were compromised, and used phones in pubs or betting agencies for what the political detectives called 'secret communications'.[295] Released files also show that the monitoring of Collins and Lake extended to surveillance of their movements and strongly suggest phone tapping, which would belie official claims that tapping had stopped and that SB lacked this capability in any case:

> On 27 March 1953, COLLINS left the 'CLUB' at 7.30 p.m. and went home where he remained until 9.50 p.m. He and another man (believed to be DOUGLAS WILLIAM LAKE) then left in COLLINS's car and the car was located outside the home of DOUGLAS WILLIAM LAKE at 195 Aro Street 11.30 o'clock that evening. [That same evening] DOUGLAS WILLIAM LAKE telephoned two different persons, one of whom he addressed as 'GEORGE' and advised or reminded them of a meeting to be held on the following Sunday at 9 a.m. ('GEORGE' may be GEORGE GODDARD, a Communist – vide attached note.)[296]

Reporter Neill Birss, who worked at *NZ Truth*'s Wellington head office in the mid-1950s, had the impression that Detective Stan Wrigley had been at the centre of an informal relationship between SB and the tabloid, which would explain the increase in publication of leaked material. He believed that electronic equipment he stumbled across in the basement belonged to Wrigley and 'looked like phone tapping gear', with 'ear phones, no mouthpiece, [and] clips at the end'.[297]

SB was also privy to information through collaboration with private agencies at home and security institutions abroad. In the emergency conditions of 1951, for example, the National Airways Corporation provided flight details of leading unionists to the political police, ensuring that the targets could be tailed on arrival even if the trip had been ordered at short notice in an attempt to evade SB attention.[298] The most important partners in the provision and receipt of information were, of course, external intelligence apparatuses. Intelligence from such sources included briefs on global Cold War issues, such as the 'atomic spy' Klaus Fuchs, arrested in 1950 in the United Kingdom; the membership of the Communist Party of the United States; the Berlin Airlift; United States–Soviet tensions; and internal rifts within the Communist world such as the Soviet–Yugoslav split.[299]

Shared intelligence could also relate to more domestic matters and concerns. For example, Police recording sheets dating to 1954–55 note that SB received intelligence from the Royal Canadian Mounted Police regarding suspicions that Canada's High Commissioner in New Zealand, Herbert Norman, was both a Communist and a Soviet agent. Canadian security's conjectures resulted from both Gouzenko's revelations and Norman's previous political associations. His posting to New Zealand in 1953 was by all accounts to marginalise him, although he was later posted to Egypt (where he committed suicide, still professing his innocence).[300] Another Western diplomat posted to New Zealand under a cloud was the American John S. Service, a 'China Hand' who had recommended the United States make some political accommodation in preparation for what he was convinced would be a Communist victory in China. Posted to Wellington between 1946 and 1949, Service had survived allegations of disloyalty in a major espionage scandal (the 'Amerasia Spy Case'). His main task was now to work on 'weaning New Zealand away from the United Kingdom' and forging closer security and trade ties with the United States. After Service's spell in New Zealand, Senator Joseph McCarthy branded him a Communist and his dismissal from the State Department was ordered.[301]

New Zealand participated in a number of efforts to foster better security cooperation and coordination within the Commonwealth. In October 1948, in the aftermath of the Commonwealth Prime Ministers' meeting, security representatives from Britain, Canada, Australia, New Zealand (Commissioner Cummings and Senior Sergeant Edward Stevenson, who had a long detective career behind him), South Africa and Southern Rhodesia met secretly at the first Commonwealth Security Conference. Their examination of the geopolitical threatscape focused on the international spread of Communism. Among other things, MI5 demonstrated 'technical aids', i.e., 'tapping, bugging, and other forms of interception'.[302]

At the conference, consensus was reached, through approval of 'Ten Points', that the major security issue for the Commonwealth were the interlinked problems of 'Russian espionage and Communist activities'. Among other things, each country agreed to establish 'a section devoted to the study of the indigenous Communist Party'. The specialist units would carry out surveillance in the following areas:

> a) the study of the structure, organisation and personnel of the Communist Party;
> b) the domestic and foreign policy of the Party and its ancillary organisations;
> c) the study of the Party in industry, with special reference to its penetration of the Trade Unions and to the employment of Party members on industrial work of national importance;
> d) the study of Communist penetration of the Civil Service and of the Armed Forces, and the investigation of Communist conspiratorial activities.[303]

At the second Commonwealth Security Conference in May 1951, convened to find better ways of pursuing the Ten Points, New Zealand's representative, Inspector Nalder, took 'considerable pride' in announcing that SB had files on all known Communist Party members – though he noted it had yet to penetrate the leadership of the Party. He stressed 'evidence that the Soviet Minister [at the Messines Road legation] was endeavouring to build up a fifth column' inside the Slavic immigrant community, and noted SB's role in overseeing a national register of assessments of aliens.[304]

This international Commonwealth network functioned as an information exchange in tracking targets. Special Branch, for example, had first surveilled Cath Eichelbaum when she was a Socialist Club member at Victoria University College in 1946, but the trail had gone cold when she went to Britain the following year. In 1951, however, MI5 reported that she was still 'an active and ardent communist', and an exchange of information between the two countries' main domestic security services about her (and her sisters) began.[305] There were larger ambitions at work, too. New Zealand, for example, contributed to a 1949, MI5-led aspiration to create an international 'who's who' of prominent Communists and fellow travellers. Initially Commissioner Young provided the names of the 18 full and reserve members of the National Committee of the CPNZ, along with that of Dick Griffin, a former member of the CPNZ's national executive who was by then active in the SCR among other causes.[306]

Compiling larger pictures out of fragments of often disparate information was fundamental to intelligence analysis. The concerns and fears induced by the Cold War added an urgency to the task of determining what, if anything, a target's statements, actions, writings or contacts might signify. Declassified files indicate the extraordinarily diverse contents of reports logged in this era. They include organisational and subject files; specialist records like a 'personality index and basic data and abbreviations of organisations that are Communist controlled';[307] reports on social functions, which include personal animosities within the Party;[308] and assessments of Communist reactions to significant events, such as the death of Stalin.[309]

Work continued on the compilation of basic data to underpin such analyses, although the definition of 'Communist' remained somewhat fluid. In September 1950, Commissioner Young requested the names of all Communists in the country and a 22-page list was submitted for Wellington alone.[310] The following year, however, Inspector Nalder argued that there were only some 50 hard-core Communists in New Zealand, although this figure might stretch to as high as a thousand if it included people with some kind of association with the CPNZ.[311]

Desk officers worked painstakingly through reports on organisations, movements and individuals, cross-referencing and drawing conclusions as they went, and their superior officers sometimes requested further investigation. Card indexes recorded those named in reports, and a general watch was kept on those individuals without a personal file. When their names appeared several times in the cards, the number of such 'traces' differing depending on the circumstances (but often fewer than a dozen), a personal file would be opened and greater scrutiny implemented.[312] Many names on the cards made only one or two appearances, such as an unidentified 'Mrs Thorne' who spoke at a public meeting in Christchurch's Latimer Square in 1951; although no extra information was ever found, this record remained until it was destroyed in a purge of redundant records by the NZSIS some three decades later.[313]

The practices of the secret world both fed on the Cold War atmosphere and stoked it, especially as vetting for the Public Service escalated. In July 1956, Lochore noted that two of SB head office's three card indexes dealt with vetting, recording those who passed and those who did not. According to Lochore, there were 'about 800 personal files on persons of particular security interest' – although the evidence indicates that this figure is the tip of the central registry iceberg. Even under Lochore's formulation, in a population of some 2,175,000, one New Zealander in 2700 was being singled out for 'particular security interest', with a great many other names coming under various degrees of surveillance.[314]

SB analysis began with the political detectives in the field, or even with their agents or informants, who often provided first-take assessments. More considered accounts were then prepared and filed. The characteristically vivid outlook of 'Call Me Dave' Paterson, as outlined in a November 1951 memorandum, is indicative of some analysis of the threatscape:

> Peacetime restrictions of the individual are regarded as unconstitutional, but may the present in New Zealand be regarded as peacetime? We have contributed a fighting force to the United Nations Organisation which engages a variety of Communist forces in Korea. At the same time, a minority of New Zealanders with impunity at least verbally support the enemy. Propaganda from countries whose troops engage in battle with our own troops, floods our mails and is disseminated among our people ... the point to be made is that here is a subtle advance of the cold war in New Zealand – a 'creeping gain' for Communism.[315]

This ideological tone characterised many political detectives' assessments in which words and deeds were inherently treated as suspicious or given excessive explanatory power. For example, a report noting critical comments allegedly made by Collins and Lake offered the following assessments:

> [C]ontemptuous references by COLLINS to the Government of the United States of America, which are completely in accord with the dictates of the Kremlin, show him in his true colours and are of

particular significance in view of the fact that he maintains a strictly neutral attitude in his employment, and has refused to comment adversely on the Government of the United States of America, when given the opportunity to do so in a private conversation with one of the senior officers in the Prime Minister's Department.[316]

In other instances, university debaters were recorded as 'pro-communist', or 'at least bitterly anti-conservative'. Conrad Bollinger had argued that John Milton had been a 'revolutionary', Hector MacNeill had 'eulogised the works of Rewi Alley in China' and Doug Foy's speech was 'a diatribe against Henry Ford'.[317] Other analyses noted Communists criticising company profits 'without taking any responsible view of their contribution' to society.[318] Canterbury Museum curator Dr Roger Duff 'appears to have the jargon of the Communists and, as mentioned before, is most probably a leftist'.[319] A 1951 speech by Jock Barnes 'was a "Hate Session" par excellence . . . calculated deliberately to stir up animosity against the Government and those responsible for law and order in the Country' and to 'inflame people of poor intelligence against authority'.[320] Some disparaging comments also reflected older policing notions about norms and deviancy. One figure was pronounced as 'a communist, and a poor specimen';[321] an investigation of a railway guard and his home found them both 'dirty [although] there was nothing to suggest that he was a Communist';[322] a film-goer in Christchurch was described as having a 'short and squat and powerful, dark and ugly, somewhat Jewish appearance'.[323]

The use of informants and agents represented a particular challenge for analysis. The veracity of their reports was always open to question, with sources potentially liable to exaggerate, or even fabricate, details. Reasons for doing so included a desire to please handlers – and possibly thereby get more money or ongoing work (or, as with Henry Guy, assistance) from the Police – or out of a zealous or scornful wish to punish targets. An internal SB report noted that 'information obtained by agents must, of course, be developed and checked by Special Branch officers on the spot, and owing to the structure and organisation of the Communist Party and the security measures adopted for its own protection the information is in the majority of cases extremely meagre'.[324]

Information supplied by agents could also be compromised by the circumstances of their penetration. George Fraser recalled the challenges of accurately recalling particulars: 'Details of those I had encountered [had to be] held in my mind until I had found a safe spot to scribble them in a notebook.'[325] In surveilling student congresses at Curious Cove in the Marlborough Sounds, for example, he recounted the 'exhausting work' of trying to 'commit 90-minute spiels' by academics and peace activists to memory before writing out 'the main gist' in downtime periods.[326] In any case, the customary alcohol consumption at social events he attended (what a Christchurch colleague of his called 'detrimental' social drinking) made accuracy difficult.[327] As he recalled, 'Special Branch was anxious for me to detail the subjects discussed [at the Vegetable Club] and the conclusions reached but, with a bellyful of booze and the camaraderie of the occasion', he continued, '[w]ho was to remember?'[328]

SB analysis, then, struggled with manichean mindsets, exaggerated and rumour-driven reports, embellishments or fabrications in the interests of job justification, drunken notebook scribblings in alleyways near targeted gatherings, and many more flaws in the material supplied. Sometimes the field operatives had to be cautioned over such matters. In one instance the Commissioner himself noted his disapproval of the tone of Detective Sergeant Paterson's reports, instructing that he provide only 'clear statement of fact' and analysis based on this.[329] Officials outside the NZPF also showed some scepticism around SB's intelligence assessments. McIntosh, for example, was far from impressed at the quality of the evidence mustered to support allegations that Lake and Collins were 'security risks'. Indeed when Nalder wrote directly to the prime minister following Petrov's allegations in 1954, McIntosh reportedly prepared a memo for the official record which essentially repeated his own assessment that SB accusations of disloyalty against the pair were misplaced. MI5's liaison officer in Wellington similarly expressed concerns about Special Branch assessments.[330]

Assessment

The first decade of the post-war world was a seminal period in the global history of state surveillance. While it was far from the strategic hotspots of the developing Cold War, New Zealand was swept up in the trends and mood of the time. Popular and official fears of Communism were renewed and greatly enlarged, and doubts around the country's defences escalated and led to endeavours to bolster state security measures, including humint and sigint surveillance capabilities.

The country's reinstatement in 1945, and reconfirmation in 1949, of a Police-based human intelligence system ran against the international current of the early Cold War (although Canada, too, continued to allocate humint to its federal police). Over the post-war decade, then, security surveillance operated within the broad parameters of the NZPF approach of the last half-century. However, these years constituted the final chapter of the NZPF holding primary responsibility for humint, before its transfer to the NZSS, now the NZSIS, where it remains today. From a longer perceptive, the removal of this mandate from the policing sphere – with its traditional public-order focus – and its assignment to a specialised security service more tightly networked with external allies was a concept first advocated after the First World War and temporarily realised during the Second.

The establishment of Special Branch in 1949 had been intended to professionalise humint within the Police. But over the course of the six years of SB's existence, a series of internal reviews, together with recommendations and expectations from external allies, had depicted it as inadequate. Such criticisms typically referenced the resources, training and specialist equipment that were becoming the hallmark of professional security intelligence apparatuses elsewhere. While these critiques were often entwined with advocacy for a stand-alone service, they were able to cite very real deficiencies.

Sheer manpower shortages may have represented SB's greatest difficulty, particularly in regard to its expanding vetting duties.[331] A report from MI5 in August 1954 noted that an 'excessive proportion of time of the personnel of Special Branch Headquarters and of the Wellington District Special Branch appears to be spent on vetting'. It saw a need 'to define carefully those posts which fall into a vettable category. Failing this there is a tendency for vetting commitments to outstrip the resources and manpower of the vetting agency, a situation which appears to be developing in Special Branch.'[332] By 1955, departmental vetting requests had reached around 6000 per annum, prompting Assistant Commissioner Nalder to protest that indiscriminate vetting was overwhelming SB with trivia.[333] A 1956 review noted that vetting consumed an estimated 40 per cent of the time of SB field staff and the employment of two record clerks.[334] By comparison, NZSIS officers employed through the 1970s–1990s note protective security duties, including vetting, as consistently constituting some 18–25 per cent of Service workloads.[335]

Shortfalls in human resources were compounded by a lack of specialist training. In an April 1948 planning document, Foss Shanahan had noted that 'it would appear essential that personnel of the [proposed] Special Branch be appointed to that Branch on a permanent basis and because of special qualifications, both [sic] of character, intellect and education'.[336] This ambition was not met, with a July 1952 report deploring 'a shortage of suitable recruits from within the Force and of qualified specialists from outside'.[337] By the time of Controller-General Barnett's review of security in 1956, there had been little progress on improving the level of expertise: 'Most of those who are in the branch now are there because they have been so instructed', he noted. The Controller-General was firm about the type of staff required: 'the organisation has to be led and leavened by people who are much better educated and of better intellectual calibre than is commonly found in a police force'.[338]

Specialist skill sets were similarly lacking. In November 1953, SB's problems in assessing attitudes in 'alien communities' were described:

> There are now 23,000 aliens in New Zealand . . . Special Branch should be studying questions of alien security but no expert with the necessary specialist knowledge of alien mentalities is available to them, and with present staffing all that can be done is to examine carefully the few hundreds of aliens who apply for naturalization each year.[339]

An assessment of the Branch in May 1956 deplored the 'totally inadequate facilities in personnel, in equipment [and] in resources', concluding that 'Special Branch has with some justice been called the Cinderella of the Police Force'.[340] Lack of technical expertise had resulted in some embarrassing episodes. When Agent Fraser borrowed the keys to CPNZ offices in order to get them duplicated, the procedure took so long and was so inept as to risk breaking his cover.[341] In one raid on a union office during the 1951 waterfront dispute, it took five hours to open a locked safe, an incident which brought mockery upon Special Branch.[342] Such episodes no doubt informed recommendations that the proposed new security service needed to employ a locksmith.[343]

New Zealand's allies added fuel to assessments that the country's security arrangements were too lax. After the 1949 formation of ASIO, the perception that Australia was the weak link in Commonwealth security was largely transferred to New Zealand. In the early 1950s Australian security is observed as harbouring 'considerable suspicions of the inadequacies' of SB.[344] In October 1955, MI5's security liaison officer in Canberra noted that ASIO would provide a photo gallery of Soviet spies identified by the Petrovs 'to both the United States and all Commonwealth countries, with the exception of New Zealand'. 'The latter omission', he wrote, 'is perhaps all to the good, in view of the danger of leakage back to the Russians, given the poor state of security in New Zealand at the present time.'[345] In March the following year, Barnett's report to ministers frankly noted, 'most certainly it cannot be denied that we are a weak link in the Commonwealth chain'.[346]

Such assessments had a considerable afterlife. Even decades later, the former head of an Australian Royal Commission into security and intelligence reflected that, during the 1970s, the other four partners in the Five Eyes maintained reservations concerning the state of New Zealand security.[347] Michael Parker's book, which drew on insider information some 20 years after SB's demise, stressed that Special Branch officers 'were not given specialised training in intelligence gathering' and claimed that they 'did not have particular political sensitivity'. Agent Fraser's memoirs liken SB operations to sailing 'a creaking flimsy-built vessel which could spring a leak at the slightest buffeting', adding that 'those at the rudder hadn't the slightest idea of how to properly steer it'.[348] Former and current NZSIS staff have made similar comments on the poor quality of pre-1956 intelligence analysis.[349]

Despite most institutions being loath to lose a function, by 1956 even some senior police officers believed that security surveillance might now best be handled by an outside body. In July 1952, the leading NZPF expert on humint, Inspector Nalder, noting that security work called for 'considerable flexibility in organisational matters and methods of work', acknowledged that SB 'as at present constituted' was 'fundamentally handicapped' by 'inelastic Police regulations and administrative machinery'.[350] Those pushing for reform came to comparable conclusions, with an August 1954 report noting – remarkably – that the head of SB was 'far too preoccupied with routine police matters allotted to him by the Commissioner of Police. On his own admission the Head of Special Branch spends over nine-tenths of his time on work unconnected with security.'[351]

Over and above questions of resources and priorities, the NZPF mission to uphold the law with 'neither fear nor favour' continued to sit uncomfortably with in-depth surveillance of large numbers of law-abiding targets. Moreover, while formally charged to operate within legal parameters, the post-war political detectives functioned towards and beyond the outer margins of the law more often than the rest of the constabulary. When a man escaped deportation in 1952 by having another person substitute for him, for example, the political detectives advised against prosecution as this might blow the cover of an informant.[352]

The early Cold War was a seminal era in embedding many of the tensions and trends that continued as major features in the ongoing confrontation between East and West, and the intelligence front remained a prominent and integral dimension in this struggle. During the Second World War, the Soviet Union had massively invested in its intelligence apparatus, and by 1945 its security agencies employed some 150,000 people and ran extensive espionage networks in the West. This effort has been assessed as possessing 'more and better intelligence [on Britain and the USA] than any power had ever had before'.[353] At this time Soviet intelligence operations were heavily entwined with diplomatic postings, and it was stating the obvious when the British advised New Zealand that it could be assumed that some of the Soviet Legation staff 'are and will continue to be spies'.[354]

RIS officers in New Zealand through the post-war decade included Vasili Urenev (1946–52); Georgi Sokolov (a Soviet Ministry of Internal Affairs/MVD official posted as a commercial attaché, 1953–56); and Yevgeni Gergel (a commercial councillor, 1956–61).[355] In early 1949 another MVD official, Nikolai Ivanovich Burov, arrived in New Zealand to take up his diplomatic posting as Second Commercial Attaché.[356] Petrov's 1954 debrief included a number of details about the RIS's presence in New Zealand, such as the information that 'Burov's successor ([Vasili] Stativkin) is a G.R.U. [Soviet military intelligence] official working in New Zealand' and that '[Alexander] Alexandrov, the former Ambassador in New Zealand, was not a permanent M.V.D. officer but while in New Zealand looked after agents and got information from them'.[357]

In January 1956, the USSR applied for permission to post Vladimir Peutin to Wellington as a First Secretary. While the British High Commission noted that he was 'known to be an active spy master', it also advised that he should be admitted, reasoning that if 'Peutin is refused entry someone else will be sent to do his work'.[358] Such a rationale reflected a standard practice in tradecraft that it is better to know who to watch, what they are doing and who they are seeing; spies were generally only outed and ousted when it was expedient to do so. British advice regarding Peutin also showcases the customary secret world etiquette in discreetly conveying an awareness of spying: 'if you don't want him, best to *not* refuse a visa, but do nothing: they will get the point and substitute another name'.[359]

A major priority of Soviet espionage efforts in New Zealand was the cultivation of contacts: informants and agents who were positioned, or who might one day be in a position, to aid Soviet interests. Burov's proposal that George Fraser could help the USSR by joining the Royal New Zealand Air Force is a case in point.[360] Agents and informants could be employed in a variety of ways within organisations – gaining access to sensitive material, assisting in building 'legends' (background material to add credence to a false identity) or acting as agents of influence who could promote Soviet policies or interests. The general secretary of the CPNZ at this time later noted that Soviet Legation officials were 'not very curious' about Party affairs, but were 'keenly interested' in the SCR and media coverage which could increase the prestige of the Soviet Union.[361]

The United States' diplomatic presence in New Zealand also carried out intelligence functions that serviced its strategic interests. The US government has released some thousand pages of reports assessing, between 1945 and 1960, New Zealand politics, current events, significant personalities and more besides. In particular, an 'inordinate interest' was displayed in the labour movement, most notably Communist influence in it and 'the personalities and political orientation of the key personalities' involved.[362] The CIA received intelligence assessments through the United States mission on such subjects as 'Communist Influence in New Zealand' and character assessments of political leaders.[363] Some of these assessments were based on information provided by official channels, but informal sources were also employed. Jack Lewin recalled one American official who attempted 'to talk to as many trade union personalities' as possible.[364] F. P. Walsh, now an ardent 'Cold Warrior', was designated by United States diplomats as 'a firm friend of the United States' and acted as a conduit between American and New Zealand officials.[365]

American interest could extend beyond analysis and into engagement in New Zealand's domestic affairs.[366] The most significant known example of direct United States involvement at this time occurred during the 1951 waterfront dispute.[367] This took the form of 'Operation Railhead', a covert mission to airlift goods between the North and South Islands. Four Curtiss Commando (C-46) transport planes were provided by Civil Air Transport, a CIA-owned front company used for supply missions across East and South-east Asia. In May and June 1951 its aircraft transported some 17 million pounds of cargo between Paraparaumu and Woodbourne airports in 1300 crossings of Cook Strait.[368]

Within the arena of Cold War espionage, several of the suspicions around the New Zealanders mentioned earlier can now be addressed. Official apprehension around Paddy and Bil Costello was revived in the decade between the former's 1954 exit from government service and his death in 1964. He came under increased scrutiny in early 1961 when MI5 arrested Soviet spies Morris and Lona Cohen, part of the Portland Spy Ring. This was because the Cohens had entered the United Kingdom under passports issued to the pseudonymous Helen and Peter Kroger in 1954 by the New Zealand Legation in Paris. British security agencies believed that Paddy Costello had facilitated the issuing of the fraudulent passports for the purposes of furthering Soviet espionage.[369]

In late 1961 KGB officer Major Anatoli Golitsyn defected and his debriefs implicated Costello in the issuing of the Kroger passports in Paris. 'At this time MI5 had begun to investigate Costello again after his wife was detected obtaining birth and death certificates for dead children': their identities were said to be 'under consideration by the [RIS] for illegal cover purposes'.[370] MI5 subsequently observed Paddy Costello making clandestine contact with KGB officers on several occasions.[371] Further information was provided by later Russian defectors, in particular Vasili Mitrokhin, a former senior KGB archivist who defected in 1992 with copious notes taken from the KGB archive. These recorded Costello as having been one of the KGB's top ten agents in Paris, operating under the code name 'Long'.[372]

Debate around Costello has generated a great deal of sometimes heated discussion. Some argue that evidence pointing to Costello being a Soviet spy has been misinterpreted, exaggerated or even fabricated.[373] The NZSIS stated, in 2002, that it possessed documentation which was 'unable to be released at this stage' indicating Costello's 'links with the intelligence service of the USSR'.[374] A recent assessment of Costello concludes that such information 'might well possess further surprises'.[375]

Suspicions around Ian Milner and Wally Clayton, which had sharpened during Australia's Royal Commission on Espionage, also possessed a long afterlife. In March 1956 Milner penned a statement declaring the allegation that he had divulged official secret information to a Soviet agent was 'entirely untrue, defamatory, and very shocking to me'. He continued to assert his innocence until his death in 1991.[376] The debate around Milner was sustained for decades, with a number of commentators asserting his innocence or questioning the case against him,[377] while others found the evidence for his involvement in Soviet espionage to be definitive.[378]

For decades after the Petrov affair, Clayton too denied having spied for the Soviets. While he was never prosecuted, he remained under ASIO monitoring ('Operation Pigeon'), partly out of fears that he might attempt to defect. In September 1996, aged 90, he was interviewed by Professor Desmond Ball, then anticipating the release of his co-authored book on the Soviet spy network in Australia, *Breaking the Codes*. Confronted with copies of Venona decryptions (which had been declassified) and extracts from the book manuscript, Clayton acknowledged that he was 'Klod', noting: 'It was an awful name they gave me, wasn't it?'[379]

During this interview Clayton identified Milner as agent 'Bur' and stated that he had received classified information from the Department of External Affairs from Milner over 1945 and 1946. Secret files released by the Czech Ministry of the Interior in 1996 reveal further details on Milner. His acceptance of an academic post in Czechoslovakia in 1950, ostensibly for his wife's health, was a pretext: Soviet intelligence had decided to relocate him out of fear that his cover had been compromised. In Prague, Milner reported to the Czechoslovakian secret service on academics and diplomatic acquaintances as agent number 9006, operating under the cover name 'Dvorak'.[380]

In the case of Bill Sutch, material released by United States, British and New Zealand governments relating to the period covered by this book reveals that, while suspicions persisted, no firm evidence was found. American files on Sutch noted only suspicions of 'pro-Communist leanings', the main concern being a lecture he gave in July 1952 on the Korean War 'that went right down the Communist line'.[381] In 1956, SB had revisited Dr Sutch's reputation in the context of his possible appointment as head of the Department of Industries and Commerce. Controller-General Barnett declared that he had 'found nothing concrete' to indicate that Sutch was disloyal to New Zealand, and that he 'could not be satisfied to condemn a man of Dr. Sutch's great ability to lose out on a promotion to which he seemed eminently deserving from a professional viewpoint merely on the basis of unsubstantiated rumor [sic] and "bar-room chatter"'.[382]

All the same, distrust continued in some quarters. A New Zealand security review in March 1957, concluded that Sutch 'is believed not to be, nor ever to have been, a member of any Communist Party or subservient organisation', nor to have 'propounded subversive doctrines such as the establishment of a dictatorship of the proletariat':

> Nevertheless, his Marxist–Leninist approach to problems, coupled with his independence of mind and his acceptance of the infallible rectitude of the policies of the Soviet State, have led him in his official work into judgments and actions which have been unacceptable to his employers and have generally been interpreted by them as indicating disloyalty to themselves and as the denial of their policies. There is no indication that such incidents will not recur. He is not considered a person to whom highly classified information can be safely entrusted.[383]

The attorney-general at the time, John Marshall, would later note that from this time onwards successive American administrations 'supplied secret information to successive New Zealand governments with the proviso that Sutch must not have access to it'.[384]

Dr Sutch did not secure the position of head of the Department of Industries and Commerce in 1956; in a move intended to block his elevation, the position went to a temporary appointee. After Labour's accession to office the following year, Prime Minister Walter Nash was informed that this decision had been made 'because the

Americans said they would regard New Zealand's security as suspect' with Sutch in the job. Nash – who had once himself been subject to security scrutiny – elected to appoint Sutch as permanent head of the department without placing security officials' objections before Cabinet.[385] Official suspicions continued to surround Sutch before and after his forced retirement in 1965. These were to be dramatically aired in a high-profile legal case in 1974, which will be covered in our subsequent volume.

Beyond this arena of Cold War espionage, the great bulk of the watching focused on the small number of Communists and the many people whose views and activities put them in the category (in the eyes of the political police) of being potential Communists or dupes thereof. The latter category was a broad one indeed, including as it did almost any form of dissent or non-conformity, and the collateral damage to many lives and careers was considerable. Much of it resulted from baseless suppositions and guilt by association – constituting a New Zealand McCarthyism, or something towards it. With regard to heightened security measures around public servants, Aaron Fox, for example, notes that 'while true McCarthyism never developed, the implacable anti-communist purges of the Public Service produced [an] appalling legacy of ruined careers, institutional paranoia, and enduring suspicion, while depriving government departments of some of the most able minds of their generation'.[386]

Information acquired by the political police often included gossip and rumour whose relationship with facts ranged from errors to distortion and outright fabrication. Over time, mistakes and flawed speculations could take on the status of assertions of fact, sometimes influencing later events. As noted earlier, the concealed status of the files, and their continuing influence, meant that their subjects could only guess at why their careers or personal lives might be suffering. In effect, the existence of a Subversive History Sheet added its subject to a blacklist. We know of no instances of subjects being recategorised as non-subversive, whatever their later personal or political trajectories.[387]

The heightened suspicions of the early Cold War, and the surveillance they generated, had a lasting impact on many lives. Dorian Saker's brush with the political police (and Peter Fraser) over his short story in Salient in 1940, for example, followed him during his medical studies and career. British security authorities were notified he was a 'radical' when he headed for Edinburgh University in 1960, although he had 'not come to our notice since 1955'.[388] Government architect Helmut Einhorn attracted similar interest from the political surveillers for his connections with peace and progressive movements. This too left a mark. In 1963, for example, his attempt to obtain clearance as a condition of his application for a UNESCO appointment in planning and architecture in New Delhi was rejected '[b]ecause of his activities in organisations of interest to [the NZSS], and his associations'. In 1952 Wolfgang Rosenberg had been targeted by union leader F. P. Walsh, who claimed he was the regular columnist 'Criticus' for The Standard, the 'Official Organ of the Labour Movement'. SB provided Walsh with information from its secret files and that October he presented a 35-page document

"That happens to be the Prime Minister holding a secret conference with Sir Percy Sillitoe."

Left: Figure 30
A cartoon parodying MI5 director-general Percy Sillitoe's 'secret conference' to advise the New Zealand prime minister on the country's security arrangements during a visit in 1951. *Otago Daily Times, October 1951, p. 8*

Below: Figure 31
The opening of the Police Training School at Trentham in 1956. The front row comprises some major figures in the history of the secret world: from left, Controller-General of Police Sam Barnett, Assistant Commissioner Peter Munro, Prime Minister Sidney Holland, Assistant Commissioner (and veteran surveiller) Percy Nalder, and Leader of the Opposition (and veteran surveillee) Walter Nash. *New Zealand Police*

Left: Figure 37
This photograph was taken at a social function in Auckland in October 1950 and acquired by Special Branch for identification purposes. It shows, from left, artist Joseph Alach, historian Willis (Bill) Airey, Soviet ambassador Alexander Alexandrov and Soviet Second Commercial Attaché Nikolai Ivanovich Burov. Burov was an intelligence officer whose duties focused on cultivating New Zealanders who might be persuaded to advance Soviet interests, while Alexandrov 'looked after' agents in New Zealand. *'NZ–USSR [New Zealand Union of Soviet Socialist Republics] Society, Auckland Branch' [ADMO 21007 W5985/7 26/17/1 pt1 (R24716792)], Archives New Zealand Te Rua Mahara o te Kāwanatanga*

Left: Figure 36
Group portrait taken at the 1948 Communist Party National Conference. Sid Scott, front row, fourth from the left, became general secretary the following year. *PAColl-4920-2-01, Alexander Turnbull Library, Wellington, New Zealand*

Right: Figure 38
A rare example in the secret files identifying anti-Communist activists, photographed at a 1955 demonstration. Number 2 is identified as Genius [Ginutis] Procuta, vice-president of the New Zealand Baltic Club. *'NZ–USSR [New Zealand Union of Soviet Socialist Republics] Society, Auckland Branch' [ADMO 21007 W5985/7 26/17/1 pt1 (R24716792)], Archives New Zealand Te Rua Mahara o te Kāwanatanga*

Left: Figure 39
A steamer once used to soften glue on envelope flaps for opening mail clandestinely. *New Zealand Security Intelligence Service*

Overleaf: Figure 40
NZ Truth's October 1953 front-page spread about phone-tapping, an escalation in the newspaper's campaign for a Royal Commission into police spying techniques. *NZ Truth, 7 October 1953, p. 1*

N.Z. Truth

Above all for New Zealand!

No. 2495 [Registered at the General Post Office, Wellington for Transmission as a Newspaper.]   **WEDNESDAY, OCTOBER 7, 1953.**   Auckland, 42-728, 42-418, Christchurch, 32-427, Dunedin, 10-582, Wellington, 54-807 (4 lines).   Price 6d.

"TRUTH" HAS EVIDENCE OF 'PHONE-TAPPING

WHEN this edition of "Truth" went to press, the Government appeared still to be hesitating about whether to order a Royal Commission of Inquiry into the Police Force. Since this newspaper has been accused of suggesting strong suspicions of telephone-tapping without a "jot of evidence" to support its statements, it says unequivocally that it has evidence in its possession which points to the present Commissioner of Police having carried out telephone-tapping as a senior-detective in Wellington.

IT also has details of how this work was done and has photographed equipment with which it is said to have been done.

THERE is no doubt that, technically, this equipment is capable of being used for telephone-tapping, both inside and outside buildings. "Truth" has been informed that it was used for this purpose on the instructions of the present Commissioner without the knowledge or authority of his superiors.

The truth of this statement can be tested by asking the Commissioner whether he has ever used the equipment and whether others used it under his instructions. A Royal Commission, and only a Royal Commission, would provide the opportunity for the necessary corroborative evidence to be brought.

"TRUTH" IS ALSO SATISFIED THAT IF A FULL INQUIRY IS ORDERED WITH IMMUNITY FOR WITNESSES, IT CAN BE SHOWN THAT TELEPHONE-TAPPING DID NOT END WITH THE PROMOTION OF MR. COMPTON.

It has ended now, but that was not the position until early last week.

AGREEMENT

Since last week the Minister of Police, Mr. Fortune, has said that he believes a full inquiry on the recent New South Wales model, to be necessary. "Truth" emphatically supports that view.

If the present Commissioner of Police, Mr. Compton, was responsible for tapping telephones before his present appointment and if this has continued since that authority since he became Commissioner, it does not square with the assurances given to the House of Representatives last week.

The House and the public are entitled to know why the Commissioner said that certain radio work had been done in his private residence so that he could keep in touch with police patrol cars when the installations are not suitable for this purpose.

"Truth's" information is that the present Commissioner, when he was senior-detective in charge of anti-bookmaking activities in Wellington, organised and, at times, personally conducted the tapping of the telephones of a number of persons suspected of bookmaking activities. There is no evidence to suggest that this tapping of telephones was authorised in any way by the then Commissioner and no evidence to suggest that it was known to the Post and Telegraph Department or the Government.

It was done, according to this newspaper's information, specifically on the instructions of Mr. Compton as the officer in charge of anti-bookmaking work in Wellington and on his own responsibility.

The apparatus used was of two kinds. One was an ordinary movable telephone set with a lengthened lead and two clip attachments which could be used to plug into the end panel of a building, the end panel being the point at which telephone lines converge and where a selection can be made of lines to be tapped. This equipment is of the type used by the P. and T. Department for correcting complaints and dealing with line faults.

The equipment used by the police was "doctored" so that there would be no backward transmission of sound from the person tapping the telephone.

"Truth" states categorically—since the need is to have the present Commissioner of Police should be asked whether the telephone set pictured on this page is not the one he used for tapping certain telephones in Wellington from 1944 onwards.

The second piece of equipment comprised, primarily, several short sections of conduit piping which could be screwed together until they were of sufficient length to reach the lead-in telephone wires on poles outside buildings. This attachment was provided with a clip which could be used to fix it to the telephone wires. The piping then became the main conductor, and the other

Hon. W. H. Fortune

lead was earthed. A line could be led from the lower end of the piping into a nearby car or building and connected to a telephone set similar to the one already mentioned.

This equipment was used at night, in cases where it was not possible to plug-in from inside buildings.

The use made of information obtained in this way, "Truth" suggests, also requires the closest examination. It was obviously impossible, in any subsequent court proceedings, to describe how information was obtained. It would, however, be possible to use relevant facts about more recent telephone operations were not reported before the matter was raised in the House last week, and whether these facts were not known to the authorities before the recent series of categorical denials was issued.

"Truth" has already said that it does not believe that either the Minister in charge of Security, Mr.

tained by telephone-tapping was always used to obtain bookmaking convictions.

While it can be argued that this system of inquiry may have been the means of bringing about a number of convictions, the methods by which the inquiries were carried out are open to the gravest abuse and should not be tolerated.

Between July and September, 1946 Senior-Detective Compton, as he was then, was concerned with 12 cases in the Wellington area in which convictions were obtained for bookmaking. In one of these cases, heard in December, 1946, counsel for the defence suggested that the police had used unfair methods of detection. Senior-Detective Compton said he would refute any such allegations.

"TRUTH" SUGGESTS THAT THIS REPUTATION SHOULD BE RE-EXAMINED IN THE LIGHT OF THE FACTS NOW EMERGING.

EQUIPMENT

"Truth" further gathers that some of the telephone-tapping equipment used by the present Commissioner when he was a detective was still in his possession when he became Commissioner and that instructions were given by Mr. Compton that it should not be broken up as it might be wanted.

It is significant that following the categorical denial of telephone tapping given by Mr. Compton when he was questioned by the Minister of Police, Mr. Fortune, by radio-telephone, a technical officer of the police force who has been closely concerned with telephone and other communications, has threatened to resign from the force.

"Truth" asks, also categorically, whether one of the reasons for this officer's protest is the fact that he had already made his objections to telephone-tapping clear when the denial of the Commissioner was repeated to the House.

It also asks whether certain very relevant facts about more recent telephone operations were not reported before the matter was raised in the House last week, and whether these facts were not known to the authorities before the recent series of categorical denials was issued.

Police Probe Urgent

COMMISSIONER OF POLICE should be asked whether he has had this telephone-tapping equipment in his possession, and whether he has used it. Canvas bag in which it was carried is at the back.

Holland, or the Minister of Police, Mr. Fortune, knew that telephone-tapping had been carried out.

It was for this reason that it was not more specific in its earlier article. It suggests that the proper reply when the matter was raised, was that it would be investigated. Instead a series of denials was issued, the chief purpose of which appeared to be to discredit the story entirely.

Since the Government now appears to favour a Royal Commission, the full facts can be examined by that body. They can, "Truth" suggests, be very simply brought to light.

Another section of the replies given

Lockers Searched

EARLY this week, when other matters were occupying the attention of the police, the lockers of six sergeants at the Central Police Station, Wellington, were broken open and the contents thoroughly examined. So far as can be ascertained nothing was removed.

by the Commissioner to the questions asked him by radio-telephone, also requires examination.

It concerns the erection of two radio masts and other radio work at the Commissioner's private residence and the suggestion by Mr. Compton that this work was done to enable him to maintain radio contacts with police patrols by short wave.

"Truth" suggests that an examination of the nature of the installations carried out for Mr. Compton will prove that they are of no use whatever for keeping

in contact with police patrol cars.

The type of aerial used for this purpose must be a certain length, usually about 30 inches. The masts at Mr. Compton's residence, apart from being unsuitable, are erected too far from the house and the aerial is 80 to 100 feet in length. With high frequencies, used by the police radio system, the lead from the aerial to the actual set must be as short as possible. A dipol aerial is the only suitable type and that it is usually attached to the house as close as possible to the receiving set.

"ALL THE TECHNICAL MODIFICATIONS KNOWN TO RADIO SCIENCE COULD NOT CONVERT THE AERIAL AT MR. COMPTON'S HOUSE FOR USE WITH THE POLICE RADIO SYSTEM." THIS NEWSPAPER WAS TOLD.

In actual fact, Mr. Compton purchased a radiogram from a Wellington commercial radio firm and he had the set overhauled by police radio technicians.

There are no external signs at Mr. Compton's residence indicating any intention of constructing a suitable aerial for police radio receiving or transmission.

"Truth" does not question the claim that the Commissioner paid for the materials, but the labour, and the diversion of it from normal police duties is a not inconsiderable factor.

If the reason for the installations given by the Commissioner to Mr. Fortune is incorrect, then he has let his Minister down very badly and misled the House of Representatives and the country.

NEW FEATURES: *Picture Serial by Pett* ● *Books, Films, Radio* ● *Snooker by Joe Davis* ● *Advice Bureau by Lou Lockheart* to *The Standard*'s board of management which denounced Rosenberg as pro-Soviet. A 1963 NZSS notation on the document states that it was 'prepared by the Info Service' (the Publicity Division) and that Walsh's intervention 'resulted in Rosenberg being denied space in the Standard.'[389]

Richard Collins was confronted with security suspicions resulting from his attendance and reported remarks at the Vegetable Club. He rejected an offer to appear before a tribunal, one which would have allowed him so few rights that he could neither be told of the charges against him nor question witnesses. He was then offered a transfer to a less sensitive departmental role, but elected to resign from External Affairs since his diplomatic future seemed compromised.[390] While subsequently building a distinguished legal career (which culminated in a number of prominent positions in both the public and private sectors) he had continued to feel the impact of the secret files. In the early 1960s, for example, as the then deputy secretary of External Affairs later recalled, the attorney-general removed Collins from consideration for appointment as a judge on grounds of the information in the files.[391] In 2009 the director of the NZSIS, Dr Warren Tucker, concluded that 'Collins' career after 1954 shows that without doubt he was a loyal New Zealander'. Founding NZSS director Brigadier Gilbert privately stated his views that the matter of the Vegetable Club had been 'badly handled at all levels'.[392]

Doug Lake resigned from the Public Service in 1954, after McIntosh had told him of the case against him (and ensured that he 'accidentally' saw his personal file).[393] His life and career now took a completely different course. He reverted to his previous occupation as a journalist, taking up a job with the Press Association before he and his family moved to the People's Republic of China in 1962. He is recorded as noting that '[t]hey got rid of me without any reason. Now I'll give them a reason.'[394] Both Lake and his wife Ruth went to work in China's Foreign Languages Institute, 'polishing' English language publications, and their daughters became 'Red Guards' in the early years of the Cultural Revolution.[395] The Lakes returned to New Zealand in 1968 where they gave positive press to the Chinese regime.[396]

Labour Party and Fabian member Nigel Taylor and his wife Nancy remained branded as 'socialist in outlook and . . . associated with the civil liberties and human rights organisations'. When Taylor was vetted by the Police for suitability for voluntary work in the Scout movement in 1960, the NZSS, on the basis of his file, opined that he 'could be a dangerous person as a Cub Master with young minds to mould' – although a decision was made to keep the report to the Police to a simple 'not recommended'. His peace movement activities continued to be watched and a 1973 entry in his file (which recorded his appointment as a magistrate) noted that he 'strongly opposed the NZSIS'.[397]

Security interest in *Newsquote*, the publication organised by Don Brown, Doug Foy and Hugh Price, brought similarly lasting consequences. In April 1953, SB concerns about the newssheet came to a head when SB officers approached Brown's employer and stated that he was 'running an undercover "front" for communists', leading to his sacking that same day.[398] The next day, *Newsquote*'s typist June Joblin (Jack Lewin's secretary, soon to be his wife) was approached and informed that her continued involvement with the periodical would see the Public Service Commission notified 'with results that would be to her disadvantage. She decided to stop.'[399]

While a new typist (Cath Eichelbaum) was found, further draconian action was taken against *Newsquote*. After a similar intervention, Foy was transferred to a less sensitive post within Treasury, but elected to resign instead. However, he was, in Agent Fraser's words, 'a marked man!', and a job offer from an exporting firm was 'mysteriously' withdrawn soon after.[400] Price, then a university student, reported no immediate repercussions, but soon found his efforts to gain employment in the Public Service were barred on security grounds (although this decision was later overturned). Moreover, in 1972 he and his family were refused permission to transit through the United States, en route to Britain, and an American consular official later affirmed that this was due to security information provided to American authorities.[401] Agent Fraser's reflections on the *Newsquote* affair indicate what seems, in retrospect, to have been the astonishing degree to which the political police saw the world through a Cold War lens. He observed that 'it is difficult to accept that the lives of these people were to be so affected – for bringing to New Zealanders news [that had been] reprinted from highly reputable publications'. But, he went on, 'at the time I believed the magazine was anti-American (and therefore communist)'.[402]

Price would subsequently become a successful publisher and remained a stalwart supporter of civil liberties and progressive causes; among his writings was a book about the Folkes debacle.[403] For some six decades, he remained puzzled as to why *Newsquote* had attracted such attention and reaction and he fought a long battle to gain access to secret files on the matter. While he was ultimately successful in gaining access to a number of such documents, they shed little light on the matter beyond indicating the thought processes of the political police during the early Cold War. He also fought for an apology. While a director of the NZSIS deemed it inappropriate to presume to apologise for the actions of SB, he noted, in a 2009 letter: 'I am of the view that hindsight shows "Newsquote" to have been misjudged, and I hope this statement will give you the closure you desire.'[404]

Our interviewees from families who had members with personal files from the period under study have struggled to find closure upon reading even the redacted files that have been released to them. Seeing such routine documentation, sometimes in extraordinarily intimate detail, of the lives of loved ones has evinced a mix of reactions: astonishment, anger, and a sense of violation and betrayal prominent among them. Some have had to live with the knowledge that informants mixed and even lived with their families. Some family memories note that members who had been subjects of surveillance, and who suspected or discovered it and found no available redress, felt the national ethos had been betrayed.

Secret surveillance over people who were neither breaking the law nor posed any threat to state security sat uncomfortably with key elements of New Zealand's dominant mythscape. The officials reviewing the state of the country's security intelligence arrangements in 1956 clearly recognised that this national narrative made covert surveillance and intrusive penetration into private lives generally taboo. In effect they considered the solution to be much greater secrecy.

CPNZ members tended to be more alert than most to the possibility of state monitoring and took some countermeasures. During the 1951 dispute, for example, the CPNZ in Auckland went underground to protect its operations and equipment.[405] In 1954, at a Communist Party street-corner election meeting in Wellington, a member with a 'flashlight camera' approached a man 'standing in the darkness', who then 'became alarmed and left the meeting in great haste'.[406] In 1955, in the context of publicity around Agent Guy, SB sources reported that some targeted organisations were investigating other members suspected of being 'snoops'. One Christchurch informant in Communist circles was outed through the wrath of his girlfriend (who 'used to be present when the man was writing up his notes') after their break-up.[407] At this same time, the front page of the *People's Voice* was given to a photograph of SB's headquarters that was captioned: 'THIS IS WHERE the security (political) police have their headquarters in Majoribanks Street, Wellington.'[408]

However, archival and oral sources now make it apparent that knowledge of the breadth and depth of the surveilling net, even in most left/progressive circles, was remarkably limited. Most certainly, the great majority of those who were surveilled would have been extremely surprised had they known they were of security interest – as some confirmed when, much later, they gained access to even sanitised copies of their personal files. A number of these former targets and their families have wryly noted that many causes upon which the political police had cast a hostile or cynical eye had eventually come to be generally accepted by public and politicians alike, and some of them given legislative protection.[409] Even committed Communists did not appear to realise the degree to which the surveillers had penetrated their political and personal lives. Looking back on his Communist days in the mid-1950s, Percy Allison felt, as he told his former comrade Rona Bailey, that the security services did a 'good hatchet job on us and [were] so subtle about it'.[410]

Conclusion

In one sense, political policing in the early Cold War reflected heightened threat perceptions of both gradual Communist encroachment and the possibility of open hostilities and potentially a nuclear war. At the same time, it also reflected the patterns and methods of state surveillance forged during interwar apprehension around Bolshevism and, more generally, the previous century's concerns with left-revolutionaries and foreign spies.

Modes of humint surveillance, too, broadly resembled those of prior decades. The surveillers attended meetings and cultivated sources, accumulated and reviewed literature, covertly followed and listened to targets, analysed reports, and carried out all the other standard processes in the intelligence cycle. The dragnet approach of surveilling broad movements and social circles that might potentially host targets, first applied systemically during the First World War, had been especially honed by the perceived security demands of the red scare, the Depression and the Second World War. In the post-war decade, this deepening surveillance of civil society can be seen in its most distilled form in the 1951 waterfront dispute. This was the most volatile moment in what now seems to be 'a lost world of political engagement', one in which large numbers participated in political movements in attempts to secure a new, fairer order.[411]

That being said, insofar as politically based surveillance and repression was known about, there was very little public questioning as to whether political policing and its consequences put a dent in New Zealand's reputation for freedom, fairness and justice. While this was generally the case through the period surveyed in this volume, such a disposition was reinforced by the zeitgeist of the early Cold War. Certainly, the political mainstream and the political police generally shared the same perspectives.

Looking forward, the decisions pursued in this era determined the broad contours of state intelligence work over the following decades. The first decade of the Cold War effectively saw the question of a professional security service outside the Police – first proposed after the First World War, tried in the Second, and shelved after the failed experiment of the SIB – resolved with the 1956 foundation of the NZSS. Accordingly, the New Zealand Police Force was instructed to begin the transfer of primary responsibility for human intelligence to the new stand-alone agency. Connectedly, signals intelligence was also reorganised in this period, with huge future ramifications. New Zealand's membership in the UKUSA alliance made it part of a vast global intelligence organisation, whose sigint interceptions 'bolstered a Commonwealth connection in a weak area for UKUSA in southeast Asia and the southwest Pacific'.[412] All such developments signalled the direction of many of the state's security considerations, policies and operations through the following decades of the Cold War and beyond. That history is the subject of the following volume.

Concluding Remarks

All histories are 'reports on progress', subject to modification and reinterpretation as new evidence comes to light and new theoretical perspectives emerge. Any study of the secret world, an environment that generally shuns the public spotlight or actively seeks to retain its secrets, is particularly open to future revision. Nevertheless, the available documentary evidence and secondary accounts reveal the broad contours and rhythms of New Zealand's system of state surveillance, and details of its operations and impacts, during the five and a half decades after 1900.

The foundations of this history build on an ancient aspect of statecraft: the search for actual or potential seditionaries, subversives and spies and the use of surveillance to underpin this. The utilisation of surveillance (from open inquiries to clandestine operations) is not an incidental development: every polity, to a greater or lesser degree, watches for subjects and outsiders attempting to undermine or overthrow both itself and the interests and values it promotes and protects. During the early decades of the nineteenth century, the application of this tradecraft to the islands of Aotearoa, which were increasingly coming within the British sphere of global influence, had been intermittent. It aimed at informing Crown authorities of conditions relevant, or potentially threatening, to their interests. This was especially so at times when they seemed to be under threat, including from Māori tribes – which had their own means of keeping appraised of issues of political and military significance.

From the beginning of the colony of New Zealand in 1840, Imperial authorities sought to inform themselves of potential or actual threats to the new colonising venture and the state which presided over it. Their surveilling was entrusted primarily to New Zealand's various police forces, often paramilitary or militarised formations whose essential mission was to impose 'peace and good order' in the colony. Major targets of surveillance included dissident Māori (although military intelligence handled this in war zones) and Pākehā activists (or, in the language of the time, 'agitators').

By the mid-1880s, the police emphasis on imposing order on both Māori and Pākehā had been superseded by a focus on maintaining the advanced state of order which had been achieved. In 1886 the New Zealand Police Force was founded as a nationwide body of police personnel divested of their former military functions. It also inherited primary responsibility for state security intelligence, a duty which sat broadly, if imperfectly, within the Force's mandate to maintain and enforce public order. Policing the newly emergent 'stable society' led to modernising and professionalising developments within the Force, including a gradual increase in the prominence of detective work. This, in turn, elevated the role of political surveillance, which was generally led by plain-clothes police. With Māori rebellion defeated, socialist revolutionaries and agents of rival powers increasingly eclipsed disaffected tribal groupings as the major concerns of official surveillance. Surveilling of such targets intensified in the first decade of the new century, with police serving as the state's eyes and ears within the labour movement and in the search for foreign spies. Police surveillance in the first decade of the twentieth century led to a stockpiling of information that subsequently informed proactive state measures to suppress labour militancy, most notably during the showdowns at Waihī in 1912 and during the Great Strike of 1913. Alarm over the possibility of foreign spies operating in New Zealand, especially at times of intensified international tension, also led to increased vigilance from the detectives.

Surveillance over society greatly intensified during the First World War. The wartime emergency meant that the definition of a threat to state security widened to include multiple potential or actual impediments to maximising New Zealand's commitment to the war. As well as this widening of the surveilling gaze, the levels of penetration into dissident elements of society deepened, aided by tightened laws and regulations seeking to counter opposition to some or all aspects of the war effort. Pacifists and pacificists, anti-conscriptionists and seditionaries, disaffected Māori, socialists and trade unionists, religious leaders deemed to be fomenting civil disruption, peace-at-any-cost 'defeatists' and supporters of the Easter Rebellion in Dublin or of the Bolshevik Revolution, and many more classes of individuals and their causes, organisations and movements: all were subject to intensive scrutiny – leading, among other things, to a heightened number of convictions for political activities.

In the years following the Bolshevik seizure of power in Russia in 1917, New Zealand's covert surveillers increasingly (re)focused on the revolutionary left and those seen to be influenced by or sympathetic to it. In the immediate aftermath of the First World War, the country entered 'a long Cold War' that would last for seven decades. Accordingly, the international Communist movement quickly superseded anarcho-syndicalism as the major perceived vector of subversion in the interwar period – a time we have termed 'the latent Cold War'. At the same time, the surveillance of dissidence within the country began to develop more systematic approaches, building upon the methods and data inherited from the four years of conflict as well as the pre-war period. Most notably, from 1920 selected detectives were instructed to undertake duties that were dedicated to political policing. The newly minted political detectives began to compile 'secret files' that were not routinely accessible by other police. This replaced the looser pre-war system under which some especially skilled detectives tended to be tasked with political surveillance when required.

State surveillance throughout the interwar period, however, broadly continued earlier patterns. The surveillers' net, for example, was cast wider and deeper during state emergencies – most notably during the social and political unrest of the early Depression years. In late 1935 the First Labour Government entered office and ministers who had once been seen as seditious (including some gaoled for that offence) took up the reins of power. Even then, little changed in the fundamentals of state surveillance, with the new government soon realising the advantages of utilising the services of the secret world. In fact, in view of their experience and knowledge base, the ministers were generally content to endorse what had now become a virtually autonomous mandate for the political police. Consistency rather than discontinuity, therefore, characterised the secret world after the political transformation of the mid-1930s, a repeat of what had happened after the Liberal–Labour alliance took up office in the early 1890s.

State surveillance on the domestic front in the Second World War period was essentially a reprise of the first global conflict, although many of the functions of the political police were temporarily handed to a new body under general military overview, the Security Intelligence Bureau. Its members, from the director down, mostly had little experience of spycraft, and the results of this experiment were mixed – and police continued to surveil those they saw as enemies of the state in any case. When the SIB's credibility was fatally undermined in 1942–43, in a bizarre episode in the history of New Zealand's secret world, it came under Police direction and, in late 1944, it was absorbed into the NZPF. It was closed at the end of hostilities, and the police detective offices in the centres of population now resumed full control of political surveillance.

After the Second World War, the broader international order within which the state surveillers operated underwent major changes. New Zealand had previously seen its security as guaranteed by British global power, and had participated in the Imperial intelligence network, contributing to transnational sigint arrangements and liaising with London-based and other Commonwealth countries on human intelligence. However, the damage to the United Kingdom's global position as a result of the war (notably after the fall of Singapore in early 1942), and the primacy of the United States in the Pacific War, saw the Americans rapidly take the lead in allied security intelligence. The US would, indeed, shortly become the centre of one of the most comprehensive sigint and security alliances in history, based upon a series of top-secret UKUSA sigint arrangements (eventually called the Five Eyes). Canada, Australia and New Zealand were viewed (and necessarily viewed themselves) as junior members of this alliance, operating initially under the cloak of the other principal partner, the United Kingdom. This five-nation sigint grouping quickly became, in effect, a broader security and intelligence alliance, based on a series of complex arrangements, treaties and understandings.

This development was propelled by the rapid and rancorous collapse of the wartime alliance of convenience with the USSR and the subsequent arrival of the Cold

War proper. Fears that tensions between East and West could escalate into a third world war (potentially involving nuclear weapons), reactions to Soviet espionage, and heated notions of Communist subversion led to ever greater numbers – notably public servants, left-wing activists and non-conformist groupings – being targeted for their political beliefs or associations. With the intelligence stakes higher than ever, pressure began to mount for a more specialist security intelligence service than the political police could provide. Such pressure came from within the New Zealand state, especially from the military, as well as from the Americans and the British, but for a time several leading officials resisted it – and MI5's head, Percy Sillitoe, a former colonial police officer, did not himself think it necessary. New Zealand did not follow Australia in setting up a stand-alone humint organisation in 1949, but instead established Special Branch late that same year, formalising the political police as a distinct unit within the NZPF. But pressure continued to build, in part because for the next half-decade the new National government followed Labour's lead and displayed reluctance to reform New Zealand security.

However, the Special Branch era proved to be the final chapter in the long story of police holding primary responsibility for domestic security intelligence. Its end came from a combination of its own shortcomings and ongoing pressure from New Zealand officials and its major external security partners. In 1956 the government accepted the thrust of the arguments for adopting an MI5-influenced model of security surveillance, and the New Zealand Security Service was established without fanfare – an appropriate beginning for the reconstitution of the country's secret world. Its officers were not tasked with the catch-all police task of imposing and maintaining peace and good order, and they lacked crucial policing powers – most notably that of arrest. Consequently, institutional priorities and the operational phase of the intelligence cycle differed considerably from that which had been carried out under policing auspices. The ramifications of this are explored in our succeeding volume.

Across the five and a half decades covered by this book, the history of New Zealand's secret world demonstrates a broad continuity. This largely reflects the NZPF's primary responsibility for state surveillance, if always in association with other departments and allied agencies (and with one interruption during the Second World War). In general, there was little fundamental change in both objectives and methods. The main targets for state surveillance at the turn of the century were the socialist and labour movements, and agents of rival powers; this remained the case in the early Cold War. It bears repeating that a detective involved in surveilling in 1900 would readily recognise what the political police of 1956 were trying to achieve and how they went about achieving it.

The broad contours of this history, then, can be relatively easily summarised. Its implications for our understanding of New Zealand's past, however, are more complex. The history of secret surveillance over civil society sits uneasily with both the nation's foundational ideals and the dominant self-image which emerged over time. New Zealand has a long history of portraying itself as an exemplary paradise. From the beginning of its existence as a colony, immigrants were said to be able to leave behind the class constraints and hardships of the Old World and 'get on' both socially and economically on the basis of 'a fair go for all'. In the late nineteenth century, interventionist state measures added an international reputation as a progressive 'social laboratory'. By 1900 it was firmly believed, in a great many quarters, that 'God's Own Country' had gone a long way in implementing the ideals proclaimed and developed since 1840: the population would enjoy freedom, prosperity, justice, good governance and security within an open, egalitarian and liberal society. The national self-image was further enhanced from the mid-1930s when the state aspired to provide social security 'from the cradle to the grave' for those in need.

Inevitably, the reality fell short of this idealised narrative. All the same, the officially proclaimed values had a sufficient degree of truth, especially vis-à-vis other societies, to persuade large sectors of the New Zealand population to accept aspirational values as real achievements. Such buy-in gained greater momentum after the introduction of the various state redistributive measures from the late nineteenth century onwards, and even more after Labour's welfare system was installed in the later 1930s. The exceptionally free, fair, just and open society, then, remained an integral part of the national mythscape of the period covered by this history.

The secret world, however, adds further complications to the tension between mythscape and reality. The surveillers spied upon large numbers of people, only a tiny number of whom could be classifiable as subversive in the sense of attempting to undermine or overthrow the state – let alone spies working for another power. The great majority of those surveilled were essentially law-abiding, swept into the surveilling net through activities which reflected their beliefs – attending meetings, signing petitions, marching in the streets, mixing in progressive circles and so on. Except for a handful of career criminals, no other sector of society was subject to such ongoing and in-depth surveillance by authorities. Many of the people subjected to surveillance saw their ideas become broadly accepted in society in the course of time – indeed, a number of causes became central pillars of state policy, their enactment presided over by formerly surveilled figures.

Quite apart from issues surrounding who and what were targeted, many of the methods of surveillance jar with New Zealand's dominant sense of itself. Special Branch's 1954 observation that 'the average law-abiding New Zealander tends to frown on anything which savours of spying or pimping' probably still holds true almost seven decades later.[1] Certainly, in the period we cover, many people would very likely have been astonished if they had known how the state penetrated civil society: how informants and agents were used, meetings were listened into, private mail was intercepted and copied, premises were covertly entered, and so on. Many of the dispositions, mistakes and confusions of those given authority to peer into personal lives would also have probably raised disquiet. Once personal files of people under surveillance in our period began to be released to themselves or their families, albeit in redacted form, recipients we have spoken to were shocked at the sheer amount and types of information collected and filed – not to mention the strong propensity of the political police to view any progressive or non-conformist interests or actions as inspired by or vulnerable to exploitation by Communism.

But the very nature of the secret world ensured that its actions, and even its existence, seldom came to public attention. Sigint provides an extreme example of this phenomenon: the existence of the UKUSA/Five Eyes alliance, for instance, remained hidden from public view for decades. In the world of humint, the exposure of political policing activities by, for example, the *People's Voice* or *NZ Truth* provided very rare glimpses of New Zealand's secret world. Had more come to light about the state's intelligence operations, the authorities would most likely have argued that state surveillance was not a violation of New Zealand's dominant mythscape but a necessary measure to secure and protect those ideals upon which it was based. Certainly, the emergencies of the two world wars and the 1951 industrial confrontation saw such arguments evoked. While the coercive measures the state deployed during such emergencies were able to find a considerable degree of public support at the time, maintaining lasting public consent for covert surveillance of large parts of the population may have been altogether another matter.

Even more astonishing to those unfamiliar with the workings of the secret world was the fact that surveillance often extended beyond recording and analysing information. It was regularly entwined with operations, formal or informal, to stymie opinions, causes and campaigns. Sometimes this occurred through seeking to dampen commitment by use of the criminal justice system, including prosecuting political targets for non-political offences. Far more often, the political police used non-judicial methods designed to lead to setbacks in campaigns, careers or relationships, such as making it difficult to secure meeting places, quietly suppressing literature, notifying employers of their employees' political activities, or passing on information to social circles.

Issues of accountability overarch the uneasy relationship between the dominant national mythscape and the secret world during the period under study. This effectively returns us to the recognition that surveillance is a key function of statecraft: in the final analysis, all states seek to protect themselves and their interests from what they perceive to be internal and external dangers, and such assessments can override formal and informal restraints. This general precept is most apparent in times of national emergency. At the outbreak of the First World War, for example, the German chancellor expressed it bluntly: 'Gentlemen, we are now in a state of necessity, and necessity knows no law!'[2] New Zealand's solicitor-general around the same time, as we have noted, enunciated this same principle: legal methods 'ended where the State's peril begins'.[3]

Insofar as there were constraints on state surveillance in New Zealand in the first half of the twentieth century, these largely reflected the fact that the surveillers worked within the context of a rules-based 'police and justice system'. Despite its paramilitary origins, the NZPF had long proclaimed its adherence to the founding principles of the London Metropolitan Police. Formulated by Robert Peel, these essentially amounted to seeking public 'consent' for policing through minimising the application of physical coercion. This is reflected in the very first of the Peelian 'Maxims for General Guidance of the Police Force in New Zealand', which held that its members were 'placed in authority to protect, not to oppress, the public'.[4] It was the government, of course, theoretically representing the people, which gave them that authority. In turn, large sectors of the New Zealand population had come to believe that consensual policing was no longer merely an aspiration but a reality. All of this meant there was, therefore, a Police imperative to avoid methods which might be seen to be oppressive, especially those of questionable ethics and even more particularly those which were of dubious legality or downright illegal; the political police operated with an acute awareness of the need to pay at least lip service to principles of freedom, fairness and 'fair go'.

Even in Peelian police forces, however, constraints were often merely theoretical. While policemen did have to be careful to be seen to be not breaking the law, they generally had scope to operate at its pliable margins – and they were not averse to moving into at least dubiously legal terrain if they felt the demands of order required it. This imperative was especially the case for political police. During the history covered by this book, accountability for the operation of the secret world rested, in theory, with the political executive, but ministers were told little – and asked little. This meant an effective lack of political accountability, compounded by the fact that there were virtually no practical processes or judicial recourses available to surveillees, assuming they were aware of the fact of their surveillance and any adverse consequences that flowed from it. The answer to Juvenal's question of 'who watches the watchers' inside the New Zealand Police Force and its surveilling partners between 1900 and 1956 was, essentially, no one.

Notes

Abbreviations

AJHR	*Appendices to the Journals of the House of Representatives*
ANZ	Archives New Zealand Te Rua Mahara o te Kāwanatanga
ATL	Alexander Turnbull Library, The National Library of New Zealand Te Puna Mātauranga o Aotearoa
CIA	Central Intelligence Agency
GCSB	Government Communications Security Bureau
NZG	*New Zealand Gazette*
NZPD	*New Zealand Parliamentary Debates*
NZS	*New Zealand Statutes*
NZSIS	New Zealand Security Intelligence Service
RHPHC	Richard Hill Police History Collection
SRCNZSSC	Stout Research Centre for New Zealand Studies Security Collection
TNA	The National Archives (United Kingdom)

Preface

1 Conor O'Reilly, 'The Pluralization of High Policing: Convergence and Divergence at the Public–Private Interface', *British Journal of Criminology*, vol. 20, no. 4 (2015), p. 705; Christopher Andrew and David Dilks (eds), *The Missing Dimension: Governments and Intelligence in the Twentieth Century* (London: Macmillan, 1984).

2 *New Zealand Herald*, 17 December 2016, p. A20.

Introduction: Theory and Practice

1 The doyen of intelligence history in the United Kingdom, Christopher Andrew, popularised this term in *The Secret World: A History of Intelligence* (New Haven: Yale University Press, 2018).

2 Stefano Musco, 'Intelligence Gathering and the Relationship between Rulers and Spies: Some Lessons from Eminent and Lesser-known Classics', *Intelligence and National Security*, vol. 31, no. 7 (2016), pp. 1025–39.

3 The state's interests range from protecting the capital-based socio-economic order over which it presides to its ideological values and the norms of social behaviour it seeks to impose and maintain; by 'ideology' we mean a system of ideas and ideals, more especially one which forms a basis for social, economic and political theory and policy.

4 For policing history in New Zealand, including security policing, see the 'History of Policing in New Zealand' series: Richard S. Hill, *Policing the Colonial Frontier: The Theory and Practice of Coercive Social and Racial Control in New Zealand, 1767–1867* (Wellington: Historical Publications Branch, Department of Internal Affairs, 1986); Richard S. Hill, *The Colonial Frontier Tamed: New Zealand Policing in Transition, 1867–1886* (Wellington: Historical Branch, Department of Internal Affairs, 1989); Richard S. Hill, *The Iron Hand in the Velvet Glove: The Modernisation of Policing in New Zealand, 1886–1917* (Palmerston North: Dunmore Press, 1995); Graeme Dunstall, *A Policeman's Paradise?: Policing a Stable Society, 1918–1945* (Palmerston North: Dunmore Press, 1999); Susan Butterworth, *More Than Law and Order: Policing a Changing Society 1945–1992* (Dunedin: University of Otago Press, 2005). The concept of 'political policing' is a flexible one in scholarship; see, for example, Tony Bunyan, *The History and Practice of the Political Police in Britain* (London: J. Friedmann, 1976) and Simon Kitson, 'Political Policing', *Crime, Histoire & Sociétés/Crime, History & Societies*, vol. 3, no. 2 (1999), pp. 95–102.

5 See, for example, SRCNZSSC, E/S/3, OPR, 'Secret Correspondence', vol. 1, 1920/1-1932/952, and 'Greymouth "Secret Files" received and despatched to Commissioner, 1932–39'.

6 For this theme in New Zealand history, see James Belich, *Making Peoples: A History of the New Zealanders from Polynesian Settlement to the End of the Nineteenth Century* (Auckland: Allen Lane, 1996), passim. For briefer coverage, see James Belich, *Paradise Reforged: A History of the New Zealanders from the 1880s to the Year 2000* (Auckland: Allen Lane, 2001), pp. 76–86 and Richard S. Hill, 'Settler Colonialism in New Zealand, 1840–1907', in Edward Cavanagh and Lorenzo Veracini (eds), *The Routledge Handbook of the History of Settler Colonialism* (Abingdon & New York: Routledge, 2017).

7 When working-class Pat Kelly, later a militant labour activist under great scrutiny by the political police, arrived in New Zealand in 1954 he wrote home of having 'found Shangri-La': Rebecca Macfie, *Helen Kelly: Her Life* (Wellington: Awa Press, 2021). For the concept of 'getting on', see Stevan Eldred-Grigg, *New Zealand Working People, 1890–1990* (Palmerston North: Dunmore Press, 1990), pp. 79–83.

8   The American historian David Hackett Fischer contrasts two 'open societies', New Zealand and the United States, through the lens of differing emphases in national identity: 'fairness' in New Zealand versus 'freedom' in the USA. This is broadly true enough, although freedom of expression forms a strong strand within New Zealand's imagery of fairness. See Fischer, *Fairness and Freedom: A History of Two Open Societies: New Zealand and the United States* (Oxford: Oxford University Press, 2012). See also Hill, 'Settler Colonialism in New Zealand', pp. 391–408, and Karl Popper, *The Open Society and Its Enemies* (London: Routledge, 1945). For critiques of notions of New Zealand exceptionalism, see Miles Fairburn, 'Is There a Good Case for New Zealand Exceptionalism?', in Tony Ballantyne and Brian Moloughney (eds), *Disputed Histories: Imagining New Zealand's Pasts* (Dunedin: University of Otago Press, 2006), pp. 143–67; Miles Fairburn, *The Ideal Society and its Enemies: The Foundations of Modern New Zealand Society, 1850–1900* (Auckland: Auckland University Press, 1989).

9   Duncan Bell, 'Mythscapes: Memory, Mythology, and National Identity', *British Journal of Sociology*, vol. 54, issue 1 (March 2003), pp. 63–81; Duncan Bell, 'Agonistic Democracy and the Politics of Memory', *Constellations*, vol. 15, no. 1 (2008), p. 151. Both hegemonic and counter-hegemonic mythscapes alter their constitutive elements over time and often intertwine elements of fact and fiction. See, for example, Belich, *Making Peoples* and *Paradise Reforged*, which offer accessible perspectives on New Zealand national narratives.

10   Brian Easton, *Not in Narrow Seas: The Economic History of Aotearoa New Zealand* (Wellington: Victoria University Press, 2020), p. 202. We use the word 'progressive' in a technical sense, to denote policies that were called such at the time. Their watchers used it too; see, for example, Saker family

papers, p. 3, Dorian Saker personal file ('he likes to obtain editing positions where he can advance progressive views').

11   James McPherson, *Reasons Why the Working Men of New Zealand Should Become Internationalists; Together with an Article entitled, Anti-Chinese Immigration* (Christchurch: J. McPherson, 1872), p. 12.

12   Ibid., p. 21.

13   Mikhail Bakunin, *Marxism, Freedom and the State* (London: Freedom Press, 1950).

14   For a range of discussion, see Mark Mazower (ed.), *The Policing of Politics in the Twentieth Century* (Providence & Oxford: Berghahn Books, 1997), especially Clive Emsley, 'Introduction: Political Police and the European Nation-State in the Nineteenth Century'; and for a country-based history, Reg Whitaker, Gregory S. Kealey and Andrew Parnaby, *Secret Service: Political Policing in Canada from the Fenians to Fortress America* (Toronto: University of Toronto Press, 2012).

15   Fugio Kano and Maurice Ward, 'Socialism is a Mission: Max Bickerton's Involvement with the Japanese Communist Party and Translation of Japanese Proletarian Literature in the 1930s', *New Zealand Journal of Asian Studies*, vol. 16, no. 2 (December 2014), p. 103.

16   See, for examples, Frank McDonough, *The Gestapo: The Myth and Reality of Hitler's Secret Police* (London: Coronet, 2015); Molly Pucci, *Security Empire: The Secret Police in Communist Eastern Europe* (New Haven: Yale University Press, 2020); George Leggett, *The Cheka: Lenin's Political Police* (New York: Oxford University Press, 1986).

17   Another way of characterising state surveillance and control of those suspected of posing political threats to the state is 'high policing', or policing of those intending to damage the machinery of state. We have avoided that concept in this book, partly because the term can be used in other senses and also because twentieth-century political

surveillance was generally conducted on people who cannot be deemed as presenting any threat to the state. Jean-Paul Brodeur, *The Policing Web* (Oxford: Oxford University Press, 2010), pp. 223–54, 346–47.

18 This also reflects a dearth of archival material from the earlier decades.

19 H. H. Gerth and C. Wright Mills (eds), *From Max Weber: Essays in Sociology* (London & New York: Routledge, 2009), p. 78; Laurence Lustgarten, 'National Security and Political Policing: Some Thoughts on Values, Ends and Law', in Jean-Paul Brodeur, Peter Gill and Dennis Töllborg (eds), *Democracy, Law and Security: Internal Security Services in Contemporary Europe* (Aldershot: Ashgate Publishing, 2003), pp. 328–29.

20 Such issues have been raised prominently in recent times by Māori claims against 'the Crown in right of New Zealand'. The Waitangi Tribunal's 2014 report *He Whakaputanga Me Te Tiriti/The Declaration and the Treaty* (Wellington: Legislation Direct) concluded that the chiefs who signed the Treaty of Waitangi in 1840, the year of annexation to Britain, 'did not [intend to] cede their sovereignty to Britain. That is, they did not cede authority to make and enforce law over their people or their territories.' The Tribunal stressed, however, that these findings drew 'no conclusions about the sovereignty the Crown exercises today', an implicit statement that the modern New Zealand state had become legitimated through time, whatever the circumstances that prevailed in 1840, pp. xxii–xxiii, 9, 529 and passim.

21 Andrew, *The Secret World*, p. 5.

22 Michael Warner, *The Rise and Fall of Intelligence: An International Security History* (Washington: Georgetown University Press, 2014), p. 6.

23 See, for example, David Lyon, *Surveillance Studies: An Overview* (Cambridge: Polity Press, 2007); Jennifer Luff, 'Covert and Overt Operations: Interwar Political Policing in the United States and the United Kingdom', *American Historical Review*, vol. 122, no. 3 (June 2017), pp. 727–57.

24 Peter Gill, *Policing Politics: Security Intelligence and the Liberal Democratic State* (London: Frank Cass & Co., 1994), p. 179.

25 David Omand, *How Spies Think: Ten Lessons in Intelligence* (London: Viking, 2020), p. 9.

26 Christopher Andrew, Richard J. Aldrich and Wesley K. Wark, 'The Intelligence Cycle', in Andrew, Aldrich and Wark (eds), *Secret Intelligence: A Reader* (London: Routledge, 2009), p. 21.

27 Gill, *Policing Politics*, p. 152.

28 Brodeur, *The Policing Web*, p. 346, identifies the 'use of infiltration and police informants on a regular basis' as one of the key characteristics of high policing.

29 An example of both relatives and neighbours supplying information can be seen in information sent by the New Zealand Police in 1954 to MI5: TNA, KV2/3922, p. 17, 'Copy of letter from Police Department, Wellington C.1., New Zealand re. Distribution of Soviet and Communist Publications in New Zealand. BICKERTON, William Maxwell'.

30 For an example of a 'secret search' for the pamphlet *Strike!: Strategy and Tactics* in a printery in 1932, see Williams/Birchfield family papers, f. 19, Albert and Constance Birchfield personal files.

31 John Hughes-Wilson, *On Intelligence* (London: Constable, 2017), pp. 74–111; C. H. Kit Bennetts, *Spy: A Former SIS Officer Unmasks New Zealand's Sensational Cold War Spy Affair* (Auckland: Random House, 2006), pp. 200–201. While the MICE acronym is used in the context of threat analysis in this book, it has wider applications in assessing motivations; for example, in recruiting informants and agents or in handling defectors. Sometimes there are variants or elaborations upon MICE; some agencies, for instance, add revenge although this can

of course overlap with or be encompassed within other categories.

32   International literature is replete with references to the conservative political and social views that prevailed within the secret world; e.g., Whitaker et al., *Secret Service*: 'the history of the political police is a secret history of conservatism', p. 11.

33   Loch K. Johnson and James J. Wirtz, 'Intelligence Analysis', in Johnson and Wirtz (eds), *Intelligence: The Secret World of Spies, An Anthology*, 3rd ed. (New York: Oxford University Press, 2011), p. 117.

34   'Dupes' was a term often utilised in official and conservative circles. See, for example, Major-General Sir Howard Kippenberger's message to the Returned Services' Association condemning the 'Communists and their dupes', undated document [1949], in SRCNZSSC, IA77, A6, 'Communist Party 5 Nov 1948–7 Dec 1950'.

35   Guy Powles, *Security Intelligence Service: Report by Chief Ombudsman* (Wellington: Government Printer, 1976), pp. 26–27.

36   Oleg Kalugin, *Spymaster: My Thirty-two Years in Intelligence and Espionage Against the West* (New York: Basic Books, 2009), pp. 341–42; Victor Marchetti and John D. Marks, *The CIA and the Cult of Intelligence* (London: Hodder & Stoughton, 1974); George Fraser, *Seeing Red: Undercover in 1950s New Zealand* (Palmerston North: Dunmore Press, 1995), pp. 96, 151.

37   See, for example, Grace Millar, 'Working Documents: Ballpoint Pen Marginalia, 1930s Police Files and Security Intelligence Practices', *Security and Surveillance History Series*, 2017/1, and Millar, 'Identifying Communists: Continuity in Political Policing, 1931–1951', *Security and Surveillance History Series*, 2017/3. The broader points here are based in our in-depth survey of declassified covert surveillance documents in the twentieth century, including personal file material released to individuals and their families which has been made available to us.

38   Lustgarten, 'National Security and Political Policing', pp. 328–29.

39   Loch K. Johnson and James J. Wirtz, 'The Danger of Intelligence Politicization', in Johnson and Wirtz, *Intelligence*, p. 165.

40   Wesley K. Wark, 'Learning to Live with Intelligence', in Andrew, Aldrich and Wark, *Secret Intelligence*, p. 526.

41   Clive Emsley, *The Great British Bobby: A History of British Policing from the 18th Century to the Present* (London: Quercus, 2009), p. 33; Ian Cobain, *The History Thieves: Secrets, Lies and the Shaping of a Modern Nation* (London: Portobello Books, 2016), pp. 1–16.

42   Charles Belton, *Outside the Law in New Zealand* (Gisborne: Gisborne Publishing Company, 1939), p. 231.

43   *New Zealand Observer and Free Lance*, 25 August 1883, p. 11.

44   Kerry Taylor, '"The Old Bolshevik": Alex Galbraith, the Communist Party and the New Zealand Revolution', in Rachael Bell (ed.), *New Zealand between the Wars* (Auckland: Massey University Press, 2017), p. 129.

45   *Evening Post*, 19 October 1965, p. 11.

46   Hill, *The Iron Hand*, pp. 98–99.

47   This phrase has been translated in several ways. The formulation we cite appears in a number of works; see, for example, Peter Edwards, 'The Impact of the Hope Royal Commissions of the 1970s and 1980s on Australia's Intelligence Agencies Today', *History Australia*, vol. 18, no. 1 (2021), p. 33.

Chapter One: Surveilling Colonial New Zealand

1   The historical context for policing draws upon Richard S. Hill, *The Colonial Frontier Tamed: New Zealand Policing in Transition, 1867–1886* (Wellington: Historical Branch, Department of Internal Affairs, 1989) and Hill, *The Iron Hand in the Velvet Glove: The Modernisation of Policing in New Zealand,*

1886–1917 (Palmerston North: Dunmore Press, 1995).

2   Andrew Peter Vayda, *Maori Warfare* (Wellington: Polynesian Society, 1960), pp. 51–52; Michael King, *Moriori: A People Rediscovered* (Auckland: Penguin, 2000), pp. 53–55; Angela Ballara, *Taua: 'Musket Wars', 'Land Wars' or Tikanga?: Warfare in Māori Society in the Early Nineteenth Century* (Auckland: Penguin, 2003), pp. 20–21.

3   Simon Burrows, *A King's Ransom: The Life of Charles Théveneau de Morande, Blackmailer, Scandalmonger and Master-Spy* (London: Bloomsbury Publishing, 2010), p. 120.

4   For pre-1840 policing and intelligence, see Richard S. Hill *Policing the Colonial Frontier: The Theory and Practice of Coercive Social and Racial Control in New Zealand, 1767–1867, Part One* (Wellington: Historical Publications Branch, Department of Internal Affairs, 1986), pp. 29–92.

5   English law was deemed to be operative in New Zealand just before the founding expedition arrived, and police patrolled upon disembarkation and presided over the first Treaty signings on 6 February 1840. All policemen held the office of constable, which was different from the rank of constable; when men progressed to the higher ranks of non-commissioned officer and commissioned officer they remained in the office of constable and retained their full constabulary powers. When detectives were appointed, this was generally (and after 1886 invariably) from within the general police, and they normally held ranks equivalent to their uniformed counterparts.

6   Hill, *Policing the Colonial Frontier*, passim. For an international dimension, see Hill, 'Policing Ireland, Policing Colonies: The Irish Constabulary "Model"', in Angela McCarthy (ed.), *Ireland in the World: Comparative, Transnational, and Personal Perspectives* (New York & London: Routledge, 2015), pp. 61–80.

7   RHPHC, Evidence of Senior Sergeant John McNamara, 'Evidence Taken at the Police Commission Held at the Central Police Station, Wellington', 7 May 1919, p. 383, typescript.

8   *Rules and Regulations of the Constabulary Force of New Zealand* (Wellington: R. Stokes, 1852), pp. 25–26.

9   Richard S. Hill, '"The Taming of Wild Man": Policing Colonial Peoples in the Nineteenth Century', in *Empire, Identity and Control: Two Inaugural Lectures, Occasional Paper Series*, no. 13 (Wellington: Stout Research Centre for New Zealand Studies, 2007), p. 5.

10   Laurie Barber, 'Map Making in Maoriland: Military Intelligence in the First New Zealand War', *New Zealand Legacy*, vol. 2, no. 2 (1990), p. 22.

11   Ibid.; 'A Pakeha Maori' [Frederick Edward Maning], *Old New Zealand: Being Incidents of Native Customs and Character in the Old Times* (London: Smith, Elder, 1863).

12   For the wars as such, see James Belich, *The New Zealand Wars and the Victorian Interpretation of Racial Conflict* (Auckland: Penguin, [1986] 1988). For intelligence, see Cliff Simons, *Soldiers, Scouts & Spies: A Military History of the New Zealand Wars 1845–1864* (Auckland: Massey University Press, 2019), pp. 49–64, 376–79. For the constabulary's role in the wars, see Hill, *The Colonial Frontier Tamed*, pp. 1–76.

13   Graeme Dunstall, 'Frontier and/or Cultural Fragment? Interpretations of Violence in Colonial New Zealand', *Social History*, vol. 29, no. 1 (2004), pp. 59–83.

14   James Belich, *Paradise Reforged: A History of the New Zealanders from the 1880s to the Year 2000* (Auckland: Allen Lane, 2001), pp. 53–68.

15   Ibid., pp. 121–88.

16   Hill, 'Policing Ireland, Policing Colonies'.

17   Margaret Nell Galt, 'Wealth and Income in New Zealand, 1870–1939' (PhD thesis, Victoria University of Wellington, 1985), p. 24.

18 Ian McGibbon, *The Path to Gallipoli: Defending New Zealand, 1840–1915* (Wellington: GP Books, 1991), pp. 54–105.

19 Glynn Barratt, *Russophobia in New Zealand, 1838–1908* (Palmerston North: Dunmore Press, 1981); Stephen Hoadley, *New Zealand and France: Politics, Diplomacy and Dispute Management* (Wellington: New Zealand Institute of International Affairs, 2005), pp. 1–13.

20 Michelle Murray, 'Identity, Insecurity, and Great Power Politics: The Tragedy of German Naval Ambition Before the First World War', *Security Studies*, vol. 19, issue 4 (2010), p. 657.

21 Hill, *The Iron Hand*, p. 110. As one study of the Irish Constabulary, which served as the initial model for the NZPF, put it, that force essentially wanted 'healthy, young men from rural backgrounds, with an elementary education and no obvious political affiliations, who could be moulded into hard-working and utterly loyal policemen'. Elizabeth Malcolm, *The Irish Policeman, 1822–1922: A Life* (Dublin: Four Courts Press, 2006), p. 69. In 1939 one New Zealand detective recalled that the majority of his fellow 15 recruits had previously been farm workers. Charles Belton, *Outside the Law in New Zealand* (Gisborne: Gisborne Publishing Company, 1939), p. 15.

22 AJHR, 1898, Session I, H-2, 'Police Force of New Zealand (Report and Evidence of the Royal Commission on the)', p. 24.

23 RHPHC, interview, Richard Hill with ex-Constable Arnold Butterworth, 17 January 1979.

24 RHPHC, Commissioner W. Gudgeon, circular 2/88, 13 March 1888, copied into Christchurch General Orders Book.

25 Hill, *The Iron Hand*, p. 84.

26 See evidence of Inspector Terence O'Brien in AJHR, 1909, H-16B, 'Police Force of New Zealand (Report and Evidence of the Royal Commission on the)', pp. 33–34.

27 Richard S. Hill, 'Surveilling the "Enemies" of Colonial New Zealand – Counter-subversion and Counter-espionage, 1840–1907', in Brad Patterson, Richard S. Hill and Kathryn Patterson (eds), *After the Treaty: The Settler State, Race Relations & the Exercise of Power in Colonial New Zealand* (Wellington: Steele Roberts, 2016), p. 280.

28 The difficulties of addressing parity issues that arose with locating a detection service inside a heavily generalist-oriented police force were extensively canvassed by a Committee of Inquiry in 1919: see its report in *New Zealand Police Gazette*, 1919, pp. 417ff.; and also RHPHC, 'Evidence Taken at the Police Commission'.

29 See evidence of Inspector Terence O'Brien in AJHR, 1909, H-16B, 'Police Force of New Zealand (Report and Evidence of the Royal Commission on the)', pp. 33–34.

30 For an example of anti-German counter-espionage measures in 1904, see RHPHC, P1/272, 04/549.

31 RHPHC, P4/20, Commissioner A. Hume to Inspectors, 20 December 1892, pp. 14–15; P5/10, p. 537A; see too, Hill, 'Surveilling the "Enemies" of Colonial New Zealand', p. 283.

32 Ruth Allen, *Nelson: A History of Early Settlement* (Wellington: A. H. & A. W. Reed, 1965).

33 For the most serious sectarian policing problem, see Hill, *The Colonial Frontier Tamed*, pp. 120–26. For a British context on the police and Fenian activism, see Phillip Thurmond Smith, *Policing Victorian London: Political Policing, Public Order, and the London Metropolitan Police* (London: Greenwood Press, 1985), pp. 183–99.

34 Hill, *The Iron Hand*, p. 72; John Crawford, 'Overt and Covert Military Involvement in the 1890 Maritime Strike and 1913 Waterfront Strike in New Zealand', *Labour History*, no. 60 (May 1991), pp. 66–83.

35 George Woodcock, *Anarchism: A History of Libertarian Ideas and Movements* (Cleveland,

OH: Meridian Books, 1962). See also Jared Davidson, *Sewing Freedom: Philip Josephs, Transnationalism & Early New Zealand Anarchism* (Edinburgh: AK Press, 2013).

36 Hill, 'Surveilling the "Enemies" of Colonial New Zealand', pp. 282–85.

37 Ibid., pp. 280–81.

38 Robert E. Weir, 'Whose Left/Who's Left?: The Knights of Labour and "Radical Progressivism"', in Pat Moloney and Kerry Taylor (eds), *On the Left: Essays on Socialism in New Zealand* (Dunedin: University of Otago Press, 2002), p. 34.

39 Graeme Dunstall, *A Policeman's Paradise?: Policing a Stable Society, 1918–1945* (Palmerston North: Dunmore Press, 1999), p. 269.

40 Hill, *The Iron Hand*, pp. 57, 125–26. For more context for this and preceding paragraphs, see Hill, 'Surveilling the "Enemies" of Colonial New Zealand', pp. 278–82. Our assessment of police monitoring of activists and their overseas contacts has been taken from a survey of copies of police reports covering the 1880s to the early twentieth century held in RHPHC.

41 Grace Millar, 'Working Documents: Ballpoint Pen Marginalia, 1930s Police Files and Security Intelligence Practices', *Security and Surveillance History Series*, 2017/1, pp. 2, 5.

42 This is a common observation by scholars of policing, although police interventions were not always successful. A magistrate, for example, dismissed 'bloody bugger' as obscene language in 1913: RHPHC, AG168/4/66, folio 5, memorandum of 15 October 1913. The capacity and propensity to charge was a powerful deterrent in police theory.

43 RHPHC, Le 1/1865/112, papers relative to the arrest of Mr. C. O. Davis for Seditious Libel, 26 July 1865. See too, *Evening Post*, 7 July 1865, p. 2, and *Daily Southern Cross*, 29 December 1865, p. 3.

44 NZS, 1868, No. 5, 'The Treason-Felony Act', pp. 19–21. Such adaptation to local circumstances was generic within the Empire. As Lord Harcourt noted in the House of Commons in 1914, South Africa's 'laws and surrounding circumstances [meant] a very different definition of sedition to our own': Arthur Berriedale Keith (ed.), *Selected Speeches and Documents on British Colonial Policy 1763–1917* [1918] (London: Oxford University Press, 1953), p. 112.

45 B. R. Hancock, 'The New Zealand Security Intelligence Service', *Auckland University Law Review*, 1973/1, p. 7.

46 NZS, 1969, No. 24, 'New Zealand Security Intelligence Service Act', pp. 284–93.

47 Reg Whitaker, 'Cold War Alchemy: How America, Britain and Canada Transformed Espionage into Subversion', *Intelligence and National Security*, vol. 15, no. 2 (2000), pp. 184–85.

48 RHPHC, Superintendent John Dwyer to Chief Detective P. Herbert, 29 October 1915.

49 ANZ, R24881820, 'Communist Party NZ, Police Raids On', Memorandum for the Commissioner of Police, 22 May 1930.

50 NZS, 1893, No. 57, 'Criminal Code Act', pp. 340–41.

51 NZS, 1908, No. 32, 'Crimes', pp. 590–92; RHPHC, Solicitor-General to Prime Minister, 23 March 1922. For a critical legal perspective on the 'ancient and unsatisfactory history' of sedition, see Law Commission, *Reforming the Law of Sedition* (Wellington: Law Commission, 2007), p. 9 and passim. See too, Dunstall, *A Policeman's Paradise?*, pp. 258–59.

52 For more extensive coverage, see Hill, 'Surveilling the "Enemies" of Colonial New Zealand', pp. 263–93.

53 Herbert Roth, 'McPherson, James', *The Dictionary of New Zealand Biography, Volume Two* (Auckland: Auckland University Press, 1996), p. 300.

54 Organisations believed to be 'communist dominated or infiltrated' constituted a major target throughout the long Cold War; for use of these terms, see, for example, Bollinger family papers, p. 163, Conrad Bollinger personal file, n.d. [but 1949].

55 A number of people who have had declassified information from their personal files released to them have expressed mystification to the authors.

Chapter Two: Searching for Spies and Seditionaries, 1900–1914

1 *Evening Post*, 8 August 1908, p. 11.

2 For the concept of 'reforging' in New Zealand history, see James Belich, *Paradise Reforged: A History of the New Zealanders from the 1880s to the Year 2000* (Auckland: Allen Lane, 2001).

3 James Bennett, 'The Contamination of Arcadia?: Class, Trans-national Interactions and the Construction of Identity, 1890–1913', *New Zealand Journal of History*, vol. 33, no. 1 (1999), pp. 20–42.

4 *Evening Post*, 6 November 1913, p. 8; *Dominion*, 30 October 1913, p. 7.

5 Arthur Berriedale Keith (ed.), *Selected Speeches and Documents on British Colonial Policy, 1763–1917* [1918] (London: Oxford University Press, 1953), pp. 217, 350.

6 Odd Arne Westad, *The Cold War: A World History* (New York: Basic Books, 2017), pp. 1, 4.

7 Michael Bassett, *Sir Joseph Ward: A Political Biography* (Auckland: Auckland University Press, 1993), pp. 154–55.

8 Belich, *Paradise Reforged*.

9 Ian McGibbon, *The Path to Gallipoli: Defending New Zealand, 1840–1915* (Wellington: GP Books, 1991), pp. 68–84.

10 Richard S. Hill, 'Surveilling the "Enemies" of Colonial New Zealand – Counter-subversion and Counter-espionage, 1840–1907', in Brad Patterson, Richard S. Hill and Kathryn Patterson (eds), *After the Treaty: The Settler State, Race Relations & the Exercise of Power in Colonial New Zealand* (Wellington: Steele Roberts, 2016), p. 283.

11 Franklyn Arthur Johnson provides a long-term perspective in *Defence by Committee: The British Committee of Imperial Defence, 1885–1959* (New York: Oxford University Press, 1960); see too, Alan Judd, *The Quest for C: Sir Mansfield Cumming and the Founding of the British Secret Service* (London: HarperCollins, 2000), p. 69.

12 Christopher Andrew, *Secret Service: The Making of the British Intelligence Community* (London: Heinemann, 1985), pp. 42–43; Jürgen Tampke (ed.), *'Ruthless Warfare': German Military Planning and Surveillance in the Australia–New Zealand Region before the Great War* (Canberra: Southern Highlands Publishers, 1998), pp. 10–13.

13 P. D. Corbett, 'Friendly Visit or Rehearsing for Attack?: The Great White Fleet in New Zealand, 1908', *Forts and Works*, no. 13 (February 2002), pp. 1–12.

14 Judd, *The Quest for C*, p. 35.

15 Andrew Francis, 'Willingly to War: British and Imperial Boys' Story Papers, 1905–1914', *Notes, Books, Authors*, no. 10 (2007); Steven Loveridge, *Calls to Arms: New Zealand Society and Commitment to the First World War* (Wellington: Victoria University Press, 2014), pp. 83–85.

16 Erik Olssen, *The Red Feds: Revolutionary Industrial Unionism and the New Zealand Federation of Labour, 1908–14* (Auckland: Oxford University Press, 1988).

17 Kerry Taylor, '"Our Motto, No Compromise": The Ideological Origins and Foundations of the Communist Party of New Zealand', *New Zealand Journal of History*, vol. 28, no. 2 (1994), p. 161; Barry Gustafson, *Labour's Path to Political Independence: The Origins and Establishment of the New Zealand Labour Party, 1900–19* (Auckland: Auckland University Press, 1980), pp. 24–26; Mark Dunick,

'Making Rebels: The New Zealand Socialist Party, 1901–1913' (MA thesis, Victoria University of Wellington, 2016), especially pp. 1–2, 13; Herbert Roth, 'Mann, Thomas', *The Dictionary of New Zealand Biography, Volume Three* (Auckland: Auckland University Press, 1996), p. 328.

18 Gustafson, *Labour's Path to Political Independence*, p. 26; Peter Steiner, *Industrial Unionism: The History of the Industrial Workers of the World in Aotearoa* (Wellington: Rebel Press, 2007), p. 2.

19 Frank Prebble, *'Troublemakers': Anarchism and Syndicalism: The Early Years of the Libertarian Movement in Aotearoa / New Zealand* (Christchurch: Libertarian Press, 1995), p. 15.

20 Gustafson, *Labour's Path to Political Independence*, pp. 26ff.; for aspects of the IWW's international influence, including in New Zealand, see Peter Cole, David Struthers and Kenyon Zimmer (eds), *Wobblies of the World: A Global History of the IWW* (London: Pluto Press, 2017).

21 Francis Shor, 'Left Labor Agitators in the Pacific Rim of the Early Twentieth Century', *International Labor and Working-Class History*, vol. 67 (Spring 2005), pp. 148–63; Steiner, *Industrial Unionism*, pp. 4–5; RHPHC, IWW folder.

22 Our account of the events at Waihī in 1912 is based on a number of sources. See especially Richard S. Hill, *The Iron Hand in the Velvet Glove: The Modernisation of Policing in New Zealand, 1886–1917* (Palmerston North, Dunmore Press, 1995), pp. 283ff. (which is based on extensive Police files, including some that had formed their own 'hidden archive' within the Police for many decades); Richard S. Hill, 'A State of Exception: Declaring "Lawless Law" in Early Twentieth Century New Zealand', *Labour History Project Bulletin*, no. 59 (December 2013), pp. 17–20; Olssen, The Red Feds, pp. 148ff.; and H. E. Holland, 'Ballot Box' and R. S. Ross, *The Tragic Story of the Waihi Strike*

(Wellington: The 'Worker' Press, 1913). See too, Stanley Roche, *The Red and the Gold: An Informal Account of the Waihi Strike, 1912* (Auckland: Oxford University Press, 1982).

23 Some of Cullen's men later affirmed that he had set up the events of Black Tuesday, in conjunction with his spies and his 'dirty thugs'; this phrase is taken from an interview by Richard Hill with ex-Constable Arnold Butterworth, 17 January 1979.

24 Taylor, '"Our Motto, No Compromise"', pp. 161ff.; Hill, *The Iron Hand*, p. 304.

25 RHPHC, telegram, PM9/13, Prime Minister W. Massey to James Gunson, 1 November 1913.

26 Mark Derby, 'Strikes and Labour Disputes – the 1912 and 1913 Strikes', *Te Ara – the Encyclopedia of New Zealand* (www.TeAra.govt. nz/en/strikes-and-labour-disputes/page-5).

27 Hill, *The Iron Hand*, pp. 309–13; John Crawford, 'Overt and Covert Military Involvement in the 1890 Maritime Strike and 1913 Waterfront Strike in New Zealand', *Labour History*, no. 60 (May 1991), pp. 66–83.

28 NZS, 1913, no. 52, 'Police Offences Amendment Act', pp. 287–88; Richard S. Hill, 'The Police, the State, and Lawless Law', in Melanie Nolan (ed.), *Revolution: The 1913 Great Strike in New Zealand* (Christchurch: Canterbury University Press in association with the Trade Union History Project, 2006), pp. 79–98; Olssen, *The Red Feds*, pp. 179ff.

29 As a retired Superintendent of Police reflected of this time, the Specials 'were a signal for disorder and bloodshed'. RHPHC, unpublished manuscript, John Dwyer, 'Fragments from the Official Career of John Dwyer Superintendent of Police 1878–1921', p. 59.

30 Crawford, 'Overt and Covert Military Involvement', pp. 82–83; H. Roth, *Trade Unions in New Zealand: Past and Present* (Wellington: A. H. & A. W. Reed, 1973), pp. 37–39.

31 Hill, *The Iron Hand*, pp. 47, 165, 363; Richard S. Hill, 'Tunbridge, John Bennett', *The Dictionary of New Zealand Biography, Volume Two* (Auckland: Auckland University Press, 1996), pp. 551–52; Richard S. Hill, 'Dinnie, Walter', *The Dictionary of New Zealand Biography, Volume Three*, pp. 134–35.

32 Bernard Porter, *The Origins of the Vigilant State: The London Metropolitan Police Special Branch Before the First World War* (London: Weidenfeld & Nicolson, 1987), pp. 114ff.

33 Christopher Andrew, *The Defence of the Realm: The Authorized History of MI5* (London: Penguin Books, 2010), pp. 4–5; Porter, *Origins of the Vigilant State*.

34 Porter, *Origins of the Vigilant State*, p. 181; AJHR, 'The Police Force of the Dominion (Annual Report on)', 1914 Session I, H-16, p. 1.

35 Hill, *The Iron Hand*, p. 169.

36 Graeme Dunstall, 'McIlveney, William Bernard', *The Dictionary of New Zealand Biography, Volume Four* (Auckland: Auckland University Press, 1998), pp. 311–12; Hill, *The Iron Hand*, p. 363.

37 AJHR, 1909, H-16B, 'Police Force of New Zealand (Report and Evidence of the Royal Commission on the)', pp. xlv, 499.

38 Hill, *The Iron Hand*, pp. 370–71.

39 AJHR, 1900, H-16, p. 1; see too, 1909, H-16B, pp. xlv, 56, 261.

40 AJHR, 1909, H-16B, pp. 170–71, 262.

41 *New Zealand Herald*, 3 April 1911, p. 7; *NZ Truth*, 17 June 1911, p. 5.

42 *Otago Daily Times*, 15 February 1913, p. 5.

43 Hill, *The Iron Hand*, pp. 273–75.

44 *NZ Truth*, 15 March 1913, p. 4. A 1919 enquiry heard extensive evidence about the uneasy relationship between the uniformed and detective branches: RHPHC, 'Evidence Taken at the Police Commission Held at the Central Police Station, Wellington', 1919.

45 For a summary of Cullen's life, see Richard S. Hill, 'Cullen, John', *The Dictionary of New Zealand Biography, Volume Three*, pp. 125–27. See too, coverage in Hill, *The Iron Hand*. For a later interpretation, see Mark Derby, *The Prophet and the Policeman: The Story of Rua Kenana and John Cullen* (Nelson: Craig Potton Publishing, 2009).

46 R. L. Weitzel, 'Pacifists and Anti-militarists in New Zealand, 1909–1914', *New Zealand Journal of History*, vol. 7, no. 2 (1973), pp. 128–47.

47 The concept of ubiquitous surveillance by unseen surveillers was famously elaborated in Michel Foucault's *Discipline and Punish: The Birth of the Prison* (London: Allen Lane, 1977), and this has been the starting point for many studies of both policing and secret surveillance.

48 Steven Loveridge and James Watson, *The Home Front: New Zealand Society and the War Effort, 1914–1919* (Auckland: Massey University Press, 2019), pp. 26, 28; Dunick, 'Making Rebels', p. 104.

49 Andrew, *Defence of the Realm*, pp. 3–28; Porter, *Origins of the Vigilant State*, p. 167.

50 For MI6, see Keith Jeffery, *MI6: The History of the Secret Intelligence Service, 1909–1949* (London: Bloomsbury Publishing, 2011).

51 McGibbon, *The Path to Gallipoli*, p. 159.

52 *Greymouth Evening Star*, 10 August 1907, p. 3. For a comparable development in Australia, see Richard Hall, *The Secret State: Australia's Spy Industry* (Stanmore: Cassell, 1978), pp. 10–12.

53 Hill, 'Surveilling the "Enemies" of Colonial New Zealand', p. 270; NZS, 1858, no. 15, 'Post Office Act', sec. XXII; NZS, 1865, no. 37, 'Electric Telegraph Act', sec. XVI, p. 112. A later privacy oriented alteration nevertheless allowed the commissioner of Electric Telegraph to authorise staff to testify in judicial proceedings on specified matters, including 'treason felony': NZS, 1874, no.2, 'Electric Telegraph Act Amendment Act',

sec. 4, p. 4. For a summary of the early telegraph system, see A. C. Wilson, *Wire and Wireless: A History of Telecommunications in New Zealand, 1860–1987* (Palmerston North: Dunmore Press, 1994), pp. 27ff.

54   The intertwining of policing and communications was so tight that a policeman's wife handling local post and telegraph duties was not considered unusual; see, for example, RHPHC, P5/5, Commissioner of Police to Inspector, Hokitika, 24 December 1881, p. 330.

55   Wilson, *Wire and Wireless*, p. 101; Howard Robinson, *A History of the Post Office in New Zealand* (Wellington: Government Printer, 1964), pp. 7–13.

56   Patrick Day, *The Radio Years: A History of Broadcasting in New Zealand, Volume One* (Auckland: Auckland University Press in association with the Broadcasting History Trust, 1994), pp. 7–13.

57   David Filer, 'Civil–Military Cooperation in Signals Intelligence in New Zealand, 1904 to 1939', *Security and Surveillance History Series*, 2017/4, p. 1; Day, *The Radio Years*, pp. 15–17.

58   Day, *The Radio Years*, pp. 17–18, 22–23.

59   Desmond Ball, Cliff Lord and Meredith Thatcher, *Invaluable Service: The Secret History of New Zealand's Signals Intelligence during Two World Wars* (Waimauku: Resource Books, 2011), p. 5; Filer, 'Civil–Military Cooperation', pp. 1–2.

60   RHPHC, Commissioner to Inspectors, 25 March 1901, p. 134; Hill, *The Iron Hand*, pp. 125–26. For an account of Irish sectarian reaction on the South Island's West Coast, which created such a severe crisis of public order that Special Police were sworn in and members of the Armed Constabulary were diverted from the North Island wars to assist the provincial police forces, see Richard S. Hill, *The Colonial Frontier Tamed: New Zealand Policing in Transition, 1867–1886* (Wellington: Historical Branch, Department of Internal Affairs, 1989), pp. 121–26, 157–61.

61   F. M. Jean Irvine, 'The Revolt of the Militant Unions' (MA thesis, Auckland University College, 1937), pp. 30–31; Dunick, 'Making Rebels', p. 51.

62   This sabotage tactic was especially associated with sections of the IWW; see Olssen, *The Red Feds*, p. 132. For an example of the advocacy of emery powder, see *Maoriland Worker*, 20 September 1912.

63   Dunick, 'Making Rebels', p. 1.

64   While such exchanges resulted from requests for specific items of information, there was an increasingly routinised tracking of individuals, including through the Finger Print (later, Criminal Registration) Branch, established in 1903 – whose foundational archives were sighted by one of the authors on police premises before they were mostly destroyed in the late 1970s. For notes from the missing files, see RHPHC, 'Finger Print Branch' folder.

65   For example, the South African Police requested such information from New Zealand: Sub-Inspector in charge, Central Identification Bureau, Johannesburg, to Commissioner of Police, 19 October 1915, 'Circulars Book', Criminal Registration Branch, Wellington, p. 43.

66   Peter Clayworth, 'Patrick Hodgens Hickey and the IWW: A Transnational Relationship', in Cole, Struthers and Zimmer, *Wobblies of the World*.

67   For extensive coverage, see Olssen, *The Red Feds*; see too, Olssen, 'Hickey, Patrick Hodgens', *The Dictionary of New Zealand Biography, Volume Three*, pp. 215–17; Len Richardson, 'Webb, Patrick Charles', in ibid., pp. 555–58; and for a fictionalised account, Eric Beardsley, *Blackball 08* (Auckland: Collins, 1984).

68   RHPHC, P 1913/1968, Superintendent Ellison to Chief Detective, 16 November [1913].

69   Hill, 'The Police, the State and Lawless Law', p. 84.

70 Ibid., p. 86; P 1913/1968, Superintendent Ellison to Commissioner, 31 October 1913.

71 Hill, 'The Police, the State and Lawless Law', pp. 79–98.

72 Hill, *The Iron Hand*, p. 323; Hill, 'The Police, the State and Lawless Law'. Mitchell in particular, along with many police of all ranks, did not welcome the 'assistance' of Specials, whose zeal for crushing the strike often promoted greater disorder. Police dislike of the use of Specials was a constant, and some police would work with strikers to defuse the problems created by Specials; see, for example, Dave Welch, *The Lucifer: A Story of Industrial Conflict in New Zealand's 1930s* (Palmerston North: Dunmore Press in association with the Trade Union History Project, 1988), pp. 184–85.

73 Olssen, *The Red Feds*, p. 198; for a list of laws used, see RHPHC, Le1/1914/248.

74 Dwyer, 'Fragments', pp. 60–65.

75 Ibid., p. 63.

76 Hill, 'The Police, the State, and Lawless Law', p. 86.

77 Dick Scott, *A Radical Writer's Life* (Auckland: Reed, 2004), p. 106.

78 E. C. Fry (ed.), *TOM BARKER AND THE I.W.W.* (Canberra: Australian Society for the Study of Labour History, 1965), pp. 12–13.

79 Crawford, 'Overt and Covert Military Involvement', pp. 82–83.

80 Papers attached to P 1913/1968. For government use of HMS *Psyche* to assist in quelling the strike, see Hill, *The Iron Hand*, pp. 309–10.

81 David Grant, 'Where Were the Peacemongers? Pacifists in New Zealand during World War One', in Steven Loveridge (ed.), *New Zealand Society at War, 1914–1918* (Wellington: Victoria University Press, 2016), pp. 220–25.

82 This was especially the case in Christchurch: see Loveridge and Watson, *The Home Front*, p. 28.

83 RHPHC, Circular 3/14, 12 February 1914, 'Police Circulars Book, 1914–1950'. The Army Department kept its own records of anti-compulsory military training and other anti-militarist activists: Jared Davidson, *Dead Letters: Censorship and Subversion in New Zealand, 1914–1920* (Dunedin: Otago University Press, 2019), pp. 46–47.

84 Richard S. Hill, 'Maori Police Personnel and the Rangatiratanga Discourse', in Barry S. Godfrey and Graeme Dunstall (eds), *Crime and Empire 1840–1940: Criminal Justice in Local and Global Context* (Cullompton: Willan Publishing, 2005), pp. 178–79; Hill, *The Iron Hand*, pp. 127–30; Raeburn Lange, *A Limited Measure of Local Self-government: Maori Councils, 1900–1920*, Rangatiratanga Series no. 5 (Wellington: Treaty of Waitangi Research Unit, 2004), pp. 58–60.

85 M. P. Lissington, *New Zealand and Japan, 1900–1941* (Wellington: Government Printer, 1972), pp. 5–10.

86 *New Zealand Herald*, 14 May 1914, p. 6.

87 Hill, *The Iron Hand*, pp. 188–89.

88 ANZ, R3885320, 'Defence scheme, expeditionary action by territorial force, August 1912–June 1913', secret memorandum for the minister of defence, 9 October 1912.

89 Tampke, 'Ruthless Warfare', p. 17.

90 Ibid., pp. 14–15, 90.

91 Ibid., pp. 90, 99, 101.

92 Steven Loveridge and Rolf W. Brednich, 'When Neighbours Became Enemy Aliens: Germans in New Zealand during World War One', in Loveridge, *New Zealand Society at War*, p. 266; Tampke, 'Ruthless Warfare', p. 103.

93 Tampke, 'Ruthless Warfare', pp. 90, 94.

94 Commissioner of Police, circular to District Inspectors, 3 March 1904, and other correspondence attached to RHPHC, PI/272, 04/549.

95 Commissioner of Police, circular to Inspectors, 28 April, 1904; Inspector,

Wellington, to Commissioner of Police, 29 April 1904; and RHPHC, P1/272, 04/549, Commissioner of Police to Minister of Justice, 29 April 1904; copies in RHPHC, Commissioner of Police, circular to Inspectors, 28 April, 1904; Inspector, Wellington, to Commissioner of Police, 29 April 1904; and P1/272, 04/549, Commissioner of Police to Minister of Justice, 29 April 1904.

96   See Detective Boddam's reports of 22 and 25 September 1904, and Inspector Ellison to Inspector Gillies, in RHPHC, P1/272, 04/549.

97   RHPHC, P5/14, p. 223, Commissioner of Police to Inspector, Napier, telegram, 10 March 1902.

98   RHPHC, P4/37, p. 342, Commissioner to General Officer Commanding New Zealand Military Forces, 8 April 1913.

99   Hill, 'The Police, the State and Lawless Law', p. 86.

100   RHPHC, P1/273, 01/811, correspondence in May 1901.

101   McGibbon, *The Path to Gallipoli*, pp. 239–40.

102   James Holt, *Compulsory Arbitration in New Zealand: The First Forty Years* (Auckland: Auckland University Press, 1986).

103   See Robert Reiner, *The Politics of the Police* (Brighton: Wheatsheaf Books), 1985, pp. 192–94, for a summary. Academic literature, both historical and contemporary, covers this extensively. See examples in Clive Emsley, *The Great British Bobby: A History of British Policing from the 18th Century to the Present* (London: Quercus, 2009), pp. 148–50, 161, 251–52, 278–79, and Hans Toch, *Cop Watch: Spectators, Social Media and Police Reform* (Washington DC: American Psychological Association, 2012). Police memoirs are often replete with the unwritten rules of policing, with violators of the law and regulations protected by their colleagues; see, for New Zealand examples, Tom Lewis, *Coverups and Copouts* (Auckland: Hodder Moa Beckett, 1998), pp. 50, 124–25, and Ray Van Beynen,

Zero-Alpha: The NZ Police Armed Offenders Squad Official History (Auckland: Howling at the Moon Productions, 1998), p. 18. 'Informal' or 'rough justice' policing is endemic in forces around the world, and continues to be reported, including recently by a former policeman who almost casually mentioned to a commission of enquiry being assaulted ('they wallop you, you know') by uniformed men when he was undercover with protesters at an anti-Vietnam War demonstration in London: Campaign Opposing Police Surveillance (2020), 'Daily Report', 13 November, testimony of 'Doug Edwards', p. 14 (http://campaignopposingpolicesurveillance.com/2020/11/14/ucpi-daily-report-13-nov-2020/).

104   Susan Butterworth, *More Than Law and Order: Policing a Changing Society 1945–1992* (Dunedin: University of Otago Press, 2005), p. 84. One of the authors of this book has been told many an anecdote by serving and retired police personnel about the reactive or proactive use of violence to address or resolve situations involving prisoners or members of the public.

105   Alex Frame, *Salmond: Southern Jurist* (Wellington: Victoria University Press, 1995), p. 167.

106   Ibid., pp. 167–68.

107   *New Zealand Times*, 4 November 1913, p. 6.

108   Crawford, 'Overt and Covert Military Involvement', p. 71; Hill, 'The Police, the State, and Lawless Law', p. 87.

Chapter Three: Surveillance and Suppression in Wartime, 1914–1918

1   Douglas Porch, *The French Secret Services: From the Dreyfus Affair to the Gulf War* (London: Basingstoke, 1996), p. 112.

2   For examples of battlefield and strategic intelligence, see Janet Morgan, *The Secrets of Rue St Roch: Intelligence Operations behind*

Enemy Lines in the First World War (London: Allen Lane, 2004); Tammy M. Proctor, *Female Intelligence: Women and Espionage in the First World War* (New York: New York University Press, 2003); Jim Beach, *Haig's Intelligence: GHQ and the German Army, 1916–1918* (Cambridge: Cambridge University Press, 2013); Nicholas Van Der Bijl, *To Complete the Jigsaw: British Military Intelligence in the First World War* (Gloucestershire: History Press, 2015); Christopher Andrew, *The Secret World: A History of Intelligence* (New Haven: Yale University Press, 2018), pp. 497–572.

3   Charles Townshend, *Making the Peace: Public Order and Public Security in Modern Britain* (Oxford: Oxford University Press, 1993), p. 56.

4   NZPD, vol. 171, 20 October 1914, p. 139.

5   *Evening Post*, 11 December 1914, p. 9.

6   *Colonist*, 20 August 1914, p. 3.

7   *New Zealand Free Lance*, 5 September 1914, p. 8.

8   *Manawatu Times*, 21 September 1914, p. 4; *Mataura Ensign*, 29 September 1914, p. 5. The *Marlborough Express* later headlined the arrested man as 'the Wellington Spy': 29 September 1914, p. 8. Experts disagreed as to how far the equipment could transmit messages, indeed whether it was capable of transmission at all, but it was suggested that with some modification a range of a hundred miles was possible.

9   *Manawatu Standard*, 5 September 1914, p. 5; *Feilding Star*, 7 September 1914, p. 2; *Wanganui Chronicle*, 7 September 1914, p. 4.

10   *Wanganui Herald*, 7 September 1914, p. 3.

11   *Auckland Star*, 15 May 1915, p. 9.

12   Peter Cooke, '"Priceless Worth": The Territorial Force and Senior Cadets in World War One', in Steven Loveridge (ed.), *New Zealand Society at War, 1914–1918* (Wellington: Victoria University Press, 2016), p. 65.

13   *Sun*, 10 August 1914, p. 7.

14   RHPHC, 'Circulars Book 1914–1937', Greytown Police Station, p. 2, Commissioner Cullen to Superintendents, 6 August 1914.

15   Steven Loveridge and Rolf W. Brednich, 'When Neighbours Became Alien Enemies: Germans in New Zealand during World War One', in Loveridge, *New Zealand Society at War*, pp. 266–80.

16   Steven Loveridge and James Watson, *The Home Front: New Zealand Society and the War Effort, 1914–1919* (Auckland: Massey University Press, 2019), p. 252.

17   Loveridge and Brednich, 'When Neighbours Became Alien Enemies', pp. 266–80.

18   ANZ, R3885393, 'Censorship of correspondence, Minister of the crown, May', Memorandum for Deputy Chief Censor, 9 May 1916.

19   ANZ, R22428979, 'Communications – Wireless apparatus – Unauthorised – Request to retain Instruments'; ANZ, R22428981, 'Communications – Wireless apparatus – Unauthorised – At Residence of Chinese Consul, Wellington'. In another example, wireless equipment at Wellington's Hotel Bristol belonging to Charles Ward was seized for the duration. See ANZ, R22428990, 'Communications – Wireless apparatus – Unauthorised – Erected by Mr Ward at Hotel Bristol'.

20   Loveridge and Watson, *The Home Front*, pp. 128–29.

21   Ian F. Grant, 'War a Daily Reminder, but Life Goes On: Newspapers during the First World War', in Loveridge, *New Zealand Society at War*, pp. 127–41.

22   John Anderson, 'Military Censorship in World War I: Its Use and Abuse in New Zealand' (MA thesis, Victoria University College, 1952), p. 9.

23   *Manual of the War Legislation of New Zealand: Comprising Acts of Parliament, Proclamations, Orders in Council, and other Instruments Passed, Issued, and Made in Consequence of the War, and in Force on 30th September, 1916*

(Wellington: Government Printer, 1916), pp. 182, 184, 188, 196.

24 NZPD, vol. 173, 8 September 1915, p. 469.

25 NZG, 20 September 1915, p. 3265; RHPHC, C6/31, 36/959, 'Prohibited Literature etc.' list of 22 August 1921; for an example of public reporting of literature, see RHPHC, P4/40, p. 461, Commissioner to G. Smith, Pahiatua, 21 December 1915.

26 RHPHC, P4/40, p. 468, Commissioner of Police to Inspectors, 30 December 1915.

27 Richard S. Hill, *The Iron Hand in the Velvet Glove: The Modernisation of Policing in New Zealand, 1886–1917* (Palmerston North: Dunmore Press, 1995), p. 359; Paul Christoffel, *Censored: A Short History of Censorship in New Zealand* (Wellington: Research Unit, Department of Internal Affairs, 1989), pp. 11–13.

28 ANZ, R3885239, 'War lectures by Ashmead Bartlett, December 1915 – May 1916', the Governor-General of New Zealand to the Governor-General of Canada, 26 May 1916; and instructions, 10 April 1916. For details regarding Ashmead-Bartlett's work as a war correspondent, see Graham Seal, *Inventing ANZAC: The Digger and National Mythology* (St Lucia: University of Queensland Press, 2004), pp. 78–79, 93, 95.

29 Jared Davidson, *Dead Letters: Censorship and Subversion in New Zealand, 1914–1920* (Dunedin: Otago University Press, 2019), p. 35.

30 Paul Baker, *King and Country Call: New Zealanders, Conscription and the Great War* (Auckland: Auckland University Press, 1988), p. 208. This duty had some pre-war antecedents in the tracking of those evading compulsory military training: ANZ, R22429370, 'Territorial Force – Reward – Payment of to Police for Arrest and Conviction of Defaulters under Defence Act'.

31 Baker, *King and Country Call*, pp. 202–9.

32 RHPHC, Lab 25/92, Inspector of Factories T. Fairhall to Chief Inspector, 30 November 1916.

33 Loveridge and Watson, *The Home Front*, pp. 293–96.

34 NZG, 4 December 1916, pp. 3751–53.

35 ANZ, R22319675, 'Miscellanous files and papers – Correspondence between J. Allen and W. F. Massey, 1st September 1916–1st August 1919 [Loose papers]', Allen to Massey, 30 December 1916; Loveridge and Watson, *The Home Front*, pp. 295–300.

36 Loveridge and Watson, *The Home Front*, pp. 368–73.

37 NZG, 26 July 1918, pp. 2759–61; Ian F. Grant, *Lasting Impressions: The Story of New Zealand's Newspapers, 1840–1920* (Masterton: Fraser Books, 2018), pp. 614–18.

38 Richard S. Hill, 'State Servants and Social Beings: The Role of the New Zealand Police Force in the Great War', in Loveridge, *New Zealand Society at War*, pp. 91–111.

39 NZS, 1914, no. 38, 'War Regulations Act', p. 128.

40 This approach reflected the solicitor-general's philosophical inclination towards the idea of an active executive as necessary to maintain order during emergencies: 'extrajudicial force may lawfully supersede the ordinary process and course of law, whenever it is needed for the protection of the state and public order against illegal violence'. Alex Frame, *Salmond: Southern Jurist* (Wellington, Victoria University Press, 1995), p. 168.

41 RHPHC, P4/40 p. 665, Commissioner of Police to Superintendent Kiely, 25 February 1916; *Evening Post*, 8 December 1918, p. 6.

42 Richard S. Hill, 'Cullen, John', *The Dictionary of New Zealand Biography, Volume Three* (Auckland: Auckland University Press, 1996), pp. 125–27. For Cullen in wartime, see Hill, *The Iron Hand*, pp. 327ff.

43 Loveridge and Watson, *The Home Front*, pp. 373–74.

44 Graeme Dunstall, 'O'Donovan, John', *The Dictionary of New Zealand Biography, Volume Three*, p. 371.

45 John O'Donovan, 'Address to the New Zealand Police Force', in *The Police Force Act, 1913, Police Force Amendment Act, 1919, and Regulations Made Thereunder for the Guidance of the Police Force of New Zealand* (Wellington: Government Printer, 1920), p. v.

46 Hill, *The Iron Hand*, pp. 395–406.

47 Hill, 'State Servants and Social Beings', pp. 107–8.

48 One example was Willy Price, who hid in his father's Christchurch shoe-repair business; his mother and father were gaoled. Richard L. N. Greenaway to Richard Hill, 19 June 2015.

49 RHPHC, P4/40, p. 477, Commissioner of Police to Superintendent, Auckland, 31 July 1916.

50 RHPHC, P4/44, p. 198, Commissioner of Police to Superintendent, Auckland, 2 December 1916.

51 ANZ, R3885342, 'Intelligence – Imperial bureau establishment in New Zealand March', cited in correspondence dated 25 March 1919.

52 David Horner, *The Spy Catchers: The Official History of ASIO, 1949–1963, Volume 1* (Crows Nest, NSW: Allen & Unwin, 2014), pp. 13–14.

53 ANZ, R3885342, 'Intelligence – Imperial bureau establishment in New Zealand March', cited in correspondence dated 25 March 1919.

54 GCSB, Colin Hanson, 'Draft Chapters for History of New Zealand Sigint', unpublished manuscript, appendix one, p. 2; Hill, *The Iron Hand*, pp. 354–55; John Fahey, *Australia's First Spies: The Remarkable Story of Australia's Intelligence Operations, 1901–45* (Sydney: Allen & Unwin, 2018), p. 39.

55 John Crawford, '"Duty Well Done": The Defence Department at War: 1914–1918', in Loveridge, *New Zealand Society at War*, pp. 36–38.

56 ANZ, R24533922, 'Date: 21 May 1915, Subject: Censorship and Press Bureau'; Anderson, 'Military Censorship in World War I', pp. 37–42; Davidson, *Dead Letters*, p. 31.

57 NZS, 1908, No. 147, 'Post and Telegraph Act', sec. 27; NZG, 17 December 1914, pp. 4361–63.

58 ANZ, R3885411, 'Censorship of German messages, August–September 1914', Memorandum for Major Gibbon, 24 August 1914.

59 Loveridge and Watson, *The Home Front*, p. 130.

60 ANZ, R22432692, 'Staff, miscellaneous – Deputy Chief Censor Wellington – Appointment of', W. H. S. Moorehouse to Defence Staff, 1 August 1914.

61 ANZ, R19162367, 'Report on Postal Censorship during the Great War', p. 37.

62 ANZ, R22428995, 'Communications – Censorship of Correspondence To and From New Zealand – Instructions re', memorandum dated 31 March 1919.

63 ANZ, R3885389, 'Censorship of correspondence, H. O'Brien to H. Duggan, February–August'; ANZ, R22430468, 'Administration and Miscellaneous – Censorship – Regulations postal', report of dispatches, 23 November 1915.

64 ANZ, R21371546, 'Consulate German: archives [with "German Consulate archives"]'. For other examples of the appointment of such personnel, see ANZ, R3885411, 'Censorship of German messages, August–September 1914'.

65 *Maoriland Worker*, 12 January 1916, p. 4.

66 ANZ, R22430468, 'Administration and Miscellaneous – Censorship – Regulations postal'.

67 Calder Walton, *Empire of Secrets: British Intelligence, the Cold War and the Twilight of Empire* (London: HarperPress, 2013), p. 8.

68 Davidson, *Dead Letters*, p. 35.

69 ANZ, R19162367, 'Report on Postal Censorship during the Great War', p. 29.

70 Anderson, 'Military Censorship in World War I', p. 103.

71   ANZ, R3885388, 'Censorship of correspondence, W. H. Webbe, April–September'; ANZ, R3885394, 'Censorship of correspondence, P. Joseph to Miss E. Goldman, July–November'; ANZ, R3885407, 'Censorship of publications re conscientious objectors in USA, July'.

72   The following paragraphs draw substantively on David Filer's research. See Filer, 'Civil–Military Cooperation in Signals Intelligence in New Zealand, 1904 to 1939', *Security and Surveillance History Series*, 2017/4, pp. 1–5.

73   John Tonkin-Covell, 'The Collectors: Naval, Army and Air Intelligence in the New Zealand Armed Forces during the Second World War' (PhD thesis, University of Waikato, 2000), p. 34.

74   Desmond Ball, Cliff Lord and Meredith Thatcher, *Invaluable Service: The Secret History of New Zealand's Signals Intelligence during Two World Wars* (Waimauku: Resource Books, 2011), pp. 13–14.

75   Laurie Barber and Cliff Lord, *Swift and Sure: A History of the Royal New Zealand Corps of Signals and Army Signalling in New Zealand* (Auckland: New Zealand Signals Incorporated, 1996), pp. 43–44.

76   Loveridge and Watson, *The Home Front*, pp. 96–97.

77   Tonkin-Covell, 'The Collectors', p. 133; Patrick Day, *The Radio Years: A History of Broadcasting in New Zealand, Volume One* (Auckland: Auckland University Press in association with the Broadcasting History Trust, 1994), p. 32.

78   Filer, 'Civil–Military Cooperation in Signals Intelligence in New Zealand', p. 2.

79   Ball et al., *Invaluable Service*, pp. 13–14.

80   Tonkin-Covell, 'The Collectors', p. 134.

81   Jürgen Tampke (ed.), *'Ruthless Warfare': German Military Planning and Surveillance in the Australia–New Zealand Region before the Great War* (Canberra: Southern Highlands Publishers, 1998), pp. 90, 99–102.

82   ANZ, R21371546, 'Consulate German: archives [with "German Consulate archives"]', Memorandum for the Minister of Internal Affairs, 11 August 1914.

83   ANZ, R22428978, 'Communications – Wireless apparatus – Suspicions Regarding a German named G. Kronfield [sic], Auckland', Gibbon to Commissioner of Police, 2 December 1914.

84   *Sun*, 24 February 1916, p. 12. Seegner was subsequently released on health grounds in mid-1916.

85   ANZ, R21371539, 'Chemists, Enemy'; ANZ, R21371431, 'Wellington: Wharves: Aliens'; ANZ, R3885352, 'Police inquiries re aliens on wharves, April'.

86   Loveridge and Watson, *The Home Front*, pp. 223, 252.

87   I. C. McGibbon, *Blue-Water Rationale: The Naval Defence of New Zealand, 1914–1942* (Wellington: Government Printer, 1981), p. 29.

88   RHPHC, P4/40, p. 571, Commissioner of Police to Superintendent, Auckland, 7 February 1916.

89   NZPD, vol. 171, 23 October 1914, p. 309.

90   ANZ, R21371431, 'Wellington: Wharves: Aliens', Commissioner of Police to the Minister of Police, 6 October 1916.

91   ANZ, R3885410, 'Censorship of correspondence, National peace conference, June 1915–July 1920', Solicitor-General's report on the censorship of Mackie's correspondence, 17 December 1915.

92   *Maoriland Worker*, 18 October 1916, p. 4.

93   ANZ, R22319675, 'Miscellaneous files and papers – Correspondence between J. Allen and W. F. Massey, 1st September 1916–1st August 1919 [Loose papers]', Allen to Massey, 28 October 1916.

94   Michael Bassett with Michael King, *Tomorrow Comes the Song: A Life of Peter Fraser* (Auckland: Penguin, 2000), p. 72.

95 Richard Boast and Richard S. Hill (eds), *Raupatu: The Confiscation of Maori Land* (Wellington: Victoria University Press, 2009).

96 Charles Belton, *Outside the Law in New Zealand* (Gisborne: Gisborne Publishing Company, 1939), p. 197.

97 Baker, *King and Country Call*, p. 220; Steven Loveridge and Basil Keane, 'Turangawaewae: Maori Relationships with the Great War', in Loveridge, *New Zealand Society at War*, pp. 289ff.

98 Judith Binney, Gillian Chaplin and Craig Wallace, *Mihaia: The Prophet Rua Kenana and His Community at Maungapohatu* (Wellington: Oxford University Press, 1979); Hill, *The Iron Hand*, pp. 382–90; Peter Webster, *Rua and the Maori Millennium* (Wellington: Price Milburn/Victoria University Press, 1979), pp. 243ff.; Mark Derby, *The Prophet and the Policeman: The Story of Rua Kenana and John Cullen* (Nelson: Craig Potton Publishing, 2009), pp. 78ff.

99 Brad Patterson, '"We Stand for the Protestant Religion, the (Protestant) King and the Empire": The Rise of the Protestant Political Association in World War One', in Loveridge, *New Zealand Society at War*, p. 250.

100 *Dominion*, 12 July 1917, p. 5. NZPD, vol. 180, 13 September 1917, p. 108 covers the texts of some of these letters.

101 AJHR, 1917 Session I, F-08, pp. 1–50.

102 NZPD, vol. 180, 13 September 1917, pp. 100–21.

103 It was ruled that '[a]s a state of war has made the establishment of censorship necessary, and as matters connected with and arising out of censorship are, for reasons of state, obviously secret, Cabinet cannot agree to allow the Commissioner to call upon any censor officer to do anything more than explain what was done by him with any letters and documents referred to in your charge . . . The censor officer can give no information and no reasons for censoring any documents or correspondence within New Zealand, or as to the scope and extent of the censorship established in New Zealand upon the outbreak of the war.' *New Zealand Herald*, 14 August 1917, p. 6.

104 Catholic groups would continue to contact the Defence Department regarding the distribution of anti-Catholic material. See ANZ, R3885381, 'Inflammatory statements by Auckland Free Press, April–May'.

105 *Auckland Star*, 18 August 1917, p. 6.

106 ANZ, R3885386, 'Censorship of correspondence, Protestant Political association. December 1916–September 1918', Solicitor-General to the Chief of the General Staff, 13 December 1916.

107 AJHR, 1917 Session I, F-08, p. 2.

108 AJHR, 1917 Session I, F-08, pp. 3–4.

109 For a full account, see Davidson, *Dead Letters*, pp. 160–77. For speculation that Dr von Dannevill may have undertaken intelligence work for the Central Powers, see Julie Glamuzina, *Spies and Lies: The Mysterious Dr Dannevill* (Mangawhai: DoubleaXe Press, 2021).

110 Frame, *Salmond*, p. 171.

111 Davidson, *Dead Letters*, p. 174.

112 Simon Johnson, 'The Home Front: Aspects of Civilian Patriotism in New Zealand during the First World War' (MA thesis, Massey University, 1975), p. 86. For further examples of members of the public reporting secret wireless operations, see ANZ, R22428977, 'Communications – Wireless apparatus – Suspicions regarding Mr J. N. Wallace of Wellington'; ANZ, R22428980, 'Communications – Wireless apparatus – Correspondence – W. H. Hildebrandt of Napier'; ANZ, R22428982, 'Communications – Wireless apparatus – Unauthorised – Alleged Wireless Station in Waikato District'; ANZ, R22428987, 'Communications – Wireless apparatus – Unauthorised – Being in Possession of German Resident in

Vicinity of Castlepoint'; ANZ, R22428991, 'Communications – Wireless apparatus – Suspicions Regarding Two Germans Engaged in Prospecting on Mt Holdsworth'; ANZ, R22428993, 'Communications – Wireless apparatus – Unauthorised – Alleged Plant at Coromandel'; ANZ, R22428994, 'Communications – Wireless apparatus – Unauthorised – St Patrick's College, Wellington'.

113 Hill, 'State Servants and Social Beings'.

114 In mid-1916 police were noted as seeking admittance to the conference held to form a united Labour Party. H. E. Holland, *Armageddon or Calvary: The Conscientious Objectors of New Zealand and 'The Process of Their Conversion'* (Wellington: The Maoriland Worker Printing and Publishing Co., 1919), p. 14. See also Bassett with King, *Tomorrow Comes the Song*, pp. 71–72.

115 ANZ, R22434535, 'Publications, instructions, etc. – Publication "Put up the Sword" Miss Pankhurst', Commissioner to Inspectors, 5 July 1916.

116 ANZ, R22434535, 'Publications, instructions, etc. – Publication "Put up the Sword" Miss Pankhurst'; ANZ, R3885386, 'Censorship of correspondence, Protestant Political association. December 1916–September 1918'.

117 ANZ, R3885386, 'Censorship of correspondence, Protestant Political association. December 1916–September 1918'; Holland, *Armageddon or Calvary*, p. 14.

118 Mitchell Library, State Library of New South Wales, A2281, Scott Family Papers, Harry Holland to Rose Scott, 14 February 1917.

119 ATL, MS-Papers-2531-4, 'New Zealand Freedom League: Minute Books', 15 November 1915.

120 Baker, *King and Country Call*, p. 77.

121 *New Zealand Herald*, 2 November 1915, p. 5.

122 *Ohinemuri Gazette*, 20 December 1916, p. 2; Bassett with King, *Tomorrow Comes the Song*, p. 73; *Maoriland Worker*, 17 January 1917, p. 4.

123 ANZ, R3885353, 'J. W. Vandann, censorship of correspondence, February', Colonel Gibbon to the Deputy Chief Censor, 28 February 1917.

124 Baker, *King and Country Call*, pp. 207–8.

125 Brook Barrington, 'New Zealand and the Search for Security 1944–54: "A Modest and Moderate Contribution"' (PhD thesis, University of Auckland, 1993), p. 4. It was through these channels that New Zealand, for example, gained intelligence reports concerning the movements of German warships in the Pacific region and the strength of German defences at Samoa. See Richard G. H. Kay, 'In Pursuit of Victory: British–New Zealand Relations during the First World War' (PhD thesis, University of Otago, 2001), pp. 59–60; Ian McGibbon, *The Path to Gallipoli: Defending New Zealand, 1840–1915* (Wellington: GP Books, 1991), p. 249.

126 RHPHC, P4/40, p. 737, Commissioner of Police to Chief Commissioner of Police, Melbourne, 8 March 1916.

127 *New Zealand Police Gazette*, 1917, p. 327.

128 Howard's correspondence came to attention due to Australian censors monitoring mail posted to Tom Walsh, a trade unionist and, incidentally, the husband of Adela Pankhurst. ANZ, R3885383, 'Censorship of correspondence, "The Wag" [sic], Christchurch, to T. Walsh, Melbourne, April–December'.

129 ANZ, R3885384, 'Censorship of correspondence, Frank Lonnigan to D. Nugent, April 1918–May 1919'.

130 ANZ, R3885396, 'Censorship of correspondence, P. Tooker to P. Green, July–September', extract from the Brisbane censor's intelligence report for the week ended 10 August 1918. For further examples of Australian censors sending copied extracts from 'of interest' individuals to New Zealand censors, see ANZ, R3885402, 'Postal censorship of J. to Mrs J. O'Brien, May'.

131 ANZ, R3885385, 'Censorship of correspondence, T. Brosnan to Mrs M. McCarthy April–December', extract from the Brisbane censor's secret intelligence report, 8 May 1918.

132 ANZ, R3885403, 'Censorship of correspondences, R. Broadhurst Hill, March–September'.

133 ANZ, R3885394, 'Censorship of correspondence, P. Joseph to Miss E. Goldman, July–November', search warrant dated 5 October 1915; Salmond to Commissioner, 20 October 1915.

134 ANZ, R3885394, 'Censorship of correspondence, P. Joseph to Miss E. Goldman, July–November', memorandum for Superintendent Dwyer, 21 October 1915. For further details on New Zealand anarchism, see Jared Davidson, *Sewing Freedom: Philip Josephs, Transnationalism & Early New Zealand Anarchism* (Edinburgh: AK Press, 2013).

135 ANZ, R3885413, 'Secret message Kiel to Guam, August 1916–May 1917'.

136 ANZ, R21371539, 'Chemists, Enemy', List of German or Austrian Chemists in the Greymouth Police District, 5 October 1917; Inspector to the Commissioner of Police, 10 October 1917.

137 ANZ, R22434535, 'Publications, instructions, etc. – Publication "Put up the Sword" Miss Pankhurst', Greymouth district report, 30 June 1916.

138 ANZ, R3885388, 'Censorship of correspondence, W. H. Webbe, April–September', London to Wellington, dispatched 8 April 1918.

139 ANZ, R3885388, 'Censorship of correspondence, W. H. Webbe, April–September', Assessment dated 27 September 1918.

140 Johnson, 'The Home Front', p. 86.

141 ANZ, R21371956, 'Signalling, Karori', memorandum dated 11 March 1916.

142 ANZ, R3885253, 'Seditious utterances from the pulpit by Rev. Dean Power, September 1916–June 1918', typed marginalia from the Commissioner on report dated 6 September 1917.

143 Johnson, 'The Home Front', pp. 96–97.

144 ANZ, R21371770, 'Lockwood, Mrs', report of Plain Clothes Constable W. Tricklebank, 5 March 1917.

145 ANZ, R3885555, 'Codes – Methods adopted by POWs [Prisoners of War], June', letter dated 18 June 1916.

146 Michael Warner, *The Rise and Fall of Intelligence: An International Security History* (Washington: Georgetown University Press, 2014), p. 334.

147 Bernard Porter, *The Origins of the Vigilant State: The London Metropolitan Police Special Branch before the First World War* (London: Weidenfeld & Nicolson, 1987), p. 179.

148 For examples, see ANZ, R3885410, 'Censorship of correspondence, National peace conference, June 1915–July 1920'; ANZ, R3885401, 'Postal censorship of J. Jackson, August 1918–May 1919'; ANZ, R3885405, 'Censorship of correspondences, B. Ubansky, October 1918–March 1919'; ANZ, R3885412, 'Censorship of correspondence, W. Eenson, October 1917–March 1918'.

149 ANZ, R3885333, 'Scheme for collection of naval intelligence for admiralty May–October'.

150 ANZ, R3885242, 'Conveyance of secret documents between England and New Zealand by transports, December 1917–January 1918'.

151 ANZ, R3885208, 'Wireless communication with British merchant vessels, August–November'.

152 Baker, *King and Country Call*, p. 78.

153 Mitchell Library, State Library of New South Wales, A2281, Scott Family Papers, Harry Holland to Rose Scott, 14 February 1917.

154 ANZ, R22434529, 'Publications, instructions, etc. – Literature (anti-militarist) – Publication of', Tanner to Gibbon, 24 November 1915.

155 ANZ, R22430468, 'Administration and Miscellaneous – Censorship – Regulations postal', report on postal censorship for the quarter ending 30 September 1917.

156 ANZ, R3885254, 'Correspondence re H. Holland and L. Glover, November 1917–January 1918', Herdman to Allen, 5 January 1918.

157 Anderson, 'Military Censorship in World War I', p. 105.

158 Ibid., pp. 106–7.

159 AJHR, 1917 Session I, F-08, pp. 15, 18, 121.

160 Loveridge and Watson, The Home Front, pp. 344–47.

161 Barry Gustafson, Labour's Path to Political Independence: The Origins and Establishment of the New Zealand Labour Party, 1900–19 (Auckland: Auckland University Press, 1980), p. 147.

Chapter Four: Searching for Subversives, 1919–1929

1 Gregory S. Kealey, Spying on Canadians: The Royal Canadian Mounted Police Security Service and the Origins of the Long Cold War (Toronto: University of Toronto Press, 2017); David McKnight, Australia's Spies and Their Secrets (St Leonards, NSW: Allen & Unwin, 1994).

2 G. J. Meyer, A World Undone: The Story of the Great War, 1914 to 1918 (New York: Delta, 2006), p. 705.

3 Robert Gerwarth, The Vanquished: Why the First World War Failed to End, 1917–1923 (London: Allen Lane, 2016); Robert Gerwarth and John Horne (eds), War in Peace: Paramilitary Violence after the Great War (Oxford: Oxford University Press, 2012); Anthony Read, The World on Fire: 1919 and the Battle with Bolshevism (London: Jonathan Cape, 2008).

4 New Zealand Official Year Book, 1921–22, p. 529.

5 Graeme Dunstall, A Policeman's Paradise?: Policing a Stable Society, 1918–1945 (Palmerston North: Dunmore Press, 1999), p. 256.

6 Evening Post, 11 October 1919, p. 4.

7 ANZ, R3885678, 'Aid to the Civil Power – 2 parts, March 1919–March 1922; March 1931–May 1935'.

8 Evening Star, 31 July 1919, p. 9.

9 Dunstall, A Policeman's Paradise?, p. 257.

10 RHPHC, AD11, part 1, Brigadier-General George Richardson to Colonels H. R. Potter et al., 26 January 1920, and other correspondence from 1920.

11 For detailed accounts, see Rory Sweetman, Bishop in the Dock: The Sedition Trial of James Liston (Auckland: Auckland University Press, 1997); Nicholas Reid, James Michael Liston: A Life (Wellington: Victoria University Press, 2006), pp. 110–26.

12 Poverty Bay Herald, 18 May 1922, p. 7.

13 For an overview of the long struggle to secure state respect for rangatiratanga/autonomy, and the Crown's ongoing efforts to contain it, see Richard S. Hill, 'Maori and State Policy', in Giselle Byrnes (ed.), The New Oxford History of New Zealand (Melbourne: Oxford University Press, 2009).

14 Raeburn Lange, In an Advisory Capacity: Maori Councils, 1919–1945, Rangatiratanga Series no. 5 (Wellington: Treaty of Waitangi Research Unit, 2005).

15 Richard S. Hill, State Authority, Indigenous Autonomy: Crown–Maori Relations in New Zealand/Aotearoa, 1900–1950 (Wellington: Victoria University Press, 2004), pp. 153–55.

16 Ibid., pp. 156–60; Richard S. Hill, 'Tōrangapū Ohaoha: Māori and the Political Economy, 1918–1945', in Michael Reilly, Suzanne Duncan, Gianna Leoni, Lachy Paterson, Lyn Carter, Matiu Rātima and Poia Rewi (eds), Te Kōparapara: An Introduction to the Māori

World (Auckland: Auckland University Press, 2018), pp. 255–56.

17   Alexander Trapeznik, 'New Zealand's Perceptions of the Russian Revolution of 1917', *Revolutionary Russia*, vol. 19, no. 1 (2006), pp. 63–77.

18   P. J. O'Farrell, 'The Russian Revolution and the Labour Movements of Australia and New Zealand, 1917–1922', *International Review of Social History*, vol. 8, issue 2 (August 1963), p. 177.

19   NZPD, vol. 186, 8 July 1920, p. 279.

20   NZPD, vol. 183, 27 November 1918, p. 442.

21   ANZ, R24118475, 'Communist Party of New Zealand: Policy on Other Political Parties in New Zealand', Report of Detective Sergeant R. Ward, 3 December 1920; Dunstall, *A Policeman's Paradise?*, p. 266.

22   O'Farrell, 'The Russian Revolution', p. 195.

23   Graeme Hunt, *Spies and Revolutionaries: A History of New Zealand Subversion* (Auckland: Reed, 2007), pp. 91, 93; O'Farrell, 'The Russian Revolution', p. 195; Peter Franks and Jim McAloon, *The New Zealand Labour Party, 1916–2016* (Wellington: Victoria University Press, 2016), p. 87.

24   Bruce Brown, *The Rise of New Zealand Labour: A History of the Labour Party from 1916 to 1940* (Wellington: Price Milburn, 1962), pp. 73, 79, 94, 222; Franks and McAloon, *The New Zealand Labour Party*, pp. 90–91.

25   Brown, *The Rise of New Zealand Labour*, p. 111.

26   Kerry Taylor, '"Our Motto, No Compromise": The Ideological Origins and Foundation of the Communist Party of New Zealand', *New Zealand Journal of History*, vol. 28, no. 2 (1994), pp. 171, 177. The Communist Party of New Zealand was interchangeably known through its existence as the New Zealand Communist Party.

27   Alexander Trapeznik, '"Agents of Moscow" at the Dawn of the Cold War: The Comintern and the Communist Party of New Zealand', *Journal of Cold War Studies*, vol. 11, no. 1 (2009), pp. 124–49.

28   Kerry Taylor, 'The Communist Party of New Zealand and the Third Period', in Matthew Worley (ed.), *In Search of Revolution: International Communist Parties in the Third Period* (London: I. B. Tauris, 2004), p. 284.

29   Trapeznik, 'New Zealand's Perceptions of the Russian Revolution of 1917', p. 71; Kerry Taylor, '"The Old Bolshevik": Alex Galbraith, the Communist Party and the New Zealand Revolution', in Rachael Bell (ed.), *New Zealand between the Wars* (Auckland: Massey University Press, 2017), p. 115.

30   O'Farrell, 'The Russian Revolution', p. 196.

31   Franks and McAloon, *The New Zealand Labour Party*, p. 87.

32   Hunt, *Spies and Revolutionaries*, p. 115.

33   Brown, *The Rise of New Zealand Labour*, p. 82.

34   *New Zealand Observer*, 28 June 1919, p. 1.

35   Barry Gustafson, *Labour's Path to Political Independence: The Origins and Establishment of the New Zealand Labour Party, 1900–19* (Auckland: Auckland University Press, 1980), p. 146.

36   For an example, see Loyalty League, *What is the Red Menace?: The Secret Forces behind Socialism and Communism: An Exposure of the So Called 'Labour' Party* (Wellington: Loyalty League, 1925).

37   Brad Patterson, '"We Stand for the Protestant Religion, the (Protestant) King and the Empire": The Rise of the Protestant Political Association in World War One', in Steven Loveridge (ed.), *New Zealand Society at War, 1914–1918* (Wellington: Victoria University Press, 2016), p. 248.

38   Paul Baker, *King and Country Call: New Zealanders, Conscription and the Great War* (Auckland: Auckland University Press, 1988), p. 231.

39   Geoffrey Troughton, 'The *Maoriland Worker* and Blasphemy in New Zealand', *Labour*

History, no. 91 (November 2006), pp. 113–29; *New Zealand Herald*, 18 March 1922, p. 10.

40   Paul Christoffel, *Censored: A Short History of Censorship in New Zealand* (Wellington: Research Unit, Department of Internal Affairs, 1989), p. 10.

41   Ibid., p. 16.

42   Patrick Day, *The Radio Years: A History of Broadcasting in New Zealand, Volume One* (Auckland: Auckland University Press in association with the Broadcasting History Trust, 1994), p. 23.

43   Ibid., pp. 34–39, 62–65, 90–94; Christoffel, *Censored*, p. 29; Peter Downes and Peter Harcourt, *Voices in the Air: Radio Broadcasting in New Zealand: A Documentary* (Wellington: Methuen/Radio New Zealand, 1976), pp. 68–70.

44   NZS, 1918, No. 9, 'Expeditionary Forces Amendment Act', p. 75.

45   NZS, 1919, No. 44, 'Undesirable Immigrants Exclusion Act', pp. 160–64.

46   NZPD, vol. 185, 24 October 1919, p. 832.

47   1st NZSIS Tranche, 'Commissioner of Police to All Districts', 29 January 1919, p. 228; Dunstall, *A Policeman's Paradise?*, pp. 253–57. For a facsimile of the confidential memorandum, see Hunt, *Spies and Revolutionaries*, p. 96.

48   1st NZSIS Tranche, 'Commissioner of Police to all Districts', 3 April 1919, p. 227.

49   Graeme Hunt, *Black Prince: The Autobiography of Fintan Patrick Walsh* (Auckland: Penguin Books, 2004), p. 167. The United States, for example, had established a filing system on known suspected subversives in 1911.

50   ANZ, R3885399, 'Rules for the censorship of the press, September 1918–May 1919', Memorandum for the Chief of the General Staff, 24 April 1919.

51   John Anderson, 'Military Censorship in World War I: Its Use and Abuse in New Zealand' (MA thesis, Victoria University College, 1952), p. 132.

52   NZS, 1920, no. 22, 'War Regulations Continuance Act', p. 56.

53   NZPD, vol. 187, 24 August 1920, p. 349.

54   Malcolm McKinnon, *The Broken Decade: Prosperity, Depression and Recovery in New Zealand, 1928–39* (Dunedin: Otago University Press, 2016), p. 148.

55   Jared Davidson, *Dead Letters: Censorship and Subversion in New Zealand, 1914–1920* (Dunedin: Otago University Press, 2019), p. 49.

56   Ibid., p. 34.

57   ANZ, R3885410, 'Censorship of correspondence, National peace conference, June 1915–July 1920', Memorandum for the Hon. Minister of Defence, 8 November 1919; Anderson, 'Military Censorship in World War I', pp. 126–27.

58   NZPD, vol. 186, 14 July 1920, p. 411; NZPD, vol. 187, 10 August 1920, p. 39; NZPD, vol. 187, 27 August 1920, p. 493; NZPD, vol. 189, 25 October 1920, p. 18; ANZ, R22183762, 'Post Office Circulars', *Post and Telegraph Official Circular*, 16 November 1920, p. 155.

59   RHPHC, AD 10, 17/31, Commissioner to Chief of General Staff, 12 June 1919.

60   Dunstall, *A Policeman's Paradise?*, p. 257; NZS, 1919, no. 19, 'Police Offences Amendment Act', p. 61.

61   RHPHC, M 15/3/477, Solicitor-General to Minister of Marine, 12 May 1921.

62   S. D. Waters, *The Royal New Zealand Navy* (Wellington: War History Branch, Department of Internal Affairs, 1956), p. 8.

63   David Filer, 'Civil–Military Cooperation in Signals Intelligence in New Zealand, 1904 to 1939', *Security and Surveillance History Series*, 2017/4, p. 3.

64   Colin Hanson, 'Draft Chapters for History of New Zealand Sigint', unpublished manuscript, 'Between the Wars 1919–1939', p. 3; Day, *The Radio Years*, p. 35.

65   ANZ, R21464478, 'Intelligence Centres – Security intelligence organisation'.

66 Filer, 'Civil–Military Cooperation in Signals Intelligence in New Zealand', p. 3; ANZ, R21465018, 'W/T stations – Direction finding stations – General'.

67 ANZ, R3885620, 'Secret memo for defence minister, July', Memorandum for the Defence Minister, July 1923.

68 ANZ, R3885342, 'Intelligence – Imperial bureau establishment in New Zealand March', Liverpool to Allen, 25 March 1919.

69 ANZ, R3885342, 'Intelligence – Imperial bureau establishment in New Zealand March', Allen to Liverpool, 5 June 1919.

70 Dunstall, *A Policeman's Paradise?*, p. 254; ANZ, R3885791, 'Intelligence – Formation and functions of intelligence branch, GHQ [General Headquarters]', secret memorandum from Brigadier-General Richardson to officers commanding all military districts, 29 August 1919; Hanson, 'Draft Chapters', unpublished manuscript, appendix one, p. 2.

71 Dunstall, *A Policeman's Paradise?*, p. 254.

72 Richard S. Hill, *The Iron Hand in the Velvet Glove: The Modernisation of Policing in New Zealand, 1886–1917* (Palmerston North: Dunmore Press, 1995), p. 306; Dunstall, *A Policeman's Paradise?*, p. 254.

73 Dunstall, *A Policeman's Paradise?*, p. 254.

74 ANZ, R3885791, 'Intelligence – Formation and functions of intelligence branch, GHQ [General Headquarters]', Memorandum for the Director of Intelligence, London, from Major-General, Commanding New Zealand Forces, 12 February 1920.

75 ANZ, R3885791, 'Intelligence – Formation and functions of intelligence branch, GHQ [General Headquarters]', Suggestions for carrying out the functions of the committee, 28 June 1920.

76 Dunstall, *A Policeman's Paradise?*, p. 255.

77 Ibid.

78 Jared Davidson, *Fighting War: Anarchists, Wobblies & the New Zealand State, 1905–1925* (Wellington: Rebel Press, 2016), p. 29.

79 ANZ, R24716774, 'Organisations: Mau Movement: Samoa', Memorandum for Commissioner W. G. Wohlmann, 12 November 1930. For further coverage of MI5's Imperial outreach, see Calder Walton, *Empire of Secrets: British Intelligence, the Cold War and the Twilight of Empire* (London: HarperPress, 2013), pp. 16–21.

80 1st NZSIS Tranche, 'Commissioner of Police to all Districts: REVOLUTIONARY ORGANISATIONS AND PROPAGANDA', 10 September 1920, pp. 222–26. For previous angles on this memorandum, see Dunstall, *A Policeman's Paradise?*, p. 257; Miriam L. Wharton, 'The Development of Security Intelligence in New Zealand, 1945–1957' (Master of Defence Studies, Massey University, 2012), pp. 10–12; and Hunt, *Spies and Revolutionaries*, pp. 95–97.

81 1st NZSIS Tranche, 'Commissioner of Police to all Districts: REVOLUTIONARY ORGANISATIONS AND PROPAGANDA', 10 September 1920, pp. 222–26.

82 Dunstall, *A Policeman's Paradise?*, p. 265. The error persists in recent accounts; see, for example, Alexander Gillespie and Claire Breen, 'The Security Intelligence Agencies in New Zealand: Evaluation, Challenges and Progress', *Intelligence and National Security*, vol. 36, no. 5 (2021), p. 677.

83 1st NZSIS Tranche, 'History of the New Zealand Security Intelligence Service and its Predecessors', p. 2.

84 See Dunstall, *A Policeman's Paradise?*, p. 265.

85 Ibid., pp. 253, 265.

86 Ibid. p. 155.

87 They were discovered by one of the present authors, after a tip-off, and are now held by Archives New Zealand.

88 1st NZSIS Tranche, 'Commissioner of Police to all Districts: REVOLUTIONARY ORGANISATIONS AND PROPAGANDA', 10 September 1920, pp. 224–25.

89 ANZ, R24716780, 'Miscellaneous Organisations: Unemployed Workers' Movement', The Commissioner of Police to the Superintendent of Police Auckland, 19 October 1927.

90 Hunt, *Spies and Revolutionaries*, p. 103; Conrad Bollinger, *Against the Wind: The Story of the New Zealand Seamen's Union* (Wellington: New Zealand Seamen's Union, 1968), p. 131.

91 Dunstall, *A Policeman's Paradise?*, p. 265.

92 Hill, *The Iron Hand*, pp. 339–40; Dunstall, *A Policeman's Paradise?*, pp. 47–49.

93 New Zealand Police College, *Police Training in New Zealand: Trentham in Retrospect* (Wellington: New Zealand Police, 1982), p. 8.

94 Dunstall, *A Policeman's Paradise?*, p. 155; Graeme Dunstall papers, 'Numbers of Detectives 1918–1941'; 'Report of Committee of Inquiry', *New Zealand Police Gazette*, 1919, pp. 417–28; *New Zealand Herald*, 28 June 1919, p. 8.

95 David Omand, 'The Cycle of Intelligence', in Robert Dover, Michael S. Goodman and Claudia Hillebrand (eds), *Routledge Companion to Intelligence Studies* (New York: Routledge, 2014), p. 63.

96 ANZ, R24881820, 'Communist Party NZ, Police Raids On', Minute Sheet: Destruction of Records, 1921–31, 10 July 1962.

97 Kerry Allan Taylor, 'Worker's Vanguard or People's Voice?: The Communist Party of New Zealand from Origins to 1946' (PhD thesis, Victoria University of Wellington, 1994), pp. 91–92.

98 This position is reflected within the NZSIS's in-house history: 'During this period [1919–40] there was no communist diplomatic missions [sic] in New Zealand and no counter-espionage work was undertaken.' 1st NZSIS Tranche, 'History of the New Zealand Security Intelligence Service and Its Predecessors', p. 2. See also Hunt, *Spies and Revolutionaries*, p. 118.

99 RHPHC, Colonel W. L. H. Sinclair-Burgess, Chief of the General Staff, to C. A. Berendsen, Prime Minister's Office, May 1927.

100 Paul Welch Behringer, 'Forewarned is Forearmed: Intelligence, Japan's Siberian Intervention, and the Washington Conference', *International History Review*, vol. 38, issue 3 (2016), p. 368; Max Everest-Phillips, 'The Pre-War Fear of Japanese Espionage: Its Impact and Legacy', *Journal of Contemporary History*, vol. 42, no. 2 (2007), p. 248.

101 Filer, 'Civil–Military Cooperation in Signals Intelligence in New Zealand', p. 3.

102 Hanson, 'Draft Chapters', unpublished manuscript, appendix one, p. 3.

103 RHPHC, Diary of Constable S. King, 'Experiences of my tour with the Police Escort to H.R.H. the Prince of Wales during his tour of New Zealand from April 24th to May 22nd 1920', 17 May 1920.

104 ANZ, R24118475, 'Communist Party of New Zealand: Policy on Other Political Parties in New Zealand', O'Donovan to the Auckland Superintendent, 7 January 1921.

105 ANZ, R24118475, 'Communist Party of New Zealand: Policy on Other Political Parties in New Zealand', Memorandum to O'Donovan from the Department of Labour, 10 September 1920.

106 ANZ, R24118475, 'Communist Party of New Zealand: Policy on Other Political Parties in New Zealand', Report of Detective John Bruce Young, 30 October 1920.

107 F. P. Walsh was among the many seamen, miners and others charged with illegal striking, and was closely watched thereafter until he changed his political stance: Hunt, *Black Prince*, pp. 77–79; Bollinger, *Against the Wind*, pp. 142–43. For a summary of the economy in the decade, see Brian Easton, *Not in Narrow Seas: The Economic History of Aotearoa New Zealand* (Wellington: Victoria University Press, 2020), pp. 229–32.

108 Dunstall, *A Policeman's Paradise?*, p. 259.

109 RHPHC, John Dwyer, 'Fragments from the Official Career of John Dwyer Superintendent of Police 1878–1921', unpublished manuscript, p. 59.

110 *New Zealand Herald*, 12 May 1926, p. 14; ANZ, R24001225, 'Old Police Records – Recording Sheets', S.1926/17.

111 ANZ, R24716775, 'Socialist Party of NZ'.

112 Dunstall, *A Policeman's Paradise?*, p. 259; Franks and McAloon, *The New Zealand Labour Party*, p. 75.

113 ANZ, R24001223, 'Old Police Records – Recording Sheets', S.1921/56.

114 Hill, *State Authority, Indigenous Autonomy*, pp. 146, 156–60.

115 Hill, *State Authority, Indigenous Autonomy*, pp. 140–46, 251–52; Taylor, '"Potential Allies of the Working Class"', pp. 103–16; Newman, *Ratana Revisited*, p. 364.

116 Hill, *State Authority, Indigenous Autonomy*, pp. 140–46; Kerry Taylor, '"Potential Allies of the Working Class": The Communist Party of New Zealand and Maori, 1921–1952', in Pat Moloney and Kerry Taylor (eds), *On the Left: Essays on Socialism in New Zealand* (Dunedin: University of Otago Press, 2002), pp. 103–16; Keith Newman, *Ratana Revisited: An Unfinished Legacy* (Auckland: Reed Books, 2006), p. 364.

117 Hill, *State Authority, Indigenous Autonomy*, pp. 140–46, 251–52; Taylor, '"Potential Allies of the Working Class"', pp. 103–16; Newman, *Ratana Revisited*, p. 364.

118 King, *Te Puea*, pp. 76–97.

119 Ann Parsonson, 'Herangi, Te Kirihaehae Te Puea', *The Dictionary of New Zealand Biography, Volume Three* (Auckland: Auckland University Press, 1996), pp. 208–11.

120 ANZ, R24001226, 'Old Police Records – Recording Sheets', S.1929/18; ANZ, R24001227, 'Old Police Records – Recording Sheets', S.1928/24.

121 ANZ, R24001223, 'Old Police Records – Recording Sheets', S.1921/33.

122 ANZ, R24001227, 'Old Police Records – Recording Sheets', S.1928/24. See also Michael J. Field, *Mau: Samoa's Struggle against New Zealand Oppression* (Wellington: A. H. & A. W. Reed, 1984), pp. 73–75.

123 RHPHC, N 8/33/1, 'NATIVE UNREST IN THE MANDATED TERRITORY OF WESTERN SAMOA', n.d.

124 RHPHC, 'Circulars and memos book, Hampden Police Station, 1877–1926', O'Donovan to Wright, 29 January 1919.

125 For New Zealand reactions to the Sacco and Vanzetti executions, see S. W. Scott, *Rebel in a Wrong Cause* (Auckland: Collins, 1960), pp. 46–47. For surveillance on these issues, see ANZ, R24001225, 'Old Police Records – Recording Sheets'; ANZ, R24001228, 'Old Police Records – Recording Sheets'; ANZ, R24118475, 'Communist Party of New Zealand: Policy on Other Political Parties in New Zealand'; ANZ, R25088001, 'Peace Organisations: Miscellaneous Peace/Disarmament Groups: Anti War Movement'; ANZ, R24716774, 'Organisations: Mau Movement: Samoa'; ANZ, R24716773, 'Protests Miscellaneous: Sacco & Vanzetti'.

126 Rachel Barrowman, *Victoria University of Wellington 1899–1999: A History* (Wellington: Victoria University Press, 1999), p. 92; TNA, KV 2/3922, p. 117. *Evening Post*, 13 October 1921, p. 4.

127 SRCNZSSC, OPR 1920 part 1, S 1921/58, 'WORKERS' EDUCATIONAL ASSOCIATION: Alleged employing Socialists 1921', and 'HUNTER, Prof.: Supports appointment W.E.A. of C. ff. Marsh-Roberts'; *Evening Post*, 26 November 1921; *Manawatu Standard*, 28 November 1921; Tim Beaglehole, 'Hunter, Thomas Anderson', *The Dictionary of New Zealand Biography, Volume Three*, pp. 241–43; W. L. Renwick, 'Sir Thomas Hunter (1876–1953)', in Vincent O'Sullivan (ed.), *Eminent Victorians: Great Teachers*

and Scholars from Victoria's First 100 Years
(Wellington: Stout Research Centre, 1999),
pp. 12, 24, 28.

128 RHPHC, Colonel W. L. H. Sinclair-Burgess,
Chief of the General Staff, to C. A. Berendsen,
Prime Minister's Office, May 1927.

129 Sweetman, *Bishop in the Dock*, pp. 146–54.

130 ANZ, R24118475, 'Communist Party of New
Zealand: Policy on Other Political Parties in
New Zealand', Emily Nichol to E. P. Lee, 28
December 1920.

131 ANZ, R24118475, 'Communist Party of New
Zealand: Policy on Other Political Parties in
New Zealand', statement attached to report
of Detective F. J. Beer, 31 October 1920.

132 Dunstall, *A Policeman's Paradise?*, p. 266.

133 Ibid., pp. 260–61.

134 ANZ, R24118475, 'Communist Party of New
Zealand: Policy on Other Political Parties in
New Zealand', Report of Detective F. J. Beer,
8 February 1921.

135 Davidson, *Fighting War*, p. 28.

136 ANZ, R24118479, 'Communist Party of New
Zealand: Wellington Branch: Sympathisers &
Contacts', report of Detective Sergeant A. E.
Andrews, 12 October 1919.

137 Dunstall, *A Policeman's Paradise?*, p. 265.

138 ANZ, R24716780, 'Miscellaneous
Organisations: Unemployed Workers'
Movement', report of Detective J. K.
Robertson, 24 February 1927.

139 ANZ, R24881820, 'Communist Party NZ,
Police Raids On', Report of Constable George
Thomas Deakin, 27 July 1929.

140 Dunstall, *A Policeman's Paradise?*, p. 267.

141 1st NZSIS Tranche, 'Commissioner of
Police to all Districts: REVOLUTIONARY
ORGANISATIONS AND PROPAGANDA',
10 September 1920, pp. 222–26; Dunstall,
A Policeman's Paradise?, p. 266.

142 Scott, *Rebel in a Wrong Cause*, pp. 53–54.

143 ANZ, R24001227, 'Old Police Records –

Recording Sheets', S.1928/59; Scott, *Rebel in a
Wrong Cause*, pp. 53–54.

144 ANZ, R24118479, 'Communist Party of New
Zealand: Wellington Branch: Sympathisers &
Contacts', Report of Detective H. Nuttall,
30 December 1926.

145 ANZ, R24881820, 'Communist Party NZ,
Police Raids On', Report of Detective N. W.
Baylis, 18 July 1929.

146 ANZ, R24881820, 'Communist Party NZ,
Police Raids On', attached to report by
Detective N. W. Baylis, 27 July 1929.

147 ANZ, R24118479, 'Communist Party of New
Zealand: Wellington Branch: Sympathisers
& Contacts', Report of Senior Sergeant G. B.
Edwards, 5 September 1929.

148 ANZ, R24118475, 'Communist Party of New
Zealand: Policy on Other Political Parties in
New Zealand', report of Detective Sergeant
R. Ward, 4 July 1921.

149 *Taranaki Daily News*, 1 March 1921, p. 4; ANZ,
R24001223, 'Old Police Records – Recording
Sheets', S.1921/56.

150 RHPHC, Customs Department Circular
36/959, memo 1921/102, 22 August 1921.

151 ANZ, R24881820, 'Communist Party NZ,
Police Raids On', Comptroller of Customs to
the Commissioner of Police, 22 May 1930.

152 Dunstall, *A Policeman's Paradise?*, p. 444, n. 14.

153 A. C. Wilson, *Wire and Wireless: A History of
Telecommunications in New Zealand, 1860–1987*
(Palmerston North: Dunmore Press, 1994), p.
212.

154 ANZ, R24118475, 'Communist Party of New
Zealand: Policy on Other Political Parties
in New Zealand', report of Constable D. J.
Hewitt, 20 October 1920.

155 ANZ, R3885401, 'Postal censorship of
J. Jackson, August 1918–May 1919', extract
from Brisbane censor's report for week
ending 19 April 1919.

156 For example, in December 1919 authorities
in London and Wellington discussed such

intelligence-sharing arrangements. ANZ,
R3885678, 'Aid to the Civil Power – 2 parts,
March 1919–March 1922; March 1931–May
1935', Mackenzie to Massey, 8 December 1919.

157   Hunt, *Spies and Revolutionaries*, pp. 117–18;
Richard J. Aldrich, *GCHQ: The Uncensored
Story of Britain's Most Secret Intelligence Agency*
(London: HarperPress, 2010), p. 18; David
Burke, *Russia and the British Left: From the
1848 Revolutions to the General Strike* (London:
I. B. Tauris, 2018), pp. 247–49.

158   Dunstall, *A Policeman's Paradise?*, p. 266.

159   Ibid., pp. 261, 447, n. 61.

160   Ibid., p. 266.

161   ANZ, R24716780, 'Miscellaneous
Organisations: Unemployed Workers'
Movement', report of Detective N. W. Baylis,
4 May 1929.

162   RHPHC, Colonel W. L. H. Sinclair-Burgess,
Chief of the General Staff, to C. A. Berendsen,
Prime Minister's Office, May 1927.

163   Taylor, '"The Old Bolshevik"', pp. 116–17.

164   ANZ, R24118477, 'Communist Party of
New Zealand: Wellington Branch: District
Committee-General: Directives & Bulletins,
District Meetings', report of Detective
Sergeant W. E. Lewis, 3 June 1921.

165   ANZ, R24118475, 'Communist Party of New
Zealand: Policy on Other Political Parties in
New Zealand', Report of Detective F. J. Beer,
4 July 1920.

166   ANZ, R24118475, 'Communist Party of New
Zealand: Policy on Other Political Parties in
New Zealand', Report of Senior Detective
R. Ward, 3 July 1924.

167   ANZ, R24716780, 'Miscellaneous
Organisations: Unemployed Workers'
Movement', report of Detective J. K.
Robertson, 10 April 1927.

168   Hunt, *Spies and Revolutionaries*, p. 104.

169   Wharton, 'The Development of Security
Intelligence in New Zealand, 1945–1957', p. 13.

170   Hunt, *Spies and Revolutionaries*, p. 104.

171   Wharton, 'The Development of Security
Intelligence in New Zealand, 1945–1957', p. 12.

172   Dunstall, *A Policeman's Paradise?*, p. 253.

173   ANZ, R24881820, 'Communist Party NZ,
Police Raids On', Minute Sheet: Destruction
of Records, 1921–31, 10 July 1962.

174   Dunstall, *A Policeman's Paradise?*, p. 260.

175   Bernard Porter, *The Origins of the Vigilant
State: The London Metropolitan Police Special
Branch before the First World War* (London:
Weidenfeld & Nicolson, 1987), pp. 182–87.

176   Dunstall, *A Policeman's Paradise?*, p. 261.

177   ANZ, R24716780, 'Miscellaneous
Organisations: Unemployed Workers'
Movement', the Commissioner of Police to
the Superintendent of Police Auckland,
19 October 1927.

178   ANZ, R24881820, 'Communist Party NZ,
Police Raids On', list of documents seized in
a 19 December 1930 police raid on 229 Cuba
Street, Wellington.

179   Lange, *In an Advisory Capacity*, pp. 26–28.

180   Kerry Taylor, '"The Old Bolshevik"',
pp. 127–28. See too, James Bennett, *'Rats
and Revolutionaries': The Labour Movement
in Australia and New Zealand, 1890–1940*
(Dunedin: University of Otago Press, 2004),
pp. 81–92.

Chapter Five: The Red Decade? 1930–1939

1   *New Zealand Official Year Book*, 1934, p. 594.

2   Malcolm McKinnon, *The Broken Decade:
Prosperity, Depression and Recovery in New
Zealand, 1928–39* (Dunedin: Otago University
Press, 2016), pp. 420–21.

3   R. T. Robertson, 'Government Responses to
Unemployment in New Zealand, 1929–35',
New Zealand Journal of History, vol. 16, no. 1
(April 1982), pp. 21–38.

4   Graeme Hunt, *Black Prince: The Autobiography
of Fintan Patrick Walsh* (Auckland: Penguin

Books, 2004), p. 121; Edward Crawford, 'Trotskyism in New Zealand', unpublished manuscript, n.d. [1993], pp. 1–2, copy in possession of Richard Hill; TNA, KV 2/3922, p. 117; Alexander Trapeznik, '"Agents of Moscow" at the Dawn of the Cold War: The Comintern and the Communist Party of New Zealand', *Journal of Cold War Studies*, vol. 11, no. 1 (2009), pp. 146–47.

5   *Evening Post*, 28 February 1933, p. 9.

6   Kerry Taylor, 'The Communist Party of New Zealand and the Third Period', in Matthew Worley (ed.), *In Search of Revolution: International Communist Parties in the Third Period* (London: I. B. Tauris, 2004), p. 284.

7   Kerry Allan Taylor, 'Worker's Vanguard or People's Voice?: The Communist Party of New Zealand from Origins to 1946' (PhD thesis, Victoria University of Wellington, 1994), p. 106.

8   Taylor, 'The Communist Party of New Zealand and the Third Period', p. 288.

9   David Burke, *Russia and the British Left: From the 1848 Revolutions to the General Strike* (London: I. B. Tauris, 2018), pp. 251–52.

10   *Strike!: Strategy and Tactics: The Lessons of the Industrial Struggles* (Wellington: Communist Party of New Zealand, 1930), p. 2; ANZ, R24716781, 'Miscellaneous Organisations: Unemployed Workers' Movement', report of Acting Detective R. H. Waterson, 1 August 1931; Herbert Roth, 'The Communist Vote in New Zealand', *Political Science*, vol. 17, no. 2 (September 1965), p. 29.

11   *Auckland Star*, 4 April 1934, p. 6.

12   Trapeznik, '"Agents of Moscow"', p. 145.

13   Taylor, 'The Communist Party of New Zealand and the Third Period', pp. 288–89.

14   Kerry Taylor, '"The Old Bolshevik": Alex Galbraith, the Communist Party and the New Zealand Revolution', in Rachael Bell (ed.), *New Zealand between the Wars* (Auckland: Massey University Press, 2017), p. 124.

15   This orientation led to some internal upheaval, and a 17 December 1932 report from the Wellington FSU announced a new FSU free of the 'impotency' of its predecessor, which was denounced as isolated from the working class and the 'plaything of intellectual adventurers, notoriety seekers and unscrupulous self-seekers'. A further charge noted that the previous incarnation had failed at 'mobilising the workers by agitation for the active defence of the Soviet Union'. ANZ, R24716797, 'Friends of the Soviet Union', report dated 17 December 1932. See too Rachel Barrowman, *Mason: The Life of R. A. K. Mason* (Wellington: Victoria University Press, 2003), p. 185.

16   Elsie Locke, *Student at the Gates* (Christchurch: Whitcoulls, 1981), p. 106.

17   *Auckland Star*, 4 April 1934, p. 6; Barrowman, *Mason*, p. 185.

18   R. T. Robertson, 'Isolation, Ideology and Impotence: Organisations for the Unemployed during the Great Depression, 1929–35', *New Zealand Journal of History*, vol. 12, no. 2 (October 1979), pp. 149–64. For regional studies of the UWM, see Paul Harris, 'The New Zealand Unemployed Workers Movement, 1931–1939 Gisborne and the Relief Workers' Strike', *New Zealand Journal of History*, vol. 10, no. 2 (1976), pp. 130–42, and Vincent O'Malley, 'A United Front against Capitalism? Unemployed Workers' Organisations in Christchurch, New Zealand, during the Depression', *Labour History Review*, vol. 73, no. 1 (April 2008), pp. 145–66.

19   *Evening Post*, 16 January 1932, p. 12.

20   Jim Edwards, *Break Down These Bars* (Auckland: Penguin, 1987); for in-depth political police penetration of CPNZ circles at this time, see Williams/Birchfield family papers, ff. 1–26, Albert and Constance Birchfield personal files. For Constance Birchfield, see Maureen Birchfield, *She Dared to Speak: Connie Birchfield's Story* (Dunedin: University of Otago Press, 1998).

21 The Labour Party newspaper, the *New Zealand Worker*, for example, attacked the UWM for its Communist leanings and for the Movement's advocacy of direct action and strikes: Rosslyn J. Noonan, 'The Riots of 1932: A Study of Social Unrest in Auckland, Wellington and Dunedin' (MA thesis, University of Auckland, 1969), pp. 56–65.

22 S. W. Scott, *Rebel in a Wrong Cause* (Auckland: Collins, 1960), p. 67.

23 W. B. Sutch, *The Quest for Security in New Zealand* (Harmondsworth: Penguin, 1942), p. 130.

24 Noonan, 'The Riots of 1932', p. 175.

25 *New Zealand Observer*, 21 April 1932, p. 1.

26 *NZ Truth*, 19 May 1932, p. 1.

27 *Evening Post*, 16 May 1932, p. 8.

28 Graeme Dunstall, *A Policeman's Paradise?: Policing a Stable Society, 1918–1945* (Palmerston North: Dunmore Press, 1999), p. 264.

29 Locke, *Student at the Gates*, p. 128.

30 *New Zealand Worker*, 18 May 1932, p. 6.

31 Tim Beaglehole, *A Life of J. C. Beaglehole: New Zealand Scholar* (Wellington: Victoria University Press, 2006), pp. 174ff.; Rachel Barrowman, *Victoria University of Wellington 1899–1999: A History* (Wellington: Victoria University Press, 1999), p. 53; George Fraser, *Ungrateful People* [1952] (Auckland: Pelorus Press, 1985), p. 53. See also Tim Beaglehole, 'Beaglehole, John Cawte', *The Dictionary of New Zealand Biography, Volume Five* (Auckland: Auckland University Press, 2000), pp. 43–44.

32 Barrowman, *Victoria University of Wellington*, p. 54; Beaglehole, *A Life*, pp. 202–8.

33 'Communism and Hysterics' was reprinted in F. A. de la Mare, *Academic Freedom in New Zealand, 1932–34: A Statement of the Facts* (Auckland: Unicorn Press, 1935), pp. 15–17.

34 Graeme Hunt, *Spies and Revolutionaries: A History of New Zealand Subversion*

(Auckland: Reed, 2007), p. 131. See also Vincent O'Sullivan, *Long Journey to the Border: A Life of John Mulgan* (Auckland: Penguin, 2003), pp. 50–52.

35 *Otago Daily Times*, 16 April 1932, p. 3.

36 This was especially so within the Douglas Social Credit movement. See Marinus Franciscus La Rooij, 'Political Antisemitism in New Zealand during the Great Depression: A Case Study in the Myth of the Jewish World Conspiracy' (MA thesis, Victoria University of Wellington, 1998). It has, however, been argued that 'anti-Semitism was not a predominant feature of monetary reform groups' in general, and was 'unlikely to provide the basis of a right-wing movement' in New Zealand: Michael C. Pugh, 'The New Zealand Legion and Conservative Protest in the Great Depression' (MA thesis, University of Auckland, 1969), p. 146.

37 Marinus F. La Rooij, 'Arthur Nelson Field: Kiwi Theoretician of the Australian Radical Right?', *Labour History*, vol. 89, no. 1 (November 2005), p. 37.

38 Of his discovery of *The Protocols*, Field noted: '[T]his made everything I had come across fit together in the most amazing way, and fairly staggered me.' He would write a foreword to a 1934 edition of the tract. La Rooij, 'Arthur Nelson Field', pp. 41, 46.

39 Marinus F. La Rooij, 'From Colonial Conservative to International Antisemite: The Life and Work of Arthur Nelson Field', *Journal of Contemporary History*, vol. 37, no. 2 (2002), pp. 229–30; La Rooij, 'Arthur Nelson Field', p. 37.

40 Noonan, 'The Riots of 1932', pp. 159–60; Matthew Cunningham, *Mobilising the Masses: Populist Conservative Movements in Australia and New Zealand during the Great Depression* (Canberra: ANU Press, 2022).

41 Matthew Cunningham, 'Conservative Protest or Conservative Radicalism? The New Zealand Legion in a Comparative Context, 1930–1935', *Journal of New Zealand Studies*,

vol. 10 (2011), pp. 139–58. See also M. C. Pugh, 'The New Zealand Legion, 1932–1935', *New Zealand Journal of History*, vol. 5, no. 1 (April 1971), pp. 49–69.

42   Paul Goldstone, 'Begg, Robert Campbell', *The Dictionary of New Zealand Biography, Volume Four* (Auckland: Auckland University Press, 1998), pp. 44–45.

43   Dunstall, *A Policeman's Paradise?*, p. 449; McKinnon, *The Broken Decade*, p. 235.

44   Patrick Day, *The Radio Years: A History of Broadcasting in New Zealand, Volume One* (Auckland: Auckland University Press in association with the Broadcasting History Trust, 1994), pp. 100, 172–80, 191, 196–201.

45   Ibid., pp. 204–8; NZPD, vol. 245, 10 June 1936, pp. 807–9; William Renwick, *Scrim: The Man with a Mike* (Wellington: Victoria University Press, 2011), pp. 97–99, 256; C. G. Scrimgeour, John A. Lee and Tony Simpson, *The Scrim Lee Papers: C. G. Scrimgeour and John A. Lee Remember the Crisis Years 1930–1940* (Wellington: A. H. & A. W. Reed, 1976), pp. 45–52.

46   Brown, *The Rise of New Zealand Labour*, p. 184.

47   Ibid., p. 221.

48   Hunt, *Spies and Revolutionaries*, p. 134.

49   Rachel Barrowman, *A Popular Vision: The Arts and the Left in New Zealand, 1930–1950* (Wellington: Victoria University Press, 1991), p. 44.

50   Charles Belton, *Outside the Law in New Zealand* (Gisborne: Gisborne Publishing Company, 1939), p. 237.

51   Erik Olssen, 'Lee, John Alfred Alexander', *The Dictionary of New Zealand Biography, Volume Four*, pp. 284–86. For a fuller account, see Erik Olssen, *John A. Lee* (Dunedin: University of Otago Press, 1977).

52   Conrad Bollinger, *Against the Wind: The Story of the New Zealand Seamen's Union* (Wellington: New Zealand Seamen's Union, 1968), p. 200.

53   Scrimgeour et al., *The Scrim–Lee Papers*, pp. 45–52.

54   John Crawford and James Watson, '"The Most Appeasing Line": New Zealand and Nazi Germany, 1935–40', *Journal of Imperial and Commonwealth History*, vol. 38, no. 1 (2010), pp. 75–97.

55   Susan Mary Skudder, '"Bringing It Home": New Zealand Responses to the Spanish Civil War, 1936–1939' (PhD thesis, University of Waikato, 1986), pp. 48–49. For commentary on how police actions caused contestation in Labour circles, see ANZ, R24716791, 'Miscellaneous Organisations: Unemployed Workers' Movement', report of Detective F. J. Brady, 25 May 1937.

56   Skudder, '"Bringing It Home"', pp. 48–49.

57   Paul Elenio, *'Alla Fine Del Mondo': To the Ends of the Earth* (Wellington: Petone Settlers Museum and the Club Garibaldi, 1995), pp. 59–60.

58   M. P. Lissington, *New Zealand and Japan, 1900–1941* (Wellington: Government Printer, 1972), pp. 115–21.

59   The *Northland Age*, 5 November 1954, has a reference by a wartime security official to I. G. Farben activities in New Zealand.

60   James N. Bade, *Von Luckner, a Reassessment: Count Felix von Luckner in New Zealand and the South Pacific, 1917–1919 and 1938* (Frankfurt am Main: Peter Lang, 2004), p. 168.

61   Graeme Dunstall papers, 'Numbers of Detectives 1918–1941'.

62   Brad Patterson, personal communication, 19 September 2018, referring to his discussion with Richard Patterson, *c*.1974.

63   Graeme Dunstall, 'Wohlmann, Ward George', *The Dictionary of New Zealand Biography, Volume Four*, p. 570.

64   See, for example, ANZ, R24716782, 'Miscellaneous Organisations: Unemployed Workers' Movement', Edwards to Sandford, n.d. [1931]. Graeme Dunstall found considerable evidence of local police

informally intercepting mail when he looked at many Police files in the 1930s while researching *A Policeman's Paradise?*. Interview, Richard Hill with Dunstall, 22 April 2016.

65 Graeme Dunstall, 'Governments, the Police and the Left, 1912–1951', in Pat Moloney and Kerry Taylor (eds), *On the Left: Essays on Socialism in New Zealand* (Dunedin: University of Otago Press, 2002), p. 95.

66 Dunstall, *A Policeman's Paradise?*, p. 267. See also Dunstall, 'Governments, the Police and the Left, 1912–1951', p. 95.

67 Dunstall, *A Policeman's Paradise?*, p. 263.

68 ANZ, R3885678, 'Aid to the Civil Power – 2 parts, March 1919–March 1922; March 1931–May 1935', Preparations for Industrial Trouble – Strikes, 24 March 1931.

69 Graeme Dunstall, 'Cummings, Denis Joseph', *The Dictionary of New Zealand Biography, Volume Four*, pp. 120–22.

70 NZS, 1932, No. 3, 'Public Safety Conservation Act', p. 18.

71 McKinnon, *The Broken Decade*, pp. 146–48.

72 NZS, 1908, No. 32, 'Crimes Act', p. 588.

73 Dunstall, *A Policeman's Paradise?*, p. 100.

74 Dunstall, 'Wohlmann, Ward George', p. 570; Len Richardson, 'Semple, Robert', *The Dictionary of New Zealand Biography, Volume Three* (Auckland: Auckland University Press, 1996), p. 467; Dunstall, 'Governments, the Police and the Left, 1912–1951', pp. 95, 229.

75 Dunstall, 'Governments, the Police and the Left', p. 96; Ormond Wilson, *An Outsider Looks Back: Reflections on Experience* (Wellington: Port Nicholson Press, 1982), p. 144; Michael Bassett with Michael King, *Tomorrow Comes the Song: A Life of Peter Fraser* (Auckland: Penguin, 2000), pp. 153–54; Leslie Hobbs, *The Thirty-year Wonders* (Christchurch: Whitcombe & Tombs, 1967), pp. 48–49.

76 ANZ, R24716797, 'Friends of the Soviet Union', examples attached to letter dated 25 October 1932.

77 ANZ, R24118479, 'Communist Party of New Zealand: Wellington Branch: Sympathisers & Contacts', memorandum for the Superintendent of Police Christchurch, 19 May 1932.

78 ANZ, R24716782, 'Miscellaneous Organisations: Unemployed Workers' Movement', report of Sub Inspector Charles William Lopdell, n.d. [September/October 1931].

79 ANZ, R24716783, 'Miscellaneous Organisations: Unemployed Workers' Movement', memorandum for the Superintendent of Police Auckland, 11 March 1932.

80 Dunstall, 'Cummings, Denis Joseph'. For a harsher assessment of Cummings' role, see Dave Welch, *The Lucifer: A Story of Industrial Conflict in New Zealand's 1930s* (Palmerston North: Dunmore Press in association with the Trade Union History Project, 1988), p. 104.

81 David McGill, *No Right to Strike: The History of the New Zealand Police Service Organisations* (Wellington: Silver Owl Press, 1992), pp. 20, 24, 29, 43, 46.

82 Barrowman, *A Popular Vision*, p. 44.

83 Dunstall, 'Cummings, Denis Joseph', pp. 120–22.

84 RHPHC, 47/14, General Manager, Department of Industries and Commerce, Tourist and Publicity to Minister in Charge of Tourist and Publicity, 14 July 1932 and other correspondence attached to 47/14.

85 W. David McIntyre, *New Zealand Prepares for War: Defence Policy, 1919–39* (Christchurch: Canterbury University Press, 1988).

86 Colin Hanson, 'Draft Chapters for History of New Zealand Sigint', unpublished manuscript, appendix one, pp. 3–5; McIntyre, *New Zealand Prepares for War*, pp. 178–79; ANZ, Civilian War Narrative CN69, 'Police Department', pp. 125–28.

87 SRCNZSSC, 'ONS W/T Committee', Memorandum on W/T Interception, [1937].

88 David Filer, 'Civil–Military Cooperation in Signals Intelligence in New Zealand, 1904 to 1939', *Security and Surveillance History Series*, 2017/4, pp. 3–4.

89 Desmond Ball, Cliff Lord and Meredith Thatcher, *Invaluable Service: The Secret History of New Zealand's Signals Intelligence during Two World Wars* (Waimauku: Resource Books, 2011), p. 14; John Tonkin-Covell, 'The Collectors: Naval, Army and Air Intelligence in the New Zealand Armed Forces during the Second World War' (PhD thesis, University of Waikato, 2000), pp. 135–37.

90 'Government Communications Security Bureau: An Overview', in Department of Prime Minister and Cabinet, *Securing our Nation's Safety: How New Zealand Manages Its Security and Intelligence Agencies* (Wellington: Domestic and External Security Secretariat, Department of the Prime Minister and Cabinet, 2000).

91 Evan Smith, 'Policing Communism across the "White Man's World": Anti-Communist Co-operation between Australia, South Africa and Britain in the Early Cold War', *Britain and the World*, vol. 10, no. 2 (2017), p. 181.

92 Hanson, 'Draft Chapters', unpublished manuscript, appendix one, pp. 4–5. For a discussion of the extension of the concept of 'joint' decision-making to intelligence in the British world from the mid-1930s, see Matthew Nicoll, 'The Concept of "Joint" Intelligence: Its Origins and Enactment, 1900–1942: From London, toward Wellington' (MA thesis, Victoria University of Wellington, 2019), pp. 61–64.

93 ANZ, R3885792, 'Intelligence – Minutes of meetings of combined intelligence committee', minute of the second meeting of the Combined Intelligence Committee, 28 April 1938.

94 ANZ, R3885792, 'Intelligence – Minutes of meetings of combined intelligence committee', minute of the fifteenth meeting of the Combined Intelligence Committee, 19 September 1938.

95 ANZ, R24716787, 'Miscellaneous Organisations: Unemployed Workers' Movement', letter dated 28 November [1933].

96 ANZ, R24716781, 'Miscellaneous Organisations: Unemployed Workers' Movement', statement attached to report of Constable G. C. Steven, 24 August 1931.

97 ANZ, R24716783, 'Miscellaneous Organisations: Unemployed Workers' Movement', statement of E. Hill, 6 April 1932.

98 ANZ, R24716787, 'Miscellaneous Organisations: Unemployed Workers' Movement', letter dated 28 November [1933].

99 ANZ, R24716783, 'Miscellaneous Organisations: Unemployed Workers' Movement', memo for the Superintendent of Police Wellington, 4 February 1932.

100 ANZ, R24001234, 'Old Police Records – Recording Sheets', declassification note, 18 June 2013.

101 ANZ, R24716784, 'Miscellaneous Organisations: Unemployed Workers' Movement', speeches delivered at May Day Demonstration, 1 May 1932.

102 ANZ, R24716785, 'Miscellaneous Organisations: Unemployed Workers' Movement', Inspector of Police to Detective Studholme re Unemployed Workers addressed by Rev. Clyde Carr, M.P., 14 October 1932. For the speech see *Timaru Herald*, 3 October 1932, p. 6.

103 J. E. Cookson, 'Pacifism and Conscientious Objection in New Zealand', in Peter Brock and Thomas P. Socknat (eds), *Challenge to Mars: Essays on Pacifism from 1918 to 1945* (Toronto: University of Toronto Press, 1999), pp. 292–311.

104 For surveillance, see ANZ, R25088001, 'Peace Organisations: Miscellaneous Peace/Disarmament Groups: Anti War Movement'.

105 Birchfield, *She Dared to Speak*, pp. 105–6.

106 ANZ, R25087993, 'Miscellaneous Organisations: Howard League for Penal Reform & Committees for the Abolition of the Death Penalty', declassification note, 10 October 2015.

107 ANZ, R24716776, 'Miscellaneous Organisations: Rationalist Association of NZ', declassification note, 1 October 2014.

108 RHPHC, Le 22/1/121, Commissioner of Police to Director of Employment, 22 March 1951.

109 ANZ, R25087988, 'Miscellaneous Organisations: NZ Council for Civil Liberties'.

110 ANZ, R24881824, 'Miscellaneous Organisations: Esperanto Association', declassification note, 31 October 2014.

111 ANZ, R24881824, 'Miscellaneous Organisations: Esperanto Association', memorandum for the Superintendent of Police Wellington, 22 December 1931.

112 Alwyn Owen, 'The Girl in Red', *New Zealand Memories*, no. 47 (April/May 2004), pp. 4–8.

113 ANZ, R24001230, 'Old Police Records – Recording Sheets', S.1931/142.

114 ANZ, R24716768, 'Communist Party NZ, Wellington District Office', Demitro Remnizov – Soviet Agent, 4 December 1932. Such investigations went extensively into personal as well as subject files, to indicate networks: see, for example, Williams/ Birchfield family papers, f. 23, Albert and Constance Birchfield personal files.

115 The resulting report noted, 'He is not a communist and does not associate with them.' ANZ, R24716774, 'Organisations: Mau Movement: Samoa', memorandum for Superintendent of Police Auckland, 12 August 1931.

116 Michael J. Field, *Mau: Samoa's Struggle against New Zealand Oppression* (Wellington: A. H. & A. W. Reed, 1984), especially pp. 147ff.

117 RHPHC, EA(PM), 84/10/1, Crown Solicitor to Permanent Head, Prime Minister's Department, 15 January 1946.

118 Peter Franks and Jim McAloon, *The New Zealand Labour Party, 1916–2016* (Wellington: Victoria University Press, 2016), p. 88; Nicholas Hoare, 'Harry Holland's "Samoan Complex"', *Journal of Pacific History*, vol. 49, no. 2 (2014), pp. 151–69.

119 RHPHC, 'Special Letter to New Zealand Comrades from the Communist International', in 'Extract from "New Zealand Labour Monthly", March 1934', cyclostyled pamphlet, p. 10.

120 Michael King, *Te Puea: A Biography* (Auckland: Hodder & Stoughton, 1977), pp. 206–7.

121 ANZ, R24716778, 'Miscellaneous Organisations: Fascist, Anti-Semitic, Extreme Right-Wing'.

122 ANZ, R12677396, 'Civilian narratives – Police Department', pp. 42–50; Dunstall, *A Policeman's Paradise?*, p. 259. See also 3rd NZSIS Tranche.

123 For examples, see ANZ, R24716774, 'Organisations: Mau Movement: Samoa'.

124 This episode continues to remain obscure; for summaries, see Tina White, 'Mystery Surrounds Assault and Movements of Victor Penny', *Stuff*, 23 March 2019 (www.stuff. co.nz/manawatu-standard/news/111449859/ mystery-surrounds-assault-and-movements-of-inventor-victor-penny), and Gerard Hindmarsh, 'Death Ray or Bedtime Story – The Curious Case of Victor Penny', *Stuff*, 10 August 2019 (www.stuff.co.nz/ national/114876175/death-ray-or-bedtime-story--the-curious-case-of-victor-penny). The mysterious episode has inspired a fictionalised account: David McGill, *The Death Ray Debacle* (Paekakariki: Silver Owl Press, 2015). For further information, see ANZ, R22497363, 'Patents: Invention – Radio Frequencies – V O M Penny'.

125 ANZ, R24881824, 'Miscellaneous Organisations: Esperanto Association', declassification note, 31 October 2014.

126 ANZ, R24716781, 'Miscellaneous Organisations: Unemployed Workers'

Movement', report of Detective N. W. Laugesen, 8 October 1931.

127 ANZ, R24716780, 'Miscellaneous Organisations: Unemployed Workers' Movement', report of Detective R. H. Waterson, 2 March 1931.

128 ANZ, R24716780, 'Miscellaneous Organisations: Unemployed Workers' Movement', report of Detective N. W. Laugesen, 2 June 1931.

129 Noonan, 'The Riots of 1932', p. 175.

130 ANZ, R24881820, 'Communist Party NZ, Police Raids On', report of Senior Sergeant H. Scott, 3 March 1931. See also ANZ, R24881821, 'Communist Party NZ, Police Raids On'.

131 ANZ, R24716780, 'Miscellaneous Organisations: Unemployed Workers' Movement', memorandum missing but evident from responses.

132 ANZ, R24716780, 'Miscellaneous Organisations: Unemployed Workers' Movement', report of Constable W. Truer, 7 April 1931.

133 ANZ, R24716782, 'Miscellaneous Organisations: Unemployed Workers' Movement', Memorandum for the Superintendent of Police Auckland, 25 January 193[2].

134 ANZ, R24716780, 'Miscellaneous Organisations: Unemployed Workers' Movement', report of N. W. Laugesen, 5 April 1931.

135 ANZ, R24716782, 'Miscellaneous Organisations: Unemployed Workers' Movement', Christchurch informant report, 14 October 1931.

136 Confidential interview, Richard Hill with confidential informant, 8 March 2022 and 16 March 2022.

137 Williams/Birchfield family papers, Albert and Constance Birchfield personal files, anonymous report, n.d. [1932], f. 14; report of 2 August 1932, f. 1.

138 Locke family papers, docs. 6–7, Elsie Locke personal file.

139 Red International of Labour Unions/ Profintern.

140 ANZ, R24716783, 'Miscellaneous Organisations: Unemployed Workers' Movement', report of [name redacted], 24 February 1932.

141 ANZ, R24716783, 'Miscellaneous Organisations: Unemployed Workers' Movement', report of [name redacted], 27 February 1932.

142 Such material made its way onto personal files. See, for example, files on Birchfield family members, which have, inter alia, references to such matters as fellow activists drinking excessively, being 'on the verge of striking each other', not passing on money from newspaper sales, quarrelling, or 'not appear[ing] to be very conversant with his subject'. Williams/Birchfield family papers, ff. 1, 3–5, 8, 11, Albert and Constance Birchfield personal files.

143 ANZ, R24716780, 'Miscellaneous Organisations: Unemployed Workers' Movement', memorandum dated 1 April 1931 attached to report of Detective P. J. Nalder, 31 March 1931.

144 ANZ, R24716780, 'Miscellaneous Organisations: Unemployed Workers' Movement', report of Detective P. J. Nalder, 31 March 1931.

145 ANZ, R24716780, 'Miscellaneous Organisations: Unemployed Workers' Movement', report of Detective N. W. Laugesen, 2 June 1931.

146 Taylor, 'The Communist Party of New Zealand and the Third Period', p. 279.

147 Williams/Birchfield family papers, memo by Baylis, 29 November 1932, f. 22, Albert and Constance Birchfield personal files.

148 Williams/Birchfield family papers, ff. 5, 7, 28, Albert and Constance Birchfield personal files.

149 This assessment is made on the basis of reading released personal files from the period; the example cited is from the Williams/Birchfield family papers, Albert and Constance Birchfield personal files.

150 ANZ, R24716781, 'Miscellaneous Organisations: Unemployed Workers' Movement', report of Detective Sergeant H. Nuttall, 1 October 1931.

151 Peter Gill, *Policing Politics: Security Intelligence and the Liberal Democratic State* (London: Frank Cass & Co., 1994), p. 162.

152 ANZ, R24716780, 'Miscellaneous Organisations: Unemployed Workers' Movement', report of Detective N. W. Laugesen, 5 April 1931.

153 ANZ, R24716783, 'Miscellaneous Organisations: Unemployed Workers' Movement', report of Detective Sergeant Nuttall, 5 November 1931. Further reports from the operation are included in ANZ, R24716782, 'Miscellaneous Organisations: Unemployed Workers' Movement'.

154 Scott, *Rebel in a Wrong Cause*, pp. 70–71.

155 Edwards, *Break Down These Bars*, pp. 47–48, 69; Noonan, 'The Riots of 1932', pp. 121–22.

156 *New Zealand Herald*, 7 June 1932, p. 12; *Patea and Waverley Press*, 1 August 1932; *New Zealand Police Gazette*, 14 September 1932, p. 586.

157 Taylor, '"The Old Bolshevik"', p. 111. For Alex Galbraith's writings on this trip, see *The Making of a New Zealand Revolutionary: Reminiscences of Alex Galbraith* (Auckland: Workers' Party, 1994), pp. 43–73.

158 ANZ, R24716780, 'Miscellaneous Organisations: Unemployed Workers' Movement', report of P. J. Nalder, 13 February 1931.

159 Bade, *Von Luckner*, pp. 151–55. In Australia the Brisbane office of the Commonwealth Investigation Branch maintained a watch on the von Luckner party during its visit, keeping records of its contacts.

In September 1939, with the declaration of war, many of these contacts were rounded up and interned: see Valdemar Robert Wake, *No Ribbons or Medals: The Story of 'Hereward', an Australian Counter Espionage Officer* (Mitcham: Jacobyte Books, 2004), pp. 90–93.

160 Alexandra Neems, '"Total Intelligence": New Zealand Signals Intelligence in Historical Context since 1945' (BA Hons thesis, University of Otago, 2014), pp. 30–31. For general reports, see ANZ, R18871181, 'Security – Intelligence – Japanese espionage'.

161 Jozef Straczek, 'The Empire is Listening: Naval Signals Intelligence in the Far East to 1942', *Journal of the Australian War Memorial*, issue 35 (2001); Neems, '"Total Intelligence"', p. 31.

162 SRCNZSSC, 'Clarkson T. R.', letter from T. R. Clarkson to GCSB Director C. M. Hanson, 9 April 1987.

163 SRCNZSSC, 'Awarua Radio W/T Intercept', Memorandum of 2 May 1939; for sigint cooperation in the later 1930s, see Filer, 'Civil–Military Cooperation in Signals Intelligence in New Zealand', pp. 3–4.

164 ANZ, R24881820, 'Communist Party NZ, Police Raids On', Senior Sergeant H. Scott to Police Headquarters, 3 March 1931.

165 For an example, see ANZ, R24716780, 'Miscellaneous Organisations: Unemployed Workers' Movement', report of Detective N. W. Laugesen, 23 April 1931.

166 ANZ, R24881821, 'Communist Party NZ, Police Raids On', memorandum for all districts, 24 June 1931.

167 ANZ, R24716768, 'Communist Party NZ, Wellington District Office'.

168 Dunstall, *A Policeman's Paradise?*, p. 266.

169 Grace Millar, 'Identifying Communists: Continuity in Political Policing, 1931–1951', *Security and Surveillance History Series*, 2017/3, pp. 1–12.

170   ANZ, R24716781, 'Miscellaneous Organisations: Unemployed Workers' Movement', memorandum for the Inspector of Police Napier, 4 August 1931.

171   ANZ, R24716782, 'Miscellaneous Organisations: Unemployed Workers' Movement', Commissioner of Police to Minister of Justice, 26 January 1932.

172   ANZ, R24716782, 'Miscellaneous Organisations: Unemployed Workers' Movement', report of Detective N. W. Laugesen, 18 January 1932.

173   ANZ, R24716782, 'Miscellaneous Organisations: Unemployed Workers' Movement', report of [name redacted], 4 November 1931.

174   Williams/Birchfield family papers, f. 11, Albert and Constance Birchfield personal files.

175   TNA, KV2/3929, 'CROSS-REFERENCE: BILL SUTCH', 29 October 1937.

176   ANZ, R24716791, 'Miscellaneous Organisations: Unemployed Workers' Movement', report of Detective E. A. Stevenson, 6 February 1938.

177   ANZ, R24716781, 'Miscellaneous Organisations: Unemployed Workers' Movement', report of Detective N. W. Laugesen, 27 September 1931.

178   ANZ, R24716768, 'Communist Party NZ, Wellington District Office', report of Detective N. W. Baylis, 4 April 1932.

179   ANZ, R24716780, 'Miscellaneous Organisations: Unemployed Workers' Movement', report of Sergeant Duncan Wilson, 22 January 1931.

180   ANZ, R24716780, 'Miscellaneous Organisations: Unemployed Workers' Movement', Memorandum for the Superintendent of Police Auckland, 20 March 1931.

181   ANZ, R24716782, 'Miscellaneous Organisations: Unemployed Workers' Movement', Memorandum for the Commissioner of Police Wellington, 21 March 1932.

182   ANZ, R24001222, 'Old Police Records – Recording Sheets', 1931/0/11.

183   Taylor, 'The Communist Party of New Zealand and the Third Period', p. 279.

184   ANZ, R24716781, 'Miscellaneous Organisations: Unemployed Workers' Movement', report of Sub-Inspector Charles Lopdell, 15 October 1931.

185   ANZ, R24716782, 'Miscellaneous Organisations: Unemployed Workers' Movement', report of Detective Laugesen, 5 November 1931.

186   ANZ, R24716780, 'Miscellaneous Organisations: Unemployed Workers' Movement', report of Sergeant W. Pender, 1 April 1931.

187   See, for example, New Zealand Herald, 13 October 1931, p. 6; New Zealand Herald, 22 October 1931, p. 12.

188   ANZ, R24716782, 'Miscellaneous Organisations: Unemployed Workers' Movement', report on alleged lawlessness at Raetihi, 23 October 1931.

189   ANZ, R24716783, 'Miscellaneous Organisations: Unemployed Workers' Movement', report of Senior Sergeant Butler, 15 February 1932.

190   Ibid.

191   NZS, 1932, No. 11, 'Finance Act', p. 15.

192   Fraser, Ungrateful People, pp. 52, 56–57; Tom Bramble (ed.), Never a White Flag: The Memoirs of Jock Barnes (Wellington: Victoria University Press, 1998), pp. 47–48.

193   Declassified NZSIS report, 'W. B. Sutch Target Assessment', 30 May 1974 (available at www.nzsis.govt.nz/assets/media/1974-05-30-Sutch-TA.pdf); ANZ, R24001243, 'Old Police Records – Recording Sheets', S.41/; Keith Sinclair, Walter Nash (Auckland: Auckland University Press, 1976), p. 148. A revisionist study raises some doubt as to whether Sutch

was the source of the leak and notes that the leaked material, which 'closely resembled the secret written record of [Prime Minister Michael] Savage's speech', was politically embarrassing to Britain rather than presenting any security danger: see Simon Emsley, 'Sutch and the State: A Progressive Marginalisation' (PhD thesis, University of New South Wales, 1998), pp. 205–7.

194 ANZ, R24716781, 'Miscellaneous Organisations: Unemployed Workers' Movement', report of Detective N. W. Laugesen, 23 April 1931.

195 Dunstall, *A Policeman's Paradise?*, pp. 268–69.

196 ANZ, R24716783, 'Miscellaneous Organisations: Unemployed Workers' Movement', report dated 29 January 1932.

197 Taylor, 'The Communist Party of New Zealand and the Third Period', p. 279.

198 ANZ, R24716782, 'Miscellaneous Organisations: Unemployed Workers' Movement', report of Detective N. W. Laugesen, 24 October 1931.

199 ANZ, R24716782, 'Miscellaneous Organisations: Unemployed Workers' Movement', memorandum from Inspector to Superintendent, 5 November 1931.

200 ANZ, R24716783, 'Miscellaneous Organisations: Unemployed Workers' Movement', report of Huntly Delegate to the UWA Conference Police Agent, 7 February 1932.

201 ANZ, R24716783, 'Miscellaneous Organisations: Unemployed Workers' Movement', report of militant workers in Dunedin, 31 December 1931.

202 ANZ, R24716782, 'Miscellaneous Organisations: Unemployed Workers' Movement', reports of Acting Detective James Gibson, and Constable J. Marsh, 5 November 1931.

203 Elsie Locke, 'Looking for Answers', *Landfall* 48 (December 1958), pp. 335–55; Locke, *Student at the Gates*, pp. 158–68.

204 Vincent O'Sullivan (ed.), *Intersecting Lines: The Memoirs of Ian Milner* (Wellington: Victoria University Press, 1993), pp. 87–88.

205 Shirley Smith, cited in Aaron Robert Jackson, 'Socialism Tells Its Own Story: Ian Milner and the Dream of a Redeemed Socialism in the Prague Spring', *New Zealand Journal of History*, vol. 55, no. 2 (2021), pp. 11–12.

206 Sillitoe to W. Hayter, 21 September 1948, FO1093/516, 'Australian Security', in *Secret Files from World Wars to Cold War: Intelligence, Strategy and Diplomacy*, online database (available at www.secretintelligencefiles.com/).

207 ATL, MS-Papers-8752-204, 'Proposed book on the Security Intelligence Service – Milner and Costello', report of Detective R. H. Waterson, 15 December 1934; Denis Lenihan, '"Different Tones of Voice": Versions of Paddy Costello', *Security and Surveillance History Series*, 2020/1, pp. 1–21.

208 Nigel West, *Mask: MI5's Penetration of the Communist Party of Great Britain* (London: Routledge, 2005), pp. 69, 73, 85, 87, 150, 153, 157, 163, 167, 179.

209 Ibid., pp. 100, 101, 102, 105, 182.

210 Ibid., pp. 46, 48, 49, 73, 106, 142–43.

211 Warwick Johnston, 'The New Zealand-born Comintern Agent', unpublished manuscript, 20 March 2022; TNA, KV2/3291, W. G. Wohlmann to Colonel Sir Vernon G. W. Kell, 31 May 1934, p. 189. See also TNA, KV2/3291, pp. 34, 81, 117, 159; *Otago Daily Times*, 9 July 1934, p. 7; Caroline Thomas, 'The Sorcerers' Apprentice: A Life of Reo Franklin Fortune, Anthropologist' (PhD thesis, University of Waikato, 2011), p. 191; Owen Matthews, *An Impeccable Spy: Richard Sorge, Stalin's Master Agent* (London: Bloomsbury Publishing, 2019), pp. 106ff., especially p. 121; John Haffenden, *William Empson: Among the Mandarins* (Oxford: Oxford University Press, 2005), pp. 349–53; West, *Mask*, pp. 49, 142–43, 159, 187.

212 Franks and McAloon, *The New Zealand Labour Party*, p. 88.

213 Barry Gustafson, *From the Cradle to the Grave: A Biography of Michael Joseph Savage* (Auckland: Reed Methuen, 1986).

214 ANZ, R24716782, 'Miscellaneous Organisations: Unemployed Workers' Movement', report of Constable C. Chesnutt, 22 November 1928.

Chapter Six: Coercion and Dissent, 1939–1945

1 John Crawford and James Watson, '"The Most Appeasing Line": New Zealand and Nazi Germany, 1935–40', *Journal of Imperial and Commonwealth History*, vol. 32, no. 1 (2010), pp. 75–97.

2 *Evening Post*, 6 September 1939, p. 8.

3 Graeme Dunstall, *A Policeman's Paradise?: Policing a Stable Society, 1918–1945* (Palmerston North: Dunmore Press, 1999), p. 310. See also ANZ, R12677280, 'Civilian narratives – Postal and Telegraphic Censorship'.

4 For accounts, see Hugh Price, *The Plot to Subvert Wartime New Zealand: The True Story of Syd Ross and His Impudent Hoax that Convulsed New Zealand and put a Shine into the Darkest Days of WWII, and that the Commissioner of Police Declared "Beyond Comprehension" A Hoax, moreover, that was Extended to Challenge the Rule of Law in the Dominion* (Wellington: Victoria University Press, 2006); Aaron Fox, '"A Formidable Responsibility": The Rise and Fall of the New Zealand Security Intelligence Bureau 1940–1945', *Security and Surveillance History Series*, 2018/1, pp. 1–32; F. L. W. Wood, *The New Zealand People at War: Political and External Affairs* (Wellington: War History Branch, Department of Internal Affairs, 1958), pp. 161–62; John Tonkin-Covell, 'The Collectors: Naval, Army and Air Intelligence in the New Zealand Armed Forces during the Second World War' (PhD thesis, University of Waikato, 2000), pp. 316–17; Dunstall, *A Policeman's Paradise?*, pp. 307–8.

5 Ian McGibbon, *Blue-Water Rationale: The Naval Defence of New Zealand, 1914–1942* (Wellington: P. D. Hasselberg, Government Printer, 1981), pp. 346–47.

6 RHPHC, N 17/1/4, 'Notes of Commander [M. H.] Burrell', 6 December 1940, and other correspondence.

7 O. A. Gillespie, *The Pacific* (Wellington: War History Branch, Department of Internal Affairs, 1952), pp. 204–7.

8 RHPHC, J-P, P.D. 1940/13/12, Prime Minister to Secretary, Mount Albert Women's Branch, New Zealand Labour Party, 4 September 1940.

9 NZPD, vol. 261, 9 July 1941, p. 502.

10 Nancy M. Taylor, *The Home Front, Volume II* (Wellington: Historical Publications Branch, 1986), pp. 893–94; *Auckland Star*, 14 June 1940, p. 7. See also Andrew Cutler, 'Tomorrow Magazine and New Zealand Politics 1934–1940', *New Zealand Journal of History*, vol. 24, no. 1 (1990), pp. 22–44.

11 Taylor, *The Home Front, Volume II*, p. 930.

12 Ibid., pp. 998–99.

13 Ibid., pp. 1002–9.

14 Graeme Hunt, *Spies and Revolutionaries: A History of New Zealand Subversion* (Auckland: Reed, 2007), pp. 139–40; Graeme Dunstall, 'Governments, the Police and the Left, 1912–1951', in Pat Moloney and Kerry Taylor (eds), *On the Left: Essays on Socialism in New Zealand* (Dunedin: University of Otago Press, 2002), p. 97.

15 *New Zealand Herald*, 5 September 1940, p. 8.

16 RHPHC, E1 29/55/2, Harold Day to Secretary, Glassworkers' Union, 1 April 1941, and other correspondence attached to E1 29/55/2.

17 Richard G. H. Kay, 'Take *That*, You Dirty Commie!: The Rise of a Cold War Consciousness in New Zealand, 1944–1949' (BA Hons thesis, University of Otago, 1994), pp. 27–37.

18 Kerry Allan Taylor, 'Worker's Vanguard or People's Voice?: The Communist Party of

New Zealand from Origins to 1946' (PhD thesis, Victoria University of Wellington, 1994), pp. 163, 184; Carl William Blackmun, 'Not the Socialism We Dreamed Of: Becoming Ex-Communists in the United States and New Zealand, 1956–58' (MA thesis, Victoria University of Wellington, 2012), p. 19; Maureen Birchfield Williams, 'Birchfield, Constance Alice', *The Dictionary of New Zealand Biography, Volume Four* (Auckland: Auckland University Press, 1998), pp. 61–32.

19   RHPHC, correspondence in CL118, 'Peoples Voice: Representations for Removal of Ban', including Minister of Justice to H. Barnes, 30 August 1942 and Solicitor-General to Frank A. Haigh, 7 May 1943.

20   Rachel Barrowman, *A Popular Vision: The Arts and the Left in New Zealand, 1930–1950* (Wellington: Victoria University Press, 1991), p. 19.

21   Dunstall, *A Policeman's Paradise?*, pp. 314–15.

22   Wood, *The New Zealand People at War*, p. 160.

23   ANZ, R12677396, 'Civilian narratives – Police Department', pp. 68–86. See also Walter Wynne Mason, *Prisoners of War* (Wellington: Department of Internal Affairs, 1954), pp. 16–18.

24   Michael King, *Tread Softly for You Tread on My Life: New & Collected Writings* (Auckland: Cape Catley Ltd, 2001), p. 69. King presents a far more sympathetic account of Lochore, seeing him as, 'at worst, a voluble and volatile eccentric of conservative inclination' who exhibited a 'characteristic brand of ethnocentrism'.

25   Fred Turnovsky, *Fifty Years in New Zealand* (Wellington: Allen & Unwin, 1990), p. 85.

26   Nancy M. Taylor, *The Home Front, Volume I* (Wellington: Historical Publications Branch, 1986), pp. 244ff., especially pp. 265–66. See also David Littlewood, '"The Debates of the Past": New Zealand's First Labour Government and the Introduction of Conscription in 1940', *War & Society*, vol. 39, no. 4 (October 2020), especially pp. 275, 285–86.

27   For accounts, see Ian Hamilton, *Till Human Voices Wake Us* [1953] (Auckland: Auckland University Press, 1984); David Grant, *Out in the Cold: Pacifists and Conscientious Objectors in New Zealand during World War II* (Auckland: Reed Methuen, 1986); Jonathan Scott, *Harry's Absence: Looking for My Father on the Mountain* (Wellington: Victoria University Press, 1997); John Pratt, *The Prison Diary of A. C. Barrington: Dissent and Conformity in Wartime New Zealand* (Dunedin: Otago University Press, 2016).

28   For official categorisations, see RHPHC, L24/1/34, National Service Department circular I.M.175, 9 June 1945, 'Release of Defaulters from Detention on Parole', p. 5.

29   For extensive coverage of pacifism in the war, based heavily on oral history, see Grant, *Out in the Cold*. See too, J. E. Cookson, 'Pacifism and Conscientious Objection in New Zealand', in Peter Brock and Thomas P. Socknat (eds), *Challenge to Mars: Essays on Pacifism from 1918 to 1945* (Toronto: University of Toronto Press, 1999), pp. 292–311.

30   Pratt, *The Prison Diary of A. C. Barrington*.

31   Grant, *Out in the Cold*, p. 95.

32   RHPHC, CL121, 'Jehovah's Witnesses', various correspondence.

33   Taylor, *The Home Front, Volume I*, p. 247.

34   Dunstall, 'Governments, the Police and the Left', p. 97.

35   Dunstall, 'Cummings, Denis Joseph', *The Dictionary of New Zealand Biography, Volume Four*, pp. 120–22.

36   Taylor, *The Home Front, Volume II*, p. 893.

37   RHPHC, J1940/35/140, Minutes, 'NEW ZEALAND CHRISTIAN PACIFIST SOCIETY: Deputation to the Prime Minister . . . 18th November, 1940', p. 6.

38   Dunstall, *A Policeman's Paradise?*, p. 304; Eunan O'Halpin, 'The Liddell Diaries and British Intelligence History', *Intelligence and National Security*, vol. 20, no. 4 (December 2005), p. 683.

39   Fox, '"A Formidable Responsibility"', p. 3.

40   Dunstall, *A Policeman's Paradise?*, pp. 305, 317; RHPHC, Police Headquarters to Richard Hill, 29 November 1994.

41   One assessment, tracing the emergence of joint military-based intelligence in an Imperial setting, finds that the concept had little success in wartime New Zealand because of historically rooted factors, including inadequate intelligence capacities within the services (with the partial exception of naval intelligence) in the first place: Matthew Nicoll, 'The Concept of "Joint" Intelligence: Its Origins and Enactment, 1900–1942: From London, toward Wellington' (MA thesis, Victoria University of Wellington, 2019), pp. 83–85.

42   Some of the fruits of the ambition to develop a capacity for irregular warfare are evident in F. Spencer Chapman, *The Jungle is Neutral* (London: Chatto & Windus, 1949), pp. 7–9; Bernard J. Callinan, *Independent Company: The 2/2 and 2/4 Australian Independent Companies in Portuguese Timor, 1941–1943* (London: Heinemann, 1953), pp. xx–xxi.

43   ANZ, R22042409, 'Intelligence Centres – Security intelligence organisation New Zealand – August 1940–March 1948', Naval Secretary, Wellington, to Secretary, Organisation for National Security, Wellington, Secret Memo 14 August 1940; Tonkin-Covell, 'The Collectors', pp. 51–78; Fox, '"A Formidable Responsibility"', p. 3.

44   John Fahey, *Traitors and Spies: Espionage and Corruption in High Places in Australia, 1901–50* (Crows Nest, NSW: Allen & Unwin, 2020), pp. 112–13.

45   Fox, '"A Formidable Responsibility"', pp. 2–4; ANZ, R21078487, 'Plans: Security Intelligence Bureau: Policy and Organisation'.

46   ANZ, R18871869, 'New Zealand Forces – Training – Para Military Training (Mawhood Mission)', Fraser, Wellington, to Menzies, Canberra, telegram 26 November 1940. See too, Fahey, *Traitors and Spies*, pp. 113, 118, 120;

Fox, '"A Formidable Responsibility"', p. 3; Dunstall, *A Policeman's Paradise?*, p. 304.

47   ANZ, R21078487, 'Plans: Security Intelligence Bureau: Policy and Organisation', Lieutenant-Colonel J. C. Mawhood, Wellington, to Chiefs of Staff, Wellington, Most Secret memo on Security Intelligence, 26 November 1940.

48   ANZ, R21078487, 'Plans: Security Intelligence Bureau: Policy and Organisation', Organisation for National Security, Chiefs of Staff Committee Paper 60 – Security Intelligence Organisation, 26 November 1940; Foss Shanahan, Secretary, Organisation for National Security, Wellington, C.O.S. 60/ note 27 November 1940; Fahey, *Traitors and Spies*, pp. 119–20.

49   Fox, '"A Formidable Responsibility"', p. 4; Wood, *The New Zealand People at War*, p. 161.

50   ATL, MS-Papers-6703, 'Price, Hugh Charles Llewellyn, 1929–2009', undated pamphlet, 'This Fair Country Now Has Its Himmler and Its S.S. Men'.

51   Fox, '"A Formidable Responsibility"', p. 5.

52   Price, *The Plot to Subvert Wartime New Zealand*, p. 40.

53   Paul Lewis with Jock McLean, *TP: The Life and Times of Sir Terry McLean* (Auckland: HarperCollins, 2010), pp. 75–78.

54   Jack Harris, *Memoirs of a Century* (Wellington: Steele Roberts, 2007), pp. 63–64.

55   Tonkin-Covell, 'The Collectors', p. 296.

56   ATL, MS-Papers-6703, 'Price, Hugh Charles Llewellyn, 1929–2009'; *New Zealand Observer*, 11 October 1944, p. 7.

57   Max Hastings, *The Secret War: Spies, Codes and Guerrillas, 1939–45* (London: William Collins, 2015), pp. 58–59.

58   Desmond Ball, Cliff Lord and Meredith Thatcher, *Invaluable Service: The Secret History of New Zealand's Signals Intelligence during Two World Wars* (Waimauku: Resource Books, 2011), especially p. 298; Jozef Straczek, 'The Empire is Listening: Naval Signals

Intelligence in the Far East to 1942', *Journal of the Australian War Memorial*, issue 35 (2001) (available at www.awm.gov.au/articles/journal/j35/straczek).

59 Dunstall, *A Policeman's Paradise?*, p. 341.

60 Ibid.; Valerie P. Redshaw, *Tact and Tenacity: New Zealand Women in Policing* (Wellington: Grantham House/New Zealand Police, 2006), pp. 53–60.

61 ATL, MS-Papers-6703, 'Price, Hugh Charles Llewellyn, 1929–2009'; *People's Voice*, 5 June 1941, and 'This Fair Country Now Has Its Himmler and Its S.S. Men'.

62 Ibid.

63 Ibid; Colin Hanson and Jim Rolfe, 'Security Intelligence 1915–1945', unpublished manuscript, p. 88.

64 Miriam L. Wharton, 'The Development of Security Intelligence in New Zealand, 1945–1957' (Master of Defence Studies, Massey University, 2012), p. 68.

65 ANZ, R22438739, 'Staff – Security Intelligence Branch – Appointments and Promotions', P. J. Nalder, Deputy Director Security Intelligence, Wellington, to Lieutenant A. S. Blaikie, Army Headquarters, Wellington, Memorandum 18 October 1945, and attached list of Security Intelligence Bureau staff; Hanson and Rolfe, 'Security Intelligence 1915–1945', p. 89.

66 Fox, '"A Formidable Responsibility"', p. 18; ATL, MS-Papers-6703, 'Price, Hugh Charles Llewellyn, 1929–2009': *People's Voice*, 5 June 1941, and 'This Fair Country Now Has Its Himmler and Its S.S. Men'.

67 Hunt, *Spies and Revolutionaries*, p. 144.

68 Fox, '"A Formidable Responsibility"', p. 18.

69 Dunstall, *A Policeman's Paradise?*, p. 307.

70 Price, *The Plot to Subvert Wartime New Zealand*, pp. 75–76.

71 Lewis and McLean, *TP: The Life and Times of Sir Terry McLean*, p. 78; ATL, MS-Papers-11459-058, 'Security Intelligence Bureau – Newspaper cuttings'.

72 Dunstall, *A Policeman's Paradise?*, pp. 305–6; Tonkin-Covell, 'The Collectors', p. 299.

73 Tonkin-Covell, 'The Collectors', p. 298.

74 Ibid., pp. 22–23.

75 Dunstall, *A Policeman's Paradise?*, p. 307.

76 ANZ, R22438739, 'Staff – Security Intelligence Branch – Appointments and Promotions', Colonel L. G. Goss, General Staff, Wellington, to The Hon. Minister of Defence, Secret Memorandum, 14 June 1941.

77 ANZ, R21078487, 'Plans: Security Intelligence Bureau: Policy and Organisation', Secret Memorandum from Kenneth Folkes to Foss Shanahan, 14 January 1942.

78 ANZ, R21078487, 'Plans: Security Intelligence Bureau: Policy and Organisation', Chiefs of Staff Committee, Organisation for National Security, Paper 119 – Security Intelligence Bureau – Increase in Establishment, 24 January 1942.

79 Ibid.

80 ANZ, R22440387, 'Security – Establishment port security patrol', Organisation for National Security memorandum, 26 February 1942.

81 Tonkin-Covell, 'The Collectors', p. 303.

82 Colin Hanson, 'Draft Chapters for History of New Zealand Sigint', unpublished manuscript, appendix one, p. 6. Military intelligence monitored external matters such as the flow of information from Fiji (which New Zealand garrisoned, and where it established an intelligence capacity in January 1941) and elsewhere in the Pacific, as well as from Australia, Singapore and further afield. Stout Street also monitored domestic matters, too: censorship and subversion, disaffected persons and aliens, 'fires and other suspicious activities' among them.

83 ATL, MS-Papers-6703, 'Price, Hugh Charles Llewellyn, 1929–2009'; 'This Fair Country Now Has Its Himmler and Its S.S. Men'; Hanson and Rolfe, 'Security Intelligence 1915–1945', p. 74.

84   Lewis and McLean, *TP: The Life and Times of Sir Terry McLean*, p. 78.

85   Price, *The Plot to Subvert Wartime New Zealand*, pp. 24–25. Another Ross associate, George Horry, assumed the identity of a British spy in 1942 to marry and murder an Auckland divorcee for her money. David Filer, 'The Great Spy Lie', *Listener*, 25 September 1982, pp. 18–19; Redmer Yska, 'Ain't Got No Body: NZ's History-making Murder Case', *New Zealand Listener*, 20 December 2014, pp. 24–28.

86   *Auckland Star*, 30 March 1942, p. 4. See also Robert Loeffel, *The Fifth Column in World War II: Suspected Subversives in the Pacific War and Australia* (London: Palgrave Macmillan, 2015), pp. 114–51.

87   Price, *The Plot to Subvert Wartime New Zealand*, p. 33.

88   Wood, *The New Zealand People at War*, p. 161; Fox, '"A Formidable Responsibility"', p. 15.

89   Fox, '"A Formidable Responsibility"', p. 15; Sherwood Young, 'Ross, Sydney Gordon', *The Dictionary of New Zealand Biography, Volume Five* (Auckland: Auckland University Press, 2000), pp. 452–53.

90   Price, *The Plot to Subvert Wartime New Zealand*, pp. 34–36.

91   Tonkin-Covell, 'The Collectors', pp. 323–24; Dunstall, *A Policeman's Paradise?*, pp. 307–8; D. J. Cummings, Commissioner of Police, Wellington, to Prime Minister Fraser, Wellington, Memorandum 9 August 1942, reproduced in Price, *The Plot to Subvert Wartime New Zealand*, p. 131; ANZ, R21124632, 'Memorandum a Security Intelligence Bureau concerning incapacities – Copy of General Puttick – 21 December 1942', Chiefs of Staff Committee, Organisation for National Security, Wellington, to Prime Minister Fraser, Wellington, draft paper on the Security Intelligence Bureau, 21 December 1942.

92   Price, *The Plot to Subvert Wartime New Zealand*, pp. 67–68.

93   Ibid., p. 76.

94   Tonkin-Covell, 'The Collectors', p. 324; Dunstall, *A Policeman's Paradise?*, p. 308; Rachel Barrowman, *Mason: The Life of R. A. K. Mason* (Wellington: Victoria University Press, 2003), p. 283.

95   Redmer Yska, *Truth: The Rise and Fall of the People's Paper* (Nelson: Craig Potton Publishing, 2010), pp. 99–100.

96   *NZ Truth*, 29 July 1942, p. 11.

97   Taylor, *The Home Front, Volume II*, pp. 884–85; Yska, *Truth*, p. 100.

98   Price, *The Plot to Subvert Wartime New Zealand*, pp. 97–99; Fox, '"A Formidable Responsibility"', p. 17.

99   ANZ, R22438739, 'Staff – Security Intelligence Branch – Appointments and Promotions', Brigadier L. G. Goss, Assistant Chief of the General Staff, Wellington, to the Minister of Defence, Wellington, Secret Memorandum, 10 July 1942.

100 Hanson and Rolfe, 'Security Intelligence 1915–1945', pp. 82–83.

101 Fox, '"A Formidable Responsibility"', p. 18.

102 ANZ, R21078487, 'Plans: Security Intelligence Bureau: Policy and Organisation', H. G. R. Mason, Attorney-General, Wellington, to the War Cabinet, Wellington, Secret Memorandum, 18 September 1942; Dunstall, *A Policeman's Paradise?*, p. 308; Fox, '"A Formidable Responsibility"', p. 17.

103 SRCNZSSC, C.O.S. Paper No. 156, 'Organisation for National Security Chiefs of Staff Committee. Security Intelligence Bureau', 22 December 1942. See too, Tonkin-Covell, 'The Collectors', pp. 332–33.

104 ANZ, R22042409, 'Intelligence Centres – Security intelligence organisation New Zealand – August 1940–March 1948', Lieutenant-Commander H. S. Barker, Intelligence Officer, Naval Intelligence, Secret Navy Office Minute 19 November 1942; Dunstall, *A Policeman's Paradise?*, p. 308.

105 ANZ, R22042409, Lieutenant-Commander F. M. Beasley, Director of Naval Intelligence, Wellington, Secret Navy Office Minute 19 November 1942; RHPHC, N8/1/18, Beasley to Director of Naval Intelligence, Melbourne, 22 March 1943.

106 Price, *The Plot to Subvert Wartime New Zealand*, pp. 113–15.

107 Ibid., p. 115.

108 Lewis and McLean, *TP: The Life and Times of Sir Terry McLean*, p. 79.

109 Fox, '"A Formidable Responsibility"', p. 21.

110 Ibid.

111 *New Zealand Observer*, 13 November 1946, as reprinted in Price, *The Plot to Subvert Wartime New Zealand*, pp. 145–57.

112 Fox, '"A Formidable Responsibility"', p. 24.

113 Dunstall, *A Policeman's Paradise?*, p. 308.

114 Fox, '"A Formidable Responsibility"', p. 20.

115 Hanson and Rolfe, 'Security Intelligence 1915–1945', pp. 69–74; Fox, '"A Formidable Responsibility"', p. 22.

116 Fox, '"A Formidable Responsibility"', p. 22; Dunstall, *A Policeman's Paradise?*, p. 309.

117 Dunstall, *A Policeman's Paradise?*, pp. 304, 307, 309, 471; Lewis and McLean, *TP: The Life and Times of Sir Terry McLean*, p. 80.

118 ANZ, R21078487, 'Plans: Security Intelligence Bureau: Policy and Organisation', H. G. R. Mason, Attorney-General, Wellington, to the War Cabinet, Wellington, Secret Memorandum, 18 September 1942, pp. 2–3.

119 Tonkin-Covell, 'The Collectors', pp. 338–39, 346–47; ANZ, R18869690, 'Visits – Superintendent J. Cummings, Director of Security Intelligence Bureau to UK and US', Secretary of State for Dominion Affairs, London, to High Commissioner for the United Kingdom, Wellington, Secret Telegram 4 August 1943.

120 ANZ, R18869690, 'Visits – Superintendent J. Cummings, Director of Security Intelligence Bureau to UK and US', Prime Minister Fraser, Wellington, to the War Cabinet, Wellington, Authority for Superintendent J. Cummings, approved 21 March 1944; Hanson and Rolfe, 'Security Intelligence 1915–1945', p. 82.

121 Fox, '"A Formidable Responsibility"', p. 22.

122 Dunstall, *A Policeman's Paradise?*, p. 308.

123 Ibid., p. 309.

124 Fox, '"A Formidable Responsibility"', p. 23.

125 His and other police careers can be traced in the *New Zealand Police Gazettes*.

126 Dunstall, *A Policeman's Paradise?*, p. 309; Fox, '"A Formidable Responsibility"', p. 23.

127 ANZ, R22438739, 'Staff – Security Intelligence Branch – Appointments and Promotions', Brigadier A. E. Conway, Adjutant-General, Wellington, Memorandum for All Districts, 30 August 1945; Hanson and Rolfe, 'Security Intelligence 1915–1945', pp. 91–93; Fox, '"A Formidable Responsibility"', p. 23.

128 ANZ, Civilian War Narrative CN69, 'Police Department', p. 128.

129 Peter Cooke, 'Home Guard', in Ian McGibbon (ed.), *The Oxford Companion to New Zealand Military History* (Auckland: Oxford University Press, 2000), p. 521–22.

130 Deborah Montgomerie, 'Women and the Second World War', in McGibbon, *The Oxford Companion to New Zealand Military History*, p. 617; Deborah Cox, 'Women in the Armed Forces', in McGibbon, *The Oxford Companion to New Zealand Military History*, pp. 622–23.

131 David Filer, 'Signals Intelligence in New Zealand during World War II', *Security and Surveillance History Series*, 2019/2, p. 4; Alexandra Neems, '"Total Intelligence": New Zealand Signals Intelligence in Historical Context since 1945' (BA Hons thesis, University of Otago, 2014), p. 32.

132 Mark McGuire, 'Army Signals', unpublished manuscript sent to authors, 2015, p. 9; Nicky Hager, 'The Origins of Signals Intelligence in New Zealand', *Centre for Peace Studies Working*

Paper, no. 5 (August 1995), pp. 1–26.

133 NZS, 1939, No. 121, 'The Censorship and Publicity Emergency Regulations', p. 567.

134 Taylor, *The Home Front, Volume II*, pp. 888–89.

135 ANZ, R18871326, 'Security – Subversion – The H. A. Ostler Case', Memorandum for the Solicitor-General, 15 February 1941; Taylor, *The Home Front, Volume II*, pp. 898–902.

136 RHPHC, EA(PM) 84/10/2 part 1, Director of Publicity to Editor, *Evening Star*, Dunedin, 21 February 1941.

137 Taylor, *The Home Front, Volume II*, p. 979.

138 For coverage of postal censorship, see ibid., pp. 979ff.

139 Ibid., pp. 981–82.

140 See, for example, *Press*, 7 August 1941, p. 6; *Press*, 8 August 1941, p. 6.

141 Taylor, *The Home Front, Volume II*, p. 989.

142 Dunstall, *A Policeman's Paradise?*, p. 305; ANZ, R12677280, 'Civilian narratives – Postal and Telegraphic Censorship', p. 5.

143 Taylor, *The Home Front, Volume II*, pp. 979–86.

144 Ibid.

145 Ibid., pp. 980–81, 997; for Lochore, see King, *Tread Softly for You Tread on My Life*, pp. 64–86.

146 Taylor, *The Home Front, Volume II*, pp. 980, 993–97.

147 Filer, 'Signals Intelligence in New Zealand During World War II', pp. 1–4; Neems, '"Total Intelligence"', pp. 31–33.

148 Nicky Hager, *Secret Power: New Zealand's Role in the International Spy Network* (Nelson: Craig Potton Publishing, 1996), pp. 277–78.

149 Hastings, *The Secret War*, p. 94.

150 James Rusbridger, 'The Sinking of the "Automedon", the Capture of the "Nankin"', *Encounter*, vol. 64, no. 5 (May 1985), p. 12.

151 Hastings, *The Secret War*, p. 95.

152 Filer, 'Signals Intelligence in New Zealand During World War II', p. 5; Hager, *Secret Power*, pp. 57ff.

153 ANZ, R18871157, 'Security – Intelligence – Intelligence summaries (Issued by the Police Department)', Intelligence Summary, 9 October 1939.

154 The same report noted that 'there is no evidence that Field has been sponsored by or belongs to any particular organisation in New Zealand' and that 'the security authorities have seen no reason to take any particular action against him'. ANZ, R18871325, 'Security – Subversion – General', Memorandum for the Chargé d'Affaires, Washington, 24 December 1943. See also Marinus F. La Rooij, 'From Colonial Conservative to International Antisemite: The Life and Work of Arthur Nelson Field', *Journal of Contemporary History*, vol. 37, no. 2 (2002), p. 238; La Rooij, 'Arthur Nelson Field: Kiwi Theoretician of the Australian Radical Right?', *Labour History*, vol. 89, no. 1 (November 2005), p. 51.

155 ANZ, R18871181, 'Security – Intelligence – Japanese espionage', Memorandum for the Prime Minister's Department, 13 October 1941.

156 Taylor, *The Home Front, Volume II*, p. 867; Dunstall, *A Policeman's Paradise?*, pp. 314–19.

157 ANZ, R12677396, 'Civilian narratives – Police Department', pp. 41–55; ANZ, R24001247, 'Old Police Records – Recording Sheets', 42/912. For coverage of Italian and Japanese expatriates/ immigrants, see ANZ, R12677396, 'Civilian narratives – Police Department', pp. 56–62.

158 ANZ, R24001246, 'Old Police Records – Recording Sheets', S42/492; ANZ, R24001249, 'Old Police Records – Recording Sheets', 43/529.

159 Tonkin-Covell, 'The Collectors', pp. 308–9; ANZ, R3885796, 'Intelligence – Japanese activities among Maoris', Report from No. 2a Home Guard Rotorua, 8 January 1942.

160 Michael King, *Te Puea: A Biography* (Auckland: Hodder & Stoughton, 1977), pp. 206–9;

Lachy Paterson, 'Were Some Māori Disloyal During the War?', *Te Hau Kāinga Māori Home Front* (www.maorihomefront.nz/en/whanau-stories/were-some-maori-disloyal-during-the-war/).

161   King, *Te Puea*, pp. 207–9.

162   Cybèle Locke, *Workers in the Margins: Union Radicals in Post-war New Zealand* (Wellington: Bridget Williams Books, 2012), pp. 25–27; King, *Te Puea*, pp. 219–20.

163   King, *Te Puea*, pp. 208–9; Kerry Taylor, '"Potential Allies of the Working Class": The Communist Party of New Zealand and Maori, 1951–52', in Moloney and Taylor, *On the Left*, pp. 106–7. SIB officers spoke with Waikato–Tainui and other tribal leaders on various occasions about the menace of Japan, generally amicably.

164   Richard S. Hill, *State Authority, Indigenous Autonomy: Crown–Maori Relations in New Zealand/Aotearoa, 1900–1950* (Wellington: Victoria University Press, 2004), pp. 184–226; Paterson, 'Were Some Māori Disloyal During the War?'.

165   Hanson and Rolfe, 'Security Intelligence 1915–1945', p. 66.

166   ANZ, R22042409, 'Intelligence Centres – Security intelligence organisation New Zealand – August 1940–March 1948', Naval Secretary, Wellington, to the Secretary, Organisation for National Security, Wellington, Secret Memo 14 August 1940.

167   RHPHC, V 12/42, Secretary, Office of the Public Service Commissioner, 3 June 1940 to Permanent Heads, and other correspondence in V12/42 and IA171/37.

168   Lewis and McLean, *TP: The Life and Times of Sir Terry McLean*, p. 78.

169   ANZ, R24001247, 'Old Police Records – Recording Sheets', 42/693. For an example of Scrimgeour's contributions to the SCR, see H. Atmore and 'Uncle Scrim', *You and the U.S.S.R.* (Wellington: Printed by Commercial Printing and Publishing Co., 1941). See too,

Patrick Day, *The Radio Years: A History of Broadcasting in New Zealand, Volume One* (Auckland: Auckland University Press in association with the Broadcasting History Trust, 1994), pp. 271–73.

170   ANZ, R24001248, 'Old Police Records – Recording Sheets', S43/39. See also Leslie M. Edwards, *Scrim: Radio Rebel in Retrospect* (Auckland: Hodder & Stoughton, 1971), pp. 132–45, 152–55.

171   Tonkin-Covell, 'The Collectors', p. 288.

172   McGibbon, *Blue-Water Rationale*, pp. 346–48, 371–76.

173   Hanson and Rolfe, 'Security Intelligence 1915–1945', p. 78.

174   See, for example, 'a treatise prepared by 100 on a group of Communists, some of whom are in the Forces', Locke family papers, doc. 220, Elsie Locke personal file.

175   Tonkin-Covell, 'The Collectors', p. 304.

176   ANZ, R22440398, 'Security – Embarkation 15 Reinforcements for 2nd NZEF', report of information contained in letters written by Army Personnel embarking at Napier, 12 March 1942.

177   Taylor, *The Home Front, Volume II*, p. 884; Hanson and Rolfe, 'Security Intelligence 1915–1945', pp. 76–80.

178   Hanson and Rolfe, 'Security Intelligence 1915–1945', pp. 69–70.

179   Ibid., p. 66.

180   Fox, '"A Formidable Responsibility"', p. 8.

181   For example, Elsie Freeman (later Locke) was surveilled by both the Police and the SIB. Maureen Birchfield, *Looking for Answers: A Life of Elsie Locke* (Christchurch: Canterbury University Press, 2009), pp. 219–25.

182   A. M. Ostler to Hon. H. T. Armstrong, 2 September 1942, and H. G. R. Mason to Ostler, 14 September 1942, in CL118, 'Peoples Voice: Representations for Removal of Ban'.

183   ANZ, R24716792, 'NZ–USSR [New Zealand–Union of Soviet Socialist Republics]

Society, Auckland Branch'; ANZ, R24716793, 'Society for Closer Relations with Russia, Christchurch Branch'; ANZ, R24716796, 'Society for Closer Relations with Russia, Wellington Branch'; ANZ, R24716794, 'Society for Closer Relations with Russia, National Society'.

184 ANZ, R24881829, 'Youth Organisations: Progressive Youth League', police agent's report, 24 March 1942.

185 ANZ, R24881824, 'Miscellaneous Organisations: Esperanto Association'.

186 ANZ, R25087986, 'Bookshops & Libraries: Christchurch Co-Operative Bookshop Society Ltd'.

187 For examples, see ANZ, R24716769, 'Communist Party NZ, Wellington City Branch'; ANZ, R24881823, 'Communist Party NZ, Wellington, Social Functions'; ANZ, R24001242, 'Old Police Records – Recording Sheets'; ANZ, R24001245, 'Old Police Records – Recording Sheets'; ANZ, R24001249, 'Old Police Records – Recording Sheets'; ANZ, R24001250, 'Old Police Records – Recording Sheets'; ANZ, R24118453, 'Old Police Records – Recording Sheets'.

188 Saker family papers, pp. 1–4, 12–13, Dorian Saker personal file.

189 Jakich family papers, pp. 2–4, Kresimir Jakich personal file.

190 ANZ, R25087995, 'Peace Organisations: NZ Peace Council: Anti Conscription', Report of Detective Samuel Craig Browne, 4 August 1944.

191 ANZ, R25087992, 'Miscellaneous Organisations: Democratic Labour Party'.

192 Littlewood, '"The Debates of the Past"', pp. 283–84.

193 Martin/Kelly family papers, p. 11, Douglas Martin personal file, 'MARTIN, DOUGLAS MURDOCH (ex Rev.)'; Elsie Locke, *Peace People: A History of Peace Activities in New Zealand* (Christchurch: Hazard Press, 1992), p. 108.

194 ANZ, R24001246, 'Old Police Records – Recording Sheets', S42/16, S42/27; ANZ, R23246723, 'Peace Organisations – Miscellaneous Peace and Disarment [sic] Groups – Christian Pacifist Society'; ANZ, R23246724, 'Peace Organisations – Miscellaneous Peace and Disarment [sic] Groups – Christian Pacifist Society'; ATL, MS-Papers-6139-1, 'Papers held by the Security Intelligence Service on A. C. Barrington'; ATL, MS-Papers-6139-2, 'Papers held by the Security Intelligence Service on A. C. Barrington'.

195 ANZ, R25087995, 'Peace Organisations: NZ Peace Council: Anti Conscription'.

196 For examples, see ANZ, R24881829, 'Youth Organisations: Progressive Youth League'; ANZ, R25087999, 'Peace Organisations: Miscellaneous Peace/Disarmament Groups: Peace Pledge Union'; ANZ, R25088000, 'Peace Organisations: Misccllaneous Peace/Disarmament Groups: Peace Pledge Union'.

197 ANZ, R23246725, 'Peace Organisations – Miscellaneous Peace and Disarment [sic] Groups – Christian Pacifist Society', report of Detective Sergeant R. H. Waterson, 26 April 1940.

198 The campaigner's son (Derek Freeman) would become a famous anthropologist.

199 ANZ, R24118479, 'Communist Party of New Zealand: Wellington Branch: Sympathisers & Contacts', report of Constable W. A. Calwell, 3 July 1940.

200 For an example, see ANZ, R24881829, 'Youth Organisations: Progressive Youth League', United Peace Front Meeting Auckland, 19 March 1940.

201 ANZ, R23246726, 'Peace Organisations – Miscellaneous Peace and Disarment [sic] Groups – Christian Pacifist Society'; ANZ, R23246727, 'Peace Organisations – Miscellaneous Peace and Disarment [sic] Groups – Christian Pacifist Society'.

202 ANZ, R23246723, 'Peace Organisations – Miscellaneous Peace and Disarment

[sic] Groups – Christian Pacifist Society';
ANZ, R23246724, 'Peace Organisations –
Miscellaneous Peace and Disarment [sic]
Groups – Christian Pacifist Society'.

203 ANZ, R24716794, 'Society for Closer Relations
with Russia, National Society'.

204 ANZ, R24716793, 'Society for Closer Relations
with Russia, Christchurch Branch', F. L.
Langley to Minister in Charge of Police,
10 March 1942.

205 ANZ, R23246723, 'Peace Organisations –
Miscellaneous Peace and Disarment [sic]
Groups – Christian Pacifist Society', report
of R. P. Thomas, 14 January 1940; David
Grant, 'Burton, Ormond Edward', *The
Dictionary of New Zealand Biography, Volume
Five*, pp. 80–82.

206 ANZ, R24881822, 'Communist Party NZ,
Police Raids On'; ANZ, R23246731, 'Peace
Organisations – Miscellaneous Peace and
Disarment [sic] Groups – Christian Pacifist
Society'.

207 For example, see ANZ, R25088002, 'Peace
Organisations: Miscellaneous Peace/
Disarmament Groups: Anti War Movement',
report of Constable K. O. Evans, 18 July 1941.

208 ANZ, R24716796, 'Society for Closer Relations
with Russia, Wellington Branch', report dated
4 November 1942.

209 Locke family papers, doc. 21, Elsie Locke
personal file.

210 Williams/Birchfield family papers, f. 28,
Albert and Constance Birchfield personal
files.

211 William L. Renwick, 'Sir Thomas Hunter
(1876–1953)', in Vincent O'Sullivan (ed.),
*Eminent Victorians: Great Teachers and Scholars
from Victoria's First 100 Years* (Wellington:
Stout Research Centre, 1999), pp. 29–32.

212 Sarah Gaitanos, *Shirley Smith: An Examined
Life* (Wellington: Victoria University Press,
2019), pp. 146–47; 'REPORT BY SGT. 170:
Dr. W. B. SUTCH', 27 Aug 1941, Sarah
Gaitanos papers.

213 Locke family papers, docs. 139, 216–220 and
passim, Elsie Locke personal file.

214 ANZ, R24716794, 'Society for Closer Relations
with Russia, National Society', report on Rev.
W. S. Rollings and New Zealand Society for
Closer Relations with Russia, 5 August 1941.

215 Locke family papers, docs. 35, 216–219, Elsie
Locke personal file.

216 Graeme Hunt, *Black Prince: The Autobiography
of Fintan Patrick Walsh* (Auckland: Penguin
Books, 2004), pp. 121–26.

217 Ibid., p. 122; Barry Gustafson, *From the Cradle
to the Grave: A Biography of Michael Joseph
Savage* (Auckland: Reed Methuen, 1986),
p. 254.

218 ANZ, R25087986, 'Bookshops & Libraries:
Christchurch Co-Operative Bookshop
Society Ltd', memorandum from the High
Commission London to the Prime Minister
Wellington, 26 April 1940.

219 ANZ, R24001247, 'Old Police Records –
Recording Sheets', 42/604.

220 ANZ, R18871181, 'Security – Intelligence
– Japanese espionage', Chinese Consulate-
General Wellington, 16 March 1943; RHPHC,
N 8/1/18, 'Secret and personal' memorandum
to Director of Naval Intelligence, Melbourne,
22 March 1943.

221 ANZ, R18871181, 'Security – Intelligence –
Japanese espionage', memorandum to the
War Cabinet Secretariat, 15 June 1943.

222 David Stevens, *U-Boat Far From Home: The
Epic Voyage of U 862 to Australia and New
Zealand* (Sydney: Allen & Unwin, 1997); Grant
Howard, *Happy in the Service: An Illustrated
History of the Women's Royal New Zealand
Naval Service, 1942–1977* (Auckland: Word
Publishers, 1985), pp. 47–50.

223 Hanson and Rolfe, 'Security Intelligence
1915–1945', pp. 79–80.

224 The most infamous incident was the
so-called Battle of Manners Street. This
almost folkloristic confrontation on 3 April
1943 supposedly saw more than 1000 US

troops square off against New Zealand troops, civilians and military police in a four-hour mêlée that began when American troops from the southern states attempted to prevent Māori servicemen from drinking at the Allied Services Club. At least two Americans were claimed to have been killed. Declassified reports provide a different account, however, stating that the disturbance originated when four or five intoxicated merchant seamen started a brawl which then escalated into a series of fights in which American marines and sailors and local servicemen and seamen became entangled. See Bernard Foster and Hebert Roth, 'Riots', in A. H. McLintock (ed.), *An Encyclopaedia of New Zealand, Volume 3* (Wellington: R. E. Owen, Government Printer, 1966), pp. 85–87; ANZ, R22438166, 'Discipline – Discipline USA troops in New Zealand'.

225 Hanson and Rolfe, 'Security Intelligence 1915–1945', p. 80.

226 Tonkin-Covell, 'The Collectors', p. 348.

227 ANZ, R23246726, 'Peace Organisations – Miscellaneous Peace and Disarment [sic] Groups – Christian Pacifist Society'; ANZ, R23246728, 'Peace Organisations – Miscellaneous Peace and Disarment [sic] Groups – Christian Pacifist Society'; ANZ, R25087986, 'Bookshops & Libraries: Christchurch Co-operative Bookshop Society Ltd'; Hunt, *Spies and Revolutionaries*, p. 145.

228 RHPHC, EA(PM) 84/1/4, part 1, Commissioner of Police to Secretary, Organisation for National Security, 9 April 1940.

229 For examples, see files on the Christian Pacifist Society (ANZ, R23246726), and the Society for Closer Relations with Russia (ANZ, R24716796, 'Society for Closer Relations with Russia, Wellington Branch').

230 Locke family papers, doc. 220 and passim, Elsie Locke personal file.

231 Einhorn family papers, pp. 126–28, 135–36, 167–69 and passim, Helmut Einhorn and Ester Einhorn personal files.

232 ATL, MS-Papers-11459-054, 'Security Intelligence Bureau – Notes on Government Ministers'.

233 Tonkin-Covell, 'The Collectors', p. 327.

234 Price, *The Plot to Subvert Wartime New Zealand*, p. 81.

235 RHPHC, E1 29/55/2, Prime Minister to Professor Horace Belshaw, 27 November 1940, and other correspondence in E1 29/55/2.

236 Bernard Smith, 'Counihan, Noel Jack', *Australian Dictionary of Biography*, vol. 17 (2007) (https://adb.anu.edu.au/biography/counihan-noel-jack-12360#); RHPHC, CL114, Solicitor-General to Attorney-General, 15 March 1940. Such aspects of wartime history were generally forgotten in post-war years. A 1974 exploration by Murray Horton in the student magazine *Canta* was headlined as a 'secret history': Murray Horton, 'The Secret History of WW2' (http://legacy.disarmsecure.org/The%20Secret%20History%20of%20WWII%20M%20Horton.pdf).

237 Day, *The Radio Years*, pp. 271–77; Allan K. Davidson, 'Scrimgeour, Colin Graham', *The Dictionary of New Zealand Biography, Volume Four*, pp. 465–66.

238 John Middleton Murry, 'Some Problems of Democracy at War, Part 1: Safeguards for the Freedom of Expression', *Times Literary Supplement*, 16 September 1939, p. 535.

239 ANZ, R21078487, 'Plans: Security Intelligence Bureau: Policy and Organisation', H. G. R. Mason, Attorney-General, Wellington, to the War Cabinet, Wellington, Secret Memorandum 18 September 1942, p. 2.

240 *New Zealand Herald*, 16 September 1944, p. 6.

241 TNA, Guy Liddell Diaries, KV4/471, pp. 121–22.

242 Wood, *The New Zealand People at War*, pp. 161–62; Taylor, *The Home Front, Volume II*, pp. 884–85; *Auckland Star*, 18 September 1944, p. 6; Dunstall, *A Policeman's Paradise?*, p. 307.

243 Price, *The Plot to Subvert Wartime New Zealand*, p. 92.

244 Tonkin-Covell, 'The Collectors', pp. 286–342; Fox, '"A Formidable Responsibility"'.

245 Tonkin-Covell, 'The Collectors', pp. 316–42.

246 SRCNZSSC, 08/1/25, 'Security Intelligence', Navy Office Minute Sheet, 20 November 1942.

247 Tonkin-Covell, 'The Collectors', p. 427.

248 Hager, 'The Origins of Signals Intelligence in New Zealand', p. iii. For sigint in New Zealand history, with an emphasis on its international dimension, see the seminal work by Nicky Hager, *Secret Power*.

249 See, for example, *Nelson Evening Mail*, 23 February 1943, p. 2; *Otago Daily Times*, 24 February 1944, p. 4; *Nelson Evening Mail*, 15 March 1944, p. 4.

250 Tonkin-Covell, 'The Collectors', p. 345.

251 Locke family papers, doc. 220, Elsie Locke personal file.

252 For examples, see ANZ, R24001242, 'Old Police Records – Recording Sheets', S.40/447, 40/313, S.40/447, 40/1513; ANZ, R24001243, 'Old Police Records – Recording Sheets', S.41/313; ANZ, R24001245, 'Old Police Records – Recording Sheets', 41/1/2; ANZ, R24001251, 'Old Police Records – Recording Sheets', S.45/127; ATL, MS-Papers-5079-426, 'Papers related to Paddy Costello'; ATL, MS-Papers-8752-204, 'Proposed book on the Security Intelligence Service – Milner and Costello'; ANZ, R24716769, 'Communist Party NZ, Wellington City Branch', report on Central Branch, 18 July 1943; Hunt, *Black Prince*, p. 127.

253 See her own version (among a number of others): Nancy Wake, *The White Mouse* (Melbourne: Sun Books, 1985).

Chapter Seven: Surveillance and Superpowers, 1945–1956

1 Ian McGibbon (ed.), *Undiplomatic Dialogue: Letters between Carl Berendsen and Alister McIntosh, 1943–1952* (Auckland: Auckland University Press, 1993), p. 205.

2 Roberto Rabel, '"A Hell of a Way to End a War": New Zealanders in Trieste, 1945', in John Crawford (ed.), *Kia Kaha: New Zealand in the Second World War* (Auckland: Oxford University Press, 2002), pp. 276–88.

3 W. David McIntyre, *Background to the ANZUS Pact: Policy-making, Strategy, and Diplomacy, 1945–55* (Christchurch: Canterbury University Press, 1995), pp. 138–43; John R. Muir, '"Our Bounden Duty": An Analysis of the Arguments Justifying the Introduction of Peacetime Compulsory Military Training in New Zealand, 1949' (BA Hons thesis, University of Otago, 1995); Ian McGibbon, *New Zealand and the Korean War, Volumes I and II* (Auckland & Wellington: Oxford University Press in association with the Historical Branch, Department of Internal Affairs, 1992–96); Christopher Pugsley, *From Emergency to Confrontation: The New Zealand Armed Forces in Malaya and Borneo, 1949–1966* (Auckland: Oxford University Press, 2003).

4 Amy Knight, *How the Cold War Began: The Igor Gouzenko Affair and the Hunt for Soviet Spies* (New York: Carroll & Graf Publishers, 2005).

5 David Horner, *The Spy Catchers: The Official History of ASIO, 1949–1963, Volume 1* (Crows Nest, NSW: Allen & Unwin, 2014), pp. 54–56; John Earl Haynes and Harvey Klehr, *Venona: Decoding Soviet Espionage in America* (New Haven: Yale University Press, 2000).

6 Horner, *The Spy Catchers*, pp. 64–67.

7 Ibid., pp. 91–99. See also David McKnight, *Australia's Spies and Their Secrets* (St Leonards, NSW: Allen & Unwin, 1994).

8 Horner, *The Spy Catchers*, pp. 56–59, 64–67. Further details on Sillitoe can be found in A. W. Cockerill, *Sir Percy Sillitoe: The Biography of the Former Head of MI5* (London: W. H. Allen, 1975), and in his autobiography, *Cloak without Dagger* (London: Cassell, 1955): see pp. xvi, 190–91 for his roving mission.

9   Georgina Sinclair, *At the End of the Line: Colonial Policing and the Imperial Endgame, 1945–80* (Manchester: Manchester University Press, 2006), pp. 198–200.

10 The term Special Branch to designate a grouping of political police within a detective office was sometimes used prior to this; see, for example, RHPHC, 'Report of Detective R. D. L. Jones', 6 March 1946, written at 'Special Branch, Auckland Detective Office'. Other terms were used too, including 'Security Service': see, for example, a memorandum from Detective Sergeant P. J. Nalder to A. D. McIntosh, 11 August 1948, in RHPHC, EA(PM) 61/281 0/6 pt 1. This book has used the common convention of the time in referring to the Special Branch; namely 'Special Branch' without the definite article.

11 McGibbon, *Undiplomatic Dialogue*, p. 210.

12 Robin Kay (ed.), *The ANZUS Pact and the Treaty of Peace with Japan* (Wellington: Historical Publications Branch, 1985), p. 525.

13 1st NZSIS Tranche, 'A Note on the Security Situation in New Zealand', 31 August 1954, p. 119.

14 For details on the Petrovs' defection and ASIO's role, see Horner, *The Spy Catchers*, pp. 318–48; for Evdokia's importance and later life, see Phillip Deery, *Spies and Sparrows: ASIO and the Cold War* (Melbourne: Melbourne University Press, 2022), pp. 110–17.

15 1st NZSIS Tranche, 'A Note on the Security Situation in New Zealand', 31 August 1954, p. 120; Geoffrey R. Weller, 'Change and Development in the New Zealand Security and Intelligence Services', *Conflict Quarterly*, vol. 21, no. 1 (Spring 2001).

16 Graeme Hunt, *Spies and Revolutionaries: A History of New Zealand Subversion* (Auckland: Reed, 2007), p. 220–21; Horner, *The Spy Catchers*, pp. 366–67; Des Ball, 'The Spy Who Came Out as Klod', *The Australian*, 24 September 2011. Percy Sillitoe relayed to the British Joint Intelligence Committee in 1948 that there was '[s]trong circumstantial evidence' that Milner passed two specified documents to the Soviet Legation in Canberra: Sillitoe to W. Hayter, 21 September 1948, FO1093/516, 'Australian Security', in *Secret Files from World Wars to Cold War: Intelligence, Strategy and Diplomacy*, online database (available at www. secretintelligencefiles.com/).

17 A. C. Wilson, *New Zealand and the Soviet Union 1950–1991: A Brittle Relationship* (Wellington: Victoria University Press, 2004), pp. 21–22, 27–28. See also the pamphlet by Minister of Public Works Bob Semple, *Why I Fight Communism* (Wellington: Hutcheson, Bowman & Stewart, 1948). Keith Sinclair observes of Prime Minister Fraser: 'Fraser had become a cold war warrior before the hot war ended; psychologically he was ready for an anti-communist crusade.' Keith Sinclair, *Walter Nash* (Auckland: Auckland University Press, 1976), p. 274.

18 Aaron Fox, 'The Price of Collective Security: State-sponsored Anti-communism in New Zealand in the Cold War', in Ian McGibbon and John Crawford (eds), *Seeing Red: New Zealand, the Commonwealth and the Cold War, 1945–91* (Wellington: NZ Military History Committee, 2012), pp. 95–124; Mark Derby, *White-collar Radical: Dan Long and the Rise of the White-collar Unions* (Nelson: Craig Potton Publishing, 2013), pp. 215–24; James McNeish, 'Hidden History: The New Zealand Cold War', *North & South* (October 2007), pp. 86–92; Michael King, *The Penguin History of New Zealand* (Auckland: Penguin, 2003), pp. 427–31; H. S. Roberts, 'A Note on the "Cold War" Period in New Zealand', in H. S. Roberts (ed.), *A History of Statistics in New Zealand* (Wellington: New Zealand Statistical Association, 1999), pp. 253–54; R. M. Campbell, 'In the Name of National Security', *New Zealand Listener*, 23 February 1974, p. 9.

19 George Fraser, *Both Eyes Open: A Memoir* (Dunedin: John McIndoe, 1990), pp. 84–90; Sinclair, *Walter Nash*, p. 269. For the pamphlet

in question, see Fraser, *Martial Plan?: An Analysis of United States Policy* (Wellington: New Zealand Fabian Society, 1948).

20　Ross Galbreath, *DSIR: Making Science Work for New Zealand: Themes from the History of the Department of Scientific and Industrial Research, 1926–1992* (Wellington: Victoria University Press in association with the Historical Branch, Department of Internal Affairs, 1998), p. 153.

21　'Organisation of Defence Science Activities in New Zealand', Annex A to 'Progress Report on Defence Research in New Zealand: Note by the New Zealand Delegation', 21 December 1948, and C.D.S. (48) 13 'Extract from a Letter from the Scientific Liaison Officer, Dominion of New Zealand', 28 September 1948, C.D.S. (48) 4, FO 1093/515, in *Secret Files from World Wars to Cold War*.

22　Sinclair, *Walter Nash*, pp. 276–77; Hunt, *Black Prince*, pp. 140–42; Dick Scott, *A Radical Writer's Life* (Auckland: Reed, 2004), p. 136; Redmer Yska, *All Shook Up: The Flash Bodgie and the Rise of the New Zealand Teenager in the Fifties* (Auckland: Penguin Books, 1993), pp. 17–20; General Secretary, PSA, to Prime Minister, 23 February 1949, 'Victimisation of Association Officials – Mr. Cecil Holmes', Ray Grover papers. Holmes wrote his own account of the affair: *One Man's Way: On the Road with a Rebel Reporter, Film-maker and Adventurer* (Auckland: Penguin Books, 1986); Fraser, *Both Eyes Open*, p. 88; Dean Parker, 'Scoundrel Times at the Film Unit', *Illusions* (7 March 1988), pp. 4–8.

23　*Public Service Journal*, vol. 41, no. 8 (September 1954), p. 51.

24　NZPD, vol. 291, 19 September 1950, p. 253.

25　Michael Bassett, *Confrontation '51: The 1951 Waterfront Dispute* (Wellington: Reed, 1972), p. 75.

26　Ibid., p. 99.

27　David Burke, 'Towards the Conception of the New Zealand Security Service: UK and US Involvement in New Zealand's Early Cold War Security Concerns', *Security and Surveillance History Series*, 2017/2, p. 6.

28　Anna Green, *British Capital, Antipodean Labour: Working the New Zealand Waterfront, 1915–1951* (Dunedin: University of Otago Press, 2001), p. 146.

29　ANZ, R10074966, 'Government and Public Order – Strikes: 1951 Strike: General', Memorandum for the Superintendent of Police, Christchurch, 13 March 1951.

30　Richard G. H. Kay, 'Take *That*, You Dirty Commie!: The Rise of a Cold War Consciousness in New Zealand, 1944–1949' (BA Hons thesis, University of Otago, 1994).

31　*NZ Truth*, 22 December 1948, p. 14.

32　NZPD, vol. 282, 21 September 1948, p. 2428.

33　Bollinger family papers, p. 25, Conrad Bollinger personal file, Report of Acting Detective T. H. Wilson, 30 November 1954.

34　Redmer Yska, 'Spies, Lies and Red Herrings', in David Grant (ed.), *The Big Blue: Snapshots of the 1951 Waterfront Lockout* (Wellington: Canterbury University Press, 2004), pp. 25–26.

35　Frances Stonor Saunders, *The Cultural Cold War: The CIA and the World of Arts and Letters* (New York: New Press, 1999).

36　Hugh Wilford, 'The Information Research Department: Britain's Secret Cold War Weapon Revealed', *Review of International Studies*, 24 (1998), pp. 353–69. Through the Information Research Department, and by other means, Commonwealth countries swapped information and intentions on such matters as legislation to combat Soviet influence: Evan Smith, 'Policing Communism across the "White Man's World": Anti-Communist Co-operation between Australia, South Africa and Britain in the Early Cold War', *Britain and the World*, vol. 10, no. 2 (2017), p. 185; David Burke, *Family Betrayal: Agent Sonya, MI5 and the Kuczynski Network* (Cheltenham: The History Press, 2021), pp. 15, 46–47; Kerry Taylor, 'The Secret State', in Nicola Legat (ed.), *The Journal of Urgent Writing*, vol. 1 (Auckland: Massey University Press, 2016), pp. 140–41.

37 Redmer Yska, 'Collaboration between *Truth* and the Police Special Branch/Security Intelligence Service during the Cold War', *Security and Surveillance History Series*, 2016/1, pp. 1–8; *People's Voice*, 18 November 1953, p. 1.

38 'Chiefs of Staff Committee: Minutes of Meeting (COS (52) M.10) held on 21 August 1952 . . .', with CAB 176/38, in *Secret Files from World Wars to Cold War*. The Dominions had been approached by Britain in 1946 about such a proposal, but New Zealand had felt then that instituting a 'system' to handle such matters was a step too far, although it was prepared to undertake ad hoc censorship decisions if the British gave guidance: J. Stephenson memo of 10 April 1947, attached to 'Issue of Defence Notices to the Press', 11 April 1947, J.I.C./330/17, CAB 176/14, in *Secret Files from World Wars to Cold War*.

39 Redmer Yska, *Truth: The Rise and Fall of the People's Paper* (Nelson: Craig Potton Publishing, 2010), pp. 114–15; Yska, *All Shook Up*, pp. 52–53; Taylor, 'The Secret State', pp. 140–41. For the 'heavy water' project, see Rebecca Priestley, *Mad on Radium: New Zealand in the Atomic Age* (Auckland: Auckland University Press, 2012), pp. 69–70.

40 Alexander Trapeznik, '"Agents of Moscow" at the Dawn of the Cold War: The Comintern and the Communist Party of New Zealand', *Journal of Cold War Studies*, vol. 11, no. 1 (2009), pp. 124–49; Herbert Roth, 'The Communist Vote in New Zealand', *Political Science*, vol. 17, no. 2 (September 1965), p. 33.

41 Rosenberg family papers, Wolfgang Rosenberg personal file, 'Communist Party and Ancillary Organisations Christchurch. Known Activities 15–27 July 1955'.

42 Marc J. Selverstone, *Constructing the Monolith: The United States, Great Britain, and International Communism, 1945–1950* (Cambridge: Harvard University Press, 2009).

43 1st NZSIS Tranche, 'History of the New Zealand Security Intelligence Service and Its Predecessors', p. 3.

44 SRCNZSSC, folder I/J/3, David Paterson to Sherwood Young, 24 June 1991.

45 Susan Butterworth, *More Than Law and Order: Policing a Changing Society, 1945–1992* (Dunedin: University of Otago Press, 2005), p. 40; Miriam L. Wharton, 'The Development of Security Intelligence in New Zealand, 1945–1957' (Master of Defence Studies, Massey University, 2012), p. 62.

46 RHPHC, WN bundle 2304, 'Report of Detective R. D. L. Jones, relative to Communist Party activities in Auckland', 6 March 1946, annexed to Commissioner to Prime Minister, 11 March 1946.

47 Rosenberg family papers, p. 22, Wolfgang Rosenberg personal file, 'WELLINGTON CO-OPERATIVE BOOK SOCIETY: EIGHTH ANNUAL REPORT', 1946; 'Documents released' compendium, no. 73.

48 Murray Horton, 'Wolfgang Rosenberg', *Watchdog*, vol. 114 (May 2007), pp. 30–31.

49 1st NZSIS Tranche, 'Security Intelligence', 2 March 1948, pp. 220–21.

50 Michael Parker, *The S.I.S.: The New Zealand Security Intelligence Service* (Palmerston North: Dunmore Press, 1979), pp. 13–14.

51 1st NZSIS Tranche, 'History of the New Zealand Security Intelligence Service and Its Predecessors', p. 4, and 'Defence of the Realm – Security Organisation', 16 April 1948, attached to Foss Shanahan to Jim Cummings, 18 May 1948, pp. 211–13; Parker, *The S.I.S.*, pp. 9–10, 13–14; Hunt, *Spies and Revolutionaries*, pp. 156–59.

52 1st NZSIS Tranche, 'Defence of the Realm – Security Organisation', 16 April 1948, attached to Foss Shanahan to Jim Cummings, 18 May 1948, pp. 211–13. See also Sillitoe, *Cloak without Dagger*, p. 192.

53 1st NZSIS Tranche, 'History of the New Zealand Security Intelligence Service and Its Predecessors', p. 3.

54 Nalder's later career was meteoric; commissioned as a Sub-Inspector on 17 May 1950, he became Assistant Commissioner within three years.

55 Wharton, 'The Development of Security Intelligence in New Zealand, 1945–1957', p. 67.

56 1st NZSIS Tranche, 'New Zealand Police Force – Special Branch', p. 107.

57 1st NZSIS Tranche, 'New Zealand Police – Special Branch', p. 196.

58 ANZ, R25087985, 'Communist Party of NZ: Wellington District: Membership & Recruitment', memorandum for the Superintendent of Police Wellington, 6 September 1950.

59 Graeme Dunstall, 'Young, John Bruce', *The Dictionary of New Zealand Biography, Volume Five* (Auckland: Auckland University Press, 2000), pp. 582–83; Graeme Dunstall, 'Governments, the Police and the Left, 1912–51', in Pat Moloney and Kerry Taylor (eds), *On the Left: Essays on Socialism in New Zealand* (Dunedin: University of Otago Press, 2002), p. 101.

60 Dunstall, 'Governments, the Police and the Left', p. 99.

61 ANZ, R10074981, 'Government and Public Order – Strikes: 1951 Strike: Wellington Districts', Detective D. S. Paterson to the Inspector CIB, 1 June 1951. See too SCRNZSSC, Grace Millar Notes, 'Government and Public Order: Wellington', no. 116, p. 68.

62 Gerard Hill to Richard Hill, 13 September 2018.

63 1st NZSIS Tranche, 'History of the New Zealand Security Intelligence Service and Its Predecessors', pp. 3–4.

64 Among them, McNeish, 'Hidden History', p. 91; J. E. Traue to Richard Hill, 21 February 2022.

65 Burke, 'Towards the Conception of the New Zealand Security Service', p. 5.

66 TNA, PREM 8/1343, top secret report by the Director General, 2 July 1951.

67 TNA, PREM 8/1343, Prime Minister Holland to Prime Minister Attlee, 6 July 1951.

68 TNA, PREM 8/1343, inward telegram from U.K. representative, Wellington, 22 August 1951. OUTWARD TELEGRAM 'To ACTING U.K.H.C. CANBERRA.' TOP SECRET AND PERSONAL, 25 September 1951.

69 1st NZSIS Tranche, 'Security Requirements in New Zealand', 12 November 1951, pp. 170–92.

70 1st NZSIS Tranche, Prime Minister to Commissioner, 12 November 1951, and Sir Percy Sillitoe to Prime Minister, 23 October 1951, pp. 170–92; Butterworth, *More Than Law and Order*, pp. 30–31, 44–45. Although operational autonomy from the political executive was not embodied in the Police Force Act of 1947, which succeeded the 1913 Act, nor in the Regulations which followed in 1950, it remained part of the national ethos.

71 Sir Percy Sillitoe to Prime Minister, 23 October 1951, Appendix A, 'Security Requirements in New Zealand', J.I.C./2538/61, CAB 176/33, in *Secret Files from World Wars to Cold War*.

72 Parker, *The S.I.S.*, pp. 16–20.

73 Redmer Yska papers, 'Dossier of Declassified NZ US Embassy documents 1945–1960', STATE OF POLITICAL PARTIES AND THEIR LEADERS, 18 May 1953; Burke, 'Towards the Conception of the New Zealand Security Service', p. 6; Butterworth, *More Than Law and Order*, pp. 45–46.

74 Prime Minister to Sir Percy Sillitoe, 5 November 1951, Appendix B to Report by Sir Percy Sillitoe to the Prime Minister of New Zealand, 'Security Arrangements in New Zealand', 23 October 1951, J.I.C./2538/51, CAB 176/33; J.I.C. (51), Item 4, 'Security Arrangements in New Zealand', Minutes of 127th Meeting, Chiefs of Staff Committee Joint Intelligence Committee, 29 November 1951, both in *Secret Files from World Wars to Cold War*.

75   1st NZSIS Tranche, 'Advisory Committee
      on Security', 11 December 1951, pp. 149–53;
      'Advisory Committee on Security', 18 January
      1952, pp. 145–48.

76   1st NZSIS Tranche, Prime Minister to
      Commissioner, 12 November 1951, p. 170.

77   Dunstall, 'Young, John Bruce', *The Dictionary
      of New Zealand Biography, Volume Five*, pp.
      582–83; Dunstall, 'Compton, Eric Henry', in
      ibid., pp. 110–11.

78   Valerie P. Redshaw, *Tact and Tenacity: New
      Zealand Women in Policing* (Wellington:
      Grantham House/New Zealand Police, 2006),
      pp. 72–75.

79   Butterworth, *More Than Law and Order*,
      pp. 54–55; Yska, *Truth*, pp. 107–8.

80   *NZ Truth*, 30 September 1953, pp. 14, 17; Yska,
      Truth, pp. 107–8.

81   Yska, *Truth*, pp. 108–11; Redmer Yska,
      'Collaboration between *Truth* and the Police
      Special Branch/Security Intelligence Service',
      pp. 1–8.

82   A. C. Wilson, *Wire and Wireless: A History of
      Telecommunications in New Zealand, 1860–1987*
      (Palmerston North: Dunmore Press, 1994),
      p. 212.

83   Butterworth, *More Than Law and Order*, p. 59.

84   Ibid.; Yska, *Truth*, p. 111.

85   Yska, *Truth*, p. 111.

86   AJHR, 1954, H-16A, pp. 3–6.

87   Butterworth, *More Than Law and Order*,
      pp. 58–59.

88   Yska, *Truth*, p. 112.

89   Ibid.; Butterworth, *More Than Law and Order*,
      pp. 64–65.

90   Butterworth, *More Than Law and Order*,
      pp. 83, 86–87; New Zealand Police College,
      *Police Training in New Zealand: Trentham in
      Retrospect* (Wellington: New Zealand Police,
      1982), pp. 114–16.

91   1st NZSIS Tranche, 'The New Zealand
      Security Service', 13 March 1956, p. 94.

92   1st NZSIS Tranche, 'Papers on Security
      Organization in New Zealand', 20 December
      1955, pp. 100–104.

93   1st NZSIS Tranche, 'The New Zealand
      Security Service', 13 March 1956, pp. 94–99.

94   1st NZSIS Tranche, 'The New Zealand
      Security Service', Holland to Marshall,
      19 March 1956, pp. 92–93.

95   1st NZSIS Tranche, Holland to Marshall, 19
      March 1956; Secret Memorandum, Marshall
      to the Prime Minster, n.d., pp. 84–91.

96   John Marshall, *Memoirs Volume One: 1912 to
      1960* (Auckland: William Collins, 1983),
      p. 243.

97   1st NZSIS Tranche, 'Directive on
      Constitution and Operation of the New
      Zealand Security Service', n.d. [*c*.18 May
      1956], pp. 65–67.

98   1st NZSIS Tranche, 'Outward telegram',
      27 May 1956, p. 64.

99   1st NZSIS Tranche, 'The Security Problem
      in New Zealand', May 1956, p. 55; 1st NZSIS
      Tranche, 'The Internal Security Problem in
      New Zealand', 23 August 1956, p. 31.

100   1st NZSIS Tranche, 'The Internal Security
      Problem in New Zealand', 23 August 1956,
      p. 33.

101   1st NZSIS Tranche, 'The Security Problem in
      New Zealand', May 1956, p. 55.

102   1st NZSIS Tranche, 'The Reorganization of
      Special Branch', pp. 73, 82.

103   Michael King, *Tread Softly for You Tread on My
      Life: New & Collected Writings* (Auckland: Cape
      Catley Ltd, 2001), p. 71.

104   A number of writers have agreed with
      disillusioned MI5 insiders that there
      was a top Soviet spy in their midst, most
      such works pinpointing Hollis, pointing
      to puzzling incidents inside MI5: see, for
      example, Ben Macintyre, *Agent Sonya:
      Moscow's Most Daring Wartime Spy* (New
      York: Random House, 2020), p. 375.
      Conversely, these rumours around Hollis

are rejected by MI5 itself, as well as by Christopher Andrew's 'authorised history' of MI5.

105 1st NZSIS Tranche, 'Directive on the Constitution and Operation of the New Zealand Security Service', pp. 10–12; Wharton, 'The Development of Security Intelligence in New Zealand, 1945–1957', pp. 96, 137–38.

106 1st NZSIS Tranche, 'Order in Council', 28 November 1956, p. 15.

107 Parker, *The S.I.S.*, pp. 24, 34–38; Denis McLean, 'Gilbert, William Herbert Ellery', *The Dictionary of New Zealand Biography, Volume Five*, pp. 187–88.

108 1st NZSIS Tranche, 'Organisation of Security Service', 26 November 1956, p. 16.

109 Nicky Hager, *Secret Power: New Zealand's Role in the International Spy Network* (Nelson: Craig Potton Publishing, 1996), p. 59.

110 John Tonkin-Covell, 'The Collectors: Naval, Army and Air Intelligence in the New Zealand Armed Forces during the Second World War' (PhD thesis, University of Waikato, 2000), p. 121; Desmond Ball, Cliff Lord and Meredith Thatcher, *Invaluable Service: The Secret History of New Zealand's Signals Intelligence during Two World Wars* (Waimauku: Resource Books, 2011), p. 306.

111 Richard J. Aldrich, *GCHQ: The Uncensored Story of Britain's Most Secret Intelligence Agency* (London: HarperPress, 2010), p. 89.

112 Ibid., p. 93; Hager, *Secret Power*, pp. 59–60.

113 Hager, *Secret Power*, p. 60.

114 Aldrich, *GCHQ*, pp. 43, 93; Hager, *Secret Power*, pp. 58–60.

115 Colin Hanson, 'Draft Chapters for History of New Zealand Sigint', unpublished manuscript, 'The post-war years, 1945–1955', p. 3.

116 Ball et al., *Invaluable Service*, p. 315.

117 Ibid., pp. 316–17.

118 Aldrich, *GCHQ*, pp. 89–90.

119 Ibid., pp. 89–90, 98; National Security Agency, 'UKUSA Agreement Release, 1940–1956' (www.nsa.gov/news-features/ declassified-documents/ukusa/). The parties agreed to share 'the collection of traffic, acquisition of communications documents, traffic analysis, cryptanalysis, decryption and translation, acquisition of information regarding communications organisations, procedures, practices and equipment': Alexandra Neems, '"Total Intelligence": New Zealand Signals Intelligence in Historical Context since 1945' (BA Hons thesis, University of Otago, 2014), pp. 6–7, 10. The origins of UKUSA and the incorporation of Australia, Canada and New Zealand remain murky, and there are many different versions, including official websites which provide information at odds with other sources; but see Jeffrey T. Richelson and Desmond Ball, *The Ties That Bind: Intelligence Cooperation between the UKUSA Countries – the United Kingdom, the United States of America, Canada, Australia, and New Zealand* [1985], 2nd ed. (Wellington: Allen & Unwin, 1990), for a sound pioneering account.

120 David Filer, 'Signals Intelligence in New Zealand during the Cold War', *Security and Surveillance History Series*, 2019/1, p. 1.

121 Evan Smith, 'Policing Communism across the "White Man's World"', pp. 20–21.

122 Hanson, 'Draft Chapters', unpublished manuscript, 'The post-war years', p. 4.

123 Hager, *Secret Power*, p. 63.

124 Hanson, 'Draft Chapters', unpublished manuscript, 'The post-war years', p. 13.

125 Ibid., pp. 14–15.

126 ANZ, R12455831, 'NZCSO [New Zealand Combined Signals Organisation]: General', Memorandum for the Minister of Defence, 31 August 1955.

127 Hager, *Secret Power*, p. 67; Filer, 'Signals Intelligence in New Zealand during the Cold War', pp. 2–3; GCSB, DSB/12/1, 'Report by

Mr J. O. H. Burrough and [name redacted] on their visit to New Zealand in November 1954 in connection with Signal Intelligence', 15 December 1954.

128 Hanson, 'Draft Chapters', unpublished manuscript, 'The post-war years', p. 14.

129 Ibid., p. 15.

130 'Report by Mr J. O. H. Burrough', p. 2; Hanson, 'Draft Chapters', unpublished manuscript, 'The post-war years', p. 15.

131 Hanson, 'Draft Chapters', unpublished manuscript, 'The post-war years', p. 17; Hager, *Secret Power*, pp. 68–75.

132 Filer, 'Signals Intelligence in New Zealand during the Cold War', pp. 2–3; Neems, '"Total Intelligence"', p. 37; Hager, *Secret Power*, pp. 69–73 for Singapore.

133 'Report by Mr J. O. H. Burrough', p. 3.

134 Hager, *Secret Power*, pp. 68, 75; Neems, '"Total Intelligence"', p. 37.

135 Michael Goodman, *The Official History of the Joint Intelligence Committee, Volume 1: From the Approach of the Second World War to the Suez Crisis* (London: Routledge, 2014). Britain's JIB had been set up in 1945.

136 SRCNZSSC, Vic Jaynes, 'Origins of the External Assessments Bureau; the first 30 years', p. 2; 'Chiefs of Staff Committee: Joint Intelligence Organisation in New Zealand', 14 March 1949, JIC/523/49, CAB 176/22, in *Secret Files from World Wars to Cold War*. For the history of the British JIB, see Huw Dylan, *Defence Intelligence and the Cold War: Britain's Joint Intelligence Bureau, 1945–1964* (Oxford: Oxford University Press, 2014).

137 ANZ, R23447132, 'Intelligence – NZ Joint Intelligence Bureau', Chief of Staff Committee, 7 March 1949. See too 'Visit to Singapore, Australia and New Zealand by the Director Joint Intelligence Bureau, 2nd to 28th January 1947'; 'Joint Intelligence Committee Report No. 28/47', CAB 176/14; and 'Chiefs of Staff Committee: Joint Intelligence Organisation in New Zealand',

14 March 1949, JIC/523/49, CAB 176/22, in *Secret Files from World Wars to Cold War*. See also Neems, '"Total Intelligence"', p. 35.

138 SRCNZSSC, Jaynes, 'Origins of the JIB/EIB', p. 1.

139 ANZ, R23447132, 'Intelligence – NZ Joint Intelligence Bureau', Prime Minister's Department, 16 February 1949; 'Joint Intelligence in New Zealand. A Report by the Joint Planning Committee', 9 March 1949, JIC/637/49, 5 April 1949, CAB 176/22, in *Secret Files from World Wars to Cold War*.

140 Jaynes, 'Origins of the External Assessments Bureau', p. 3; Neems, '"Total Intelligence"', p. 34. In 1952 Holland noted that the JIO had, since its founding, 'come entirely under the Prime Minister's Office' and provided, inter alia, 'information that would be necessary in the event of trouble coming to New Zealand': NZPD, vol. 298, 9 September 1952, p. 1349. See too 'Chiefs of Staff Committee: Joint Intelligence Organisation in New Zealand', 14 March 1949, JIC/523/49, CAB 176/22, in *Secret Files from World Wars to Cold War*.

141 David Filer, 'The Joint Intelligence Office, the Joint Intelligence Bureau and the External Intelligence Bureau, 1949–1980: An Insider's Account of the First Three Decades of a Small Intelligence Agency', *Security and Surveillance History Series*, 2016/3, p. 1.

142 Hager, 'The Origins of Signals Intelligence in New Zealand', *Centre for Peace Studies, Working Paper*, no. 5 (August 1995), p. 21; Neems, '"Total Intelligence"', p. 36. The first task for the JIO staff was to build a library of reports, publications, maps and photographs about the South Pacific islands in the New Zealand area of responsibility. When the Korean War began and stimulated fears of a wider conflagration, the JIO was commissioned to prepare a register of 'Key Points' in New Zealand (including power stations, oil storage tanks, reservoirs, railway bridges, tunnels and wireless/telegraph stations) that may have required protection

from possible sabotage. A register was compiled but, as Jaynes later noted, this undertaking 'faded away with the end of hostilities in Korea'. Jaynes, 'Origins of the External Assessments Bureau', pp. 3–4.

143 'Joint Intelligence in New Zealand. A Report by the Joint Planning Committee', 9 March 1949, JIC/637/49, 5 April 1949, CAB 176/22, in *Secret Files from World Wars to Cold War*.

144 Hanson, 'Draft Chapters', unpublished manuscript, appendix one, p. 8.

145 ANZ, R23447132, 'Intelligence – NZ Joint Intelligence Bureau', Joint Intelligence office report covering the period 4th April 1949 to 31st March 1950, 5 May 1950.

146 ANZ, R23447132, 'Intelligence – NZ Joint Intelligence Bureau', report on the Joint Intelligence Office, 21 July 1950.

147 SRCNZSSC, [Vic Jaynes], 'The Problems of a Small Bureau', Research Methods Conference, Melbourne, November 1958, p. 8.

148 Jaynes, 'Origins of the External Assessments Bureau', p. 6; Filer, 'The Joint Intelligence Office', p. 3; NZPD, vol. 298, 9 September 1952, p. 1350; Neems, '"Total Intelligence"', p. 35.

149 Filer, 'The Joint Intelligence Office', pp. 3–4.

150 Ibid., p. 5.

151 Eric Morgan, 'The History of Communications Security in New Zealand, Part 1', unpublished manuscript, n.d., p. 10.

152 Pugsley, *From Emergency to Confrontation*, pp. 88–89, 121; Ian McGibbon, 'Special Air Service (SAS)', in Ian McGibbon (ed.), *The Oxford Companion to New Zealand Military History* (Auckland: Oxford University Press, 2009), p. 505.

153 1st NZSIS Tranche, 'Memorandum for the Superintendent of Police, Wellington', 21 November 1951, p. 159.

154 1st NZSIS Tranche, 'New Zealand Police, Special Branch, Christchurch', 24 November 1951, p. 160.

155 1st NZSIS Tranche, 'A Note on the Security Situation in New Zealand', 31 August 1954, p. 121.

156 1st NZSIS Tranche, 'The security problem in New Zealand', May 1956, p. 44.

157 1st NZSIS Tranche, 'A Note on the Security Situation in New Zealand', 31 August 1954, p. 120.

158 Ibid., p. 121.

159 NZPD, vol. 280, 6 July 1948, p. 335.

160 RHPHC, CAB 43/201/1 pt. 1, 'Public Service Legislation – Security Positions', memorandum for Cabinet by Attorney-General T. C. Webb; NZS, 1951, 'Public Service Amendment', no. 72, pp. 458–65.

161 NZS, 1951, No. 77, 'Official Secrets Act', pp. 555–68.

162 C. H. Kit Bennetts, *Spy: A Former SIS Officer Unmasks New Zealand's Sensational Cold War Spy Affair* (Auckland: Random House New Zealand, 2006), p. 123.

163 1st NZSIS Tranche, 'History of the New Zealand Security Intelligence Service and Its Predecessors', p. 4.

164 Butterworth, *More Than Law and Order*, p. 43; 1st NZSIS Tranche, 'History of the New Zealand Security Intelligence Service and Its Predecessors', p. 4; ANZ, R24118466, 'Old Police Record – Recording Sheets', S54/76.

165 ANZ, R10074966, 'Government and Public Order – Strikes: 1951 Strike: General', Memorandum for W. H. Fortune, 2 April 1951.

166 Ibid.

167 Ruth Lake, *My Years in Mrs Boswell's Moscow* (Wellington: N.Z. Society for Closer Relations with U.S.S.R., 1950). For further details, see Douglas Lake's 1955 unpublished memoir, ATL, MS-Papers-8661-2, 'Goodbye Diplomacy', pp. 25–26 and, for context, Redmer Yska, 'Spying on New Zealand's "Vegetable Club": A Cold War Episode', *Security and Surveillance History Series*, 2016/2, p. 4.

168 ANZ, R24118462, 'Old Police Record – Recording Sheets', S.52/108. For further details, see McGibbon, *Undiplomatic Dialogue*, p. 264; ATL, MS-Papers-8661-1, 'Ruth and Doug Lake: A Narrative of Recollections, Reminiscences and Material from Various Sources'.

169 Frank Corner, in Malcolm Templeton (ed.), *An Eye, An Ear and A Voice: 50 Years in New Zealand's External Relations, 1943–1993* (Wellington: Ministry of Foreign Affairs, 1993), p. 99; Ian McGibbon, 'Costello, Desmond Patrick', *The Dictionary of New Zealand Biography, Volume Five*, pp. 118–19.

170 Further details on Costello's background and the suspicions surrounding him are available in Malcolm Templeton, *Top Hats Are Not Being Taken: A Short History of the New Zealand Legation in Moscow, 1944–1950* (Wellington: New Zealand Institute of International Affairs, 1988), pp. 20–24; Denis Lenihan, '"Different Tones of Voice": Versions of Paddy Costello', *Security and Surveillance History Series*, 2020/1, pp. 1–21; James McNeish, *The Sixth Man: The Extraordinary Life of Paddy Costello* (Auckland: Vintage, 2007), p. 146.

171 Lenihan, '"Different Tones of Voice"', pp. 5–8. For an example of Hollis's reasoning: 'we know from very secret sources that certain of the Communist Party leaders [in Britain] were aware [in advance] of COSTELLO's departure from this country in July [1944], and it is possible that COSTELLO was seen by one or more of the leaders'. TNA, KV2/4328, Hollis to [Peter] Loxley, 18 October 1944.

172 McNeish, *The Sixth Man*, p. 182.

173 His arrest for drunk and disorderly behaviour in 1950 led to the Commissioner initiating a chain of events that ended up in Cabinet and the prime minister 'reprimanded Paddy severely'. ANZ, R24118459, 'Old Police Record – Recording Sheets', S.50/485; ANZ, R24118462, 'Old Police Record – Recording Sheets', S.52/108; McNeish, *The Sixth Man*, pp. 235–39.

174 Lenihan, '"Different Tones of Voice"', pp. 11–12.

175 Hunt, *Spies and Revolutionaries*, p. 227. Other New Zealanders domiciled overseas would also come under MI5 and/or FBI suspicion from time to time, including scientist (and future Nobel Prize winner) Maurice Wilkins in the early 1950s: Alan Travis, 'Nobel-winning British Scientist Accused of Spying by MI5, Papers Reveal', *Guardian*, 26 August 2010. For MI5 records on Wilkins, see TNA, UK, KV2/3922.

176 See 'W. B. Sutch – Target Assessment', 30 May 1974, released by the NZSIS 15 May 2008 (available at www.nzsis.govt.nz/assets/media/1974-05-30-Sutch-TA.pdf).

177 Sarah Gaitanos, *Shirley Smith: An Examined Life* (Wellington: Victoria University Press, 2019), pp. 86–104, 156.

178 Timothy Bollinger, 'The Administrative Career of Dr W. B. Sutch 1958–1965: A Study in New Zealand Bureaucratic Politics' (PhD thesis, Victoria University of Wellington, 2001), p. 46; Sinclair, *Walter Nash*, p. 342.

179 Aaron Fox papers, 'SUBJECT: WILLIAM BALL SUTCH', FBI file 62-HQ-84363-144p.9a.

180 Sinclair, *Walter Nash*, p. 342.

181 ANZ, R24118463, 'Old Police Record – Recording Sheets', S.52/770; Wharton, 'The Development of Security Intelligence in New Zealand, 1945–1957', p. 47.

182 NZS, 1951, No. 67, 'Police Force Amendment Act', pp. 391–407. The Act was opposed by liberal-minded lawyers such as Nigel Taylor (personal file, pp. 15, 28–32), among others such as unionists, academics, politicians and public servants, and meetings drew large crowds. For a broader discussion of civil liberties versus 'the maintenance of political system of the state, and public order' (p. 50), see K. J. Keith, 'The Right to Protest', in K. J. Keith (ed.), *Essays on Human Rights*

(Wellington: Sweet & Maxwell, 1968), pp. 49–69.

183   ANZ, R10074981, 'Government and Public Order – Strikes: 1951 Strike: Wellington Districts', report of Detective D. S. Paterson Wellington, 8 March 1951.

184   Matthews family papers, p. 94, 'VEGETABLE CLUB: Associations and Activities of Members', report of 6 May 1953.

185   ANZ, R24716772, 'Protests Miscellaneous: Japanese Peace Treaty', report of [name redacted], 11 October 1951.

186   ANZ, R24881832, 'Peace Organizations: NZ Peace Council: Policy'.

187   ANZ, R24118472, 'Old Police Record – Recording Sheets', 55/807.

188   Kelly family papers, Annex 1, p. 4, Director General of Security to Max Kelly, 2 June 2020.

189   2nd NZSIS Tranche, 'Ministerial Correspondence with Communist Front Organisations', 10 July 1951, p. 144.

190   ANZ, R24881830, 'Youth Organisations: Progressive Youth League'; ANZ, R24881831, 'Youth Organisations: Progressive Youth League'.

191   ANZ, R24881831, 'Youth Organisations: Progressive Youth League', extract from the biography of S. W. Scott, November 1959.

192   George Fraser, *Seeing Red: Undercover in 1950s New Zealand* (Palmerston North: Dunmore Press, 1995), p. 60.

193   ANZ, R24118469, 'Old Police Record – Recording Sheets', S.55/376.

194   ANZ, R24118467, 'Old Police Record – Recording Sheets', S.54/588.

195   ANZ, R24118474, 'Old Police Record – Recording Sheets', S.56/238; S.56/302.

196   For a consideration of the Police position in regard to the strike, examining strategies, tactics, regulations, logistics, intelligence and field leadership, see Sherwood Young,

'The Activities and Problems of the Police in the 1951 Waterfront Dispute' (MA thesis, University of Canterbury, 1975). Perhaps the quickest indication of the scale of 1951-related intelligence work is how it created hefty, specialised regional files as well as more general records relating to the situation. Declassified records include Auckland (ANZ, R10074967, 'Government and Public Order – Strikes: 1951 Strike: Auckland Districts'), Christchurch (ANZ, R10074968, 'Government and Public Order – Strikes: 1951 Strike: Christchurch Districts'; ANZ, R10074969, 'Government and Public Order – Strikes: 1951 Strike: Christchurch Districts'), Dunedin (ANZ, R10074970, 'Government and Public Order – Strikes: 1951 Strike: Dunedin District'), Napier (ANZ, R10074971, 'Government and Public Order – Strikes: 1951 Strike: Napier Districts'), Nelson (ANZ, R10074972, 'Government and Public Order – Strikes: 1951 Strike: Nelson Districts'), the West Coast (ANZ, R10074982, 'Government and Public Order – Strikes: 1951 Strike: West Coast Districts') and Wellington (ANZ, R10074981, 'Government and Public Order – Strikes: 1951 Strike: Wellington Districts').

197   ANZ, R24118460, 'Old Police Record – Recording Sheets', S.51/344.

198   ANZ, R25088000, 'Peace Organisations: Miscellaneous Peace/Disarmament Groups: Peace Pledge Union'.

199   ANZ, R25087988, 'Miscellaneous Organisations: NZ Council for Civil Liberties', report of Detective D. S. Paterson, 21 August 1952; Taylor family papers, p. 21, Nigel Taylor personal file, 'Report relative to NEW ZEALAND COUNCIL FOR CIVIL LIBERTIES', 20 August 1952. For further discussion of security interest in the Council for Civil Liberties, see Tim Beaglehole, *A Life of J. C. Beaglehole: New Zealand Scholar* (Wellington: Victoria University Press, 2006), p. 430.

200   In 1958 a newspaper report of a 1950 Summer School was placed on the file of one of the

speakers, Wolfgang Rosenberg's personal file. See Rosenberg family papers, Wolfgang Rosenberg personal file, vol. 1, p. 24.

201 ANZ, R24118467, 'Old Police Record – Recording Sheets', S.54/473.

202 2nd NZSIS Tranche, 'Ministerial Correspondence with Communist Front Organizations', 23 October 1951, p. 151.

203 ANZ, R25087989, 'Miscellaneous Organisations: NZ Seamen's Social Club'.

204 Kelly family papers, Tranche Two, Annex 1, p. 5, Director-General of Security to Max Kelly, 2 June 2020.

205 ANZ, R24716770, 'Protests Miscellaneous: The Rosenbergs'.

206 ANZ, R24716771, 'Protests Miscellaneous: Extension of Korean War'; ANZ, R24118468, 'Old Police Record – Recording Sheets', S.55/98.

207 ANZ, R24716772, 'Protests Miscellaneous: Japanese Peace Treaty'; ANZ, R24118459, 'Old Police Record – Recording Sheets', S.50/357; ANZ, R24118461, 'Old Police Record – Recording Sheets', S.51/461; S.51/469.

208 ANZ, R24118473, 'Old Police Record – Recording Sheets', S.56/78.

209 Rosenberg family papers, f. 81, Special Branch Report, 13 September 1950.

210 ANZ, R24118480, 'Old Police Record – Recording Sheets', S.56/547; ANZ, R24118481, 'Old Police Record – Recording Sheets', S.57/73.

211 ATL, MS-Papers 6218-06, 'Security Intelligence Service – Cuttings and Articles'.

212 Matthews family papers, p. 58, report by C.1., 22 November 1952.

213 SRCNZSSC, folder I/J/3, OPR 1/1/1, vol. 1, P. J. Nalder to S. G. Holland, 20 December 1954, and attached memos.

214 Yska, *All Shook Up*, pp. 51–52.

215 Megan C. Woods, 'Integrating the Nation: Gendering Maori Urbanisation and Integration, 1942–1969' (PhD thesis, University of Canterbury, 2002), pp. 82–83.

216 ANZ, R24118454, 'Old Police Record – Recording Sheets', S.47/130; ANZ, R24118460, 'Old Police Record – Recording Sheets', S.51/387; 2nd NZSIS Tranche, 'Report of Detective Sergeant R. Jones relative to Yugoslavs and Communism', 14 June 1947, pp. 257–83.

217 RHPHC, Le 22/1/121-3, Commissioner of Police to Director of Employment, 7 September 1951.

218 Steven Loveridge, 'Discerning "the Fascist Creed": Counter-subversion and Fascistic Activity in New Zealand, 1950s–1960s', *Security and Surveillance History Series*, 2015/2, pp. 1–18.

219 ANZ, R24716778, 'Miscellaneous Organisations: Fascist, Anti-Semitic, Extreme Right-Wing', memorandum for the Director of Special Branch from Secretary for Internal Affairs, 4 December 1953.

220 Peter Bland, *Sorry, I'm a Stranger Here Myself: A Memoir* (Auckland: Vintage, 2004), p. 98. In the early 1990s, after research by the Simon Wiesenthal Center, the New Zealand government set up a task force to examine reports that several dozen Nazis, including war criminals, had slipped into post-war New Zealand posing as refugees. While there were leads, the government concluded that there was insufficient evidence to prosecute. Perry Trotter, 'Nazi Hunter Reacts to Death of Local "Hero" SS-Waffen Officer', Holocaust and Anti-Semitism Foundation New Zealand, 18 August 2020 (https://holocaustfoundation. com/blog/2020/8/18/nazi-hunter-reacts-to-death-of-local-hero-ss-waffen-soldier); Neil Reid, 'Nazi War Criminals Tracked on NZ Film', *Stuff*, 30 October 2011 (www.stuff. co.nz/entertainment/film/5876440/Nazi-war-criminals-tracked-on-NZ-film).

221 Andrew Macdonald and Naomi Arnold, 'The Nazi Who Built Mount Hutt', *North & South*

(June 2021), pp. 28–47; 8th NZSIS Tranche, p. 3, Director General of Security to Richard Hill, 15 February 2021.

222 ANZ, R10074973, 'Government and Public Order – Strikes: 1951 Strike: Newspaper Reports'; ANZ, R10074974, 'Government and Public Order – Strikes: 1951 Strike: Newspaper Reports'.

223 ANZ, R24716792, 'NZ–USSR [New Zealand–Union of Soviet Socialist Republics] Society, Auckland Branch'; ANZ, R24716796, 'Society for Closer Relations with Russia, Wellington Branch'; ANZ, R24118467, 'Old Police Record – Recording Sheets', S.54/736; ANZ, R24118471, 'Old Police Record – Recording Sheets'.

224 ANZ, R25087994, 'Peace Organisations: NZ Peace Council: Official Publication "Peace"'; ANZ, R24881839, 'Peace Organisations: NZ Peace Council: National Newsletters'.

225 For examples, see ANZ, R24118468, 'Old Police Record – Recording Sheets', S.55/13; S.55/33.

226 This was told to Sherwood Young (later a Chief Inspector) by Toby Hill in 1975 when the former was writing his MA thesis on the policing of the waterfront dispute; personal communication, Young to Richard Hill, 12 December 2020.

227 ANZ, R10074975, 'Government and Public Order – Strikes: 1951 Strike: Open Letter to Government: Signatures', Commissioner of Police to the Solicitor-General, n.d.

228 See numerous examples in ANZ, R24716770, 'Protests Miscellaneous: The Rosenbergs'.

229 ANZ, R25087986, 'Bookshops & Libraries: Christchurch Co-Operative Bookshop Society Ltd'.

230 Fraser, *Seeing Red*, p. 30.

231 ANZ, R24118465, 'Old Police Record – Recording Sheets', S.53/689; ANZ, R24118472, 'Old Police Record – Recording Sheets', 55/641.

232 ANZ, R10074981, 'Government and Public Order – Strikes: 1951 Strike: Wellington Districts'. Much of this literature was collected for analysis (see ANZ, R10074976, 'Government and Public Order – Strikes: 1951 Strike: Pamphlets'; ANZ, R10074977, 'Government and Public Order – Strikes: 1951 Strike: Pamphlets'; ANZ, R10074978, 'Government and Public Order – Strikes: 1951 Strike: Pamphlets'). The many publications illegally produced sometimes allege phone tapping and mail tampering; see, for example, 'Who Uses Violence?: The Facts & a Warning: Lawless "Law and Order"', leaflet addressed 'To the People of Wellington' and 'Issued by the W.W.W.U. 5 May, 1951'.

233 Rona Bailey, 'Telling the World "the Other Side of the Story"', in David Grant (ed.), *The Big Blue: Snapshots of the 1951 Waterfront Lockout* (Wellington: Canterbury University Press, 2004), pp. 43–44. Not all raids were as inconsiderate. For example, Kay Bollinger, wife of watersiders' cartoonist Max, refused to let the constables into her sons' bedroom and Paterson agreed that this was not necessary: Grace Millar, 'Families and the 1951 New Zealand Waterfront Lockout' (PhD thesis, Victoria University of Wellington, 2013), p. 132.

234 Noel Hilliard, 'Max Bollinger – The Man behind those 1951 Cartoons', *Sites*, 16 (Autumn 1988), p. 40.

235 ANZ, R24118461, 'Old Police Record – Recording Sheets', S.51/533.

236 ANZ, R25087990, 'Miscellaneous Organisations: William Morris Group', report of [name redacted], 15 December 1953.

237 Loveridge, 'Discerning "the Fascist Creed"', pp. 11–13.

238 ANZ, R24881824, 'Miscellaneous Organisations: Esperanto Association'.

239 Fraser, *Seeing Red*, p. 68.

240 ANZ, R6721934, 'Papers about the "Newsquote" Affair of 1952', Special Branch report relative to Newsquote, 19 December 1952. For extensive coverage of the *Newsquote* affair and its aftermath,

including a compendium compiled by Hugh Price in 2004 and subsequent developments, see ATL, MS-Group-1411; MS-Papers-11453; MS-Papers-8354; and MS-Papers-8200.

241 Matthews family papers, p. 21, Keith Matthews personal file; ANZ, R6721934, 'Papers about the "Newsquote" Affair of 1952', p. 77.

242 Richard S. Hill, *State Authority, Indigenous Autonomy: Crown–Maori Relations in New Zealand/Aotearoa, 1900–1950* (Wellington: Victoria University Press, 2004), pp. 212–15, 252–53; Richard S. Hill, *Māori and the State: Crown–Māori Relations in New Zealand/ Aotearoa, 1950–2000* (Wellington: Victoria University Press, 2009), pp. 20–21, 37, 123–26, 130, 251–52; Augie Fleras, 'From Village Runanga to the New Zealand Maori Wardens', *He Whakariwhare*, no. 1 (July 1980), p. 24; Raeburn Lange, *To Promote Maori Well-Being: Tribal Committees and Executives under the Maori Social and Economic Advancement Act, 1945–1962*, Rangatiratanga Series no. 6 (Wellington: Treaty of Waitangi Research Unit, 2006), p. 23; Bryan Gilling, *Paddling Their Own Waka or Rowing the Government's Boat? The Official System for Maori Socio-Economic Development in the Post-1945 Period*, Rangatiratanga Series no. 15 (Wellington: Treaty of Waitangi Research Unit, 2008), p. 27; Graham and Susan Butterworth, *Policing and the Tangata Whenua, 1935–85*, Rangatiratanga Series no. 16 (Wellington: Treaty of Waitangi Research Unit, 2008), p. 17.

243 ANZ, R24881834, 'Peace Organisations: NZ Peace Council: History'; ANZ, R24881835, 'Peace Organisations: NZ Peace Council: Administration'.

244 ANZ, R24716792, 'NZ–USSR [New Zealand–Union of Soviet Socialist Republics] Society, Auckland Branch'.

245 ANZ, R24881829, 'Youth Organisations: Progressive Youth League'.

246 ANZ, R10074981, 'Government and Public Order – Strikes: 1951 Strike: Wellington Districts', Det-Sgt R. Jones to Insp P. J. Nalder, 6 July 1951, 9.20 am (telephone message).

247 Birchfield, *Looking for Answers*, pp. 305–7; Locke family papers, doc. 83, Elsie Locke personal file.

248 ANZ, R24118468, 'Old Police Record – Recording Sheets', S.55/235.

249 ANZ, R10074968, 'Government and Public Order – Strikes: 1951 Strike: Christchurch Districts'; ANZ, R10074981, 'Government and Public Order – Strikes: 1951 Strike: Wellington Districts'.

250 Redshaw, *Tact and Tenacity*, pp. 72–75.

251 Kelly family papers, Special Branch report, S.53/444, 25 June 1953.

252 Fraser, *Seeing Red*, pp. 110–11.

253 1st NZSIS Tranche, 'The reorganization of Special Branch', 25 July 1956, p. 73.

254 ANZ, R10074981, 'Government and Public Order – Strikes: 1951 Strike: Wellington Districts', report of Acting Detective R. Q. Petherick, Wellington, 1 June 1951.

255 ANZ, R10074966, 'Government and Public Order – Strikes: 1951 Strike: Christchurch Districts', Senior Detective J. J. Halcrow, Activities for the week ended 26 April 1951.

256 ANZ, R24881831, 'Youth Organisations: Progressive Youth League', report of Detective D. S. Paterson, 3 November 1954.

257 ANZ, R10074968, 'Government and Public Order – Strikes: 1951 Strike: Christchurch Districts', Memorandum for the Superintendent of Police Wellington, 1 June 1951.

258 1st NZSIS Tranche, 'New Zealand Police Force – Special Branch', 20 December 1954, p. 108.

259 Ibid.

260 Ibid.

261 Deery, *Spies and Sparrows*, p. 162.

262 Fraser, *Seeing Red*.

263 Ibid, passim.

264 Ibid, pp. 110–11, 114–16. For further material relating to agent George Fraser, see Hugh Price papers (box 2) in the Beaglehole Room, Victoria University of Wellington Library.

265 Fraser, *Seeing Red*, pp. 70–78.

266 Ibid., pp. 93ff.

267 Ibid., p. 65.

268 Matthews family papers, p. 58, report by C.1., 22 November 1952.

269 Fraser, *Seeing Red*, p. 113.

270 Bollinger family papers, p. 16, Conrad Bollinger personal file, memorandum of 30 April 1953; Fraser, *Seeing Red*, p. 82.

271 Conrad Bollinger's personal file provides official summaries of secret reports relating to Bollinger in the period covered by this book. Examples include C1's (Fraser's) report of 4 June 1951 noting access to his correspondence and the same agent's report of 2 June 1953 noting Bollinger's application for a position in the public service. See Bollinger family papers, pp. 30–46.

272 Fraser, *Seeing Red*, pp. 50–2.

273 In a 29 June 2009 letter, Dr Warren Tucker, director of the NZSIS, noted that Special Branch's assessment of Collins 'as a security risk was based on a suspicion that he had been an undercover member of the Communist Party in 1948 (he had been a member of the Victoria University Socialist Club) and more particularly knowledge of his continued association with "leftists" at the Vegetable Club'. Matthews family papers, pp. 20–21, Tucker to Keith Matthews.

274 Matthews family papers, p. 94, 'VEGETABLE CLUB: Associations and Activities of Members', 6 May 1953; interview, Richard Hill and Steven Loveridge with Jackie Matthews, 18 January 2022; interview, Richard Hill and Steven Loveridge with Nicola Saker, 24 April 2022.

275 For an analysis of the club and the way SB saw it, see Yska, 'Spying on New Zealand's "Vegetable Club"', pp. 1–9. See also Nicola Saker, 'The Forever Files', *North & South* (May 2022), pp. 26–35.

276 Taylor family papers, pp. 3–5, Keith Matthews to Nigel Taylor, 4 March 1951, attached to Detective Sergeant [name redacted] to Officer-in-charge, Special Branch, Wellington, 6 February 1957.

277 Matthews family papers, pp. 42ff., Assistant Commissioner, Metropolitan Police Office (Special Branch) to Commissioner of Police, Wellington, 9 October 1950; 'KEITH TAYLOR MATTHEWS LL. B', report 5 May 1953; Matthews to Taylor, 4 March 1951.

278 Matthews family papers, pp. 59, 68, report of D. S. Paterson, 29 October 1951. In later years Nancy Taylor wrote the official New Zealand War History of service on the home front.

279 Matthews family papers, 'Summary of activity – Veg. Club File to 3rd February 1955'; report of D. S. Paterson, 5 June 1952.

280 Matthews family papers, p. 94, 'VEGETABLE CLUB: Associations and Activities of Members', report of 6 May 1953.

281 Interviews with Clare Taylor and Nicola Saker by Richard Hill and Steven Loveridge on 1 and 10 February 2022 respectively. See too, Taylor family papers, pp. 62–63, Nigel Taylor personal file. There are contradictions in different reports of the same meetings with regard to lists of attendees, possibly due to informants leaving themselves out of the listings. Comparing reports and their lists later helped members or their families identify those they believed to be most likely to be informants. This paragraph is also partly based on Richard Hill's discussions with former Vegetable Club members, including Jackie Matthews and the late Dorian Saker, and with the late Hugh Price, Zygmunt Frankel and Hector MacNeill.

282 Matthews family papers, p. 96, 'VEGETABLE CLUB', 6 May 1953 report. List of attendees

and dates of attendance were accumulated (see, for example, 'VEGETABLE CLUB: Associations and Activities of Members', 30 April 1954 report, Matthews family papers, p. 70).

283   1st NZSIS Tranche, 'New Zealand Police Force – Special Branch', 20 December 1954, p. 108.

284   Fraser, *Seeing Red*, pp. 100–101.

285   1st NZSIS Tranche, 'The New Zealand Security Service', 13 March 1956, p. 95.

286   1st NZSIS Tranche, 'New Zealand Police Force – Special Branch', 20 December 1954, p. 108.

287   *People's Voice*, 29 June 1955, pp. 1, 4–5.

288   7th NZSIS Tranche, 'Henry Togson GUY – employed as undercover agent from 15th September, 1954 to 22nd June, 1955, and known as Samuel LEE or "S.1"', 20 March 1956, pp. 8–9; 'report of D. S. Paterson relative to Police Undercover Source in Communist Party – S.1', 29 June 1955, pp. 36–37.

289   ATL, MS-Papers 6218-06, 'Security Intelligence Service – Cuttings and articles'; *Subversive Activity: A Statement by the New Zealand Council for Civil Liberties* (Petone: Valley Printing Company, 1955).

290   ANZ, R24118469, 'Old Police Record – Recording Sheets', S.55/413.

291   NZPD, vol. 308, 2 May 1956, p. 574.

292   Fraser, *Seeing Red*, pp. 99–101.

293   1st NZSIS Tranche, 'New Zealand Police Force – Special Branch', 20 December 1954, p. 108.

294   NZPD, vol. 305, 3 May 1955, p. 730. From time to time, the CPNZ provided accounts of phone tapping and covert eavesdropping dating back to the 1951 waterfront dispute. For examples, see *People's Voice*, 29 June 1955, p. 3 and 21 July 1980, p. 7. Some unionists claimed police awareness of knowledge that had only been shared over phones. See, for example, *The Building Worker*, 5 August 1951, p. 6.

295   See, for example, Bollinger family papers, p. 37, Conrad Bollinger personal file.

296   Matthews family papers, p. 96, 'VEGETABLE CLUB', 6 May 1953.

297   Yska, 'Collaboration between *Truth* and the Police Special Branch/Security Intelligence Service', p. 4.

298   ANZ, R10074981, 'Government and Public Order – Strikes: 1951 Strike: Wellington Districts', report of Acting Detective J. W. McGuire, 25 May 1951.

299   ANZ, R24118458, 'Old Police Record – Recording Sheets'; ANZ, R24118455, 'Old Police Record – Recording Sheets'.

300   ANZ, R24118468, 'Old Police Record – Recording Sheets', S.55/134. There is a large literature on Norman. For contrasting views, see James Barros, *No Sense of Evil: Espionage: The Case of Herbert Norman* (Toronto: Deneau Publishers, 1986) and Roger Bowen, *Innocence Is Not Enough: The Life and Death of Herbert Norman* (Vancouver: Douglas & McIntyre, 1986).

301   Lynne Joiner, *Honorable Survivor: Mao's China, McCarthy's America, and the Persecution of John S. Service* (Annapolis: Naval Institute Press, 2009), pp. 211–12, 218, 297.

302   Gregory S. Kealey and Kerry A. Taylor, 'After Gouzenko and "The Case": Canada, Australia and New Zealand at the Secret Commonwealth Security Conferences of 1948 and 1951', in Dennis G. Molinaro (ed.), *The Bridge in the Parks: The Five Eyes and Cold War Counter-Intelligence* (Toronto: University of Toronto Press, 2022), p. 34.

303   TNA, PREM 8/1343, summary report of the 1951 Commonwealth Security Conference. See too, Kealey and Taylor, 'After Gouzenko', pp. 23–25.

304   Kealey and Taylor, 'After Gouzenko', pp. 31–33. David Paterson later recalled that Todor Kremic ran the national Aliens Register in the premises shared by the Wellington District and Head Offices of

SB: SRCNZSSC, folder I/J/3, Paterson to Sherwood Young, 24 June 1991.

305 Kelly family papers, Tranche Two, report on 'CATHERINE VERA EICHELBAUM, B.A.', 1 May 1953, S 52/398; and Sir Percy Sillitoe to J. Bruce Young, 4 April 1952.

306 Hunt, *Spies and Revolutionaries*, p. 311.

307 ANZ, R24118466, 'Old Police Record – Recording Sheets', S54/77.

308 ANZ, R24881823, 'Communist Party NZ, Wellington, Social Functions'.

309 ANZ, R24118464, 'Old Police Record – Recording Sheets'.

310 ANZ, R25087985, 'Communist Party of NZ: Wellington District: Membership & Recruitment', memorandum for the Superintendent of Police Wellington, 6 September 1950.

311 Butterworth, *More Than Law and Order*, pp. 30, 43–45; Parker, *The S.I.S.*, pp. 16–20. The Joint Intelligence Sub-Committee in London felt that the CPNZ's 'influence in New Zealand politics is said to be remarkable considering its number, and to be growing': 'The Spread of Communism Throughout the World and the Extent of its Direction from Moscow: Report by the Joint Intelligence Sub-Committee', J.I.C. (46) 70 (Final), CAB 81/133, 23 September 1946, in *Secret Files From World Wars to Cold War*.

312 Sometimes personal files were opened on a married couple, but these were generally later split into individual files if both parties were politically active.

313 ANZ, R10074969, 'Government and Public Order – Strikes: 1951 Strike: Christchurch Districts', report of Senior Detective J. J. Halcrow, 17 May 1951.

314 1st NZSIS Tranche, 'The Reorganization of Special Branch', 25 July 1956, p. 80.

315 1st NZSIS Tranche, 'Report of D. S. Paterson relative to threats to New Zealand Security', p. 156.

316 Matthews family papers, p. 98, 'VEGETABLE CLUB', 6 May 1953.

317 Bollinger family papers, p. 11, Conrad Bollinger personal file, 'REPORT of Constable A. E. V. Lane relative to VICTORIA UNIVERSITY COLLEGE', 9 July 1952.

318 ANZ, R10074981, 'Government and Public Order – Strikes: 1951 Strike: Wellington Districts', report of Detective D. S. Paterson, 14 March 1951.

319 Locke family papers, doc. 98, Elsie Locke personal file, 're COMMUNISTS and LEFTISTS, CHRISTCHURCH: General information acquired during period 2nd to 27th June, 1956'.

320 ANZ, R10074969, 'Government and Public Order – Strikes: 1951 Strike: Christchurch Districts', report of J. C. Fletcher Senior Sergeant, Christchurch Police Station, 7 June 1951.

321 ANZ, R10074981, 'Government and Public Order – Strikes: 1951 Strike: Wellington Districts', report of Detective D. S. Paterson, 4 April 1951.

322 ANZ, R10074981, 'Government and Public Order – Strikes: 1951 Strike: Wellington Districts', report of Detective A. W. Baker, 15 June 1951.

323 Locke family papers, doc. 99, Elsie Locke personal file, 'COMMUNIST PARTY and ANCILLARY ORGANISATIONS, CHRISTCHURCH: activities during the period 30/6/55 to 6/7/55'.

324 1st NZSIS Tranche, 'New Zealand Police Force – Special Branch', 20 December 1954, p. 108.

325 Fraser, *Seeing Red*, p. 31.

326 Ibid., p. 80.

327 ANZ, R24118470, 'Old Police Record – Recording Sheets', S.55/505.

328 Fraser, *Seeing Red*, p. 96.

329 ANZ, R10074981, 'Government and Public Order – Strikes: 1951 Strike: Wellington

Districts', Commissioner of Police to the Superintendent of Police Wellington, 6 April 1951.

330 Yska, 'Spying on New Zealand's "Vegetable Club"', p. 6; J. E. Traue to Richard Hill, 1 February 2022.

331 'Four officers are employed on records and two officers on vetting work.' 1st NZSIS Tranche, 'The Reorganization of Special Branch', 25 July 1956, p. 80.

332 1st NZSIS Tranche, 'The Security Organisation in New Zealand', 31 August 1954, p. 126.

333 Butterworth, *More Than Law and Order*, p. 43.

334 1st NZSIS Tranche, 'The Reorganization of Special Branch', 25 July 1956, p. 69.

335 Interview, Richard Hill and Steven Loveridge with former NZSIS officer 'A', 7 November 2017. Furthermore, it was noted that 75 per cent of vetting relates to Defence personnel, with the remainder constituted by Foreign Affairs, Customs and Cabinet.

336 1st NZSIS Tranche, 'Defence of the Realm – Security Organisation', 18 May 1948, p. 213.

337 1st NZSIS Tranche, 'Notes on the Security Service', 4 July 1952, p. 141.

338 1st NZSIS Tranche, 'The New Zealand Security Service', 13 March 1956, p. 95.

339 1st NZSIS Tranche, 'The Work of Special Branch', 5 November 1953, p. 137.

340 1st NZSIS Tranche, 'The Security Problem in New Zealand', May 1956, p. 55.

341 Fraser, *Seeing Red*, pp. 115–16.

342 Dick Scott, 'The Propaganda War', in Grant, *The Big Blue*, p. 34.

343 1st NZSIS Tranche, 'The Reorganization of Special Branch', 25 July 1956, p. 69.

344 Kealey and Taylor, 'After Gouzenko', p. 32.

345 Cited in Lenihan, '"Different Tones of Voice"', p. 11.

346 1st NZSIS Tranche, 'The New Zealand Security Service', 13 March 1956, p. 94.

347 Lenihan, '"Different Tones of Voice"', p. 13.

348 Fraser, *Seeing Red*, p. 45.

349 Parker, *The S.I.S.*, p. 15; Interview, Richard Hill and Steven Loveridge with former NZSIS officers 'A' and 'B', 12 October 2017.

350 1st NZSIS Tranche, 'Notes on the Security Service', 4 July 1952, p. 141.

351 1st NZSIS Tranche, 'The Security Organisation in New Zealand', 31 August 1954, p. 125.

352 ANZ, R10074969, 'Government and Public Order – Strikes: 1951 Strike: Christchurch Districts', report of Detective Sergeant A. R. Grant, Special Branch Christchurch, 29 August 1952.

353 Ernest Volkman, *The History of Espionage: The Clandestine World of Surveillance, Spying and Intelligence, from Ancient Times to the Post-9/11 World* (London: Carlton Books, 2007), p. 177; Christopher Andrew and Julius Green, *Stars and Spies: Intelligence Operations and the Entertainment Business* (London: The Bodley Head, 2021), p. 247.

354 RHPHC, EA(PM) 61/20/4 pt. 1, High Commissioner to Minister of External Affairs, telegram of 23 January 1956.

355 Christopher Andrew and Oleg Gordievsky, *KGB: The Inside Story of its Foreign Operations from Lenin to Gorbachev* (New York: HarperCollins Publishers, 1990), p. 662.

356 Parker, *The S.I.S.*, p. 23; S. W. Scott, *Rebel in a Wrong Cause* (Auckland: Collins, 1960), pp. 200–201.

357 1st NZSIS Tranche, 'A Note on the Security Situation in New Zealand', 31 August 1954, p. 120.

358 High Commissioner to Minister of External Affairs, telegrams of 20 and 23 January 1956, and other papers in RHPHC, EA(PM) 61/20/4 pt. 1; see too, RHPHC, EA(PM) 61/280/5, Secretary of External Affairs to Minister of External Affairs, 10 July 1950 and other papers.

359 RHPHC, High Commissioner to Minister of External Affairs, telegrams of 23 January 1956.

360 Fraser, *Seeing Red*, p. 78.

361 Scott, *Rebel in a Wrong Cause*, pp. 200–201.

362 Yska papers, Dossier of Declassified NZ US Embassy documents 1945–1960; Burke, 'Towards the Conception of the New Zealand Security Service', p. 6.

363 Central Intelligence Agency, 'Communist Influence in New Zealand', sanitised copy approved for release, 30 June 1949. Available at www.cia.gov/readingroom/document/cia-rdp78-01617a003600030002-7

364 Francis Wevers and Dean Parker (directors), *Shattered Dreams* (Trade Union History Project, 1990). Available online from Ngā Taonga Sound & Vision (https://ngataonga.org.nz/collections/catalogue/catalogue-item?record_id=72458).

365 Burke, 'Towards the Conception of the New Zealand Security Service', p. 6; Taylor, 'The Secret State', pp. 140–41.

366 Further details regarding ongoing CIA interest in New Zealand can be seen in sanitised releases: https://www.cia.gov/readingroom/home

367 Dick Scott, *151 Days: History of the Great Waterfront Lockout and Supporting Strikes, February 15–July 15 1951* (Auckland: New Zealand Waterside Workers' Union Deregistered, 1952), p. 196.

368 See 'Clandestine Services History: Civil Air Transport (CAT): A Proprietary Airline, 1946–1955', available at Scribd (www.scribd.com/document/341923971/Clandestine-Services-History#from_embed).

369 Hunt, *Spies and Revolutionaries*, pp. 195–200; Lenihan, 'Paddy Costello: What the Papers Say' (June 2012), pp. 37–42, available at Kiwi Spies (http://kiwispies.com/pdfs/Costello-August14-2.pdf).

370 Lenihan, '"Different Tones of Voice"', p. 4; Ian McGibbon, 'The MI5 Verdict', *New Zealand International Review*, vol. 42, no. 6 (November/December 2017), p. 10.

371 Lenihan, '"Different Tones of Voice"', pp. 1–21.

372 Christopher Andrew and Vasili Mitrokhin, *The Mitrokhin Archive: The KGB in Europe and the West* (London: Allen Lane at the Penguin Press, 1999), pp. 534, 600, 864, 878; Lenihan, '"Different Tones of Voice"', pp. 3–6. See also Trevor Barnes, *Dead Doubles: The Extraordinary Worldwide Hunt for One of the Cold War's Most Notorious Spy Rings* (New York: Harper, 2020), pp. 202–5, 253; Lenihan, 'Paddy Costello: What the Papers Say'.

373 McNeish, *The Sixth Man*; Ken Ross, 'Alister McIntosh's "Best" Diplomat', *New Zealand International Review*, vol. 42, no. 6 (November/December 2017), pp. 2–5; Rita Ricketts, 'Esprit de Contradiction', *New Zealand International Review*, vol. 42, no. 6 (November/December 2017), pp. 6–9.

374 McNeish, *The Sixth Man*, p. 367.

375 Lenihan, '"Different Tones of Voice"', p. 1.

376 Vincent O'Sullivan (ed.), *Intersecting Lines: The Memoirs of Ian Milner* (Wellington: Victoria University Press, 1993), p. 188.

377 Frank Cain, 'The Making of a Cold War Victim', *Overland*, vol. 134 (Autumn 1994), pp. 60–66; James McNeish, *Dance of the Peacocks: New Zealanders in Exile in the Time of Hitler and Mao Tse-Tung* (Auckland: Vintage, 2003), pp. 321–29; O'Sullivan, *Intersecting Lines*, pp. 23–30; Aaron Fox, 'The Pedigree of Truth: Western Intelligence Agencies *versus* Ian Frank George Milner and William Ball Sutch', in Alexander Trapeznik and Aaron Fox (eds), *Lenin's Legacy Down Under: New Zealand's Cold War* (Dunedin: University of Otago Press, 2004), pp. 116–24.

378 Robert Manne, *The Petrov Affair: Politics and Espionage* (Sydney: Pergamon Press, 1987); Denis Lenihan, 'Was Ian Milner a Spy? A Review of the Evidence', *Kōtare* (2008), pp. 1–18; Mike Hanley, 'Ian Milner: A New

Zealand Traitor', *New Zealand Defence Quarterly* (Winter 1999), pp. 31–33; Richard Hall, *The Rhodes Scholar Spy* (Milsons Point, NSW: Random House, 1991); Desmond Ball and David Horner, *Breaking the Codes: Australia's KGB Network, 1944–1950* (St Leonards, NSW: Allen & Unwin, 1998); Horner, *The Spy Catchers*, p. 99; Hunt, *Spies and Revolutionaries*, pp. 218–26.

379 Horner, *The Spy Catchers*, pp. 471–75; Desmond Ball, 'The Spy Who Came Out as Klod', *The Australian*, 24 December 2011, p. 5.

380 Horner, *The Spy Catchers*, pp. 295–96. See too, Phillip Deery, 'Cold War Victim or Rhodes Scholar Spy?', *Overland*, vol. 147 (June 1997), pp. 9–12.

381 Gaitanos, *Shirley Smith*, p. 232.

382 Fox, 'The Pedigree of Truth', p. 127.

383 Gaitanos, *Shirley Smith*, p. 235.

384 John Marshall, *Memoirs Volume Two: 1960–1988* (Auckland: William Collins, 1989), p. 145.

385 Sinclair, *Walter Nash*, pp. 341–42.

386 Fox, 'The Price of Collective Security', p. 123.

387 RHPHC, WN bundle 2304, 'Report of Detective R. D. L. Jones, relative to Communist Party activities in Auckland', 6 March 1946, annexed to Commissioner to Prime Minister, 11 March 1946.

388 Saker family papers, Dorian Saker personal file.

389 Einhorn family papers, pp. 28, 74, 76 and passim, Helmut Einhorn and Ester Einhorn personal file; information from Barbara Einhorn. For details on the Criticus affair see Murray Horton, 'Wolfgang Rosenberg', *Watchdog*, vol. 114 (May 2007), p. 30; Murray Horton, 'F. P. Walsh, Special Branch & Wolf Rosenberg', *Watchdog*, vol. 69 (April 1992), p. 27.

390 McNeish, 'Hidden History', p. 89; Yska, 'Spying on New Zealand's "Vegetable Club"', pp. 6–7.

391 Yska, 'Spying on New Zealand's "Vegetable Club"', p. 7. Matthews' Law Society obituary records: 'In addition to being a fine lawyer, Dick served his profession as President of the Wellington District Law Society in 1970 (he was involved with the WDLS Council in various roles for 10 years), and as a member of the New Zealand Law Practitioners' Disciplinary Tribunal for six years. He was Vice-President of the New Zealand Law Society for three years. He was chairman of Television One, the forerunner of Television New Zealand, and a member of the Board of the New Zealand Broadcasting Corporation and the Crown Forestry Rental Trust. He was chairman of the NZLS ethics committee, and president of the Wellington Medico-Legal Society. He was awarded the CBE in 1987.' See New Zealand Law Society, 'Richard Gray Collins CBE, 1921–2007' (www.lawsociety. org.nz/news-and-communications/people-in-the-law/obituaries/obituaries-list/richard-gray-collins-cbe,-1921-2007).

392 Matthews family papers, p. 21, Dr Warren Tucker to Keith Matthews, 29 June 2009.

393 ATL, MS-Papers-8661-2, 'Goodbye Diplomacy', pp. 36–41; there are several versions of how McIntosh allowed Lake to see his file. One, narrated by Conrad Bollinger to Brian Easton, has McIntosh arranging to leave his own office unattended for a considerable period of time while Lake was awaiting his return (personal communication, Brian Easton to Richard Hill, 19 October 2021).

394 McNeish, 'Hidden History', pp. 88–89.

395 Alistair Shaw, 'Telling the Truth About People's China' (PhD thesis, Victoria University of Wellington, 2010), p. 200.

396 See, for example, *New Zealand Weekly News*, 10 February 1969, pp. 12–13; *Canta*, March 1972, p. 8. Lake's positions on Mao's China also received some critical responses. See *Truth*, 10 December 1968, pp. 1, 13; Brian Edwards, *The Public Eye* (Wellington: A. H. & A. W. Reed, 1971), p. 68.

397 Taylor family papers, especially pp. 75, 80, 92–97, Nigel Taylor personal file.

398 Fraser, *Seeing Red*, p. 69.

399 ANZ, R6721934, 'Papers about the "Newsquote" Affair of 1952', p. 7.

400 Fraser, *Seeing Red*, p. 69.

401 ANZ, R6721934, 'Papers about the "Newsquote" Affair of 1952', pp. 85–86.

402 Fraser, *Seeing Red*, p. 70.

403 Hugh Price, *The Plot to Subvert Wartime New Zealand: The True Story of Syd Ross and His Impudent Hoax that Convulsed New Zealand and put a Shine into the Darkest Days of WWII, and that the Commissioner of Police Declared "Beyond Comprehension" A Hoax, moreover, that was Extended to Challenge the Rule of Law in the Dominion* (Wellington: Victoria University Press, 2006).

404 ANZ, R6721934, 'Papers about the "Newsquote" Affair of 1952', p. 43 and passim; ATL, MS-Papers-11453, 'Further papers relating to the Newsquote affair', Dr Warren Tucker to Hugh Price, 6 November 2009.

405 ANZ, R10074968, 'Government and Public Order – Strikes: 1951 Strike: Christchurch Districts', report of Detective Sergeant R. Jones, 4 March 1951; various sources supplied information about safeguarding union funds.

406 Williams/Birchfield family papers, f. 53, Albert and Constance Birchfield personal files.

407 Locke family papers, docs. 99–102, Elsie Locke personal file, Christchurch informant reports covering the period 13 June to 11 August 1955.

408 *People's Voice*, 6 July 1955, p. 1.

409 This is based on conversations and interviews with a great many people who had personal files established on them. A similar reaction has occurred in allied jurisdictions; see, for example, accounts by 'leading Australians' in Meredith Burgmann (ed.), *Dirty Secrets: Our ASIO Files* (Sydney: UNSW Press, 2014).

410 RHPHC, Percy Allison to Rona Bailey, 7 May 1988, attached to Rona Bailey's note to Richard Hill, n.d.

411 Stuart Macintyre, *The Party: The Communist Party of Australia from Heyday to Reckoning* (Crows Nest, NSW: Allen & Unwin, 2022), p. 23.

412 John Ferris, *Behind the Enigma: The Authorised History of GCHQ, Britain's Secret Cyber-Intelligence Agency* (London: Bloomsbury Publishing, 2020), pp. 324, 376.

Concluding Remarks

1 1st NZSIS Tranche, 'New Zealand Police Force – Special Branch', 20 December 1954, p. 108.

2 Editorial Comment, 'The Neutrality of Belgium', *American Journal of International Law*, vol. 9, no. 3 (July 1915), p. 709.

3 Alex Frame, *Salmond: Southern Jurist* (Wellington: Victoria University Press, 1995), p. 167 and passim.

4 These are reproduced as endpapers in Richard S. Hill, *Policing the Colonial Frontier: The Theory and Practice of Coercive Social and Racial Control in New Zealand, 1767–1867* (Wellington: Historical Publications Branch, Department of Internal Affairs, 1986).

Bibliography

PRIMARY SOURCES

Archives and Official Papers

Alexander Turnbull Library, The National Library of New Zealand Te Puna Mātauranga o Aotearoa

Archives New Zealand Te Rua Mahara o te Kāwanatanga

Beaglehole Room, Victoria University of Wellington Library Te Pātaka Kōrero

Government Communications Security Bureau Te Tira Tiaki: Papers released to the authors

Mitchell Library, State Library of New South Wales, Australia

New Zealand Security Intelligence Service Te Pā Whakamarumaru: papers released to the authors in tranches

The National Archives, United Kingdom

The New Zealand Police Museum

Official Publications

Appendices to the Journals of the House of Representatives

Manual of the War Legislation of New Zealand: Comprising Acts of Parliament, Proclamations, Orders in Council, and other Instruments Passed, Issued, and Made in Consequence of the War, and in Force on 30th September, 1916 (Wellington: Government Printer, 1916)

New Zealand Gazette

New Zealand Official Year Book

New Zealand Parliamentary Debates

New Zealand Police Gazette

New Zealand Statutes

Rules and Regulations of the Constabulary Force of New Zealand (Wellington: R. Stokes, 1852)

The Police Force Act, 1913, Police Force Amendment Act, 1919, and Regulations Made Thereunder for the Guidance of the Police Force of New Zealand (Wellington: Government Printer, 1920)

Newspapers and Periodicals

Auckland Star

Canta

Colonist

Daily Southern Cross

Dominion

Evening Post

Evening Star

Feilding Star

Greymouth Evening Star

Manawatu Standard

Manawatu Times

Maoriland Worker

Mataura Ensign

Nelson Evening Mail

New Zealand Free Lance

New Zealand Herald

New Zealand Listener

New Zealand Observer

New Zealand Observer and Free Lance

New Zealand Weekly News

New Zealand Worker

Northland Age

NZ Truth

Ohinemuri Gazette

Otago Daily Times

Patea and Waverley Press

People's Voice

Poverty Bay Herald

Public Service Journal

Sun

Taranaki Daily News

The Australian

The Building Worker

The Guardian

The Marlborough Express

The Times Literary Supplement

Timaru Herald

Wanganui Chronicle

Wanganui Herald

Interviews

Retired NZSIS officer 'A'; retired NZSIS officer 'B'; Arnold Butterworth; Graeme Dunstall; Jackie Matthews; Tina Matthews; Nicola Saker; Clare Taylor; and other confidential interviewees.

Family Papers
(including personal files released by the NZSIS)

Bollinger family papers

Einhorn family papers

Jakich family papers

Kelly family papers

Locke family papers

Martin/Kelly family papers

Matthews family papers

Rosenberg family papers

Saker family papers

Taylor family papers

Williams/Birchfield family papers

Private Collections

Graeme Dunstall papers

David Filer papers

Aaron Fox papers

Sarah Gaitanos papers

Ray Grover papers

Richard Hill Police History Collection

Hugh Price papers

Stout Research Centre for New Zealand Studies Security Collection

Sherwood Young papers

Redmer Yska papers

SECONDARY SOURCES

Articles

Ball, Des, 'The Spy Who Came Out as Klod', *The Australian*, 24 September 2011.

Barber, Laurie, 'Map Making in Maoriland: Military Intelligence in the First New Zealand War', *New Zealand Legacy*, vol. 2, no. 2 (1990), pp. 22–24.

Beaglehole, Tim, 'Beaglehole, John Cawte', *The Dictionary of New Zealand Biography, Volume Five* (Auckland: Auckland University Press, 2000), pp. 43–45.

———, 'Hunter, Thomas Anderson', *The Dictionary of New Zealand Biography, Volume Three* (Auckland: Auckland University Press, 1996), pp. 241–43.

Behringer, Paul Welch, 'Forewarned is Forearmed: Intelligence, Japan's Siberian Intervention, and the Washington Conference', *International History Review*, vol. 38, issue 3 (2016), pp. 367–93.

Bell, Duncan, 'Agnostic Democracy and the Politics of Memory', *Constellations*, vol. 15, no. 1 (2008), pp. 148–66.

———, 'Mythscapes: Memory, Mythology, and National Identity', *British Journal of Sociology*, vol. 54, issue 1 (March 2003), pp. 63–81.

Bennett, James, 'The Contamination of Arcadia?: Class, Trans-national Interactions and the Construction of Identity, 1890–1913', *New Zealand Journal of History*, vol. 33, no. 1 (1999), pp. 20–42.

Burke, David, 'Towards the Conception of the New Zealand Security Service: UK and US Involvement in New Zealand's Early Cold War Security Concerns', *Security and Surveillance History Series*, 2017/2, pp. 1–10.

Butterworth, Graham and Susan, *Policing and the Tangata Whenua, 1935–85*, Rangatiratanga Series no. 16 (Wellington: Treaty of Waitangi Research Unit, 2008).

Cain, Frank, 'The Making of a Cold War Victim', *Overland*, vol. 134 (Autumn 1994), pp. 60–66.

Campbell, R. M., 'In the Name of National Security', *Listener*, 23 February 1974, p. 9.

Cooke, Peter, 'Home Guard', in Ian McGibbon (ed.), *The Oxford Companion to New Zealand Military History* (Auckland: Oxford University Press, 2000), pp. 220–23.

Corbett, P. D., 'Friendly Visit or Rehearsing for Attack?: The Great White Fleet in New Zealand, 1908', *Forts and Works*, no. 13 (February 2002), pp. 1–12.

Cox, Deborah, 'Women in the Armed Forces', in Ian McGibbon (ed.), *The Oxford Companion to New Zealand Military History* (Auckland: Oxford University Press, 2000), pp. 620–24.

Crawford, John, 'Overt and Covert Military Involvement in the 1890 Maritime Strike and 1913 Waterfront Strike in New Zealand', *Labour History*, no. 60 (May 1991), pp. 66–83.

Crawford, John, and James Watson, '"The Most Appeasing Line": New Zealand and Nazi Germany, 1935–40', *Journal of Imperial and Commonwealth History*, vol. 38, no. 1 (2010), pp. 75–97.

Cunningham, Matthew, 'Conservative Protest or Conservative Radicalism? The New Zealand Legion in a Comparative Context, 1930–1935', *Journal of New Zealand Studies*, vol. 10 (2011), pp. 139–58.

Cutler, Andrew, '*Tomorrow* Magazine and New Zealand Politics 1934–1940', *New Zealand Journal of History*, vol. 24, no. 1 (1990), pp. 22–44.

Davidson, Allan K., 'Scrimgeour, Colin Graham', *The Dictionary of New Zealand Biography, Volume Four* (Auckland: Auckland University Press, 1998), pp. 465–66.

Deery, Phillip, 'Cold War Victim or Rhodes Scholar Spy?', *Overland*, vol. 147 (June 1997), pp. 9–12.

Derby, Mark, 'Strikes and Labour Disputes – the 1912 and 1913 Strikes', *Te Ara – the Encyclopedia of New Zealand* (www.TeAra.govt.nz/en/strikes-and-labour-disputes/page-5).

Dunstall, Graeme, 'Frontier and/or Cultural Fragment? Interpretations of Violence in Colonial New Zealand', *Social History*, vol. 29, no. 1 (2004), pp. 59–83.

———, 'Compton, Eric Henry', *The Dictionary of New Zealand Biography, Volume Five* (Auckland: Auckland University Press, 2000), pp. 110–11.

———, 'Young, John Bruce', *The Dictionary of New Zealand Biography, Volume Five* (Auckland: Auckland University Press, 2000), pp. 582–83.

———, 'Cummings, Denis Joseph', *The Dictionary of New Zealand Biography, Volume Four* (Auckland: Auckland University Press, 1998), pp. 120–22.

———, 'McIlveney, William Bernard', *The Dictionary of New Zealand Biography, Volume Four* (Auckland: Auckland University Press, 1998), pp. 311–12.

———, 'Wohlmann, Ward George', *The Dictionary of New Zealand Biography, Volume Four* (Auckland: Auckland University Press, 1998), pp. 570–71.

———, 'O'Donovan, John', *The Dictionary of New Zealand Biography, Volume Three* (Auckland: Auckland University Press, 1996), pp. 370–71.

Editorial Comment, 'The Neutrality of Belgium', *American Journal of International Law*, vol. 9, no. 3 (July 1915), pp. 707–20.

Edwards, Peter, 'The Impact of the Hope Royal Commissions of the 1970s and 1980s on Australia's Intelligence Agencies Today', *History Australia*, vol .18, no. 1 (2021), pp. 32–41.

Everest-Phillips, Max, 'The Pre-War Fear of Japanese Espionage: Its Impact and Legacy', *Journal of Contemporary History*, vol. 42, no. 2 (2007), pp. 243–65.

Filer, David, 'Signals Intelligence in New Zealand during World War II', *Security and Surveillance History Series*, 2019/2, pp. 1–6.

———, 'Signals Intelligence in New Zealand during the Cold War', *Security and Surveillance History Series*, 2019/1, pp. 1–9.

———, 'Civil–Military Cooperation in Signals Intelligence in New Zealand, 1904 to 1939', *Security and Surveillance History Series*, 2017/4, pp. 1–5.

———, 'The Joint Intelligence Office, the Joint Intelligence Bureau and the External Intelligence Bureau, 1949–1980: An Insider's Account of the First Three Decades of a Small Intelligence Agency', *Security and Surveillance History Series*, 2016/3, pp. 1–7.

———, 'The Great Spy Lie', *New Zealand Listener*, 25 September 1982, pp. 18–19.

Fleras, Augie, 'From Village Runanga to the New Zealand Maori Wardens', *He Whakariwhare*, no. 1 (July 1980).

Foster, Bernard and Hebert Roth, 'Riots', in A. H. McLintock (ed.), *An Encyclopaedia of New Zealand, Volume 3* (Wellington: R. E. Owen, Government Printer, 1966), pp. 85–87.

Fox, Aaron, '"A Formidable Responsibility": The Rise and Fall of the New Zealand Security Intelligence Bureau 1940–1945', *Security and Surveillance History Series*, 2018/1, pp. 1–32.

Francis, Andrew, 'Willingly to War: British and Imperial Boys' Story Papers, 1905–1914', *Notes, Books, Authors*, no. 10 (2007).

Gillespie, Alexander, and Claire Breen, 'The Security Intelligence Agencies in New Zealand: Evaluation, Challenges and Progress', *Intelligence and National Security*, vol. 36, no. 5 (2021), pp. 676–95.

Gilling, Bryan, *Paddling Their Own Waka or Rowing the Government's Boat? The Official System for Maori Socio-Economic Development in the Post-1945 Period*, Rangatiratanga Series no. 15 (Wellington: Treaty of Waitangi Research Unit, 2008).

Goldstone, Paul, 'Begg, Robert Campbell', *The Dictionary of New Zealand Biography, Volume Four* (Auckland: Auckland University Press, 1998), pp. 44–45.

Grant, David, 'Burton, Ormond Edward', *The Dictionary of New Zealand Biography, Volume Five* (Auckland: Auckland University Press, 2000), pp. 80–82.

Hager, Nicky, 'The Origins of Signals Intelligence in New Zealand', *Centre for Peace Studies Working Paper*, no. 5 (August 1995), pp. 1–26.

Hancock, B. R., 'The New Zealand Security Intelligence Service', *Auckland University Law Review*, 1973/1, pp. 1–34.

Hanley, Mike, 'Ian Milner: A New Zealand Traitor', *New Zealand Defence Quarterly* (Winter 1999), pp. 31–33.

Harris, Paul, 'The New Zealand Unemployed Workers Movement, 1931–1939: Gisborne and the Relief Workers' Strike', *New Zealand Journal of History*, vol. 10, no. 2 (1976), pp. 130–42.

Hill, Richard S., 'A State of Exception: Declaring "Lawless Law" in Early Twentieth Century New Zealand', *Labour History Project Bulletin*, no. 59 (December 2013), pp. 17–20.

———, '"The Taming of Wild Man": Policing Colonial Peoples in the Nineteenth Century', in *Empire, Identity and Control: Two Inaugural Lectures, Occasional Paper Series*, no. 13 (Wellington: Stout Research Centre for New Zealand Studies, 2007).

———, 'Cullen, John', *The Dictionary of New Zealand Biography, Volume Three* (Auckland: Auckland University Press, 1996), pp. 125–27.

———, 'Dinnie, Walter', *The Dictionary of New Zealand Biography, Volume Three* (Auckland: Auckland University Press, 1996), pp. 134–35.

———, 'Tunbridge, John Bennett', *The Dictionary of New Zealand Biography, Volume Two* (Auckland: Auckland University Press, 1996), pp. 551–52.

Hilliard, Noel, 'Max Bollinger – The Man behind those 1951 Cartoons', *Sites*, 16 (Autumn 1988), pp. 37–43.

Hindmarsh, Gerard, 'Death Ray or Bedtime Story – The Curious Case of Victor Penny', *Stuff* (www.stuff.co.nz/national/114876175/death-ray-or-bedtime-story--the-curious-case-of-victor-penny).

Hoare, Nicholas, 'Harry Holland's "Samoan Complex"', *Journal of Pacific History*, vol. 49, no. 2 (2014), pp. 151–69.

Horton, Murray, 'Wolfgang Rosenberg', *Watchdog*, vol. 114 (May 2007).

———, 'F. P. Walsh, Special Branch & Wolf Rosenberg', *Watchdog*, vol. 69 (April 1992).

———, 'The Secret History of WW2' (http://legacy.disarmsecure.org/The%20Secret%20History%20of%20WWII%20M%20Horton.pdf).

Jackson, Aaron Robert, 'Socialism Tells Its Own Story: Ian Milner and the Dream of a Redeemed Socialism in the Prague Spring', *New Zealand Journal of History*, vol. 55, no. 2 (2021), pp. 3–31.

Kano, Fugio, and Maurice Ward, 'Socialism is a Mission: Max Bickerton's Involvement with the Japanese Communist Party and Translation of Japanese Proletarian Literature in the 1930s', *New Zealand Journal of Asian Studies*, vol. 16, no. 2 (December 2014), pp. 99–120.

Kitson, Simon, 'Political Policing', *Crime, Histoire & Sociétés/Crime, History & Societies*, vol. 3, no. 2 (1999), pp. 95–102.

La Rooij, Marinus F., 'Arthur Nelson Field: Kiwi Theoretician of the Australian Radical Right?', *Labour History*, vol. 89, no. 1 (November 2005), pp. 37–54.

———, 'From Colonial Conservative to International Antisemite: The Life and Work of Arthur Nelson Field', *Journal of Contemporary History*, vol. 37, no. 2 (2002), pp. 223–39.

Lange, Raeburn, *To Promote Maori Well-Being: Tribal Committees and Executives under the Maori Social and Economic Advancement Act, 1945–1962*, Rangatiratanga Series no. 6 (Wellington: Treaty of Waitangi Research Unit, 2006).

———, *In an Advisory Capacity: Maori Councils, 1919–1945*, Rangatiratanga Series no. 5 (Wellington: Treaty of Waitangi Research Unit, 2005).

———, *A Limited Measure of Local Self-government: Maori Councils, 1900–1920*,

Rangatiratanga Series no. 2 (Wellington: Treaty of Waitangi Research Unit, 2004).

Lenihan, Denis, '"Different Tones of Voice": Versions of Paddy Costello', *Security and Surveillance History Series*, 2020/1, pp. 1–21.

———, 'Paddy Costello: What the Papers Say' (http://kiwispies.com/pdfs/Costello-August14-2.pdf).

———, 'Was Ian Milner a Spy? A Review of the Evidence', *Kōtare* (2008), pp. 1–18.

Littlewood, David, '"The Debates of the Past": New Zealand's First Labour Government and the Introduction of Conscription in 1940', *War & Society*, vol. 39, no. 4 (October 2020), pp. 273–89.

Locke, Elsie, 'Looking for Answers', *Landfall* 48 (December 1958), pp. 335–55.

Loveridge, Steven, 'Discerning "the Fascist Creed": Counter-subversion and Fascistic Activity in New Zealand, 1950s–1960s', *Security and Surveillance History Series*, 2015/2, pp. 1–18.

Luff, Jennifer, 'Covert and Overt Operations: Interwar Political Policing in the United States and the United Kingdom', *American Historical Review*, vol. 122, no. 3 (June 2017), pp. 727–57.

Macdonald, Andrew, and Naomi Arnold, 'The Nazi Who Built Mount Hutt', *North & South* (June 2021), pp. 28–47.

McGibbon, Ian, 'The MI5 Verdict', *New Zealand International Review*, vol. 42, no. 6 (November/December 2017), p. 10.

———, 'Costello, Desmond Patrick', *The Dictionary of New Zealand Biography, Volume Five* (Auckland: Auckland University Press, 2000), pp. 118–19.

———, 'Special Air Service (SAS)', in Ian McGibbon (ed.), *The Oxford Companion to New Zealand Military History* (Auckland: Oxford University Press, 2000), pp. 505–6.

McLean, Denis, 'Gilbert, William Herbert Ellery', *The Dictionary of New Zealand Biography, Volume Five* (Auckland: Auckland University Press, 2000), pp. 187–88.

McNeish, James, 'Hidden History: The New Zealand Cold War', *North & South* (October 2007), pp. 86–92.

Millar, Grace, 'Identifying Communists: Continuity in Political Policing, 1931–1951', *Security and Surveillance History Series*, 2017/3, pp. 1–12.

———, 'Working Documents: Ballpoint Pen Marginalia, 1930s Police Files and Security Intelligence Practices', *Security and Surveillance History Series*, 2017/1, pp. 1–14.

Montgomerie, Deborah, 'Women and the Second World War', in Ian McGibbon (ed.), *The Oxford Companion to New Zealand Military History* (Auckland: Oxford University Press, 2000), pp. 615–20.

Murray, Michelle, 'Identity, Insecurity, and Great Power Politics: The Tragedy of German Naval Ambition Before the First World War', *Security Studies*, vol. 19, issue 4 (2010), pp. 656–88.

Murry, John Middleton, 'Some Problems of Democracy at War, Part 1: Safeguards for the Freedom of Expression', *Times Literary Supplement*, 16 September 1939, p. 535.

Musco, Stefano, 'Intelligence Gathering and the Relationship between Rulers and Spies: Some Lessons from Eminent and Lesser-known Classics', *Intelligence and National Security*, vol. 31, no. 7 (2016), pp. 1025–39.

New Zealand Law Society, 'Richard Gray Collins CBE, 1921–2007' (www.lawsociety. org.nz/news/people-in-the-law/obituaries/obituaries-list/richard-gray-collins-cbe-1921-2007/).

O'Farrell, P. J., 'The Russian Revolution and the Labour Movements of Australia and New Zealand, 1917–1922', *International Review of Social History*, vol. 8, issue 2 (August 1963), pp. 177–97.

O'Halpin, Eunan, 'The Liddell Diaries and British Intelligence History', *Intelligence and National Security*, vol. 20, no. 4 (December 2005), pp. 670–86.

O'Malley, Vincent, 'A United Front against Capitalism? Unemployed Workers' Organisations in Christchurch, New Zealand, during the Depression', *Labour History Review*, vol. 73, no. 1 (April 2008), pp. 145–66.

O'Reilly, Conor, 'The Pluralization of High Policing: Convergence and Divergence at the Public–Private Interface', *British Journal of Criminology*, vol. 20, no. 4 (2015), pp. 688–710.

Olssen, Erik, 'Lee, John Alfred Alexander', *The Dictionary of New Zealand Biography*, *Volume Four* (Auckland: Auckland University Press, 1998), pp. 284–86.

———, 'Hickey, Patrick Hodgens', *The Dictionary of New Zealand Biography*, *Volume Three* (Auckland: Auckland University Press, 1996), pp. 215–17.

Owen, Alwyn, 'The Girl in Red', *New Zealand Memories*, no. 47 (April/May 2004), pp. 4–8.

Parker, Dean, 'Scoundrel Times at the Film Unit', *Illusions* (7 March 1988), pp. 4–8.

Parsonson, Ann, 'Herangi, Te Kirihaehae Te Puea', *The Dictionary of New Zealand Biography*, *Volume Three* (Auckland: Auckland University Press, 1996), pp. 208–11.

Paterson, Lachy, 'Were Some Māori Disloyal During the War?', *Te Hau Kāinga Māori Home Front* (www.maorihomefront.nz/en/whanau-stories/were-some-maori-disloyal-during-the-war/).

Pugh, M. C., 'The New Zealand Legion, 1932–1935', *New Zealand Journal of History*, vol. 5, no. 1 (April 1971), pp. 49–69.

Reid, Neil, 'Nazi War Criminals Tracked on NZ Film', *Stuff* (www.stuff.co.nz/entertainment/film/5876440/Nazi-war-criminals-tracked-on-NZ-film).

Richardson, Len, 'Semple, Robert', *The Dictionary of New Zealand Biography*, *Volume Three* (Auckland: Auckland University Press, 1996), pp. 466–68.

———, 'Webb, Patrick Charles', *The Dictionary of New Zealand Biography*, *Volume Three* (Auckland: Auckland University Press, 1996), pp. 555–58.

Ricketts, Rita, 'Esprit de Contradiction', *New Zealand International Review*, vol. 42, no. 6 (November/December 2017), pp. 6–9.

Robertson, R. T., 'Government Responses to Unemployment in New Zealand, 1929–35', *New Zealand Journal of History*, vol. 16, no. 1 (April 1982), pp. 21–38.

———, 'Isolation, Ideology and Impotence: Organisations for the Unemployed during the Great Depression, 1929–35', *New Zealand Journal of History*, vol. 12, no. 2 (October 1979), pp. 149–64.

Ross, Ken, 'Alister McIntosh's "Best" Diplomat', *New Zealand International Review*, vol. 42, no. 6 (November/December 2017), pp. 2–5.

Roth, Herbert, 'McPherson, James', *The Dictionary of New Zealand Biography, Volume Two* (Auckland: Auckland University Press, 1996), p. 300.

———, 'Mann, Thomas', *The Dictionary of New Zealand Biography, Volume Three* (Auckland: Auckland University Press, 1996), p. 328.

———, 'The Communist Vote in New Zealand', *Political Science*, vol. 17, no. 2 (September 1965), pp. 26–35.

Rusbridger, James, 'The Sinking of the "Automedon", the Capture of the "Nankin"', *Encounter*, vol. 64, no. 5 (May 1985), pp. 8–14.

Saker, Nicola, 'The Forever Files', *North & South* (May 2022), pp. 26–35.

Shor, Francis, 'Left Labor Agitators in the Pacific Rim of the Early Twentieth Century', *International Labor and Working-Class History*, vol. 67 (Spring 2005), pp. 148–63.

Smith, Bernard, 'Counihan, Noel Jack', *Australian Dictionary of Biography*, vol. 17 (2007) (https://adb.anu.edu.au/biography/counihan-noel-jack-12360#).

Smith, Evan, 'Policing Communism across the "White Man's World": Anti-Communist Co-operation between Australia, South Africa and Britain in the Early Cold War', *Britain and the World*, vol. 10, no. 2 (2017), pp. 170–96.

Straczek, Jozef, 'The Empire is Listening: Naval Signals Intelligence in the Far East to 1942', *Journal of the Australian War Memorial*, issue 35 (2001).

Taylor, Kerry, 'The Secret State', in Nicola Legat (ed.), *The Journal of Urgent Writing*, vol. 1 (Auckland: Massey University Press, 2016), pp. 140–53.

———, '"Our Motto, No Compromise": The Ideological Origins and Foundations of the Communist Party of New Zealand', *New Zealand Journal of History*, vol. 28, no. 2 (1994), pp. 160–77.

Trapeznik, Alexander, '"Agents of Moscow" at the Dawn of the Cold War: The Comintern and the Communist Party of New Zealand', *Journal of Cold War Studies*, vol. 11, no. 1 (2009), pp. 124–49.

———, 'New Zealand's Perceptions of the Russian Revolution of 1917', *Revolutionary Russia*, vol. 19, no. 1 (2006), pp. 63–77.

Trotter, Perry, 'Nazi Hunter Reacts to Death of Local "Hero" SS-Waffen Officer', *Holocaust and Anti-Semitism Foundation New Zealand* (https://holocaustfoundation.com/blog/2020/8/18/nazi-hunter-reacts-to-death-of-local-hero-ss-waffen-soldier).

Troughton, Geoffrey, 'The *Maoriland Worker* and Blasphemy in New Zealand', *Labour History*, no. 91 (November 2006), pp. 113–29.

Weitzel, R. L., 'Pacifists and Anti-militarists in New Zealand, 1909–1914', *New Zealand Journal of History*, vol. 7, no. 2 (1973), pp. 128–47.

Weller, Geoffrey R., 'Change and Development in the New Zealand Security and Intelligence Services', *Conflict Quarterly*, vol. 21, no. 1 (Spring 2001).

Whitaker, Reg, 'Cold War Alchemy: How America, Britain and Canada Transformed Espionage into Subversion', *Intelligence and National Security*, vol. 15, no. 2 (2000), pp. 177–210.

White, Tina, 'Mystery Surrounds Assault and Movements of Victor Penny', *Stuff* (www.stuff.co.nz/manawatu-standard/news/111449859/mystery-surrounds-assault-and-movements-of-inventor-victor-penny).

Wilford, Hugh, 'The Information Research Department: Britain's Secret Cold War Weapon Revealed', *Review of International Studies*, 24 (1998), pp. 353–69.

Williams, Maureen Birchfield, 'Birchfield, Constance Alice', *The Dictionary of New Zealand Biography, Volume Four* (Auckland: Auckland University Press, 1998), pp. 61–62.

Young, Sherwood, 'Ross, Sydney Gordon', *The Dictionary of New Zealand Biography, Volume Five* (Auckland: Auckland University Press, 2000), pp. 452–53.

Yska, Redmer, 'Spying on New Zealand's "Vegetable Club": A Cold War Episode', *Security and Surveillance History Series*, 2016/2, pp. 1–10.

———, 'Collaboration between *Truth* and the Police Special Branch/Security Intelligence Service during the Cold War', *Security and Surveillance History Series*, 2016/1, pp. 1–8.

———, 'Ain't Got No Body: NZ's History-making Murder Case', *New Zealand Listener*, 20 December 2014, pp. 24–28.

Books

Aldrich, Richard J., *GCHQ: The Uncensored Story of Britain's Most Secret Intelligence Agency* (London: HarperPress, 2010).

Allen, Ruth, *Nelson: A History of Early Settlement* (Wellington: A. H. & A. W. Reed, 1965).

Andrew, Christopher, *The Secret World: A History of Intelligence* (New Haven: Yale University Press, 2018).

———, *The Defence of the Realm: The Authorized History of MI5* (London: Penguin Books, 2010).

———, *Secret Service: The Making of the British Intelligence Community* (London: Heinemann, 1985).

Andrew, Christopher, and David Dilks (eds), *The Missing Dimension: Governments and Intelligence in the Twentieth Century* (London: Macmillan, 1984).

Andrew, Christopher, and Oleg Gordievsky, *KGB: The Inside Story of its Foreign Operations from Lenin to Gorbachev* (New York: HarperCollins Publishers, 1990).

Andrew, Christopher, and Julius Green, *Stars and Spies: Intelligence Operations and the*

Entertainment Business (London: The Bodley Head, 2021).

Andrew, Christopher, and Vasili Mitrokhin, *The Mitrokhin Archive: The KGB in Europe and the West* (London: Allen Lane at the Penguin Press, 1999).

Atmore, H., and 'Uncle Scrim', *You and the U.S.S.R.* (Wellington: Printed by Commercial Printing and Publishing Co., 1941).

Bade, James N., *Von Luckner, a Reassessment: Count Felix von Luckner in New Zealand and the South Pacific, 1917–1919 and 1938* (Frankfurt am Main: Peter Lang, 2004).

Baker, Paul, *King and Country Call: New Zealanders, Conscription and the Great War* (Auckland: Auckland University Press, 1988).

Bakunin, Mikhail, *Marxism, Freedom and the State* (London: Freedom Press, 1950).

Ball, Desmond, and David Horner, *Breaking the Codes: Australia's KGB Network, 1944–1950* (St Leonards, NSW: Allen & Unwin, 1998).

Ball, Desmond, Cliff Lord and Meredith Thatcher, *Invaluable Service: The Secret History of New Zealand's Signals Intelligence during Two World Wars* (Waimauku: Resource Books, 2011).

Ballara, Angela, *Taua: 'Musket Wars', 'Land Wars' or Tikanga?: Warfare in Māori Society in the Early Nineteenth Century* (Auckland: Penguin Books, 2003).

Barber, Laurie, and Cliff Lord, *Swift and Sure: A History of the Royal New Zealand Corps of Signals and Army Signalling in New Zealand* (Auckland: New Zealand Signals Incorporated, 1996).

Barnes, Trevor, *Dead Doubles: The Extraordinary Worldwide Hunt for One of the Cold War's Most Notorious Spy Rings* (New York: Harper, 2020).

Barratt, Glynn, *Russophobia in New Zealand, 1838–1908* (Palmerston North: Dunmore Press, 1981).

Barros, James, *No Sense of Evil: Espionage: The Case of Herbert Norman* (Toronto: Deneau Publishers, 1986).

Barrowman, Rachel, *Mason: The Life of R. A. K. Mason* (Wellington: Victoria University Press, 2003).

———, *Victoria University of Wellington 1899–1999: A History* (Wellington: Victoria University Press, 1999).

———, *A Popular Vision: The Arts and the Left in New Zealand, 1930–1950* (Wellington: Victoria University Press, 1991).

Bassett, Michael, *Sir Joseph Ward: A Political Biography* (Auckland: Auckland University Press, 1993).

———, *Confrontation '51: The 1951 Waterfront Dispute* (Wellington: Reed, 1972).

Bassett, Michael, with Michael King, *Tomorrow Comes the Song: A Life of Peter Fraser* (Auckland: Penguin, 2000).

Beach, Jim, *Haig's Intelligence: GHQ and the German Army, 1916–1918* (Cambridge: Cambridge University Press, 2013).

Beaglehole, Tim, *A Life of J. C. Beaglehole: New Zealand Scholar* (Wellington: Victoria

University Press, 2006).

Beardsley, Eric, *Blackball 08* (Auckland: Collins, 1984).

Belich, James, *Paradise Reforged: A History of the New Zealanders from the 1880s to the Year 2000* (Auckland: Allen Lane, 2001).

———, *Making Peoples: A History of the New Zealanders From Polynesian Settlement to the End of the Nineteenth Century* (Auckland: Allen Lane, 1996).

———, *The New Zealand Wars and the Victorian Interpretation of Racial Conflict* (Auckland: Penguin, [1986] 1988).

Belton, Charles, *Outside the Law in New Zealand* (Gisborne: Gisborne Publishing Company, 1939).

Bennett, James, *'Rats and Revolutionaries': The Labour Movement in Australia and New Zealand, 1890–1940* (Dunedin: University of Otago Press, 2004).

Bennetts, C. H. Kit, *Spy: A Former SIS Officer Unmasks New Zealand's Sensational Cold War Spy Affair* (Auckland: Random House, 2006).

Binney, Judith, Gillian Chaplin and Craig Wallace, *Mihaia: The Prophet Rua Kenana and His Community at Maungapohatu* (Wellington: Oxford University Press, 1979).

Birchfield, Maureen, *Looking for Answers: A Life of Elsie Locke* (Christchurch: University of Canterbury Press, 2009).

———, *She Dared to Speak: Connie Birchfield's Story* (Dunedin: University of Otago Press, 1998).

Bland, Peter, *Sorry, I'm a Stranger Here Myself: A Memoir* (Auckland: Vintage, 2004).

Boast, Richard, and Richard S. Hill (eds), *Raupatu: The Confiscation of Maori Land* (Wellington: Victoria University Press, 2009).

Bollinger, Conrad, *Against the Wind: The Story of the New Zealand Seamen's Union* (Wellington: New Zealand Seamen's Union, 1968).

Bowen, Roger, *Innocence Is Not Enough: The Life and Death of Herbert Norman* (Vancouver: Douglas & McIntyre, 1986).

Bramble, Tom (ed.), *Never a White Flag: The Memoirs of Jock Barnes* (Wellington: Victoria University Press, 1998).

Brodeur, Jean-Paul, *The Policing Web* (Oxford: Oxford University Press, 2010).

Brown, Bruce, *The Rise of New Zealand Labour: A History of the Labour Party from 1916 to 1940* (Wellington: Price Milburn, 1962).

Bunyan, Tony, *The History and Practice of the Political Police in Britain* (London: J. Friedmann, 1976).

Burgmann, Meredith (ed.), *Dirty Secrets: Our ASIO Files* (Sydney: UNSW Press, 2014).

Burke, David, *Family Betrayal: Agent Sonya, MI5 and the Kuczynski Network* (Cheltenham: The History Press, 2021).

———, *Russia and the British Left: From the 1848 Revolutions to the General Strike* (London: I. B. Tauris, 2018).

Burrows, Simon, *A King's Ransom: The Life of Charles Théveneau de Morande, Blackmailer,*

Scandalmonger and Master-Spy (London: Bloomsbury Publishing, 2010).

Butterworth, Susan, *More Than Law and Order: Policing a Changing Society 1945–1992* (Dunedin: University of Otago Press, 2005).

Callinan, Bernard J., *Independent Company: The 2/2 and 2/4 Australian Independent Companies in Portuguese Timor, 1941–1943* (London: Heinemann, 1953).

Chapman, F. Spencer, *The Jungle is Neutral* (London: Chatto & Windus, 1949).

Christoffel, Paul, *Censored: A Short History of Censorship in New Zealand* (Wellington: Research Unit, Department of Internal Affairs, 1989).

Cobain, Ian, *The History Thieves: Secrets, Lies and the Shaping of a Modern Nation* (London: Portobello Books, 2016).

Cockerill, A. W., *Sir Percy Sillitoe: The Biography of the Former Head of MI5* (London: W. H. Allen, 1975).

Cole, Peter, David Struthers and Kenyon Zimmer (eds), *Wobblies of the World: A Global History of the IWW* (London: Pluto Press, 2017).

Corner, Frank, in Malcolm Templeton (ed.), *An Eye, An Ear and A Voice: 50 Years in New Zealand's External Relations, 1943–1993* (Wellington: Ministry of Foreign Affairs, 1993), pp. 64–126.

Cunningham, Matthew, *Mobilising the Masses: Populist Conservative Movements in Australia and New Zealand during the Great Depression* (Canberra: ANU Press, 2022).

Davidson, Jared, *Dead Letters: Censorship and Subversion in New Zealand, 1914–1920* (Dunedin: Otago University Press, 2019).

———, *Fighting War: Anarchists, Wobblies & the New Zealand State, 1905–1925* (Wellington: Rebel Press, 2016).

———, *Sewing Freedom: Philip Josephs, Transnationalism & Early New Zealand Anarchism* (Edinburgh: AK Press, 2013).

Day, Patrick, *The Radio Years: A History of Broadcasting in New Zealand, Volume One* (Auckland: Auckland University Press in association with the Broadcasting History Trust, 1994).

De la Mare, F. A., *Academic Freedom in New Zealand, 1932–34: A Statement of the Facts* (Auckland: Unicorn Press, 1935).

Deery, Phillip, *Spies and Sparrows: ASIO and the Cold War* (Melbourne: Melbourne University Press, 2022).

Department of the Prime Minister and Cabinet, *Securing our Nation's Safety: How New Zealand Manages Its Security and Intelligence Agencies* (Wellington: Domestic and External Security Secretariat, Department of the Prime Minister and Cabinet, 2000).

Derby, Mark, *White-collar Radical: Dan Long and the Rise of the White-collar Unions* (Nelson: Craig Potton Publishing, 2013).

———, *The Prophet and the Policeman: The Story of Rua Kenana and John Cullen* (Nelson: Craig Potton Publishing, 2009).

Downes, Peter, and Peter Harcourt, *Voices in the Air: Radio Broadcasting in New Zealand: A Documentary* (Wellington: Methuen/Radio New Zealand, 1976).

Dunstall, Graeme, *A Policeman's Paradise?: Policing a Stable Society, 1918–1945* (Palmerston North: Dunmore Press, 1999).

Dylan, Huw, *Defence Intelligence and the Cold War: Britain's Joint Intelligence Bureau, 1945–1964* (Oxford: Oxford University Press, 2014).

Easton, Brian, *Not in Narrow Seas: The Economic History of Aotearoa New Zealand* (Wellington: Victoria University Press, 2020).

Edwards, Brian, *The Public Eye* (Wellington: A. H. & A. W. Reed, 1971).

Edwards, Jim, *Break Down These Bars* (Auckland: Penguin, 1987).

Edwards, Leslie M., *Scrim: Radio Rebel in Retrospect* (Auckland: Hodder & Stoughton, 1971).

Eldred-Grigg, Stevan, *New Zealand Working People, 1890–1990* (Palmerston North: Dunmore Press, 1990).

Elenio, Paul, *'Alla Fine del Mondo': To the Ends of the Earth* (Wellington: Petone Settlers Museum and the Club Garibaldi, 1995).

Emsley, Clive, *The Great British Bobby: A History of British Policing from the 18th Century to the Present* (London: Quercus, 2009).

Fahey, John, *Traitors and Spies: Espionage and Corruption in High Places in Australia, 1901–50* (Crows Nest, NSW: Allen & Unwin, 2020).

———, *Australia's First Spies: The Remarkable Story of Australia's Intelligence Operations, 1901–45* (Sydney: Allen & Unwin, 2018).

Fairburn, Miles, *The Ideal Society and its Enemies: The Foundations of Modern New Zealand Society, 1850–1900* (Auckland: Auckland University Press, 1989).

Ferris, John, *Behind the Enigma: The Authorised History of GCHQ, Britain's Secret Cyber-Intelligence Agency* (London: Bloomsbury Publishing, 2020).

Field, Michael J., *Mau: Samoa's Struggle against New Zealand Oppression* (Wellington: A. H. & A. W. Reed, 1984).

Fischer, David Hackett, *Fairness and Freedom: A History of Two Open Societies: New Zealand and the United States* (Oxford: Oxford University Press, 2012).

Foucault, Michel, *Discipline and Punish: The Birth of the Prison* (London: Allen Lane, 1977).

Frame, Alex, *Salmond: Southern Jurist* (Wellington: Victoria University Press, 1995).

Franks, Peter, and Jim McAloon, *The New Zealand Labour Party, 1916–2016* (Wellington: Victoria University Press, 2016).

Fraser, George [A.], *Seeing Red: Undercover in 1950s New Zealand* (Palmerston North: Dunmore Press, 1995).

Fraser, George [F.], *Both Eyes Open: A Memoir* (Dunedin: John McIndoe, 1990).

———, *Ungrateful People* [1952] (Auckland: Pelorus Press, 1985).

———, *Martial Plan?: An Analysis of United States Policy* (Wellington: New Zealand

Fabian Society, 1948).

Fry, E. C. (ed.), *TOM BARKER AND THE I.W.W.* (Canberra: Australian Society for the Study of Labour History, 1965).

Gaitanos, Sarah, *Shirley Smith: An Examined Life* (Wellington: Victoria University Press, 2019).

Galbraith, Alex, *The Making of a New Zealand Revolutionary: Reminiscences of Alex Galbraith* (Auckland: Workers' Party, 1994).

Galbreath, Ross, *DSIR: Making Science Work for New Zealand: Themes from the History of the Department of Scientific and Industrial Research, 1926–1992* (Wellington: Victoria University Press in association with the Historical Branch, Department of Internal Affairs, 1998).

Gerth, H. H., and C. Wright Mills (eds), *From Max Weber: Essays in Sociology* (London & New York: Routledge, 2009).

Gerwarth, Robert, *The Vanquished: Why the First World War Failed to End, 1917–1923* (London: Allen Lane, 2016).

Gerwarth, Robert, and John Horne (eds), *War in Peace: Paramilitary Violence after the Great War* (Oxford: Oxford University Press, 2012).

Gill, Peter, *Policing Politics: Security Intelligence and the Liberal Democratic State* (London: Frank Cass & Co., 1994).

Gillespie, O. A., *The Pacific* (Wellington: War History Branch, Department of Internal Affairs, 1952).

Glamuzina, Julie, *Spies and Lies: The Mysterious Dr Dannevill* (Mangawhai: DoubleaXe Press, 2021).

Goodman, Michael, *The Official History of the Joint Intelligence Committee, Volume 1: From the Approach of the Second World War to the Suez Crisis* (London: Routledge, 2014).

Grant, David, *Out in the Cold: Pacifists and Conscientious Objectors in New Zealand during World War II* (Auckland: Reed Methuen, 1986).

Grant, Ian F., *Lasting Impressions: The Story of New Zealand's Newspapers, 1840–1920* (Masterton: Fraser Books, 2018).

Green, Anna, *British Capital, Antipodean Labour: Working the New Zealand Waterfront, 1915–1951* (Dunedin: University of Otago Press, 2001).

Gustafson, Barry, *From the Cradle to the Grave: A Biography of Michael Joseph Savage* (Auckland: Reed Methuen, 1986).

———, *Labour's Path to Political Independence: The Origins and Establishment of the New Zealand Labour Party, 1900–19* (Auckland: Auckland University Press, 1980).

Haffenden, John, *William Empson: Among the Mandarins* (Oxford: Oxford University Press, 2005).

Hager, Nicky, *Secret Power: New Zealand's Role in the International Spy Network* (Nelson: Craig Potton Publishing, 1996).

Hall, Richard, *The Rhodes Scholar Spy* (Milsons Point, NSW: Random House, 1991).

———, *The Secret State: Australia's Spy Industry* (Stanmore: Cassell, 1978).

Hamilton, Ian, *Till Human Voices Wake Us* [1953] (Auckland: Auckland University Press, 1984).

Harris, Jack, *Memoirs of a Century* (Wellington: Steele Roberts, 2007).

Hastings, Max, *The Secret War: Spies, Codes and Guerrillas, 1939–1945* (London, William Collins, 2015).

Haynes, John Earl, and Harvey Klehr, *Venona: Decoding Soviet Espionage in America* (New Haven: Yale University Press, 2000).

Henderson, J. McLeod, *Ratana: The Man, the Church, the Political Movement* [1963], 2nd ed. (Wellington: A. H. & A. W. Reed/Polynesian Society, 1972).

Hill, Richard S., *Maori and the State: Crown–Maori Relations in New Zealand/Aotearoa, 1950–2000* (Wellington: Victoria University Press, 2009).

———, *State Authority, Indigenous Autonomy: Crown–Maori Relations in New Zealand/ Aotearoa, 1900–1950* (Wellington: Victoria University Press, 2004).

———, *The Iron Hand in the Velvet Glove: The Modernisation of Policing in New Zealand, 1886–1917* (Palmerston North: Dunmore Press, 1995).

———, *The Colonial Frontier Tamed: New Zealand Policing in Transition, 1867–1886* (Wellington: Historical Branch, Department of Internal Affairs, 1989).

———, *Policing the Colonial Frontier: The Theory and Practice of Coercive Social and Racial Control in New Zealand, 1767–1867, Parts One and Two* (Wellington: Historical Publications Branch, Department of Internal Affairs, 1986).

Hoadley, Stephen, *New Zealand and France: Politics, Diplomacy and Dispute Management* (Wellington: New Zealand Institute of International Affairs, 2005).

Hobbs, Leslie, *The Thirty-year Wonders* (Christchurch: Whitcombe & Tombs, 1967).

Holland, H. E., *Armageddon or Calvary: The Conscientious Objectors of New Zealand and 'The Process of Their Conversion'* (Wellington: Maoriland Worker Printing and Publishing Co., 1919).

Holland, H. E., 'Ballot Box' and R. S. Ross, *The Tragic Story of the Waihi Strike* (Wellington: 'Worker' Press, 1913).

Holmes, Cecil, *One Man's Way: On the Road with a Rebel Reporter, Film-maker and Adventurer* (Auckland: Penguin Books, 1986).

Holt, James, *Compulsory Arbitration in New Zealand: The First Forty Years* (Auckland: Auckland University Press, 1986).

Horner, David, *The Spy Catchers: The Official History of ASIO, 1949–1963, Volume 1* (Crows Nest, NSW: Allen & Unwin, 2014).

Howard, Grant, *Happy in the Service: An Illustrated History of the Women's Royal New Zealand Naval Service, 1942–1977* (Auckland: Word Publishers, 1985).

Hughes-Wilson, John, *On Intelligence* (London: Constable, 2017).

Hunt, Graeme, *Spies and Revolutionaries: A History of New Zealand Subversion* (Auckland: Reed, 2007).

———, *Black Prince: The Autobiography of Fintan Patrick Walsh* (Auckland: Penguin Books, 2004).

Jeffery, Keith, *MI6: The History of the Secret Intelligence Service, 1909–1949* (London: Bloomsbury Publishing, 2011).

Johnson, Franklyn Arthur, *Defence by Committee: The British Committee of Imperial Defence, 1885–1959* (New York: Oxford University Press, 1960).

Joiner, Lynne, *Honorable Survivor: Mao's China, McCarthy's America, and the Persecution of John S. Service* (Annapolis: Naval Institute Press, 2009).

Judd, Alan, *The Quest for C: Sir Mansfield Cumming and the Founding of the British Secret Service* (London: HarperCollins, 2000).

Kalugin, Oleg, *Spymaster: My Thirty-two Years in Intelligence and Espionage Against the West* (New York: Basic Books, 2009).

Kay, Robin (ed.), *The ANZUS Pact and the Treaty of Peace with Japan* (Wellington: Historical Publications Branch, 1985).

Kealey, Gregory S., *Spying on Canadians: The Royal Canadian Mounted Police Security Service and the Origins of the Long Cold War* (Toronto: University of Toronto Press, 2017).

Keith, Arthur Berriedale (ed.), *Selected Speeches and Documents on British Colonial Policy 1763–1917* [1918] (London: Oxford University Press, 1953).

King, Michael, *The Penguin History of New Zealand* (Auckland: Penguin, 2003).

———, *Tread Softly for You Tread on My Life: New & Collected Writings* (Auckland: Cape Catley Ltd, 2001).

———, *Moriori: A People Rediscovered* (Auckland: Penguin, 2000).

———, *Te Puea: A Biography* (Auckland: Hodder & Stoughton, 1977).

Knight, Amy, *How the Cold War Began: The Igor Gouzenko Affair and the Hunt for Soviet Spies* (New York: Carroll & Graf Publishers, 2005).

Lake, Ruth, *My Years in Mrs Boswell's Moscow* (Wellington: N.Z. Society for Closer Relations with U.S.S.R., 1950).

Law Commission, *Reforming the Law of Sedition* (Wellington: Law Commission, 2007).

Leggett, George, *The Cheka: Lenin's Political Police* (New York: Oxford University Press, 1986).

Lewis, Paul, with Jock McLean, *TP: The Life and Times of Sir Terry McLean* (Auckland: HarperCollins, 2010).

Lewis, Tom, *Coverups and Copouts* (Auckland: Hodder Moa Beckett, 1998).

Lissington, M. P., *New Zealand and Japan, 1900–1941* (Wellington: Government Printer, 1972).

Locke, Cybèle, *Workers in the Margins: Union Radicals in Post-war New Zealand* (Wellington: Bridget Williams Books, 2012).

Locke, Elsie, *Peace People: A History of Peace Activities in New Zealand* (Christchurch: Hazard Press, 1992).

————, *Student at the Gates* (Christchurch: Whitcoulls, 1981).

Loeffel, Robert, *The Fifth Column in World War II: Suspected Subversives in the Pacific War and Australia* (London: Palgrave Macmillan, 2015).

Loveridge, Steven, *Calls to Arms: New Zealand Society and Commitment to the First World War* (Wellington: Victoria University Press, 2014).

Loveridge, Steven, and James Watson, *The Home Front: New Zealand Society and the War Effort, 1914–1919* (Auckland: Massey University Press, 2019).

Loyalty League, *What is the Red Menace?: The Secret Forces behind Socialism and Communism: An Exposure of the So Called 'Labour' Party* (Wellington: Loyalty League, 1925).

Lyon, David, *Surveillance Studies: An Overview* (Cambridge: Polity Press, 2007).

McDonough, Frank, *The Gestapo: The Myth and Reality of Hitler's Secret Police* (London: Coronet, 2015).

Macfie, Rebecca, *Helen Kelly: Her Life* (Wellington: Awa Press, 2021).

McGibbon, Ian (ed.), *Undiplomatic Dialogue: Letters between Carl Berendsen & Alister McIntosh, 1943–1952* (Auckland: Auckland University Press, 1993).

————, *New Zealand and the Korean War, Volumes I and II* (Auckland & Wellington: Oxford University Press in association with the Historical Branch, Department of Internal Affairs, 1992–96).

————, *The Path to Gallipoli: Defending New Zealand, 1840–1915* (Wellington: GP Books, 1991).

————, *Blue-Water Rationale: The Naval Defence of New Zealand, 1914–1942* (Wellington: P. D. Hasselberg, Government Printer, 1981).

McGill, David, *The Death Ray Debacle* (Paekakariki: Silver Owl Press, 2015).

————, *No Right to Strike: The History of the New Zealand Police Service Organisations* (Wellington: Silver Owl Press, 1992).

Macintyre, Ben, *Agent Sonya: Moscow's Most Daring Wartime Spy* (New York: Random House, 2020).

Macintyre, Stuart, *The Party: The Communist Party of Australia from Heyday to Reckoning* (Crows Nest, NSW: Allen & Unwin, 2022).

McIntyre, W. David, *Background to the ANZUS Pact: Policy-making, Strategy, and Diplomacy, 1945–55* (Christchurch: Canterbury University Press, 1995).

————, *New Zealand Prepares for War: Defence Policy, 1919–39* (Christchurch: Canterbury University Press, 1988).

McKinnon, Malcolm, *The Broken Decade: Prosperity, Depression and Recovery in New Zealand, 1928–39* (Dunedin: Otago University Press, 2016).

McKnight, David, *Australia's Spies and Their Secrets* (St Leonards, NSW: Allen & Unwin, 1994).

McNeish, James, *The Sixth Man: The Extraordinary Life of Paddy Costello* (Auckland: Vintage, 2007).

———, *Dance of the Peacocks: New Zealanders in Exile in the Time of Hitler and Mao Tse-Tung* (Auckland: Vintage, 2003).

McPherson, James, *Reasons Why the Working Men of New Zealand Should Become Internationalists; Together with an Article entitled, Anti-Chinese Immigration* (Christchurch: J. McPherson, 1872).

Malcolm, Elizabeth, *The Irish Policeman, 1822–1922: A Life* (Dublin: Four Courts Press, 2006).

Manne, Robert, *The Petrov Affair: Politics and Espionage* (Sydney: Pergamon Press, 1987).

[Maning, Frederick Edward], 'A Pakeha Maori', *Old New Zealand: Being Incidents of Native Customs and Character in the Old Times* (London: Smith, Elder, 1863).

Marchetti, Victor, and John D. Marks, *The CIA and the Cult of Intelligence* (London: Hodder & Stoughton, 1974).

Marshall, John, *Memoirs Volume Two: 1960–1988* (Auckland: William Collins, 1989).

———, *Memoirs Volume One: 1912 to 1960* (Auckland: William Collins, 1983).

Mason, Walter Wynne, *Prisoners of War* (Wellington: Department of Internal Affairs, 1954).

Matthews, Owen, *An Impeccable Spy: Richard Sorge, Stalin's Master Agent* (London: Bloomsbury Publishing, 2019).

Mazower, Mark (ed.), *The Policing of Politics in the Twentieth Century* (Providence & Oxford: Berghahn Books, 1997).

Meyer, G. J., *A World Undone: The Story of the Great War, 1914 to 1918* (New York: Delta, 2006).

Morgan, Janet, *The Secrets of Rue St Roch: Intelligence Operations behind Enemy Lines in the First World War* (London: Allen Lane, 2004).

Newman, Keith, *Ratana Revisited: An Unfinished Legacy* (Auckland: Reed Books, 2006).

New Zealand Police College, *Police Training in New Zealand: Trentham in Retrospect* (Wellington: New Zealand Police, 1982).

O'Sullivan, Vincent, *Long Journey to the Border: A Life of John Mulgan* (Auckland: Penguin, 2003).

———, (ed.), *Intersecting Lines: The Memoirs of Ian Milner* (Wellington: Victoria University Press, 1993).

Olssen, Erik, *The Red Feds: Revolutionary Industrial Unionism and the New Zealand Federation of Labour, 1908–14* (Auckland: Oxford University Press, 1988).

———, *John A. Lee* (Dunedin: University of Otago Press, 1977).

Omand, David, *How Spies Think: Ten Lessons in Intelligence* (London: Viking, 2020).

Parker, Michael, *The S.I.S.: The New Zealand Security Intelligence Service* (Palmerston North: Dunmore Press, 1979).

Popper, Karl, *The Open Society and Its Enemies* (London: Routledge, 1945).

Porch, Douglas, *The French Secret Services: From the Dreyfus Affair to the Gulf War* (London: Basingstoke, 1996).

Porter, Bernard, *The Origins of the Vigilant State: The London Metropolitan Police Special Branch Before the First World War* (London: Weidenfeld & Nicolson, 1987).

Powles, Guy, *Security Intelligence Service: Report by Chief Ombudsman* (Wellington: Government Printer, 1976).

Pratt, John, *The Prison Diary of A. C. Barrington: Dissent and Conformity in Wartime New Zealand* (Dunedin: Otago University Press, 2016).

Prebble, Frank, 'Troublemakers': *Anarchism and Syndicalism: The Early Years of the Libertarian Movement in Aotearoa / New Zealand* (Christchurch: Libertarian Press, 1995).

Price, Hugh, *The Plot to Subvert Wartime New Zealand: The True Story of Syd Ross and His Impudent Hoax that Convulsed New Zealand and put a Shine into the Darkest Days of WWII, and that the Commissioner of Police Declared "Beyond Comprehension" A Hoax, moreover, that was Extended to Challenge the Rule of Law in the Dominion* (Wellington: Victoria University Press, 2006).

Priestley, Rebecca, *Mad on Radium: New Zealand in the Atomic Age* (Auckland: Auckland University Press, 2012).

Proctor, Tammy M., *Female Intelligence: Women and Espionage in the First World War* (New York: New York University Press, 2003).

Pucci, Molly, *Security Empire: The Secret Police in Communist Eastern Europe* (New Haven: Yale University Press, 2020).

Pugsley, Christopher, *From Emergency to Confrontation: The New Zealand Armed Forces in Malaya and Borneo, 1949–1966* (Auckland: Oxford University Press, 2003).

Read, Anthony, *The World on Fire: 1919 and the Battle with Bolshevism* (London: Jonathan Cape, 2008).

Redshaw, Valerie P., *Tact and Tenacity: New Zealand Women in Policing* (Wellington: Grantham House/New Zealand Police, 2006).

Reid, Nicholas, *James Michael Liston: A Life* (Wellington: Victoria University Press, 2006).

Reiner, Robert, *The Politics of the Police* (Brighton: Wheatsheaf Books, 1985).

Renwick, William, *Scrim: The Man with a Mike* (Wellington: Victoria University Press, 2011).

Richelson, Jeffrey T., and Desmond Ball, *The Ties That Bind: Intelligence Cooperation between the UKUSA Countries, the United Kingdom, the United States of America, Canada, Australia, and New Zealand* [1985], 2nd ed. (Wellington: Allen & Unwin, 1990).

Robinson, Howard, *A History of the Post Office in New Zealand* (Wellington: Government Printer, 1964).

Roche, Stanley, *The Red and the Gold: An Informal Account of the Waihi Strike, 1912* (Auckland: Oxford University Press, 1982).

Roth, H., *Trade Unions in New Zealand: Past and Present* (Wellington: A. H. & A. W. Reed, 1973).

Saunders, Frances Stonor, *The Cultural Cold War: The CIA and the World of Arts and Letters* (New York: New Press, 1999).

Scott, Dick, *A Radical Writer's Life* (Auckland: Reed, 2004).

———, *151 Days: History of the Great Waterfront Lockout and Supporting Strikes, February 15–July 15 1951* (Auckland: New Zealand Waterside Workers' Union Deregistered, 1952).

Scott, Jonathan, *Harry's Absence: Looking for My Father on the Mountain* (Wellington: Victoria University Press, 1997).

Scott, S. W., *Rebel in a Wrong Cause* (Auckland: Collins, 1960).

Scrimgeour, C. G., John A. Lee and Tony Simpson, *The Scrim–Lee Papers: C. G. Scrimgeour and John A. Lee Remember the Crisis Years, 1930–1940* (Wellington: A. H. & A. W. Reed, 1976).

Seal, Graham, *Inventing ANZAC: The Digger and National Mythology* (St Lucia: University of Queensland Press, 2004).

Selverstone, Marc J., *Constructing the Monolith: The United States, Great Britain, and International Communism, 1945–1950* (Cambridge: Harvard University Press, 2009).

Semple, Bob, *Why I Fight Communism* (Wellington: Hutcheson, Bowman & Stewart, 1948).

Sillitoe, Percy, *Cloak without Dagger* (London: Cassell, 1955).

Simons, Cliff, *Soldiers, Scouts & Spies: A Military History of the New Zealand Wars 1845–1864* (Auckland: Massey University Press, 2019).

Sinclair, Georgina, *At the End of the Line: Colonial Policing and the Imperial Endgame, 1945–80* (Manchester: Manchester University Press, 2006).

Sinclair, Keith, *Walter Nash* (Auckland: Auckland University Press, 1976).

Smith, Phillip Thurmond, *Policing Victorian London: Political Policing, Public Order, and the London Metropolitan Police* (London: Greenwood Press, 1985).

Steiner, Peter, *Industrial Unionism: The History of the Industrial Workers of the World in Aotearoa* (Wellington: Rebel Press, 2007).

Stevens, David, *U-Boat Far From Home: The Epic Voyage of U 862 to Australia and New Zealand* (Sydney: Allen & Unwin, 1997).

Strike!: Strategy and Tactics: The Lessons of the Industrial Struggles (Wellington: Communist Party of New Zealand, 1930).

Subversive Activity: A Statement by the New Zealand Council for Civil Liberties (Petone: Valley Printing Company, 1955).

Sutch, W. B., *The Quest for Security in New Zealand* (Harmondsworth: Penguin, 1942).

Sweetman, Rory, *Bishop in the Dock: The Sedition Trial of James Liston* (Auckland: Auckland University Press, 1997).

Tampke, Jürgen (ed.), *'Ruthless Warfare': German Military Planning and Surveillance in the Australia–New Zealand Region before the Great War* (Canberra: Southern Highlands Publishers, 1998).

Taylor, Nancy M., *The Home Front, Volumes I and II* (Wellington: Historical Publications Branch, 1986).

Templeton, Malcolm, *Top Hats Are Not Being Taken: A Short History of the New Zealand Legation in Moscow, 1944–1950* (Wellington: New Zealand Institute of International Affairs, 1988).

Toch, Hans, *Cop Watch: Spectators, Social Media and Police Reform* (Washington DC: American Psychological Association, 2012).

Townshend, Charles, *Making the Peace: Public Order and Public Security in Modern Britain* (Oxford: Oxford University Press, 1993).

Turnovsky, Fred, *Fifty Years in New Zealand* (Wellington: Allen & Unwin, 1990).

Van Beynen, Ray, *Zero-Alpha: The NZ Police Armed Offenders Squad Official History* (Auckland: Howling at the Moon Productions, 1998).

Van Der Bijl, Nicholas, *To Complete the Jigsaw: British Military Intelligence in the First World War* (Gloucestershire: History Press, 2015).

Vayda, Andrew Peter, *Maori Warfare* (Wellington: Polynesian Society, 1960).

Volkman, Ernest, *The History of Espionage: The Clandestine World of Surveillance, Spying and Intelligence, from Ancient Times to the Post-9/11 World* (London: Carlton Books, 2007).

Waitangi Tribunal, *He Whakaputanga Me Te Tiriti/The Declaration and the Treaty* (Wellington: Legislation Direct, 2014).

Wake, Nancy, *The White Mouse* (Melbourne: Sun Books, 1985).

Wake, Valdemar Robert, *No Ribbons or Medals: The Story of 'Hereward', an Australian Counter Espionage Officer* (Mitcham: Jacobyte Books, 2004).

Walton, Calder, *Empire of Secrets: British Intelligence, the Cold War and the Twilight of Empire* (London: HarperPress, 2013).

Warner, Michael, *The Rise and Fall of Intelligence: An International Security History* (Washington: Georgetown University Press, 2014).

Waters, S. D., *The Royal New Zealand Navy* (Wellington: War History Branch, Department of Internal Affairs, 1956).

Webster, Peter, *Rua and the Maori Millennium* (Wellington: Price Milburn/Victoria University Press, 1979).

Welch, Dave, *The Lucifer: A Story of Industrial Conflict in New Zealand's 1930s* (Palmerston North: Dunmore Press in association with the Trade Union History Project, 1988).

West, Nigel, *Mask: MI5's Penetration of the Communist Party of Great Britain* (London: Routledge, 2005).

Westad, Odd Arne, *The Cold War: A World History* (New York: Basic Books, 2017).

Whitaker, Reg, Gregory S. Kealey and Andrew Parnaby, *Secret Service: Political Policing in Canada from the Fenians to Fortress America* (Toronto: University of Toronto Press, 2012).

Wilson, A. C., *New Zealand and the Soviet Union 1950–1991: A Brittle Relationship* (Wellington: Victoria University Press, 2004).

———, *Wire and Wireless: A History of Telecommunications in New Zealand, 1860–1987* (Palmerston North: Dunmore Press, 1994).

Wilson, Ormond, *An Outsider Looks Back: Reflections on Experience* (Wellington: Port Nicholson Press, 1982).

Wood, F. L. W., *The New Zealand People at War: Political and External Affairs* (Wellington: War History Branch, Department of Internal Affairs, 1958).

Woodcock, George, *Anarchism: A History of Libertarian Ideas and Movements* (Cleveland, OH: Meridian Books, 1962).

Yska, Redmer, *Truth: The Rise and Fall of the People's Paper* (Nelson: Craig Potton Publishing, 2010).

———, *All Shook Up: The Flash Bodgie and the Rise of the New Zealand Teenager in the Fifties* (Auckland: Penguin Books, 1993).

Book Chapters

Andrew, Christopher, Richard J. Aldrich and Wesley K. Wark, 'The Intelligence Cycle', in Christopher Andrew, Richard J. Aldrich and Wesley K. Wark (eds), *Secret Intelligence: A Reader* (London: Routledge, 2009), pp. 21–25.

Bailey, Rona, 'Telling the World "the Other Side of the Story"', in David Grant (ed.), *The Big Blue: Snapshots of the 1951 Waterfront Lockout* (Wellington: Canterbury University Press, 2004), pp. 38–44.

Clayworth, Peter, 'Patrick Hodgens Hickey and the IWW: A Transnational Relationship', in Peter Cole, David Struthers and Kenyon Zimmer (eds), *Wobblies of the World: A Global History of the IWW* (London: Pluto Press, 2017), pp. 204–11.

Cooke, Peter, '"Priceless Worth": The Territorial Force and Senior Cadets in World War One', in Steven Loveridge (ed.), *New Zealand Society at War, 1914–1918* (Wellington: Victoria University Press, 2016), pp. 64–76.

Cookson, J. E., 'Pacifism and Conscientious Objection in New Zealand', in Peter Brock and Thomas P. Socknat (eds), *Challenge to Mars: Essays on Pacifism from 1918 to 1945* (Toronto: University of Toronto Press, 1999), pp. 292–311.

Crawford, John, '"Duty Well Done": The Defence Department at War: 1914–1918', in Steven Loveridge (ed.), *New Zealand Society at War, 1914–1918* (Wellington: Victoria University Press, 2016), pp. 34–48.

Dunstall, Graeme, 'Governments, the Police and the Left, 1912–1951', in Pat Moloney and Kerry Taylor (eds), *On the Left: Essays on Socialism in New Zealand* (Dunedin: University of Otago Press, 2002), pp. 87–102.

Emsley, Clive, 'Introduction: Political Police and the European Nation-State in the Nineteenth Century', in Mark Mazower (ed.), *The Policing of Politics in the Twentieth Century* (Providence & Oxford: Berghahn Books, 1997), pp. 1–25.

Fairburn, Miles, 'Is There a Good Case for New Zealand Exceptionalism?', in Tony Ballantyne and Brian Moloughney (eds), *Disputed Histories: Imagining New Zealand's Pasts* (Dunedin: University of Otago Press, 2006), pp. 143–67.

Fox, Aaron, 'The Price of Collective Security: State-sponsored Anti-communism in New Zealand in the Cold War', in Ian McGibbon and John Crawford (eds), *Seeing Red: New Zealand, the Commonwealth and the Cold War, 1945–91* (Wellington: NZ Military History Committee, 2012), pp. 95–124.

———, 'The Pedigree of Truth: Western Intelligence Agencies *versus* Ian Frank George Milner and William Ball Sutch', in Alexander Trapeznik and Aaron Fox (eds), *Lenin's Legacy Down Under: New Zealand's Cold War* (Dunedin: University of Otago Press, 2004), pp. 115–30.

Grant, David, 'Where Were the Peacemongers? Pacifists in New Zealand during World War One', in Steven Loveridge (ed.), *New Zealand Society at War, 1914–1918* (Wellington: Victoria University Press, 2016), pp. 220–34.

Grant, Ian F., 'War a Daily Reminder, but Life Goes On: Newspapers during the First World War', in Steven Loveridge (ed.), *New Zealand Society at War, 1914–1918* (Wellington: Victoria University Press, 2016), pp. 127–41.

Hill, Richard S., 'Tōrangapū Ohaoha: Māori and the Political Economy, 1918–1945', in Michael Reilly, Suzanne Duncan, Gianna Leoni, Lachy Paterson, Lyn Carter, Matiu Rātima and Poia Rewi (eds), *Te Kōparapara: An Introduction to the Māori World* (Auckland: Auckland University Press, 2018), pp. 245–65.

———, 'Settler Colonialism in New Zealand, 1840–1907', in Edward Cavanagh and Lorenzo Veracini (eds), *The Routledge Handbook of the History of Settler Colonialism* (Abingdon & New York: Routledge, 2017), pp. 391–408.

———, 'State Servants and Social Beings: The Role of the New Zealand Police Force in the Great War', in Steven Loveridge (ed.), *New Zealand Society at War, 1914–1918* (Wellington: Victoria University Press, 2016), pp. 91–111.

———, 'Surveilling the "Enemies" of Colonial New Zealand – Counter-subversion and Counter-espionage, 1840–1907', in Brad Patterson, Richard S. Hill and Kathryn Patterson (eds), *After the Treaty: The Settler State, Race Relations & the Exercise of Power in Colonial New Zealand* (Wellington: Steele Roberts, 2016), pp. 263–93.

———, 'Policing Ireland, Policing Colonies: The Irish Constabulary "Model"', in Angela McCarthy (ed.), *Ireland in the World: Comparative, Transnational, and Personal Perspectives* (New York & London: Routledge, 2015), pp. 61–80.

———, 'Maori and State Policy', in Giselle Byrnes (ed.), *The New Oxford History of New Zealand* (Melbourne: Oxford University Press, 2009), pp. 513–36.

———, 'The Police, the State, and Lawless Law', in Melanie Nolan (ed.), *Revolution:*

The 1913 Great Strike in New Zealand (Christchurch: Canterbury University Press in association with the Trade Union History Project, 2006), pp. 79–98.

———, 'Maori Police Personnel and the Rangatiratanga Discourse', in Barry S. Godfrey and Graeme Dunstall (eds), *Crime and Empire 1840–1940: Criminal Justice in Local and Global Context* (Cullompton: Willan Publishing, 2005), pp. 174–88.

Johnson, Loch K., and James J. Wirtz, 'Intelligence Analysis', in Loch K. Johnson and James J. Wirtz (eds), *Intelligence: The Secret World of Spies, An Anthology*, 3rd ed. (New York: Oxford University Press, 2011), pp. 117–22.

———, 'The Danger of Intelligence Politicization', in Loch K. Johnson and James J. Wirtz (eds), *Intelligence: The Secret World of Spies, An Anthology*, 3rd ed. (New York: Oxford University Press, 2011), pp. 165–68.

Kealey, Gregory S., and Kerry A. Taylor, 'After Gouzenko and "The Case": Canada, Australia and New Zealand at the Secret Commonwealth Security Conferences of 1948 and 1951', in Dennis G. Molinaro (ed.), *The Bridge in the Parks: The Five Eyes and Cold War Counter-Intelligence* (Toronto: University of Toronto Press, 2022), pp. 22–44.

Keith, K. J., 'The Right to Protest', in K. J. Keith (ed.), *Essays on Human Rights* (Wellington: Sweet & Maxwell, 1968), pp. 49–69.

Loveridge, Steven, and Rolf W. Brednich, 'When Neighbours Became Alien Enemies: Germans in New Zealand during World War One', in Steven Loveridge (ed.), *New Zealand Society at War, 1914–1918* (Wellington: Victoria University Press, 2016), pp. 266–80.

Loveridge, Steven, and Basil Keane, 'Turangawaewae: Maori Relationships with the Great War', in Steven Loveridge (ed.), *New Zealand Society at War, 1914–1918* (Wellington: Victoria University Press, 2016), pp. 281–96.

Lustgarten, Laurence, 'National Security and Political Policing: Some Thoughts on Values, Ends and Law', in Jean-Paul Brodeur, Peter Gill and Dennis Töllborg (eds), *Democracy, Law and Security: Internal Security Services in Contemporary Europe* (Aldershot: Ashgate Publishing, 2003), pp. 319–34.

Omand, David, 'The Cycle of Intelligence', in Robert Dover, Michael S. Goodman and Claudia Hillebrand (eds), *Routledge Companion to Intelligence Studies* (New York: Routledge, 2014), pp. 59–70.

Patterson, Brad, '"We Stand for the Protestant Religion, the (Protestant) King and the Empire": The Rise of the Protestant Political Association in World War One', in Steven Loveridge (ed.), *New Zealand Society at War, 1914–1918* (Wellington: Victoria University Press, 2016), pp. 235–51.

Rabel, Roberto, '"A Hell of a Way to End a War": New Zealanders in Trieste, 1945', in John Crawford (ed.), *Kia Kaha: New Zealand in the Second World War* (Auckland: Oxford University Press, 2002), pp. 276–88.

Renwick, William, 'Sir Thomas Hunter (1876–1953)', in Vincent O'Sullivan (ed.), *Eminent*

Victorians: Great Teachers and Scholars from Victoria's First 100 Years (Wellington: Stout Research Centre, 1999), pp. 9–48.

Roberts, H. S., 'A Note on the "Cold War" Period in New Zealand', in H. S. Roberts (ed.), *A History of Statistics in New Zealand* (Wellington: New Zealand Statistical Association, 1999), pp. 253–54.

Scott, Dick, 'The Propaganda War', in David Grant (ed.), *The Big Blue: Snapshots of the 1951 Waterfront Lockout* (Wellington: Canterbury University Press, 2004), pp. 30–37.

Taylor, Kerry, '"The Old Bolshevik": Alex Galbraith, the Communist Party and the New Zealand Revolution', in Rachael Bell (ed.), *New Zealand between the Wars* (Auckland: Massey University Press, 2017), pp. 108–31.

———, 'The Communist Party of New Zealand and the Third Period', in Matthew Worley (ed.), *In Search of Revolution: International Communist Parties in the Third Period* (London: I. B. Tauris, 2004), pp. 270–300.

———, '"Potential' Allies of the Working Class": The Communist Party of New Zealand and Maori, 1921–1952', in Pat Moloney and Kerry Taylor (eds), *On the Left: Essays on Socialism in New Zealand* (Dunedin: University of Otago Press, 2002), pp. 103–16.

Wark, Wesley K., 'Learning to Live with Intelligence', in Christopher Andrew, Richard J. Aldrich and Wesley K. Wark (eds), *Secret Intelligence: A Reader* (London: Routledge, 2009), pp. 522–32.

Weir, Robert E., 'Whose Left/Who's Left?: The Knights of Labour and "Radical Progressivism"', in Pat Moloney and Kerry Taylor (eds), *On the Left: Essays on Socialism in New Zealand* (Dunedin: University of Otago Press, 2002), pp. 21–38.

Yska, Redmer, 'Spies, Lies and Red Herrings', in David Grant (ed.), *The Big Blue: Snapshots of the 1951 Waterfront Lockout* (Wellington: Canterbury University Press, 2004), pp. 22–29.

Theses

Anderson, John, 'Military Censorship in World War I: Its Use and Abuse in New Zealand' (MA thesis, Victoria University College, 1952).

Barrington, Brook, 'New Zealand and the Search for Security 1944–54: "A Modest and Moderate Contribution"' (PhD thesis, University of Auckland, 1993).

Blackmun, Carl William, 'Not the Socialism We Dreamed Of: Becoming Ex-Communists in the United States and New Zealand, 1956–58' (MA thesis, Victoria University of Wellington, 2012).

Bollinger, Timothy, 'The Administrative Career of Dr W. B. Sutch 1958–1965: A Study in New Zealand Bureaucratic Politics' (PhD thesis, Victoria University of Wellington, 2001).

Dunick, Mark, 'Making Rebels: The New Zealand Socialist Party, 1901–1913' (MA thesis, Victoria University of Wellington, 2016).

Emsley, Simon, 'Sutch and the State: A Progressive Marginalisation' (PhD thesis, University of New South Wales, 1998).

Galt, Margaret Nell, 'Wealth and Income in New Zealand, 1870–1939' (PhD thesis, Victoria University of Wellington, 1985).

Irvine, F. M. Jean, 'The Revolt of the Militant Unions' (MA thesis, Auckland University College, 1937).

Johnson, Simon, 'The Home Front: Aspects of Civilian Patriotism in New Zealand during the First World War' (MA thesis, Massey University, 1975).

Kay, Richard G. H., 'In Pursuit of Victory: British–New Zealand Relations During the First World War' (PhD thesis, University of Otago, 2001).

———, 'Take *That*, You Dirty Commie!: The Rise of a Cold War Consciousness in New Zealand, 1944–1949' (BA Hons thesis, University of Otago, 1994).

La Rooij, Marinus Franciscus, 'Political Antisemitism in New Zealand during the Great Depression: A Case Study in the Myth of the Jewish World Conspiracy' (MA thesis, Victoria University of Wellington, 1998).

Millar, Grace, 'Families and the 1951 New Zealand Waterfront Lockout' (PhD thesis, Victoria University of Wellington, 2013).

Muir, John R., '"Our Bounden Duty": An Analysis of the Arguments Justifying the Introduction of Peacetime Compulsory Military Training in New Zealand, 1949' (BA Hons thesis, University of Otago, 1995).

Neems, Alexandra, '"Total Intelligence": New Zealand Signals Intelligence in Historical Context since 1945' (BA Hons thesis, University of Otago, 2014).

Nicoll, Matthew, 'The Concept of "Joint" Intelligence: Its Origins and Enactment, 1900–1942: From London, toward Wellington' (MA thesis, Victoria University of Wellington, 2019).

Noonan, Rosslyn J., 'The Riots of 1932: A Study of Social Unrest in Auckland, Wellington and Dunedin' (MA thesis, University of Auckland, 1969).

Pugh, Michael C., 'The New Zealand Legion and Conservative Protest in the Great Depression' (MA thesis, University of Auckland, 1969).

Shaw, Alistair, 'Telling the Truth About People's China' (PhD thesis, Victoria University of Wellington, 2010).

Skudder, Susan Mary, '"Bringing It Home": New Zealand Responses to the Spanish Civil War, 1936–1939' (PhD thesis, University of Waikato, 1986).

Taylor, Kerry Allan, 'Worker's Vanguard or People's Voice?: The Communist Party of New Zealand from Origins to 1946' (PhD thesis, Victoria University of Wellington, 1994).

Thomas, Caroline, 'The Sorcerers' Apprentice: A Life of Reo Franklin Fortune, Anthropologist' (PhD thesis, University of Waikato, 2011).

Tonkin-Covell, John, 'The Collectors: Naval, Army and Air Intelligence in the New Zealand Armed Forces during the Second World War' (PhD thesis, University of Waikato, 2000).

Wharton, Miriam L., 'The Development of Security Intelligence in New Zealand, 1945–1957' (Master of Defence Studies, Massey University, 2012).

Woods, Megan C., 'Integrating the Nation: Gendering Maori Urbanisation and Integration, 1942–1969' (PhD thesis, University of Canterbury, 2002).

Young, Sherwood, 'The Activities and Problems of the Police in the 1951 Waterfront Dispute' (MA thesis, University of Canterbury, 1975).

Unpublished Manuscripts

Crawford, Edward, 'Trotskyism in New Zealand', n.d. [1993].

Dwyer, John, 'Fragments from the Official Career of John Dwyer Superintendent of Police 1878–1921', n.d.

Hanson, Colin, 'Draft Chapters for History of New Zealand Sigint', n.d.

Hanson, Colin, and Jim Rolfe, 'Security Intelligence 1915–1945', n.d.

Johnston, Warwick, 'The New Zealand-born Comintern Agent', 2022.

McGuire, Mark, 'Army Signals', 2015.

Morgan, Eric, 'The History of Communications Security in New Zealand, Part 1', n.d.

Online Sources

Central Intelligence Agency (https://www.cia.gov/readingroom/home)

'Clandestine Services History: Civil Air Transport (CAT): A Proprietary Airline, 1946-1955' (www.scribd.com/document/341923971/Clandestine-Services-History#from_embed)

'Communist Influence in New Zealand published 30 June 1949', sanitised copy approved for release (www.cia.gov/readingroom/document/cia-rdp78-01617a00360003 0002-7)

'Daily Report', 13 November (2020), testimony of 'Doug Edwards' (http://campaign opposingpolicesurveillance.com/2020/11/14/ucpi-daily-report-13-nov-2020/)

Kiwi Spies (http://kiwispies.com)

New Zealand Security Intelligence Service Te Pā Whakamarumaru (www.nzsis.govt.nz)

Secret Files from World Wars to Cold War: Intelligence, Strategy and Diplomacy (www.secretintelligencefiles.com/)

Te Ara – the Encyclopedia of New Zealand (https://teara.govt.nz)

Te Hau Kāinga Māori Home Front (www.maorihomefront.nz)

'UKUSA Agreement Release' (www.nsa.gov/news-features/declassified-documents/ukusa/)

'W.B. Sutch Target Assessment', 30 May 1974 (www.nzsis.govt.nz/assets/media/1974-05-30-Sutch-TA.pdf)

Film

Wevers, Francis, and Dean Parker (directors), *Shattered Dreams* (Trade Union History Project, 1990). Available online at Ngā Taonga Sound & Vision (https://ngataonga.org.nz/collections/catalogue/catalogue-item?record_id=72458).

Index

An endnote is indicated by a page number followed by n and then the note number. A plate and its caption are indicated by *Fig.* followed by the number of the figure.

sigint (signals intelligence) operations

definition of, ix, 6

direction-finding, 104, 144–45, 192, 195–97, 239

intercept activities, 47, 49, 74, 76–77, 194, 102, 104, 112, 144, 157, 192, 195–96, 197, 239, 240–41, 278

radio-finger-printing ('Z' intelligence), 192

radio transmitting and receiving stations, 48–49, 64, 65, 77, 104, 148, 157, 192, 194, 195, 238, 240–41, 242

'Ultra secret' intelligence, 196–97, 215

Sillitoe, Sir Percy, 220, 227, 230–31, 234, 282, *Fig. 30*

Silverstone, Harold, 172

Sim, Leo, 133, 140, 160, 164

Sim Commission, 96

Simon Wiesenthal Center, 348n220

Singapore, 144, 157, 241, 242, 243, 281, 329n82

Sinn Féin, 99, 115, 121

six o'clock closing, 67, 70, 100

Smith, Shirley, 163, 248

Social Credit, 170, 202, 317n36

Social Democratic Party, 41, 116

Social Security Act (1938), 137

socialism/socialist movement, ix, 12, 23, 24, 27, 29, 36, 37, 39, 41, 42, 43, 46, 48, 50–52, 54, 59, 62, 70, 79–80, 85, 87, 89–90, 94–99, 101, 102, 111, 114–16, 118, 120, 121, 127, 130, 132, 136, 137, 158, 159, 160, 163, 164, 168, 171, 202, 251, 253, 255, 258, 264, 275, 280, 282, 351n273

see also CPNZ; Democratic Labour Party; Labour Party; NZSP; Social Democratic Party

Soldiers' Mothers League, 116

South-East Asia Treaty Organization (SEATO), 219, 243

Sokolov, Georgi, 270

Solidarity, 67

South Africa, 38, 58, 239, 263, 294n44, 298n65

Soviet Union (USSR), vii, ix, 69, 94, 96, 97, 98, 111, 122, 130, 132, 135, 138, 141, 148, 156, 172, 214, 216, 219, 221, 224, 225, 245, 247, 248, 256, 270–73

espionage, 111, 163–64, 219–22, 224, 245, 257–58, 263–64, 270–71, 270, 272, 282, 312n98, *Fig. 37*

Legation, 221, 233, 245, 256, 258, 264, 270, 271, 338n16

see also Comintern; KGB; Messines Road; RIS

Soviet Union Review, 122

Spanish Civil War, 138, 318n55

Special Air Service, 244

Special Branch (NZPF), *see* NZPF Special Branch (SB)

Special Branch (UK), 10, 43, 46, 89, 106, 107, 109, 126, 182, 227

Special Constables ('Specials'), 27, 41–42, 53, 69, 99, 134, 141–42, 229, 296n29, 298n60, 299n72, *Fig. 6*

Special Intelligence Bureaus, 74, 105

Special Wireless Section, 192, 196

Spee, Maximilian Reichsgraf von, 77

spies/spying, *see* agents for foreign powers, suspected or actual; counter-espionage

Stalin, Joseph/Stalinism, 32, 130, 132, 214, 216, 219, 225, 247, 264, *Fig. 22*

The Standard, 274–75

Stativkin, Vasili, 270

state, definition of, 6

Steele, Captain, 108

Stevens, W. G., 112, 144

Stevenson, Edward, 263

Stout Street, Wellington, 183, 228, 329n82

strikes, *see* industrial disputes

Strong, Kenneth, 241–42

subversion, definitions of, x, 30, 31, 89, 103, 129

Subversive History Sheets, 226, 274

Sullivan, Daniel, 102